W9-BXX-082

RACE,
CLASS, and GENDER

An Anthology
Fourth Edition

Margaret L. Andersen
University of Delaware

Patricia Hill Collins
University of Cincinnati

Wadsworth
Thomson Learning

Australia • Canada • Mexico • Singapore • Spain • United Kingdom • United States

Publisher: Eve Howard
Sociology Editor: Lin Marshall
Assistant Editor: Dee Dee Zobian
Marketing Manager: Matthew Wright
Signing Representative: Ron Shelly
Project Editor: Jerilyn Emori
Print Buyer: Karen Hunt
Permissions Editor: Joohee Lee
Production Service: Gretchen Otto /
G & S Typesetters, Inc.

Text Designer: Cynthia Schultz
Copy Editor: John Mulvihill
Illustrator: Glenda Hassinger
Cover Designer: Laurie Anderson
Cover Art: *Bound,* by Mike Shea (oil and wax
on canvas), © Mike Shea. Courtesy Froelick
Adelhart Gallery, Portland, Oregon
Text and Cover Printer: Von Hoffmann
Press, Inc. / Custom
Compositor: G&S Typesetters, Inc.

For permission to use material from this text, contact
us by **Web:** http://www.thomsonrights.com
Fax: 1-800-730-2215
Phone: 1-800-730-2214

Wadsworth/Thomson Learning
10 Davis Drive
Belmont, CA 94002-3098
USA

For more information about our products, contact us:
Thomson Learning Academic Resource Center
1-800-423-0563
http://www.wadsworth.com

International Headquarters
Thomson Learning
International Division
290 Harbor Drive, 2nd Floor
Stamford, CT 06902-7477
USA

UK/Europe/Middle East/South Africa
Thomson Learning
Berkshire House
168-173 High Holborn
London WC1V 7AA
United Kingdom

Asia
Thomson Learning
60 Albert Street, #15-01
Albert Complex
Singapore 189969

Canada
Nelson Thomson Learning
1120 Birchmount Road
Toronto, Ontario M1K 5G4
Canada

Library of Congress Cataloging-in-Publication Data
Race, class, and gender: an anthology / [compiled by]
Margaret L. Andersen, Patricia Hill Collins—4th ed.
p. cm.
Includes bibliographical references and index.
ISBN 0-534-56890-4 (pbk.)
1. United States—Social conditions—1980   2. United States—
Race relations.   3. Social classes—United States.   4. Sex role—
United States.   5. Homosexuality—United States.   6. Discrimination—
United States. I. Andersen, Margaret L. II. Collins, Patricia Hill
HN59.2.R32 2000
305—dc21   00—029018

This book is printed on acid-free recycled paper.

Contents

Preface

Race, Class, and Gender is an anthology that introduces students to how race, class, and gender shape the experiences of diverse groups in the United States. We want the book to help students see how the lives of different groups develop in the context of their race, class, and gender position in society. Central to the book is the idea that race, class, and gender are interrelated—and as a result, experience depends on the particular configuration of these factors in a given group's experience. We are aware that people often interpret this to mean that groups are only victimized by race, class, and gender. Students and faculty often understandably resist that characterization, wanting instead to affirm group identity, especially those who have been silenced, made invisible, and defined as "other." We are sympathetic to the resistance to a victimization perspective, and we do not want to make people appear to have no agency or choice in the formation of their lives; however, we also know that the structure of race, class, and gender in society has significant consequences for different groups, and we do not think this should be ignored. Thus, although our book is not just about victimization and while we want to affirm the value of diversity, our primary goal is for students to understand the structural arrangements in society and how they result in different systems of privilege and disadvantage. At the same time, we want students to learn how they can make a difference in their own lives and how they can help society at large.

Our introductory essay develops these ideas further and situates this book in the race, class, gender studies of which we are a part. The introductory essay distinguishes models of race, class, and gender studies that are strictly additive from those that see race, class, and gender as interlocking systems of societal relationships. We want readers to conceptualize race, class, and gender as interactive systems, not merely as variables in sociological equations or separate cultural experiences. We want readers to see race, class, and gender in an analytical, not merely a descriptive way, although we recognize that description of group experience (both historical and current) is an important part of this process.

About the Fourth Edition

We have been pleased by the success of *Race, Class, and Gender* because it represents the commitment of many people to become more inclusive in their teaching and thinking. We appreciate the reactions people have shared with us, particularly those who have reviewed the book for Wadsworth.

One of the challenges of creating an anthology in a field so rich with new research and new writing is to include articles that will provide a full portrait of the complexity of race, class, and gender. We cannot cover every topic that might be included in such a book. We know that one book cannot do everything people want, but we hope that the fourth edition builds on the strengths of the first three editions and furthers people's thinking in race, class, gender studies. We want the book to influence students and help teachers with the hard work of building a more inclusive curriculum. We have expanded our original editorial introduction to develop the model of inclusive thinking that we hope we have established.

In selecting articles for the new edition, we found we had to replace some that were dated—for example, those that focused on the now-eliminated AFDC welfare system. We also included several new articles that strengthen the historical context in which race, class, and gender systems have emerged. We find that many students have little sense of the history of diverse groups, even though knowing this history is critical to understanding the present. We have added a new section on "Cultural Institutions and the Production of Ideas" (in part III), including within this section material on language, popular culture, sports, and education. We think these are key sources of the ideological frames that influence people's consciousness about race, class, and gender, and we wanted students to think, not just about the images produced within these institutional structures but about who produces them and why.

In creating this new section, we moved some of our earlier articles on education to a new section on "State Institutions and Social Policy." Our goal here is to help students see how systems of state power, as manifested in law, education, policy, welfare tax structures, and prisons, regulate race, class, and gender relations and how they operate as systems of social control.

In other new selections, we have included pieces that we think better show the interlocking connections between race, class, and gender, including how sexuality and forms of heterosexual privilege are linked to race, gender, and class. As in the earlier editions, we do not want readers to conclude that heterosexual privilege is only significant when thinking about sexuality per se; thus, we include several authors who discuss sexuality in the context of race, gender, and class. In the end, however, we want students to understand that studying race, class, and gender is not just a question of learning about differences, but is fundamentally a matter of social justice.

We have deliberately not revised our final section on political activism. Contemporary students often conclude that, even if they begin to understand the complexities of race, class, and gender relations, there is little they can do to change current realities. Our students often seem overwhelmed by the problems they see in society, and they feel powerless to do much about it. Books like ours, however well intended, often present examples of activism that actually contribute to students' impressions that they can be a significant agent of change only by dedicating their entire lives to change. We want students to think about social change differently, recognizing that people work for change in multiple ways—including in the context of their everyday lives. We also want students to understand that the responsibility for change does not fall exclusively on exceptionally committed individuals. Rather, all people share collective responsibility for change, including institutional change. One of the problems we see currently is the government's abandonment of social support for those in need, even while the state increases its support for wealthy individuals and corporate entities. We would like students to learn that creating social change is not just a matter of putting themselves on the line, but of insisting on a new model of social responsibility for society as a whole.

In this revision, we hope we have maintained the strengths of the first three editions—a strong sociological foundation, a historical perspective provided by many authors, a conceptual grounding supplied in our introductions, inclusive attention to the interlocking dynamics of race, class, and gender, and a balance of different group experiences. Although not every group can be covered on every subject, we hope that our inclusion of different selections conveys a sense of the multiple but related ways that race, class, and gender shape U.S. society and culture. We have maintained the theme of linking personal narratives with the analytical study of race, class, and gender. We are pleased when we hear that students enjoy the readings and find that they illuminate perspectives they had not thought about before in quite the same way.

We have added some new pedagogical features to help faculty who teach with this book and to give students additional resources from which to build their understanding of race, class, and gender. Students who purchase the book are given a password to Wadsworth's InfoTrac College Edition feature. We have included terms at the end of the introduction to each major part that students can use on InfoTrac College Edition to find additional information on subjects that interest them. These terms can also be used as the basis for in-class discussion, exercises, exams, or research projects. In addition, we have included lists of suggested readings at the conclusion of each introductory essay for students and faculty who want to explore these topics further. We have selected these books based on their currency and their accessibility to undergraduate students. This edition also includes an *Instructor's Manual* with suggestions for class exercises, discussion and examination questions, and course assignments. We have also included a Subject Index to help students and faculty locate material in the book.

This edition also includes online support via the Wadsworth Sociology Resource Center, representing how electronic technology is transforming the teaching profession. We encourage people to browse the Race, Class, & Gender page at the Wadsworth Web site for related resources. The address is http://sociology.wadsworth.com.

A Note on Language

The reconstruction of existing ways of thinking to make them more inclusive requires many transformations. One transformation needed involves the language we use to describe and define different groups. This language reflects many assumptions about race, class, and gender; and for that reason, language changes and evolves as knowledge changes. The term *minority*, for example, marginalizes groups, making them seem somehow outside the mainstream or majority culture. Even worse, the phrase *non-White*, routinely used by social scientists, defines groups in terms of what they are not and assumes that Whites have the universal experiences against which the experiences of all other groups are measured. We have consciously avoided using both of these terms throughout this book.

We have capitalized *Black* in our writing because of the specific historical experience, varied as it is, of African Americans in the United States. We also capitalize *White* when referring to a particular group experience; however, we recognize that *White American* is no more a uniform experience than is *African American*. We realize that these are arguable points, but we want to make our decision apparent and explicit. For the benefit of purists who like to follow the rules, we note that the fourteenth edition of the *Chicago Manual of Style* recognizes that these grammatical questions are also political ones; this edition suggests that writers might want to capitalize *Black* and *White* to reflect the fact that they are referring to proper names of groups. We use "Hispanic" and "Latino" interchangeably, though we recognize that is not how groups necessarily define themselves. When citing data from other sources (typically government documents), we use "Hispanic," since that is how such data are reported.

Language becomes especially problematic when we want to talk about features of experience that different groups share. Using shortcut terms like *Hispanic, Latino, Native American,* and *women of color* homogenizes distinct historical experiences. Even the term *White* falsely unifies experiences across such factors as ethnicity, region, class, and gender, to name a few. At times, though, we want to talk of common experiences across different groups, so we have used labels like *Latino, Asian American, Native American* and *women of color* to do so. Unfortunately, describing groups in this way reinforces basic categories of oppression. We do not know how to resolve this problem, but want readers to be aware of the limitations and significance of language as they try to think more inclusively about diverse group experiences.

Acknowledgments

An anthology rests on the efforts of more people than the editors alone. This book has been inspired by our work with scholars and teachers from around the country who are working to make their teaching and writing more inclusive and sensitive to the experiences of all groups. Over the years of our own collaboration, we have each been enriched by the work of those trying to make higher education a more equitable and fair institution. This book has grown from several of those projects, most notably the University of Memphis Center for Research on Women Curriculum Workshops and the American Sociological Association Minority Opportunity Summer Training Program, now the Minority Opportunity through School Transformation Program. These two programs provided the context for many of our early discussions about this book. Over the years, the networks that have emerged from these associations continue to sustain us. We thank Maxine Baca Zinn, Chuck Bonjean, Marion Coleman, Patrice Dickerson, Bonnie Thornton Dill, Valerie Hans, Elizabeth Higginbotham, Clarence Lo, Lionel Maldonado, Carole Marks, Cora Marrett, Howard Taylor, and Lynn Weber for inspiring our work and, in many cases, suggesting new ideas and articles to consider here. We also thank them for the companionship, encouragement, and vision that inspires our work.

Many other people contributed to the development of this book. We especially thank Cathleen Brooks at the University of Delaware and Tina Beyene and Robin Deisher at the University of Cincinnati for their expert research assistance. We appreciate the support given by our two institutions, with special thanks to Lisa Huber and Jeffrey Quirico at the University of Delaware and to John Brackett, former head of the Department of African American Studies, and Robin Sheets, former Head of the Center for Women's Studies, at the University of Cincinnati. Thanks as well to Al Camarillo, Margarita Ibarra, and Monica Wheeler of the Stanford University Center for Comparative Studies in Race and Ethnicity for their support during the production of this book. We also thank Sadie Wright Oliver and Tiffaney Livingston for their invaluable secretarial support.

Eve Howard has supported this project with great enthusiasm and commitment, and we appreciate her guidance and support in helping us complete the fourth edition. She, Dee Dee Zobian, and Bridget Schulte all provided ideas and work that helped us complete the new edition. We sincerely appreciate their hard work and vision for the book and look forward to continued collaboration with them.

Developing this book has been an experience based on friendship, hard work, travel, and fun. We especially thank Valerie, Roger, and Richard for giving us the support, love, and time we needed to do this work well. This book has deepened our friendship, as we have grown more committed to transformed ways of thinking and being. We are lucky to be working on a project that draws us closer together.

About the Editors

Margaret L. Andersen is professor of sociology and women's studies at the University of Delaware. She is the author of *Thinking about Women, Sociology: Understanding a Diverse Society* (with Howard F. Taylor), *Understanding Society: Readings in the Sociological Perspective* (with Kim A. Logio and Howard F. Taylor), and *Social Problems* (with Frank R. Scarpitti and Laura L. O'Toole). She has recently served as president of the Eastern Sociological Society and was a visiting scholar at Stanford University's Center for Comparative Studies in Race and Ethnicity while completing this edition.

Patricia Hill Collins is professor of African American studies and sociology at the University of Cincinnati, where she is currently chair of the Department of African American Studies. She is the author of *Fighting Words* (1998) and *Black Feminist Thought: Knowledge, Consciousness, and the Politics of Empowerment,* which won the C. Wright Mills Award of the Society for the Study of Social Problems. A revised edition of *Black Feminist Thought* was published in 2000 to mark its ten-year anniversary.

About the Contributors

Paula Gunn Allen is professor of English at UCLA. She was awarded the Native American Prize for Literature in 1990. That same year her anthology of short stories, *Spider Woman's Granddaughters*, was awarded the American Book Award, sponsored by the Before Columbus Foundation, and the Susan Koppleman Award. A major Native American poet, writer, and scholar, she has published numerous volumes of poetry, a novel, a collection of essays, and several anthologies. Her prose and poetry appear widely in anthologies, journals, and scholarly publications.

Teresa Amott is on the faculty in economics at Bucknell University. She is the author of *Race, Gender, and Work: A Multicultural Economic History of Women in the United States* (with Julie Matthaei) and *Caught in the Crisis: Women in the U.S. Economy Today*, along with numerous articles. She is an editorial associate with *Dollars and Sense* magazine, and is committed to sharing economic analysis with unions, welfare rights organizations, women's organizations, and other progressive groups.

Elijah Anderson is the Charles and William L. Day Professor of the Social Sciences, professor of sociology, and director of the Philadelphia Ethnography Project at the University of Pennsylvania. An expert on the sociology of Black America, he is the author of the highly regarded sociological work *A Place on the Corner: A Study of Black Street Corner Men*, numerous articles on the Black experience, and *The Code of the Streets: Decency, Violence, and the Moral Life of the Inner City* (Norton 1999). For his recently published ethnographic study, *Streetwise: Race, Class and Change in an Urban Community*, he was honored with the Robert E. Park Award by the American Sociological Association. An associate editor of *Qualitative Sociology*, he is a member of the Board of Directors of the American Academy of Political and Social Science.

John Anner is the founding editor and publisher of *Third Force*, a magazine that reports on and evaluates grass-roots labor and community organizing in communities of color. He is the editor of *Beyond Identity Politics: Emerging Social Justice Movements in Communities of Color*, and writes frequently about successful organizing.

Charon Asetoyer is the founder and executive director of the Native American Women's Health Education Resource Center, based on the Yankton Sioux Reservation in Lake Andes, South Dakota. She has been involved in community organizing and activism on women's health issues for the past twenty years.

Magdoline Asfahani was an undergraduate political science student at the time she published her essay "Time to Look and Listen" in *Newsweek*. Her plans at the time were to work for government so that she could inspire others and further the cause against prejudice and discrimination.

Alan Berkman is a political activist and physician who was imprisoned for anti-imperialist activities in the 1980s. While in prison, he wrote a number of articles reporting on his life as a prisoner. He is currently identified on the Web as assistant professor of psychiatry at Columbia Presbyterian Medical Center.

Peter Blood is a marriage and family therapist for the Institute for Christian Counseling and Therapy. He writes about and leads retreats that focus on men's issues. He is the editor of *Rise Up Singing* and is editorial director for the *Sing Out* publication.

Tim Blunk became a student activist in the late 1970s. In 1986, he was sent to a maximum security federal penitentiary, accused by the FBI of escape conspiracy with other political activists. As a revolutionary, artist, and poet, he contributed to *Hauling Up the Morning* and *Cages of Steel*. He received Honorable Mention for his poetry in the 1990 Larry Neal Writers' Competition.

Sucheng Chan is professor of Asian American studies and global studies at the University of California at Santa Barbara. She is the author of *This Bittersweet Soil: The Chinese in California Agriculture, 1860–1910; Asian Californians;* and *Asian Americans: An Interpretive History*. She has also edited eight books and written dozens of articles.

Sumi K. Cho is assistant professor at the DePaul University College of Law in Chicago where she pursues her research on Asian Pacific Americans and critical race theory. She teaches courses on remedies and employment discrimination, as well as a course called "Race, Racism & U.S. Law." As a campus-community organizer on issues of affirmative action, racial/gender discrimination, and sexual harassment, she strives to bring a multidisciplinary approach and community-based orientation to the study of race, gender, and law.

Ward Churchill (enrolled Keetoowah Band Cherokee) is a long-time native rights activist, acclaimed public speaker, and award-winning writer. A member of the Governing Council of the Colorado chapter of the American Indian Movement, he also serves as professor of ethnic studies and coordinator of American Indian studies for the University of Colorado. His many books include *Marxism and Native Americans, Agents of Repression, The COINTEL-PRO Papers, Critical Issues in Native North America, Fantasies of the Master Race, Struggle for the Land, Since Predator Came, From a Native Son,* and *A Little Matter of Genocide: Holocaust and Denial in the Americas.*

Judith Ortiz Cofer is the author of a novel, *The Line of the Sun,* of *Silent Dancing,* a collection of essays and poetry, of two books of poetry, *Terms of Survival* and *Reaching for the Mainland,* and of *The Latin Deli: Prose and Poetry.* Her work has appeared in *Glamour, The Georgia Review, Kenyon Review,* and other journals. She has been anthologized in *The Best American Essays, The Norton Book of Women's Lives, The Pushcart Prize,* and the *O. Henry Prize Stories.* A PEN/Martha Albrand Special Citation in nonfiction was awarded to her for *Silent Dancing,* the Anisfield Wolf Book Award for *The Latin Deli,* and her work has been selected for the Syndicated Fiction Project. She has received fellowships from the NEA and the Witter Bynner Foundation for poetry. Her most recent book is a collection of short stories, *An Island Like You: Stories of the Barrio,* (Orchard Books, 1995; Penguin U.S.A., 1996) which was named a Best Book of the Year, 1995–96, by the American Library Association. She is the 1998 recipient of the Christ-Janner Award in Creative Research from the University of Georgia. A native of Puerto Rico, she now resides in Georgia and is professor of English and creative writing at the University of Georgia.

Chuck Collins is the coordinator of the Share the Wealth Project and works with the Tax Equity Alliance of Massachusetts. He contributes to the *Directory of Socially Responsible Investment* and writes regularly for *Dollars and Sense.*

Dalton Conley is currently associate professor of sociology and director of the Center for Advanced Social Science Research at New York University. Prior to joining the ranks of NYU, he was a faculty member of the departments of sociology and African American studies at Yale University. He is author of *Being Black, Living in the Red: Race, Wealth and Social Policy in America* (University of California Press, 1999). This study was based on Conley's doctoral dissertation research, which received the award for best in the field from the American Sociological Association (1996). He is also author of *Honky* (University of California Press, fall 2000), a memoir of growing up white in a predominantly minority, inner-city housing project. Conley has written extensively on issues of race and socioeconomic status for both academic journals and the mainstream press and is currently working on a project that examines how siblings from the same family of origin end up in different class positions as adults. Conley is a recipient of a Robert Wood Johnson Foundation Investigator Award.

Marc Cooper is a contributing editor for *The Nation,* and host and executive producer of RadioNation. He is the author of *Roll Over, Che Guevara: Travels of a Radical Reporter* (Verso, 1994) and a PBS video, *Our Forgotten War.*

Deirdre E. Davis received her B.A. from Wesleyan University and J.D. from Boalt Hall School of Law at the University of California, Berkeley. While in law school, she edited the *Berkeley Women's Law Journal* and is now in private practice.

Bonnie Thornton Dill, professor of women's studies and director of the Research Consortium on Gender, Race, and Ethnicity at the University of Maryland, College Park, conducts research on African American women, work, and family and is currently studying coping and survival strategies of low-income single mothers in several rural southern communities. Her books include: *Women of Color in U.S. Society,* coedited with Maxine Baca Zinn (Temple University Press, 1994) and *Across the Boundaries of Race and Class: Work and Family Among Black Female Domestic Servants,* (Garland Press, 1994). Recent articles have been published in *Signs, Feminist Studies,* and *Journal of Comparative Family Studies,* among others, and have been reprinted extensively.

Michael Dyson, who has taught at Hartford Seminary, Chicago Theological Seminary, and Brown University, is presently a professor of communication studies at the University of North Carolina, Chapel Hill. He is the author of the widely acclaimed *Reflecting Black: African-American Cultural Criticism.*

Barbara Ehrenreich writes feature articles, reviews, essays, and humor that have appeared in a wide range of publications, including *The Nation, The New York Times Magazine, The Atlantic Monthly, Harper's, The New Republic,* and *Time.* Her most recent book is *The Snarling Citizen.* She is currently a teaching fellow in the Graduate School of Journalism, University of California, Berkeley.

D. Stanley Eitzen is professor emeritus of sociology at Colorado State University. With Maxine Baca Zinn, he has written *Diversity in Families, In Conflict and Order,* and *Social Problems.* He has also written *Elite Deviance* (with David R. Simon), *Sociology of North American Sport* (with George H. Sage), *Criminology* (with Doug A. Timmer), and *Paths to Homelessness* (with Doug A. Timmer and Kathryn Talley). His current book projects include *Demythologizing Sport* and *Where the Welfare State Works.*

Yen Le Espiritu is professor in the department of ethnic studies at U.C. San Diego. She is the author of *Asian American Panethnicity* (1992); *Filipino American Lives* (1994); and *Asian American Women and Men: Labor, Laws, and Love* (1997). Her current research examines the lives of second-generation Asian Americans.

Abby L. Ferber is assistant professor and codirector of the graduate program in sociology at the University of Colorado at Colorado Springs, where she teaches in the areas of race, gender, and social theory. She is the author of *White Man Falling: Race, Gender and White Supremacy*, (Rowman and Littlefield, 1998), "What White Supremacists Taught a Jewish Scholar About Identity," *Chronicle of Higher Education*, May 7, 1999, and numerous articles exploring the intersections of race and gender. She is also the coauthor of a forthcoming manuscript exploring the experiences of university students of color.

Marilyn Frye teaches philosophy and women's studies at Michigan State University. She received her Ph.D. at Cornell University in 1969 and is the author of two books of essays, *The Politics of Reality* and *Willful Virgin*. Her current work is a critical analysis of the nature of *categories*—what they are and how they work ("The Necessity of Differences," *Signs*, Summer 1996). With her partner Carolyn Shafer, she created and manages Bare Bones Studios for Women's Art—space and facilities for art-making in a wide range of media.

John Garvey works at the City University of New York and is a long-time political activist.

Rose Campbell Gibson is faculty associate at the Institute for Social Research and Institute of Gerontology, and professor emerita at the University of Michigan. She is the author of several books, including *Different Worlds: Inequality in The Aging Experience* (with Eleanor Palo Stoller); *Blacks in an Aging Society;* and *Health in Black America* (with James Jackson); and numerous articles and chapters on sociocultural issues in aging. She is a past editor-in-chief of *The Gerontologist*. Her research on sociocultural factors in aging has been funded by the National Institute of Aging, the Administration on Aging, and private foundations. She has been a distinguished visiting professor/scholar at several universities, including Yonsei, Dong-A and Yeungnam Universities in South Korea, University of California at Berkeley, University of Georgia, and University of Iowa, where she was the Ida I. Beam Distinguished Visiting Professor.

Amy Gluckman is a social studies teacher in an alternative high school in Lowell, Massachusetts. She is part of an editorial collective that publishes the progressive economics magazine, *Dollars and Sense* and, with Betsy Reed, is the editor of a book, *Homo Economics*, a collection of articles about capitalism, economics, and gay and lesbian life.

Elizabeth Higginbotham grew up in a working-class family in New York City. She is a professor of sociology and Black American studies at the University of Delaware and a cofounder of the University of Memphis Center for Research on Women. Higginbotham has published widely on issues of race, class, and gender. She is coeditor of *Women and Work: Exploring Race, Ethnicity, and Class* and has articles in *American Behavioral Scientist, Gender & Society, Women's Studies Quarterly*, and many edited collections. She is currently completing a book on social class differences in the experiences of college-educated Black women titled *Too Much to Ask: The Cost of Black Female Success*.

Pierrette Hondagneu-Sotelo is associate professor of sociology, American studies, and ethnicity at the University of Southern California. Her research and activism centers on immigration, immigrant rights and gender. She is author of *Gendered Transitions: Mexican Experiences of Immigration*, and a forthcoming book based on research conducted with Latina immigrant women who work as house cleaners and nannies, and the women who employ them.

James Jennings is professor of political science and senior fellow at the Trotter Institute, University of Massachusetts, Boston. He teaches courses on race and public policy in the Africana Studies Department. He has published and lectured on urban affairs and politics. He works extensively on a range of community and economic development issues in Boston and other cities. Currently, Jennings is completing a study on the institutional effects of welfare reform on predominantly Black and Latino neighborhoods, and another study examining the civic involvement of faith-based institutions in Boston. His books include *Blacks, Latinos, and Asians: Status and Prospects for Activism; The Politics of Black Empowerment;* and *Race and Politics*. Jennings is editor of the *Trotter Review*, the annual journal of the Trotter Institute.

June Jordan is a poet and activist and the most published African American writer in history. Her 26th book, *Soldier, A Poet's Childhood*, is published by Basic Books (2000). Internationally acclaimed for her creative accomplishments in many genres, she is professor of African American studies at U.C. Berkeley, where she directs the enormously popular Poetry for the People program. Her most recent titles are *Affirmative Acts* (new political essays) and *Kissing God Good-bye* (new poems).

Robin D. G. Kelley is a professor of history and African studies at New York University. He is the author of *Hammer and Hoe: Alabama Communists During the Great Depression* (1990); *Race Rebels: Culture Politics and the Black Working*

Class (1994); *Into the Fire: African Americans Since 1970* (1996); *Yo' Mama's Dis-Funktional!: Fighting the Culture Wars in Urban America* (1997). His edited works include *Imagining Home: Class, Culture, and Nationalism in the African Diaspora* (with Sidney Lemelle); *To Make Our World Anew: A History of African Americans* (2000) (with Earl Lewis); and the eleven-volume *Young Oxford History of African Americans* (Oxford University Press) (also with Earl Lewis). His articles have appeared in *The Nation, Monthly Review, The Voice Literary Supplement, labor History, Journal of American History, The American Historical Review, New York Newsday, New York Daily Challenge, New York times Magazine, Color Lines, One World, Black Renaissance/Renaissance Noir, Boston Review, Social Text,* and *Radical History Review,* among others. Kelley is currently finishing a book titled *Misterioso: In Search of Thelonious Monk.*

Nazli Kibria is assistant professor of sociology at Boston University. She has written widely on the sociology of families, race and ethnicity, and gender. She is the author of *Family Tightrope: The Changing Lives of Vietnamese Americans,* and is currently completing a book on the racial and ethnic identities of second-generation Chinese and Korean Americans.

Bruce Kokopeli is the author of *Leadership for Change: Toward a Feminist Model* (with George Lakey).

Celene Krauss is professor of sociology and women's studies at Kean University. She has written extensively on women's issues and toxic waste protests, with a focus on race, ethnicity, and class. Her work has appeared in *Sociological Forum, Qualitative Sociology,* and other journals and books.

Louis Kushnick is a senior lecturer in sociology at the University of Manchester, and is director of the Ahmen Iqbal Ullah Race Relations Archive. He has been vice chairman of the Institute of Race Relations and editor of the *Sage Race Relations Abstracts* since 1980. He is author of *Race, Class, and Struggle: Essays on Racism and Inequality in Britain, the U.S. and Western Europe* (Rivers Oram Press) and coeditor with James Jennings of *A New Introduction to Poverty: The Role of Race, Power and Politics* (NYU Press).

George Lakey is a consultant and trainer, an activist and college teacher, and author of five books. He has conducted over 1000 workshops on five continents. He began leading men's conferences in the mid-1970s. He has initiated social change projects in civil rights, neighborhood development, economic conversion, and peace, and was a founder of the Movement for a New Society. An openly gay grandfather of four, he frequently lectures at major colleges and universities.

Donna Langston is coeditor of *Changing Our Power* and professor of women's studies at Mankato State University.

Audre Lorde, who passed away in 1992, grew up in the West Indian community of Harlem in the 1930s, the daughter of immigrants from Grenada. She attended Hunter College (later becoming professor of English there), ventured to the American expatriate community in Mexico, and participated in the Greenwich Village scene of the early 1950s. She was a major figure in the lesbian and feminist movements. Among her works are *Sister Outsider, Zami: A New Spelling of My Name, Uses of the Erotic, Chosen Poems Old and New, The Black Unicorn,* and *From a Land Where Other People Live.*

Arturo Madrid is Murchison Distinguished Professor of the Humanities at Trinity University and the recipient of the Charles Frankel Prize in the Humanities, National Endowment for the Humanities, in 1996. From 1984 until 1993 he served as founding president of The Tomás Rivera Center, a national institute for policy studies on Latino issues.

Gregory Mantsios is the director of worker education at Queens College, the City University of New York.

Elizabeth (Betita) Martinez is an activist, author, and educator, and has published five books and many articles on social movements in the Americas. After working for the United Nations and as Books & Arts editor of *The Nation* in New York, she served full-time in the black civil rights movement with the Student Nonviolent Coordination Committee (SNCC), then with the Chicano movement in New Mexico, where she initiated a newspaper and the Chicano Communications Center. She has lectured at dozens of campuses and conferences across the country. Her bilingual book *500 Years of Chicano History in Pictures* is the basis for the video "Viva la Causa!" which she co-directed; such work reflects her goal of providing educational resources for youth. Her most recent book is a collection of essays *De Colores Means All of Us: Latino Views for a Multi-Colored Century.* In northern California, she teaches ethnic studies and women's studies part-time, works with the Women of Color Resource Center, and is chair of the Institute for Multiracial Justice to link peoples of color. She has received many awards for community leadership and serving Latino youth; most recently, she was named Scholar of the Year 2000 by the National Association of Chicano/Chicana Studies (NACCS) for its national conference in March.

Julie Matthaei is a fellow at the Radcliffe Public Policy Center and professor of economics at Wellesley College. She has been active in the anti-war, feminist, anti-racist, lesbian and gay rights, and ecology movements over the past thirty years. Her books include *An Economic History of Women in America: Women's Work, The Sexual Division of Labor, and the Development of Capitalism* (1982) and, with Teresa Amott, *Race, Gender, and Work: A Multicultural Economic History of Women in the United States* (1992, 1996). She is currently writing a book with Barbara Brandt on the next stage of feminist economic transformation, which she calls integrative feminism, tentatively titled *Healing Ourselves, Healing Our Economy.*

Peggy McIntosh is associate director of the Wellesley College Center for Research on Women. She is founder and codirector of the National SEED Project on Inclusive Curriculum and consults throughout the country and the world with college and school faculty who are creating gender-fair and multicultural curricula. She has written many articles on women's studies, curriculum change, and systems of unearned privilege. She has also taught at the Bearley School, Harvard University, Trinity College (Washington, D.C.), the University of Denver, the University of Durham (England), and Wellesley College. She is contributing editor to *Women's Studies Quarterly* and a consulting editor to *SAGE: A Scholarly Journal on Black Women.*

Michael Messner is associate professor of sociology and gender studies at the University of Southern California. He is past president of the North American Society for the Sociology of Sport. His books include *Power at Play: Sports and the Problem of Masculinity; Sex, Violence, and Power in Sports: Rethinking Masculinity* (with Donald F. Sabo); and *Politics of Masculinities: Men in Movements.*

Roslyn Arlin Mickelson is professor of sociology and adjunct professor of women's studies at the University of North Carolina at Charlotte. Her research examines the political economy of schooling, in particular how race, class, and gender shape educational processes and outcomes.

Barbara Miner is coauthor of *Selling Out Our Schools: Vouchers, Markets, and the Future of Public Education* and *False Choice: Why School Vouchers Threaten our Children's Future.* She is also managing editor of *Rethinking Schools,* a journal providing a grass-roots look at educational reform in urban schools.

Joan Moore, Distinguished Professor Emerita of Sociology at the University of Wisconsin in Milwaukee, has written extensively about urban poverty and about Latinos, with a particular concern for youth gangs.

Cherríe Moraga is a poet, playwright, and essayist. She is the coeditor of *This Bridge Called My Back: Writing by Radical Women of Color,* which won the Before Columbus American Book Award in 1986. She is the author of numerous plays including *Shadow of a Man,* winner of the 1990 Fund for New American Plays Award and *Heroes and Saints,* winner of the Will Glickman Prize and the Pen West Award in 1992. She is also a recipient of the National Endowment for the Arts' Theatre Playwrights' Fellowship.

Katherine Newman is Malcolm Wiener Professor of Urban Studies at the John F. Kennedy School of Government, Harvard University. She is the author, most recently, of *No Shame in My Game: The Working Poor in the Inner City* (Knopf, 1999) and *Falling from Grace: Downward Mobility in the Age of Affluence* (University of California Press, 1999). She received the Anthropology in Media Award from the American Anthropological Association in 1993.

Raquel Pinderhughes is associate professor and director of the urban studies program at San Francisco State University. She is the editor (with Joan Moore) of *In the Barrios: Latinos and the Underclass Debate.* Her research focus is on community-level impacts of social inequality and poverty in the United States. Within this framework, she has conducted research on urban restructuring; urban poverty; the socioeconomic condition of Latino populations in the United States; the relationship between race, poverty, and environmental quality; environmental hazards in residential communities; inequality in local food systems; and the role of urban agriculture in reducing poverty.

Valerie Polakow is professor of education at Eastern Michigan University. She is the author of *The Erosion of Childhood* and *Lives on the Edge: Single Mothers and their Children in the Other America.* Her research is on women and children in poverty, homelessness, and welfare policy.

Bernice Johnson Reagon, Distinguished Professor of History at American University and Curator Emerita at the Smithsonian Institution, is also a composer and singer performing with Sweet Honey in the Rock, the ensemble she founded in 1973. Her recent works include *We Who Believe in Freedom: Sweet Honey in the Rock, Still On The Journey, We'll Understand it Better By and By: African American Pioneering Gospel Composers,* and the re-mastered *Voices of the Civil Rights Movement, 1960–1965,* a two-CD collection with booklet anthology. Reagon was conceptual producer and narrator of the Peabody Award-winning radio series "Wade in the Water: African American Sacred Music Traditions" produced by the Smithsonian Institution and National Public Radio and curator for a traveling exhibition of the same title. She received the 1995 Charles Frankel Prize, a Presidential medal, in recognition of her outstanding contribution to public understanding of the humanities. Most recently, Reagon created the sound score for the Peabody Award-winning 1998 PBS film series, "Africans in America," produced by WGBH-TV. She was also the producer of the sound score recordings of the "Africans in America" series released by Rykodisc/WGBH Recordings.

Betsy Reed, a former editor of *Dollars and Sense*, is a senior editor at *The Nation.* She is coeditor with Amy Gluckman of the anthology *Homo Economics: Capitalism, Community and Lesbian and Gay Life* (Routledge).

Adrienne Rich's most recent books are *What Is Found There: Notebooks on Poetry and Politics* (1993), *Dark Fields of the Republic: Poems 1991–1995*, and *Midnight Salvage: Poems 1995–1998* (Norton). Her awards for poetry include the Lenore Marshall/*Nation* Award, a MacArthur Fellowship, the Dorothea Tanning Prize, and the Lannan Foundation Lifetime Achievement Award. She has lived in California since 1984.

Lillian Rubin is the author of numerous books and articles, including *Families on the Fault Line* and *Worlds of Pain.*

Virginia Rutter is finishing her Ph.D. in sociology at the University of Washington, where she teaches on topics related to gender, sexuality, families, women in the social structure, research methodology, and writing. Prior to teaching she worked as a journalist and in public affairs and Congress in Washington, D.C. She writes for academic and general audiences and is the author of two books, *The Gender of Sexuality* and *The Love Test.*

Jason Schultz is the director of special projects for Stir Fry Productions, an organization specializing in diversity training and racial conflict resolution. He was also the coordinator of the Duke Men's Project, a group for college men working on issues of gender and sexuality.

Pepper Schwartz is a professor of sociology at the University of Washington in Seattle, Washington. She is past president of the Society for the Scientific Study of Sexuality and a member of the International Academy of Sex Research. She is the author of eleven books, among them *American Couples* (with Philip Blumstein), *Peer Marriage*, and *The Gender of Sexuality* (with Virginia Rutter). She writes for many popular magazines and Web sites and does expert testimony on marriage, family, sexuality, and gender issues. She testified for Llambda in the "Don't Ask, Don't Tell" case on gays in the military and in the gay marriage case in Hawaii. She lives with her family on a horse and llama ranch in Snoqualmie, Washington.

Stephen Samuel Smith is associate professor of political science at Winthrop University in Rock Hill, South Carolina. His interests include the politics of education, urban political economy, social movements, and program evaluation.

C. Matthew Snipp is a professor of sociology at Stanford University. He also has been a professor of rural sociology and sociology, and director of the American Indian studies program, at the University of Wisconsin in Madison. He has been a research fellow at the U.S. Bureau of the Census and a fellow at the Center for Advanced Study in the Behavioral Sciences. Snipp has published numerous works on American Indian demography, economic development, poverty, and unemployment. He is the author of *American Indians: The First of This Land* and *Public Policy Impacts on American Indian Economic Development*. His current research and writing deals with poverty and unemployment on American Indian reservations, and American Indian ethnic identity. His tribal heritage is Oklahoma Cherokee and Choctaw.

Gloria Steinem is one of the most influential writers, editors, and activists of our time. She travels in this and other countries as a lecturer and feminist organizer, and is a frequent media interviewer and spokeswoman on issues of equality. Currently, she is a writer and consulting editor for *Ms. Magazine*, the international feminist bimonthly that she cofounded in 1972. Several of her books—*Moving Beyond Words, Revolution from Within: A Book of Self-Esteem*, and *Outrageous Acts and Everyday Rebellions*—have been best-sellers. As an organizer, she has helped to found many associations and projects that empower women and girls. In 1993, her concern with child abuse led her to coproduce and narrate an Emmy-winning TV documentary, "Multiple Personalities: The Search for Deadly Memories." As both a writer and an activist, she remains especially interested in the shared origins of caste systems based on sex and race; in gender roles and child abuse as the roots of violence; in nonviolent conflict resolution; in the cultures of indigenous people; and in organizing across national boundaries for peace and justice.

Eleanor Palo Stoller, Ph.D., is the Selah Chamberlain Professor of Sociology at Case Western Reserve University. Her research explores how older people and their families cope with health declines. She is the author of over forty articles and book chapters and coauthor (with Rose Campbell Gibson) of *Worlds of Difference, Inequality and the Aging Experience*.

Dana Y. Takagi is associate professor of sociology at the University of California at Santa Cruz. Her book *The Retreat from Race: Asian American Admissions and Racial Politics* examines how discursive politics about Asian Americans can significantly shape contemporary debates about affirmative action. Her current work examines the politics of sovereignty in Hawaii.

Ronald T. Takaki is professor of ethnic studies at the University of California at Berkeley. He served as departmental chairperson and also the graduate advisor of the ethnic studies Ph.D. program. He is the author of several books, including *Iron Cages: Race and Culture in 19th Century America, Strangers from* *a Different Shore: A History of Asian Americans,* and *A Different Mirror: A History of Multicultural America.* He helped to establish Berkeley's multicultural requirement for graduation.

Cooper Thompson has been a consultant, writer, and teacher in the field of oppression since 1978. He is a founder and former National Coordinator of the Campaign to End Homophobia. As a heterosexual white man, he is the author of numerous articles on the dynamics of oppression, and he is a coproducer of "Finding Our Way," a unique video on men and sexuality, distributed by New Day Films. Currently, he is conducting interviews across the United States with white men who have committed their lives to challenging racism. Cooper lives in Cambridge, Massachusetts, where he is a member of the Cambridge Human Rights Commission. In 1995 he was awarded the Drylongso Award for his work to challenge racism in the metropolitan Boston area.

Alan Tuttle is a contributor to *Off Our Backs* and *On Our Own Two Feet,* publications on men and feminism.

Lynet Uttal is an assistant professor in the Department of Child and Family Studies at the University of Wisconsin, Madison. She uses in-depth interviewing to study employed mothers and their child care arrangements and racial ethnic families.

Steven VanderStaay is associate professor of English at Western Washington University. He is the author of *Street Lives: An Oral History of Homeless Americans* (Philadelphia: New Society Publishers), and a forthcoming book, *School Rules: Juvenile (In)Justice and the Promise of Schooling.*

Mary C. Waters is professor of sociology and Harvard College Professor at Harvard University. She is the author of *Black Identities: West Indian Immigrant Dreams and American Realities, Ethnic Options: Choosing Identities in America,* and numerous articles on race, ethnicity, and immigration.

Lynn Weber is the director of the women's studies program at the University of South Carolina and a professor of sociology. Her research and teaching explore the intersections of race, class, gender, and sexuality particularly as they are manifest in the process of upward social mobility, in the work world, in women's mental health, and in the creation of an inclusive classroom environment. She is the coauthor of *The American Perception of Class* and is currently writing a book on race, class, gender, and sexuality in everyday life.

Cornel West is professor of Afro-American studies and the philosophy of religion at Harvard University. He is the author of numerous books and essays, including *Restoring Hope: Conversations on the Future of Black America* (with Shawn Sealey) and *Race Matters.*

Patricia J. Williams is the author of *the Alchemy of Race and Rights* and *The Diary of a Law Professor.* She is a regular contributor to *The Nation.*

Naomi Wolf was born in San Francisco in 1962. She was educated at Yale University and New College, Oxford University, where she was a Rhodes Scholar. Her essays have appeared in various publications including *The New Republic, Wall Street Journal, Glamour, Ms. Magazine, Esquire, The Washington Post,* and *The New York Times.* She lectures on college campuses and is the author of *The Beauty Myth* and *Fire with Fire.* Currently she is writing *Promiscuities,* a history and memoir of female desire.

Deborah Woo is a sociologist on the faculty in the Community Studies Department at the University of California at Santa Cruz. Her research has revolved around issues of cultural diversity and racial/ethnic inequality in the areas of health/mental health, education, and work, with primary concern with uncovering how the claim to institutional "objectivity" can often camouflage biases which reinforce social inequities. In 1994 she completed a research monograph commissioned by the Department of Labor's Federal Glass Ceiling Commission (Barriers to Work Place Advancement Experienced by Asian Americans). This work became the basis for a more extensive analysis of mobility barriers, published in her new book, *Glass Ceilings and Asian Americans: The New Face of Workplace Barriers* (AltaMira Press, A Division of Rowman and Littlefield Publishers, Inc., 2000).

Gloria Yamato is currently the community relations associate for the Pacific Northwest Regional Office of the American Friends Service Committee. She is also the acting Executive Director for ACT/fra, an organization for community-based social/economic change. She has contributed essays to *Changing Our Power* and *Making Face, Making Soul/Haciendo Caras.*

Helen Zia is a former executive editor of *Ms. Magazine* and is the author of *Asian American Dreams: The Emergence of an American People.* She resides in the San Francisco Bay Area.

Maxine Baca Zinn is professor of sociology at Michigan State University and senior research associate in the Julian Samora Research Institute. She is co-editor of *Women of Color in U.S. Society* (with Bonnie Thornton Dill), coauthor of *Diversity in Families, in Conflict and Order,* and *Social Problems* (with D. Stanley Eitzen), and the coeditor of *Gender Through the Prism of Difference: A Sex and Gender Reader* (with Pierrette Hondagneu-Sotelo and Michael A. Messner).

Introduction

TOWARD INCLUSIVE THINKING THROUGH THE STUDY OF RACE, CLASS, AND GENDER

Anyone who takes even a cursory look at the contemporary United States has to acknowledge that this is one of the most diverse nations in the world. Different racial and ethnic groups populate American cities, suburbs, and small towns. In schools, students speak a variety of languages. At work, although different groups are still segregated into specific jobs, the presence of women, new immigrants, and racial minorities is growing. African Americans, Latinos, Asian Americans, and Native Americans together account for an increasing proportion of the total population—so much so that even the term *minority* is misleading, at least in the numerical sense. Furthermore, as shown in Figure 1, the population of the United States will become even more diverse in years to come, as African Americans, Latinos, Asian Americans, and American Indians become a larger proportion of the total population.

What does diversity mean? Because the public has become more conscious of the many differences among us, *diversity* has become a buzzword—a word popularly used, but loosely defined. People use diversity to mean cultural variety, numerical representation, changing social norms, and the inequalities that characterize the status of different groups. In thinking about diversity, people have recognized that gender, age, race, sexual orientation, and ethnicity matter; thus, groups who have previously been invisible, including people of color, gays and lesbians, old people, and immigrants, are now in some ways more visible. At the same time that diversity is more commonly recognized, however, these same groups continue to be defined as "other"; that is, they are perceived through dominant group values, treated in exclusionary ways, and subjected to social injustice and economic inequality. Moreover, dominant ways of thinking remain centered in the experiences of a few. As a result, groups who in total are the majority are still rendered invisible. Thus, while diversity is widely acknowledged, there is still a need to reconstruct how we think—and how we behave—if we are to create a more just society.

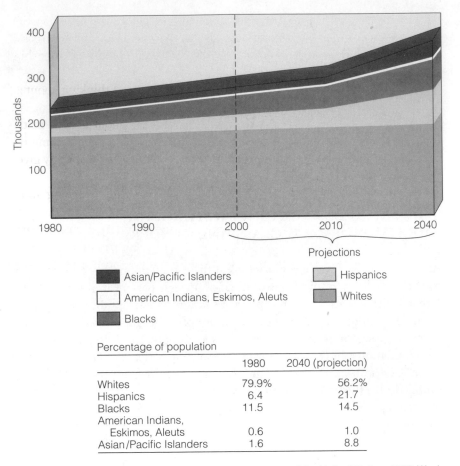

Source: U.S. Census Bureau. 1998. *Statistical Abstracts of the United States, 1998.* Washington, D.C.: U.S. Department of Commerce, p. 19.

FIGURE 1 Share of Minorities in the U.S. Population, 1980–2040.

Understanding the social dynamics of race, class, and gender is central to this new vision. Studying race, class, and gender brings new facts and new perspectives to light, and it illuminates familiar things in new ways. For example, as we explore in the introduction to part II, college basketball can be seen as pure entertainment, but it can also be seen as a social system in which race, class, and gender play a significant part. Also, places that appear to be all-White or all-men can be understood as products of a social system that is premised on certain race, class, and gender arrangements. Understanding the significance of race, class, and gender puts the experience of all groups in the United States in a broader context. Furthermore, knowing how race, class, and gender operate within American national borders helps you see beyond those borders, developing an awareness of how the increasingly global basis of society influences the configuration of race, class, and gender relationships at home.

Thinking about race, class, and gender need not entail thinking about all groups at one time. Rather, it means understanding the experience of any group in context. So, even though writing exclusively about groups in the United States can be seen as writing from a singular place, understanding the United States in a global context means seeing the factors that shape any given experience more completely.

In this vein, studying diversity is not simply a matter of learning about other people's cultures, values, and ways of being; it involves discovering how race, class, and gender—along with factors like age, ethnicity, sexual orientation, and religion—frame people's lives. The point is not just that people are diverse, as if that were a nice and interesting fact of life, but that race, class, and gender are fundamental axes of society and, as such, are critical to understanding people's lives, institutional systems, contemporary social issues, and the possibilities for social change.

This book is part of the new effort to transform thinking by seeing how race, class, and gender operate together to create the experiences of diverse groups in society. In this introduction, we provide a partial framework for approaching the articles in this book. We want students and faculty—as well as our other readers—to understand fundamentally that race, class, and gender are linked experiences, no one of which is more important than the others; the three are interrelated and together configure the structure of this society.

NEW RACE, CLASS, AND GENDER STUDIES

Race, class, and gender shape the experiences of all people in the United States. This fact has been widely documented in research and, to some extent, is commonly understood. Thus, for years, social scientists have studied the consequences of race, class, and gender inequality for diverse groups in society. New race, class, and gender studies, however, have produced new understandings of how race, class, and gender operate together in people's lives. Fundamentally, these studies interpret race, class, and gender as interlocking categories of experience that affect all aspects of human life; thus, they simultaneously structure the experiences of all people in this society. At any moment, race, class, or gender may feel more salient or meaningful in a given person's life, but they are overlapping and cumulative in their effect on people's experience.

Because of their simultaneity in people's lives, in this book we conceptualize race, class, and gender as different but interrelated axes of social structure.

We use the approach of a "matrix of domination" to analyze race, class, and gender. A matrix of domination posits multiple, interlocking levels of domination that stem from the societal configuration of race, class, and gender relations. This structural pattern affects individual consciousness, group interaction, and group access to institutional power and privileges (Collins 2000).

Approaching the study of race, class, and gender from this perspective differs from employing the usual "additive model," which focuses on the independent effects of race, class, and gender on human experience. The additive model is reflected in terms like *double* and *triple jeopardy*—terms used to describe the oppression of women of color by race, as well as by gender and class. We do not think of race and gender oppression in the simple additive terms implied by phrases like *double* and *triple jeopardy*. The effects of race, class, and gender do "add up," both over time and in intensity of impact, but seeing race, class, and gender only in additive terms misses the social structural connections between them and the particular ways in which different configurations of race, class, and gender affect group experience.

The additive model also tends to assess the impact of race, class, and gender exclusively on the experience of women and people of color, rather than seeing them as an integral part of social structures that shape the experience of all groups. The additive model also places people in "either/or" categories, as if one is either Black or White, oppressed or oppressor, powerful or powerless. We do not think that people can be dichotomized so easily. To begin with, race is not a fixed category, but a socially constructed category whose meaning shifts over time. This is not well understood, particularly in the United States, where race has been construed as a biological phenomenon. In other places, such as Great Britain, race is more typically understood as a political construct—as is ethnicity in national contexts where ethnicity is the basis for significant social conflict.

Although socially constructed, race nonetheless has actual consequences for different groups. Consider the U.S. census, a practice that involves counting and categorizing groups for purposes of representation in government, allocating of federal and state resources, and drawing political boundaries. How one is counted—indeed, whether one is counted—is of enormous importance. Underestimating the number of homeless, for example, affects the resources made available to assist them. Yet, many people do not see themselves as fitting neatly into the defined categories, as is the case for the growing number of multiracial people. Whether one even has the choice to define one's group membership is a question of state policy, which can change. The point is that race is a fluid, not a fixed, concept that develops in specific historical contexts, that defines power relations in society, and that develops within the particular circumstances faced by diverse groups.

New race, class, and gender studies also interpret the division between powerful and powerless, or between oppressor and oppressed, as not being clear cut. White women, for example, may be disadvantaged because of gender, but privileged by race and perhaps (but not necessarily) by class. Increasing class differentiation within racial-ethnic groups reminds us that race is not a monolithic category. Rather, race *and* class shape the experiences of, for example, Asian Americans, African Americans, and White Americans. For that matter, White Americans do not fit in "either/or" categories—either oppressor or oppressed. Isolating White Americans as if their experience stands alone ignores how White experience is intertwined with that of other groups.

Race, class, and gender are manifested differently, depending on their configuration with the others. Thus, although from the perspective of an additive model, one might say Black men are privileged as men, this makes no sense when their race *and* gender *and* class are taken into account. Otherwise, how can we possibly explain the particular disadvantages African American men experience *as men*—in the criminal justice system, in education, and in the labor market? For that matter, how can we explain the experience that Native American women experience *as Native American women*—disadvantaged by the unique experiences that they have based on race, class, and gender—none of which is isolated from the effects of the others?

DIVERSITY AND MULTICULTURALISM

Approaching the study of race, class, and gender from the perspective of the matrix of domination means that we see our work as differing somewhat from the concepts implicit in the language of "diversity" or "multiculturalism." Clearly, our work is part of these movements, but we find the framework of multiculturalism and diversity to be limited. Why do we find this problematic?

Diversity has become a catchword for trying to understand the complexities of race, class, and gender in the United States. The movement to promote diversity has made people more sensitive and aware of the intersections of race, class, and gender, and we are glad to be part of this. Thinking about diversity has also encouraged students and activists to see linkages to other forms of oppression, including sexuality, age, region, physical disability, national identity, and ethnicity; but "understanding diversity" is not the only point. The very term *diversity* implies that understanding race, class, and gender is simply a matter of recognizing the plurality of views and experiences in society—as if race, class, and gender oppression were just the sum total of different experiences. We want readers to be more analytical. Analyzing race, class, and gender involves more than "appreciating cultural diversity." It requires analysis and criticism of existing systems of power and privilege; otherwise, understanding diversity becomes just one more privilege for those with the greatest access to education—something that has always been a mark of the elite class. Analyzing race, class, and gender as they shape different group experiences also involves addressing issues of power, privilege, and equity. This means more than just knowing the cultures of an array of human groups. It means recognizing and analyzing the hierarchies and systems of domination that permeate society and that systematically exploit and control people.

In this sense, we distinguish "thinking comparatively" from "thinking relationally." People think comparatively when they learn about experiences other than their own and begin comparing and contrasting the experiences of different groups. This is a step beyond centering one's thinking in a single group (typically one's own), but it is nonetheless limited. For example, when students encounter studies of race, class, and gender for the first time, they often ask, "How is this group's experience like or not like my own?" This is an important question and a necessary first step, but it is not enough. For one thing, it tends to promote groups ranking one anothers' oppression, as if the important thing were to determine who is most victimized. Furthermore, it frames one's understanding of different groups only within the context of other groups' experiences; thus, it can assume an artificial norm against which different groups are judged. Although thinking comparatively is an important step toward thinking more inclusively, we must go further.

Relational thinking involves seeing the interrelationships among diverse group experiences. When you think relationally, you see the social structures that simultaneously generate unique group histories and link them together in society. This does not mean that one group's experience is the same as another's, although finding commonalities is an important step toward more inclusive thinking. In thinking relationally, you untangle the workings of social systems that shape the experiences of different people and groups, and you move beyond just comparing (for example) gender oppression with race oppression, or the oppression of gays and lesbians with that of racial groups. When you recognize the systems of power that mark different groups' experiences, you possess the conceptual apparatus to think about changing the system, not just about documenting the effects of that system on different people.

This process also differs from simply adding up all the experiences of groups who have been defined as "other." Certainly, opening our awareness of distinct group experiences is important, but one need not know the experience of every single combination of oppressions to understand how the social system works. For example, some people in recent years have tended to think of race, class, and gender in terms of a "voices" metaphor—a metaphor that appropriately arose from challenging the silence surrounding many group experiences. In this framework, people think about diversity as "listening to the voices" of a multitude of previously silenced groups. This is an important part of coming to understand race, class, and gender, but it is not enough.

One problem is that people may begin hearing the voices as if they were disembodied from particular historical and social conditions—a framework that has been exacerbated by postmodernist trends in feminist theory. This perspective sees experience as a matter of competing discourses, personifying "voice" as if the voice or discourse itself constituted lived experience. Second, the "voices" framework suggests that any analysis is incomplete unless every voice is heard. In a sense, of course, this is true, since inclusion of silenced people is one of the goals of multicultural work. But an analysis grounded in race, class, and gender can be complete even if centered on the experience of a single group—as long as that group's experience is situated within a framework that recognizes the influence of race, class, and gender on group experience.

Finally, we see limits to the multicultural movement because we think it is important to challenge the idea that diversity is important only at the level of culture—an implication of the term *multiculturalism. Culture* is traditionally defined as the "total way of life" of a group of people. It encompasses both material and symbolic components and is an important dimension of understanding human life. Analysis of culture per se, however, tends to look at the group itself, rather than at the broader conditions within which the group lives. Of course, as anthropologists know, a sound analysis of culture situates group experience within these external conditions. Nonetheless, the focus on culture tends to ignore social conditions of power, privilege, and prestige. The result is that multicultural studies often seem tangled up with notions of cultural pluralism—as if knowing a culture other than one's own is the goal of a multicultural education.

We think it is important to see the diversity and plurality of different cultural forms; but in our view this perspective, taken in and of itself, misses the broader point of understanding how racism, sexism, homophobia, and class relations have shaped the experience of groups. Imagine, for example, trying to study the oppression of gays and lesbians in terms of gay culture only. Obviously, doing this turns attention onto the group itself, and away from the dominant society. Likewise, studying race in terms of Latino culture or Asian American culture or African American culture, or studying women's oppression only by looking at women's culture, encourages thinking that blames the victims for their own oppression. For all of these reasons, the focus of this book is on the institutional, or structural, bases for race, class, and gender relations.

ORGANIZATION OF THE BOOK

We have organized the book to follow this thinking. Part I, "Shifting the Center and Reconstructing Knowledge," contains personal reflections on how race, class, and gender shape individual and collective experiences. These articles provide a fresh beginning point for social thought by putting those who have traditionally been excluded at the center of our thought. These different accounts are not meant to represent everyone who has been excluded, but to ground readers in the practice of thinking about the lives of people who rarely occupy the center of dominant group thinking. When excluded groups are placed in the forefront of thought, they are typically stereotyped and distorted. When you look at society through the different perspectives of persons reflecting on their location within systems of race, class, and gender oppression, you begin to see just how much race, class, and gender really matter.

In part II of the book, "Conceptualizing Race, Class, and Gender," we provide a basic conceptual grounding for these three major concepts. Although we do not consider them separate systems, we treat them separately here for analytical purposes, so students will understand how each operates and then be better able to see their interlocking nature. We also want students to see the continuing effects of race, class, and gender on people's experiences: our introduction to this section and the articles within document those effects and point to the interrelationships between them.

In part III, "Rethinking Institutions," we examine how race, class, and gender shape the organization of social institutions and how, as a result, these institutions affect group experience. Social scientists routinely document how different race, class, and gender groups are affected by institutional structures. We know this is true, but want to go beyond these analyses to scrutinize how institutions are constructed through race, class and gender relations. As contemporary feminist scholars argue, institutions are "gendered" (Acker 1992). We should add that they are also "racially formed" (Omi and Winant 1994) and organized as class systems.

Part IV, "Analyzing Social Issues," uses the inclusive perspective gained by understanding race, class, and gender to analyze contemporary social issues. We examine American identity, sexuality, and violence—social issues that are hotly contested in public discourse and that we think can be properly understood only if they are located within a race, class, and gender analysis. Indeed, we think that these social issues are hotly contested *because* they evolve from contemporary race, class, and gender politics. Although specific social issues may change from time to time, contemporary discussions of American identity and culture, sexual politics, and the causes and consequences of violence are framed by implicit and explicit assumptions that stem from competing ideologies of race, class, and gender. Understanding the social issues on the public agenda requires an analysis of race, class, and gender relations.

Finally, in part V, "Making a Difference," we look at social change. When studying the effects of race, class, and gender, a person can all too easily think only in terms of how people are victimized and oppressed by these systems. Throughout the book, we have avoided a "social problems approach" because we want readers to move away from thinking exclusively in a problem-centered framework. Race, class, and gender do indeed form the basis of many social problems, but a problems-based approach has three serious limitations: it tends to portray people primarily as victims, while ignoring their independent views of themselves and their society; it tends to see oppressed groups only from the perspective of the more privileged, relegating those who most suffer under race, class, and gender oppression to the status of "others," thereby reproducing the hierarchical viewpoints that have permeated traditional thinking; and it tends to leave students feeling that they have no power to make changes in the society.

People are not just victims; they are creative and visionary. As a result, people organize to resist oppression and to make liberating social changes. In fact, oppression generates resistance. In part V we examine the meaning of activism and its connection to the conditions in which people live. We see these articles as providing a basis for understanding how people can make a difference—something that we find often puzzles students. These articles suggest that change takes place through new actions and new social structures, and sometimes through existing channels; but unless one has an inclusive framework from which to make change, one's action is limited. Resistance to oppression on behalf of one's own group is not enough. Truly multicultural change takes place only when people and groups build coalitions with others. Change also takes place over the long run. Short-term actions are needed, but the dedication needed to achieve long-term, institutional changes must be sustained by new visions. We hope the articles in this volume provide a visionary approach to the future.

In selecting articles for the anthology, we tried to find pieces that would show the intersections of race, class, and gender. Not every article does this, but we consider it equally important for students to learn to recognize connections between groups and social structural conditions even when these are not obvious. We searched for articles that are conceptually and theoretically informed, and at the same time accessible to undergraduate readers. Although it is important to think of race, class, and gender as analytical categories, we do not want to lose sight of how they affect human experiences and feelings; thus, we have included personal narratives that are reflective and analytical. We think that personal accounts generate empathy and also help us connect personal experiences to social structural conditions.

We have tried to be as inclusive of all groups as possible, representing the richness of difference and diversity within the United States. It is impossible to include all historically and presently marginalized groups in one book, so we encourage readers to explore the many other works available. We have selected materials that explain the relationships among race, class, and gender and that illuminate the experiences of many groups, not just the groups about whom an article is specifically written. As we begin to untangle the structure of race, class, and gender relations, we can better see both the commonalities and differences that various historical and contemporary experiences have generated.

We also want students to learn that thinking about race, class, and gender is not just a matter of studying victims. We remind students that race, class, and gender have affected the experiences of all groups. As a result, we do not think we should talk only about women when talking about gender, or only about people of color when talking about race. Because race, class, and gender affect the experience of all, it is important to study men when analyzing gender, to study whites when analyzing race, and to study the experience of the affluent when analyzing class. If we are thinking in an inclusive way, we will think about women, not just men, when studying race; Latinos and other people of color, when thinking about class; and women and men of color when studying gender.

In addition, we should not relegate the study of racial-ethnic groups, the working class, and women only to subjects marked explicitly as race, class, or gender studies. As categories of social experience, race, class, and gender shape all social institutions and systems of meaning; thus, it is important to think about people of color, different class experiences, and women in analyzing all social institutions and belief systems.

Developing truly inclusive thinking and teaching is a long-term process that involves personal, intellectual, and political change. We do not claim to be models of perfection in this regard. We have been pleased by the strong response to the first three editions of this book, and we are fascinated by how race, class, and gender studies have developed in the short period of time since the publication of the first edition. We know further work is needed. Our own teaching and thinking has been transformed by developing this book. We imagine many changes still to come.

References

Acker, Joan. 1992. "Gendered Institutions: From Sex Roles to Gendered Institutions." *Contemporary Sociology* 21 (September): 565–69.

Collins, Patricia Hill. 2000. *Black Feminist Thought: Knowledge, Consciousness, and Empowerment.* 2d ed. New York: Routledge.

Omi, Michael, and Howard Winant. 1994. *Racial Formation in the United States: From the 1960s to the 1990s.* 2d ed. New York: Routledge.

Suggested Readings

Anzaldua, Gloria. 1990. *Making Face, Making Soul. Haciendo Caras: Creative and Critical Perspectives by Women of Color.* San Francisco: Aunt Lute Books.

Baca Zinn, Maxine, Pierrette Hondagneu-Sotelo, and Michael A. Messner. 1999. *Gender through the Prism of Difference.* 2d ed. Needham Heights, MA: Allyn & Bacon.

Chow, Esther Ngan-Ling, Doris Wilkinson, and Maxine Baca Zinn, eds. 1996. *Race, Class, & Gender: Common Bonds, Different Voices.* Thousand Oaks, CA: Sage.

Davis, Angela. 1981. *Women, Race, and Class.* New York: Random House.

Delgado, Richard. 1998. *The Latino Condition: A Critical Reader.* New York: New York University Press.

Dill, Bonnie Thornton, and Maxine Baca Zinn, eds. 1994. *Women of Color in U.S. Society*. Philadelphia: Temple University Press.

Guy-Sheftall, Beverly, ed. 1995. *Words of Fire: An Anthology of African-American Feminist Thought*. New York: New Press.

Schneider, Beth E., and Peter M. Nardi, eds. 1998. *Social Perspectives in Lesbian and Gay Studies: A Reader*. New York: Routledge.

Segrest, Mab. 1994. *Memoir of a Race Traitor*. Boston: South End Press.

InfoTrac College Edition: Search Terms

Use your access to the online library, InfoTrac College Edition, to learn more about subjects covered in this section. The following are some suggested terms for searches:

African American studies
antimiscegenation
anti-Semitism
Chicano studies (and Latino studies)
critical race theory
de jure/de facto segregation
lesbian identity
marginality
Native American studies
segregation
women's studies

Wadsworth Sociology Resource Center: Virtual Society

For additional links, quizzes, and learning tools related to this section, see the Wadsworth Sociology Resource Center, Virtual Society, at **http://sociology.wadsworth.com**.

I

Shifting the Center and Reconstructing Knowledge

We begin this book by asking, Who has been excluded from what is known, and how might we see the world differently if we were to acknowledge and value the experiences and thoughts of those who have been excluded? Many groups whose experiences have been vital in the formation of American society and culture have been silenced in the construction of knowledge about this society. The result is that what we know—about the experiences of both these silenced groups and the dominant culture—is distorted and incomplete.

As examples, think about the large number of social science studies that routinely make general conclusions about *the* population, when they have been based on research done only about and by men. Or, think about the content of history courses (and, for that matter, music, art, and literature courses) and how little the work of women, Asian Americans, Latinos, African Americans, Native Americans, gays, and lesbians is included. By excluding or marginalizing these groups, do we not communicate that they have no history or that their history is less important and less central to the development of American culture than is the history of White American men? What false conclusions does this exclusionary thinking generate? One example is the claim that democracy and egalitarianism were central cultural beliefs in the early history of the United States. If this is true, how do we explain the enslavement of millions of African Americans? the genocide of Native Americans? the laws against intermarriage between Asian Americans and White Americans? Without more inclusive thinking, our knowledge of American society and history is limited or wrong, and we are left only with contemporary stereotypes and misleading information as the basis for our knowledge about each other.

"Shifting the center" means putting at the center of our thinking the experiences of groups who have formerly been excluded. Without doing so, many groups simply remain invisible. When they are seen, they are typically judged through the experiences of White people, rather than understood on their own terms; this establishes a false norm through which all groups are judged. This is well expressed by Scott Kurashige, who writes, "The public view of Asian Americans is a lot like that of Casper the Ghost: we're either white or we're invisible" (Kurashige 1994).

Shifting the center is a shift in stance that illuminates the experiences not only of the oppressed groups but also of those in the dominant culture. For example, the development of women's studies has changed what we know and how we think about women; at the same time, it has changed what we know and how we think about men. This does not mean that women's studies is about "male-bashing." It means that we take the experiences of women and men seriously and analyze the way that gender, race, and class have shaped the experiences of both—although in different but interrelated ways. Likewise, the study of racial-ethnic groups begins by learning the diverse histories and experiences of these groups, but in doing so, we transform our understanding of White experiences, too. The exclusionary thinking we have relied upon in the past simply does not reveal the intricate interconnections that exist between the different groups composing American society.

Exclusionary thinking is increasingly being challenged by scholars and teachers who want to include the diversity of human experience in the construction and transmission of knowledge. Thinking more inclusively opens up the way the world is viewed, making the experience of previously excluded groups more visible and central in the construction of knowledge. Inclusive thinking shifts our perspective from the White, male-centered forms of thinking that have characterized much of Western thought, helping us better understand the intersections of race, class, and gender in the experiences of all groups, including those with privilege and power.

Why would we want to do this? Does reconstructing knowledge matter? To begin with, knowledge is not just some abstract thing—good to have, but not all that important. There are real consequences to having partial or distorted knowledge. First, learning about other groups helps you realize the partiality of your own perspective; furthermore, this is true for both dominant and subordinate groups. Knowing only the history of African Americans, for example, or seeing that history only in single-minded terms will not reveal the historical linkages between the oppression of African Americans and the exclusionary and exploitative treatment of other groups. This is well pointed out by Ronald Takaki in his essay on the multicultural history of American society included here.

Second, having misleading and incorrect knowledge gives us a poor social analysis and leads to the formation of bad social policy—policy that then reproduces, rather than solves, social problems. Finally, knowledge is not just about content and information; it provides an orientation to the world. What you know frames how you behave and how you think about yourself and others. If what you know is wrong because it is based on exclusionary thought, you are likely to act in exclusionary ways, thereby reproducing the racism, anti-Semitism, sexism, class oppression, and homophobia of society. This may not be because you are overtly racist, anti-Semitic, sexist, elitist, or homophobic (although it may encourage these beliefs); it may simply be because you do not know any better. Challenging oppressive race, class, and gender relations in society requires a reconstruction of knowledge so that we have some basis from which to change these damaging and dehumanizing systems of oppression.

As we said in the preface, developing inclusive thinking is more than just "understanding diversity" or valuing cultural pluralism. Inclusive thinking begins with the recognition that the United States is a multicultural and diverse society. Population data reveal that simple truth, but inclusive thinking is more than recognizing the plurality of experiences in this society. Understanding race, class, and gender means coming to see the systematic exclusion and exploitation of different groups. This is more than just adding in different group experiences to already established frameworks of thought. It means constructing new analyses that are focused on the centrality of race, class, and gender in the experiences of us all.

You can begin to develop a more inclusive perspective by asking, How does the world look different if we put the experiences of those who have been excluded at the center of our thinking? At first, people might be tempted to simply assert the perspective and experience of their own group. Nationalist movements of different kinds have done this. They are valuable because they recognize the contributions and achievements of oppressed groups, but ultimately they are unidimensional frameworks because they are centered in a single group experience and they encourage, rather than discourage, exclusionary thought.

Seeing inclusively is more than just seeing the world through the perspective of any one group whose views have been distorted or ignored. Remember that group membership cuts across race, class, and gender categories: for example, one may be a working-class, Asian American woman or a Black, middle-class man or a gay, White, working-class woman. Inclusive thinking means seeing the interconnections between these experiences and not reducing a given person's or group's life to a single factor. In addition, developing inclusive thinking is more than just summing up the experiences of individual groups. Race, class, and gender are social structural categories. This means that they are embedded in the institutional structure of society. Understanding them requires a social structural analysis—by which we mean revealing the race, class, and gender patterns and processes that form the very framework of society.

We believe that shifting our perspective by thinking about the experiences of those who have been excluded from knowledge changes how we think about society, history, and culture. No longer do different groups seem just "different" or "deviant." Rather, specific patterns of the intersections of race, class, and gender are revealed, as are the connections that exist between groups. We then learn how our different experiences are linked, both historically and now.

Once we understand that race, class, and gender are simultaneous and intersecting systems of relationship and meaning, we come to see the different ways that other categories of experience intersect in society. Age, religion, sexual orientation, physical ability, region, and ethnicity also shape systems of privilege and inequality. We have tried to integrate these different experiences throughout the book, although we could not include as much as we would have liked.

Seeing these connections is what we think is most important about analyzing race, class, and gender. It is the reason for taking the perspective of people other than those like you. The purpose of the articles in "Shifting the Center" is not to appropriate others' experiences but to begin uncovering the structures of race, class, and gender that are embedded in the experiences of all people.

By providing personal accounts of what exclusion means and how it feels, the articles in part I show the limits of existing knowledge. We have selected personal accounts that reflect the diverse experiences of race, class, gender, and/or sexual orientation. We intend for the personal nature of these accounts to build empathy between groups—an emotional stance that we think is critical to seeing linkages and connections. By describing how exclusion shapes individual and collective consciousness, these accounts also document the diversity of experience within the United States. As a result, we begin to see how diverse experiences can shape the concepts and theories we develop in the academy. Together, they suggest new possibilities for thinking inclusively and imagining a society that would be more enabling for everyone.

In "Missing People and Others," Arturo Madrid tells how exclusion and marginalization in the educational curriculum have affected us all. Madrid describes his schooling as a process of denial of the specific experience of Latinos, Asian Americans, Native Americans, and all other groups together considered to be "other." He asks us to consider what it feels like to be the missing person. As we read his account, we see how education has contributed to exclusion by marginalizing the history of Chicanos and groups considered to be "other."

In "La Güera," Cherríe Moraga writes about her developing awareness of her class, race, and sexual identity. Like the other authors here, Moraga tells us what exclusion has meant in her experience and how it feels. Her essay also reveals the intersections of race, class, and gender with the system of compulsory heterosexuality—that is, the institutionalized structures and beliefs that define and enforce heterosexual behavior as the only natural and permissible form of sexual expression. For Moraga, acknowledging her lesbian identity deepened her understanding of her mother's oppression as a poor Chicana. Moraga reminds us of the importance of breaking the silences that protect oppression.

Readers should keep the accounts of Madrid and Moraga in mind as they read the remainder of this book. What new experiences, understandings, theories, histories, and analyses do these readings inspire? What does it take for a member of one group (say a White male) to be willing to learn from and value the experiences of another (for example, a Chicana lesbian)? June Jordan's essay, "Report from the Bahamas" is a model of this inclusive thinking. In it she begins from her own experience as a Black, middle-class, well-educated woman and reflects on her connections with other women in different locations in the race, class, gender system. In doing so, she finds connections in surprising places, while also understanding the differences that distinguish our experiences. She also shows her student, a White Catholic Irish woman, finding common ground with her South African classmate. There are no simple or singular answers to these questions, but recentering our frame of reference can reshape what we know, both formally and in everyday life. These essays show that, although we are caught in multiple systems, we can learn to see our connection to others. This is not just an intellectual exercise. As Paula Gunn Allen shows in her article on Native American women, "Angry Women Are Building," it is a matter of survival. Resisting systems of oppression means revising the ideas about ourselves and others that have been created as a part of a system of social control.

Reading these articles shows us the radical shift that thinking inclusively requires. Such a shift begins with valuing the experiences of those who have been excluded and questioning the assumptions made about all groups. When we begin to take a more inclusive perspective, divisions between privileged and underprivileged, oppressor and oppressed are challenged because we start to see race, class, and gender as intersecting systems of experience. For example, White women and women of color share some common experiences based on their gender, but their racial experiences are quite distinct; moreover, experiences within the race/gender system are further conditioned by one's class.

Engaging oneself at the personal level is critical to this process of thinking inclusively. Changing one's mind is not just a matter of assessing facts and data, though that is important; it also requires examining one's feelings. That is why we begin with several personal narratives. Unlike more conventional forms of sociological data (such as surveys, interviews, and even direct observations), personal accounts are more likely to elicit emotional responses. Traditionally, social science has defined emotional engagement as an impediment to objectivity. Sociology, for example, has emphasized rational thought as the basis for social action and has often discouraged more personalized reflection, but the capacity to reflect on one's experience makes us distinctly human. Personal documents tap the private, reflective dimension of life, enabling us to see the inner lives of others and, in the process, revealing our own lives more completely. The idea that objectivity is best reached only through rational thought is a specifically Western and masculine way of thinking—one that we challenge throughout this book.

Including personal narratives is not meant to limit our level of understanding only to individuals. As sociologists, we study individuals in groups as a way of revealing the social structures shaping collective experiences. Through doing so, we discover our common experiences and see the impact of the social structures of race, class, and gender on our experiences. Marilyn Frye's article, "Oppression," introduces the structural perspective that lies at the heart of this book. She distinguishes oppression from suffering, pointing out that many individuals suffer in society, but that oppression is structured into the fabric of social institutions. Using the metaphor of a birdcage, Frye artfully explains the concept of social structure. Looking only at an individual wire in a cage does not reveal the network of wires that forms a cage; likewise, social structure refers to the patterns of behavior, belief, resource distribution, and social control that constitute society.

Analysis of the multicultural basis of society is critical to understanding who we are as a society and a culture. The new focus on multiculturalism is, as Ronald Takaki says in "A Different Mirror," a debate over our national identity. Takaki makes a point of showing the common connections in the histories of African Americans, Chicanos, Irish Americans, Jews, and Native Americans. He argues that only when we understand this multidimensional history will we see ourselves in the full complexity of our humanity.

As all of the authors in this section show, the strength and richness of our society lies in its diversity, but the potential of this diversity will be realized only through social structures that value and protect all human experiences. To reconstruct what we know, we begin with the experiences of those who have been excluded. In so doing, we begin to build a system of knowledge that ensures the survival of us all.

Reference

Kurashige, Scott. 1994. Cited in Karin Aguilar-San Juan, "Linking the Issues: From Identity to Activism." In Karin Aguilar-San Juan, ed., *The State of Asian America: Activism and Resistance in the 1990s*, pp. 1–15. Boston: South End Press.

Suggested Readings

Berry, Mary Frances, and John Blassingame. 1982. *Long Memory: The Black Experience in America*. New York: Oxford University Press.

Collins, Patricia Hill. 2000. *Black Feminist Thought: Knowledge, Consciousness, and Empowerment*. 2d ed. New York: Routledge.

Feagin, Joe R., and Melvin P. Sykes. 1994. *Living with Racism: The Black Middle-Class Experience*. Boston: Beacon Press.

Lorde, Audre. 1984. *Sister Outsider*. Trumansburg, NY: The Crossing Press.

Romero, Mary, Pierrette Hodagneu-Sotelo, and Vilma Ortiz, eds. 1997. *Challenging Fronteras: Structuring Latina and Latino Lives in the U.S.* New York: Routledge.

Takaki, Ronald. 1993. *A Different Mirror: A History of Multicultural America*. Boston: Little, Brown.

Vicinus, Martha, George Chauncey, and Martin Bauml Duberman, eds. 1990. *Hidden from History*. New York: Meridian Books.

InfoTrac College Edition: Search Terms

Use your access to the online library, InfoTrac College Edition, to learn more about subjects covered in this section. The following are some suggested terms for searches:

Chinese Exclusion Act
discrimination
diversity
ethnic studies
immigration
matrix of domination
multicultural studies/multiculturalism
U.S. census and multiracial categories

Wadsworth Sociology Resource Center: Virtual Society

For additional links, quizzes, and learning tools related to this section, see the Wadsworth Sociology Resource Center, Virtual Society, at **http://sociology.wadsworth.com**.

Shifting the Center

MISSING PEOPLE AND OTHERS

Joining Together to Expand the Circle

Arturo Madrid

1

I am a citizen of the United States, as are my parents and as were their parents, grandparents, and great-grandparents. My ancestors' presence in what is now the United States antedates Plymouth Rock, even without taking into account any American Indian heritage I might have.

I do not, however, fit those mental sets that define America and Americans. My physical appearance, my speech patterns, my name, my profession (a professor of Spanish) create a text that confuses the reader. My normal experience is to be asked, "And where are *you* from?"

My response depends on my mood. Passive-aggressive, I answer, "From here." Aggressive-passive, I ask, "Do you mean where am I originally from?" But ultimately my answer to those follow-up questions that ask about origins will be that we have always been from here.

Overcoming my resentment I will try to educate, knowing that nine times out of ten my words fall on inattentive ears. I have spent most of my adult life explaining who I am not. I am exotic, but—as Richard Rodriguez of *Hunger of Memory* fame so painfully found out—not exotic enough . . . not Peruvian, or Pakistani, or Persian, or whatever.

I am, however, very clearly *the other*, if only your everyday, garden-variety, domestic *other*. I've always known that I was *the other*, even before I knew the vocabulary or understood the significance of being *the other*.

I grew up in an isolated and historically marginal part of the United States, a small mountain village in the state of New Mexico, the eldest child of par-

From: *Change* 20 (May/June 1988): 55–59. Reprinted by permission.

ents native to that region and whose ancestors had always lived there. In those vast and empty spaces, people who look like me, speak as I do, and have names like mine predominate. But the *americanos* lived among us: the descendants of those nineteenth-century immigrants who dispossessed us of our lands; missionaries who came to convert us and stayed to live among us; artists who became enchanted with our land and humanscape and went native; refugees from unhealthy climes, crowded spaces, unpleasant circumstances; and, of course, the inhabitants of Los Alamos, whose socio-cultural distance from us was moreover accentuated by the fact that they occupied a space removed from and proscribed to us. More importantly, however, they—*los americanos*—were omnipresent (and almost exclusively so) in newspapers, newsmagazines, books, on radio, in movies and, ultimately, on television.

Despite the operating myth of the day, school did not erase my otherness. It did try to deny it, and in doing so only accentuated it. To this day, schooling is more socialization than education, but when I was in elementary school— and given where I was—socialization was everything. School was where one became an American. Because there was a pervasive and systematic denial by the society that surrounded us that we were Americans. That denial was both explicit and implicit. My earliest memory of the former was that there were two kinds of churches: theirs and ours. The more usual was the implicit denial, our absence from the larger cultural, economic, political and social spaces— the one that reminded us constantly that we were *the other*. And school was where we felt it most acutely.

Quite beyond saluting the flag and pledging allegiance to it (a very intense and meaningful action, given that the U.S. was involved in a war and our brothers, cousins, uncles, and fathers were on the front lines) becoming American was learning English and its corollary—not speaking Spanish. Until very recently ours was a proscribed language—either *de jure* (by rule, by policy, by law) or *de facto* (by practice, implicitly if not explicitly; through social and political and economic pressure). I do not argue that learning English was not appropriate. On the contrary. Like it or not, and we had no basis to make any judgments on that matter, we were Americans by virtue of having been born Americans, and English was the common language of Americans. And there was a myth, a pervasive myth, that said that if we only learned to speak English well—and particularly without an accent—we would be welcomed into the American fellowship.

Senator Sam Hayakawa notwithstanding, the true text was not our speech, but rather our names and our appearance, for we would always have an accent, however perfect our pronunciation, however excellent our enunciation, however divine our diction. That accent would be heard in our pigmentation, our physiognomy, our names. We were, in short, *the other*.

Being *the other* means feeling different; is awareness of being distinct; is consciousness of being dissimilar. It means being outside the game, outside the circle, outside the set. It means being on the edges, on the margins, on the periphery. Otherness means feeling excluded, closed out, precluded, even disdained and scorned. It produces a sense of isolation, of apartness, of disconnectedness, of alienation.

Being *the other* involves a contradictory phenomenon. On the one hand being *the other* frequently means being invisible. Ralph Ellison wrote eloquently about that experience in his magisterial novel *The Invisible Man*. On the other hand, being *the other* sometimes involves sticking out like a sore thumb. What is she/he doing here?

If one is *the other*, one will inevitably be perceived unidimensionally; will be seen stereotypically; will be defined and delimited by mental sets that may not bear much relation to existing realities. There is a darker side to otherness as well. *The other* disturbs, disquiets, discomforts. It provokes distrust and suspicion. *The other* makes people feel anxious, nervous, apprehensive, even fearful. *The other* frightens, scares.

For some of us being *the other* is only annoying; for others it is debilitating; for still others it is damning. Many try to flee otherness by taking on protective colorations that provide invisibility, whether of dress or speech or manner or name. Only a fortunate few succeed. For the majority, otherness is permanently sealed by physical appearance. For the rest, otherness is betrayed by ways of being, speaking or of doing.

I spent the first half of my life downplaying the significance and consequences of otherness. The second half has seen me wrestling to understand its complex and deeply ingrained realities; striving to fathom why otherness denies us a voice or visibility or validity in American society and its institutions; struggling to make otherness familiar, reasonable, even normal to my fellow Americans.

I am also a missing person. Growing up in northern New Mexico I had only a slight sense of our being missing persons. *Hispanos*, as we called (and call) ourselves in New Mexico, were very much a part of the fabric of the society and there were Hispano professionals everywhere about me: doctors, lawyers, school teachers, and administrators. My people owned businesses, ran organizations and were both appointed and elected public officials.

To be sure, we did not own the larger businesses, nor at the time were we permitted to be part of the banking world. Other than that, however, people who looked like me, spoke like me, and had names like mine, predominated. There was, to be sure, Los Alamos, but as I have said, it was removed from our realities.

My awareness of our absence from the larger institutional life of society became sharper when I went off to college, but even then it was attenuated by the circumstances of history and geography. The demography of Albuquerque still strongly reflected its historical and cultural origins, despite the influx of Midwesterners and Easterners. Moreover, many of my classmates at the University of New Mexico in Albuquerque were Hispanos, and even some of my professors were.

I thought that would obtain at UCLA, where I began graduate studies in 1960. Los Angeles already had a very large Mexican population, and that population was visible even in and around Westwood and on the campus. Many of the groundskeepers and food-service personnel at UCLA were Mexican. But Mexican-American students were few and mostly invisible, and I do not recall seeing or knowing a single Mexican-American (or, for that matter, black, Asian, or American Indian) professional on the staff or faculty of that institution during the five years I was there.

Needless to say, persons like me were not present in any capacity at Dartmouth College—the site of my first teaching appointment—and, of course, were not even part of the institutional or individual mind-set. I knew then that we—a "we" that had come to encompass American Indians, Asian Americans, black Americans, Puerto Ricans, and women—were truly missing persons in American institutional life.

Over the past three decades, the *de jure* and *de facto* segregations that have historically characterized American institutions have been under assault. As a consequence, minorities and women have become part of American institutional life, and although there are still many areas where we are not to be found, the missing persons phenomenon is not as pervasive as it once was.

However, the presence of *the other*, particularly minorities, in institutions and in institutional life, is, as we say in Spanish, *a flor de tierra;* spare plants whose roots do not go deep, a surface phenomenon, vulnerable to inclemencies of an economic, political, or social nature.

Our entrance into and our status in institutional life is not unlike a scenario set forth by my grandmother's pastor when she informed him that she and her family were leaving their mountain village to relocate in the Rio Grande Valley. When he asked her to promise that she would remain true to the faith and continue to involve herself in the life of the church, she assured him that she would and asked him why he thought she would do otherwise.

"Doña Trinidad," he told her, "in the Valley there is no Spanish church. There is only an American church." "But," she protested, "I read and speak English and would be able to worship there." Her pastor's response was: "It is possible that they will not admit you, and even if they do, they might not accept you. And that is why I want you to promise me that you are going to go to church. Because if they don't let you in through the front door, I want you to go in through the back door. And if you can't get in through the back door, go in the side door. And if you are unable to enter through the side door I want you to go in through the window. What is important is that you enter and that you stay."

Some of us entered institutional life through the front door; others through the back door; and still others through side doors. Many, if not most of us, came in through windows and continue to come in through windows. Of those who entered through the front door, some never made it past the lobby; others were ushered into corners and niches. Those who entered through back and side doors inevitably have remained in back and side rooms. And those who entered through windows found enclosures built around them. For despite the lip service given to the goal of the integration of minorities into institutional life, what has occurred instead is ghettoization, marginalization, isolation.

Not only have the entry points been limited: in addition, the dynamics have been singularly conflictive. Gaining entry and its corollary—gaining space—have frequently come as a consequence of demands made on institutions and institutional officers. Rather than entering institutions more or less passively, minorities have, of necessity, entered them actively, even aggressively. Rather than taking, they have demanded. Institutional relations have thus been adversarial, infused with specific and generalized tensions.

The nature of the entrance and the nature of the space occupied have greatly influenced the view and attitudes of the majority population within those institutions. All of us are put into the same box; that is, no matter what the individual reality, the assessment of the individual is inevitably conditioned by a perception that is held of the class. Whatever our history, whatever our record, whatever our validations, whatever our accomplishments, by and large we are perceived unidimensionally and are dealt with accordingly.

My most recent experience in this regard is atypical only in its explicitness. A few years ago I allowed myself to be persuaded to seek the presidency of a large and prestigious state university. I was invited for an interview and presented myself before the selection committee, which included members of the board of trustees. The opening question of the brief but memorable interview was directed at me by a member of that august body. "Dr. Madrid," he asked, "why does a one-dimensional person like you think he can be the president of a multi-dimensional institution like ours?"

If, as I happen to believe, the well-being of a society is directly related to the degree and extent to which all of its citizens participate in its institutions, we have a challenge before us. One of the strengths of our society—perhaps its main strength—has been a tradition of struggle against clubbishness, exclusivity, and restriction.

Today, more than ever, given the extraordinary changes that are taking place in our society, we need to take up that struggle again—irritating, grating, troublesome, unfashionable, unpleasant as it is. As educated and educator members of this society, we have a special responsibility for leading the struggle against marginalization, exclusion, and alienation.

Let us work together to assure that all American institutions, not just its precollegiate educational and penal institutions, reflect the diversity of our society. Not to do so is to risk greater alienation on the part of a growing segment of our society. It is to risk increased social tension in an already conflictive world. And ultimately it is to risk the survival of a range of institutions that, for all their defects and deficiencies, permit us the space, the opportunity, and the freedom to improve our individual and collective lot; to guide the course of our government, and to redress whatever grievances we have. Let us join together to expand, not to close the circle.

LA GÜERA   2

Cherríe Moraga

It requires something more than personal experience to gain a philosophy or point of view from any specific event. It is the quality of our response to the event and our capacity to enter into the lives of others that help us to make their lives and experiences our own.

Emma Goldman[1]

I am the very well-educated daughter of a woman who, by the standards in this country, would be considered largely illiterate. My mother was born in Santa Paula, Southern California, at a time when much of the central valley there was still farm land. Nearly thirty-five years later, in 1948, she was the only daughter of six to marry an anglo, my father.

I remember all of my mother's stories, probably much better than she realizes. She is a fine story-teller, recalling every event of her life with the vividness of the present, noting each detail right down to the cut and color of her dress. I remember stories of her being pulled out of school at the ages of five, seven, nine, and eleven to work in the fields, along with her brothers and sisters; stories of her father drinking away whatever small profit she was able to make for the family; of her going the long way home to avoid meeting him on the street, staggering toward the same destination. I remember stories of my mother lying about her age in order to get a job as a hat-check girl at Agua Caliente Racetrack in Tijuana. At fourteen, she was the main support of the

---

1. Alix Kates Shulman, "Was My Life Worth Living?" *Red Emma Speaks* (New York: Random House, 1972), p. 388.

family. I can still see her walking home alone at 3 a.m., only to turn all of her salary and tips over to her mother, who was pregnant again.

The stories continue through the war years and on: walnut-cracking factories, the Voit Rubber factory, and then the computer boom. I remember my mother doing piecework for the electronics plant in our neighborhood. In the late evening, she would sit in front of the T.V. set, wrapping copper wires into the backs of circuit boards, talking about "keeping up with the younger girls." By that time, she was already in her mid-fifties.

Meanwhile, I was college-prep in school. After classes, I would go with my mother to fill out job applications for her, or write checks for her at the supermarket. We would have the scenario all worked out ahead of time. My mother would sign the check before we'd get to the store. Then, as we'd approach the checkstand, she would say—within earshot of the cashier—"oh honey, you go 'head and make out the check," as if she couldn't be bothered with such an insignificant detail. No one asked any questions.

I was educated, and wore it with a keen sense of pride and satisfaction, my head propped up with the knowledge, from my mother, that my life would be easier than hers. I was educated; but more than this, I was "la güera": fair-skinned. Born with the features of my Chicana mother, but the skin of my Anglo father, I had it made.

No one ever quite told me this (that light was right), but I knew that being light was something valued in my family (who were all Chicano, with the exception of my father). In fact, everything about my upbringing (at least what occurred on a conscious level) attempted to bleach me of what color I did have. Although my mother was fluent in it, I was never taught much Spanish at home. I picked up what I did learn from school and from over-heard snatches of conversation among my relatives and mother. She often called other lower-income Mexicans "braceros," or "wet-backs," referring to herself and her family as "a different class of people." And yet, the real story was that my family, too, had been poor (some still are) and farmworkers. My mother can remember this in her blood as if it were yesterday. But this is something she would like to forget (and rightfully), for to her, on a basic economic level, being Chicana meant being "less." It was through my mother's desire to protect her children from poverty and illiteracy that we became "anglocized"; the more effectively we could pass in the white world, the better guaranteed our future.

From all of this, I experience, daily, a huge disparity between what I was born into and what I was to grow up to become. Because, (as Goldman suggests) these stories my mother told me crept under my "güera" skin. I had no choice but to enter into the life of my mother. *I had no choice.* I took her life into my heart, but managed to keep a lid on it as long as I feigned being the happy, upwardly mobile heterosexual.

When I finally lifted the lid to my lesbianism, a profound connection with my mother reawakened in me. It wasn't until I acknowledged and confronted my own lesbianism in the flesh, that my heartfelt identification with and empathy for my mother's oppression—due to being poor, uneducated, and Chicana—was realized. My lesbianism is the avenue through which I have learned the most about silence and oppression, and it continues to be the most tactile reminder to me that we are not free human beings.

You see, one follows the other. I had known for years that I was a lesbian, had felt it in my bones, had ached with the knowledge, gone crazed with the knowledge, wallowed in the silence of it. Silence *is* like starvation. Don't be fooled. It's nothing short of that, and felt most sharply when one has had a full belly most of her life. When we are not physically starving, we have the luxury to realize psychic and emotional starvation. It is from this starvation that other starvations can be recognized—if one is willing to take the risk of making the connection—if one is willing to be responsible to the result of the connection. For me, the connection is an inevitable one.

What I am saying is that the joys of looking like a white girl ain't so great since I realized I could be beaten on the street for being a dyke. If my sister's being beaten because she's Black, it's pretty much the same principle. We're both getting beaten any way you look at it. The connection is blatant; and in the case of my own family, the difference in the privileges attached to looking white instead of brown are merely a generation apart.

In this country, lesbianism is a poverty—as is being brown, as is being a woman, as is being just plain poor. The danger lies in ranking the oppressions. *The danger lies in failing to acknowledge the specificity of the oppression.* The danger lies in attempting to deal with oppression purely from a theoretical base. Without an emotional, heartfelt grappling with the source of our own oppression, without naming the enemy within ourselves and outside of us, no authentic, nonhierarchical connection among oppressed groups can take place.

When the going gets rough, will we abandon our so-called comrades in a flurry of racist/heterosexist/what-have-you panic? To whose camp, then, should the lesbian of color retreat? Her very presence violates the ranking and abstraction of oppression. Do we merely live hand to mouth? Do we merely struggle with the "ism" that's sitting on top of our own heads?

The answer is: yes, I think first we do; and we must do so thoroughly and deeply. But to fail to move out from there will only isolate us in our own oppression—will only insulate, rather than radicalize us.

To illustrate: a gay male friend of mine once confided to me that he continued to feel that, on some level, I didn't trust him because he was male; that he felt, really, if it ever came down to a "battle of the sexes," I might kill him. I admitted that I might very well. He wanted to understand the source of my distrust. I responded, "You're not a woman. Be a woman for a day. Imagine being a woman." He confessed that the thought terrified him because, to him, being a woman meant being raped by men. He *had* felt raped by men; he wanted to forget what that meant. What grew from that discussion was the realization that in order for him to create an authentic alliance with me, he must deal with the primary source of his own sense of oppression. He must, first, emotion-ally come to terms with what it feels like to be a victim. If he— or anyone— were to truly do this, it would be impossible to discount the oppression of oth-ers, except by again forgetting how we have been hurt.

And yet, oppressed groups are forgetting all the time. There are instances of this in the rising Black middle class, and certainly an obvious trend of such "unconsciousness" among white gay men. Because to remember may mean giving up whatever privileges we have managed to squeeze out of this society by virtue of our gender, race, class, or sexuality.

Within the women's movement, the connections among women of dif-ferent backgrounds and sexual orientations have been fragile, at best. I think this phenomenon is indicative of our failure to seriously address ourselves to some very frightening questions: How have I internalized my own oppres-sion? How have I oppressed? Instead, we have let rhetoric do the job of po-etry. Even the word "oppression" has lost its power. We need a new language, better words that can more closely describe women's fear of and resistance to one another; words that will not always come out sounding like dogma.

What prompted me in the first place to work on an anthology by radical women of color was a deep sense that I had a valuable insight to contribute, by virtue of my birthright and background. And yet, I don't really understand first-hand what it feels like being shitted on for being brown. I understand much more about the joys of it—being Chicana and having family are syn-onymous for me. What I know about loving, singing, crying, telling stories, speaking with my heart and hands, even having a sense of my own soul comes from the love of my mother, aunts, cousins. . . .

But at the age of twenty-seven, it is frightening to acknowledge that I have internalized a racism and classism, where the object of oppression is not only someone outside of my skin, but the someone inside my skin. In fact, to a large degree, the real battle with such oppression, for all of us, begins under the skin. I have had to confront the fact that much of what I value about be-ing Chicana, about my family, has been subverted by anglo culture and my own cooperation with it. This realization did not occur to me overnight. For example, it wasn't until long after my graduation from the private college I'd attended in Los Angeles, that I realized the major reason for my total alien-ation from and fear of my classmates was rooted in class and culture. CLICK.

Three years after graduation, in an apple-orchard in Sonoma, a friend of mine (who comes from an Italian Irish working-class family) says to me, "Che-rríe, no wonder you felt like such a nut in school. Most of the people there were white and rich." It was true. All along I had felt the difference, but not until I had put the words "class" and "color" to the experience, did my feel-ings make any sense. For years, I had berated myself for not being as "free" as my classmates. I completely bought that they simply had more guts than I did—to rebel against their parents and run around the country hitch-hiking, reading books and studying "art." They had enough privilege to be atheists, for chrissake. There was no one around filling in the disparity for me between their parents, who were Hollywood filmmakers, and my parents, who wouldn't know the name of a filmmaker if their lives depended on it (and precisely because their lives didn't depend on it, they couldn't be bothered). But I knew nothing about "privilege" then. White was right. Period. I could pass. If I got educated enough, there would never be any telling.

Three years after that, another CLICK. In a letter to Barbara Smith, I wrote:

> I went to a concert where Ntosake Shange was reading. There, everything exploded for me. She was speaking a language that I knew—in the deepest parts of me—existed, and that I had ignored in my own feminist studies and even in my own writing. What Ntosake caught in me is the realization that in my development as a poet, I have, in many ways, denied the voice of my brown mother—the brown in me. I have acclimated to the sound of a white language which, as my father represents it, does not speak to the emotions in my poems—emotions which stem from the love of my mother.
>
> The reading was agitating. Made me uncomfortable. Threw me into a week-long terror of how deeply I was affected. I felt that I had to start all over again. That I turned only to the perceptions of white middle-class women to speak for me and all women. I am shocked by my own ignorance.

Sitting in that auditorium chair was the first time I had realized to the core of me that for years I had disowned the language I knew best—ignored the words and rhythms that were the closest to me. The sounds of my mother and aunts gossiping—half in English, half in Spanish—while drinking cerveza in the kitchen. And the hands—I had cut off the hands in my poems. But not in conversation; still the hands could not be kept down. Still they insisted on moving.

The reading had forced me to remember that I knew things from my roots. But to remember puts me up against what I don't know. Shange's reading agitated me because she spoke with power about a world that is both alien and common to me: "the capacity to enter into the lives of others." But you can't just take the goods and run. I knew that then, sitting in the Oakland auditorium (as I know in my poetry), that the only thing worth writing about is what seems to be unknown and, therefore, fearful.

The "unknown" is often depicted in racist literature as the "darkness" within a person. Similarly, sexist writers will refer to fear in the form of the vagina, calling it "the orifice of death." In contrast, it is a pleasure to read works such as Maxine Hong Kingston's *Woman Warrior*, where fear and alienation are described as "the white ghosts." And yet, the bulk of literature in this country reinforces the myth that what is dark and female is evil. Consequently, each of us—whether dark, female, or both—has in some way *internalized* this oppressive imagery. What the oppressor often succeeds in doing is simply *externalizing* his fears, projecting them into the bodies of women, Asians, gays, disabled folks, whoever seems most "other."

call me
roach and presumptuous
nightmare on your white pillow
your itch to destroy
the indestructible
part of yourself

Audre Lorde[2]

But it is not really difference the oppressor fears so much as similarity. He fears he will discover in himself the same aches, the same longings as those of the people he has shitted on. He fears the immobilization threatened by his own incipient guilt. He fears he will have to change his life once he has seen himself in the bodies of the people he has called different. He fears the hatred, anger, and vengeance of those he has hurt.

This is the oppressor's nightmare, but it is not exclusive to him. We women have a similar nightmare, for each of us in some way has been both oppressed and the oppressor. We are afraid to look at how we have failed each other. We are afraid to see how we have taken the values of our oppressor into our hearts and turned them against ourselves and one another. We are afraid to admit how deeply "the man's" words have been ingrained in us.

To assess the damage is a dangerous act. I think of how, even as a feminist lesbian, I have so wanted to ignore my own homophobia, my own hatred of myself for being queer. I have not wanted to admit that my deepest personal sense of myself has not quite "caught up" with my "woman-identified" politics. I have been afraid to criticize lesbian writers who choose to "skip over" these issues in the name of feminism. In 1979, we talk of "old gay" and "butch and femme" roles as if they were ancient history. We toss them aside as merely patriarchal notions. And yet, the truth of the matter is that I have sometimes taken society's fear and hatred of lesbians to bed with me. I have sometimes hated my lover for loving me. I have sometimes felt "not woman enough" for her. I have sometimes felt "not man enough." For a lesbian trying to survive in a heterosexist society, there is no easy way around these emotions. Similarly, in a white-dominated world, there is little getting around racism and our own internalization of it. It's always there, embodied in some one we least expect to rub up against.

When we do rub up against this person, *there* then is the challenge. *There* then is the opportunity to look at the nightmare within us. But we usually shrink from such a challenge.

Time and time again, I have observed that the usual response among white women's groups when the "racism issue" comes up is to deny the difference. I have heard comments like, "Well, we're open to *all* women; why

---

2. From "The Brown Menace or Poem to the Survival of Roaches," *The New York Head Shop and Museum* (Detroit: Broadside, 1974), p. 48.

don't they (women of color) come? You can only do so much . . . ." But there is seldom any analysis of how the very nature and structure of the group itself may be founded on racist or classist assumptions. More importantly, so often the women seem to feel no loss, no lack, no absence when women of color are not involved; therefore, there is little desire to change the situation. This has hurt me deeply. I have come to believe that the only reason women of a privileged class will dare to look at *how* it is that *they* oppress, is when they've come to know the meaning of their own oppression. And understand that the oppression of others hurts them personally.

The other side of the story is that women of color and working-class women often shrink from challenging white middle-class women. It is much easier to rank oppressions and set up a hierarchy, rather than take responsibility for changing our own lives. We have failed to demand that white women, particularly those who claim to be speaking for all women, be accountable for their racism.

The dialogue has simply not gone deep enough.

I have many times questioned my right to even work on an anthology which is to be written "exclusively by Third World women." I have had to look critically at my claim to color, at a time when, among white feminist ranks, it is a "politically correct" (and sometimes peripherally advantageous) assertion to make. I must acknowledge the fact that, physically, I have had a *choice* about making that claim, in contrast to women who have not had such a choice, and have been abused for their color. I must reckon with the fact that for most of my life, by virtue of the very fact that I am white-looking, I identified with and aspired toward white values, and that I rode the wave of that Southern California privilege as far as conscience would let me.

Well, now I feel both bleached and beached. I feel angry about this—the years when I refused to recognize privilege, both when it worked against me, and when I worked it, ignorantly, at the expense of others. These are not settled issues. That is why this work feels so risky to me. It continues to be discovery. It has brought me into contact with women who invariably know a hell of a lot more than I do about racism, as experienced in the flesh, as revealed in the flesh of their writing.

I think: what is my responsibility to my roots—both white and brown, Spanish-speaking and English? I am a woman with a foot in both worlds; and I refuse the split. I feel the necessity for dialogue. Sometimes I feel it urgently.

But one voice is not enough, nor two, although this is where dialogue begins. It is essential that radical feminists confront their fear of and resistance to each other, because without this, there *will* be no bread on the table. Simply, we will not survive. If we could make this connection in our heart of hearts, that if we are serious about a revolution—better—if we seriously believe there should be joy in our lives (real joy, not just "good times"), then we need one another. We women need each other. Because my/your solitary, self-asserting "go-for-the-throat-of-fear" power is not enough. The real power, as you and I well know, is collective. I can't afford to be afraid of you, nor you of me. If it takes head-on collisions, let's do it: this polite timidity is killing us.

As Lorde suggests in the passage I cited earlier, it is in looking to the nightmare that the dream is found. There, the survivor emerges to insist on a future, a vision, yes, born out of what is dark and female. The feminist movement must be a movement of such survivors, a movement with a future.

REPORT FROM THE BAHAMAS

3

June Jordan

I am staying in a hotel that calls itself The Sheraton British Colonial. One of the photographs advertising the place displays a middle-aged Black man in a waiter's tuxedo, smiling. What intrigues me most about the picture is just this: while the Black man bears a tray full of "colorful" drinks above his left shoulder, both of his feet, shoes and trouserlegs, up to ten inches above his ankles, stand in the also "colorful" Caribbean salt water. He is so delighted to serve you he will wade into the water to bring you Banana Daquiris while you float! More precisely, he will wade into the water, fully clothed, oblivious to the ruin of his shoes, his trousers, his health, and he will do it with a smile.

I am in the Bahamas. On the phone in my room, a spinning complement of plastic pages offers handy index clues such as CAR RENTAL and CASINOS. A message from the Ministry of Tourism appears among these travelers' tips. Opening with a paragraph of "WELCOME," the message then proceeds to "A PAGE OF HISTORY," which reads as follows:

> New World History begins on the same day that modern Bahamian history begins—October 12, 1492. That's when Columbus stepped ashore—British influence came first with the Eleutherian Adventurers of 1647—After the Revolutions, American Loyalists fled from the newly independent states and settled in the Bahamas. Confederate blockade-runners used the island as a haven during the War between the States, and after the War, a number of Southerners moved to the Bahamas . . .

There it is again. Something proclaims itself a legitimate history and all it does is track white Mr. Columbus to the British Eleutherians through the

From: June Jordan, *On Call: Political Essays* (Boston: South End Press, 1985), pp. 39–49. Reprinted by permission of the author.

Confederate Southerners as they barge into New World surf, land on New World turf, and nobody saying one word about the Bahamian people, the Black peoples, to whom the only thing new in their island world was this weird succession of crude intruders and its colonial consequences.

This is my consciousness of race as I unpack my bathing suit in the Sheraton British Colonial. Neither this hotel nor the British nor the long ago Italians nor the white Delta airline pilots belong here, of course. And every time I look at the photograph of that fool standing in the water with his shoes on I'm about to have a West Indian fit, even though I know he's no fool; he's a middle-aged Black man who needs a job and this is his job—pretending himself a servile ancillary to the pleasures of the rich. (Compared to his options in life, I am a rich woman. Compared to most of the Black Americans arriving for this Easter weekend on a three nights four days' deal of bargain rates, the middle-aged waiter is a poor Black man.)

We will jostle along with the other (white) visitors and join them in the tee shirt shops or, laughing together, learn ruthless rules of negotiation as we, Black Americans as well as white, argue down the price of handwoven goods at the nearby straw market while the merchants, frequently toothless Black women seated on the concrete in their only presentable dress, humble themselves to our careless games:

"Yes? You like it? Eight dollar."

"Five."

"I give it to you. Seven."

And so it continues, this weird succession of crude intruders that, now, includes me and my brothers and my sisters from the North.

This is my consciousness of class as I try to decide how much money I can spend on Bahamian gifts for my family back in Brooklyn. No matter that these other Black women incessantly weave words and flowers into the straw hats and bags piled beside them on the burning dusty street. No matter that these other Black women must work their sense of beauty into these things that we will take away as cheaply as we dare, or they will do without food.

We are not white, after all. The budget is limited. And we are harmlessly killing time between the poolside rum punch and "The Native Show on the Patio" that will play tonight outside the hotel restaurant.

This is my consciousness of race and class and gender identity as I notice the fixed relations between these other Black women and myself. They sell and I buy or I don't. They risk not eating. I risk going broke on my first vacation afternoon.

We are not particularly women anymore; we are parties to a transaction designed to set us against each other.

"Olive" is the name of the Black woman who cleans my hotel room. On my way to the beach I am wondering what "Olive" would say if I told her why I chose The Sheraton British Colonial; if I told her I wanted to swim. I wanted to sleep. I did not want to be harassed by the middle-aged waiter, or his nephew. I did not want to be raped by anybody (white or Black) at all and I calculated that my safety as a Black woman alone would best be assured by a multinational hotel corporation. In my experience, the big guys take customer complaints more seriously than the little ones. I would suppose that's one reason why they're big; they don't like to lose money anymore than I like to be bothered when I'm trying to read a goddamned book underneath a palm tree I paid $264 to get next to. A Black woman seeking refuge in a multinational corporation may seem like a contradiction to some, but there you are. In this case it's a co-incidence of entirely different self-interests: Sheraton/cash = June Jordan's short run safety.

Anyway, I'm pretty sure "Olive" would look at me as though I came from someplace as far away as Brooklyn. Then she'd probably allow herself one indignant query before righteously removing her vacuum cleaner from my room; "and why in the first place you come down you without your husband?"

I cannot imagine how I would begin to answer her.

My "rights" and my "freedom" and my "desire" and a slew of other New World values; what would they sound like to this Black woman described on the card atop my hotel bureau as "Olive the Maid"? "Olive" is older than I am and I may smoke a cigarette while she changes the sheets on my bed. Whose rights? Whose freedom? Whose desire?

And why should she give a shit about mine unless I do something, for real, about hers?

It happens that the book that I finished reading under a palm tree earlier today was the novel, *The Bread Givers*, by Anzia Yezierska. Definitely autobiographical, Yezierska lays out the difficulties of being both female and "a person" inside a traditional Jewish family at the start of the 20th century. That any Jewish woman became anything more than the abused servant of her father or her husband is really an improbable piece of news. Yet Yezierska managed such an unlikely outcome for her own life. In *The Bread Givers*, the heroine also manages an important, although partial, escape from traditional Jewish female destiny. And in the unpardonable, despotic father, the Talmudic scholar of that Jewish family, did I not see my own and hate him twice, again? When the heroine, the young Jewish child, wanders the streets with a filthy pail she borrows to sell herring in order to raise the ghetto rent and when she cries, "Nothing was before me but the hunger in our house, and no bread for the next meal if I didn't sell the herring. No longer like a fire engine, but like a houseful of hungry mouths my heart cried, 'herring—herring! Two cents apiece!'" who would doubt the ease, the sisterhood of conversation possible between that white girl and the Black women selling straw bags on the streets of paradise because they do not want to die? And is it not obvious that the wife of that Talmudic scholar and "Olive," who cleans my room here at the hotel, have more in common than I can claim with either one of them?

This is my consciousness of race and class and gender identity as I collect wet towels, sunglasses, wristwatch, and head towards a shower.

I am thinking about the boy who loaned this novel to me. He's white and he's Jewish and he's pursuing an independent study project with me, at the State University where I teach whether or not I feel like it, where I teach without stint because, like the waiter, I am no fool. It's my job and either I work or I do without everything you need money to buy. The boy loaned me the novel because he thought I'd be interested to know how a Jewish-American writer used English so that the syntax, and therefore the cultural habits of mind expressed by the Yiddish language, could survive translation. He did this because he wanted to create another connection between us on the basis of language, between his knowledge/his love of Yiddish and my knowledge/my love of Black English.

He has been right about the forceful survival of the Yiddish. And I had become excited by this further evidence of the written voice of spoken language protected from the monodrone of "standard" English, and so we had grown closer on this account. But then our talk shifted to student affairs more generally, and I had learned that this student does not care one way or the other about currently jeopardized Federal Student Loan Programs because, as he explained it to me, they do not affect him. He does not need financial help outside his family. My own son, however, is Black. And I am the only family help available to him and that means, if Reagan succeeds in eliminating Federal programs to aid minority students, he will have to forget about furthering his studies, or he or I or both of us will have to hit the numbers pretty big. For these reasons of difference, the student and I had moved away from each other, even while we continued to talk.

My consciousness turned to race, again, and class.

Sitting in the same chair as the boy, several weeks ago, a graduate student came to discuss her grade. I praised the excellence of her final paper; indeed it had seemed to me an extraordinary pulling together of recent left brain/right brain research with the themes of transcendental poetry.

She told me that, for her part, she'd completed her reading of my political essays. "You are so lucky!" she exclaimed.

"What do you mean by that?"

"You have a cause. You have a purpose to your life."

I looked carefully at this white woman; what was she really saying to me?

"What do you mean?" I repeated.

"Poverty. Police violence. Discrimination in general."

(Jesus Christ, I thought: Is that her idea of lucky?)

"And how about you?" I asked.

"Me?"

"Yeah, you. Don't you have a cause?"

"Me? I'm just a middle-aged woman: a housewife and a mother. I'm a nobody."

For a while, I made no response.

First of all, speaking of race and class and gender in one breath, what she said meant that those lucky preoccupations of mine, from police violence to nuclear wipe-out, were not shared. They were mine and not hers. But here she sat, friendly as an old stuffed animal, beaming good will or more "luck" in my direction.

In the second place, what this white woman said to me meant that she did not believe she was "a person" precisely because she had fulfilled the traditional female functions revered by the father of that Jewish immigrant, Anzia Yezierska. And the woman in front of me was not a Jew. That was not the connection. The link was strictly female. Nevertheless, how should that woman and I, another female, connect, beyond this bizarre exchange?

If she believed me lucky to have regular hurdles of discrimination then why shouldn't I insist that she's lucky to be a middle-class white Wasp female who lives in such well-sanctioned and normative comfort that she even has the luxury to deny the power of the privileges that paralyze her life?

If she deserts me and "my cause" where we differ, if, for example, she abandons me to "my" problems of race, then why should I support her in "her" problems of housewifely oblivion?

Recollection of this peculiar moment brings me to the shower in the bathroom cleaned by "Olive." She reminds me of the usual Women's Studies curriculum because it has nothing to do with her or her job: you won't find "Olive" listed anywhere on the reading list. You will likewise seldom hear of Anzia Yezierska. But yes, you will find, from Florence Nightingale to Adrienne Rich, a white procession of independently well-to-do women writers. (Gertrude Stein/Virginia Woolf/Hilda Doolittle are standard names among the "essential" women writers.)

In other words, most of the women of the world—Black and First World and white who work because we must—most of the women of the world persist far from the heart of the usual Women's Studies syllabus.

Similarly, the typical Black history course will slide by the majority experience it pretends to represent. For example, Mary McLeod Bethune will scarcely receive as much attention as Nat Turner, even though Black women who bravely and efficiently provided for the education of Black people hugely outnumber those few Black men who led successful or doomed rebellions against slavery. In fact, Mary McLeod Bethune may not receive even honorable mention because Black history too often apes those ridiculous white history courses which produce such dangerous gibberish as The Sheraton British Colonial "history" of the Bahamas. Both Black and white history courses exclude from their central consideration those people who neither killed nor conquered anyone as the means to new identity, those people who took care of every one of the people who wanted to become "a person," those people who still take care of the life at issue: the ones who wash and who feed and who teach and who diligently decorate straw hats and bags with all of their historically unrequired gentle love—the women.

> *Oh the old rugged cross*
> *on a hill far away*
> *Well I cherish the old rugged cross*

It's Good Friday in the Bahamas. Seventy-eight degrees in the shade. Except for Sheraton territory, everything's closed.

It so happens that for truly secular reasons I've been fasting for three days. My hunger has now reached nearly violent proportions. In the hotel sandwich shop, the Black woman handling the counter complains about the tourists; why isn't the shop closed and why don't the tourists stop eating for once in their lives. I'm famished and I order chicken salad and cottage cheese and lettuce and tomato and a hard boiled egg and a hot cross bun and apple juice.

She eyes me with disgust.

To be sure, the timing of my stomach offends her serious religious practices. Neither one of us apologizes to the other. She seasons the chicken salad to the peppery max while I listen to the loud radio gospel she plays to console herself. It's a country Black version of "The Old Rugged Cross."

As I heave much chicken into my mouth, tears start. It's not the pepper. I am, after all, a West Indian daughter. It's the Good Friday music that dominates the humid atmosphere.

> *Well I cherish the old rugged cross*

And I am back, faster than a 747, in Brooklyn, in the home of my parents where we are wondering, as we do every year, if the sky will darken until Christ has been buried in the tomb. The sky should darken if God is in His heavens. And then, around 3 p.m., at the conclusion of our mournful church service at the neighborhood St. Phillips, and even while we dumbly stare at the black cloth covering the gold altar and the slender unlit candles, the sun should return through the high gothic windows and vindicate our waiting faith that the Lord will rise again, on Easter.

How I used to bow my head at the very name of Jesus: ecstatic to abase myself in deference to His majesty.

My mouth is full of salad. I can't seem to eat quickly enough. I can't think how I should lessen the offense of my appetite. The other Black woman on the premises, the one who disapprovingly prepared this very tasty break from my fast, makes no remark. She is no fool. This is a job that she needs. I suppose she notices that at least I included a hot cross bun among my edibles. That's something in my favor. I decide that's enough.

I am suddenly eager to walk off the food. Up a fairly steep hill I walk without hurrying. Through the pastel desolation of the little town, the road brings me to a confectionary pink and white plantation house. At the gates, an unnecessarily large statue of Christopher Columbus faces me down, or tries to. His hand is fisted to one hip. I look back at him, laugh without deference, and turn left.

It's time to pack it up. Catch my plane. I scan the hotel room for things not to forget. There's that white report card on the bureau.

"Dear Guests:" it says, under the name "Olive." "I am your maid for the day. Please rate me: Excellent. Good. Average. Poor. Thank you."

I tuck this memento from the Sheraton British Colonial into my notebook. How would "Olive" rate *me*? What would it mean for us to seem "good" to each other? What would that rating require?

But I am hastening to leave. Neither turtle soup nor kidney pie nor any conch shell delight shall delay my departure. I have rested, here, in the Bahamas, and I'm ready to return to my usual job, my usual work. But the skin on my body has changed and so has my mind. On the Delta flight home I realize I am burning up, indeed.

So far as I can see, the usual race and class concepts of connection, or gender assumptions of unity, do not apply very well. I doubt that they ever did. Otherwise why would Black folks forever bemoan our lack of solidarity when the deal turns real. And if unity on the basis of sexual oppression is something natural, then why do we women, the majority people on the planet, still have a problem?

The plane's ready for takeoff. I fasten my seatbelt and let the tumult inside my head run free. Yes: race and class and gender remain as real as the weather. But what they must mean about the contact between two individuals is less obvious and, like the weather, not predictable.

And when these factors of race and class and gender absolutely collapse is whenever you try to use them as automatic concepts of connection. They may serve well as indicators of commonly felt conflict, but as elements of connection they seem about as reliable as precipitation probability for the day after the night before the day.

It occurs to me that much organizational grief could be avoided if people understood that partnership in misery does not necessarily provide for partnership for change: *When we get the monsters off our backs all of us may want to run in very different directions.*

And not only that: even though both "Olive" and "I" live inside a conflict neither one of us created, and even though both of us therefore hurt inside that conflict, I may be one of the monsters she needs to eliminate from her universe and, in a sense, she may be one of the monsters in mine.

I am reaching for the words to describe the difference between a common identity that has been imposed and the individual identity any one of us will choose, once she gains that chance.

That difference is the one that keeps us stupid in the face of new, specific information about somebody else with whom we are supposed to have a connection because a third party, hostile to both of us, has worked it so that the two of us, like it or not, share a common enemy. *What happens beyond the idea of that enemy and beyond the consequences of that enemy?*

I am saying that the ultimate connection cannot be the enemy. The ultimate connection must be the need that we find between us. It is not only who you are, in other words, but what we can do for each other that will determine the connection.

I am flying back to my job. I have been teaching contemporary women's poetry this semester. One quandary I have set myself to explore with my students is the one of taking responsibility without power. We had been wrestling ideas to the floor for several sessions when a young Black woman, a South African, asked me for help, after class.

Sokutu told me she was "in a trance" and that she'd been unable to eat for two weeks.

"What's going on?" I asked her, even as my eyes startled at her trembling and emaciated appearance.

"My husband. He drinks all the time. He beats me up. I go to the hospital. I can't eat. I don't know what/anything."

In my office, she described her situation. I did not dare to let her sense my fear and horror. She was dragging about, hour by hour, in dread. Her husband, a young Black South African, was drinking himself into more and more deadly violence against her.

Sokutu told me how she could keep nothing down. She weighed 90 lbs. at the outside, as she spoke to me. She'd already been hospitalized as a result of her husband's battering rage.

I knew both of them because I had organized a campus group to aid the liberation struggles of Southern Africa.

Nausea rose in my throat. What about this presumable connection: this husband and this wife fled from that homeland of hatred against them, and now what? He was destroying himself. If not stopped, he would certainly murder his wife.

She needed a doctor, right away. It was a medical emergency. She needed protection. It was a security crisis. She needed refuge for battered wives and personal therapy and legal counsel. She needed a friend.

I got on the phone and called every number in the campus directory that I could imagine might prove helpful. Nothing worked. There were no institutional resources designed to meet her enormous, multifaceted, and ordinary woman's need.

I called various students. I asked the Chairperson of the English Department for advice. I asked everyone for help.

Finally, another one of my students, Cathy, a young Irish woman active in campus IRA activities, responded. She asked for further details. I gave them to her.

"Her husband," Cathy told me, "is an alcoholic. You have to understand about alcoholics. It's not the same as anything else. And it's a disease you can't treat any old way."

I listened, fearfully. Did this mean there was nothing we could do?

"That's not what I'm saying," she said. "But you have to keep the alcoholic part of the thing central in everybody's mind, otherwise her husband will kill her. Or he'll kill himself."

She spoke calmly. I felt there was nothing to do but to assume she knew what she was talking about.

"Will you come with me?" I asked her, after a silence. "Will you come with me and help us figure out what to do next?"

Cathy said she would but that she felt shy: Sokutu comes from South Africa. What would she think about Cathy?

"I don't know," I said. "But let's go."

We left to find a dormitory room for the young battered wife.

It was late, now, and dark outside.

On Cathy's VW that I followed behind with my own car, was the sticker that reads BOBBY SANDS FREE AT LAST. My eyes blurred as I read and re-read the words. This was another connection: Bobby Sands and Martin Luther King Jr. and who would believe it? I would not have believed it; I grew up terrorized by Irish kids who introduced me to the word "nigga."

And here I was following an Irish woman to the room of a Black South African. We were going to that room to try to save a life together.

When we reached the little room, we found ourselves awkward and large. Sokutu attempted to treat us with utmost courtesy, as though we were honored guests. She seemed surprised by Cathy, but mostly Sokutu was flushed with relief and joy because we were there, with her.

I did not know how we should ever terminate her heartfelt courtesies and address, directly, the reason for our visit: her starvation and her extreme physical danger.

Finally, Cathy sat on the floor and reached out her hands to Sokutu.

"I'm here," she said quietly, "because June has told me what has happened to you. And I know what it is. Your husband is an alcoholic. He has a disease. I know what it is. My father was an alcoholic. He killed himself. He almost killed my mother. I want to be your friend."

"Oh," was the only small sound that escaped from Sokutu's mouth. And then she embraced the other student. And then everything changed and I watched all of this happen so I know that this happened: this connection.

And after we called the police and exchanged phone numbers and plans were made for the night and for the next morning, the young South African woman walked down the dormitory hallway, saying goodbye and saying thank you to us.

I walked behind them, the young Irish woman and the young South African, and I saw them walking as sisters walk, hugging each other, and whispering and sure of each other and I felt how it was not who they were but what they both know and what they were both preparing to do about what they know that was going to make them both free at last.

And I look out the windows of the plane and I see clouds that will not kill me and I know that someday soon other clouds may erupt to kill us all.

And I tell the stewardess No thanks to the cocktails she offers me. But I look about the cabin at the hundred strangers drinking as they fly and I think even here and even now I must make the connection real between me and these strangers everywhere before those other clouds unify this ragged bunch of us, too late.

ANGRY WOMEN ARE BUILDING

Issues and Struggles Facing American Indian
Women Today

Paula Gunn Allen

4

The central issue that confronts American Indian women throughout the hemisphere is survival, *literal survival*, both on a cultural and biological level. According to the 1980 census, population of American Indians is just over one million. This figure, which is disputed by some American Indians, is probably a fair estimate, and it carries certain implications.*

Some researchers put our pre-contact population at more than 45 million, while others put it at around 20 million. The U.S. government long put it at 450,000—a comforting if imaginary figure, though at one point it was put at around 270,000. If our current population is around one million; if, as some researchers estimate, around 25 percent of Indian women and 10 percent of Indian men in the United States have been sterilized without informed con-

---

*Editors' note: The 1995 population is over two million.

From: Paula Gunn Allen, *The Sacred Hoop: Recovering the Feminism in American Indian Traditions* (Boston: Beacon Press, 1986), pp. 189–93. Reprinted with permission.

sent; if our average life expectancy is, as the best-informed research presently says, 55 years; if our infant mortality rate continues at well above national standards; if our average unemployment for all segments of our population—male, female, young, adult, and middle-aged—is between 60 and 90 percent; if the U.S. government continues its policy of termination, relocation, removal, and assimilation along with the destruction of wilderness, reservation land, and its resources, and severe curtailment of hunting, fishing, timber harvesting and water-use rights—then existing tribes are facing the threat of extinction which for several hundred tribal groups has already become fact in the past five hundred years.

In this nation of more than 200 million, the Indian people constitute less than one-half of one percent of the population.* In a nation that offers refuge, sympathy, and billions of dollars in aid from federal and private sources in the form of food to the hungry, medicine to the sick, and comfort to the dying, the indigenous subject population goes hungry, homeless, impoverished, cut out of the American deal, new, old, and in between. Americans are daily made aware of the worldwide slaughter of native peoples such as the Cambodians, the Palestinians, the Armenians, the Jews—who constitute only a few groups faced with genocide in this century. . . . The American Indian people are in a situation comparable to the imminent genocide in many parts of the world today. The plight of our people north and south of us is no better; to the south it is considerably worse. Consciously or unconsciously, deliberately, as a matter of national policy, or accidentally as a matter of "fate," *every single government,* right, left, or centrist in the western hemisphere is consciously or subconsciously dedicated to the extinction of those tribal people who live within its borders.

Within this geopolitical charnel house, American Indian women struggle on every front for the survival of our children, our people, our self-respect, our value systems, and our way of life. The past five hundred years testify to our skill at waging this struggle: for all the varied weapons of extinction pointed at our heads, we endure.

We survive war and conquest; we survive colonization, acculturation, assimilation; we survive beating, rape, starvation, mutilation, sterilization, abandonment, neglect, death of our children, our loved ones, destruction of our land, our homes, our past, and our future. We survive, and we do more than just survive. We bond, we care, we fight, we teach, we nurse, we bear, we feed, we earn, we laugh, we love, we hang in there, no matter what.

Of course, some, many of us, just give up. Many are alcoholics, many are addicts. Many abandon the children, the old ones. Many commit suicide. Many become violent, go insane. Many go "white" and are never seen or heard from again. But enough hold on to their traditions and their ways so that even after almost five hundred brutal years, we endure. And we even write songs and

---

* Editors' note: In 2000, this figure was one percent.

poems, make paintings and drawings that say "We walk in beauty. Let us continue."

Currently our struggles are on two fronts: physical survival and cultural survival. For women this means fighting alcoholism and drug abuse (our own and that of our husbands, lovers, parents, children); [1] poverty; affluence—a destroyer of people who are not traditionally socialized to deal with large sums of money; rape, incest, battering by Indian men; assaults on fertility and other health matters by the Indian Health Service and the Public Health Service; high infant mortality due to substandard medical care, nutrition, and health information; poor educational opportunities or education that takes us away from our traditions, language, and communities; suicide, homicide, or similar expressions of self-hatred; lack of economic opportunities; substandard housing; sometimes violent and always virulent racist attitudes and behaviors directed against us by an entertainment and educational system that wants only one thing from Indians: our silence, our invisibility, and our collective death.

A headline in the *Navajo Times* . . . reported that rape was the number one crime on the Navajo reservation. In a professional mental health journal of the Indian Health Services, Phyllis Old Dog Cross reported that incest and rape are common among Indian women seeking services and that their incidence is increasing. "It is believed that at least 80 percent of the Native Women seen at the regional psychiatric service center (five state area) have experienced some sort of sexual assault." [2] Among the forms of abuse being suffered by Native American women, Old Dog Cross cites a recent phenomenon, something called "training." This form of gang rape is "a punitive act of a group of males who band together and get even or take revenge on a selected woman." [3]

These and other cases of violence against women are powerful evidence that the status of women within the tribes has suffered grievous decline since contact, and the decline has increased in intensity in recent years. The amount of violence against women, alcoholism, and violence, abuse, and neglect by women against their children and their aged relatives have all increased. These social ills were virtually unheard of among most tribes fifty years ago, popular American opinion to the contrary. As Old Dog Cross remarks:

> Rapid, unstable and irrational change was required of the Indian people if they were to survive. Incredible loss of all that had meaning was the norm. Inhuman treatment, murder, death, and punishment was a typical experience for all the tribal groups and some didn't survive.
>
> The dominant society devoted its efforts to the attempt to change the Indian into a white-Indian. No inhuman pressure to effect this change was overlooked. These pressures included starvation, incarceration and enforced education. Religious and healing customs were banished.
>
> In spite of the years of oppression, the Indian and the Indian spirit survived. Not, however, without adverse effect. One of the major effects was the loss of cultured values and the concomitant loss of personal identity . . . The Indian was taught to be ashamed of being Indian and to emulate the non-

Indian. In short, "white was right." For the Indian male, the only route to be successful, to be good, to be right, and to have an identity was to be as much like
the white man as he could.[4]

Often it is said that the increase of violence against women is a result of
various sociological factors such as oppression, racism, poverty, hopelessness,
emasculation of men, and loss of male self-esteem as their own place within traditional society has been systematically destroyed by increasing urbanization,
industrialization, and institutionalization, but seldom do we notice that for
the past forty to fifty years, American popular media have depicted American
Indian men as bloodthirsty savages devoted to treating women cruelly. While
traditional Indian men seldom did any such thing—and in fact among most
tribes abuse of women was simply unthinkable, as was abuse of children or the
aged—the lie about "usual" male Indian behavior seems to have taken root
and now bears its brutal and bitter fruit.

Image casting and image control constitute the central process that American Indian women must come to terms with, for on that control rests our sense
of self, our claim to a past and to a future that we define and that we build. Images of Indians in media and educational materials profoundly influence how
we act, how we relate to the world and to each other, and how we value ourselves. They also determine to a large extent how our men act toward us, toward
our children, and toward each other. The popular American media image of
Indian people as savages with no conscience, no compassion, and no sense of
the value of human life and human dignity was hardly true of the tribes—
however true it was of the invaders. But as Adolf Hitler noted a little over fifty
years ago, if you tell a lie big enough and often enough, it will be believed. Evidently, while Americans and people all over the world have been led into a
deep and unquestioned belief that American Indians are cruel savages, a number of American Indian men have been equally deluded into internalizing that
image and acting on it. Media images, literary images, and artistic images,
particularly those embedded in popular culture, must be changed before Indian women will see much relief from the violence that destroys so many lives.

To survive culturally, American Indian women must often fight the United
States government, the tribal governments, women and men of their tribe or
their urban community who are virulently misogynist or who are threatened
by attempts to change the images foisted on us over the centuries by whites.
The colonizers' revisions of our lives, values, and histories have devastated us
at the most critical level of all—that of our own minds, our own sense of who
we are.

Many women express strong opposition to those who would alter our life
supports, steal our tribal lands, colonize our cultures and cultural expressions,
and revise our very identities. We must strive to maintain tribal status; we must
make certain that the tribes continue to be legally recognized entities, sovereign nations within the larger United States, and we must wage this struggle in

many ways—political, educational, literary, artistic, individual, and communal. We are doing all we can: as mothers and grandmothers; as family members and tribal members; as professionals, workers, artists, shamans, leaders, chiefs, speakers, writers, and organizers, we daily demonstrate that we have no intention of disappearing, of being silent, or of quietly acquiescing in our extinction.

NOTES

1. It is likely, say some researchers, that fetal alcohol syndrome, which is serious among many Indian groups, will be so serious among the White Mountain Apache and the Pine Ridge Sioux that if present trends continue, by the year 2000 some people estimate that almost one-half of all children born on those reservations will in some way be affected by FAS. (Michael Dorris, Native American Studies, Dartmouth College, private conversation. Dorris has done extensive research into the syndrome as it affects native populations in the United States as well as in New Zealand.)

2. Phyllis Old Dog Cross, "Sexual Abuse, a New Threat to the Native American Woman: An Overview," *Listening Post: A Periodical of the Mental Health Programs of Indian Health Services,* vol. 6, no. 2 (April 1982), p. 18.

3. Old Dog Cross, p. 18.

4. Old Dog Cross, p. 20.

OPPRESSION   5

Marilyn Frye

It is a fundamental claim of feminism that women are oppressed. The word "oppression" is a strong word. It repels and attracts. It is dangerous and dangerously fashionable and endangered. It is much misused, and sometimes not innocently.

The statement that women are oppressed is frequently met with the claim that men are oppressed too. We hear that oppressing is oppressive to those who oppress as well as to those they oppress. Some men cite as evidence of their oppression their much-advertised inability to cry. It is tough, we are told, to be masculine. When the stresses and frustrations of being a man are

From: Marilyn Frye, *The Politics of Reality* (Trumansburg, NY: Crossing Press, 1983), pp. 1–16. Reprinted by permission.

cited as evidence that oppressors are oppressed by their oppressing, the word "oppression" is being stretched to meaninglessness; it is treated as though its scope includes any and all human experience of limitation or suffering, no matter the cause, degree, or consequence. Once such usage has been put over on us, then if ever we deny that any person or group is oppressed, we seem to imply that we think they never suffer and have no feelings. We are accused of insensitivity; even of bigotry. For women, such accusation is particularly intimidating, since sensitivity is one of the few virtues that has been assigned to us. If we are found insensitive, we may fear we have no redeeming traits at all and perhaps are not real women. Thus are we silenced before we begin: the name of our situation drained of meaning and our guilt mechanisms tripped.

But this is nonsense. Human beings can be miserable without being oppressed, and it is perfectly consistent to deny that a person or group is oppressed without denying that they have feelings or that they suffer. . . .

The root of the word "oppression" is the element "press." *The press of the crowd; pressed into military service; to press a pair of pants; printing press; press the button.* Presses are used to mold things or flatten them or reduce them in bulk, sometimes to reduce them by squeezing out the gases or liquids in them. Something pressed is something caught between or among forces and barriers which are so related to each other that jointly they restrain, restrict or prevent the thing's motion or mobility. Mold. Immobilize. Reduce.

The mundane experience of the oppressed provides another clue. One of the most characteristic and ubiquitous features of the world as experienced by oppressed people is the double bind—situations in which options are reduced to a very few and all of them expose one to penalty, censure, or deprivation. For example, it is often a requirement upon oppressed people that we smile and be cheerful. If we comply, we signal our docility and our acquiescence in our situation. We need not, then, be taken note of. We acquiesce in being made invisible, in our occupying no space. We participate in our own erasure. On the other hand, anything but the sunniest countenance exposes us to being perceived as mean, bitter, angry, or dangerous. This means, at the least, that we may be found "difficult" or unpleasant to work with, which is enough to cost one one's livelihood; at worst, being seen as mean, bitter, angry, or dangerous has been known to result in rape, arrest, beating, and murder. One can only choose to risk one's preferred form and rate of annihilation.

Another example: It is common in the United States that women, especially younger women, are in a bind where neither sexual activity nor sexual inactivity is all right. If she is heterosexually active, a woman is open to censure and punishment for being loose, unprincipled, or a whore. The "punishment" comes in the form of criticism, snide and embarrassing remarks, being treated as an easy lay by men, scorn from her more restrained female friends. She may have to lie and hide her behavior from her parents. She must juggle the risks of unwanted pregnancy and dangerous contraceptives. On the other hand, if she refrains from heterosexual activity, she is fairly constantly harassed by men who try to persuade her into it and pressure her to "relax" and "let her hair down"; she is threatened with labels like "frigid," "uptight," "man-hater," "bitch" and "cocktease." The same parents who would be disapproving of her sexual activity may be worried by her inactivity because it suggests she is not or will not be popular, or is not sexually normal. She may be charged with lesbianism. If a woman is raped, then if she has been heterosexually active she is subject to the presumption that she liked it (since her activity is presumed to show that she likes sex), and if she has not been heterosexually active, she is subject to the presumption that she liked it (since she is supposedly "repressed and frustrated"). Both heterosexual activity and heterosexual nonactivity are likely to be taken as proof that you wanted to be raped, and hence, of course, weren't *really* raped at all. You can't win. You are caught in a bind, caught between systematically related pressures.

Women are caught like this, too, by networks of forces and barriers that expose one to penalty, loss, or contempt whether one works outside the home or not, is on welfare or not, bears children or not, raises children or not, marries or not, stays married or not, is heterosexual, lesbian, both, or neither. Economic necessity; confinement to racial and/or sexual job ghettos; sexual harassment; sex discrimination; pressures of competing expectations and judgments about *women*, *wives*, and *mothers* (in the society at large, in racial and ethnic subcultures, and in one's own mind); dependence (full or partial) on husbands, parents, or the state; commitment to political ideas; loyalties to racial or ethnic or other "minority" groups; the demands of self-respect and responsibilities to others. Each of these factors exists in complex tension with every other, penalizing or prohibiting all of the apparently available options. And nipping at one's heels, always, is the endless pack of little things. If one dresses one way, one is subject to the assumption that one is advertising one's sexual availability; if one dresses another way, one appears to "not care about oneself" or to be "unfeminine." If one uses "strong language," one invites categorization as a whore or slut; if one does not, one invites categorization as a "lady"—one too delicately constituted to cope with robust speech or the realities to which it presumably refers.

The experience of oppressed people is that the living of one's life is confined and shaped by forces and barriers which are not accidental or occasional and hence avoidable, but are systematically related to each other in such a way as to catch one between and among them and restrict or penalize motion in any direction. It is the experience of being caged in: all avenues, in every direction, are blocked or booby trapped.

Cages. Consider a birdcage. If you look very closely at just one wire in the cage, you cannot see the other wires. If your conception of what is before you is determined by this myopic focus, you could look at that one wire, up and down the length of it, and be unable to see why a bird would not just fly around the wire any time it wanted to go somewhere. Furthermore, even if, one day at a time, you myopically inspected each wire, you still could not see why a bird would have trouble going past the wires to get anywhere. There is no physical property of any one wire, *nothing* that the closest scrutiny could discover, that will reveal how a bird could be inhibited or harmed by it except in the most accidental way. It is only when you step back, stop looking at the wires one by one, microscopically, and take a macroscopic view of the whole cage, that you can see why the bird does not go anywhere; and then you will see it in a moment. It will require no great subtlety of mental powers. It is perfectly *obvious* that the bird is surrounded by a network of systematically related barriers, no one of which would be the least hindrance to its flight, but which, by their relations to each other, are as confining as the solid walls of a dungeon.

It is now possible to grasp one of the reasons why oppression can be hard to see and recognize: one can study the elements of an oppressive structure with great care and some good will without seeing the structure as a whole, and hence without seeing or being able to understand that one is looking at a cage and that there are people there who are caged, whose motion and mobility are restricted, whose lives are shaped and reduced.

The arresting of vision at a microscopic level yields such common confusion as that about the male door-opening ritual. This ritual, which is remarkably widespread across classes and races, puzzles many people, some of whom do and some of whom do not find it offensive. Look at the scene of the two people approaching a door. The male steps slightly ahead and opens the door. The male holds the door open while the female glides through. Then the male goes through. The door closes after them. "Now how," one innocently asks, "can those crazy womenslibbers say that is oppressive? The guy *removed* a barrier to the lady's smooth and unruffled progress." But each repetition of this ritual has a place in a pattern, in fact in several patterns. One has to shift the level of one's perception in order to see the whole picture.

The door-opening pretends to be a helpful service, but the helpfulness is false. This can be seen by noting that it will be done whether or not it makes any practical sense. Infirm men and men burdened with packages will open doors for able-bodied women who are free of physical burdens. Men will impose themselves awkwardly and jostle everyone in order to get to the door first. The act is not determined by convenience or grace. Furthermore, these very numerous acts of unneeded or even noisome "help" occur in counterpoint to a pattern of men not being helpful in many practical ways in which women might welcome help. What *women* experience is a world in which gallant princes charming commonly make a fuss about being helpful and providing small services when help and services are of little or no use, but in which there are rarely ingenious and adroit princes at hand when substantial assistance is really wanted either in mundane affairs or in situations of threat, assault, or terror. There is no help with the (his) laundry; no help typing a report at 4:00 a.m.; no help in mediating disputes among relatives or children. There is nothing but advice that women should stay indoors after dark, be chaperoned by a man, or when it comes down to it, "lie back and enjoy it."

The gallant gestures have no practical meaning. Their meaning is symbolic. The door-opening and similar services provided are services which really are needed by people who are for one reason or another incapacitated—unwell, burdened with parcels, etc. So the message is that women are incapable. The detachment of the acts from the concrete realities of what women need and do not need is a vehicle for the message that women's actual needs and interests are unimportant or irrelevant. Finally, these gestures imitate the behavior of servants toward masters and thus mock women, who are in most respects the servants and caretakers of men. The message of the false helpfulness of male gallantry is female dependence, the invisibility or insignificance of women, and contempt for women.

One cannot see the meanings of these rituals if one's focus is riveted upon the individual event in all its particularity, including the particularity of the individual man's present conscious intentions and motives and the individual woman's conscious perception of the event in the moment. It seems sometimes that people take a deliberately myopic view and fill their eyes with things seen microscopically in order not to see macroscopically. At any rate, whether it is deliberate or not, people can and do fail to see the oppression of women because they fail to see macroscopically and hence fail to see the various elements of the situation as systematically related in larger schemes.

As the cageness of the birdcage is a macroscopic phenomenon, the oppressiveness of the situations in which women live their various and different lives is a macroscopic phenomenon. Neither can be *seen* from a microscopic perspective. But when you look macroscopically you can see it—a network of forces and barriers which are systematically related and which conspire to the immobilization, reduction, and molding of women and the lives we live. . . .

A DIFFERENT MIRROR   6

Ronald T. Takaki

I had flown from San Francisco to Norfolk and was riding in a taxi to my hotel to attend a conference on multiculturalism. Hundreds of educators from

From: Ronald T. Takaki, *A Different Mirror: A History of Multicultural America* (Boston: Little, Brown, 1993), pp. 1–17. Copyright © 1993 by Ronald Takaki. Reprinted by permission of the publisher.

across the country were meeting to discuss the need for greater cultural diversity in the curriculum. My driver and I chatted about the weather and the tourists. The sky was cloudy, and Virginia Beach was twenty minutes away. The rearview mirror reflected a white man in his forties. "How long have you been in this country?" he asked. "All my life," I replied, wincing. "I was born in the United States." With a strong southern drawl, he remarked: "I was wondering because your English is excellent!" Then, as I had many times before, I explained: "My grandfather came here from Japan in the 1880s. My family has been here, in America, for over a hundred years." He glanced at me in the mirror. Somehow I did not look "American" to him; my eyes and complexion looked foreign.

Suddenly, we both became uncomfortably conscious of a racial divide separating us. An awkward silence turned my gaze from the mirror to the passing landscape, the shore where the English and the Powhatan Indians first encountered each other. Our highway was on land that Sir Walter Raleigh had renamed "Virginia" in honor of Elizabeth I, the Virgin Queen. In the English cultural appropriation of America, the indigenous peoples themselves would become outsiders in their native land. Here, at the eastern edge of the continent, I mused, was the site of the beginning of multicultural America. Jamestown, the English settlement founded in 1607, was nearby: the first twenty Africans were brought here a year before the Pilgrims arrived at Plymouth Rock. Several hundred miles offshore was Bermuda, the "Bermoothes" where William Shakespeare's Prospero had landed and met the native Caliban in *The Tempest*. Earlier, another voyager had made an Atlantic crossing and unexpectedly bumped into some islands to the south. Thinking he had reached Asia, Christopher Columbus mistakenly identified one of the islands as "Cipango" (Japan). In the wake of the admiral, many peoples would come to America from different shores, not only from Europe but also Africa and Asia. One of them would be my grandfather. My mental wandering across terrain and time ended abruptly as we arrived at my destination. I said good-bye to my driver and went into the hotel, carrying a vivid reminder of why I was attending this conference.

Questions like the one my taxi driver asked me are always jarring, but I can understand why he could not see me as American. He had a narrow but widely shared sense of the past—a history that has viewed American as European in ancestry. "Race," Toni Morrison explained, has functioned as a "metaphor" necessary to the "construction of Americanness": in the creation of our national identity, "American" has been defined as "white."[1]

But America has been racially diverse since our very beginning on the Virginia shore, and this reality is increasingly becoming visible and ubiquitous. Currently, one-third of the American people do not trace their origins to Europe; in California, minorities are fast becoming a majority. They already predominate in major cities across the country—New York, Chicago, Atlanta, Detroit, Philadelphia, San Francisco, and Los Angeles.

This emerging demographic diversity has raised fundamental questions about America's identity and culture. In 1990, *Time* published a cover story on "America's Changing Colors." "Someday soon," the magazine announced, "white Americans will become a minority group." How soon? By 2056, most Americans will trace their descent to "Africa, Asia, the Hispanic world, the Pacific Islands, Arabia—almost anywhere but white Europe." This dramatic change in our nation's ethnic composition is altering the way we think about ourselves. "The deeper significance of America's becoming a majority non-white society is what it means to the national psyche, to individuals' sense of themselves and their nation—their idea of what it is to be American." . . .[2]

What is fueling the debate over our national identity and the content of our curriculum is America's intensifying racial crisis. The alarming signs and symptoms seem to be everywhere—the killing of Vincent Chin in Detroit, the black boycott of a Korean grocery store in Flatbush, the hysteria in Boston over the Carol Stuart murder, the battle between white sportsmen and Indians over tribal fishing rights in Wisconsin, the Jewish-black clashes in Brooklyn's Crown Heights, the black-Hispanic competition for jobs and educational resources in Dallas, which *Newsweek* described as "a conflict of the have-nots," and the Willie Horton campaign commercials, which widened the divide between the suburbs and the inner cities.[3]

This reality of racial tension rudely woke America like a fire bell in the night on April 29, 1992. Immediately after four Los Angeles police officers were found not guilty of brutality against Rodney King, rage exploded in Los Angeles. Race relations reached a new nadir. During the nightmarish rampage, scores of people were killed, over two thousand injured, twelve thousand arrested, and almost a billion dollars' worth of property destroyed. The live televised images mesmerized America. The rioting and the murderous melee on the streets resembled the fighting in Beirut and the West Bank. The thousands of fires burning out of control and the dark smoke filling the skies brought back images of the burning oil fields of Kuwait during Desert Storm. Entire sections of Los Angeles looked like a bombed city. "Is this America?" many shocked viewers asked. "Please, can we get along here," pleaded Rodney King, calling for calm. "We all can get along. I mean, we're all stuck here for a while. Let's try to work it out."[4]

But how should "we" be defined? Who are the people "stuck here" in America? One of the lessons of the Los Angeles explosion is the recognition of the fact that we are a multiracial society and that race can no longer be defined in the binary terms of white and black. "We" will have to include Hispanics and Asians. While blacks currently constitute 13 percent of the Los Angeles population, Hispanics represent 40 percent. The 1990 census revealed that South Central Los Angeles, which was predominantly black in 1965 when the Watts rebellion occurred, is now 45 percent Hispanic. A majority of the first 5,438 people arrested were Hispanic, while 37 percent were black. Of the fifty-eight people who died in the riot, more than a third were

Hispanic, and about 40 percent of the businesses destroyed were Hispanic-owned. Most of the other shops and stores were Korean-owned. The dreams of many Korean immigrants went up in smoke during the riot: two thousand Korean-owned businesses were damaged or demolished, totaling about $400 million in losses. There is evidence indicating they were targeted. "After all," explained a black gang member, "we didn't burn our community, just *their* stores."[5]

"I don't feel like I'm in America anymore," said Denisse Bustamente as she watched the police protecting the firefighters. "I feel like I am far away." Indeed, Americans have been witnessing ethnic strife erupting around the world—the rise of neo-Nazism and the murder of Turks in Germany, the ugly "ethnic cleansing" in Bosnia, the terrible and bloody clashes between Muslims and Hindus in India. Is the situation here different, we have been nervously wondering, or do ethnic conflicts elsewhere represent a prologue for America? What is the nature of malevolence? Is there a deep, perhaps primordial, need for group identity rooted in hatred for the other? Is ethnic pluralism possible for America? But answers have been limited. Television reports have been little more than thirty-second sound bites. Newspaper articles have been mostly superficial descriptions of racial antagonisms and the current urban malaise. What is lacking is historical context; consequently, we are left feeling bewildered.[6]

How did we get to this point, Americans everywhere are anxiously asking. What does our diversity mean, and where is it leading us? How do we work it out in the post–Rodney King era?

Certainly one crucial way is for our society's various ethnic groups to develop a greater understanding of each other. For example, how can African Americans and Korean Americans work it out unless they learn about each other's cultures, histories, and also economic situations? This need to share knowledge about our ethnic diversity has acquired new importance and has given new urgency to the pursuit for a more accurate history. . . .

While all of America's many groups cannot be covered [here], the English immigrants and their descendants require attention, for they possessed inordinate power to define American culture and make public policy. What men like John Winthrop, Thomas Jefferson, and Andrew Jackson thought as well as did mattered greatly to all of us and was consequential for everyone. A broad range of groups [is important]: African Americans, Asian Americans, Chicanos, Irish, Jews, and Indians. While together they help to explain general patterns in our society, each has contributed to the making of the United States.

African Americans have been the central minority throughout our country's history. They were initially brought here on a slave ship in 1619. Actually, these first twenty Africans might not have been slaves; rather, like most of the white laborers, they were probably indentured servants. The transformation of Africans into slaves is the story of the "hidden" origins of slavery. How and when was it decided to institute a system of bonded black labor?

What happened, while freighted with racial significance, was actually conditioned by class conflicts within white society. Once established, the "peculiar institution" would have consequences for centuries to come. During the nineteenth century, the political storm over slavery almost destroyed the nation. Since the Civil War and emancipation, race has continued to be largely defined in relation to African Americans—segregation, civil rights, the underclass, and affirmative action. Constituting the largest minority group in our society, they have been at the cutting edge of the Civil Rights Movement. Indeed, their struggle has been a constant reminder of America's moral vision as a country committed to the principle of liberty. Martin Luther King clearly understood this truth when he wrote from a jail cell: "We will reach the goal of freedom in Birmingham and all over the nation, because the goal of America is freedom. Abused and scorned though we may be, our destiny is tied up with America's destiny."[7]

Asian Americans have been here for over one hundred and fifty years, before many European immigrant groups. But as "strangers" coming from a "different shore," they have been stereotyped as "heathen," exotic, and unassimilable. Seeking "Gold Mountain," the Chinese arrived first, and what happened to them influenced the reception of the Japanese, Koreans, Filipinos, and Asian Indians as well as the Southeast Asian refugees like the Vietnamese and the Hmong. The 1882 Chinese Exclusion Act was the first law that prohibited the entry of immigrants on the basis of nationality. The Chinese condemned this restriction as racist and tyrannical. "They call us 'Chink,'" complained a Chinese immigrant, cursing the "white demons." "They think we no good! America cuts us off. No more come now, too bad!" This precedent later provided a basis for the restriction of European immigrant groups such as Italians, Russians, Poles, and Greeks. The Japanese painfully discovered that their accomplishments in America did not lead to acceptance, for during World War II, unlike Italian Americans and German Americans, they were placed in internment camps. Two-thirds of them were citizens by birth. "How could I as a 6-month-old child born in this country," asked Congressman Robert Matsui years later, "be declared by my own Government to be an enemy alien?" Today, Asian Americans represent the fastest-growing ethnic group. They have also become the focus of much mass media attention as "the Model Minority" not only for blacks and Chicanos, but also for whites on welfare and even middle-class whites experiencing economic difficulties.[8]

Chicanos represent the largest group among the Hispanic population, which is projected to outnumber African Americans. They have been in the United States for a long time, initially incorporated by the war against Mexico. The treaty had moved the border between the two countries, and the people of "occupied" Mexico suddenly found themselves "foreigners" in their "native land." As historian Albert Camarillo pointed out, the Chicano past is an integral part of America's westward expansion, also known as "manifest destiny." But while the early Chicanos were a colonized people, most of them today have immigrant roots. Many began the trek to El Norte in the early twentieth century. "As I had heard a lot about the United States," Jesus Garza recalled, "it was my dream to come here." "We came to know families from Chihuahua, Sonora, Jalisco, and Durango," stated Ernesto Galarza. "Like ourselves, our Mexican neighbors had come this far moving step by step, working and waiting, as if they were feeling their way up a ladder." Nevertheless, the Chicano experience has been unique, for most of them have lived close to their homeland—a proximity that has helped reinforce their language, identity, and culture. This migration to El Norte has continued to the present. Los Angeles has more people of Mexican origin than any other city in the world, except Mexico City. A mostly mestizo people of Indian as well as African and Spanish ancestries, Chicanos currently represent the largest minority group in the Southwest, where they have been visibly transforming culture and society.[9]

The Irish came here in greater numbers than most immigrant groups. Their history has been tied to America's past from the very beginning. Ireland represented the earliest English frontier: the conquest of Ireland occurred before the colonization of America, and the Irish were the first group that the English called "savages." In this context, the Irish past foreshadowed the Indian future. During the nineteenth century, the Irish, like the Chinese, were victims of British colonialism. While the Chinese fled from the ravages of the Opium Wars, the Irish were pushed from their homeland by "English tyranny." Here they became construction workers and factory operatives as well as the "maids" of America. Representing a Catholic group seeking to settle in a fiercely Protestant society, the Irish immigrants were targets of American nativist hostility. They were also what historian Lawrence J. McCaffrey called "the pioneers of the American urban ghetto," "previewing" experiences that would later be shared by the Italians, Poles, and other groups from southern and eastern Europe. Furthermore, they offer contrast to the immigrants from Asia. The Irish came about the same time as the Chinese, but they had a distinct advantage: the Naturalization Law of 1790 had reserved citizenship for "whites" only. Their compatible complexion allowed them to assimilate by blending into American society. In making their journey successfully into the mainstream, however, these immigrants from Erin pursued an Irish "ethnic" strategy: they promoted "Irish" solidarity in order to gain political power and also to dominate the skilled blue-collar occupations, often at the expense of the Chinese and blacks.[10]

Fleeing pogroms and religious persecution in Russia, the Jews were driven from what John Cuddihy described as the "Middle Ages into the Anglo-American world of the *goyim* 'beyond the pale.'" To them, America represented the Promised Land. This vision led Jews to struggle not only for themselves but also for other oppressed groups, especially blacks. After the 1917 East St. Louis race riot, the Yiddish *Forward* of New York compared this anti-black violence to a 1903 pogrom in Russia: "Kishinev and St. Louis—the same soil, the same people." Jews cheered when Jackie Robinson broke into the

Brooklyn Dodgers in 1947. "He was adopted as the surrogate hero by many of us growing up at the time," recalled Jack Greenberg of the NAACP Legal Defense Fund. "He was the way we saw ourselves triumphing against the forces of bigotry and ignorance." Jews stood shoulder to shoulder with blacks in the Civil Rights Movement: two-thirds of the white volunteers who went south during the 1964 Freedom Summer were Jewish. Today Jews are considered a highly successful "ethnic" group. How did they make such great socioeconomic strides? This question is often reframed by neoconservative intellectuals like Irving Kristol and Nathan Glazer to read: if Jewish immigrants were able to lift themselves from poverty into the mainstream through self-help and education without welfare and affirmative action, why can't blacks? But what this thinking overlooks is the unique history of Jewish immigrants, especially the initial advantages of many of them as literate and skilled. Moreover, it minimizes the virulence of racial prejudice rooted in American slavery.[11]

Indians represent a critical contrast, for theirs was not an immigrant experience. The Wampanoags were on the shore as the first English strangers arrived in what would be called "New England." The encounters between Indians and whites not only shaped the course of race relations, but also influenced the very culture and identity of the general society. The architect of Indian removal, President Andrew Jackson told Congress: "Our conduct toward these people is deeply interesting to the national character." Frederick Jackson Turner understood the meaning of this observation when he identified the frontier as our transforming crucible. At first, the European newcomers had to wear Indian moccasins and shout the war cry. "Little by little," as they subdued the wilderness, the pioneers became "a new product" that was "American." But Indians have had a different view of this entire process. "The white man," Luther Standing Bear of the Sioux explained, "does not understand the Indian for the reason that he does not understand America." Continuing to be "troubled with primitive fears," he has "in his consciousness the perils of this frontier continent. . . . The man from Europe is still a foreigner and an alien. And he still hates the man who questioned his path across the continent." Indians questioned what Jackson and Turner trumpeted as "progress." For them, the frontier had a different "significance": their history was how the West was lost. But their story has also been one of resistance. As Vine Deloria declared, "Custer died for your sins."[12]

By looking at these groups from a multicultural perspective, we can comparatively analyze their experiences in order to develop an understanding of their differences and similarities. Race, we will see, has been a social construction that has historically set apart racial minorities from European immigrant groups. Contrary to the notions of scholars like Nathan Glazer and Thomas Sowell, race in America has not been the same as ethnicity. A broad comparative focus also allows us to see how the varied experiences of different racial and ethnic groups occurred within shared contexts.

During the nineteenth century, for example, the Market Revolution employed Irish immigrant laborers in New England factories as it expanded cotton fields worked by enslaved blacks across Indian lands toward Mexico. Like blacks, the Irish newcomers were stereotyped as "savages," ruled by passions rather than "civilized" virtues such as self-control and hard work. The Irish saw themselves as the "slaves" of British oppressors, and during a visit to Ireland in the 1840s, Frederick Douglass found that the "wailing notes" of the Irish ballads reminded him of the "wild notes" of slave songs. The United States annexation of California, while incorporating Mexicans, led to trade with Asia and the migration of "strangers" from Pacific shores. In 1870, Chinese immigrant laborers were transported to Massachusetts as scabs to break an Irish immigrant strike; in response, the Irish recognized the need for interethnic working-class solidarity and tried to organize a Chinese lodge of the Knights of St. Crispin. After the Civil War, Mississippi planters recruited Chinese immigrants to discipline the newly freed blacks. During the debate over an immigration exclusion bill in 1882, a senator asked: If Indians could be located on reservations, why not the Chinese? [13]

Other instances of our connectedness abound. In 1903, Mexican and Japanese farm laborers went on strike together in California: their union officers had names like Yamaguchi and Lizarras, and strike meetings were conducted in Japanese and Spanish. The Mexican strikers declared that they were standing in solidarity with their "Japanese brothers" because the two groups had toiled together in the fields and were now fighting together for a fair wage. Speaking in impassioned Yiddish during the 1909 "uprising of twenty thousand" strikers in New York, the charismatic Clara Lemlich compared the abuse of Jewish female garment workers to the experience of blacks: "[The bosses] yell at the girls and 'call them down' even worse than I imagine the Negro slaves were in the South." During the 1920s, elite universities like Harvard worried about the increasing numbers of Jewish students, and new admissions criteria were instituted to curb their enrollment. Jewish students were scorned for their studiousness and criticized for their "clannishness." Recently, Asian-American students have been the targets of similar complaints: they have been called "nerds" and told there are "too many" of them on campus. [14]

Indians were already here, while blacks were forcibly transported to America, and Mexicans were initially enclosed by America's expanding border. The other groups came here as immigrants: for them, America represented liminality—a new world where they could pursue extravagant urges and do things they had thought beyond their capabilities. Like the land itself, they found themselves "betwixt and between all fixed points of classification." No longer fastened as fiercely to their old countries, they felt a stirring to become new people in a society still being defined and formed. [15]

These immigrants made bold and dangerous crossings, pushed by political events and economic hardships in their homelands and pulled by America's demand for labor as well as by their own dreams for a better life. "By all means let me go to America," a young man in Japan begged his parents. He had calculated that in one year as a laborer here he could save almost a thousand yen — an amount equal to the income of a governor in Japan. "My dear Father," wrote an immigrant Irish girl living in New York, "Any man or woman without a family are fools that would not venture and come to this plentyful Country where no man or woman ever hungered." In the shtetls of Russia, the cry "To America!" roared like "wildfire." "America was in everybody's mouth," a Jewish immigrant recalled. "Businessmen talked [about] it over their accounts; the market women made up their quarrels that they might discuss it from stall to stall; people who had relatives in the famous land went around reading their letters." Similarly, for Mexican immigrants crossing the border in the early twentieth century, El Norte became the stuff of overblown hopes. "If only you could see how nice the United States is," they said, "that is why the Mexicans are crazy about it." [16]

The signs of America's ethnic diversity can be discerned across the continent — Ellis Island, Angel Island, Chinatown, Harlem, South Boston, the Lower East Side, places with Spanish names like Los Angeles and San Antonio or Indian names like Massachusetts and Iowa. Much of what is familiar in America's cultural landscape actually has ethnic origins. The Bing cherry was developed by an early Chinese immigrant named Ah Bing. American Indians were cultivating corn, tomatoes, and tobacco long before the arrival of Columbus. The term *okay* was derived from the Choctaw word *oke*, meaning "it is so." There is evidence indicating that the name *Yankee* came from Indian terms for the English — from *eankke* in Cherokee and *Yankwis* in Delaware. Jazz and blues as well as rock and roll have African-American origins. The "Forty-Niners" of the Gold Rush learned mining techniques from the Mexicans; American cowboys acquired herding skills from Mexican *vaqueros* and adopted their range terms — such as *lariat* from *la reata*, *lasso* from *lazo*, and *stampede* from *estampida*. Songs like "God Bless America," "Easter Parade," and "White Christmas" were written by a Russian-Jewish immigrant named Israel Baline, more popularly known as Irving Berlin. [17]

Furthermore, many diverse ethnic groups have contributed to the building of the American economy, forming what Walt Whitman saluted as "a vast, surging, hopeful army of workers." They worked in the South's cotton fields, New England's textile mills, Hawaii's canefields, New York's garment factories, California's orchards, Washington's salmon canneries, and Arizona's copper mines. They built the railroad, the great symbol of America's industrial triumph. . . .

Moreover, our diversity was tied to America's most serious crisis: the Civil War was fought over a racial issue — slavery. . . .

. . . The people in our study have been actors in history, not merely victims of discrimination and exploitation. They are entitled to be viewed as subjects — as men and women with minds, wills, and voices.

In the telling and retelling
of their stories,
They create communities
of memory.

They also re-vision history. "It is very natural that the history written by the victim," said a Mexican in 1874, "does not altogether chime with the story of the victor." Sometimes they are hesitant to speak, thinking they are only "little people." "I don't know why anybody wants to hear my history," an Irish maid said apologetically in 1900. "Nothing ever happened to me worth the tellin'." [18]

But their stories are worthy. Through their stories, the people who have lived America's history can help all of us, including my taxi driver, understand that Americans originated from many shores, and that all of us are entitled to dignity. "I hope this survey do a lot of good for Chinese people," an immigrant told an interviewer from Stanford University in the 1920s. "Make American people realize that Chinese people are humans. I think very few American people really know anything about Chinese." But the remembering is also for the sake of the children. "This story is dedicated to the descendants of Lazar and Goldie Glauberman," Jewish immigrant Minnie Miller wrote in her autobiography. "My history is bound up in their history and the generations that follow should know where they came from to know better who they are." Similarly, Tomo Shoji, an elderly Nisei woman, urged Asian Americans to learn more about their roots: "We got such good, fantastic stories to tell. All our stories are different." Seeking to know how they fit into America, many young people have become listeners; they are eager to learn about the hardships and humiliations experienced by their parents and grandparents. They want to hear their stories, unwilling to remain ignorant or ashamed of their identity and past. [19]

The telling of stories liberates. By writing about the people on Mango Street, Sandra Cisneros explained, "the ghost does not ache so much." The place no longer holds her with "both arms. She sets me free." Indeed, stories may not be as innocent or simple as they seem to be. Native-American novelist Leslie Marmon Silko cautioned:

> *I will tell you something about stories . . .*
> *They aren't just entertainment.*
> *Don't be fooled.*

Indeed, the accounts given by the people in this study vibrantly re-create moments, capturing the complexities of human emotions and thoughts. They also provide the authenticity of experience. After she escaped from slavery, Harriet Jacobs wrote in her autobiography: "[My purpose] is not to tell you what I have heard but what I have seen—and what I have suffered." In their sharing of memory, the people in this study offer us an opportunity to see ourselves reflected in a mirror called history. [20]

In his recent study of Spain and the New World, *The Buried Mirror*, Carlos Fuentes points out that mirrors have been found in the tombs of ancient Mexico, placed there to guide the dead through the underworld. He also tells us about the legend of Quetzalcoatl, the Plumed Serpent: when this god was given a mirror by the Toltec deity Tezcatlipoca, he saw a man's face in the mirror and realized his own humanity. For us, the "mirror" of history can guide the living and also help us recognize who we have been and hence are. In *A Distant Mirror*, Barbara W. Tuchman finds "phenomenal parallels" between the "calamitous fourteenth century" of European society and our own era. We can, she observes, have "greater fellow-feeling for a distraught age" as we painfully recognize the "similar disarray," "collapsing assumptions," and "unusual discomfort."[21]

But what is needed in our own perplexing times is not so much a "distant" mirror, as one that is "different." While the study of the past can provide collective self-knowledge, it often reflects the scholar's particular perspective or view of the world. What happens when historians leave out many of America's peoples? What happens, to borrow the words of Adrienne Rich, "when someone with the authority of a teacher" describes our society, and "you are not in it"? Such an experience can be disorienting—"a moment of psychic disequilibrium, as if you looked into a mirror and saw nothing."[22]

Through their narratives about their lives and circumstances, the people of America's diverse groups are able to see themselves and each other in our common past. They celebrate what Ishmael Reed has described as a society "unique" in the world because "the world is here"—a place "where the cultures of the world crisscross." Much of America's past, they point out, has been riddled with racism. At the same time, these people offer hope, affirming the struggle for equality as a central theme in our country's history. At its conception, our nation was dedicated to the proposition of equality. What has given concreteness to this powerful national principle has been our coming together in the creation of a new society. "Stuck here" together, workers of different backgrounds have attempted to get along with each other.

> People harvesting
> Work together unaware
> Of racial problems,

wrote a Japanese immigrant describing a lesson learned by Mexican and Asian farm laborers in California.[23]

Finally, how do we see our prospects for "working out" America's racial crisis? Do we see it as through a glass darkly? Do the televised images of racial hatred and violence that riveted us in 1992 during the days of rage in Los Angeles frame a future of divisive race relations—what Arthur Schlesinger Jr., has fearfully denounced as the "disuniting of America"? Or will Americans of diverse races and ethnicities be able to connect themselves to a larger narrative? Whatever happens, we can be certain that much of our society's future will be influenced by which "mirror" we choose to see ourselves. America does not belong to one race or one group . . . Americans have been constantly redefining their national identity from the moment of first contact on the Virginia shore. By sharing their stories, they invite us to see ourselves in a different mirror.[24]

NOTES

1. Toni Morrison, *Playing in the Dark: Whiteness in the Literary Imagination* (Cambridge, Mass., 1992), p. 47.

2. William A. Henry III, "Beyond the Melting Pot," in "America's Changing Colors," *Time*, vol. 135, no. 15 (April 9, 1990), pp. 28–31.

3. "A Conflict of the Have-Nots," *Newsweek*, December 12, 1988, pp. 28–29.

4. Rodney King's statement to the press, *New York Times*, May 2, 1992, p. 6.

5. Tim Rutten, "A New Kind of Riot," *New York Times Review of Books*, June 11, 1992, pp. 52–53; Maria Newman, "Riots Bring Attention to Growing Hispanic Presence in South-Central Area," *New York Times*, May 11, 1992, p. A10; Mike Davis, "In L.A. Burning All Illusions," *The Nation*, June 1, 1992, pp. 744–745; Jack Viets and Peter Fimrite, "S.F. Mayor Visits Riot-Torn Area to Buoy Businesses," *San Francisco Chronicle*, May 6, 1992, p. A6.

6. Rick DelVecchio, Suzanne Espinosa, and Carl Nolte, "Bradley Ready to Lift Curfew," *San Francisco Chronicle*, May 4, 1992, p. A1.

7. Abraham Lincoln, "The Gettysburg Address," in *The Annals of America*, vol. 9, *1863–1865: The Crisis of the Union* (Chicago, 1968), pp. 462–463; Martin Luther King, *Why We Can't Wait* (New York, 1964), pp. 92–93.

8. Interview with old laundryman, in "Interviews with Two Chinese," circa 1924, Box 326, folder 325, Survey of Race Relations, Stanford University, Hoover Institution Archives; Congressman Robert Matsui, speech in the House of Representatives on the 442 bill for redress and reparations, September 17, 1987, *Congressional Record* (Washington, D.C., 1987), p. 7584.

9. Camarillo, *Chicanos in a Changing Society*, p. 2; Juan Nepornuceno Seguín, in David J. Weber (ed.), *Foreigners in Their Native Land: Historical Roots of the Mexican Americans* (Albuquerque, N. M., 1973), p. vi; Jesus Garza, in Manuel Garnio, *The Mexican Immigrant: His Life Story* (Chicago, 1931), p. 15; Ernesto Galarza, *Barrio Boy: The Story of a Boy's Acculturation* (Notre Dame, Ind., 1986), p. 200.

10. Lawrence J. McCaffrey, *The Irish Diaspora in America* (Washington, D.C., 1984), pp. 6, 62.

11. John Murray Cuddihy, *The Ordeal of Civility: Freud, Marx, Levi Strauss, and the Jewish Struggle with Modernity* (Boston, 1987), p. 165; Jonathan Kaufman, *Broken Alliance: The Turbulent Times between Blacks and Jews in America* (New York, 1989), pp. 28, 82, 83–84, 91, 93, 106.

12. Andrew Jackson, First Annual Message to Congress, December 8, 1829, in James D. Richardson (ed.), *A Compilation of the Messages and Papers of the Presidents,*

1789–1897 (Washington, D.C., 1897), vol. 2, p. 457; Frederick Jackson Turner, "The Significance of the Frontier in American History," in *The Early Writings of Frederick Jackson Turner* (Madison, Wis., 1938), pp. 185ff.; Luther Standing Bear, "What the Indian Means to America," in Wayne Moquin (ed.), *Great Documents in American Indian History* (New York, 1973), p. 307; Vine Deloria, Jr., *Custer Died for Your Sins: An Indian Manifesto* (New York, 1969).

13. Nathan Glazer, *Affirmative Discrimination: Ethnic Inequality and Public Policy* (New York, 1978); Thomas Sowell, *Ethnic America: A History* (New York, 1981); David R. Roediger, *The Wages of Whiteness: Race and the Making of the American Working Class* (London, 1991), pp. 134–136; Dan Caldwell, "The Negroization of the Chinese Stereotype in California," *Southern California Quarterly*, vol. 33 (June 1971), pp. 123–131.

14. Thomas Almaguer, "Racial Domination and Class Conflict in Capitalist Agriculture: The Oxnard Sugar Beet Workers' Strike of 1903," *Labor History*, vol. 25, no. 3 (summer 1984), p. 347; Howard M. Sachar, *A History of the Jews in America* (New York, 1992), p. 183.

15. For the concept of liminality, see Victor Turner, *Dramas, Fields, and Metaphors: Symbolic Action in Human Society* (Ithaca, N.Y., 1974), pp. 232, 237; and Arnold Van Gennep, *The Rites of Passage* (Chicago, 1960). What I try to do is to apply liminality to the land called America.

16. Kazuo Ito, *Issei: A History of Japanese Immigrants in North America* (Seattle, 1973), p. 33; Arnold Schrier, *Ireland and the American Emigration, 1850–1900* (New York, 1970), p. 24; Abraham Cahan, *The Rise of David Levinsky* (New York, 1960; originally published in 1917), pp. 59–61; Mary Antin, quoted in Howe, *World of Our Fathers* (New York, 1983), p. 27; Lawrence A. Cardoso, *Mexican Emigration to the United States, 1897–1931* (Tucson, Ariz., 1981), p. 80.

17. Ronald Takaki, *Strangers from a Different Shore: A History of Asian Americans* (Boston, 1989), pp. 88–89; Jack Weatherford, *Native Roots: How the Indians Enriched America* (New York, 1991), pp. 210, 212; Carey McWilliams, *North from Mexico: The Spanish-Speaking People of the United States* (New York, 1968), p. 154; Stephan Themstrom (ed.), *Harvard Encyclopedia of American Ethnic Groups* (Cambridge, Mass., 1980), p. 22; Sachar, *A History of the Jews in America*, p. 367.

18. Weber (ed.), *Foreigners in Their Native Land*, p. vi; Hamilton Holt (ed.), *The Life Stories of Undistinguished Americans as Told by Themselves* (New York, 1906), p. 143.

19. "Social Document of Pany Lowe, interviewed by C. H. Burnett, Seattle, July 5, 1924," p. 6, Survey of Race Relations, Stanford University, Hoover Institution Archives; Minnie Miller, "Autobiography," private manuscript, copy from Richard Balkin; Tomo Shoji, presentation, Obana Cultural Center, Oakland, California, March 4, 1988.

20. Sandra Cisneros, *The House on Mango Street* (New York, 1991), pp. 109–110; Leslie Marmon Silko, *Ceremony* (New York, 1978), p. 2; Harriet A. Jacobs, *Incidents in the Life of a Slave Girl, written by herself* (Cambridge, Mass., 1987; originally published in 1857), p. xiii.

21. Carlos Fuentes, *The Buried Mirror: Reflections on Spain and the New World* (Boston, 1992), pp. 10, 11, 109; Barbara W. Tuchman, *A Distant Mirror: The Calamitous 14th Century* (New York, 1978), pp. xiii, xiv.

22. Adrienne Rich, *Blood, Bread, and Poetry: Selected Prose, 1979–1985* (New York, 1986), p. 199.

23. Ishmael Reed, "America: The Multinational Society," in Rick Simonson and Scott Walker (eds.), *Multi-cultural Literacy* (St. Paul, 1988), p. 160; Ito, *Issei*, p. 497.

24. Arthur M. Schlesinger Jr., *The Disuniting of America: Reflections on a Multicultural Society* (Knoxville, Tenn., 1991); Carlos Bulosan, *America Is in the Heart: A Personal History* (Seattle, 1981), pp. 188–189.

II

Conceptualizing Race, Class, and Gender

Picture a typical college basketball game. It all seems pretty familiar: the players on the court, the cheerleaders arrayed at the side, the band playing, fans cheering, boosters watching from the best seats, and—if the team is ranked—perhaps a television crew. Everybody seems to have a place in the game. Everybody seems to be following the rules. But what are the "rules" of this game? What explains the patterns that we see and don't see?

Race clearly matters. The predominance of young African American men on many college basketball teams is noticeable. Why do so many young Black men play basketball? Some people argue that African Americans are better in areas requiring physical skills such as sports and are less capable of doing intellectual work in fields such as physics, law, and medicine. Others look to Black culture for explanations, suggesting that African Americans would be perfectly happy just playing ball and partying. But these perspectives fail to take into account the continuing effects of institutional racism. Lack of access to decent jobs, adequate housing, high-quality education, and adequate health care has resulted in higher rates of poverty for African Americans. In 1998, 26 percent of African Americans, 26 percent of Hispanics, and 13 percent of Asian Americans were poor, as compared to 9 percent of Whites who are not Hispanic

(U.S. Census Bureau 1999b). For young Black men growing up in communities with few opportunities, sports like basketball become attractive as a way out of poverty.

Despite the importance of institutionalized racism, does a racial analysis fully explain the "rules" of the game of college basketball? Not really, because Black men are not the only players. White men also play college basketball, also raising questions about the significance of social class in explaining a basketball game. Who benefits from college basketball? Some observers argue that, because the players get scholarships and are offered a chance to earn college degrees, the players reap the rewards; but this misses the point of who really benefits. College athletics is big business, and the players make far less from it than many people believe. As amateur athletes, they are forbidden to take any payment for their skills. They are offered the hope of an NBA contract when they turn pro, or at least a college degree if they graduate. But, as Michael Messner shows in his "Masculinities and Athletic Careers" (printed in part IV), few actually turn pro. Indeed, among Division I Black basketball players, only 31 percent graduate from college, compared to 57 percent of White male basketball players. Interestingly, however, graduation rates among Black college athletes are higher than among nonathletes, perhaps because of the scholarship support they receive. The same is true for women athletes, who have higher graduation rates than nonathletes and higher graduation rates than male athletes. This is true for both Black and White women student athletes (National Collegiate Athletic Association, 1999; http://www.ncaa.org/).

So who actually benefits from college basketball? The colleges that recruit the athletes certainly benefit. For the university, winning teams garner increased admissions applications, alumni giving, corporate support, and television revenues. In athletics as a business, corporate sponsors want their names and products identified with winning teams and athletes; advertisers want their products promoted by members of winning teams. Even though the athletes themselves are forbidden to promote the products, corporations create and market products in conjunction with prevailing excitement about basketball, sustained by the players' achievements. Products such as athletic shoes, workout clothing, cars, and beer all target the consumer dollars of those who enjoy watching basketball. Also, consider how many full-time jobs are supported by the revenues generated from the enterprise of college basketball. Referees, sports reporters—both at the games and on local media outlets—athletic trainers, coaches, and health personnel all benefit. Unlike the players, these people all get paid for their contributions to college basketball.

Do race and class fully explain the "rules" of basketball? Sometimes what we *don't* see can be just as revealing as what we do see. One other feature of the game on the court may escape attention because it is so familiar and, therefore, so unquestioned. Although women's basketball is increasingly popular, men's basketball is generally the public's focal point. Most of the coaches and support personnel are men, as are most of the camera crew and announcers. Where are the women? A few are coaches, rarely paid what the men receive. Those closest to the action on the court may be cheerleaders—tumbling, dancing, and being thrown into the air in support of the exploits of the athletes. Others may be in the band. Some women are in the stands, cheering on the team—many of them accompanied by their husbands, boyfriends, parents, and children. Many work in the concession stands, fulfilling women's traditional roles of serving others. Still others are even more invisible, left to clean the restrooms, locker rooms, and stands after the crowd goes home. Women remain on the sidelines in other ways as well. The treatment of women basketball players markedly differs from that of their male counterparts: women have many fewer opportunities for scholarships and professional careers in athletics. The centrality of men's activities in basketball mirrors the centrality afforded men's activities in the society as a whole; thus, women's seeming invisibility in basketball ironically highlights the salience of gender.

Men's behavior, too, can reveal a gendered dimension to basketball, as in other sports. Where else are men able to put their arms around each other, slap one another's buttocks, hug each other, or cry in public without having their "masculinity" questioned? Sportscasters, too, bring gender into the play of sports, such as when they talk about men's heroic athletic achievements, but talk about women athletes' looks or their connection to children. For that matter, look at the prominence given to men's teams in sports pages of the daily newspaper, compared to sports news about women, who are typically relegated to the back pages—if their athletic accomplishments are reported at all.

This brief discussion of college basketball demonstrates how race, class, and gender each provide an important, yet partial, perspective on the action on the court. Race, class, and gender are so inextricably intertwined that gaining a comprehensive understanding of one basketball game requires that we think inclusively. If race, class, and gender relations are embedded in something as familiar and widespread as college basketball, we might ask to what extent other social practices, institutions, relations, and social issues are similarly structured.

Although some people believe that race, gender, and class divisions are relics of the past, we see them as deeply embedded in the structure of social institutions such as work, family, education, and the state. Race, class, and gender in turn shape the social issues that emerge from within the institutions themselves. As we discussed in the introduction, they are interlocking systems of experience. In this part, however, we focus on each one to provide a basic grounding in how each operates, keeping in mind that they are connected and overlapping. Before you understand the intricacy of these intersections, though, you need to have a basic understanding of each concept.

Our purpose in this section is to conceptualize how each—race, class, and gender—shapes society and people's experience within it and how they are connected. We want readers to understand how race and class structure gender relations, as well as how gender and race structure class relations and how class and race structure gender relations. We look at each distinctly only to provide a foundation for understanding their interlocking nature.

RACE

In this volume we examine race, class, and gender relations from an institutional or structural perspective. Locating racial oppression in the structure of social institutions provides a different frame of analysis from what would be obtained by analyzing individuals only. *Individual racism* is one person's belief in the superiority of one race over another. Individual racism is related to *prejudice*, a hostile attitude toward a person who is presumed to have negative characteristics associated with a group to which he or she belongs.

Institutional racism is more systematic than this. Institutions such as work, family, education, the state, and sports are "fairly stable social arrangements and practices" that persist over time (Knowles and Prewitt 1970: 5). *Institutional racism* is a system of behavior and beliefs by which a group defined as a race is oppressed, controlled, and exploited because of presumed cultural or biological characteristics (Blauner 1972). Racism is not the same thing as prejudice. Prejudice refers to people's attitudes. Racism is a system of power and privilege; it can be manifested in people's attitudes but is rooted in society's structure and is reflected in the different advantages and disadvantages that groups experience, based on their location in this societal system. The concept of institutional racism reminds us that racism is structured into society, not just into people's minds.

In this definition of institutional racism, notice first that racism is systematic: it is part of society's structure, not just present in individual bigots. As Gloria Yamato discusses in "Something about the Subject Makes It Hard to Name," racism can be intentional or unintentional. In a racist system, well-meaning White people benefit from racism even if they have no intention of acting or thinking like a "racist." Thus, institutional racism creates a built-in system of privilege. As Yamato suggests, different groups internalize it in different forms of consciousness. Peggy McIntosh's essay, "White Privilege and Male Privilege," describes how the system of racial privilege becomes invisible to those who benefit from it, even though it structures the everyday life of both White people and people of color.

Second, institutional racism shapes everyday social relations. In other words, despite its systematic nature, institutional racism depends on the presence of individual racists acting daily in order to continue. If you are a person of color, even being middle class does not protect you from the everyday realities of racism (Feagin and Sikes 1994). According to sociologist Philomena Essed (1991), it is important to identify practices, rather than individuals, as racist. Essed identifies numerous practices engaged in by White people as examples of everyday racism. For example, White people deny racism by failing to take a stand against racism, by refusing to admit racism, by acknowledging only extreme racism, and by expressing anger at Black people who point out racism, among other strategies. Although each act of everyday racism in and of itself may be relatively benign, institutional racism operates in our everyday lives as a sustained pattern of everyday actions such as these.

Patricia Williams, a noted African American legal scholar, shows this in her discussion of persistent discrimination in housing. Despite her middle-class status, systemic racism confronts her—and other African Americans—in daily encounters. The experience Michael Dyson describes in "The Plight of Black Men" offers another example of the practice of everyday racism. Dyson, an African American professor and philosopher, was using his credit card to get a cash advance when a bank manager in Princeton questioned him, cut his card in half, and called the police. Dyson's experience is a familiar one to many African American men, who, given the dynamics of racism, are often perceived by Whites to be dangerous and threatening.

Practices of everyday racism are part of the edifice of institutional racism; yet we often misread their meaning. Many people believe that being nonracist means being color-blind—that is, refusing to recognize or treat as significant a person's racial background and identity. But to ignore the significance of race in a society where racial groups have distinct historical and contemporary experiences is to deny the reality of their group experience. Being color-blind in a society structured on racial privilege means assuming that everybody is "White," which is why people of color might be offended by friends who say, for example, "But I never think of you as Black." Such practices of everyday racism are powerful because, instead of seeing them as components of patterns of institutional racism, we experience these interactions as ordinary occurrences.

Another dimension of institutional racism is that its forms change over time. Racial discrimination is no longer legal, but racism is present nonetheless and continues to structure relations between groups and to differentiate the power that different groups have. The changing character of racism is also evident in the fact that specific racial group histories differ, but different racial groups share common experiences of racial oppression. Thus, Chinese Americans were never enslaved, but they experienced forced residential segregation and economic exploitation based on their presumed racial characteristics. Mexican Americans were never placed on federal reservations as Native Americans have been, but in some regards both groups share the experience of colonization by White settlers.

In a racist society, the very meaning of *race* reflects institutionalized racist practices and beliefs. Most people assume that race is biologically fixed, an assumption that has been fueled recently by popular arguments about the presumed biological basis for different forms of inequality. But the concept of race is more social than biological: it is given meaning and significance in specific social, historical, and political contexts. The significance of race comes from this context, not from whatever physical differences may exist between groups. This is what it means to say that race is a social-historical-political concept.

To understand this, think about how racial categories are created, by whom, and for what purposes. Racial classification systems reflect prevailing views of race, thereby establishing groups that are presumed to be "natural." These constructed racial categories then serve as the basis for allocating resources; furthermore, once defined, the categories frame political issues and conflicts (Omi and Winant 1994). Omi and Winant define *racial formation* as "the sociohistorical process by which racial categories are created, inhabited, transformed, and destroyed" (1994: 55). In Nazi Germany, Jews were considered to be a race—a social construction that became the basis for the Holocaust. Abby Ferber's essay shows the complexities that evolve in the social construction of race. As someone who studies White supremacist groups, she sees how White racism defiles her as Jewish, even while she lives in the society as

White. Her reflections reveal, too, the interconnections between racism and anti-Semitism (the hatred of Jewish people), reminding us of the interplay between different systems of oppression.

In understanding racial formation, we see that societies construct race and that racial meanings constantly change as different groups contest prevailing racial definitions that empower some groups at the expense of others. Consider, for example, the changing definitions of race in the U.S. census. Given the large number of multiracial groups and the increasing diversity brought about by immigration, we can no longer think of race in terms of mutually exclusive categories. Persons of mixed racial heritage, a small but growing group, present a challenge to the current system. In 1860, only three "races" were presumed to exist—Whites, Blacks, and mulattoes. By 1890, however, these original three "races" had been joined by five others—quadroon, octoroon, Chinese, Japanese, and Indian. Ten short years later, this list shrank to five "races"—White, Black, Chinese, Japanese, and Indian—a situation reflecting the growth of strict segregation in the South (O'Hare 1996). In the 1990 census, the U.S. government distinguished between race and ethnicity; thus, a person could be classified in one of five "racial" groups—White; Black African American; Asian or Pacific Islander; American Indian, Eskimo, or Aleut; and other—and one of two ethnicities, Hispanic or non-Hispanic. In this scheme, Hispanics may be of any race, even though many Hispanics do not identify with any of the racial categories established by the census. In fact, in the 1990 census, 43 percent of Hispanics identified their race as "other"; most people (96 percent) in the "other" race category were Hispanic (O'Hare 1996: 6).

In the year 2000 census, the racial categories to be included were the subject of dispute. The growing number of multiracial people in the United States poses a significant challenge for categorizing people. This is not just a matter of accurate statistics; it has significant consequences in the apportionment of societal resources. Data on racial groups are used to enforce voting rights, to regulate equal employment opportunities, and to determine various governmental supports, among other things. Although it may be easy for some people to say, "Race doesn't matter; we should be a color-blind society," Cornel West argues that race clearly matters and it matters a lot.

Shifting definitions of race are grounded in shifting relations of power. Recent decades have seen additional revisions to definitions of race. In particular, the experiences of Latino groups in the United States challenge long-standing racial categories of "Black" and "White." Elizabeth Martinez (in "Seeing More Than Black & White") notes that White-Black relations have defined racism in the United States for centuries, but that a rapidly changing population that includes diverse Latino groups is forcing Americans to reconsider the nature of racism. Color, she argues, has been the marker of race, but she challenges the dualistic thinking that has promoted this racist thinking.

The overarching structure of racial power relations means that placement in this structure leads to differences in outlook regarding the very presence of racism and what can be done about it. The reappearance of racial hostilities on college campuses is certainly evidence of the continuation of racist practices and beliefs; yet despite this and other evidence, Whites continue to be optimistic in their assessment of racial progress. They say that they are tired of hearing about racism and that they have done all they can to eliminate racial discrimination. Blacks are less sanguine about racial progress and are more aware of the nuances of racism. Although overt discrimination has been lessened, marked differences by race are still evident in employment, political representation, schooling, and other basic measures of group well-being.

Racism does not exist in a vacuum. As we have said, race, gender, and class are intersecting systems—experienced simultaneously, not separately. It is a mistake to think of any one category in the absence of the others. People's experiences with race and racism are framed by their location in this overarching system of race, class, and gender privileges and penalties. Race possesses not only objective dimensions that result from institutional racism; it also has subjective dimensions that relate to how people experience it. For example, some people of color grow up with class privilege; yet this does not eliminate racism, as Dyson's experience in the bank shows us. Although class differentiation has increased within racial groups and such class difference is significant, this does not mean that some people are immune from the effects of racism. Class differences within racial groups show how race and class together configure group experiences differently. As a consequence, the experiences of poor Black men in Michael Dyson's discussion differ from those of the Black women in Elizabeth Higginbotham's and Lynn Weber's analysis of differing mobility experiences ("Moving Up with Kin and Community"). All people of color encounter institutional racism, but their actual experiences with racism vary, depending on social class, gender, age, sexuality, and other markers of social position.

CLASS

Like institutional racism, the social class system is grounded in social institutions and practices. Rather than thinking of social class as an identity owned by an individual, think of social class as a series of relations that pervade the entire society and shape our social institutions and relationships with one another. While class shapes identity, importantly the social class system differentially structures group access to material resources, including economic, political, and social resources. This system results from patterns of capitalist development, especially as those patterns intersect with institutional racism and gender oppression.

In the United States, the social class system is marked by striking differences in wealth and income. *Wealth*, or net worth, is determined by adding all of one's financial assets and subtracting all debt. In 1993, White households had an average net worth of $45,740, as compared to $4,418 for Black households (U.S. Census Bureau 1997). Household income data show similar patterns. In 1998, median income was $42,439 for White non-Hispanic households; $25,351 for Blacks; $28,330 for Hispanics; and $46,637 for Asian Americans/Pacific Islanders (U.S. Census Bureau 1999a: 1; see Figure 1).

Wealth is especially significant because it provides a *cumulative* advantage to those who have it. Wealth helps pay for college costs for children and down payments on houses; it can cushion the impact of emergencies, such as unex-

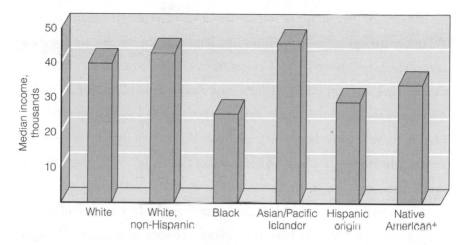

Source: U.S. Census Bureau. 1999a. *Money Income in the United States: 1998.* Washington, D.C.: U.S. Department of Commerce, p. vi.
*Data on Native Americans available only for 1989; this is an approximation based on changes in the CPI (consumer price index).

FIGURE 1 Median Income (All Households), 1998.

pected unemployment or sudden health problems. The median net worth of White households is more than ten times that of African American and Latino households. Buying a home, investing, being free of debt, sending one's children to college, and transferring economic assets to the next generation are all instances of class advantage that add up over time and produce advantage even beyond one's current income level. Sociologists Melvin Oliver and Thomas Shapiro (1995) have found, for example, that Black and White Americans with the same educational and occupational assets still have a substantial difference in their financial assets—an average difference of $43,143 per year! This means that, even when earning the same income, the two groups are in quite different class situations, as reflected in tax breaks, the possibility of home ownership, the benefits of inheritance, and the accumulation of investments. Given these facts, Oliver and Shapiro conclude that "the long-term life prospects of black households are substantially poorer than those of whites in similar income brackets" (1995: 101). Furthermore, wealth produces more wealth, as perhaps best reflected in the ability—through inheritance—to transmit economic status from one generation to the next. Dalton Conley shows us the difference this makes in the experiences of Black and White families.

Aggregate data showing wide differences in economic status between Whites and people of color are revealing, but they can also obscure the workings of the social class system. We must be careful not to generalize from such data and see, for example, all Whites and Asians as wealthy and all African Americans and Latinos as poor. Consider the range of social class experiences just among Whites. Although on the average White households possess higher accumulated wealth and have higher incomes than Black and Hispanic households, large numbers of White households do not. Even though 8.2 percent of Whites were poor in 1998 (a figure lower than the 26.1 percent of African Americans, 12.5 percent of Asian Americans and Pacific Islanders, and 25.6 percent of Hispanics who are poor), White people account for 46 percent of the nation's poor (U.S. Census Bureau 1999b). Imagine what the range in White wealth must be to produce such a high White median income while so many White people remain in poverty.

Likewise, the aggregate data on Asian Americans show them as a group to be relatively well off. Stereotypes of the "model minority," however, obscure serious problems of poverty among many Asian Americans: 13 percent of Asian American/Pacific Islanders were poor in 1998, almost twice the percentage of White non-Hispanics (U.S. Census Bureau 1999b). The proportion of Asian Americans living in poverty has also increased substantially since the 1980s, particularly among the most recent immigrant groups, including Laotians, Cambodians, Vietnamese, Chinese, and Korean immigrants. Filipino and Asian Indian families had lower rates of poverty (Lee 1995).

In the U.S. class system, poverty is a problem for many, as the rates of poverty illustrated in Figure 2 show. Women and their children are especially hard hit by poverty; although they are not the only people who are poor, poverty in this group has reached alarming rates. Poverty rates among children are especially disturbing: 37 percent of African American children, 34 percent of Hispanic children, 18 percent of Asian/Pacific Islander children, and 11 percent of White children (those under 18 years of age) are poor—astonishing figures for one of the most affluent nations in the world (U.S. Census Bureau

1999b). Simplistic solutions suggested by current welfare policy imply that women would not be poor if they would just get married or get a job. As James Jennings and Louis Kushnick argue in "Poverty as Race, Power, and Wealth," the root causes of poverty lie in the distribution of wealth and capital, coupled with low wages and high unemployment among certain groups—groups whose social location is the result of race, gender, and class stratification.

In the United States, the social class system is also marked by differences in *power*. Social class is not just a matter of material difference; it is a pattern of domination in which some groups have more power than others. Power is the ability to influence and in some cases dominate others. This means not just interpersonal power but also the structural power that some groups hold because of their position of domination over others. Power is, of course, influenced by material well-being. Groups with vast amounts of wealth, for example, have the ability to influence systems like the media and the political process in ways that less powerful groups cannot. The power held by different

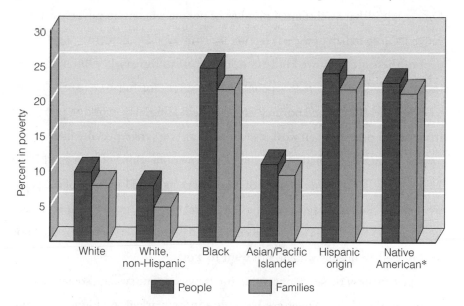

Source: U.S. Census Bureau. 1999c. *Poverty in the United States: 1998.*
Washington, D.C.: U.S. Department of Commerce, p. vi.
*Poverty data for Native Americans available only for 1989.

FIGURE 2 Poverty in the United States, 1998.

groups varies enormously, depending on each group's position in the class system. Privilege in social class thus encompasses both a position of material advantage and the ability to control and influence others.

Like the system of institutional racism, the system of social class undergoes change. Changes in class are intimately linked to patterns of economic transformation in the U.S. political economy. Increasingly, these changes occur in a global context. Jobs are exported overseas as vast multinational corporations seek to enhance their profits by promoting new markets and cutting the cost of labor. Within the United States, specific economic changes include a shift from a manufacturing economy to a service economy, with corresponding changes in the types of jobs available and the wages attached to these jobs. As a result of mechanization, job export, deskilling of work, and other changes in the workplace, fewer skilled, high-paying manufacturing jobs exist today than in the past. This situation in turn has benefited some but left many people in jobs that do not pay enough, in part-time work, or without any work at all. One result is that a substantial number of people who are in poverty are employed. Close to half of the adult poor are employed (41 percent), and 13 percent of these are employed full-time (U.S. Census Bureau 1999b); moreover, the number of *working poor*—people whose wages for full-time work are below the federally defined poverty line—is increasing. The working poor now make up 25 percent of all workers, with young workers especially likely to be among them. Nearly half of all women and over one-third of men aged 18 to 24 are in this group. One-quarter of Black workers and 31 percent of Hispanic workers (including all ages) earn poverty-level incomes, even though they are working full-time. This is in sharp contrast to popular stereotypes of the poor as lazy welfare queens who do not want to work.

As a result of these changes affecting the economic system, social class divisions in the United States are becoming more marked. As Figure 3 shows, looking at the growth of income in different quintiles of the population (i.e., fifths) reveals a growing gap between the "haves" and "have-nots," with the top 20 percent (and the top 5 percent) reaping enormous income gains in recent years, while the income growth of those in the middle and at the bottom has remained relatively flat. Furthermore, these patterns hold for all racial groups (U.S. Census Bureau 1999a). In the nation's cities and towns, homelessness has become increasingly apparent even to casual observers. A recent report by the U.S. Census Bureau found that of the nation's homeless (470,000 people on an average night), almost half (44 percent) had worked in the past month, an indication of the connection between low wages and poverty (Bernstein 1999). Middle-class people feel that their way of life is slipping away—a feeling supported by data showing increasing economic polarization. Yet as Barbara Ehrenreich points out in "The Silenced Majority," the remaining professional middle class is insulated from the realities of working-class experience. Dominant ideology renders the working class invisible, even though this group is the largest segment of the population.

If social class is so important in shaping life chances, why don't more people realize its significance? The answer lies in how dominant groups use ideology to explain the social class system and other systems of inequality.

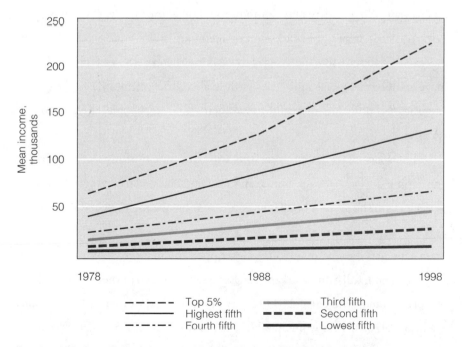

Source: U.S. Census Bureau. 1999. *Historical Income Tables—Households.* Web site: http://www.census.gov/hhes/income/histinc/h03.html

FIGURE 3 Income Growth by Income Group, 1978–1998.

Ideology created by dominant groups refers to a system of beliefs that simultaneously distort reality and justify the status quo. As we learn in "Tired of Playing Monopoly?" by Donna Langston, the class system in the United States has been supported through the myth that we live in a classless society. This myth serves the dominant class, making class privilege seem like something that one earns, not something that is deeply embedded in the institutions of society. Langston also suggests that the system of privilege and inequality (by race, class, and gender) is least visible to those who are most privileged and who, in turn, control the resources to define the dominant cultural belief systems. Perhaps this is why the privileged, not the poor, are more likely to believe that one gets ahead through hard work. It may also explain why men more than women deny that patriarchy exists, and why Whites more than Blacks believe racism is disappearing.

In addition to giving some groups more privileges than others, class shapes social relationships. As Elizabeth Higginbotham and Lynn Weber point out in "Moving Up with Kin and Community," one of the best ways of seeing how social class shapes relationships among members of the same class and among people of different social classes is to examine the experiences of people who have undergone social mobility. As they also observe, mobility experiences significantly differ for men and for women—and for people of color and for Whites.

The social class system intersects with the system of institutional racism in shaping the experiences of men and women. The social class system also intersects with the system of gender oppression by placing men and women differently within this same overarching structure. For example, in 1998, White men's median income of $37,196 outstripped the income of all other groups of year-round, full-time workers (see Figure 4). Arrayed in the figure are Asian American men, who earned $34,682; Asian American women, $27,782; Black men, $27,472; White women, $27,304; Latino men, $22,505; Black women, $23,864; and Latinas, $19,817—most groups' earnings falling substantially below White men's earnings (U.S. Census Bureau 1999a; U.S. Census Bureau

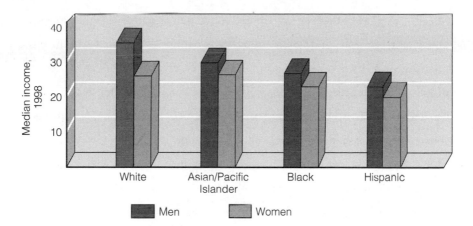

Source: U.S. Census Bureau. 1999a. *Money Income in the United States: 1998.*
Washington, D.C.: U.S. Department of Commerce, pp. 28–29; U.S. Census Bureau.
1999c. *Historical Income Tables*, Table 4.
Web site: http://www.census.gov/population/socdemo/race/api98/table04.txt

FIGURE 4 Income for Full-Time Workers (by Race and Gender).

1999c). We should point out, however, that men's wages (in all racial groups)
have been falling, especially among bottom-level jobs and entry-level positions. One result is that people have to work more just to stay in place (Mishel,
Bernstein, and Schmitt 1999).

Overall, the effects of race, class, and gender manifest themselves in variable patterns of advantage or disadvantage. For example, in some ways—such
as in rates of poverty and the racial gap in earnings in the labor market—
women of color share a class position with men of color. In other ways, women
of different races share a common class position: they all make less on average
than men of their racial group. Together, these trends point to the need for
inclusive thinking in developing a social class analysis.

GENDER

Gender, like race, is a socially constructed experience, not a biological imper-
ative. Sociologists distinguish between the terms *sex* and *gender* to emphasize
this point. *Sex* refers to one's biological identity as male or female; *gender*

refers to the social identities attributed to women and men. Gender is rooted in social institutions and results in patterns within society that structure the relationships between women and men and that give them differing positions of advantage and disadvantage within institutions. As an identity, gender is learned; that is, through gender socialization, people construct definitions of themselves and others that are marked by gender. Like race, however, gender cannot be understood at the individual level alone. Gender is structured in social institutions, including work, families, mass media, and education. Changing gender relations is not just a matter of changing individual attitudes. As with race relations, change requires transformation of institutional structures.

The ideology of sexism supports the system of gender relations, just as the ideology of racism supports the system of race relations. Like racism, *sexism* is a system of beliefs and behaviors by which a group is oppressed, controlled, and exploited because of presumed gender differences. Sexism is manifested in individually held beliefs and in social behaviors, and it is embedded in cultural symbols. It supports the gender inequalities that are structured into social institutions.

Gender, however, is not a monolithic category. Maxine Baca Zinn, Pierrette Hondagneu-Sotelo, and Michael Messner argue that, although gender is grounded in specific power relations, it is important to understand gender as constructed differently depending on the specific social locations of diverse groups. Thus race, class, nationality, sexual orientation, and other factors produce varying social and economic consequences that cannot be understood by looking at gender differences alone. They ask us to move beyond studying differences and instead to use multiple "prisms" to see and comprehend the complexities of multiple systems of domination—each of which shapes and is shaped by gender. This point is also argued by Audre Lorde, who discusses the different realities for women that stem from their racial group membership, their social class location, and their sexual orientation. Despite their similar status as women, women are not oppressed in the same ways by gender.

Seen in this way, men's lives appear less monolithic as well. Although, as Peter Blood, Alan Tuttle, and George Lakey show, patriarchy is the power structure by which men dominate women, not all men benefit equally from this arrangement. Patriarchy is joined with capitalism and systems of racial subordination; thus, not all men benefit equally from the patriarchal system. Blood, Tuttle, and Lakey also show how these systems of domination penetrate people's consciousness.

As long as some groups of people are ideologically defined as "the other," systems of exploitation persist, as Yen Le Espiritu argues in "Ideological Racism and Cultural Resistance." Her discussion of the controlling images of Asian American men and women explains how such images result in racialized, sexualized, and unidimensional views of Asian American men and women. Importantly, she locates the construction of such images in the institutions that produce popular culture, thereby showing how such institutions have a stake in perpetuating race, gender, and sexual domination.

Likewise, gender stereotypes take unique forms for particular groups. Ruth Atkin and Adrienne Rich document the pernicious stereotyping of Jewish women, explaining that the process of scapegoating deflects understanding of the persecution of Jews and of other forms of critical analysis. Thus, they point out the irony of the "JAP" label as directed against women, arguing that this term simultaneously promotes anti-Asian racism, anti-Semitism, and misogyny (defined as the hatred of women).

Gender oppression also works with another major system of oppression, that of sexuality. *Homophobia*—the fear and hatred of homosexuality—is part of the system of social control that legitimates and enforces gender oppression. It supports the institutionalized power and privilege accorded to heterosexual behavior and identification. If only heterosexual forms of gender identity are labeled "normal," then gays, lesbians, and bisexuals become ostracized, oppressed, and defined as "socially deviant." Homophobia affects heterosexuals as well because it is part of gender ideology used to define "normal" men and women from those deemed deviant. Cooper Thompson's essay, "A New Vision of Masculinity," shows this well, as he discusses how young boys learn a rigid view of masculinity—one often associated with violence, bullying, and degrading others—to avoid being perceived as a "fag." Thus, oppression of lesbians and gay men is linked to the structure of gender in everyone's lives, even though the specific forms of oppression that stem from heterosexism are also shaped by race and class.

Throughout part II, you should keep the concept of social structure in mind. Remembering Marilyn Frye's analogy of the birdcage, be aware that race, class, and gender form a structure of social relations. This structure is supported by ideological beliefs that make it appear "normal" and "acceptable" and that often cloud our awareness of how the structure operates. Contemporary ideology leads many to believe that women are now equal to men and that sexism is disappearing. Seeing more White women in the labor force and seeing more women in jobs traditionally reserved for men can give the appearance that women are doing well. Indeed, some are. But how real are these gains and who do they benefit?

The gap between women's and men's income has closed some; however, most analysts agree that the narrowing of the gap reflects a drop in men's wages more than an increase in women's wages. The most dramatic gains in economic status have been made by younger women in professional jobs— those who become defined as the stereotypical "working woman." Despite this new image, though, most women remain concentrated in gender-segregated occupations with low wages, little opportunity for mobility, and stressful conditions. This is particularly true for women of color, who are more likely to be in occupations that are race and gender segregated. For women heading their own households, poverty persists at alarmingly high rates. Close to half of all Black and Latino families (40.8 percent and 43.7 percent, respectively) and 20.7 percent of White families headed by women are officially categorized as poor; that is, they earn incomes below the federal poverty line—$16,813 for a family of four in 1998 (U.S. Census Bureau 1999b). Female-headed households with children under age eighteen are even more in jeopardy, as shown in Figure 5. Income and occupational data, however, do not tell the full story for women. High rates of violence against women—whether in the home, on campus, in the workplace, or on the streets—indicate the continuing devaluation of and danger for women in this society.

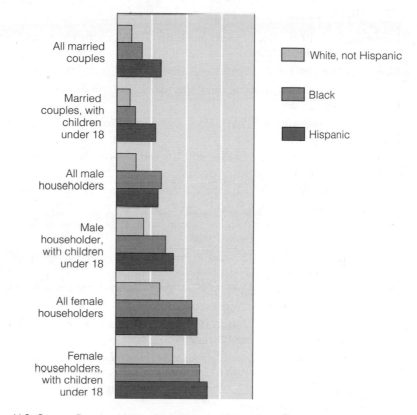

Source: U.S. Census Bureau. 1999b. *Poverty in the United States: 1998.*
Washington, D.C.: U.S. Department of Commerce, pp. B11–B17.

FIGURE 5 Families in Poverty, 1998 (by Race, Household Type, and Presence of Children).

As you read the articles in this section (and others), continue to ask yourself how different groups of women are experiencing the changes in gender relations that have characterized recent history. And, remember that although race, class, and gender are often discussed in terms of cultural difference, they are part of the institutional framework of society. A structural analysis studies the intersections of race, class, and gender within institutions and within individual's experiences in those institutions. Although we have divided the articles into sections on race, class, and gender, many theoretically fit in multiple categories. Thinking inclusively means recognizing that practices rarely belong to only one category. A more accurate way of viewing the world and the articles in part II is to see them as interconnected.

References

Bernstein, Nina. 1999. "Deep Poverty and Illness Found among Homeless." *New York Times*, December 8, p. A13.

Blauner, Robert. 1972. *Racial Oppression in America*. New York: Harper & Row.

Essed, Philomena. 1991. *Understanding Everyday Racism: An Interdisciplinary Theory*. Newbury Park, CA: Sage.

Feagin, Joe R., and Melvin P. Sikes. 1994. *Living with Racism: The Black Middle-Class Experience*. Boston: Beacon Press.

Knowles, Louis L., and Kenneth Prewitt. 1970. *Institutional Racism in America*. Englewood Cliffs, NJ: Prentice-Hall.

Lee, Sharon M. 1995. "Poverty and the U.S. Asian Population." *Social Science Quarterly* 75 (September): 541–59.

Mishel, Lawrence, Jared Bernstein, and John Schmitt. 1999. *The State of Working America*. Ithaca, NY: Cornell University Press.

O'Hare, William P. 1996. *A New Look at Poverty in America*. Washington, DC: Population Reference Bureau.

Oliver, Melvin L., and Thomas M. Shapiro. 1995. *Black Wealth/White Wealth: A New Perspective on Racial Inequality*. New York: Routledge.

Omi, Michael, and Howard Winant. 1994. *Racial Formation in the United States: From the 1960s to the 1990s*. 2d ed. New York: Routledge.

U.S. Census Bureau. 1997. *Table F. Asset Ownership of Households: 1993*. http://www.census.gov:80/hhes/www/wealth/wlth93f.html

U.S. Census Bureau. 1999a. *Money Income in the United States: 1998*. Washington, DC: U.S. Department of Commerce.

———. 1999b. *Poverty in the United States: 1998*. Washington, DC: U.S. Department of Commerce.

———. 1999c. Detailed Historical Tables, Table 4. "Selected Characteristics of Households, by Type, Region and Race of Householder: March 1998." Census Bureau Web site: http://www.census.gov/population/socdemo/race/api98/table04.txt

Suggested Readings

Andersen, Margaret L. 2000. *Thinking about Women: Sociological Perspectives on Sex and Gender*. 5th ed. Needham Heights, MA: Allyn & Bacon.

Espiritu, Yen Le. 1997. *Asian American Women and Men*. Thousand Oaks, CA: Sage.

Essed, Philomena. 1991. *Understanding Everyday Racism: An Interdisciplinary Theory*. Newbury Park, CA: Sage.

Frankenberg, Ruth. 1993. *White Women, Race Matters: The Social Construction of Whiteness*. Minneapolis: University of Minnesota Press.

Jhally, Sut, and Justin Lewis. 1992. *Enlightened Racism*. Boulder, CO: Westview Press.

Kushnick, Louis, and James Jennings, eds. 1999. *A New Introduction to Poverty: The Role of Race, Power, and Politics*. New York: New York University Press.

Oliver, Melvin, and Thomas Shapiro. 1995. *Black Wealth/White Wealth: A New Perspective on Racial Inequality*. New York: Routledge.

Omi, Michael, and Howard Winant. 1994. *Racial Formation in the United States: From the 1960s to the 1990s*. 2d ed. New York: Routledge.

Shapiro, Thomas M., ed. 1998. *Great Divides: Readings in Social Inequality in the United States*. Mountain View, CA: Mayfield.

Vanneman, Reeve, and Lynn Weber Cannon. 1987. *The American Perception of Class*. Philadelphia: Temple University Press.

InfoTrac College Edition: Search Terms

Use your access to the online library, InfoTrac College Edition, to learn more about subjects covered in this section. The following are some suggested terms for searches:

economic restructuring
gender segregation
gendered institutions
glass ceiling
heterosexism
homelessness
homophobia
income gap
institutional racism
"model minority"
Personal Responsibility and Work Opportunity
    Reconciliation Act of 1996
racial formation
social mobility
wealth
White privilege
working poor

Wadsworth Sociology Resource Center: Virtual Society

For additional links, quizzes, and learning tools related to this section, see the Wadsworth Sociology Resource Center, Virtual Society, at **http://sociology. wadsworth.com**.

Race and Racism

![segment divider]

SOMETHING ABOUT THE SUBJECT
MAKES IT HARD TO NAME

7

Gloria Yamato

Racism—simple enough in structure, yet difficult to eliminate. Racism—pervasive in the U.S. culture to the point that it deeply affects all the local town folk and spills over, negatively influencing the fortunes of folk around the world. Racism is pervasive to the point that we take many of its manifestations for granted, believing "that's life." Many believe that racism can be dealt with effectively in one hellifying workshop, or one hour-long heated discussion. Many actually believe this monster, racism, that has had at least a few hundred years to take root, grow, invade our space and develop subtle variations . . . this mind-funk that distorts thought and action, can be merely wished away. I've run into folks who really think that we can beat this devil, kick this habit, be healed of this disease in a snap. In a sincere blink of a well-intentioned eye, presto—poof—racism disappears. "I've dealt with my racism . . . (envision a laying on of hands) . . . Hallelujah! Now I can go to the beach." Well, fine. Go to the beach. In fact, why don't we all go to the beach and continue to work on the sucker over there? Cuz you can't even shave a little piece off this thing called racism in a day, or a weekend, or a workshop.

When I speak of *oppression*, I'm talking about the systematic, institutionalized mistreatment of one group of people by another for whatever reason. The oppressors are purported to have an innate ability to access economic

From: Jo Whitehorse Cochran, Donna Langston, and Carolyn Woodward, eds., *Changing Our Power: An Introduction to Women's Studies* (Dubuque, IA: Kendall-Hunt, 1988), pp. 3–6. Reprinted by permission.

resources, information, respect, etc., while the oppressed are believed to have a corresponding negative innate ability. The flip side of oppression is *internalized oppression*. Members of the target group are emotionally, physically, and spiritually battered to the point that they begin to actually believe that their oppression is deserved, is their lot in life, is natural and right, and that it doesn't even exist. The oppression begins to feel comfortable, familiar enough that when mean ol' Massa lay down de whip, we got's to pick up and whack ourselves and each other. Like a virus, it's hard to beat racism, because by the time you come up with a cure, it's mutated to a "new cure-resistant" form. One shot just won't get it. Racism must be attacked from many angles.

The forms of racism that I pick up on these days are 1) aware/blatant racism, 2) aware/covert racism, 3) unaware/unintentional racism, and 4) unaware/self-righteous racism. I can't say that I prefer any one form of racism over the others, because they all look like an itch needing a scratch. I've heard it said (and understandably so) that the aware/blatant form of racism is preferable if one must suffer it. Outright racists will, without apology or confusion, tell us that because of our color we don't appeal to them. If we so choose, we can attempt to get the hell out of their way before we get the sweat knocked out of us. Growing up, aware/covert racism is what I heard many of my elders bemoaning "up north," after having escaped the overt racism "down south." Apartments were suddenly no longer vacant or rents were outrageously high, when black, brown, red, or yellow persons went to inquire about them. Job vacancies were suddenly filled, or we were fired for very vague reasons. It still happens, though the perpetrators really take care to cover their tracks these days. They don't want to get gummed to death or slobbered on by the toothless laws that supposedly protect us from such inequities.

Unaware/unintentional racism drives usually tranquil white liberals wild when they get called on it, and confirms the suspicions of many people of color who feel that white folks are just plain crazy. It has led white people to believe that it's just fine to ask if they can touch my hair (while reaching). They then exclaim over how soft it is, how it does not scratch their hand. It has led whites to assume that bending over backwards and speaking to me in high-pitched (terrified), condescending tones would make up for all the racist wrongs that distort our lives. This type of racism has led whites right to my doorstep, talking 'bout, "We're sorry/we love you and want to make things right," which is fine, and further, "We're gonna give you the opportunity to fix it while we sleep. Just tell us what you need. 'Bye!!"—which *ain't* fine. With the best of intentions, the best of educations, and the greatest generosity of heart, whites, operating on the misinformation fed to them from day one, will behave in ways that are racist, will perpetuate racism by being "nice" the way we're taught to be nice. You can just "nice" somebody to death with naïveté and lack of awareness of privilege. Then there's guilt and the desire to end racism and how the two get all tangled up to the point that people, morbidly fascinated with their guilt, are immobilized. Rather than deal with ending racism, they sit and ponder their guilt and hope nobody notices how awful they are. Meanwhile, racism picks up momentum and keeps on keepin' on.

Now, the newest form of racism that I'm hip to is unaware/self-righteous racism. The "good white" racist attempts to shame Blacks into being blacker, scorns Japanese-Americans who don't speak Japanese, and knows more about the Chicano/a community than the folks who make up the community. They assign themselves as the "good whites," as opposed to the "bad whites," and are often so busy telling people of color what the issues in the Black, Asian, Indian, Latino/a communities should be that they don't have time to deal with their errant sisters and brothers in the white community. Which means that people of color are still left to deal with what the "good whites" don't want to . . . racism.

Internalized racism is what really gets in my way as a Black woman. It influences the way I see or don't see myself, limits what I expect of myself or others like me. It results in my acceptance of mistreatment, leads me to believe that being treated with less than absolute respect, at least this once, is to be expected because I am Black, because I am not white. "Because I am (*you fill in the color*), you think, "Life is going to be hard." The fact is life may be hard, but the color of your skin is not the cause of the hardship. The color of your skin may be used as an excuse to mistreat you, but there is no reason or logic involved in the mistreatment. If it seems that your color is the reason, if it seems that your ethnic heritage is the cause of the woe, it's because you've been deliberately beaten down by agents of a greedy system until you swallowed the garbage. That is the internalization of racism.

Racism is the systematic, institutionalized mistreatment of one group of people by another based on racial heritage. Like every other oppression, racism can be internalized. People of color come to believe misinformation about their particular ethnic group and thus believe that their mistreatment is justified. With that basic vocabulary, let's take a look at how the whole thing works together. Meet "the Ism Family," racism, classism, ageism, adultism, elitism, sexism, heterosexism, physicalism, etc. All these ism's are systematic, that is, not only are these parasites feeding off our lives, they are also dependent on one another for foundation. Racism is supported and reinforced by classism, which is given a foothold and a boost by adultism, which also feeds sexism, which is validated by heterosexism, and so it goes on. You cannot have the "ism" functioning without first effectively installing its flip-side, the internalized version of the ism. Like twins, as one particular form of the ism grows in potency, there is a corresponding increase in its internalized form within the population. Before oppression becomes a specific ism like racism, usually all hell breaks loose. War. People fight attempts to enslave them, or to subvert their will, or to take what they consider theirs, whether that is territory or dignity. It's true that the various elements of racism, while repugnant, would not be able to do very much damage, but for one generally overlooked key piece: power/ privilege.

While in one sense we all have power we have to look at the fact that, in our society, people are stratified into various classes and some of these classes have more privilege than others. The owning class has enough power and privilege to not have to give a good whinney what the rest of the folks have on their minds. The power and privilege of the owning class provides the ability to pay off enough of the working class and offer that paid-off group, the middle class, just enough privilege to make it agreeable to do various and sundry oppressive things to other working-class and outright disenfranchised folk, keeping the lid on explosive inequities, at least for a minute. If you're at the bottom of this heap, and you believe the line that says you're there because that's all you're worth, it is at least some small solace to believe that there are others more worthless than you, because of their gender, race, sexual preference . . . whatever. The specific form of power that runs the show here is the power to intimidate. The power to take away the most lives the quickest, and back it up with legal and "divine" sanction, is the very bottom line. It makes the difference between who's holding the racism end of the stick and who's getting beat with it (or beating others as vulnerable as they are) on the internalized racism end of the stick. What I am saying is, while people of color are welcome to tear up their own neighborhoods and each other, everybody knows that you cannot do that to white folks without hell to pay. People of color can be prejudiced against one another and whites, but do not have an ice-cube's chance in hell of passing laws that will get whites sent to relocation camps "for their own protection and the security of the nation." People who have not thought about or refuse to acknowledge this imbalance of power/privilege often want to talk about the racism of people of color. But then that is one of the ways racism is able to continue to function. You look for someone to blame and you blame the victim, who will nine times out of ten accept the blame out of habit.

So, what can we do? Acknowledge racism for a start, even though and especially when we've struggled to be kind and fair, or struggled to rise above it all. It is hard to acknowledge the fact that racism circumscribes and pervades our lives. Racism must be dealt with on two levels, personal and societal, emotional and institutional. It is possible—and most effective—to do both at the same time. We must reclaim whatever delight we have lost in our own ethnic heritage or heritages. This so-called melting pot has only succeeded in turning us into fast-food gobbling "generics" (as in generic "white folks" who were once Irish, Polish, Russian, English, etc. and "black folks," who were once Ashanti, Bambara, Baule, Yoruba, etc.). Find or create safe places to actually *feel* what we've been forced to repress each time we were a victim of, witness to or perpetrator of racism, so that we do not continue, like puppets, to act out the past in the present and future. Challenge oppression. Take a stand against it. When you are aware of something oppressive going down, stop the show. At least call it. We become so numbed to racism that we don't even think twice about it, unless it is immediately life-threatening.

Whites who want to be allies to people of color: You can educate yourselves via research and observation rather than rigidly, arrogantly relying solely on interrogating people of color. Do not expect that people of color should teach you how to behave non-oppressively. Do not give into the pull to be lazy. Think, hard. Do not blame people of color for your frustration about racism, but do appreciate the fact that people of color will often help you get in touch with that frustration. Assume that your effort to be a good friend is appreciated, but don't expect or accept gratitude from people of color. Work on racism for your sake, not "their" sake. Assume that you are needed and capable of being a good ally. Know that you'll make mistakes and commit yourself to correcting them and continuing on as an ally, no matter what. Don't give up.

People of color, working through internalized racism: Remember always that you and others like you are completely worthy of respect, completely capable of achieving whatever you take a notion to do. Remember that the term "people of color" refers to a variety of ethnic and cultural backgrounds. These various groups have been oppressed in a variety of ways. Educate yourself about the ways different peoples have been oppressed and how they've resisted that oppression. Expect and insist that whites are capable of being good allies against racism. Don't give up. Resist the pull to give out the "people of color seal of approval" to aspiring white allies. A moment of appreciation is fine, but more than that tends to be less than helpful. Celebrate yourself. Celebrate yourself. Celebrate the inevitable end of racism.

WHITE PRIVILEGE AND MALE PRIVILEGE

A Personal Account of Coming to See
Correspondences through Work
in Women's Studies (1988)

8

Peggy McIntosh

Through work to bring materials and perspectives from Women's Studies into the rest of the curriculum, I have often noticed men's unwillingness to grant that they are overprivileged in the curriculum, even though they may grant that women are disadvantaged. Denials that amount to taboos surround the subject of advantages that men gain from women's disadvantages. These denials protect male privilege from being fully recognized, acknowledged, lessened, or ended.

Thinking through unacknowledged male privilege as a phenomenon with a life of its own, I realized that since hierarchies in our society are interlocking, there was most likely a phenomenon of white privilege that was similarly denied and protected, but alive and real in its effects. As a white person, I realized I had been taught about racism as something that puts others at a disadvantage, but had been taught not to see one of its corollary aspects, white privilege, which puts me at an advantage.

I think whites are carefully taught not to recognize white privilege, as males are taught not to recognize male privilege. So I have begun in an untutored way to ask what it is like to have white privilege. This paper is a partial record of my personal observations and not a scholarly analysis. It is based on my daily experiences within my particular circumstances.

I have come to see white privilege as an invisible package of unearned assets that I can count on cashing in each day, but about which I was "meant" to remain oblivious. White privilege is like an invisible weightless knapsack of special provisions, assurances, tools, maps, guides, codebooks, passports, visas, clothes, compass, emergency gear, and blank checks.

I have appreciated commentary on this paper from the Working Papers Committee of the Wellesley College Center for Research on Women, from members of the Dodge seminar, and from many individuals, including Margaret Andersen, Sorel Berman, Joanne Braxton, Johnnella Butler, Sandra Dickerson, Marnie Evans, Beverly Guy-Sheftall, Sandra Harding, Eleanor Hinton Hoytt, Pauline Houston, Paul Lauter, Joyce Miller, Mary Norris, Gloria Oden, Beverly Smith, and John Walter.

Since I have had trouble facing white privilege, and describing its results in my life, I saw parallels here with men's reluctance to acknowledge male privilege. Only rarely will a man go beyond acknowledging that women are disadvantaged to acknowledging that men have unearned advantage, or that unearned privilege has not been good for men's development as human beings, or for society's development, or that privilege systems might ever be challenged and *changed*.

I will review here several types or layers of denial that I see at work protecting, and preventing awareness about, entrenched male privilege. Then I will draw parallels, from my own experience, with the denials that veil the facts of white privilege. Finally, I will list forty-six ordinary and daily ways in which I experience having white privilege, by contrast with my African American colleagues in the same building. This list is not intended to be generalizable. Others can make their own lists from within their own life circumstances.

Writing this paper has been difficult, despite warm receptions for the talks on which it is based.[1] For describing white privilege makes one newly accountable. As we in Women's Studies work reveal male privilege and ask men to give up some of their power, so one who writes about having white privilege must ask, "Having described it, what will I do to lessen or end it?"

The denial of men's overprivileged state takes many forms in discussions of curriculum change work. Some claim that men must be central in the curriculum because they have done most of what is important or distinctive in life or in civilization. Some recognize sexism in the curriculum but deny that it makes male students seem unduly important in life. Others agree that certain *individual* thinkers are male oriented but deny that there is any *systemic* tendency in disciplinary frameworks or epistemology to overempower men as a group. Those men who do grant that male privilege takes institutionalized and embedded forms are still likely to deny that male hegemony has opened doors for them personally. Virtually all men deny that male overreward alone can explain men's centrality in all the inner sanctums of our most powerful institutions. Moreover, those few who will acknowledge that male privilege systems have overempowered them usually end up doubting that we could dismantle these privilege systems. They may say they will work to improve women's status, in the society or in the university, but they can't or won't support the idea of lessening men's. In curricular terms, this is the point at which they say that they regret they cannot use any of the interesting new scholarship on women because the syllabus is full. When the talk turns to giving men less cultural room, even the most thoughtful and fair-minded of the men I know will tend to reflect, or fall back on, conservative assumptions about the inevitability of present gender relations and distributions of power, calling on precedent or sociobiology and psychobiology to demonstrate that male domination is natural and follows inevitably from evolutionary pressures. Others resort to arguments from "experience" or religion or social responsibility or wishing and dreaming.

After I realized, through faculty development work in Women's Studies, the extent to which men work from a base of unacknowledged privilege, I understood that much of their oppressiveness was unconscious. Then I remembered the frequent charges from women of color that white women whom they encounter are oppressive. I began to understand why we are justly seen as oppressive, even when we don't see ourselves that way. At the very least, obliviousness of one's privileged state can make a person or group irritating to be with. I began to count the ways in which I enjoy unearned skin privilege and have been conditioned into oblivion about its existence, unable to see that it put me "ahead" in any way, or put my people ahead, overrewarding us and yet also paradoxically damaging us, or that it could or should be changed.

My schooling gave me no training in seeing myself as an oppressor, as an unfairly advantaged person, or as a participant in a damaged culture. I was taught to see myself as an individual whose moral state depended on her individual moral will. At school, we were not taught about slavery in any depth; we were not taught to see slaveholders as damaged people. Slaves were seen as the only group at risk of being dehumanized. My schooling followed the pattern which Elizabeth Minnich has pointed out: whites are taught to think of their lives as morally neutral, normative, and average, and also ideal, so that when we work to benefit others, this is seen as work that will allow "them" to be more like "us." I think many of us know how obnoxious this attitude can be in men.

After frustration with men who would not recognize male privilege, I decided to try to work on myself at least by identifying some of the daily effects of white privilege in my life. It is crude work, at this stage, but I will give here a list of special circumstances and conditions I experience that I did not earn but that I have been made to feel are mine by birth, by citizenship, and by virtue of being a conscientious law-abiding "normal" person of goodwill. I have chosen those conditions that I think in my case *attach somewhat more to skin-color privilege* than to class, religion, ethnic status, or geographical location, though these other privileging factors are intricately intertwined. As far as I can see, my Afro-American co-workers, friends, and acquaintances with whom I come into daily or frequent contact in this particular time, place, and line of work cannot count on most of these conditions.

1. I can, if I wish, arrange to be in the company of people of my race most of the time.
2. I can avoid spending time with people whom I was trained to mistrust and who have learned to mistrust my kind or me.
3. If I should need to move, I can be pretty sure of renting or purchasing housing in an area which I can afford and in which I would want to live.
4. I can be reasonably sure that my neighbors in such a location will be neutral or pleasant to me.

5. I can go shopping alone most of the time, fairly well assured that I will not be followed or harassed by store detectives.

6. I can turn on the television or open to the front page of the paper and see people of my race widely and positively represented.

7. When I am told about our national heritage or about "civilization," I am shown that people of my color made it what it is.

8. I can be sure that my children will be given curricular materials that testify to the existence of their race.

9. If I want to, I can be pretty sure of finding a publisher for this piece on white privilege.

10. I can be fairly sure of having my voice heard in a group in which I am the only member of my race.

11. I can be casual about whether or not to listen to another woman's voice in a group in which she is the only member of her race.

12. I can go into a book shop and count on finding the writing of my race represented, into a supermarket and find the staple foods that fit with my cultural traditions, into a hairdresser's shop and find someone who can deal with my hair.

13. Whether I use checks, credit cards, or cash, I can count on my skin color not to work against the appearance that I am financially reliable.

14. I could arrange to protect our young children most of the time from people who might not like them.

15. I did not have to educate our children to be aware of systemic racism for their own daily physical protection.

16. I can be pretty sure that my children's teachers and employers will tolerate them if they fit school and workplace norms; my chief worries about them do not concern others' attitudes toward their race.

17. I can talk with my mouth full and not have people put this down to my color.

18. I can swear, or dress in secondhand clothes, or not answer letters, without having people attribute these choices to the bad morals, the poverty, or the illiteracy of my race.

19. I can speak in public to a powerful male group without putting my race on trial.

20. I can do well in a challenging situation without being called a credit to my race.

21. I am never asked to speak for all the people of my racial group.

22. I can remain oblivious to the language and customs of persons of color who constitute the world's majority without feeling in my culture any penalty for such oblivion.

23. I can criticize our government and talk about how much I fear its policies and behavior without being seen as a cultural outsider.

24. I can be reasonably sure that if I ask to talk to "the person in charge," I will be facing a person of my race.

25. If a traffic cop pulls me over or if the IRS audits my tax return, I can be sure I haven't been singled out because of my race.
26. I can easily buy posters, postcards, picture books, greeting cards, dolls, toys, and children's magazines featuring people of my race.
27. I can go home from most meetings of organizations I belong to feeling somewhat tied in, rather than isolated, out of place, outnumbered, unheard, held at a distance, or feared.
28. I can be pretty sure that an argument with a colleague of another race is more likely to jeopardize her chances for advancement than to jeopardize mine.
29. I can be fairly sure that if I argue for the promotion of a person of another race, or a program centering on race, this is not likely to cost me heavily within my present setting, even if my colleagues disagree with me.
30. If I declare there is a racial issue at hand, or there isn't a racial issue at hand, my race will lend me more credibility for either position than a person of color will have.
31. I can choose to ignore developments in minority writing and minority activist programs, or disparage them, or learn from them, but in any case, I can find ways to be more or less protected from negative consequences of any of these choices.
32. My culture gives me little fear about ignoring the perspectives and powers of people of other races.
33. I am not made acutely aware that my shape, bearing, or body odor will be taken as a reflection on my race.
34. I can worry about racism without being seen as self-interested or self-seeking.
35. I can take a job with an affirmative action employer without having my co-workers on the job suspect that I got it because of my race.
36. If my day, week, or year is going badly, I need not ask of each negative episode or situation whether it has racial overtones.
37. I can be pretty sure of finding people who would be willing to talk with me and advise me about my next steps, professionally.
38. I can think over many options, social, political, imaginative, or professional, without asking whether a person of my race would be accepted or allowed to do what I want to do.
39. I can be late to a meeting without having the lateness reflect on my race.
40. I can choose public accommodation without fearing that people of my race cannot get in or will be mistreated in the places I have chosen.
41. I can be sure that if I need legal or medical help, my race will not work against me.
42. I can arrange my activities so that I will never have to experience feelings of rejection owing to my race.
43. If I have low credibility as a leader, I can be sure that my race is not the problem.

44. I can easily find academic courses and institutions that give attention only to people of my race.
45. I can expect figurative language and imagery in all of the arts to testify to experiences of my race.
46. I can choose blemish cover or bandages in "flesh" color and have them more or less match my skin.

I repeatedly forgot each of the realizations on this list until I wrote it down. For me, white privilege has turned out to be an elusive and fugitive subject. The pressure to avoid it is great, for in facing it I must give up the myth of meritocracy. If these things are true, this is not such a free country; one's life is not what one makes it; many doors open for certain people through no virtues of their own. These perceptions mean also that my moral condition is not what I had been led to believe. The appearance of being a good citizen rather than a troublemaker comes in large part from having all sorts of doors open automatically because of my color.

A further paralysis of nerve comes from literary silence protecting privilege. My clearest memories of finding such analysis are in Lillian Smith's unparalleled *Killers of the Dream* and Margaret Andersen's review of Karen and Mamie Fields' *Lemon Swamp.* Smith, for example, wrote about walking toward black children on the street and knowing they would step into the gutter; Andersen contrasted the pleasure that she, as a white child, took on summer driving trips to the south with Karen Fields' memories of driving in a closed car stocked with all necessities lest, in stopping, her black family should suffer "insult, or worse." Adrienne Rich also recognizes and writes about daily experiences of privilege, but in my observation, white women's writing in this area is far more often on systemic racism than on our daily lives as light-skinned women.[2]

In unpacking this invisible knapsack of white privilege, I have listed conditions of daily experience that I once took for granted, as neutral, normal, and universally available to everybody, just as I once thought of a male-focused curriculum as the neutral or accurate account that can speak for all. Nor did I think of any of these perquisites as bad for the holder. I now think that we need a more finely differentiated taxonomy of privilege, for some of these varieties are only what one would want for everyone in a just society, and others give license to be ignorant, oblivious, arrogant, and destructive. Before proposing some more finely tuned categorization, I will make some observations about the general effects of these conditions on my life and expectations.

In this potpourri of examples, some privileges make me feel at home in the world. Others allow me to escape penalties or dangers that others suffer. Through some, I escape fear, anxiety, insult, injury, or a sense of not being welcome, not being real. Some keep me from having to hide, to be in disguise, to feel sick or crazy, to negotiate each transaction from the position of being an outsider or, within my group, a person who is suspected of having too close links with a dominant culture. Most keep me from having to be angry.

I see a pattern running through the matrix of white privilege, a pattern of assumptions that were passed on to me as a white person. There was one main piece of cultural turf; it was my own turf, and I was among those who could control the turf. I could measure up to the cultural standards and take advantage of the many options I saw around me to make what the culture would call a success of my life. *My skin color was an asset for any move I was educated to want to make.* I could think of myself as "belonging" in major ways and of making social systems work for me. I could freely disparage, fear, neglect, or be oblivious to anything outside of the dominant cultural forms. Being of the main culture, I could also criticize it fairly freely. My life was reflected back to me frequently enough so that I felt, with regard to my race, if not to my sex, like one of the real people.

Whether through the curriculum or in the newspaper, the television, the economic system, or the general look of people in the streets, I received daily signals and indications that my people counted and that others *either didn't exist or must be trying, not very successfully, to be like people of my race.* I was given cultural permission not to hear voices of people of other races or a tepid cultural tolerance for hearing or acting on such voices. I was also raised not to suffer seriously from anything that darker-skinned people might say about my group, "protected," though perhaps I should more accurately say *prohibited*, through the habits of my economic class and social group, from living in racially mixed groups or being reflective about interactions between people of differing races.

In proportion as my racial group was being made confident, comfortable, and oblivious, other groups were likely being made unconfident, uncomfortable, and alienated. Whiteness protected me from many kinds of hostility, distress, and violence, which I was being subtly trained to visit in turn upon people of color.

For this reason, the word "privilege" now seems to me misleading. Its connotations are too positive to fit the conditions and behaviors which "privilege systems" produce. We usually think of privilege as being a favored state, whether earned, or conferred by birth or luck. School graduates are reminded they are privileged and urged to use their (enviable) assets well. The word "privilege" carries the connotation of being something everyone must want. Yet some of the conditions I have described here work to systemically overempower certain groups. Such privilege simply *confers dominance*, gives permission to control, because of one's race or sex. The kind of privilege that gives license to some people to be, at best, thoughtless and, at worst, murderous should not continue to be referred to as a desirable attribute. Such "privilege" may be widely desired without being in any way beneficial to the whole society.

Moreover, though "privilege" may confer power, it does not confer moral strength. Those who do not depend on conferred dominance have traits and qualities that may never develop in those who do. Just as Women's Studies courses indicate that women survive their political circumstances to lead lives that hold the human race together, so "underprivileged" people of color who are the world's majority have survived their oppression and lived survivors' lives from which the white global minority can and must learn. In some groups, those dominated have actually become strong through *not* having all of these unearned advantages, and this gives them a great deal to teach the others. Members of so-called privileged groups can seem foolish, ridiculous, infantile, or dangerous by contrast.

I want, then, to distinguish between earned strength and unearned power conferred systemically. Power from unearned privilege can look like strength when it is, in fact, permission to escape or to dominate. But not all of the privileges on my list are inevitably damaging. Some, like the expectation that neighbors will be decent to you, or that your race will not count against you in court, should be the norm in a just society and should be considered as the entitlement of everyone. Others, like the privilege not to listen to less powerful people, distort the humanity of the holders as well as the ignored groups. Still others, like finding one's staple foods everywhere, may be a function of being a member of a numerical majority in the population. Others have to do with not having to labor under pervasive negative stereotyping and mythology.

We might at least start by distinguishing between positive advantages that we can work to spread, to the point where they are not advantages at all but simply part of the normal civic and social fabric, and negative types of advantage that unless rejected will always reinforce our present hierarchies. For example, the positive "privilege" of belonging, the feeling that one belongs within the human circle, as Native Americans say, fosters development and should not be seen as privilege for a few. It is, let us say, an entitlement that none of us should have to earn; ideally it is an *unearned entitlement*. At present, since only a few have it, it is an *unearned advantage* for them. The negative "privilege" that gave me cultural permission not to take darker-skinned Others seriously can be seen as arbitrarily conferred dominance and should not be desirable for anyone. This paper results from a process of coming to see that some of the power that I originally saw as attendant on being a human being in the United States consisted in *unearned advantage* and *conferred dominance*, as well as other kinds of special circumstance not universally taken for granted.

In writing this paper I have also realized that white identity and status (as well as class identity and status) give me considerable power to choose whether to broach this subject and its trouble. I can pretty well decide whether to disappear and avoid and not listen and escape the dislike I may engender in other people through this essay, or interrupt, answer, interpret, preach, correct, criticize, and control to some extent what goes on in reaction to it. Being white,

I am given considerable power to escape many kinds of danger or penalty as well as to choose which risks I want to take.

There is an analogy here, once again, with Women's Studies. Our male colleagues do not have a great deal to lose in supporting Women's Studies, but they do not have a great deal to lose if they oppose it either. They simply have the power to decide whether to commit themselves to more equitable distributions of power. They will probably feel few penalties whatever choice they make; they do not seem, in any obvious short-term sense, the ones at risk, though they and we are all at risk because of the behaviors that have been rewarded in them.

Through Women's Studies work I have met very few men who are truly distressed about systemic, unearned male advantage and conferred dominance. And so one question for me and others like me is whether we will be like them, or whether we will get truly distressed, even outraged, about unearned race advantage and conferred dominance and if so, what we will do to lessen them. In any case, we need to do more work in identifying how they actually affect our daily lives. We need more down-to-earth writing by people about these taboo subjects. We need more understanding of the ways in which white "privilege" damages white people, for these are not the same ways in which it damages the victimized. Skewed white psyches are an inseparable part of the picture, though I do not want to confuse the kinds of damage done to the holders of special assets and to those who suffer the deficits. Many, perhaps most, of our white students in the United States think that racism doesn't affect them because they are not people of color; they do not see "whiteness" as a racial identity. Many men likewise think that Women's Studies does not bear on their own existences because they are not female; they do not see themselves as having gendered identities. Insisting on the universal "effects" of "privilege" systems, then, becomes one of our chief tasks, and being more explicit about the *particular* effects in particular contexts is another. Men need to join us in this work.

In addition, since race and sex are not the only advantaging systems at work, we need to similarly examine the daily experience of having age advantage, or ethnic advantage, or physical ability, or advantage related to nationality, religion, or sexual orientation. Professor Marnie Evans suggested to me that in many ways the list I made also applies directly to heterosexual privilege. This is a still more taboo subject than race privilege: the daily ways in which heterosexual privilege makes some persons comfortable or powerful, providing supports, assets, approvals, and rewards to those who live or expect to live in heterosexual pairs. Unpacking that content is still more difficult, owing to the deeper imbeddedness of heterosexual advantage and dominance and stricter taboos surrounding these.

But to start such an analysis I would put this observation from my own experience: the fact that I live under the same roof with a man triggers all kinds of societal assumptions about my worth, politics, life, and values and triggers a host of unearned advantages and powers. After recasting many elements from the original list I would add further observations like these:

1. My children do not have to answer questions about why I live with my partner (my husband).
2. I have no difficulty finding neighborhoods where people approve of our household.
3. Our children are given texts and classes that implicitly support our kind of family unit and do not turn them against my choice of domestic partnership.
4. I can travel alone or with my husband without expecting embarrassment or hostility in those who deal with us.
5. Most people I meet will see my marital arrangements as an asset to my life or as a favorable comment on my likability, my competence, or my mental health.
6. I can talk about the social events of a weekend without fearing most listeners' reactions.
7. I will feel welcomed and "normal" in the usual walks of public life, institutional and social.
8. In many contexts, I am seen as "all right" in daily work on women because I do not live chiefly with women.

Difficulties and dangers surrounding the task of finding parallels are many. Since racism, sexism, and heterosexism are not the same, the advantages associated with them should not be seen as the same. In addition, it is hard to isolate aspects of unearned advantage that derive chiefly from social class, economic class, race, religion, region, sex, or ethnic identity. The oppressions are both distinct and interlocking, as the Combahee River Collective statement of 1977 continues to remind us eloquently.[3]

One factor seems clear about all of the interlocking oppressions. They take both active forms that we can see and embedded forms that members of the dominant group are taught not to see. In my class and place, I did not see myself as racist because I was taught to recognize racism only in individual acts of meanness by members of my group, never in invisible systems conferring racial dominance on my group from birth. Likewise, we are taught to think that sexism or heterosexism is carried on only through intentional, individual acts of discrimination, meanness, or cruelty, rather than in invisible systems conferring unsought dominance on certain groups. Disapproving of the systems won't be enough to change them. I was taught to think that racism could end if white individuals changed their attitudes; many men think sexism can be ended by individual changes in daily behavior toward women. But a man's sex provides advantage for him whether or not he approves of the way in which dominance has been conferred on his group. A "white" skin in the United States opens many doors for whites whether or not we approve of the way dominance has been conferred on us. Individual acts can palliate, but cannot end, these problems. To redesign social systems, we need first to acknowledge their colossal unseen dimensions. The silences and denials surrounding privilege are the key political tool here. They keep the thinking about equality or equity incomplete, protecting unearned advantage and conferred dominance by making these taboo subjects. Most talk by whites about equal opportunity seems to me now to be about equal opportunity to try to get into a position of dominance while denying that *systems* of dominance exist.

Obliviousness about white advantage, like obliviousness about male advantage, is kept strongly inculturated in the United States so as to maintain the myth of meritocracy, the myth that democratic choice is equally available to all. Keeping most people unaware that freedom of confident action is there for just a small number of people props up those in power and serves to keep power in the hands of the same groups that have most of it already. Though systemic change takes many decades, there are pressing questions for me and I imagine for some others like me if we raise our daily consciousness on the perquisites of being light-skinned. What will we do with such knowledge? As we know from watching men, it is an open question whether we will choose to use unearned advantage to weaken invisible privilege systems and whether we will use any of our arbitrarily awarded power to try to reconstruct power systems on a broader base.

NOTES

1. This paper was presented at the Virginia Women's Studies Association conference in Richmond in April, 1986, and the American Educational Research Association conference in Boston in October, 1986, and discussed with two groups of participants in the Dodge seminars for Secondary School Teachers in New York and Boston in the spring of 1987.

2. Andersen, Margaret, "Race and the Social Science Curriculum: A Teaching and Learning Discussion." *Radical Teacher*, November, 1984, pp. 17–20. Smith, Lillian, *Killers of the Dream*, New York: W. W. Norton, 1949.

3. "A Black Feminist Statement," The Combahee River Collective, pp. 13–22 in G. Hull, P. Scott, B. Smith, Eds., *All the Women Are White, All the Blacks Are Men, But Some of Us Are Brave: Black Women's Studies*, Old Westbury, NY: The Feminist Press, 1982.

OF RACE AND RISK   9

Patricia J. Williams

Several years ago, at a moment when I was particularly tired of the unstable lifestyle that academic careers sometimes require, I surprised myself and bought a real house. Because the house was in a state other than the one where I was living at the time, I obtained my mortgage by telephone. I am a prudent little squirrel when it comes to things financial, always tucking away stores of nuts for the winter, and so I meet the criteria of a quite good credit risk. My loan was approved almost immediately.

A little while later, the contract came in the mail. Among the papers the bank forwarded were forms documenting compliance with the Fair Housing Act, which outlaws racial discrimination in the housing market. The act monitors lending practices to prevent banks from redlining—redlining being the phenomenon whereby banks circle certain neighborhoods on the map and refuse to lend in those areas. It is a practice for which the bank with which I was dealing, unbeknownst to me, had been cited previously—as well as since. In any event, the act tracks the race of all banking customers to prevent discrimination. Unfortunately, and with the creative variability of all illegality, some banks also use the racial information disclosed on the fair housing forms to engage in precisely the discrimination the law seeks to prevent.

I should repeat that to this point my entire mortgage transaction had been conducted by telephone. I should also note that I speak a Received Standard English, regionally marked as Northeastern perhaps, but not easily identifiable as black. With my credit history, my job as a law professor and, no doubt, with my accent, I am not only middle class but apparently match the cultural stereotype of a good white person. It is thus, perhaps, that the loan officer of the bank, whom I had never met, had checked off the box on the fair housing form indicating that I *was* white.

Race shouldn't matter, I suppose, but it seemed to in this case, so I took a deep breath, crossed out "white" and send the contract back. That will teach them to presume too much, I thought. A done deal, I assumed. But suddenly the transaction came to a screeching halt. The bank wanted more money, more points, a higher rate of interest. Suddenly I found myself facing great resistance and much more debt. To make a long story short, I threatened to sue under the act in question, the bank quickly backed down and I procured the loan on the original terms.

From: *The Nation*, December 29, 1997, p. 10.

What was interesting about all this was that the reason the bank gave for its new-found recalcitrance was not race, heaven forbid. No, it was all about economics and increased risk: The reason they gave was that property values in that neighborhood were suddenly falling. They wanted more money to buffer themselves against the snappy winds of projected misfortune.

Initially, I was surprised, confused. The house was in a neighborhood that was extremely stable. I am an extremely careful shopper; I had uncovered absolutely nothing to indicate that prices were falling. It took my realtor to make me see the light. "Don't you get it," he sighed. "This is what always happens." And even though I suppose it was a little thick of me, I really hadn't gotten it: For of course, I was the reason the prices were in peril.

The bank's response was driven by demographic data that show that any time black people move into a neighborhood, whites are overwhelmingly likely to move out. In droves. In panic. In concert. Pulling every imaginable resource with them, from school funding to garbage collection to social workers who don't want to work in black neighborhoods. The imagery is awfully catchy, you had to admit: the neighborhood just tipping on over like a terrible accident, whoops! Like a pitcher, I suppose. All that nice fresh wholesome milk spilling out, running away . . . leaving the dark, echoing, upended urn of the inner city.

In retrospect, what has remained so fascinating to me about this experience was the way it so exemplified the problems of the new rhetoric of racism. For starts, the new rhetoric of race never mentions race. It wasn't race but risk with which the bank was so considered.

Second, since financial risk is all about economics, my exclusion got reclassified as just a consideration of class. There's no law against class discrimination, goes the argument, because that would represent a restraint on that basic American freedom, the ability to contract or not. If schools, trains, buses, swimming pools and neighborhoods remain segregated, it's no longer a racial problem if someone who just happens to be white keeps hiking up the price for someone who accidentally and purely by the way happens to be black. Black people end up paying higher prices for the attempt to integrate, even as the integration of oneself threatens to lower the value of one's investment.

By this measure of mortgage-worthiness, the ingredient of blackness is cast not just as a social toll but as an actual tax. A fee, an extra contribution at the door, an admission charge for the high costs of handling my dangerous propensities, my inherently unsavory properties. I was not judged based on my independent attributes or financial worth; not even was I judged by statistical profiles of what my group actually does. (For in fact, anxiety-stricken, middle-class people make grovelingly good cake-baking neighbors when not made to feel defensive by the unfortunate historical strategies of bombs, burnings or abandonment.) Rather, I was being evaluated based on what an abstraction of White Society writ large thinks we—or I—do, and that imagined "doing" was treated and thus established as a self-fulfilling prophecy. It is a dispiriting message: that some in society apparently not only devalue black people but devalue *themselves* and their homes just for having us as part of their landscape.

"I bet you'll keep your mouth shut the next time they plug you into the computer as white," laughed a friend when he heard my story. It took me aback, this postmodern pressure to "pass," even as it highlighted the intolerable logic of it all. For by these "rational" economic measures, an investment in my property suggests the selling of myself.

SEEING MORE THAN BLACK & WHITE   **10**
Latinos, Racism, and the Cultural Divides

Elizabeth Martinez

A certain relish seems irresistible to this Latina as the mass media has been compelled to sit up, look south of the border, and take notice. Probably the Chiapas uprising and Mexico's recent political turmoil have won us no more than a brief day in the sun. Or even less: liberal Ted Koppel still hadn't noticed the historic assassination of presidential candidate Colosio three days afterward. But it's been sweet, anyway.

When Kissinger said years ago "nothing important ever happens in the south," he articulated a contemptuous indifference toward Latin America, its people, and their culture, which has long dominated U.S. institutions and attitudes. Mexico may be great for a vacation, and some people like burritos but the usual image of Latin America combines incompetence with absurdity in loud colors. My parents, both Spanish teachers, endured decades of being told kids were better off learning French.

U.S. political culture is not only Anglo-dominated but also embraces an exceptionally stubborn national self-centeredness, with no global vision other than relations of domination. The U.S. refuses to see itself as one nation sitting on a continent with 20 others all speaking languages other than English and having the right not to be dominated.

Such arrogant indifference extends to Latinos within the U.S. The mass media complain, "people can't relate to Hispanics"—or Asians, they say. Such

From: *Z Magazine* 7 (May 1994): 56–60. Reprinted with permission.

arrogant indifference has played an important role in invisibilizing La Raza (except where we become a serious nuisance or a handy scapegoat). It is one reason the U.S. harbors an exclusively white-on-Black concept of racism. It is one barrier to new thinking about racism which is crucial today. There are others.

GOOD-BYE WHITE MAJORITY

In a society as thoroughly and violently racialized as the United States, white-Black relations have defined racism for centuries. Today the composition and culture of the U.S. are changing rapidly. We need to consider seriously whether we can afford to maintain an exclusively white/Black model of racism when the population will be 32 percent Latin/Asian/Pacific American and Native American—in short, neither Black nor white—by the year 2050. We are challenged to recognize that multi-colored racism is mushrooming, and then strategize how to resist it. We are challenged to move beyond a dualism comprised of two white supremacist inventions: Blackness and Whiteness.

At stake in those challenges is building a united anti-racist force strong enough to resist contemporary racist strategies of divide-and-conquer. Strong enough in the long run to help defeat racism itself. Doesn't an exclusively Black/white model of racism discourage the perception of common interests among people of color and thus impede a solidarity that can challenge white supremacy? Doesn't it encourage the isolation of African Americans from potential allies? Doesn't it advise all people of color to spend too much energy understanding our lives in relation to Whiteness, and thus freeze us in a defensive, often self-destructive mode?

NO "OPPRESSION OLYMPICS"

For a Latina to talk about recognizing the multi-colored varieties of racism is not, and should not be, yet another round in the Oppression Olympics. We don't need more competition among different social groupings for that "Most Oppressed" gold. We don't need more comparisons of suffering between women and Blacks, the disabled and the gay, Latino teenagers and white seniors, or whatever. We don't need more surveys like the recent much publicized Harris Poll showing that different peoples of color are prejudiced toward each other—a poll patently designed to demonstrate that us coloreds are no better than white folk. (The survey never asked people about positive attitudes.)

Rather, we need greater knowledge, understanding, and openness to learning about each other's histories and present needs as a basis for working together. Nothing could seem more urgent in an era when increasing impoverishment encourages a self-imposed separatism among people of color as a desperate attempt at community survival. Nothing could seem more important as we search for new social change strategies in a time of ideological confusion.

My call to rethink concepts of racism in the U.S. today is being sounded elsewhere. Among academics, liberal foundation administrators, and activist-intellectuals, you can hear talk of the need for a new "racial paradigm" or model. But new thinking seems to proceed in fits and starts, as if dogged by a fear of stepping on toes, of feeling threatened, or of losing one's base. With a few notable exceptions, even our progressive scholars of color do not make the leap from perfunctorily saluting a vague multi-culturalism to serious analysis. We seem to have made little progress, if any, since Bob Blauner's 1972 book *Racial Oppression in America.* Recognizing the limits of the white-Black axis, Blauner critiqued White America's ignorance of and indifference to the Chicano/a experience with racism.

Real opposition to new paradigms also exists. There are academics scrambling for one flavor of ethnic studies funds versus another. There are politicians who cultivate distrust of others to keep their own communities loyal. When we hear, for example, of Black/Latino friction, dismay should be quickly followed by investigation. In cities like Los Angeles and New York, it may turn out that political figures scrapping for patronage and payola have played a narrow nationalist·game, whipping up economic anxiety and generating resentment that sets communities against each other.

So the goal here, in speaking about moving beyond a bipolar concept of racism is to build stronger unity against white supremacy. The goal is to see our similarities of experience and needs. If that goal sounds naive, think about the hundreds of organizations formed by grassroots women of different colors coming together in recent years. Their growth is one of today's most energetic motions and it spans all ages. Think about the multicultural environmental justice movement. Think about the coalitions to save schools. Small rainbows of our own making are there, to brighten a long road through hellish times.

It is in such practice, through daily struggle together, that we are most likely to find the road to greater solidarity against a common enemy. But we also need a will to find it and ideas about where, including some new theory.

THE WEST GOES EAST

Until very recently, Latino invisibility—like that of Native Americans and Asian/Pacific Americans—has been close to absolute in U.S. seats of power, major institutions, and the non-Latino public mind. Having lived on both the

East and West Coasts for long periods, I feel qualified to pronounce: an especially myopic view of Latinos prevails in the East. This, despite such data as a 24.4 percent Latino population of New York City alone in 1991, or the fact that in 1990 more Puerto Ricans were killed by New York police under suspicious circumstances than any other ethnic group. Latino populations are growing rapidly in many eastern cities and the rural South, yet remain invisible or stigmatized—usually both.

Eastern blinders persist. I've even heard that the need for a new racial paradigm is dismissed in New York as a California hangup. A black Puerto Rican friend in New York, when we talked about experiences of racism common to Black and brown, said "People here don't see Border Patrol brutality against Mexicans as a form of police repression," despite the fact that the Border Patrol is the largest and most uncontrolled police force in the U.S. It would seem that an old ignorance has combined with new immigrant bashing to sustain divisions today.

While the East (and most of the Midwest) usually remains myopic, the West Coast has barely begun to move away from its own denial. Less than two years ago in San Francisco, a city almost half Latino or Asian/Pacific American, a leading daily newspaper could publish a major series on contemporary racial issues and follow the exclusively Black-white paradigm. Although millions of TV viewers saw massive Latino participation in the April 1992 Los Angeles uprising, which included 18 out of 50 deaths and the majority of arrests, the mass media and most people labeled that event "a Black riot."

If the West Coast has more recognition of those who are neither Black nor white, it is mostly out of fear about the proximate demise of its white majority. A second, closely related reason is the relentless campaign by California Gov. Pete Wilson to scapegoat immigrants for economic problems and pass racist, unconstitutional laws attacking their health, education, and children's future. Wilson has almost single-handedly made the word "immigrant" mean Mexican or other Latino (and sometimes Asian). Who thinks of all the people coming from the former Soviet Union and other countries? The absolute racism of this has too often been successfully masked by reactionary anti-immigrant groups like FAIR blaming immigrants for the staggering African-American unemployment rate. . . .

As this suggests, what has been a regional issue mostly limited to western states is becoming a national issue. If you thought Latinos were just "Messicans" down at the border, wake up—they are all over North Carolina, Pennsylvania and 8th Avenue Manhattan now. A qualitative change is taking place. With the broader geographic spread of Latinos and Asian/Pacific Islanders has come a nationalization of racist practices and attitudes that were once regional. The west goes east, we could say.

Like the monster Hydra, racism is growing some ugly new heads. We will have to look at them closely.

THE ROOTS OF RACISM AND LATINOS

A bipolar model of racism—racism as white on Black—has never really been accurate. Looking for the roots of racism in the U.S. we can begin with the genocide against American Indians which made possible the U.S. land base, crucial to white settlement and early capitalist growth. Soon came the massive enslavement of African people which facilitated that growth. As slave labor became economically critical, "blackness" became ideologically critical; it provided the very source of "whiteness" and the heart of racism. Franz Fanon would write, "colour is the most outward manifestation of race."

If Native Americans had been a crucial labor force during those same centuries, living and working in the white man's sphere, our racist ideology might have evolved differently. "The tawny," as Ben Franklin dubbed them, might have defined the opposite of what he called "the lovely white." But with Indians decimated and survivors moved to distant concentration camps, they became unlikely candidates for this function. Similarly, Mexicans were concentrated in the distant West; elsewhere Anglo fear of them or need to control was rare. They also did not provide the foundation for a definition of whiteness.

Some anti-racist left activists have put forth the idea that only African Americans experience racism as such and that the suffering of other people of color results from national minority rather than racial oppression. From this viewpoint, the exclusively white/Black model for racism is correct. Latinos, then, experience exploitation and repression for reasons of culture and nationality—not for their "race." (It should go without saying in *Z* that while racism is an all-too-real social fact, race has no scientific basis.)

Does the distinction hold? This and other theoretical questions call for more analysis and more expertise than one article can offer. In the meantime, let's try on the idea that Latinos do suffer for their nationality and culture, especially language. They became part of the U.S. through the 1846–48 war on Mexico and thus a foreign population to be colonized. But as they were reduced to cheap or semi-slave labor, they quickly came to suffer for their "race"—meaning, as non-whites. In the Southwest of a super-racialized nation the broad parallelism of race and class embrace Mexicans ferociously.

The bridge here might be a definition of racism as "the reduction of the cultural to the biological," in the words of French scholar Christian Delacampagne now working in Egypt. Or: "racism exists wherever it is claimed that a given social status is explained by a given natural characteristic." We know that line: Mexicans are just naturally lazy and have too many children, so they're poor and exploited.

The discrimination, oppression and hatred experienced by Native Americans, Mexicans, Asian/Pacific Islanders, and Arab Americans are forms of racism. Speaking only of Latinos, we have seen in California and the Southwest, especially along the border, almost 150 years of relentless repression which today includes Central Americans among its targets. That history reveals hundreds of lynchings between 1847 and 1935, the use of counter-insurgency armed forces beginning with the Texas Rangers, random torture and murder by Anglo ranchers, forced labor, rape by border lawmen, and the prevailing Anglo belief that a Mexican life doesn't equal a dog's in value.

But wait. If color is so key to racial definition, as Fanon and others say, perhaps people of Mexican background experience racism less than national minority oppression because they are not dark enough as a group. For White America, shades of skin color are crucial to defining worth. The influence of those shades has also been internalized by communities of color. Many Latinos can and often want to pass for whites; therefore, White America may see them as less threatening than darker sisters and brothers.

Here we confront more of the complexity around us today, with questions like: What about the usually poor, very dark Mexican or Central American of strong Indian or African heritage? (Yes, folks, 200,000–300,000 Africans were brought to Mexico as slaves, which is far, far more than the Spaniards who came.) And what about the effects of accented speech or foreign name, characteristics that may instantly subvert "passing"?

What about those cases where a Mexican-American is never accepted, no matter how light-skinned, well-dressed or well-spoken? A Chicano lawyer friend coming home from a professional conference in suit, tie and briefcase found himself on a bus near San Diego that was suddenly stopped by the Border Patrol. An agent came on board and made a beeline through the all-white rows of passengers direct to my friend. "Your papers." The agent didn't believe Jose was coming from a U.S. conference and took him off the bus to await proof. Jose was lucky; too many Chicanos and Mexicans end up killed.

In a land where the national identity is white, having the "wrong" nationality becomes grounds for racist abuse. Who would draw a sharp line between today's national minority oppression in the form of immigrant-bashing, and racism?

None of this aims to equate the African American and Latino experiences; that isn't necessary even if it were accurate. Many reasons exist for the persistence of the white/Black paradigm of racism; they include numbers, history, and the psychology of whiteness. In particular they include centuries of slave revolts, a Civil War, and an ongoing resistance to racism that cracked this society wide open while the world watched. Nor has the misery imposed on Black people lessened in recent years. New thinking about racism can and should keep this experience at the center.

A DEADLY DUALISM

The exclusively white/Black concept of race and racism in the U.S. rests on a western, Protestant form of dualism woven into both race and gender relations from earliest times. In the dualist universe there is only black and white.

A disdain, indeed fear, of mixture haunts the Yankee soul; there is no room for any kind of multi-faceted identity, any hybridism.

As a people, La Raza combines three sets of roots—indigenous, European, and African—all in widely varying degrees. In short we represent a profoundly un-American concept: *mestizaje* (pronounced mess-tee-zah-hey), the mixing of peoples and emergence of new peoples. A highly racialized society like this one cannot deal with or allow room for *mestizaje*. It has never learned to do much more than hiss "miscegenation!" Or, like that Alabama high school principal who recently denied the right of a mixed-blood pupil to attend the prom, to say: "your parents made a mistake." Apparently we, all the millions of La Raza, are just that—a mistake.

Mexicans in the U.S. also defy the either-or, dualistic mind in that, on the one hand, we are a colonized people displaced from the ancestral homeland with roots in the present-day U.S. that go back centuries. Those ancestors didn't cross the border; the border crossed them. At the same time many of us have come to the U.S. more recently as "immigrants" seeking work. The complexity of Raza baffles and frustrates most Anglos; they want to put one neat label on us. It baffles many Latinos too, who often end up categorizing themselves racially as "Other" for lack of anything better. For that matter, the term "Latino" which I use here is a monumental simplification; it refers to 20-plus nationalities and a wide range of classes.

But we need to grapple with the complexity, for there is more to come. If anything, this nation will see more *mestizaje* in future, embracing innumerable ethnic combinations. What will be its effects? Only one thing seems certain: "white" shall cease to be the national identity.

A glimpse at the next century tells us how much we need to look beyond the white/Black model of race relations and racism. White/Black are real poles, central to the history of U.S. racism. We can neither ignore them nor stop there. But our effectiveness in fighting racism depends on seeing the changes taking place, trying to perceive the contours of the future. From the time of the Greeks to the present, racism around the world has had certain commonalties but no permanently fixed character. It is evolving again today, and we'd best labor to read the new faces of this Hydra-headed monster. Remember, for every head that Hydra lost it grew two more.

Sometimes the problem seems so clear. Last year I showed slides of Chicano history to an Oakland high school class with 47 African Americans and three Latino students. The images included lynchings and police beatings of Mexicans and other Latinos, and many years of resistance. At the end one Black student asked, "Seems like we have had a lot of experiences in common—so why can't Blacks and Mexicans get along better?" No answers, but there was the first step: asking the question.

WHAT WHITE SUPREMACISTS TAUGHT A JEWISH SCHOLAR ABOUT IDENTITY

11

Abby L. Ferber

A few years ago, my work on white supremacy led me to the neo-Nazi tract *The New Order*, which proclaims: "The single serious enemy facing the white man is the Jew." I must have read that statement a dozen times. Until then, I hadn't thought of myself as the enemy.

When I began my research for a book on race, gender, and white su premacy, I could not understand why white supremacists so feared and hated Jews. But after being immersed in newsletters and periodicals for months, I learned that white supremacists imagine Jews as the masterminds behind a great plot to mix races and, thereby, to wipe the white race out of existence.

The identity of white supremacists, and the white racial purity they espouse, requires the maintenance of secure boundaries. For that reason, the literature I read described interracial sex as "the ultimate abomination." White supremacists see Jews as threats to racial purity, the villains responsible for desegregation, integration, the civil-rights movement, the women's movement, and affirmative action—each depicted as eventually leading white women into the beds of black men. Jews are believed to be in control everywhere, staging a multipronged attack against the white race. For *WAR*, the newsletter of White Aryan Resistance, the Jew "promotes a thousand social ills . . . [f]or which you'll have to foot the bills."

Reading white-supremacist literature is a profoundly disturbing experience, and even more difficult if you are one of those targeted for elimination. Yet, as a Jewish woman, I found my research to be unsettling in unexpected ways. I had not imagined that it would involve so much self-reflection. I knew white supremacists were vehemently anti-Semitic, but I was ambivalent about my Jewish identity and did not see it as essential to who I was. Having grown up in a large Jewish community, and then having attended a college with a large Jewish enrollment, my Jewishness was invisible to me—something I mostly ignored. As I soon learned, to white supremacists, that is irrelevant.

Contemporary white supremacists define Jews as non-white: "not a religion, they are an Asiatic *race*, locked in a mortal conflict with Aryan man," according to *The New Order*. In fact, throughout white-supremacist tracts, Jews are described not merely as a separate race, but as an impure race, the

---

From: *The Chronicle of Higher Education*, May 7, 1999, pp. B6–B7. Reprinted with permission of the author.

product of mongrelization. Jews, who pose the ultimate threat to racial boundaries, are themselves imagined as the product of mixed-race unions.

Although self-examination was not my goal when I began, my research pushed me to explore the contradictions in my own racial identity. Intellectually, I knew that the meaning of race was not rooted in biology or genetics, but it was only through researching the white-supremacist movement that I gained a more personal understanding of the social construction of race. Reading white-supremacist literature, I moved between two worlds: one where I was white, another where I was the non-white seed of Satan; one where I was privileged, another where I was despised; one where I was safe and secure, the other where I was feared and thus marked for death.

According to white-supremacist ideology, I am so dangerous that I must be eliminated. Yet, when I put down the racist, anti-Semitic newsletters, leave my office, and walk outdoors, I am white.

Growing up white has meant growing up privileged. Sure, I learned about the historical persecutions of Jews, overheard the hushed references to distant relatives lost in the Holocaust. I knew of my grandmother's experiences with anti-Semitism as a child of the only Jewish family in a Catholic neighborhood. But those were just stories to me. Reading white supremacists finally made the history real.

While conducting my research, I was reminded of the first time I felt like an "other." Arriving in the late 1980s for the first day of graduate school in the Pacific Northwest, I was greeted by a senior graduate student with the welcome: "Oh, you're the Jewish one." It was a jarring remark, for it immediately set me apart. This must have been how my mother felt, I thought, when, a generation earlier, a college classmate had asked to see her horns. Having lived in predominantly Jewish communities, I had never experienced my Jewishness as "otherness." In fact, I did not even *feel* Jewish. Since moving out of my parents' home, I had not celebrated a Jewish holiday or set foot in a synagogue. So it felt particularly odd to be identified by this stranger as a Jew. At the time, I did not feel that the designation described who I was in any meaningful sense.

But whether or not I define myself as Jewish, I am constantly defined by others that way. Jewishness is not simply a religious designation that one may choose, as I once naïvely assumed. Whether or not I see myself as Jewish does not matter to white supremacists.

I've come to realize that my own experience with race reflects the larger historical picture for Jews. As whites, Jews today are certainly a privileged group in the United States. Yet the history of the Jewish experience demonstrates precisely what scholars mean when they say that race is a social construction.

At certain points in time, Jews have been defined as a non-white minority. Around the turn of the last century, they were considered a separate, inferior race, with a distinguishable biological identity justifying discrimination and even genocide. Today, Jews are generally considered white, and Jewishness is largely considered merely a religious or ethnic designation. Jews, along with other European ethnic groups, were welcomed into the category of "white" as beneficiaries of one of the largest affirmative-action programs in history—the 1944 GI Bill of Rights. Yet, when I read white-supremacist discourse, I am reminded that my ancestors were expelled from the dominant race, persecuted, and even killed.

Since conducting my research, having heard dozens of descriptions of the murders and mutilations of "race traitors" by white supremacists, I now carry with me the knowledge that there are many people out there who would still wish to see me dead. For a brief moment, I think that I can imagine what it must feel like to be a person of color in our society. . . but then I realize that, as a white person, I cannot begin to imagine that.

Jewishness has become both clearer and more ambiguous for me. And the questions I have encountered in thinking about Jewish identity highlight the central issues involved in studying race today. I teach a class on race and ethnicity, and usually, about midway through the course, students complain of confusion. They enter my course seeking answers to the most troubling and divisive questions of our time, and are disappointed when they discover only more questions. If race is not biological or genetic, what is it? Why, in some states, does it take just one black ancestor out of 32 to make a person legally black, yet those 31 white ancestors are not enough to make that person white? And, always, are Jews a race?

I have no simple answers. As Jewish history demonstrates, what is and is not a racial designation, and who is included within it, is unstable and changes over time—and that designation is always tied to power. We do not have to look far to find other examples: The Irish were also once considered non-white in the United States, and U.S. racial categories change with almost every census.

My prolonged encounter with the white-supremacist movement forced me to question not only my assumptions about Jewish identity, but also my assumptions about whiteness. Growing up "white," I felt raceless. As it is for most white people, my race was invisible to me. Reflecting the assumption of most research on race at the time, I saw race as something that shaped the lives of people of color—the victims of racism. We are not used to thinking about whiteness when we think about race. Consequently, white people like myself have failed to recognize the ways in which our own lives are shaped by race. It was not until others began identifying me as the Jew, the "other," that I began to explore race in my own life.

Ironically, that is the same phenomenon shaping the consciousness of white supremacists: They embrace their racial identity at the precise moment when they feel their privilege and power under attack. Whiteness historically has equaled power, and when that equation is threatened, their own whiteness becomes visible to many white people for the first time. Hence, white supremacists seek to make racial identity, racial hierarchies, and white power part of the natural order again. The notion that race is a social construct threatens that order. While it has become an academic commonplace to assert that race is socially constructed, the revelation is profoundly unsettling to many, especially those who benefit most from the constructs.

My research on hate groups not only opened the way for me to explore my own racial identity, but also provided insight into the question with which I began this essay: Why do white supremacists express such hatred and fear of Jews? This ambiguity in Jewish racial identity is precisely what white supremacists find so threatening. Jewish history reveals race as a social designation, rather than a God-given or genetic endowment. Jews blur the boundaries between whites and people of color, failing to fall securely on either side of the divide. And it is ambiguity that white supremacists fear most of all.

I find it especially ironic that, today, some strict Orthodox Jewish leaders also find that ambiguity threatening. Speaking out against the high rates of intermarriage among Jews and non-Jews, they issue dire warnings. Like white supremacists, they fear assaults on the integrity of the community and fight to secure its racial boundaries, defining Jewishness as biological and restricting it only to those with Jewish mothers. For both white supremacists and such Orthodox Jews, intermarriage is tantamount to genocide.

For me, the task is no longer to resolve the ambiguity, but to embrace it. My exploration of white-supremacist ideology has revealed just how subversive doing so can be: Reading white-supremacist discourse through the lens of Jewish experience has helped me toward new interpretations. White supremacy is not a movement just about hatred, but even more about fear: fear of the vulnerability and instability of white identity and privilege. For white supremacists, the central goal is to naturalize racial identity and hierarchy, to establish boundaries.

Both my own experience and Jewish history reveal that to be an impossible task. Embracing Jewish identity and history, with all their contradictions, has given me an empowering alternative to white-supremacist conceptions of race. I have found that eliminating ambivalence does not require eliminating ambiguity.

RACE MATTERS

Cornel West

12

Since the beginning of the nation, white Americans have suffered from a deeper inner uncertainty as to who they really are. One of the ways that has been used to simplify the answer has been to seize upon the presence of black Americans and use them as a marker, a symbol of limits, a metaphor for the "outsider." Many whites could look at the social position of blacks and feel that color formed an easy and reliable gauge for determining to what extent one was or was not American. Perhaps that is why one of the first epithets that many European immigrants learned when they got off the boat was the term "nigger"—it made them feel instantly American. But this is tricky magic. Despite his racial difference and social status, something indisputably American about Negroes not only raised doubts about the white man's value system but aroused the troubling suspicion that whatever else the true American is, he is also somehow black.

Ralph Ellison, "What America Would Be Like Without Blacks" (1970)

What happened in Los Angeles in April of 1992 was neither a race riot nor a class rebellion. Rather, this monumental upheaval was a multiracial, trans-class, and largely male display of justified social rage. For all its ugly, xenophobic resentment, its air of adolescent carnival, and its downright barbaric behavior, it signified the sense of powerlessness in American society. Glib attempts to reduce its meaning to the pathologies of the black underclass, the criminal actions of hoodlums, or the political revolt of the oppressed urban masses miss the mark. Of those arrested, only 36 percent were black, more than a third had full-time jobs, and most claimed to shun political affiliation. What we witnessed in Los Angeles was the consequence of a lethal linkage of economic decline, cultural decay, and political lethargy in American life. Race was the visible catalyst, not the underlying cause.

The meaning of the earthshaking events in Los Angeles is difficult to grasp because most of us remain trapped in the narrow framework of the dominant liberal and conservative views of race in America, which with its worn-out vocabulary leaves us intellectually debilitated, morally disempowered, and personally depressed. The astonishing disappearance of the event from public dialogue is testimony to just how painful and distressing a serious engagement with race is. Our truncated public discussions of race suppress the best of who and what we are as a people because they fail to confront the complexity of the issue in a candid and critical manner. The predictable pitting of liberals against conservatives, Great Society Democrats against self-help Republicans, reinforces intellectual parochialism and political paralysis.

The liberal notion that more government programs can solve racial problems is simplistic—precisely because it focuses *solely* on the economic dimension. And the conservative idea that what is needed is a change in the moral behavior of poor black urban dwellers (especially poor black men, who, they say, should stay married, support their children, and stop committing so much crime) highlights immoral actions while ignoring public responsibility for the immoral circumstances that haunt our fellow citizens.

The common denominator of these views of race is that each still sees black people as a "problem people," in the words of Dorothy I. Height, president of the National Council of Negro Women, rather than as fellow American citizens with problems. Her words echo the poignant "unasked question" of W. E. B. Du Bois, who, in *The Souls of Black Folk* (1903), wrote:

> They approach me in a half-hesitant sort of way, eye me curiously or compassionately, and then instead of saying directly, How does it feel to be a problem? they say, I know an excellent colored man in my town. . . . Do not these Southern outrages make your blood boil? At these I smile, or am interested, or reduce the boiling to a simmer, as the occasion may require. To the real question, How does it feel to be a problem? I answer seldom a word.

Nearly a century later, we confine discussions about race in America to the "problems" black people pose for whites rather than consider what this way of viewing black people reveals about us as a nation.

This paralyzing framework encourages liberals to relieve their guilty consciences by supporting public funds directed at "the problems"; but at the same time, reluctant to exercise principled criticism of black people, liberals deny them the freedom to err. Similarly, conservatives blame the "problems" on black people themselves—and thereby render black social misery invisible or unworthy of public attention.

Hence, for liberals, black people are to be "included" and "integrated" into "our" society and culture, while for conservatives they are to be "well behaved" and "worthy of acceptance" by "our" way of life. Both fail to see that the presence and predicaments of black people are neither additions to nor defections from American life, but rather *constitutive elements of that life*.

To engage in a serious discussion of race in America, we must begin not with the problems of black people but with the flaws of American society—flaws rooted in historic inequalities and longstanding cultural stereotypes. How we set up the terms for discussing racial issues shapes our perception and response to these issues. As long as black people are viewed as a "them," the burden falls on blacks to do all the "cultural" and "moral" work necessary for healthy race relations. The implication is that only certain Americans can define what it means to be American—and the rest must simply "fit in."

The emergence of strong black-nationalist sentiments among blacks, especially among young people, is a revolt against this sense of having to "fit in." The variety of black-nationalist ideologies, from the moderate views of Supreme Court Justice Clarence Thomas in his youth to those of Louis Farrakhan today, rest upon a fundamental truth: white America has been historically weak-willed in ensuring racial justice and has continued to resist fully accepting the humanity of blacks. As long as double standards and differential treatment abound—as long as the rap performer Ice-T is harshly condemned while former Los Angeles Police Chief Daryl F. Gates's antiblack comments are received in polite silence, as long as Dr. Leonard Jeffries's anti-Semitic statements are met with vitriolic outrage while presidential candidate Patrick J. Buchanan's anti-Semitism receives a genteel response—black nationalisms will thrive.

Afrocentrism, a contemporary species of black nationalism, is a gallant yet misguided attempt to define an African identity in a white society perceived to be hostile. It is gallant because it puts black doings and sufferings, not white anxieties and fears, at the center of discussion. It is misguided because—out of fear of cultural hybridization and through silence on the issue of class, retrograde views on black women, gay men, and lesbians, and a reluctance to link race to the common good—it reinforces the narrow discussions about race.

To establish a new framework, we need to begin with a frank acknowledgement of the basic humanness and Americanness of each of us. And we must acknowledge that as a people—*E Pluribus Unum*—we are on a slippery slope toward economic strife, social turmoil, and cultural chaos. If we go down, we go down together. The Los Angeles upheaval forced us to see not only that we are not connected in ways we would like to be but also, in a more profound sense, that this failure to connect binds us even more tightly together. The paradox of race in America is that our common destiny is more pronounced and imperiled precisely when our divisions are deeper. The Civil War and its legacy speak loudly here. And our divisions are growing deeper. Today, 86 percent of white suburban Americans live in neighborhoods that are less than 1 percent black, meaning that the prospects for the country depend largely on how its cities fare in the hands of a suburban electorate. There is no escape from our interracial interdependence, yet enforced racial hierarchy dooms us as a nation to collective paranoia and hysteria—the unmaking of any democratic order.

The verdict in the Rodney King case which sparked the incidents in Los Angeles was perceived to be wrong by the vast majority of Americans. But whites have often failed to acknowledge the widespread mistreatment of black people, especially black men, by law enforcement agencies, which helped ignite the spark. The verdict was merely the occasion for deep-seated rage to come to the surface. This rage is fed by the "silent" depression ravaging the country—in which real weekly wages of all American workers since 1973 have declined nearly 20 percent, while at the same time wealth has been upwardly distributed.

The exodus of stable industrial jobs from urban centers to cheaper labor markets here and abroad, housing policies that have created "chocolate cities and vanilla suburbs" (to use the popular musical artist George Clinton's memorable phrase), white fear of black crime, and the urban influx of poor Spanish-speaking and Asian immigrants—all have helped erode the tax base of American cities just as the federal government has cut its supports and programs. The result is unemployment, hunger, homelessness, and sickness for millions.

And a pervasive spiritual impoverishment grows. The collapse of meaning in life—the eclipse of hope and absence of love of self and others, the breakdown of family and neighborhood bonds—leads to the social deracination and cultural denudement of urban dwellers, especially children. We have created rootless, dangling people with little link to the supportive networks—family, friends, school—that sustain some sense of purpose in life. We have witnessed the collapse of the spiritual communities that in the past helped Americans face despair, disease, and death and that transmit through the generations dignity and decency, excellence and elegance.

The result is lives of what we might call "random nows," of fortuitous and fleeting moments preoccupied with "getting over"—with acquiring pleasure, property, and power by any means necessary. (This is not what Malcolm X meant by this famous phrase.) Post-modern culture is more and more a market culture dominated by gangster mentalities and self-destructive wantonness. This culture engulfs all of us—yet its impact on the disadvantaged is devastating, resulting in extreme violence in everyday life. Sexual violence against women and homicidal assaults by young black men on one another are only the most obvious signs of this empty quest for pleasure, property, and power.

Last, this rage is fueled by a political atmosphere in which images, not ideas, dominate, where politicians spend more time raising money than debating issues. The functions of parties have been displaced by public polls, and politicians behave less as thermostats that determine the climate of opinion than as thermometers registering the public mood. American politics has been rocked by an unleashing of greed among opportunistic public officials—who have followed the lead of their counterparts in the private sphere, where, as of 1989, 1 percent of the population owned 37 percent of the wealth and 10 percent of the population owned 86 percent of the wealth—leading to a profound cynicism and pessimism among the citizenry.

And given the way in which the Republican Party since 1968 has appealed to popular xenophobic images—playing the black, female, and homophobic cards to realign the electorate along race, sex, and sexual-orientation lines—it is no surprise that the notion that we are all part of one garment of destiny is discredited. Appeals to special interests rather than to public interests reinforce this polarization. The Los Angeles upheaval was an expression of utter fragmentation by a powerless citizenry that includes not just the poor but all of us.

What is to be done? How do we capture a new spirit and vision to meet the challenges of the post-industrial city, post-modern culture, and post-party politics?

First, we must admit that the most valuable sources for help, hope, and power consist of ourselves and our common history. As in the ages of Lincoln, Roosevelt, and King, we must look to new frameworks and languages to understand our multilayered crisis and overcome our deep malaise.

Second, we must focus our attention on the public square—the common good that undergirds our national and global destinies. The vitality of any public square ultimately depends on how much we *care* about the quality of our lives together. The neglect of our public infrastructure, for example—our water and sewage systems, bridges, tunnels, highways, subways, and streets— reflects not only our myopic economic policies, which impede productivity, but also the low priority we place on our common life.

The tragic plight of our children clearly reveals our deep disregard for public well-being. About one out of every five children in this country lives in poverty, including one out of every two black children and two out of every five Hispanic children. Most of our children—neglected by overburdened parents and bombarded by the market values of profit-hungry corporations— are ill-equipped to live lives of spiritual and cultural quality. Faced with these facts, how do we expect ever to constitute a vibrant society?

One essential step is some form of large-scale public intervention to ensure access to basic social goods—housing, food, health care, education, child care, and jobs. We must invigorate the common good with a mixture of government, business, and labor that does not follow any existing blueprint. After a period in which the private sphere has been sacralized and the public square gutted, the temptation is to make a fetish of the public square. We need to resist such dogmatic swings.

Last, the major challenge is to meet the need to generate new leadership. The paucity of courageous leaders—so apparent in the response to the events in Los Angeles—requires that we look beyond the same elites and voices that recycle the older frameworks. We need leaders—neither saints nor sparkling television personalities—who can situate themselves within a larger historical narrative of this country and our world, who can grasp the complex dynamics of our peoplehood and imagine a future grounded in the best of our past, yet who are attuned to the frightening obstacles that now perplex us. Our ideals of freedom, democracy, and equality must be invoked to invigorate all of us, especially the landless, propertyless, and luckless. Only a visionary leadership that can motivate "the better angels of our nature," as Lincoln said, and activate possibilities for a freer, more efficient, and stable America—only that leadership deserves cultivation and support.

This new leadership must be grounded in grass-roots organizing that highlights democratic accountability. Whoever *our* leaders will be as we approach the twenty-first century, their challenge will be to help Americans determine whether a genuine multiracial democracy can be created and sustained in an era of global economy and a moment of xenophobic frenzy.

Let us hope and pray that the vast intelligence, imagination, humor, and courage of Americans will not fail us. Either we learn a new language of empathy and compassion, or the fire this time will consume us all.

Class and Inequality

TIRED OF PLAYING MONOPOLY?

13

Donna Langston

I. Magnin, Nordstrom, The Bon, Sears, Penneys, K mart, Goodwill, Salvation Army. If the order of this list of stores makes any sense to you, then we've begun to deal with the first question which inevitably arises in any discussion of class here in the U.S.—huh? Unlike our European allies, we in the U.S. are reluctant to recognize class differences. This denial of class divisions functions to reinforce ruling class control and domination. America is, after all, the supposed land of equal opportunity where, if you just work hard enough, you can get ahead, pull yourself up by your bootstraps. What the old bootstraps theory overlooks is that some were born with silver shoe horns. Female-headed households, communities of color, the elderly, disabled and children find themselves, disproportionately, living in poverty. If hard work were the sole determinant of your ability to support yourself and your family, surely we'd have a different outcome for many in our society. We also, however, believe in luck and, on closer examination, it certainly is quite a coincidence that the "unlucky" come from certain race, gender and class backgrounds. In order to perpetuate racist, sexist and classist outcomes, we also have to believe that the current economic distribution is unchangeable, has always existed, and probably exists in this form throughout the known universe; i.e., it's "natural." Some people explain or try to account for poverty or class position by focusing on the personal and moral merits of an individual. If people are poor, then it's something they did or didn't do; they were lazy, unlucky, didn't try hard enough, etc. This has the familiar ring of blaming the victims. Alternative explanations focus on the ways

From: Jo Whitehorse Cochran, Donna Langston, and Carolyn Woodward, eds., *Changing Our Power: An Introduction to Women's Studies* (Dubuque, IA: Kendall-Hunt, 1988). Reprinted by permission.

in which poverty and class position are due to structural, systematic, institu-tionalized economic and political power relations. These power relations are based firmly on dynamics such as race, gender, and class.

In the myth of the classless society, ambition and intelligence alone are responsible for success. The myth conceals the existence of a class society, which serves many functions. One of the main ways it keeps the working class and poor locked into a class-based system in a position of servitude is by cru-elly creating false hope. It perpetuates the false hope among the working class and poor that they can have different opportunities in life. The hope that they can escape the fate that awaits them due to the class position they were born into. Another way the rags-to-riches myth is perpetuated is by creating enough visible tokens so that oppressed persons believe they, too, can get ahead. The creation of hope through tokenism keeps a hierarchical structure in place and lays the blame for not succeeding on those who don't. This keeps us from re-sisting and changing the class-based system. Instead, we accept it as inevitable, something we just have to live with. If oppressed people believe in equality of opportunity, then they won't develop class consciousness and will internalize the blame for their economic position. If the working class and poor do not recognize the way false hope is used to control them, they won't get a chance to control their lives by acknowledging their class position, by claiming that identity and taking action as a group.

The myth also keeps the middle class and upper class entrenched in the privileges awarded in a class-based system. It reinforces middle- and upper-class beliefs in their own superiority. If we believe that anyone in society really can get ahead, then middle- and upper-class status and privileges must be de-served, due to personal merits, and enjoyed—and defended at all costs. Ac-cording to this viewpoint, poverty is regrettable but acceptable, just the out-come of a fair game: "There have always been poor people, and there always will be."

Class is more than just the amount of money you have; it's also the pres-ence of economic security. For the working class and poor, working and eat-ing are matters of survival, not taste. However, while one's class status can be defined in important ways in terms of monetary income, class is also a whole lot more—specifically, class is also culture. As a result of the class you are born into and raised in, class is your understanding of the world and where you fit in; it's composed of ideas, behavior, attitudes, values, and language; class is how you think, feel, act, look, dress, talk, move, walk; class is what stores you shop at, restaurants you eat in; class is the schools you attend, the education you at-tain; class is the very jobs you will work at throughout your adult life. Class even determines when we marry and become mothers. Working-class women become mothers long before middle-class women receive their bachelor's degrees. We experience class at every level of our lives; class is who our friends are, where we live and work, even what kind of car we drive, if we own one, and what kind of health care we receive, if any. Have I left anything out? In other words, class is socially constructed and all-encompassing. When we experience classism, it will be because of our lack of money (i.e., choices and power in this society) and because of the way we talk, think, act, move—because of our culture.

Class affects what we perceive as and what we have available to us as choices. Upon graduation from high school, I was awarded a scholarship to attend any college, private or public, in the state of California. Yet it never occurred to me or my family that it made any difference which college you went to. I ended up just going to a small college in my town. It never would have occurred to me to move away from my family for school, because no one ever had and no one would. I was the first person in my family to go to college. I had to figure out from reading college catalogs how to apply—no one in my family could have sat down and said, "Well, you take this test and then you really should think about . . ." Although tests and high school performance had shown I had the ability to pick up white middle-class lingo, I still had quite an adjustment to make—it was lonely and isolating in college. I lost my friends from high school—they were at the community college, vo-tech school, working, or married. I lasted a year and a half in this foreign environment before I quit college, married a factory worker, had a baby and resumed living in a community I knew. One middle-class friend in college had asked if I'd like to travel to Europe with her. Her father was a college professor and people in her family had actually travelled there. My family had seldom been able to take a vacation at all. A couple of times my parents were able—by saving all year—to take the family over to the coast on their annual two-week vacation. I'd seen the time and energy my parents invested in trying to take a family vacation to some place a few hours away; the idea of how anybody ever got to Europe was beyond me.

If class is more than simple economic status but one's cultural background as well, what happens if you're born and raised middle class, but spend some of your adult life with earnings below a middle-class income bracket—are you then working-class? Probably not. If your economic position changes, you still have the language, behavior, educational background, etc., of the middle class, which you can bank on. You will always have choices. Men who consciously try to refuse male privilege are still male; whites who want to challenge white privilege are still white. I think those who come from middle-class backgrounds need to recognize that their class privilege does not float out with the rinse water. Middle-class people can exert incredible power just by being nice and polite. The middle-class way of doing things is the standard— they're always right, just by being themselves. Beware of middle-class people who deny their privilege. Many people have times when they struggle to get shoes for the kids, when budgets are tight, etc. This isn't the same as long-term economic conditions without choices. Being working class is also generational. Examine your family's history of education, work, and standard of living. It may not be a coincidence that you share the same class status as your parents and grandparents. If your grandparents were professionals, or your parents were professionals, it's much more likely you'll be able to grow up to become a yuppie, if your heart so desires, or even if you don't think about it.

How about if you're born and raised poor or working class, yet through struggle, usually through education, you manage to achieve a different economic level: do you become middle class? Can you pass? I think some working-class people may successfully assimilate into the middle class by learning to dress, talk, and act middle class—to accept and adopt the middle-class way of doing things. It all depends on how far they're able to go. To succeed in the middle-class world means facing great pressures to abandon working-class friends and ways.

Contrary to our stereotype of the working class—white guys in overalls—the working class is not homogeneous in terms of race or gender. If you are a person of color, if you live in a female-headed household, you are much more likely to be working class or poor. The experience of Black, Latino, American Indian or Asian American working classes will differ significantly from the white working classes, which have traditionally been able to rely on white privilege to provide a more elite position within the working class. Working-class people are often grouped together and stereotyped, but distinctions can be made among the working class, working poor, and poor. Many working-class families are supported by unionized workers who possess marketable skills. Most working-poor families are supported by non-unionized, unskilled men and women. Many poor families are dependent on welfare for their income.

Attacks on the welfare system and those who live on welfare are a good example of classism in action. We have a "dual welfare" system in this country whereby welfare for the rich in the form of tax-free capital gain, guaranteed loans, oil depletion allowances, etc., is not recognized as welfare. Almost everyone in America is on some type of welfare; but, if you're rich, it's in the form of tax deductions for "business" meals and entertainment, and if you're poor, it's in the form of food stamps. The difference is the stigma and humiliation connected to welfare for the poor, as compared to welfare for the rich, which is called "incentives." . . . A common focal point for complaints about "welfare" is the belief that most welfare recipients are cheaters—goodness knows there are no middle-class income tax cheaters out there. Imagine focusing the same anger and energy on the way corporations and big business cheat on their tax revenues. Now, there would be some dollars worth quibbling about. The "dual welfare" system also assigns a different degree of stigma to programs that benefit women and children . . . and programs whose recipients are primarily male, such as veterans' benefits. The implicit assumption is that mothers who raise children do not work and therefore are not deserving of their daily bread crumbs.

Anti-union attitudes are another prime example of classism in action. At best, unions have been a very progressive force for workers, women and people of color. At worst, unions have reflected the same regressive attitudes which are out there in other social structures: classism, racism, and sexism. Classism exists within the working class. The aristocracy of the working class—unionized, skilled workers—have mainly been white and male and have viewed themselves as being better than unskilled workers, the unemployed, and the poor, who are mostly women and people of color. The white working class must commit itself to a cultural and ideological transformation of racist attitudes. The history of working people, and the ways we've resisted many types of oppressions, are not something we're taught in school. Missing from our education is information about workers and their resistance.

Working-class women's critiques have focused on the following issues:

Education: White middle-class professionals have used academic jargon to rationalize and justify classism. The whole structure of education is a classist system. Schools in every town reflect class divisions: like the store list at the beginning of this article, you can list schools in your town by what classes of kids attend, and in most cities you can also list by race. The classist system is perpetuated in schools with the tracking system, whereby the "dumbs" are tracked into homemaking, shop courses and vocational school futures, while the "smarts" end up in advanced math, science, literature, and college-prep courses. If we examine these groups carefully, the coincidence of poor and working-class backgrounds with "dumbs" is rather alarming. The standard measurement of supposed intelligence is white middle-class English. If you're other than white middle class, you have to become bilingual to succeed in the educational system. If you're white middle class, you only need the language and writing skills you were raised with, since they're the standard. To do well in society presupposes middle-class background, experiences and learning for everyone. The tracking system separates those from the working class who can potentially assimilate to the middle class from all our friends, and labels us "college bound."

After high school, you go on to vocational school, community college, or college—public or private—according to your class position. Apart from the few who break into middle-class schools, the classist stereotyping of the working class as being dumb and inarticulate tracks most into vocational and low-skilled jobs. A few of us are allowed to slip through to reinforce the idea that equal opportunity exists. But for most, class position is destiny—determining our educational attainment and employment. Since we must overall abide by middle-class rules to succeed, the assumption is that we go to college in order to "better ourselves"—i.e., become more like them. I suppose it's assumed we have "yuppie envy" and desire nothing more than to be upwardly mobile individuals. It's assumed that we want to fit into their world. But many of us remain connected to our communities and families. Becoming college educated doesn't mean we have to, or want to, erase our first and natural language and value system. It's important for many of us to remain in and return to our communities to work, live, and stay sane.

Jobs: Middle-class people have the privilege of choosing careers. They can decide which jobs they want to work, according to their moral or political commitments, needs for challenge or creativity. This is a privilege denied the working class and poor, whose work is a means of survival, not choice (see Hartsock). Working-class women have seldom had the luxury of choosing between work in the home or market. We've generally done both, with little ability to purchase services to help with this double burden. Middle- and upper-class women can often hire other women to clean their houses, take care of their children, and cook their meals. Guess what class and race those "other" women are? Working a double or triple day is common for working-class women. Only middle-class women have an array of choices such as: parents put you through school, then you choose a career, then you choose when and if to have babies, then you choose a support system of working-class women to take care of your kids and house if you choose to resume your career. After the birth of my second child, I was working two part-time jobs—one loading trucks at night—and going to school during the days. While I was quite privileged because I could take my colicky infant with me to classes and the daytime job, I was in a state of continuous semi-consciousness. I had to work to support my family; the only choice I had was between school or sleep: Sleep became a privilege. A white middle-class feminist instructor at the university suggested to me, all sympathetically, that I ought to hire someone to clean my house and watch the baby. Her suggestion was totally out of my reality, both economically and socially. I'd worked for years cleaning other peoples' houses. Hiring a working-class woman to do the shit work is a middle-class woman's solution to any dilemma which her privileges, such as a career, may present her.

Mothering: The feminist critique of families and the oppressive role of mothering has focused on white middle-class nuclear families. This may not be an appropriate model for communities of class and color. Mothering and families may hold a different importance for working-class women. Within this context, the issue of coming out can be a very painful process for working-class lesbians. Due to the homophobia of working-class communities, to be a lesbian is most often to be excommunicated from your family, neighborhood, friends and the people you work with. If you're working class, you don't have such clearly demarcated concepts of yourself as an individual, but instead see yourself as part of a family and community that forms your survival structure. It is not easy to be faced with the risk of giving up ties which are so central to your identity and survival.

Individualism: Preoccupation with one's self—one's body, looks, relationships—is a luxury working-class women can't afford. Making an occupation out of taking care of yourself through therapy, aerobics, jogging, dressing for success, gourmet meals and proper nutrition, etc., may be responses that are directly rooted in privilege. The middle class has the leisure time to be preoccupied with their own problems, such as their waistlines, planning their vacations, coordinating their wardrobes, or dealing with what their mother said to them when they were five—my!

The white middle-class women's movement has been patronizing to working-class women. Its supporters think we don't understand sexism. What we don't understand is white middle-class feminism. They act as though they invented the truth, the light, and the way, which they merely need to pass along to us lower-class drudges. What they invented is a distorted form of what working-class women already know—if you're female, life sucks. Only at least we were smart enough to know that it's not just being female, but also being a person of color or class, which makes life a quicksand trap. The class system weakens all women. It censors and eliminates images of female strength. The idea of women as passive, weak creatures totally discounts the strength, self-dependence and inter-dependence necessary to survive as working-class and poor women. My mother and her friends always had a less-than-passive, less-than-enamoured attitude toward their spouses, male bosses, and men in general. I know from listening to their conversations, jokes and what they passed on to us, their daughters, as folklore. When I was five years old, my mother told me about how Aunt Betty had hit Uncle Ernie over the head with a skillet and knocked him out because he was raising his hand to hit her, and how he's never even thought about doing it since. This story was told to me with a good amount of glee and laughter. All the men in the neighborhood were told of the event as an example of what was a very acceptable response in the women's community for that type of male behavior. We kids in the neighborhood grew up with these stories of women giving husbands, bosses, the welfare system, schools, unions and men in general hell, whenever they deserved it. For me there were many role models of women taking action, control and resisting what was supposed to be their lot. Yet many white middle-class feminists continue to view feminism like math homework, where there's only supposed to be one answer. Never occurs to them that they might be talking algebra while working-class women might be talking metaphysics.

Women with backgrounds other than white middle-class experience compounded, simultaneous oppressions. We can't so easily separate our experiences by categories of gender, or race, or class, i.e., "I remember it well: on Saturday, June 3, I was experiencing class oppression, but by Tuesday, June 6, I was caught up in race oppression, then all day Friday, June 9, I was in the middle of gender oppression. What a week!" Sometimes, for example, gender and class reinforce each other. When I returned to college as a single parent after a few years of having kids and working crummy jobs—I went in for vocational testing. Even before I was tested, the white middle-class male vocational counselor looked at me, a welfare mother in my best selection from the Salvation Army racks, and suggested I quit college, go to vo-tech school and become a grocery clerk. This was probably the highest paying female working-class occupation he could think of. The vocational test results suggested I become an attorney. I did end up quitting college once again, not because of his suggestion, but because I was tired of supporting my children in ungenteel poverty. I entered vo-tech school for training as an electrician and, as one of the first women in a non-traditional field, was able to earn a living wage at a job which had traditionally been reserved for white working-class males. But this is a story for another day. Let's return to our little vocational counselor example. Was he suggesting the occupational choice of grocery clerk to me because of my gender or my class? Probably both. Let's imagine for a moment what this same vocational counselor might have advised, on sight only, to the following people:

1. A white middle-class male: doctor, lawyer, engineer, business executive.
2. A white middle-class female: close to the same suggestion as #1 if the counselor was not sexist, or, if sexist, then: librarian, teacher, nurse, social worker.
3. A middle-class man of color: close to the same suggestions as #1 if the counselor was not racist, or, if racist, then: school principal, sales, management, technician.
4. A middle-class woman of color: close to the same suggestions as #3 if counselor was not sexist; #2 if not racist; if not racist or sexist, then potentially #1.
5. A white working-class male: carpenter, electrician, plumber, welder.
6. A white working-class female—well, we already know what he told me, although he could have also suggested secretary, waitress and dental hygienist (except I'd already told him I hated these jobs).
7. A working-class man of color: garbage collector, janitor, fieldhand.
8. A working-class woman of color: maid, laundress, garment worker.

Notice anything about this list? As you move down it, a narrowing of choices, status, pay, working conditions, benefits and chances for promotions occurs. To be connected to any one factor, such as gender or class or race, can make life difficult. To be connected to multiple factors can guarantee limited economic status and poverty.

WAYS TO AVOID FACING CLASSISM

Deny Deny Deny: Deny your class position and the privileges connected to it. Deny the existence or experience of the working class and poor. You can even set yourself up (in your own mind) as judge and jury in deciding who qualifies as working class by your white middle-class standards. So if someone went to college, or seems intelligent to you, not at all like your stereotypes, they must be middle class.

Guilt Guilt Guilt: "I feel so bad, I just didn't realize!" is not helpful, but is a way to avoid changing attitudes and behaviors. Passivity—"Well, what can I do about it, anyway?"—and anger—"Well, what do they want!"—aren't too helpful either. Again, with these responses, the focus is on you and absolving the white middle class from responsibility. A more helpful remedy is to take action. Donate your time and money to local foodbanks. Don't cross picket lines. Better yet, go join a picket line.

HOW TO CHALLENGE CLASSISM

If you're middle class, you can begin to challenge classism with the following:

1. Confront classist behavior in yourself, others and society. Use and share the privileges, like time or money, which you do have.
2. Make demands on working-class and poor communities' issues—anti-racism, poverty, unions, public housing, public transportation, literacy and day care.
3. Learn from the skills and strength of working people—study working and poor people's history; take some Labor Studies, Ethnic Studies, Women Studies classes. Challenge elitism. There are many different types of intelligence: white middle-class, academic, professional intellectualism being one of them (reportedly). Finally, educate yourself, take responsibility and take action.

If you're working class, just some general suggestions (it's cheaper than therapy—free, less time-consuming and I won't ask you about what your mother said to you when you were five):

1. Face your racism! Educate yourself and others, your family, community, any organizations you belong to; take responsibility and take action. Face your classism, sexism, heterosexism, ageism, able-bodiness, adultism. . . .
2. Claim your identity. Learn all you can about your history and the history and experience of all working and poor peoples. Raise your children to be anti-racist, anti-sexist and anti-classist. Teach them the language and culture of working peoples. Learn to survive with a fair amount of anger and lots of humor, which can be tough when this stuff isn't even funny.
3. Work on issues which will benefit your community. Consider remaining in or returning to your communities. If you live and work in white middle-class environments, look for working-class allies to help you survive with your humor and wits intact. How do working-class people spot each other? We have antennae.

We need not deny or erase the differences of working-class cultures but can embrace their richness, their variety, their moral and intellectual heritage. We're not at the point yet where we can celebrate differences—not having money for a prescription for your child is nothing to celebrate. It's not time yet to party with the white middle class, because we'd be the entertainment ("Aren't they quaint? Just love their workboots and uniforms and the way they cuss!"). We need to overcome divisions among working people, not by ignoring the multiple oppressions many of us encounter, or by oppressing each other, but by becoming committed allies on all issues which affect working people: racism, sexism, classism, etc. An injury to one is an injury to all. Don't play by ruling-class rules, hoping that maybe you can live on Connecticut Avenue instead of Baltic, or that you as an individual can make it to Park Place and Boardwalk. Tired of Monopoly? Always ending up on Mediterranean Avenue? How about changing the game?

WEALTH MATTERS

14

Dalton Conley

Property is theft.

Pierre Joseph Proudhon, 1809–65

... In 1994, the median white family held assets worth more than seven times those of the median nonwhite family. Even when we compare white and minority families at the same income level, whites enjoy a huge advantage in wealth. For instance, at the lower end of the income spectrum (less than $15,000 per year), the median African American family has no assets, while the equivalent white family holds $10,000 worth of equity. At upper income levels (greater than $75,000 per year), white families have a median net worth of $308,000, almost three times the figure for upper-income African American families ($114,600).[1] ...

From: Dalton Conley, *Being Black, Living in the Red: Race, Wealth, and Social Policy in America* (Berkeley, CA: University of California Press, 1999). Reprinted with permission of the author and the publisher.

. . . Contrast the situations of two hypothetical families. Let's say that both households consist of married parents, in their thirties, with two young children.[2] Both families are low-income—that is, the total household income of each family is approximately the amount that the federal government has "declared" to be the poverty line for a family of four (with two children). In 1996, this figure was $15,911.

Brett and Samantha Jones (family 1) earned about $12,000 that year. Brett earned this income from his job at a local fast-food franchise (approximately two thousand hours at a rate of $6 per hour). He found himself employed at this low-wage job after being laid off from his relatively well-paid position as a sheet metal worker at a local manufacturing plant, which closed because of fierce competition from companies in Asia and Latin America. After six months of unemployment, the only work Brett could find was flipping burgers alongside teenagers from the local high school.

Fortunately for the Jones family, however, they owned their own home. Fifteen years earlier, when Brett graduated from high school, married Samantha, and landed his original job as a sheet metal worker, his parents had lent the newlyweds money out of their retirement nest egg that enabled Brett and Samantha to make a 10 percent down payment on a house. With Samantha's parents cosigning—backed by the value of their own home—the newlyweds took out a fifteen-year mortgage for the balance of the cost of their $30,000 home. Although money was tight in the beginning, they were nonetheless thrilled to have a place of their own. During those initial, difficult years, an average of $209 of their $290.14 monthly mortgage payment was tax deductible as a home mortgage interest deduction. In addition, their annual property taxes of $800 were completely deductible, lowering their annual taxable income by a total of $3,308 per year. This more than offset the payments they were making to Brett's parents for the $3,000 they had borrowed for the down payment.

After four years, Brett and Samantha had paid back the $3,000 loan from his parents. At that point, the total of their combined mortgage payment ($290.14), monthly insurance premium ($50), and monthly property tax payment ($67), minus the tax savings from the deductions for mortgage interest and local property taxes, was less than the $350 that the Smiths (family 2) were paying to rent a unit the same size as the Joneses' house on the other side of town.

That other neighborhood, on the "bad" side of town, where David and Janet Smith lived, had worse schools and a higher crime rate and had just been chosen as a site for a waste disposal center. Most of the residents rented their housing units from absentee landlords who had no personal stake in the community other than profit. A few blocks from the Smiths' apartment was a row of public housing projects. Although they earned the same salaries and paid more or less the same monthly costs for housing as the Joneses did, the Smiths and their children experienced living conditions that were far inferior on every dimension, ranging from the aesthetic to the functional (buses ran less frequently, large supermarkets were nowhere to be found, and class size at the local school was well over thirty).

Like Brett Jones, David Smith had been employed as a sheet metal worker at the now-closed manufacturing plant. Unfortunately, the Smiths had not been able to buy a home when David was first hired at the plant. With little in the way of a down payment, they had looked for an affordable unit at the time, but the real estate agents they saw routinely claimed that there was nothing available at the moment, although they promised to "be sure to call as soon as something comes up. . . ." The Smiths never heard back from the agents and eventually settled into a rental apartment.

David spent the first three months after the layoffs searching for work, drawing down the family's savings to supplement unemployment insurance— savings that were not significantly greater than those of the Joneses, since both families had more or less the same monthly expenses. After several months of searching, David managed to land a job. Unfortunately, it was of the same variety as the job Brett Jones found: working as a security guard at the local mall, for about $12,000 a year. Meanwhile, Janet Smith went to work part time, as a nurse's aide for a home health care agency, grossing about $4,000 annually.

After the layoffs, the Joneses experienced a couple of rough months, when they were forced to dip into their small cash savings. But they were able to pay off the last two installments of their mortgage, thus eliminating their single biggest living expense. So, although they had some trouble adjusting to their lower standard of living, they managed to get by, always hoping that another manufacturing job would become available or that another company would buy out the plant and reopen it. If worst came to worst, they felt that they could always sell their home and relocate in a less expensive locale or an area with a more promising labor market.

The Smiths were a different case entirely. As renters, they had no latitude in reducing their expenses to meet their new economic reality, and they could not afford their rent on David's reduced salary. The financial strain eventually proved too much for the Smiths, who fought over how to structure the family budget. After a particularly bad row when the last of their savings had been spent, they decided to take a break; both thought life would be easier and better for the children if Janet moved back in with her mother for a while, just until things turned around economically—that is, until David found a better-paying job. With no house to anchor them, this seemed to be the best course of action.

Several years later, David and Janet Smith divorced, and the children began to see less and less of their father, who stayed with a friend on a "temporary" basis. Even though together they had earned more than the Jones family (with total incomes of $16,000 and $12,000, respectively), the Smiths had a rougher financial, emotional, and family situation, which, we may infer, resulted from a lack of property ownership.

What this comparison of the two families illustrates is the inadequacy of relying on income alone to describe the economic and social circumstances of families at the lower end of the economic scale. With a $16,000 annual income, the Smiths were just above the poverty threshold. In other words, they were not defined as "poor," in contrast to the Joneses, who were.[3] Yet the Smiths were worse off than the Joneses, despite the fact that the U.S. government and most researchers would have classified the Jones family as the one who met the threshold of neediness, based on that family's lower income.

These income-based poverty thresholds differ by family size and are adjusted annually for changes in the average cost of living in the United States. In 1998, more than two dozen government programs—including food stamps, Head Start, and Medicaid—based their eligibility standards on the official poverty threshold. Additionally, more than a dozen states currently link their needs standard in some way to this poverty threshold. The example of the Joneses and the Smiths should tell us that something is gravely wrong with the way we are measuring economic hardship—poverty—in the United States. By ignoring assets, we not only give a distorted picture of life at the bottom of the income distribution but may even create perverse incentives.

Of course, we must be cautious and remember that the Smiths and the Joneses are hypothetically embellished examples that may exaggerate differences. Perhaps the Smiths would have divorced regardless of their economic circumstances. The hard evidence linking modest financial differences to a propensity toward marital dissolution is thin; however, a substantial body of research shows that financial issues are a major source of marital discord and relationship strain.[4] It is also possible that the Smiths, with nothing to lose in the form of assets, might have easily slid into the world of welfare dependency. A wide range of other factors, not included in our examples, affect a family's well-being and its trajectory. For example, the members of one family might have been healthier than those of the other, which would have had important economic consequences and could have affected family stability. Perhaps one family might have been especially savvy about using available resources and would have been able to take in boarders, do under-the-table work, or employ another strategy to better its standard of living. Nor do our examples address educational differences between the two households.

But I have chosen not to address all these confounding factors for the purpose of illustrating the importance of asset ownership *per se*. Of course, homeownership, savings behavior, and employment status all interact with a variety of other measurable and unmeasurable factors. This interaction, however, does not take away from the importance of property ownership itself.

. . . In order to understand a family's well-being and the life chances of its children—in short, to understand its class position—we not only must consider income, education, and occupation but also must take into account accumulated wealth (that is, property, assets, or net worth). . . . As you might have guessed, an important detail is missing from the preceding descriptions of the two families: the Smiths are black and have fewer assets than the Joneses, who are white.

At all income, occupational, and education levels, black families on average have drastically lower levels of wealth than similar white families. The situation of the Smiths may help us to understand the reason for this disparity of wealth between blacks and whites. For the Smiths, it was not discrimination in hiring or education that led to a family outcome vastly different from that of the Joneses; rather, it was a relative lack of assets from which they could draw. In contemporary America, race and property are intimately linked and form the nexus for the persistence of black-white inequality.

Let us look again at the Smith family, this time through the lens of race. Why did real estate agents tell the Smiths that nothing was available, thereby hindering their chances of finding a home to buy? This well-documented practice is called "steering," in which agents do not disclose properties on the market to qualified African American home seekers, in order to preserve the racial makeup of white communities—with an eye to maintaining the property values in those neighborhoods. Even if the Smiths had managed to locate a home in a predominantly African American neighborhood, they might well have encountered difficulty in obtaining a home mortgage because of "redlining," the procedure by which banks code such neighborhoods "red"—the lowest rating—on their loan evaluations, thereby making it next to impossible to get a mortgage for a home in these districts. Finally, and perhaps most important, the Smiths' parents were more likely to have been poor and without assets themselves (being black and having been born early in the century), meaning that it would have been harder for them to amass enough money to loan their children a down payment or to cosign a loan for them. The result is that while poor whites manage to have, on average, net worths of over $10,000, impoverished blacks have essentially no assets whatsoever.[5]

Since wealth accumulation depends heavily on intergenerational support issues such as gifts, informal loans, and inheritances, net worth has the ability to pick up both the current dynamics of race and the legacy of past inequalities that may be obscured in simple measures of income, occupation, or education. This thesis has been suggested by the work of sociologists Melvin Oliver and Thomas Shapiro in their recent book *Black Wealth, White Wealth*.[6] They claim that wealth is central to the nature of black-white inequality and that wealth—as opposed to income, occupation, or education—represents the "sedimentation" of both a legacy of racial inequality as well as contemporary, continuing inequalities. . . .

NOTES

1. Data from the Panel Study of Income Dynamics (PSID), 1994 Wealth Supplement. The PSID is an ongoing study conducted by the Survey Research Center, Institute for Social Research, at the University of Michigan; see the PSID Web site at *www.isr.umich. edu/src/psid.*

2. These family descriptions were extrapolated from profiles of specific families who were interviewed for this study. The age, racial, income, family size, wealth, housing tenure, and divorce descriptions of these families come directly from cases 4348 and 1586 of the PSID 1984 wave (inflation-adjusted to 1996 dollars). The names and other details are fictitious but are in line with previous research that would suggest such profiles.

3. Neither family received health insurance from an employer. Since the Smiths' income was under 185 percent of the poverty line, their children were eligible for Medicaid. (In most states, the Joneses' children would also have been eligible for Medicaid since that family's wealth was in the form of a home, which is excluded from the asset limits of many states.)

4. See, e.g., G. Levinger and O. Moles, eds., *Divorce and Separation: Contexts, Causes, and Consequences* (New York: Basic Books, 1979); and R. Conger, G. H. Elder, et al., "Linking Economic Hardship to Marital Quality and Instability," *Journal of Marriage and the Family* 52 (1990): 643–56.

5. The terms "black" and "African American" are used interchangeably, as are the terms "Hispanic" and "Latino." Black people of Caribbean origin make up a negligible portion of the data sample.

6. M. Oliver and T. Shapiro, *Black Wealth/White Wealth: A New Perspective on Racial Inequality* (New York: Routledge, 1995).

POVERTY AS RACE, POWER, AND WEALTH   15

James Jennings and Louis Kushnick

. . . Racial and gender hierarchies are important features for the maintenance of wealth and political power in this country. In addition, . . . poor people are not politically passive. . . . The persistence of poverty cannot be understood completely, nor can it be reduced significantly, without also examining the

From: Louis Kushnick and James Jennings, eds., *A New Introduction to Poverty: The Role of Race, Power, and Politics* (New York: New York University Press, 1999). Reprinted with permission of the publisher.

question of who has political influence in the United States. . . . The unchanging distribution of wealth and power is the greatest determinant in the persistence of massive impoverization of some sectors in this society. Furthermore, the racializing of poverty serves to strengthen institutional arrangements and social relations that generally keep high proportions of women and people of color in economically vulnerable and impoverished positions.

. . . The problem of poverty cannot be analyzed or responded to effectively if it is perceived simply as a behavioral issue for poor people or, in what William Ryan described several decades ago as a "blaming-the-victim" approach. We believe that persistent poverty, and poverty that is highly concentrated in some communities, reflects the interplay of an array of national and international factors, as well as specific economic arrangements that support social relations at least partially defined by race and gender. At a broad level, three factors contribute to continuing poverty and high rates of impoverization among certain groups: the increasing imbalance in the distribution of wealth, with the rich continually becoming richer; the unbridled mobility of capital, both in finance and in production; and the prevalence of low wages coupled with levels of relatively high unemployment among certain groups. These are the root causes of poverty in many societies.

These causes of poverty are exacerbated by national policies that allow corporate leaders to pursue profits without consideration of the social costs incurred by their strategies. Militarization also aggravates the causes of poverty by appropriating resources that could be utilized to expand socially beneficial productivity and using them instead to produce tools for human destruction. The major causes of poverty also contribute to the fiscal incapacity of national and local governments, at times raising the level of political and social tensions and popular dissatisfaction as a result. . . .

In the United States, at least three mechanisms work to mute class tensions that arise from the subsidization of the rich by the working- and middle-class sectors of the population. One ideological mechanism is the belief that diligent individuals can make it economically and achieve the good life if they work hard and put God and country above everything; this is the popular Horatio Alger myth. Second is the supply-side proposition, which maintains that economic development and progress will result from allowing wealthy interests to accumulate more wealth; policies that result in lower taxes and less regulation of income mean, according to this thinking, that the wealthy will have more resources to save and invest, raising the standard of living for everyone by producing a healthier economy.

Race is the third mechanism by which class tensions and popular dissatisfaction with economic policies have been managed by wealthy and powerful interests. Certain racial mechanisms have been manipulated by some interests to divide poor and working-class people who are black from poor and working-class people who are not black. Tools used for this purpose throughout U.S. history include segregation and discrimination; the belief and practices associated with the presumption of white cultural superiority; political and racial scapegoating; and even the public presentation and dialogue of welfare reform in the contemporary period. The media also contribute to this process by aggressively racializing poverty. Journalists and commentators frequently present the faces of poor people as black, Puerto Rican, or of other minority racial heritage, and focus on problems like teen births, family instability, crime and drug use, low educational achievement, and poor health attributes—as if poor whites did not exhibit similar characteristics. The racialization of poverty is strengthened and facilitated by private and public policies that continue to result in residential and educational segregation.

Indeed, there are significant historical and contemporary differences among black, white, Latino, Asian, and Native American poverty in this country. Black poverty tends to be more highly concentrated, and black people tend to be impoverished for longer periods of times than whites or some Latino groups. Black poor people also tend to be poorer than white poor people. Black children and youth, as well as some groups of Latino children, remain the most impoverished in this society. But the root causes of long-lasting and persistent poverty are linked directly to the political and economic factors suggested here. If poor people were politically capable of raising and sustaining alliances on the basis of their poverty, then these issues would be highlighted. In a few episodic cases, such alliances have actually been forged. . . . It is precisely this political possibility, however, that is discouraged and resisted by political and economic leadership in response to the interests of wealth and corporate power.

To a large extent, the current literature and the public dialogue on poverty in the United States ignore the possibility that the poor might forge political alliances. There is generally an absence of a perspective that considers power or the relationship between racial hierarchy and divisions, poverty, and the distribution and management of wealth. The connection between wealth and power, on the one hand, and poverty and homelessness, on the other, has been ignored or overlooked by politicians, the media, and academe. . . .

The work of some poverty researchers is myopic regarding political factors that have led to and that sustain persistent impoverishment for many Americans. But politics . . . is a major factor requiring examination by those seeking to determine the causes of poverty, as well as the means for its resolution, especially among communities of color in the United States. As James Jennings writes, . . . politics is not "explored for its explanatory possibilities; it is merely assumed by some researchers that poverty has more to do with pathology among groups like Puerto Ricans and blacks, or with politically irrelevant structural cataclysmic changes in the economy, than with the lack of political power that characterizes impoverished groups in this nation."[1] . . . The lack of political analysis regarding the problem of poverty on the part of the research community and the media encourages the use of the notion of dependency as a major, yet undefined, variable in explaining the nature of poverty. And yet his unexamined concept . . . is consistently used in devising policy responses to poverty.

The myth of a dependency culture as created by income-transfer programs that benefit poor people became the new orthodoxy in mainstream media and intellectual circles, as reflected in the work of Thomas Sowell, George Gilder, Mickey Kaus, Charles Murray, and others. Yet, the policy initiatives of the current Democratic administration reflect the ideas and suggestions of these very same conservative writers. In fact, there has been little fundamental difference between Republicans and Democrats in how they approach the notions of work and personal responsibility. Both electoral camps ignore the basic causes of poverty and instead propose that this problem reflects the lack of a work ethic or a sense of personal responsibility among poor people. Although the problem of poverty has been presented and discussed in many sectors in terms of dependency or the absence of a work ethic, domestic poverty in the United States is in fact much more complex, reflecting the interplay of political and economic factors, rather than the particular behavior of poor people. . . .

. . . Race has been utilized to detract attention from wealth inequality and from the consequence of poverty and economic dislocation for significant numbers of people. Thus, although poverty is not solely a "black" problem, it is politically effective (and perhaps even methodologically neater) to represent it as such because it serves to divert dialogue from issues related to the accumulation, management, and distribution of wealth. . . . Historically, race and racial divisions have been fomented in order to keep people from realizing the political, or class, nature of persistent poverty in the United States.

The use of race and ethnicity as political dividers of working-class and poor people is also a common tactic in the current period. Some evidence for the usefulness of highlighting race and ethnicity to keep people divided is found in a *CBS News/New York Times Poll* reported on December 6–9, 1994:

> attitudes about the poor and about welfare recipients have a racial element: Americans are more likely to think that people on welfare (and all those who are poor in this country) are more likely to be black than they are to be white. And the characterizations of welfare recipients differ dramatically based on the racial images one has of them. Those who say welfare recipients are mostly white (18% say this) are more likely to think people on welfare want to work, that they are on welfare because of circumstances beyond their control, and that they really need help. On the other hand, people who think most welfare recipients are black (44%) say they're on welfare because of lack of effort, that they don't want to work, and that they could get along without welfare benefits.

. . . Distorted media images have been central to the attack on poor people and the few programs that even slightly benefit them, images of black and

Puerto Rican women with loads of "illegitimate" children and of black and Latino men, lazy and dangerous, as suggested by Edward C. Banfield in *The Unheavenly City*;[2] frequent photos of poor black women with babies bolstering these myths in the *New York Times* and other major news outlets; and similar images that will continue to pervade the literature. . . . This catalog of distorted images was crucial in Ronald Reagan's presidential campaigns, as it was in the Ku Klux Klan spokesperson David Duke's gubernatorial and senatorial campaigns in Louisiana and in the right-wing politician Oval Fordyce's gubernatorial campaign in Mississippi. And such images continue to be useful for both Republicans and Democrats. The portrait of the *underclass*, a pejorative term used by conservatives and liberals alike, has been created as another myth to prove the deleterious consequences of programs that benefit the poor, thereby justifying policies and containment and reminding good, normal, hard-working middle-class citizens that they have nothing in common with "them." . . .

NOTES

1. James Jennings, "Missing Links in the Study of Puerto Rican Poverty in the United States," in *A New Introduction to Poverty: The Role of Race, Power, and Politics*, Louis Kushnick and James Jennings, eds., pp. 89–101 (New York: New York University Press, 1999).

2. Edward C. Banfield, *The Unheavenly City* (Boston: Little, Brown, 1968).

THE SILENCED MAJORITY   16
Why the Average Working Person Has Disappeared from American Media and Culture

Barbara Ehrenreich

It is possible for a middle-class person today to read the papers, watch television, even go to college, without suspecting that America has any inhabitants other than white-collar people—and, of course, the annoyingly persistent

From: *Zeta Magazine* 2 (September 1989): 22. Reprinted by permission.

"black underclass." The average American has disappeared—from the media, from intellectual concern, and from the mind of the American middle class. The producers of public affairs talk shows do not blush to serve up four upper-income professionals (all, incidentally, white, male, and conservative) to ponder the minimum wage or the possible need for national health insurance. Never, needless to say, an uninsured breadwinner or an actual recipient of the minimum wage. Working-class people are likely to cross the screen only as witnesses to crimes or sports events, never as commentators or—even when their own lives are under discussion—as "experts."

A quick definition: By "working class" I mean not only industrial workers in hard hats, but all those people who are not professionals, managers, or entrepreneurs; who work for wages rather than salaries; and who spend their working hours variously lifting, bending, driving, monitoring, typing, keyboarding, cleaning, providing physical care for others, loading, unloading, cooking, serving, etc. The working class so defined makes up 60 to 70 percent of the U.S. population.

By "middle class" I really mean the "professional middle class," or the "professional-managerial class." This group includes the journalists, professors, media executives, etc. who are responsible, in a day-to-day sense, for what we do or do not see or read about in the media. By this definition, the middle class amounts to no more than 20 percent of the U.S. population.

So when I say the working class is disappearing, I do not mean just a particular minority group favored, for theoretical reasons, by leftists. I mean the American majority. And I am laying the blame not only on the corporate sponsors of the media, but on many less wealthy and powerful people. Media people for example. People who are, by virtue of their lifestyles and expectations, not too different from me, and possibly also you.

The disappearance of the working class reflects—and reinforces—the long-standing cultural insularity of the professional middle class. Compared to, say, a decade ago, the classes are less likely to mix in college (due to the decline of financial aid), in residential neighborhoods (due to the rise in real estate prices), or even in the malls (due to the now almost universal segmentation of the retail industry into upscale and downscale components).

In the absence of real contact or communication, stereotypes march on unchallenged; prejudices easily substitute for knowledge. The most intractable stereotype is of the working class (which is, in imagination, only white) as a collection of reactionaries and bigots—reflected, for example, in the use of the terms "hard hat" or "redneck" as class slurs. Even people who call themselves progressives are not immune to this prejudice.

The truth is that, statistically and collectively, the working class is far more reliably liberal than the professional middle class. It was more, not less, opposed to the war in Vietnam. It is more, not less, disposed to vote for a Democrat for president. And thanks to the careful, quantitative studies of Canadian historian Richard F. Hamilton, we know that the white working class (at least outside the South) is no more racist, and by some measures less so, than the white professional class.

Even deeper-rooted than the stereotype of the hard-hat bigot is the middle-class suspicion that the working class is dumb, inarticulate, and mindlessly loyal to old-fashioned values. In the entertainment media, for example, the working class is usually portrayed by macho exhibitionism (from *Saturday Night Fever* to *Working Girl*) or mental inferiority (*Married, with Children*). Mainstream sociologists have reinforced this prejudice with their emphasis on working-class "parochialism," as illustrated by this quote from a 1976 beginning sociology textbook: "The limited education, reading habits and associations isolate the lower class. . . . and this ignorance, together with their class position, makes them suspicious of [the] middle- and upper-class 'experts' and 'do-gooders'. . . ."

Finally, there is a level of prejudice that grows out of middle-class moralism about matters of taste and lifestyle. All privileged classes seek to differentiate themselves from the less-privileged through the ways they dress, eat, entertain themselves, and so on, and tend to see their own choices in these matters as inherently wiser, better, and more aesthetically inspired. In the middle-class stereotype, the white working class, for example, is addicted to cigarettes, Budweiser, polyester, and network television. (In part this is true, and it is true in part because Bud is cheaper than Dos Equis and polyester is cheaper than linen.) Furthermore in the middle-class view, polyester and the like is "tacky"—a common code word for "lower class." Health concerns, plus a certain reverence for the "natural" in food and fiber, infuse these middle-class prejudices with a high-minded tone of moral indignation.

But I am alarmed by what seems to me to be the growing parochialism of the professional middle class—living in its own social and residential enclaves, condemned to hear only the opinions of its own members (or, of course, the truly rich), and cut off from the lives and struggles and insights of the American majority. This middle-class parochialism is insidiously self-reinforcing: The less "we" know about "them," the more likely "we" are to cling to our stereotypes—or forget "them" altogether.

THE PLIGHT OF BLACK MEN   17

Michael Dyson

On a recent trip to Knoxville, I visited Harold's barber shop, where I had gotten my hair cut during college, and after whenever I had the chance. I had developed a friendship with Ike, a local barber who took great pride in this work. I popped my head inside the front door, and after exchanging friendly greetings with Harold, the owner, and noticing Ike missing, I inquired about his return. It had been nearly two years since Ike had cut my hair, and I was hoping to receive the careful expertise that comes from familiarity and repetition.

"Man, I'm sorry to tell you, but Ike got killed almost two years ago," Harold informed me. "He and his brother, who was drunk, got into a fight, and he stabbed Ike to death."

I was shocked, depressed, and grieved, these emotions competing in rapid-fire fashion for the meager psychic resources I was able to muster. In a daze of retreat from the fierce onslaught of unavoidable absurdity, I half-consciously slumped into Harold's chair, seeking solace through his story of Ike's untimely and brutal leave-taking. Feeling my pain, Harold filled in the details of Ike's last hours, realizing that for me Ike's death had happened only yesterday. Harold proceeded to cut my hair with a methodical precision that was itself a temporary and all-too-thin refuge from the chaos of arbitrary death, a protest against the nonlinear progression of miseries that claim the lives of too many black men. After he finished, I thanked Harold, both of us recognizing that we would not soon forget Ike's life, or his terrible death.

This drama of tragic demise, compressed agony, nearly impotent commiseration, and social absurdity is repeated countless times, too many times, in American culture for black men. Ike's death forced to the surface a painful awareness that provides the chilling sound track to most black men's lives: it is still hazardous to be a human being of African descent in America.

Not surprisingly, much of the ideological legitimation for the contemporary misery of African-Americans in general, and black men in particular, derives from the historical legacy of slavery, which continues to assert its brutal presence in the untold suffering of millions of everyday black folk. For instance, the pernicious commodification of the black body during slavery was underwritten by the desire of white slave owners to completely master black life. The desire for mastery also fueled the severe regulation of black sexual

From: Michael Dyson, *Reflecting Black: African-American Cultural Criticism* (Minneapolis: University of Minnesota Press, 1993), pp. 182–94. Reprinted by permission of the author.

activity, furthering the telos of southern agrarian capital by reducing black men to studs and black women to machines of production. Black men and women became sexual and economic property. Because of the arrangement of social relations, slavery was also the breeding ground for much of the mythos of black male sexuality that survives to this day: that black men are imagined as peripatetic phalluses with unrequited desire for their denied object—white women.

Also crucial during slavery was the legitimation of violence toward blacks, especially black men. Rebellion in any form was severely punished, and the social construction of black male image and identity took place under the disciplining eye of white male dominance. Thus healthy black self-regard and self-confidence were outlawed as punitive consequences were attached to their assertion in black life. Although alternative forms of resistance were generated, particularly those rooted in religious praxis, problems of self-hatred and self-abnegation persisted. The success of the American political, economic, and social infrastructure was predicated in large part upon a squelching of black life by white modes of cultural domination. The psychic, political, economic, and social costs of slavery, then, continue to be paid, but mostly by the descendants of the oppressed. The way in which young black men continue to pay is particularly unsettling.

Black men are presently caught in a web of social relations, economic conditions, and political predicaments that portray their future in rather bleak terms.[1] For instance, the structural unemployment of black men has reached virtually epidemic proportions, with black youth unemployment double that of white youth.* Almost one-half of young black men have had no work experience at all. Given the permanent shift in the U.S. economy from manufacturing and industrial jobs to high-tech and service employment and the flight of these jobs from the cities to the suburbs, the prospects for eroding the stubborn unemployment of black men appear slim.[2]

The educational front is not much better. Young black males are dropping out of school at alarming rates, due to a combination of severe economic difficulties, disciplinary entanglements, and academic frustrations. Thus the low level of educational achievement by young black men exacerbates their already precarious employment situation. Needless to say, the pool of high-school graduates eligible for college has severely shrunk, and even those who go on to college have disproportionate rates of attrition. . . .

Even with all this, a contemporary focus on the predicament of black males is rendered problematical and ironic for two reasons. First, what may be termed the "Calvin Klein" character of debate about social problems—which

---

*Editors' note: *Structural unemployment* is a technical term used by economists; here, Dyson is using the term only to refer to unemployment that is the result of societal conditions.

amounts to a "designer" social consciousness—makes it very difficult for the concerns of black men to be taken seriously. Social concern, like other commodities, is subject to cycles of production, distribution, and consumption. With the dwindling of crucial governmental resources to address a range of social problems, social concern is increasingly relegated to the domain of private philanthropic and nonprofit organizations. Furthermore, the selection of which problems merit scarce resources is determined, in part, by such philanthropic organizations, which highlight special issues, secure the services of prominent spokespersons, procure capital for research, and distribute the benefits of their information.

Unfortunately, Americans have rarely been able to sustain debate about pressing social problems over long periods of time. Even less have we been able to conceive underlying structural features that bind complex social issues together. Such conceptualization of the intricate relationship of social problems would facilitate the development of broadly formed coalitions that address a range of social concerns. As things stand, problems like poverty, racism, and sexism go in and out of style. Black men, with the exception of star athletes and famous entertainers, are out of style.

Second, the irony of the black male predicament is that it has reached its nadir precisely at the point when much deserved attention has been devoted to the achievements of black women like Alice Walker, Toni Morrison, and Terry McMillan.

The identification and development of the womanist tradition in African-American culture has permitted the articulation of powerful visions of black female identity and liberation. Michele Wallace, bell hooks, Alice Walker, Audre Lorde, and Toni Morrison have written in empowering ways about the disenabling forms of racism and patriarchy that persist in white and black communities. They have expressed the rich resources for identity that come from maintaining allegiances to multiple kinship groups defined by race, gender, and sexual orientation, while also addressing the challenges that arise in such membership.

Thus discussions about black men should not take place in an ahistorical vacuum, but should be informed by sensitivity to the plight of black women. To isolate and examine the pernicious problems of young black men does not privilege their perspectives or predicament. Rather, it is to acknowledge the decisively deleterious consequences of racism and classism that plague black folk, particularly young black males.

The aim of my analysis is to present enabling forms of consciousness that may contribute to the reconstitution of the social, economic, and political relations that continually consign the lives of black men to psychic malaise, social destruction, and physical death. It does not encourage or dismiss the sexism of black men, nor does it condone the patriarchal behavior that sometimes manifests itself in minority communities in the form of misdirected machismo.

Above all, African-Americans must avoid a potentially hazardous situation that plays musical chairs with scarce resources allocated to black folk and threatens to inadvertently exacerbate already deteriorated relations between black men and women. The crisis of black inner-city communities is so intense that it demands our collective resources to stem the tide of violence and catastrophe that has besieged them.

I grew up as a young black male in Detroit in the 1960s and 1970s. I witnessed firsthand the social horror that is entrenched in inner-city communities, the social havoc wreaked from economic hardship. In my youth, Detroit had been tagged the "murder capital of the world," and many of those murders were of black men, many times by other black men. Night after night, the news media in Detroit painted the ugly picture of a homicide-ridden city caught in the desperate clutches of death, depression, and decay. I remember having recurring nightmares of naked violence, in which Hitchcockian vertigo emerged in Daliesque perspective to produce gun-wielding perpetrators of doom seeking to do me in.

And apart from those disturbing dreams, I was exercised by the small vignettes of abortive violence that shattered my circle of friends and acquaintances. My next-door neighbor, a young black man, was stabbed in the jugular vein by an acquaintance and bled to death in the midst of a card game. (Of course, one of the ugly statistics involving black-on-black crime is that many black men are killed by those whom they know.) Another acquaintance murdered a businessman in a robbery; another executed several people in a gangland-style murder.

At fourteen, I was at our corner store at the sales counter, when suddenly a jolt in the back revealed a young black man wielding a sawed-off, double-barreled shotgun, requesting, along with armed accomplices stationed throughout the store, that we hit the floor. We were being robbed. At the age of eighteen I was stopped one Saturday night at 10:30 by a young black man who ominously materialized out of nowhere, much like the .357 Magnum revolver that he revealed to me in a robbery attempt. Terror engulfed my entire being in the fear of imminent death. In desperation I hurled a protest against the asphyxiating economic hardships that had apparently reduced him to desperation, too, and appealed to the conscience I hoped was buried beneath the necessity that drove him to rob me. I proclaimed, "Man, you don't look like the type of brother that would be doin' something like this."

"I wouldn't be doin' this, man," he shot back, "but I got a wife and three kids, and we ain't got nothin' to eat. And besides, last week somebody did the same thing to me that I'm doin' to you." After convincing him that I really only had one dollar and thirty-five cents, the young man permitted me to leave with my life intact.

The terrain for these and so many other encounters that have shaped the lives of black males was the ghetto. Much social research and criticism has been generated in regard to the worse-off inhabitants of the inner city, the so-called underclass. From the progressive perspective of William Julius Wilson to the archconservative musings of Charles Murray, those who dwell in ghettos, or enclaves of civic, psychic, and social terror, have been the object of recrudescent interest within hallowed academic circles and governmental policy rooms.[3] In most cases they have not fared well and have borne the brunt of multifarious "blame the victim" social logics and policies.

One of the more devastating developments in inner-city communities is the presence of drugs and the criminal activity associated with their production, marketing, and consumption. Through the escalation of the use of the rocklike form of cocaine known as "crack" and intensified related gang activity, young black men are involved in a vicious subculture of crime. This subculture is sustained by two potent attractions: the personal acceptance and affirmation gangs offer and the possibility of enormous economic reward.

U.S. gang life had its genesis in the Northeast of the 1840s, particularly in the depressed neighborhoods of Boston and New York, where young Irishmen developed gangs to sustain social solidarity and to forge a collective identity based on common ethnic roots.[4] Since then, youth of every ethnic and racial origin have formed gangs for similar reasons, and at times have even functioned to protect their own ethnic or racial group from attack by harmful outsiders. Overall, a persistent reason for joining gangs is the sense of absolute belonging and unsurpassed social love that results from gang membership. Especially for young black men whose lives hold a low premium in America, gangs have fulfilled a primal need to possess a sense of social cohesion through group identity. Particularly when traditional avenues for the realization of personal growth, esteem, and self-worth, usually gained through employment and career opportunities, have been closed, young black men find gangs a powerful alternative.

Gangs also offer immediate material gratification through a powerful and lucrative underground economy. This underground economy is supported by exchanging drugs and services for money, or by barter. The lifestyle developed and made possible by the sale of crack presents often irresistible economic alternatives to young black men frustrated by their own unemployment. The death that can result from involvement in such drug- and gang-related activity is ineffective in prohibiting young black men from participating.

To understand the attraction such activity holds for black men, one must remember the desperate economic conditions of urban black life. The problems of poverty and joblessness have loomed large for African-American men, particularly in the Rust Belt, including New York, Chicago, Philadelphia, Detroit, Cleveland, Indianapolis, and Baltimore. From the 1950s to the 1980s, there was severe decline in manufacturing and in retail and wholesale trade, attended by escalating unemployment and a decrease in labor-force participation by black males, particularly during the 1970s.

During this three-decade decline of employment, however, there was not an expansion of social services or significant increase in entry-level service jobs. As William Julius Wilson rightly argues, the urban ghettos then became more socially isolated than at any other time. Also, with the mass exodus of black working- and middle-class families from the ghetto, the inner city's severe unemployment and joblessness became even more magnified. With black track from the inner city mimicking earlier patterns of white flight, severe class changes have negatively affected black ghettos. Such class changes have depleted communities of service establishments, local businesses, and stores that could remain profitable enough to provide full-time employment so that persons could support families, or even to offer youths part-time employment in order to develop crucial habits of responsibility and work. Furthermore, ghetto residents are removed from job networks that operate in more affluent neighborhoods. Thus, they are deprived of the informal contact with employers that results in finding decent jobs. All of these factors create a medium for the development of criminal behavior by black men in order to survive, ranging from fencing stolen goods to petty thievery to drug dealing. For many black families, the illegal activity of young black men provides their only income.

Predictably, then, it is in these Rust Belt cities, and other large urban and metropolitan areas, where drug and gang activity has escalated in the past decade. Detroit, Philadelphia, and New York have had significant gang and drug activity, but Chicago and Los Angeles have dominated of late. . . .

Of course, L.A.'s gang scene has generated mythic interpretation in the Dennis Hopper film *Colors*. In the past decade, gang membership in L.A. has risen from 15,000 to almost 60,000 (with some city officials claiming as much as 80,000), as gang warfare claims one life per day. The ethnic composition of the groups include Mexicans, Armenians, Samoans, and Fijians. But gang life is dominated by South Central L.A. black gangs, populated by young black men willing to give their lives in fearless fidelity to their group's survival. The two largest aggregates of gangs, composed of several hundred microgangs, are the Bloods and the Crips, distinguished by the colors of their shoelaces, T-shirts, and bandannas.

The black gangs have become particularly dangerous because of their association with crack. The gangs control more than 150 crack houses in L.A., each of which does over five thousand dollars of business per day, garnering over half a billion dollars per year. Crack houses, which transform powdered cocaine into crystalline rock form in order to be smoked, offer powerful material rewards to gang members. Even young teens can earn almost a thousand dollars a week, often outdistancing what their parents, if they work at all, can earn in two months.

So far, most analyses of drug gangs and the black youth who comprise their membership have repeated old saws about the pathology of black culture and weak family structure, without accounting for the pressing economic realities and the need for acceptance that help explain such activity. As long as the poverty of young black men is ignored, the disproportionate number of black unemployed males is overlooked, and the structural features of racism and classism are avoided, there is room for the proliferation of social explanations that blame the victim. Such social explanations reinforce the misguided efforts of public officials to stem the tide of illegal behavior by state repression aimed at young blacks, such as the sweeps of L.A. neighborhoods resulting in mass arrests of more than four thousand black men, more than at any time since the Watts rebellion of 1965.

Helpful remedies must promote the restoration of job training (such as Neighborhood Youth Corps [NYC] and the Comprehensive Employment and Training Act [CETA]); the development of policies that support the family, such as child-care and education programs; a full employment policy; and dropout prevention in public schools. These are only the first steps toward the deeper structural transformation necessary to improve the plight of African-American men, but they would be vast improvements over present efforts.

Not to be forgotten, either, are forms of cultural resistance that are developed and sustained within black life and are alternatives to the crack gangs. An example that springs immediately to mind is rap music. Rap music provides space for cultural resistance to the criminal-ridden ethos that pervades segments of many underclass communities. Rap was initially a form of musical play that directed the creative urges of its producers into placing often humorous lyrics over the music of well-known black hits.

As it evolved, however, rap became a more critical and conscientious forum for visiting social criticism upon various forms of social injustice, especially racial and class oppression. For instance, Grandmaster Flash and the Furious Five pioneered the social awakening of rap with two rap records, "The Message" and "New York, New York." These rap records combined poignant descriptions of social misery and trenchant criticism of social problems as they remarked upon the condition of black urban America. They compared the postmodern city of crime, deception, political corruption, economic hardship, and cultural malaise to a "jungle." These young savants portrayed a chilling vision of life that placed them beyond the parameters of traditional African-American cultural resources of support: religious faith, communal strength, and familial roots. Thus, they were creating their own aesthetic of survival, generated from the raw material of their immediate reality, the black ghetto. This began the vocation of the rap artist, in part, as urban grist dispensing social and cultural critique.

Although rap music has been saddled with a reputation for creating violent outbursts by young blacks, especially at rap concerts, most of rap's participants have repeatedly spurned violence and all forms of criminal behavior as useless alternatives for black youth. Indeed rap has provided an alternative to patterns of identity formation provided by gang activity and has created musical vehicles for personal and cultural agency. A strong sense of self-confidence permeates the entire rap genre, providing healthy outlets for young blacks to assert, boast, and luxuriate in a rich self-conception based upon the achievement that their talents afford them. For those reasons alone, it deserves support. Even more, rap music, although its increasing expansion means being influenced by the music industry's corporate tastes and decisions, presents an economic alternative to the underground economy of crack gangs and the illegal activity associated with them.

However, part of the enormous difficulty in discouraging illegal activity among young black men has to do, ironically, with their often correct perception of the racism and classism still rampant in employment and educational opportunities open to upwardly mobile blacks. The subtle but lethal limits continually imposed upon young black professionals, for instance, as a result of the persistence of racist ideologies operating in multifarious institutional patterns and personal configurations, send powerful signals to young black occupants of the underclass that education and skill do not ward off racist, classist forms of oppression.

This point was reiterated to me upon my son's recent visit with me at Princeton near Christmas. Excited about the prospect of spending time together catching up on new movies, playing video games, reading, and the like, we dropped by my bank to get a cash advance on my MasterCard. I presented my card to the young service representative, expecting no trouble since I had just paid my bill a couple of weeks before. When he returned, he informed me that not only could I not get any money, but that he would have to keep my card. When I asked for an explanation, all he could say was that he was following the instructions of my card's bank, since my MasterCard was issued by a different bank.

After we went back and forth a few times about the matter, I asked to see the manager. "He'll just tell you the same thing that I've been telling you," he insisted. But my persistent demand prevailed, as he huffed away to the manager's office, resentfully carrying my request to his boss. My son, sitting next to me the whole time, asked what the problem was, and I told him that there must be a mistake, and that it would all be cleared up shortly. He gave me that confident look that says, "My dad can handle it." After waiting for about seven or eight minutes, I caught the manager's figure peripherally, and just as I turned, I saw him heading with the representative to an empty desk, opening the drawer and pulling out a pair of scissors. I could feel the blood begin to boil in my veins as I beseeched the manager, "Sir, if you're about to do what I fear you will, can we please talk first?" Of course, my request was to no avail, as he sliced my card in two before what had now become a considerable crowd. I immediately jumped up and followed him into his office, my son trailing close behind, crying now, tearfully pumping me with "Daddy, what's going on?"

I rushed into the manager's office and asked for the privacy of a closed door, to which he responded, "Don't let him close the door," as he beckoned three other employees into his office. I angrily grabbed the remnants of my card from his hands and proceeded to tell him that I was a reputable member of the community and a good customer of the bank and that if I had been wearing a three-piece suit (instead of the black running suit I was garbed in) and if I had been a white male (and not a black man) I would have been at least accorded the respect of a conversation, prior to a private negotiation of an embarrassing situation, which furthermore was the apparent result of a mistake on the bank's part.

His face flustered, the manager then prominently positioned his index finger beneath his desk drawer, and pushed a button, while declaring, "I'm calling the police on you." My anger now piqued, I was tempted to vent my rage on his defiant countenance, arrested only by the vision terrible that flashed before my eyes as a chilling premonition of destruction: I would assault the manager's neck; his co-workers would join the fracas, as my son stood by horrified by his helplessness to aid me; the police would come, and abuse me even further, possibly harming my son in the process. I retreated under the power of this proleptic vision, grabbing my son's hand as I marched out of the bank. Just as we walked through the doors, the policemen were pulling up.

Although after extensive protests, phone calls, and the like, I eventually received an apology from the bank's board and a MasterCard from their branch, this incident seared an indelible impression onto my mind, reminding me that regardless of how much education, moral authority, or personal integrity a black man possesses, he is still a "nigger," still powerless in many ways to affect his destiny.

The tragedy in all of this, of course, is that even when articulate, intelligent black men manage to rise above the temptations and traps of "the ghetto," they are often subject to continuing forms of social fear, sexual jealousy, and obnoxious racism. More pointedly, in the 1960s, during a crucial stage in the development of black pride and self-esteem, highly educated, deeply conscientious black men were gunned down in cold blood. This phenomenon finds paradigmatic expression in the deaths of Medgar Evers, Malcolm X, and Martin Luther King, Jr. These events of public death are structured deep in the psyches of surviving black men, and the ways in which these horrible spectacles of racial catastrophe represent and implicitly sanction lesser forms of social evil against black men remains hurtful to black America.

I will never forget the effect of King's death on me as a nine-year-old boy in Detroit. For weeks I could not be alone at night before an open door or window without fearing that someone would kill me, too. I thought that if they killed this man who taught justice, peace, forgiveness, and love, then they would kill all black men. For me, Martin's death meant that no black man in America was safe, that no black man could afford the gift of vision, that no black man could possess an intelligent fire that would sear the fierce edges of ignorance and wither to ashes the propositions of hate without being extinguished. Ultimately Martin's death meant that all black men, in some way, are perennially exposed to the threat of annihilation.

As we move toward the last decade of this century, the shadow of Du Bois's prophetic declaration that the twentieth century's problem would be the color line continues to extend itself in foreboding manner. The plight of black men, indeed, is a microcosmic reflection of the problems that are at the throat of all black people, an idiomatic expression of hurt drawn from the larger discourse of racial pain. Unless, however, there is vast reconstitution of our social, economic, and political policies and practices, most of which target black men with vicious specificity, Du Bois's words will serve as the frontispiece to the racial agony of the twenty-first century, as well.

NOTES

1. For a look at the contemporary plight of black men, especially black juvenile males, see *Young, Black, and Male in America: An Endangered Species*, ed. Jewelle Taylor Gibbs (Dover, Mass.: Auburn House, 1988).

2. See William Julius Wilson, *The Truly Disadvantaged: The Inner City, the Underclass, and Public Policy* (Chicago: University of Chicago Press, 1987).

3. See Wilson, *The Truly Disadvantaged*. For Charles Murray's views on poverty, welfare, and the ghetto underclass, see his influential book, *Losing Ground: American Social Policy, 1950–1980* (New York: Basic Books, 1984).

4. This section on gangs is informed by the work of Mike Davis in his *City of Quartz* (New York: Verso Press, 1991).

MOVING UP WITH KIN AND COMMUNITY

18

Upward Social Mobility for Black and White Women

Elizabeth Higginbotham and Lynn Weber

. . . When women and people of color experience upward mobility in America, they scale steep structural as well as psychological barriers. The long process of moving from a working-class family of origin to the professional-managerial class is full of twists and turns: choices made with varying degrees of information and varying options; critical junctures faced with support and encouragement or disinterest, rejection, or active discouragement; and interpersonal relationships in which basic understandings are continuously negotiated and renegotiated. It is a fascinating process that profoundly shapes the lives of those who experience it, as well as the lives of those around them. Social mobility is also a process engulfed in myth. One need only pick up any newspaper or turn on the television to see that the myth of upward mobility remains firmly entrenched in American culture: With hard work, talent, determination, and some luck, just about anyone can "make it." . . .

The image of the isolated and detached experience of mobility that we have inherited from past scholarship is problematic for anyone seeking to understand the process for women or people of color. Twenty years of scholarship in the study of both race and gender has taught us the importance of interpersonal attachments to the lives of women . . . and a commitment to racial uplift among people of color. . . .

. . . Lacking wealth, the greatest gift a Black family has been able to give to its children has been the motivation and skills to succeed in school. Aspirations for college attendance and professional positions are stressed as *family* goals, and the entire family may make sacrifices and provide support. . . . Black women have long seen the activist potential of education and have sought it as a cornerstone of community development—a means of uplifting the race. When women of color or white women are put at the center of the analysis of upward mobility, it is clear that different questions will be raised about social mobility and different descriptions of the process will ensue. . . .

Authors' note: The research reported here was supported by National Institute for Mental Health Grant MH38769. All the names used in this article are pseudonyms.

RESEARCH DESIGN

These data are from a study of full-time employed middle-class women in the Memphis metropolitan area. This research is designed to explore the processes of upward social mobility for Black and white women by examining differences between women professionals, managers, and administrators who are from working- and middle-class backgrounds—that is, upwardly mobile and middle-class stable women. In this way, we isolate subjective processes shared among women who have been upwardly mobile from those common to women who have reproduced their family's professional-managerial class standing. Likewise, we identify many experiences in the attainment process that are shared by women of the same race, be they upwardly mobile or stable middle class. Finally, we specify some ways in which the attainment process is unique for each race-class group. . . .

. . . We rely on a model of social class basically derived from the work of Poulantzas (1974), Braverman (1974), Ehrenreich and Ehrenreich (1979), and elaborated in Vanneman and Cannon (1987). These works explicate a basic distinction between social class and social status. Classes represent bounded categories of the population, groups set in a relation of opposition to one another by their roles in the capitalist system. The middle class, or professional-managerial class, is set off from the working class by the power and control it exerts over workers in three realms: economic (power through ownership), political (power through direct supervisory authority), and ideological (power to plan and organize work; Poulantzas 1974; Vanneman and Cannon 1987).

In contrast, education, prestige, and income represent social statuses—hierarchically structured relative rankings along a ladder of economic success and social prestige. Positions along these dimensions are not established by social relations of dominance and subordination but, rather, as rankings on scales representing resources and desirability. In some respects, they represent both the justification for power differentials vested in classes and the rewards for the role that the middle class plays in controlling labor.

Our interest is in the process of upward social class mobility, moving from a working-class family of origin to a middle-class destination—from a position of working-class subordination to a position of control over the working class. Lacking inherited wealth or other resources, those working-class people who attain middle-class standing do so primarily by obtaining a college education and entering a professional, managerial, or administrative occupation. Thus we examine carefully the process of educational attainment not as evidence of middle-class standing but as a necessary part of the mobility process for most working-class people.

Likewise, occupation alone does not define the middle class, but professional, managerial, and administrative occupations capture many of the supervisory and ideologically based positions whose function is to control workers' lives. Consequently, we defined subjects as *middle class* by virtue of their employment in either a professional, managerial, or administrative occupa-tion. . . . Classification of subjects as either professional or managerial-administrative was made on the basis of the designation of occupations in the U.S. Bureau of the Census's (1983) "Detailed Population Characteristics: Tennessee." Managerial occupations were defined as those in the census cate-gories of managers and administrators; professionals were defined as those oc-cupations in the professional category, excluding technicians, whom Braver-man (1974) contends are working class.

Upwardly mobile women were defined as those women raised in families where neither parent was employed as a professional, manager, or adminis-trator. Typical occupations for working-class fathers were postal clerk, crafts-man, semi-skilled manufacturing worker, janitor, and laborer. Some working-class mothers had clerical and sales positions, but many of the Black mothers also worked as private household workers. *Middle-class stable* women were defined as those women raised in families where *either* parent was employed as a professional, manager, or administrator. Typical occupations of middle-class parents were social worker, teacher, and school administrator as well as high-status professionals such as attorneys, physicians, and dentists. . . .

FAMILY EXPECTATIONS
FOR EDUCATIONAL ATTAINMENT

Four questions assess the expectations and support among family members for the educational attainment of the subjects. First, "Do you recall your father or mother stressing that you attain an education?" Yes was the response of 190 of the 200 women. Each of the women in this study had obtained a college de-gree, and many have graduate degrees. It is clear that for Black and white women, education was an important concern in their families. . . .

The comments of Laura Lee, a 39-year-old Black woman who was raised middle class, were typical:

> Going to school, that was never a discussable issue. Just like you were born to live and die, you were going to go to school. You were going to prepare your-self to do something.

It should be noted, however, that only 86 percent of the white working-class women answered yes, compared to 98 percent of all other groups. Al-though this difference is small, it foreshadows a pattern where white women raised in working-class families received the least support and encouragement for educational and career attainment.

"When you were growing up, how far did your father expect you to go in school?" While most fathers expected college attendance from their daughters, differences also exist by class of origin. Only 70 percent of the working-class fathers, both Black and white, expected their daughters to attend college. In contrast, 94 percent of the Black middle-class and 88 percent of the white middle-class women's fathers had college expectations for their daughters.

When asked the same question about mother's expectations, 88 percent to 92 percent of each group's mothers expected their daughters to get a college education, except the white working-class women, for whom only 66 percent of mothers held such expectations. In short, only among the white working-class women did a fairly substantial proportion (about one-third) of both mothers and fathers expect less than a college education from their daughters. About 30 percent of Black working-class fathers held lower expectations for their daughters, but not the mothers; virtually all middle-class parents expected a college education for their daughters.

Sara Marx is a white, 33-year-old director of counseling raised in a rural working-class family. She is among those whose parents did not expect a college education for her. She was vague about the roots of attending college:

> It seems like we had a guest speaker who talked to us. Maybe before our exams somebody talked to us. I really can't put my finger on anything. I don't know where the information came from exactly.

"Who provided emotional support for you to make the transition from high school to college?" While 86 percent of the Black middle-class women indicated that family provided that support, 70 percent of the white middle class, 64 percent of the Black working class, and only 56 percent of the white working class received emotional support from family.

"Who paid your college tuition and fees?" Beyond emotional support, financial support is critical to college attendance. There are clear class differences in financial support for college. Roughly 90 percent of the middle-class respondents and only 56 percent and 62 percent of the Black and white working-class women, respectively, were financially supported by their families. These data also suggest that working-class parents were less able to give emotional or financial support for college than they were to hold out the expectation that their daughters should attend.

FAMILY EXPECTATIONS
FOR OCCUPATION OR CAREER

When asked, "Do you recall your father or mother stressing that you should have an occupation to succeed in life?", racial differences appear. Ninety-four percent of all Black respondents said yes. In the words of Julie Bird, a Black woman raised-middle-class junior high school teacher:

> My father would always say, "You see how good I'm doing? Each generation should do more than the generation before." He expects me to accomplish more than he has.

Ann Right, a 36-year-old Black attorney whose father was a janitor, said:

> They wanted me to have a better life than they had. For all of us. And that's why they emphasized education and emphasized working relationships and how you get along with people and that kind of thing.

Ruby James, a Black teacher from a working-class family, said:

> They expected me to have a good-paying job and to have a family and be married. Go to work every day. Buy a home. That's about it. Be happy.

In contrast, only 70 percent of the white middle-class and 56 percent of the white working-class women indicated that their parents stressed that an occupation was needed for success. Nina Pentel, a 26-year-old white medical social worker, expressed a common response: "They said 'You're going to get married but get a degree, you never know what's going to happen to you.' They were pretty laid back about goals."

When the question focuses on a career rather than an occupation, the family encouragement is lower and differences were not significant, but similar patterns emerged. We asked respondents, "Who, if anyone, encouraged you to think about a career?" Among Black respondents, 60 percent of the middle-class and 56 percent of the working-class women answered that family encouraged them. Only 40 percent of the white working-class women indicated that their family encouraged them in their thinking about a career, while 52 percent of the white middle-class women did so. . . .

When working-class white women seek to be mobile through their own attainments, they face conflicts. Their parents encourage educational attainment, but when young women develop professional career goals, these same parents sometimes become ambivalent. This was the case with Elizabeth Marlow, who is currently a public interest attorney—a position her parents never intended her to hold. She described her parents' traditional expectations and their reluctance to support her career goals fully.

> My parents assumed that I would go to college and meet some nice man and finish, but not necessarily work after. I would be a good mother for my children. I don't think that they ever thought I would go to law school. Their attitude about my interest in law school was, "You can do it if you want to, but we don't think it is a particularly practical thing for a woman to do."

Elizabeth is married and has three children, but she is not the traditional housewife of her parents' dreams. She received more support outside the family for her chosen life-style.

Although Black families are indeed more likely than white families to encourage their daughters to prepare for careers, like white families, they frequently steer them toward highly visible traditionally female occupations, such as teacher, nurse, and social worker. Thus many mobile Black women are directed toward the same gender-segregated occupations as white women. . . .

MARRIAGE

Although working-class families may encourage daughters to marry, they recognize the need for working-class women to contribute to family income or to support themselves economically. To achieve these aims, many working-class girls are encouraged to pursue an education as preparation for work in gender-segregated occupations. Work in these fields presumably allows women to keep marriage, family, and child rearing as life goals while contributing to the family income and to have "something to fall back on" if the marriage does not work out. This interplay among marriage, education, financial need, and class mobility is complex (Joslin 1979).

We asked, "Do you recall your mother or father emphasizing that marriage should be your primary life goal?" While the majority of all respondents did not get the message that marriage was the *primary life goal,* Black and white women's parents clearly saw this differently. Virtually no Black parents stressed marriage as the primary life goal (6 percent of the working class and 4 percent of the middle class), but significantly more white parents did (22 percent of the working class and 18 percent of the middle class).

Some white women said their families expressed active opposition to marriage, such as Clare Baron, a raised-working-class nursing supervisor, who said, "My mother always said, 'Don't get married and don't have children!'"

More common responses recognized the fragility of marriage and the need to support oneself. For example, Alice Page, a 31-year-old white raised-middle-class librarian, put it this way:

> I feel like I am really part of a generation that for the first time is thinking, "I don't want to have to depend on somebody to take care of me because what if they say they are going to take care of me and then they are not there? They die, or they leave me or whatever." I feel very much that I've got to be able to support myself and I don't know that single women in other eras have had to deal with that to the same degree.

While white working-class women are often raised to prepare for work roles so that they can contribute to family income and, if necessary, support themselves, Black women face a different reality. Unlike white women, Black women are typically socialized to view marriage separately from economic security, because it is not expected that marriage will ever remove them from the labor market. As a result, Black families socialize all their children—girls and boys—for self-sufficiency (Clark 1986; Higginbotham and Cannon 1988). . . .

. . . Fairly substantial numbers of each group had never married by the time of the interview, ranging from 20 percent of the white working-class to 34 percent of the Black working-class and white middle-class respondents. Some of the women were pleased with their singlehood, like Alice Page, who said:

> I am single by choice. That is how I see myself. I have purposely avoided getting into any kind of romantic situation with men. I have enjoyed going out but never wanted to get serious. If anyone wants to get serious, I quit going out with him.

Other women expressed disappointment and some shock that they were not yet married. When asked about her feeling about being single, Sally Ford, a 32-year-old white manager, said:

> That's what I always wanted to do: to be married and have children. To me, that is the ideal. I want a happy, good marriage with children. I do not like being single at all. It is very, very lonesome. I don't see any advantages to being single. None! . . .

SUBJECTIVE SENSE OF DEBT TO KIN AND FRIENDS

McAdoo (1978) reports that upwardly mobile Black Americans receive more requests to share resources from their working-class kin than do middle-class Black Americans. Many mobile Black Americans feel a "social debt" because their families aided them in the mobility process and provided emotional support. When we asked the white women in the study the following question: "Generally, do you feel you owe a lot for the help given to you by your family and relatives?" many were perplexed and asked what the question meant. In contrast, both the working- and middle-class Black women tended to respond immediately that they felt a sense of obligation to family and friends in return for the support they had received. Black women, from both the working class and the middle class, expressed the strongest sense of debt to family, with 86 percent and 74 percent, respectively, so indicating. White working-class women were least likely to feel that they owed family (46 percent), while 68 percent of white middle-class women so indicated. In short, upwardly mobile Black women were almost twice as likely as upwardly mobile white women to express a sense of debt to family.

Linda Brown, an upwardly mobile Black woman, gave a typical response, "Yes, they are there when you need them." Similar were the words of Jean

Marsh, "Yes, because they have been supportive. They're dependable. If I need them I can depend upon them."

One of the most significant ways in which Black working-class families aided their daughters and left them with a sense of debt related to care for their children. Dawn March expressed it thus:

> They have been there more so during my adult years than a lot of other families that I know about. My mother kept all of my children until they were old enough to go to day care. And she not only kept them, she'd give them a bath for me during the daytime and feed them before I got home from work. Very, very supportive people. So, I really would say I owe them for that.

Carole Washington, an upwardly mobile Black woman occupational therapist, also felt she owed her family. She reported:

> I know the struggle that my parents have had to get me where I am. I know the energy they no longer have to put into the rest of the family even though they want to put it there and they're willing. I feel it is my responsibility to give back some of that energy they have given to me. It's self-directed, not required.

White working-class women, in contrast, were unlikely to feel a sense of debt and expressed their feelings in similar ways. Irma Cox, part owner of a computer business, said, "I am appreciative of the values my parents instilled in me. But I for the most part feel like I have done it on my own." Carey Mink, a 35-year-old psychiatric social worker, said, "No, they pointed me in a direction and they were supportive, but I've done a lot of the work myself." Debra Beck, a judge, responded, "No, I feel that I've gotten most places on my own." . . .

COMMITMENT TO COMMUNITY

The mainstream "model of community stresses the rights of individuals to make decisions in their own self-interest, regardless of the impact on the larger society" (Collins 1990, 52). This model may explain relations to community of origin for mobile white males but cannot be generalized to other racial and gender groups. In the context of well-recognized structures of racial oppression, America's racial-ethnic communities develop collective survival strategies that contrast with the individualism of the dominant culture but ensure the community's survival. . . . Widespread community involvement enables mobile people of color to confront and challenge racist obstacles in credentialing institutions, and it distinguishes the mobility process in racial-ethnic communities from mobility in the dominant culture. For example, Lou Nelson, now a librarian, described the support she felt in her southern, segregated, inner-city school. She said:

> There was a closeness between people and that had a lot to do with neighbor-hood schools. I went to Tubman High School with people that lived in the Tub-man area. I think that there was a bond, a bond between parents, the PTA . . . I think that it was just that everybody felt that everybody knew everybody. And that was special.

Family and community involvement and support in the mobility process means that many Black professionals and managers continue to feel linked to their communities of origin. Lillian King, a high-ranking city official who was raised working class, discussed her current commitment to the Black community. She said:

> Because I have more opportunities, I've got an obligation to give more back and to set a positive example for Black people and especially for Black women. I think we've got to do a tremendous job in building self-esteem and giving people the desire to achieve.

Judith Moore is a 34-year-old single parent employed as a health investigator. She has been able to maintain her connection with her community, and that is a source of pride.

> I'm proud that I still have a sense of who I am in terms of Black people. That's very important to me. No matter how much education or professional status I get, I do not want to lose touch with where I've come from. I think that you need to look back and that kind of pushes you forward. I think the degree and other things can make you lose sight of that, especially us Black folks, but I'm glad that I haven't and I try to teach that [commitment] to my son.

For some Black women, their mobility has enabled them to give to an even broader community. This is the case with Sammi Lewis, a raised-working-class woman who is a director of a social service agency. She said, "I owe a responsibility to the entire community, and not to any particular group." . . .

CROSSING THE COLOR LINE

Mobility for people of color is complex because in addition to crossing class lines, mobility often means crossing racial and cultural ones as well. Since the 1960s, people of color have increasingly attended either integrated or predominantly white schools. Only mobile white ethnics have a comparable experience of simultaneously crossing class and cultural barriers, yet even this experience is qualitatively different from that of Black and other people of color. White ethnicity can be practically invisible to white middle-class school peers and co-workers, but people of color are more visible and are subjected to harsher treatment. Our research indicates that no matter when people of color first encounter integrated or predominantly white settings, it is always a shock. The experience of racial exclusion cannot prepare people of color to deal with the racism in daily face-to-face encounters with white people.

For example, Lynn Johnson was in the first cohort of Black students at Regional College, a small private college in Memphis. The self-confidence and stamina Lynn developed in her supportive segregated high school helped her withstand the racism she faced as the first female and the first Black to graduate in economics at Regional College. Lynn described her treatment:

> I would come into class and Dr. Simpson (the Economics professor) would al-phabetically call the roll. When he came to my name, he would just jump over it. He would not ask me any questions, he would not do anything. I stayed in that class I struggled through. When it was my turn, I'd start talking. He would say, "Johnson, I wasn't talking to you" [because he never said *Miss* Johnson). I'd say, "That's all right, Dr. Simpson, it was my turn. I figured you just over-looked me. I'm just the littlest person in here. Wasn't that the right answer?" He would say, "Yes, that was the right answer." I drove him mad, I really did. He finally got used to me and started to help me.

. . . Learning to live in a white world was an additional hurdle for all Black women in this age cohort. Previous generations of Black people were more likely to be educated in segregated colleges and to work within the confines of the established Black community. They taught in segregated schools, pro-vided dental and medical care to the Black communities, and provided social services and other comforts to members of their own communities. They also lived in the Black community and worshiped on Sunday with many of the people they saw in different settings. As the comments of our respondents re-veal, both Black and white people had to adjust to integrated settings, but it was more stressful for the newcomers.

SUMMARY AND CONCLUSIONS

Our major aim in this research was to reopen the study of the subjective ex-perience of upward social mobility and to begin to incorporate race and gen-der into our vision of the process. In this exploratory work, we hope to raise issues and questions that will cast a new light on taken-for-granted assump-tions about the process and the people who engage in it. The experiences of these women have certainly painted a different picture from the one we were left some twenty years ago. First and foremost, these women are not detached, isolated, or driven solely by career goals. Relationships with family of origin, partners, children, friends, and the wider community loom large in the way they envision and accomplish mobility and the way they sustain themselves as professional and managerial women.

Several of our findings suggest ways that race and gender shape the mobility process for baby boom Black and white women. Education was stressed as important in virtually all of the families of these women; however, they differed in how it was viewed and how much was desired. The upwardly mobile women, both Black and white, shared some obstacles to attainment. More mobile women had parents who never expected them to achieve a college education. They also received less emotional and financial support for college attendance from their families than the women in middle-class families received. Black women also faced the unique problem of crossing racial barriers simultaneously with class barriers.

There were fairly dramatic race differences in the messages that the Black and white women received from family about what their lives should be like as adults. Black women clearly received the message that they needed an occupation to succeed in life and that marriage was a secondary concern. Many Black women also expressed a sense that their mobility was connected to an entire racial uplift process, not merely an individual journey.

White upwardly mobile women received less clear messages. Only one-half of these women said that their parents stressed the need for an occupation to succeed, and 20 percent said that marriage was stressed as the primary life goal. The most common message seemed to suggest that an occupation was necessary, because marriage could not be counted on to provide economic survival. Having a career, on the other hand, could even be seen as detrimental to adult happiness.

Upward mobility is a process that requires sustained effort and emotional and cognitive, as well as financial, support. The legacy of the image of mobility that was built on the white male experience focuses on credentialing institutions, especially the schools, as the primary place where talent is recognized and support is given to ensure that the talented among the working class are mobile. Family and friends are virtually invisible in this portrayal of the mobility process.

Although there is a good deal of variation in the roles that family and friends play for these women, they are certainly not invisible in the process. Especially among many of the Black women, there is a sense that they owe a great debt to their families for the help they have received. Black upwardly mobile women were also much more likely to feel that they give more than they receive from kin. Once they have achieved professional managerial employment, the sense of debt combines with their greater access to resources to put them in the position of being asked to give and of giving more to both family and friends. Carrington (1980) identifies some potential mental health hazards of such a sense of debt in upwardly mobile Black women's lives.

White upwardly mobile women are less likely to feel indebted to kin and to feel that they have accomplished alone. Yet even among this group, connections to spouses and children played significant roles in defining how women were mobile, their goals, and their sense of satisfaction with their life in the middle class.

These data are suggestive of a mobility process that is motivated by a desire for personal, but also collective, gain and that is shaped by interpersonal commitments to family, partners and children, community, and the race. Social mobility involves competition, but also cooperation, community support, and personal obligations. Further research is needed to explore fully this new image of mobility and to examine the relevance of these issues for white male mobility as well.

References

Braverman, Harry. 1974. *Labor and monopoly capital.* New York: Monthly Review Press.

Carrington, Christine. 1980. Depression in Black women: A theoretical appraisal. In *The Black woman,* edited by La Frances Rodgers Rose. Beverly Hills, CA: Sage.

Clark, Reginald. 1986. *Family life and school achievement.* Chicago: University of Chicago Press.

Collins, Patricia Hill. 1990. *Black feminist thought: Knowledge, consciousness, and the politics of empowerment.* Boston: Routledge.

Ehrenreich, Barbara, and John Ehrenreich. 1979. The professional-managerial class. In *Between labor and capital,* edited by Pat Walker. Boston: South End Press.

Higginbotham, Elizabeth, and Lynn Weber Cannon. 1988. *Rethinking mobility: Towards a race and gender inclusive theory.* Research Paper no. 8. Center for Research on Women, Memphis State University.

Joslin, Daphne. 1979. Working-class daughters, middle-class wives: Social identity and self-esteem among women upwardly mobile through marriage. Ph.D. diss., New York University, New York.

McAdoo, Harriette Pipes. 1978. Factors related to stability in upwardly mobile Black families. *Journal of Marriage and the Family* 40:761–76.

Poulantzas, Nicos. 1974. *Classes in contemporary capitalism.* London: New Left Books.

U.S. Bureau of the Census. 1983. Detailed population characteristics: Tennessee. Census of the Population, 1980. Washington, D.C.: GPO.

Vanneman, Reeve, and Lynn Weber Cannon. 1987. *The American perception of class.* Philadelphia: Temple University Press.

Gender and Sexism

GENDER THROUGH THE PRISM OF DIFFERENCE

19

Maxine Baca Zinn, Pierrette Hondagneu-Sotelo, and Michael A. Messner

"Men can't cry." "Women are victims of patriarchal oppression." "After divorce, single mothers are downwardly mobile, often moving into poverty." "Men don't do their share of housework and childcare." "Professional women face barriers such as sexual harassment and a 'glass ceiling' that prevent them from competing equally with men for high-status positions and high salaries." "Heterosexual intercourse is an expression of men's power over women." Sometimes, the students in our sociology and gender studies courses balk at these kinds of generalizations. And they are right to do so. After all, some men are more emotionally expressive than some women, some women have more power and success than some men, some men do their share—or more—of housework and childcare, and some women experience sex with men as both pleasurable and empowering. Indeed, contemporary gender relations are complex, changing in various directions, and, as such, we need to be wary of simplistic, if handy, slogans that seem to sum up the essence of relations between women and men.

On the other hand, we think it is a tremendous mistake to conclude that "all individuals are totally unique and different" and that therefore all generalizations about social groups are impossible or inherently oppressive. In fact, we are convinced that it is this very complexity, this multifaceted nature of contemporary gender relations that fairly begs for a sociological analysis of gender. . . . We use the image of "the prism of difference" to illustrate our approach to developing this sociological perspective on contemporary gender relations. *The American Heritage Dictionary* defines *prism*, in part, as "a homogeneous transparent solid, usually with triangular bases and rectangular sides, used to produce or analyze a continuous spectrum." Imagine a ray of light—which to the naked eye, appears to be only one color—refracted through a prism onto a white wall. To the eye, the result is not an infinite, disorganized scatter of individual colors. Rather, the refracted light displays an order, a structure of relationships among the different colors—a rainbow. Similarly, we propose to use the "prism of difference" . . . to analyze a continuous spectrum of people, in order to show how gender is organized and experienced differently when refracted through the prism of sexual, racial/ethnic, social class, physical abilities, age, and national citizenship differences.

EARLY WOMEN'S STUDIES: CATEGORICAL VIEWS OF "WOMEN" AND "MEN"

. . . It is possible to make good generalizations about women and men. But these generalizations should be drawn carefully, by always asking the questions "*which* women?" and "*which* men?" Scholars of sex and gender have not always done this. In the 1960s and 1970s, women's studies focused on the differences *between* women and men rather than *among* women and men. The very concept of gender, women's studies scholars demonstrated, is based on socially defined difference between women and men. From the macro level of social institutions like the economy, politics, and religion, to the micro level of interpersonal relations, distinctions between women and men structure social relations. Making males and females *different* from one another is the essence of gender. It is also the basis of men's power and domination. Understanding this was profoundly illuminating. Knowing that difference produced domination enabled women to name, analyze, and set about changing their victimization.

In the 1970s, riding the wave of a resurgent feminist movement, colleges and universities began to develop women's studies courses that aimed first and foremost to make women's lives visible. The texts that were developed for these courses tended to stress the things that women shared under patriarchy—having the responsibility for housework and childcare, the experience or fear of men's sexual violence, a lack of formal or informal access to education, exclusion from high-status professional and managerial jobs, political office, and religious leadership positions (Brownmiller, 1976; Kanter, 1977).

The study of women in society offered new ways of seeing the world. But the 1970s approach was limited in several ways. Thinking of gender primarily in terms of differences between women and men led scholars to overgeneralize about both. The concept of patriarchy led to a dualistic perspective of male privilege and female subordination. Women and men were cast as opposites. Each was treated as a homogeneous category with common characteristics and experiences. This approach *essentialized* women and men. Essentialism, simply put, is the notion that women's and men's attributes are categorically different. From this perspective, male control and coercion of women produced conflict between the sexes. The feminist insight originally introduced by Simone de Beauvoir in 1953—that women, as a group, had been socially defined as the "other" and that men had constructed themselves as the subjects of history, while constructing women as their objects—fueled an energizing sense of togetherness among many women. As college students read books like *Sisterhood Is Powerful* (Morgan, 1970), many of them joined organizations that fought, with some success, for equality and justice for women.

THE VOICES OF "OTHER" WOMEN

Although this view of women as an oppressed "other" was empowering for certain groups of women, some women began to claim that the feminist view of universal sisterhood ignored and marginalized their major concerns. It soon became apparent that treating women as a group united in its victimization by patriarchy was biased by too narrow a focus on the experiences and perspectives of women from more privileged social groups. "Gender" was treated as a generic category, uncritically applied to women. Ironically, this analysis, which was meant to unify women, instead produced divisions between and among them. The concerns projected as "universal" were removed from the realities of many women's lives. For example, it became a matter of faith in second-wave feminism that women's liberation would be accomplished by breaking down the "gendered public–domestic split." Indeed, the feminist call for women to move out of the kitchens and into the workplaces resonated in the experiences of many of the college-educated white women who were inspired by Betty Friedan's 1963 book, *The Feminine Mystique*. But the idea that women's movement into workplaces was itself empowering or liberating seemed absurd or irrelevant to many working-class women and women of color. They were already working for wages, as had many of their mothers and grandmothers, and did not consider access to jobs and public life as "liberating." For many of these women, liberation had more to do with organizing in communities and workplaces—often alongside men—for better schools, better pay, decent benefits, and other policies to benefit their neighborhoods, jobs, and families. The feminism of the 1970s did not seem to address these issues.

As more and more women analyzed their own experiences, they began to address the power relations creating differences among women and the part that privileged women played in the oppression of others. For many women of color, working-class women, lesbians, and women in contexts outside the United States (especially women in non-Western societies), the focus on male domination was a distraction from other oppressions. Their lived experiences could support neither a unitary theory of gender nor an ideology of universal sisterhood. As a result, finding common ground in a universal female victim-ization was never a priority for many groups of women.

Challenges to gender stereotypes soon emerged. Women of varied races, classes, national origins, and sexualities insisted that the concept of gender be broadened to take their differences into account (Baca Zinn et al., 1986; Hartman, 1976; Rich, 1980; Smith, 1977). Many women began to argue that their lives are affected by their location in a number of different hierarchies: as African Americans, Latinas, Native Americans, or Asian Americans in the race hierarchy; as young or old in the age hierarchy; as heterosexual, gay, les-bian, or bisexual in the sexual orientation hierarchy; and as women outside of the Western, industrialized nations, in subordinated geopolitical contexts. These arguments make it clear that women were not victimized by gender alone but by the historical and systematic denial of rights and privileges based on other differences as well.

MEN AS GENDERED BEINGS

As the voices of "other" women in the mid- to late 1970s began to challenge and expand the parameters of women's studies, a new area of scholarly inquiry was beginning to stir—a critical examination of men and masculinity. To be sure, in those early years of gender studies, the major task was to conduct studies and develop courses about the lives of women in order to begin to cor-rect centuries of scholarship that rendered women's lives, problems, and ac-complishments invisible. But the core idea of feminism—that "femininity" and women's subordination is a social construction—logically led to an ex-amination of the social construction of "masculinity" and men's power. Many of the first scholars to take on this task were psychologists, who were con-cerned with looking at the social construction of "the male sex role" (e.g., Pleck, 1981). By the late 1980s, there was a growing interdisciplinary collec-tion of studies of men and masculinity, much of it by social scientists (Brod, 1987; Kaufman, 1987; Kimmel, 1987; Kimmel & Messner, 1989).

Reflecting developments in women's studies, the scholarship on men's lives tended to develop three themes: First, what we think of as "masculinity" is not a fixed, biological essence of men but, rather, is a social construction that shifts and changes over time, as well as between and among various na-tional and cultural contexts. Second, power is central to understanding gen-der as a relational construct, and the dominant definition of masculinity is largely about expressing difference from—and superiority over—anything considered "feminine." Third, there is no singular "male sex role." Rather, at any given time there are various masculinities. R. W. Connell (1987, 1995) has been among the most articulate advocates of this perspective. Connell argues that hegemonic masculinity (the dominant form of masculinity at any given moment) is constructed in relation to femininities *as well as* in relation to various subordinated or marginalized masculinities. For example, in the United States, various racialized masculinities (e.g., as represented by African American men, Latino immigrant men, etc.) have been central to the construction of hegemonic (White, middle-class) masculinity. . . . This "othering" of racialized masculinities helps to shore up the material privileges that have been historically connected to hegemonic masculinity. When viewed this way, we can better understand hegemonic masculinity as part of a system that includes gender, as well as racial, class, sexual, and other relations of power.

The new literature on men and masculinities also begins to move us beyond the simplistic, falsely categorical, and pessimistic view of men simply as a privileged sex class. When race, social class, sexual orientation, physical abilities, and immigrant or national status are taken into account, we can see that in some circumstances, "male privilege" is partly—sometimes substantially—muted (Kimmel & Messner, 1998). Although it is unlikely that we will soon see a "men's movement" that aims to undermine the power and privileges that are connected with hegemonic masculinity, when we begin to look at "masculinities" through the prism of difference, we can begin to see similarities and possible points of coalition between and among certain groups of women and men (Messner, 1998). Certain kinds of changes in gender relations—for instance, a national family leave policy for working parents—might serve as a means of uniting particular groups of women and men.

GENDER IN INTERNATIONAL CONTEXTS

It is an increasingly accepted truism that late twentieth-century increases in transnational trade, international migration, and global systems of production and communication have diminished both the power of nation-states and the significance of national borders. A much more ignored issue is the extent to which gender relations—in the United States and elsewhere in the world— are increasingly linked to patterns of global economic restructuring. Decisions made in corporate headquarters located in Los Angeles, Tokyo, or London may have immediate repercussions in how women and men thousands of miles away organize their work, community, and family lives (Sassen, 1991). It is no longer possible to study gender relations without attention to global processes and inequalities. . . .

Around the world, women's paid and unpaid labor is key to global development strategies. Yet it would be a mistake to conclude that gender is molded from the "top down." What happens on a daily basis in families and workplaces simultaneously constitutes and is constrained by structural transnational institutions. For instance, in the second half of the twentieth century young, single women, many of them from poor rural areas, have been recruited for work in export assembly plants along the U.S.–Mexico border, in East and Southeast Asia, in Silicon Valley, in the Caribbean, and in Central America. While the profitability of these multinational factories depends, in part, on management's ability to manipulate the young women's ideologies of gender, the women . . . do not respond passively or uniformly, but they actively resist, challenge, and accommodate. At the same time, the global diversion of the assembly line has concentrated corporate facilities in many U.S. cities, making available myriad managerial, administrative, and clerical jobs for college educated women. Women's paid labor is used at various points along this international system of production. Not only employment, but also consumption, embodies global interdependencies. There is a high probability that the clothes you wear and the computer you use originated in multinational corporate headquarters and in assembly plants scattered around third-world nations. And if these items were actually manufactured in the United States, they were probably assembled by Latin American and Asian-born women.

Worldwide, international labor migration and refugee movements are creating new types of multiracial societies. Although these developments are often discussed and analyzed with respect to racial differences, gender typically remains absent. As several commentators have noted, the White feminist movement in the United States has not addressed issues of immigration and nationality. Gender, however, has been fundamental in shaping immigration policies (Chang, 1994; Hondagneu-Sotelo, 1994). Direct labor recruitment programs generally solicit either male or female labor (e.g., Filipina nurses, Mexican male farm workers); national disenfranchisement has particular repercussions for women and men; and current immigrant laws are based on very gendered notions of what constitutes "family unification." As Chandra Mohanty suggests, "analytically these issues are the contemporary metropolitan counterpart of women's struggles against colonial occupation in the geographical third world" (1991: 23). Moreover, immigrant and refugee women's daily lives often challenge familiar feminist paradigms. The occupations in which immigrant and refugee women concentrate—paid domestic work, informal sector street vending, assembly or industrial piece work performed in the home—often blur the ideological distinction between work and family and between public and private spheres.

FROM PATCHWORK QUILT TO PRISM

All of these developments—the voices of "other" women, the study of men and masculinities, and the examination of gender in transnational contexts— have helped redefine the study of gender. By working to develop knowledge that is inclusive of the experiences of all groups, new insights about gender have begun to emerge. Examining gender in the context of other differences makes it clear that nobody experiences themselves as solely gendered. Instead, gender is configured through cross-cutting forms of difference that carry deep social and economic consequences.

By the mid-1980s, thinking about gender had entered a new stage that was more carefully grounded in the experiences of diverse groups of women and men. This perspective is a general way of looking at women and men and understanding their relationships to the structure of society. Gender is no longer viewed simply as a matter of two opposite categories of people—males and females—but as a range of social relations among differently situated people. Because centering on difference is a radical challenge to the conventional gender framework, it raises several concerns. Does the recognition that gender can only be understood contextually (meaning that there is no singular "gender" per se) make women's studies and gender studies newly vulnerable to critics in the academy? Does the immersion in difference throw us into a whirlwind of "spiraling diversity" (Hewitt, 1992: 316) where multiple identities and locations shatter the categories *women* and *men?*

. . . We take a position directly opposed to an empty pluralism. Although the categories *woman* and *man* have multiple meanings, this does not reduce gender to a "postmodern kaleidoscope of lifestyles. Rather, it points to the *relational* character of gender" (Connell, 1992: 736). Not only are masculinity and femininity relational, but different masculinities and femininities are interconnected also through other social structures such as race, class, and nation. Groups are created by their relationships with each other. The meaning of *woman* is defined by the existence of women of different races and classes. Being a White woman in the United States is meaningful only insofar as it is set apart from and in contradistinction to women of color.

Just as masculinity and femininity each depend on the definitions of the other to produce domination, differences *among* women and *among* men are also created in the context of structured relationships. Some women derive benefits from their race and class position, and from their location in the global economy, while they are simultaneously restricted by gender. In other words, such women are subordinated by patriarchy, yet their relatively privileged positions within hierarchies of race, class, and the global political economy intersect to create for them an expanded range of opportunities, choices, and ways of living. They may even use their race and class advantage to minimize some of the consequences of patriarchy and/or to oppose other women. Similarly, one can become a man in opposition to other men. For example, "the relation between heterosexual and homosexual men is central, carrying heavy symbolic freight. To many people, homosexuality is the *negation* of masculinity. . . . Given that assumption, antagonism toward homosexual men may be used to define masculinity" (Connell, 1992: 736).

In the past decade, viewing gender through the prism of difference has profoundly reoriented the field (Acker, 1999; Glenn, 1999; Messner, 1996; West & Fenstermaker, 1995). Yet analyzing the multiple constructions of gender does not mean studying just groups of women and groups of men as different. It is clearly time to go beyond what we call the "patchwork quilt" phase in the study of women and men—that is, the phase in which we have acknowledged the importance of examining differences within constructions of gender, but do so largely by collecting a study here on African American women, a study there on gay men, and a study on working-class Chicanas. This patchwork quilt approach too often amounts to no more than "adding difference and stirring." The result may be a lovely mosaic, but like a patchwork quilt it still tends to overemphasize boundaries, rather than highlighting bridges of interdependency. In addition, this approach too often does not explore the ways that social constructions of femininities and masculinities are based on, and reproduce relations of, power. In short, we think that the substantial quantity of research that has now been done on various groups and subgroups needs to be analyzed within a framework that emphasizes differences and inequalities not as discrete areas of separation, but as interrelated bands of color that together make up a spectrum.

References

Acker, Joan. 1999. "Rewriting Class, Race and Gender: Problems in Feminist Rethinking." Pp. 44–69 in Myra Marx Ferree, Judith Lorber, and Beth B. Hess (eds.), *Revisioning Gender*. Thousand Oaks, CA: Sage.

Baca Zinn, M., Weber Cannon, L., Higginbotham, E., Thornton Dill, B. 1986. "The Costs of Exclusionary Practices in Women's Studies," *Signs: Journal of Women in Culture and Society 11:* 290–303.

Brod, Harry (ed.). 1987. *The Making of Masculinities: The New Men's Studies*. Boston: Allen & Unwin.

Brownmiller, Susan. 1975 *Against Our Will: Men, Women, and Rape*. New York: Simon and Schuster.

Chang, Grace. 1994 "Undocumented Latinas: The New 'Employable Mothers.'" Pp. 259–285 in Evelyn Nakano Glenn, Grace Chang, and Linda Rennie Forcey (eds.), *Mothering, Ideology, Experience, and Agency*. New York and London: Routledge.

Connell, R. W. 1987. *Gender and Power*. Stanford, CA: Stanford University Press.

Connell, R. W. 1992. "A Very Straight Gay: Masculinity, Homosexual Experience, and the Dynamics of Gender," *American Sociological Review 57:* 735–751.

Connell, R. W. 1995. *Masculinities*. Berkeley: University of California Press.

De Beauvoir, Simone. 1953. *The Second Sex*. New York: Knopf.

Glenn, Evelyn Nakano. 1999. "The Social Construction and Institutionalization of Gender and Race: An Integrative Framework." Pp. 3–43 in Myra Marx Ferree, Judith Lorber, and Beth B. Hess (eds.), *Revisioning Gender*. Thousand Oaks, CA: Sage.

_176_ _Gender and Sexism_

Hartmann, Heidi. 1976. "Capitalism, Patriarchy, and Job Segregation by Sex," _Signs: Journal of Women in Culture and Society 1:_ (3), part 2, Spring: 137–167.

Hewitt, Nancy A. 1992 "Compounding Differences," _Feminist Studies 18:_ 313–326.

Hondagneu-Sotelo, Pierrette. 1994. _Gendered Transitions: Mexican Experiences of Immigration._ Berkeley: University of California Press.

Kanter, Rosabeth Moss. 1977. _Men and Women of the Corporation._ New York: Basic Books.

Kaufman, Michael. 1987. _Beyond Patriarchy: Essays by Men on Pleasure, Power, and Change._ Toronto and New York: Oxford University Press.

Kimmel, Michael S. (ed.). 1987. _Changing Men: New Directions in Research on Men and Masculinity._ Newbury Park, CA: Sage.

Kimmel, Michael S., & Michael A. Messner (eds.). 1989. _Men's Lives._ New York: Macmillan.

Kimmel, Michael S., & Michael A. Messner (eds.). 1998. _Men's Lives,_ 4th edition. Allyn & Bacon.

Messner, Michael A. 1996. "Studying Up on Sex," _Sociology of Sport Journal 13:_ 221–237.

Messner, Michael A. 1998. _Politics of Masculinities: Men in Movements._ Thousand Oaks, CA: Sage.

Mohanty, Chandra Talpade. 1991. "Cartographies of Struggle: Third World Women and the Politics of Feminism." Pp. 51–80 in Chandra Talpade Mohanty, Ann Russo, and Lourdes Torres (eds.), _Third World Women and the Politics of Feminism._ Bloomington: Indiana University Press.

Morgan, Robin. 1970. _Sisterhood Is Powerful: An Anthology of Writing from the Women's Liberation Movement._ New York: Vintage Books.

Pleck, Joseph. 1981. _Thy Myth of Masculinity._ Cambridge, MA: MIT Press.

Rich, Adrienne. 1980. "Compulsory Heterosexuality and the Lesbian Experience," _Signs: Journal of Women in Culture and Society 5:_ 631–660.

Sassen, Saskia. 1991. _The Global City: New York, London, Tokyo._ Princeton, NJ: Princeton University Press.

Smith, Barbara. 1977. _Toward a Black Feminist Criticism._ Freedom, CA: Crossing Press.

West, Candace, & Sarah Fenstermaker. 1995. "Doing Difference," _Gender & Society 9:_ 8–37.

AGE, RACE, CLASS, AND SEX

20

Women Redefining Difference

Audre Lorde

Much of Western European history conditions us to see human differences in simplistic opposition to each other: dominant/subordinate, good/bad, up/down, superior/inferior. In a society where the good is defined in terms of profit rather than in terms of human need, there must always be some group of people who, through systematized oppression, can be made to feel surplus, to occupy the place of the dehumanized inferior. Within this society, that group is made up of Black and Third World people, working-class people, older people, and women.

As a forty-nine-year-old Black lesbian feminist socialist mother of two, including one boy, and a member of an interracial couple, I usually find myself a part of some group defined as other, deviant, inferior, or just plain wrong. Traditionally, in American society, it is the members of oppressed, objectified groups who are expected to stretch out and bridge the gap between the actualities of our lives and the consciousness of our oppressor. For in order to survive, those of us for whom oppression is as american as apple pie have always had to be watchers, to become familiar with the language and manners of the oppressor, even sometimes adopting them for some illusion of protection. Whenever the need for some pretense of communication arises, those who profit from our oppression call upon us to share our knowledge with them. In other words, it is the responsibility of the oppressed to teach the oppressors their mistakes. I am responsible for educating teachers who dismiss my children's culture in school. Black and Third World people are expected to educate white people as to our humanity. Women are expected to educate men. Lesbians and gay men are expected to educate the heterosexual world. The oppressors maintain their position and evade responsibility for their own actions. There is a constant drain of energy which might be better used in redefining ourselves and devising realistic scenarios for altering the present and constructing the future.

Institutionalized rejection of difference is an absolute necessity in a profit economy which needs outsiders as surplus people. As members of such an

---

Paper delivered at the Copeland Colloquium, Amherst College, April 1980.

From: Audre Lorde, *Sister Outsider* (Freedom, CA: Crossing Press, 1984), pp. 114–23. Reprinted by permission.

economy, we have *all* been programmed to respond to the human differences between us with fear and loathing and to handle that difference in one of three ways: ignore it, and if that is not possible, copy it if we think it is dominant, or destroy it if we think it is subordinate. But we have no patterns for relating across our human differences as equals. As a result, those differences have been misnamed and misused in the service of separation and confusion.

Certainly there are very real differences between us of race, age, and sex. But it is not those differences between us that are separating us. It is rather our refusal to recognize those differences, and to examine the distortions which result from our misnaming them and their effects upon human behavior and expectation.

Racism, the belief in the inherent superiority of one race over all others and thereby the right to dominance. Sexism, the belief in the inherent superiority of one sex over the other and thereby the right to dominance. Ageism. Heterosexism. Elitism. Classism.

It is a lifetime pursuit for each one of us to extract these distortions from our living at the same time as we recognize, reclaim, and define those differences upon which they are imposed. For we have all been raised in a society where those distortions were endemic within our living. Too often, we pour the energy needed for recognizing and exploring difference into pretending those differences are insurmountable barriers, or that they do not exist at all. This results in a voluntary isolation, or false and treacherous connections. Either way, we do not develop tools for using human difference as a springboard for creative change within our lives. We speak not of human difference, but of human deviance.

Somewhere, on the edge of consciousness, there is what I call a *mythical norm*, which each one of us within our hearts knows "that is not me." In america, this norm is usually defined as white, thin, male, young, heterosexual, christian, and financially secure. It is with this mythical norm that the trappings of power reside within this society. Those of us who stand outside that power often identify one way in which we are different, and we assume that to be the primary cause of all oppression, forgetting other distortions around difference, some of which we ourselves may be practicing. By and large within the women's movement today, white women focus upon their oppression as women and ignore differences of race, sexual preference, class, and age. There is a pretense to a homogeneity of experience covered by the word *sisterhood* that does not in fact exist.

Unacknowledged class differences rob women of each others' energy and creative insight. Recently a women's magazine collective made the decision for one issue to print only prose, saying poetry was a less "rigorous" or "serious" art form. Yet even the form our creativity takes is often a class issue. Of all the art forms, poetry is the most economical. It is the one which is the most secret, which requires the least physical labor, the least material, and the one which can be done between shifts, in the hospital pantry, on the subway, and on scraps of surplus paper. Over the last few years, writing a novel on tight finances, I came to appreciate the enormous differences in the material demands between poetry and prose. As we reclaim our literature, poetry has been the major voice of poor, working class, and Colored women. A room of one's own may be a necessity for writing prose, but so are reams of paper, a typewriter, and plenty of time. The actual requirements to produce the visual arts also help determine, along class lines, whose art is whose. In this day of inflated prices for material, who are our sculptors, our painters, our photographers? When we speak of a broadly based women's culture, we need to be aware of the effect of class and economic differences on the supplies available for producing art.

As we move toward creating a society within which we can each flourish, ageism is another distortion of relationship which interferes without vision. By ignoring the past, we are encouraged to repeat its mistakes. The "generation gap" is an important social tool for any repressive society. If the younger members of a community view the older members as contemptible or suspect or excess, they will never be able to join hands and examine the living memories of the community, nor ask the all important question, "Why?" This gives rise to a historical amnesia that keeps us working to invent the wheel every time we have to go to the store for bread.

We find ourselves having to repeat and relearn the same old lessons over and over that our mothers did because we do not pass on what we have learned, or because we are unable to listen. For instance, how many times has this all been said before? For another, who would have believed that once again our daughters are allowing their bodies to be hampered and purgatoried by girdles and high heels and hobble skirts?

Ignoring the differences of race between women and the implications of those differences presents the most serious threat to the mobilization of women's joint power.

As white women ignore their built-in privilege of whiteness and define *woman* in terms of their own experience alone, then women of Color become "other," the outsider whose experience and tradition is too "alien" to comprehend. An example of this is the signal absence of the experience of women of Color as a resource for women's studies courses. The literature of women of Color is seldom included in women's literature courses and almost never in other literature courses, nor in women's studies as a whole. All too often, the excuse given is that the literatures of women of Color can only be taught by Colored women, or that they are too difficult to understand, or that classes cannot "get into" them because they come out of experiences that are "too different." I have heard this argument presented by white women of otherwise quite clear intelligence, women who seem to have no trouble at all teaching and reviewing work that comes out of the vastly different experiences of

Shakespeare, Molière, Dostoyefsky, and Aristophanes. Surely there must be some other explanation.

This is a very complex question, but I believe one of the reasons white women have such difficulty reading Black women's work is because of their reluctance to see Black women as women and different from themselves. To examine Black women's literature effectively requires that we be seen as whole people in our actual complexities—as individuals, as women, as human—rather than as one of those problematic but familiar stereotypes provided in this society in place of genuine images of Black women. And I believe this holds true for the literatures of other women of Color who are not Black.

The literatures of all women of Color re-create the textures of our lives, and many white women are heavily invested in ignoring the real differences. For as long as any difference between us means one of us must be inferior, then the recognition of any difference must be fraught with guilt. To allow women of Color to step out of stereotypes is too guilt provoking, for it threatens the complacency of those women who view oppression only in terms of sex.

Refusing to recognize difference makes it impossible to see the different problems and pitfalls facing us as women.

Thus, in a patriarchal power system where whiteskin privilege is a major prop, the entrapments used to neutralize Black women and white women are not the same. For example, it is easy for Black women to be used by the power structure against Black men, not because they are men, but because they are Black. Therefore, for Black women, it is necessary at all times to separate the needs of the oppressor from our own legitimate conflicts within our communities. This same problem does not exist for white women. Black women and men have shared racist oppression and still share it, although in different ways. Out of that shared oppression we have developed joint defenses and joint vulnerabilities to each other that are not duplicated in the white community, with the exception of the relationship between Jewish women and Jewish men.

On the other hand, white women face the pitfall of being seduced into joining the oppressor under the pretense of sharing power. This possibility does not exist in the same way for women of Color. The tokenism that is sometimes extended to us is not an invitation to join power; our racial "otherness" is a visible reality that makes that quite clear. For white women there is a wider range of pretended choices and rewards for identifying with patriarchal power and its tools.

Today, with the defeat of ERA, the tightening economy, and increased conservatism, it is easier once again for white women to believe the dangerous fantasy that if you are good enough, pretty enough, sweet enough, quiet enough, teach the children to behave, hate the right people, and marry the right men, then you will be allowed to co-exist with patriarchy in relative peace, at least until a man needs your job or the neighborhood rapist happens along. And true, unless one lives and loves in the trenches it is difficult to remember that the war against dehumanization is ceaseless.

But Black women and our children know the fabric of our lives is stitched with violence and with hatred, that there is no rest. We do not deal with it only on the picket lines, or in dark midnight alleys, or in the places where we dare to verbalize our resistance. For us, increasingly, violence weaves through the daily tissues of our living—in the supermarket, in the classroom, in the elevator, in the clinic and the schoolyard, from the plumber, the baker, the saleswoman, the bus driver, the bank teller, the waitress who does not serve us.

Some problems we share as women, some we do not. You fear your children will grow up to join the patriarchy and testify against you, we fear our children will be dragged from a car and shot down in the street, and you will turn your backs upon the reasons they are dying.

The threat of difference has been no less blinding to people of Color. Those of us who are Black must see that the reality of our lives and our struggle does not make us immune to the errors of ignoring and misnaming difference. Within Black communities where racism is a living reality, differences among us often seem dangerous and suspect. The need for unity is often misnamed as a need for homogeneity, and a Black feminist vision mistaken for betrayal of our common interests as a people. Because of the continuous battle against racial erasure that Black women and Black men share, some Black women still refuse to recognize that we are also oppressed as women, and that sexual hostility against Black women is practiced not only by the white racist society, but implemented within our Black communities as well. It is a disease striking the heart of Black nationhood, and silence will not make it disappear. Exacerbated by racism and the pressures of powerlessness, violence against Black women and children often becomes a standard within our communities, one by which manliness can be measured. But these woman-hating acts are rarely discussed as crimes against Black women.

As a group, women of Color are the lowest paid wage earners in america. We are the primary targets of abortion and sterilization abuse, here and abroad. In certain parts of Africa, small girls are still being sewed shut between their legs to keep them docile and for men's pleasure. This is known as female circumcision, and it is not a cultural affair as the late Jomo Kenyatta insisted, it is a crime against Black women.

Black women's literature is full of the pain of frequent assault, not only by a racist patriarchy, but also by Black men. Yet the necessity for and history of shared battle have made us, Black women, particularly vulnerable to the false accusation that anti-sexist is anti-Black. Meanwhile, womanhating as a recourse of the powerless is sapping strength from Black communities, and our very lives. Rape is on the increase, reported and unreported, and rape is not aggressive sexuality, it is sexualized aggression. As Kalamu ya Salaam, a Black male writer points out, "As long as male domination exists, rape will exist. Only women revolting and men made conscious of their responsibility to fight sexism can collectively stop rape."*

Differences between ourselves as Black women are also being misnamed and used to separate us from one another. As a Black lesbian feminist comfortable with the many different ingredients of my identity, and a woman committed to racial and sexual freedom from oppression, I find I am constantly being encouraged to pluck out some one aspect of myself and present this as the meaningful whole, eclipsing or denying the other parts of self. But this is a destructive and fragmenting way to live. My fullest concentration of energy is available to me only when I integrate all the parts of who I am, openly, allowing power from particular sources of my living to flow back and forth freely through all my different selves, without the restrictions of externally imposed definition. Only then can I bring myself and my energies as a whole to the service of those struggles which I embrace as part of my living.

A fear of lesbians, or of being accused of being a lesbian, has led many Black women into testifying against themselves. It has led some of us into destructive alliances, and others into despair and isolation. In the white women's communities, heterosexism is sometimes a result of identifying with the white patriarchy, a rejection of that interdependence between women-identified women which allows the self to be, rather than to be used in the service of men. Sometimes it reflects a die-hard belief in the protective coloration of heterosexual relationships, sometimes a self-hate which all women have to fight against, taught us from birth.

Although elements of these attitudes exist for all women, there are particular resonances of heterosexism and homophobia among Black women. Despite the fact that woman-bonding has a long and honorable history in the African and African-american communities, and despite the knowledge and accomplishments of many strong and creative women-identified Black women in the political, social and cultural fields, heterosexual Black women often tend to ignore or discount the existence and work of Black lesbians. Part of this attitude has come from an understandable terror of Black male attack within the close confines of Black society, where the punishment for any female self-assertion is still to be accused of being a lesbian and therefore unworthy of the attention or support of the scarce Black male. But part of this need to misname and ignore Black lesbians comes from a very real fear that openly women-identified Black women who are no longer dependent upon men for their self-definition may well reorder our whole concept of social relationships.

---

*From "Rape: A Radical Analysis, An African-American Perspective" by Kalamu ya Salaam in *Black Books Bulletin*, vol. 6, no. 4 (1980).

Black women who once insisted that lesbianism was a white woman's problem now insist that Black lesbians are a threat to Black nationhood, are consorting with the enemy, are basically un-Black. These accusations, coming from the very women to whom we look for deep and real understanding, have served to keep many Black lesbians in hiding, caught between the racism of white women and the homophobia of their sisters. Often, their work has been ignored, trivialized, or misnamed, as with the work of Angelina Grimke, Alice Dunbar-Nelson, Lorraine Hansberry. Yet women-bonded women have always been some part of the power of Black communities, from our unmarried aunts to the amazons of Dahomey.

And it is certainly not Black lesbians who are assaulting women and raping children and grandmothers on the streets of our communities.

Across this country, as in Boston during the spring of 1979 following the unsolved murders of twelve Black women, Black lesbians are spearheading movements against violence against Black women.

What are the particular details within each of our lives that can be scrutinized and altered to help bring about change? How do we redefine difference for all women? It is not our differences which separate women, but our reluctance to recognize those differences and to deal effectively with the distortions which have resulted from the ignoring and misnaming of those differences.

As a tool of social control, women have been encouraged to recognize only one area of human difference as legitimate, those differences which exist between women and men. And we have learned to deal across those differences with the urgency of all oppressed subordinates. All of us have had to learn to live or work or coexist with men, from our fathers on. We have recognized and negotiated these differences, even when this recognition only continued the old dominant/subordinate mode of human relationship, where the oppressed must recognize the masters' difference in order to survive.

But our future survival is predicated upon our ability to relate within equality. As women, we must root out internalized patterns of oppression within ourselves if we are to move beyond the most superficial aspects of social change. Now we must recognize differences among women who are our equals, neither inferior nor superior, and devise ways to use each others' difference to enrich our visions and our joint struggles.

The future of our earth may depend upon the ability of all women to identify and develop new definitions of power and new patterns of relating across difference. The old definitions have not served us, nor the earth that supports us. The old patterns, no matter how cleverly rearranged to imitate progress, still condemn us to cosmetically altered repetitions of the same old exchanges, the same old guilt, hatred, recrimination, lamentation, and suspicion.

For we have, built into all of us, old blueprints of expectation and response, old structures of oppression, and these must be altered at the same time as we alter the living conditions which are a result of those structures. For the master's tools will never dismantle the master's house.

As Paulo Freire shows so well in *The Pedagogy of the Oppressed*,* the true focus of revolutionary change is never merely the oppressive situations which we seek to escape, but that piece of the oppressor which is planted deep within each of us, and which knows only the oppressors' tactics, the oppressors' relationships.

Change means growth, and growth can be painful. But we sharpen self-definition by exposing the self in work and struggle together with those whom we define as different from ourselves, although sharing the same goals. For Black and white, old and young, lesbian and heterosexual women alike, this can mean new paths to our survival.

> We have chosen each other
> and the edge of each others battles
> the war is the same
> if we lose
> someday women's blood will congeal
> upon a dead planet
> if we win
> there is no telling
> we seek beyond history
> for a new and more possible meeting.**

---

*Seabury Press, New York, 1970.
**From "Outlines," unpublished poem.

UNDERSTANDING AND FIGHTING SEXISM

21

A Call to Men

Peter Blood, Alan Tuttle, and George Lakey

PART 1: UNDERSTANDING THE ENEMY: HOW SEXISM WORKS IN THE U.S.A.

What Is Sexism?

Sexism is much more than a problem with the language we use, our personal attitudes, or individual hurtful acts toward women. Sexism in our country is a complex mesh of practices, institutions, and ideas which have the overall effect of giving more power to men than to women. By "power" we mean the ability to influence important decisions—political decisions of government on every level, economic decisions (jobs, access to money, choice of priorities), and a wide variety of other life areas down to the most personal concerns, such as whether two people are going to make love on a given night or not. The word "patriarchy" is sometimes used to refer to the actual power structure built around men's domination of women. Two key areas where women are denied power are the area of jobs and the area of violence directed toward women.

Women have much less earning power in our labor market than men do. Reasons for this include the fact that much of women's labor is unwaged (housecleaning, childrearing, little services to please bosses or lovers); the low status and pay of most of the traditionally women's jobs that are waged (secretary, sales clerk, childcare, nursing home attendant); the non-union status of most women workers; and the discriminatory practices such as the recent Supreme Court decision allowing companies to exclude pregnancy from their medical insurance and sick leave benefits.

Women face a constant threat of physical violence and sexual aggression in our society. As men we are rarely aware of how pervasive this is or the powerful effect it has on women's outlook on themselves and the world. Actual rape

From: *Off Their Backs . . . and on Our Own Two Feet* (Philadelphia: New Society Publishers, 1983), pp. 1–8. Reprinted by permission.

or sadistic violence is the tip of the iceberg. Physical abuse of wives and lovers is common and rarely publicized. A majority of women have probably experienced some form of sexual abuse as children. The memory of these experiences often gets suppressed because they feel so humiliated and scared, and because adults deny repeatedly that such a thing could happen. Society is filled with messages pressuring women to provide men with sexual pleasure.

All of the above combine with differences in physical strength, voice, acculturated ways of dealing with anger, and the very concrete power men hold in other areas of life to keep many women intimidated, passive, and unable to even acknowledge their own fear openly. The rapist is the shock trooper for an overall system of unequal power.

Patriarchy is not just a power structure "out there"; it is mainly enforced by our own acceptance of its character ideals for our lives. The character ideal which is held up for men to reach toward is "masculinity." A masculine man is supposed to be tough, good at abstract reasoning, hard-working, unfeeling except for anger and sexual desire, and habitually taking the initiative. Masculinity exists only in contrast to femininity, the model for women. Feminine characteristics include cooperativeness, emotionality, patience, passivity, nurturance, and sexual appeal.

We all know that human characteristics are *not* distributed neatly between the sexes that way. A nursery school will often include girls who do abstract reasoning and get into fights and boys who cry easily. We also know that the culture does not leave them alone—the tomboy usually learns to become a lady, and the gentle boy develops armor to protect him from the jibes of his mates. They also learn that masculinity is valued in our culture more than femininity, especially when it comes to gaining power. In fact, the characteristics which are assigned to men by the patriarchy are the power-linked characteristics. In other words, by accepting masculinity as an ideal for ourselves, men buy into a system which keeps women down.

SEXISM AND OUR ECONOMIC SYSTEM

Why does sexism exist? Why is it so hard to root it out? Who really benefits from it? There is a variety of theories as to where sexism originated. Some say it started with the advent of class society; others say it preceded all other forms of oppression.

Regardless of its historic roots, it is clear that sexism today is intimately connected with our economic system, which is called "corporate capitalism."

In our society, a small group of people own and control almost all of the factories, financial institutions, networks of transport and sales of food and clothing. What this means, first of all, is that though we as men generally have more power than women do, the great majority of us have relatively little real power. Most of us are given very little chance to make the major decisions which affect our lives (for example, whether society will emphasize public transportation or private cars, how decisions are made at the factory where we work, what quality air we breathe, what is taught to our children in school). In fact, this kind of power is concentrated in the hands of a relatively small number of white, middle-aged to older men.

However much power the system has given to each of us, this power is only useful in keeping things going according to the present rules, not in changing things in any basic way. The moment one of us tries to use power conveyed by the system to make fundamental changes, we find it taken away from us by that system. (All of us do possess the power to influence the course of history and bring about fundamental changes if we work together. This power comes from a very different source: from our power to work collectively to change the world around us, by "grass roots" power.)

Corporate capitalism is supported by sexism in many ways. Perhaps the most important way is that women function as a surplus labor force, where they can be pushed in and out of employment in keeping with current needs of the economy (depression, expansion, wartime, or a period of union-busting). In effect, the prevalent attitude in this society might be: "A woman's place is in the home . . . *until she's needed in the factory.*" Women's low wages keep wages lower for all: our boss holds the implicit threat that he can replace us with lower-paid women workers if we get too uppity or demand too high wages. Job role stereotyping also helps get women to do unpleasant forms of work which men would rather not do.

There are other ways sexism helps maintain capitalism. Women's unwaged labor of reproducing and taking care of the work force is called "women's work" and taken for granted. Women's servicing of men at home keeps our feelings of alienation and frustration concerning our jobs in check, which might otherwise lead to rebellion or burnout. Men's role as sole breadwinner in many families makes them reluctant to take militant stands on safety, wages, or other issues at work. It is threatening for a man not to be filling the breadwinner role—and he knows his wife will have a very difficult time finding work that pays enough to support a family. Women and men are played off against each other in competing for scarce jobs rather than sharing the fruits of a non-competitive, non-wasteful economy. Finally, excess consumption is encouraged by the lifeless, unsatisfying sex roles which we get shunted into on the job and at home.

The capitalist economic-political structure works to preserve sexism through indoctrination in our schools, a constant flow of brainwashing (subtle or otherwise) in advertising, and through its control of the mass media (what news gets reported and what does not, what programs get chosen for airing . . .). It also maintains it through control of legislation (influence through money), through the policies of our large corporations, and through failure to make use of leadership positions to educate people about the ways sexism affects us and ways it can be overcome.

Sexism and capitalism are so intertwined, in fact, that we believe there is no way that sexism can be thoroughly uprooted from our society without the total remaking of our economic system. . . .

Setting up a socialist society in no way guarantees an end to sexism (as can also be seen in the persistence of sexism to one degree or another in [many] countries). The patriarchy is a power arrangement which has a life of its own independent of capitalism's indoctrination. The struggle against sexism, therefore, must be a high priority for any movement which is offering leadership in creating a new society. The style pervading socialist movements in this country and the groups which are leading socialist countries is all too often determined by the masculine conditioning of domination and competition. This conditioning needs to be struggled against much more forcefully than it has been if we are ever to achieve a world free from sexism.

ARE WE MEN THE ENEMY?

Some people say that men are the enemy when it comes to fighting sexism. We do not agree; blame and guilt don't help in understanding why people function as they do or in getting them to change.

Does this mean we are not responsible for what is happening? Not at all! As men, we are all involved in the oppression women experience, and we benefit from it each day. Yet this is no reason to fix blame on ourselves as "the oppressor" (or, for that matter, to place blame on any woman for "failing to fight back"). Over many years society has forced men and women into these roles of domination and submission.

How did society do this? It is clear we were pushed into these roles when we were young children and especially vulnerable. At that time, all of us were hurt in many ways through the expectations put on our sex. These hurts came through ridicule and threats directed at us and also through having to watch others get hurt while feeling ourselves incapable (because of lack of information or strength) of stopping that hurt. This experience of powerlessness in turn has reduced our ability to see the world clearly and act accordingly. The ingrained fear from these experiences tends to lead to either of two responses: feeling powerless and playing the victim role, or turning the experience around and acting out an oppressor role.

These dynamics do not just happen between men and women, but also between races, age groups, gays and non-gays, healthy and physically challenged people, and a number of other groups. As a matter of fact, everyone in our society has probably ended up playing both of these roles at one time or another. Even the richest, most powerful man was once powerless as a child in relation to his parents. Even a poor black woman could experience some privilege in relation to a very young person or a gay person.

The point is that we were all taught very early not to go beyond the expected stereotyped behavior. The sooner we recognize the effects of this kind of conditioning on us, the sooner we can effectively change the way things happen. This may mean stopping our domination of others or ceasing to accept oppression ourselves. It is good to recognize that stepping out of the old roles usually feels uncomfortable and may well require years of painful struggle, but to give up before the process is over is to miss the rich rewards that are down the road. We can travel that road successfully if we join with others for strength and support.

WHY CHANGE?

What rewards are there for us in this process? Much of what society thinks of as being manly is really a way of hardening up so we can dominate or coerce other people. We pay a high price for this hardening, however; it means giving up much of our humanity. We men are conditioned to suppress our feelings and don't learn how to give and receive support, nurturance, and affection awarely. We are taught to take all the responsibility for a situation on our own shoulders. We are taught to have heavy expectations of accomplishment for ourselves and for others. The direct result of this is a high level of tension and anxiety; the indirect result is a high disease rate and early death.

So, as men we have a lot to gain by fighting sexism. From what we have seen and experienced, men (at least in the long run) feel relief and joy just from being freed from the roles that lead to the oppression of women.

But this in no way means that we change easily. Conditioning is far too strong, and the temptation to keep the privilege too great. Nor does it mean, as some people suggest, that "men and women are both oppressed equally by sexism." However much men are hurt or limited by sex roles in this country, the fact remains that they are *not* systematically denied power simply because of being born a certain sex, as women are. Tremendous amounts of struggle will be required—as well as lots of loving support, especially from other men— to undergo the process of change.

RACISM, AGEISM, AND THE OPPRESSION OF LESBIANS AND GAY MEN

All forms of oppression in our society are closely connected both to each other and to our economic system. Racism, for example, has many close parallels with sexism. Racial minorities, like women, function as a "reserve labor force," shunted into unattractive jobs with little reward or decision-making power, pushed in and out of employment as benefits the system. Racism, like sexism, divides working people from one another, preventing them from looking at who holds most of the power in our country. Racial minorities, like women, are thought to be unintelligent and to have less motivation to achieve and work hard than white males. Both groups are kept in place by violent intimidation and are referred to with abusive words. Both frequently get deflected from militant struggle against the oppression of their group by co-optation of a few of their leaders into the lower levels of the power structure. In addition, sexual myths and paranoia about blacks and Latinos play an especially vicious role in undergirding white people's racial fears and stereotypes.

People are just beginning to have a glimpse of what oppression based on age involves. The fact is that our society is almost totally blind to the dignity and capacities of the very young and the very old. Children are like women in being considered helpless, dependent, and cute—creatures to be cherished and taken care of, but not full human beings to be deeply respected and trusted with significant power. They experience 10–15 years of unpaid labor and brainwashing in our current form of education. Older people are looked at as children—except that they often find themselves without anyone interested in cherishing or taking care of them. For men, growing up is associated with taking on more and more of the hard masculine traits we mentioned before. Crying, acting afraid, and showing too much tenderness are all considered shameful because they are "childish" or "woman-like." ("You gotta stop that crying—don't be a sissy.")

Most of us know gay people, but usually we do not know who they are! Lesbians and gay men are so frequently hurt in this society that they usually do not feel safe to come out, even to their friends. An invisible colony of 20,000,000 people in our midst, lesbians and gay men generally work to service the status quo—even the Hollywood illusions of heterosexual romance—while their own dignity and security are denied.

People are still beaten and even killed for being homosexual in America, and the memory of the mass deaths of gays in Nazi concentration camps remains vivid. Now the "new right" is cutting back some recent gains lesbians and gay men have made in rights to jobs and housing. The fact that the same forces are opposing the Equal Rights Amendment and gay rights is a tip-off to the intimate connection between sexism and heterosexism. For one thing, gay men are mistakenly seen as taking the role of women in heterosexual relationships, and therefore not being "real men." For another, lesbians are seen as "uppity" because they act with a freedom not usually found when dependent upon men for loving.

Gay oppression is one of the ways the potential unity of all workers is prevented. It is also one of the cornerstones of the American nuclear family, which in turn is used to promote consumption and to teach sexist division of labor and sex roles. Lesbians and gay men are also exploited by being forced into ghettos and by the commercialized culture which profits from them.

Everyone is hurt by gay oppression. The fear of being considered gay limits and distorts everyone's life choices and relationships. Men are often afraid to get close to their male friends because it might imply gayness—and might even reveal a half-suspected gay dimension of themselves. An essential prop for sexism, in keeping people within their accustomed sex roles, is this fear of homosexuality, or homophobia. Because of this, women's liberation and men's liberation depend partly on gay liberation. . . .

IDEOLOGICAL RACISM AND CULTURAL RESISTANCE

22

Constructing Our Own Images

Yen Le Espiritu

. . . A central aspect of racial exploitation centers on defining people of color as "the other" (Said, 1979). The social construction of Asian American "otherness"—through such controlling images as the Yellow Peril, the model minority, the Dragon Lady, and the China Doll—is "the precondition for their cultural marginalization, political impotence, and psychic alienation from mainstream American society" (Hamamoto, 1994, p. 5). As indicated by these stereotypes, representations of gender and sexuality figure strongly in the articulation of racism. These racist stereotypes collapse gender and sexuality: Asian men have been constructed as hypermasculine, in the image of the "Yellow Peril," but also as effeminate, in the image of the "model minority," and Asian women have been depicted as superfeminine, in the image of the "China Doll," but also as castrating, in the image of the "Dragon Lady" (Mullings, 1994, pp. 279–280; Okihiro, 1995). As Mary Ann Doane (1991) suggested, sexuality is "indissociable from the effects of polarization and differentiation, often linking them to structures of power and domination" (p. 217). In the

From: Yen Le Espiritu, *Asian American Women and Men* (Thousand Oaks, CA: Sage, 1997). Reprinted by permission of Sage Publications, Inc.

Asian American case, the gendering of ethnicity—the process whereby white ideology assigns selected gender characteristics to various ethnic "others"—cast Asian American men and women as simultaneously masculine and feminine but also as neither masculine nor feminine. On the one hand, as part of the Yellow Peril, Asian American men and women have been depicted as a *masculine* threat that needs to be contained. On the other hand, both sexes have been skewed toward the female side: an indication of the group's marginalization in U.S. society and its role as the compliant "model minority" in contemporary U.S. cultural ideology. Although an apparent disjunction, both the feminization and masculinization of Asian men and women exist to define and confirm the white man's superiority (Kim, 1990).

THE YELLOW PERIL

In the United States, Asia and America—East and West—are viewed as mutually exclusive binaries (Kim, 1993, p. viii). Within this exclusive binary system, Asian Americans, even as citizens, are designated Asians, not Americans. Characterizing Asian Americans as "permanent houseguests in the house of America," Sau-Ling Cynthia Wong (1993) stated that "Asian Americans are put in the niche of the 'unassimilable alien': . . . they are alleged to be self-disqualified from full American membership by materialistic motives, questionable political allegiance, and, above all, outlandish, overripe, 'Oriental' cultures" (p. 6). Sonia Shah (1994) defined this form of "cultural discrimination" as a "peculiar blend of cultural and sexist oppression based on our accents, our clothes, our foods, our values and our commitments" (p. 182). This cultural discrimination brands Asians as perpetual foreigners and thus perpetuates the notion of their alleged racial unassimilability. For example, although Japanese Americans have lived in the United States since the turn of the century, many television programs, such as *Happy Days* (1974–1984) and *Gung Ho* (1986–1987), have continued to portray them as newly arrived foreigners (Hamamoto, 1994, p. 13).

As the unassimilable alien, Asian Americans embody for many other Americans the "Yellow Peril"—the threat that Asians will one day unite and conquer the world. This threat includes military invasion and foreign trade from Asia, competition to white labor from Asian labor, the alleged moral degeneracy of Asian people, and potential miscegenation between whites and Asians (Wu, 1982, p. 1). Between 1850 and 1940, U.S. popular media consistently portrayed Asian men as a military threat to the security and welfare of the United States *and* as a sexual danger to innocent white women (Wu, 1982). In numerous dime novels, movies, and comic strips, Asians appeared as feral, rat-faced men lusting after virginal white women. Arguing for racial purity, these popular media depicted Asian-white sexual union as "at best, a form of beastly sodomy, and, at worst, a Satanic marriage" (Hoppenstand, 1983, p. 174). In these popular depictions, the white man was the desirable sexual partner and the hero who rescued the white woman from "a fate worse than death" (Hoppenstand, 1983, pp. 174–175). By the mid-1880s, hundreds of garishly illustrated and garishly written dime novels were being disseminated among a wide audience, sporting such sensational titles as *The Bradys and the Yellow Crooks, The Chase for the Chinese Diamonds, The Opium Den Detective,* and *The Stranglers of New York.* As portrayed in these dime novels, the Yellow Peril was the Chinatown district of a big city "in which decent, honest white folk never ventured" (Hoppenstand, 1983, p. 177).

In 20th-century U.S. popular media, the Japanese joined the Chinese as a perceived threat to Europe and the United States (Wu, 1982, p. 2). In 1916, William Randolph Hearst produced and distributed *Petria,* a movie about a group of fanatical Japanese who invade the United States and attempt to rape a white woman (Quinsaat, 1976, p. 265). After the Japanese bombing of Pearl Harbor on December 7, 1941, the entire Yellow Peril stereotype became incorporated in the nation's war propaganda, quickly whipping white Americans into a war fever. Along with the print media, Hollywood cranked up its anti-Japanese propaganda and produced dozens of war films that centered on the Japanese menace. The fiction of the Yellow Peril stereotype became intertwined with the fact of the United States' war with Japan, and the two became one in the mind-set of the American public (Hoppenstand, 1983, pp. 182–183). It was fear of the Yellow Peril—fear of the rise of nonwhite people and their contestation of white supremacy—that led to the declaration of martial law in Hawaii on December 7, 1941, and to the internment of over 110,000 Japanese on the mainland in concentration camps (Okihiro, 1994, p. 137). In subsequent decades, reflecting changing geopolitical concerns, U.S. popular media featured a host of new yellow peril stereotypes. During the 1950s Cold War years, in television programs as well as in movies, the Communist Chinese evildoers replaced the Japanese monster; during the Vietnam war of the 1970s, the Vietnamese Communists emerged as the new Oriental villains.

Today, Yellow Perilism takes the forms of the greedy, calculating, and clever Japanese businessman aggressively buying up U.S. real estate and cultural institutions *and* the superachieving but nonassimilating Asian Americans (Hagedorn, 1993, p. xxii). In a time of rising economic powers in Asia, declining economic opportunities in the United States, and growing diversity among America's people, this new Yellow Perilism—the depiction of Asian and Asian Americans as economic and cultural threats to mainstream United States—supplies white Americans with a united identity and provides ideological justification for U.S. isolationist policy toward Asia, increasing restrictions against Asian (and Latino) immigration, and the invisible institutional racism and visible violence against Asians in the United States (Okihiro, 1994, pp. 138–139).

THE RACIAL CONSTRUCTION
OF ASIAN AMERICAN MANHOOD

Like other men of color, Asian American men have been excluded from white-based cultural notions of the masculine. Whereas white men are depicted both as virile and as protectors of women, Asian men have been characterized both as asexual *and* as threats to white women. It is important to note the historical contexts of these seemingly divergent representations of Asian American manhood. The racist depictions of Asian men as "lascivious and predatory" were especially pronounced during the nativist movement against Asians at the turn of the century (Frankenberg, 1993, pp. 75–76). The exclusion of Asian women from the United States and the subsequent establishment of bachelor societies eventually reversed the construction of Asian masculinity from "hypersexual" to "asexual" and even "homosexual." The contemporary model-minority stereotype further emasculates Asian American men as passive and malleable. Disseminated and perpetuated through the popular media, these stereotypes of the emasculated Asian male construct a reality in which social and economic discrimination against these men appears defensible. As an example, the desexualization of Asian men naturalized their inability to establish conjugal families in pre-World War II United States. Gliding over race-based exclusion laws that banned the immigration of most Asian women and antimiscegenation laws that prohibited men of color from marrying white women, these dual images of the eunuch and the rapist attributed the "womanless households" characteristics of pre-war Asian America to Asian men's lack of sexual prowess and desirability.

A popular controlling image applied to Asian American men is that of the sinister Oriental—a brilliant, powerful villain who plots the destruction of Western civilization. Personified by the movie character of Dr. Fu Manchu, this Oriental mastermind combines Western science with Eastern magic and commands an army of devoted assassins (Hoppenstand, 1983, p. 178). Though ruthless, Fu Manchu lacks masculine heterosexual prowess (Wang, 1988, p. 19), thus privileging heterosexuality. Frank Chin and Jeffrey Chan (1972), in a critique of the desexualization of Asian men in Western culture, described how the Fu Manchu character undermines Chinese American virility:

> Dr. Fu, a man wearing a long dress, batting his eyelashes, surround by muscular black servants in loin cloths, and with his habit of caressingly touching white men on the leg, wrist, and face with his long fingernails is not so much a threat as he is a frivolous offense to white manhood. (p. 60)

In another critique that glorifies male aggression, Frank Chin (1972) contrasted the neuterlike characteristics assigned to Asian men to the sexually aggressive images associated with other men of color. "Unlike the white stereo-type of the evil black stud, Indian rapist, Mexican macho, the evil of the evil Dr. Fu Manchu was not sexual, but homosexual" (p. 66). However, Chin failed to note that as a homosexual, Dr. Fu (and by extension, Asian men) threatens and offends white masculinity—and therefore needs to be contained ideolog-ically and destroyed physically.

Whereas the evil Oriental stereotype marks Asian American men as the white man's enemy, the stereotype of the sexless Asian sidekick—Charlie Chan, the Chinese laundryman, the Filipino houseboy—depicts Asian men as devoted and impotent, eager to please. William Wu (1982) reported that the Chinese servant "is the most important single image of the Chinese immi-grants" in American fiction about Chinese Americans between 1850 and 1940 (p. 60). More recently, such diverse television programs as *Bachelor Father* (1957–1962), *Bonanza* (1959–1973), *Star Trek* (1966–1969), and *Falcon Crest* (1981–1990) all featured the stock Chinese bachelor domestic who dispenses sage advice to his superiors in addition to performing traditional female func-tions within the household (Hamamoto, 1994, p. 7). By trapping Chinese men (and by extension, Asian men) in the stereotypical "feminine" tasks of serving white men, American society erases the figure of the Asian "masculine" planta-tion worker in Hawaii or railroad construction worker in the western United States, thus perpetuating the myth of the androgynous and effeminate Asian man (Goellnicht, 1982, p 198). This feminization, in turn, confines Asian im-migrant men to the segment of the labor force that performs women's work.

The motion picture industry has been key in the construction of Asian men as sexual deviants. In a study of Asians in the U.S. motion pictures, Eu-gene Franklin Wong (1978) maintained that the movie industry filmically cas-trates Asian males to magnify the superior sexual status of white males (p. 27). As on-screen sexual rivals of whites, Asian males are neutralized, unable to sexually engage Asian women and prohibited from sexually engaging white women. By saving the white women from sexual contact with the racial "other," the motion picture industry protects the Anglo-American, bourgeois male es-tablishment from any challenges to its hegemony (Marchetti, 1993, p. 218). At the other extreme, the industry has exploited on the most potent aspects of the Yellow Peril discourses—the sexual danger of contact between the races— by concocting a sexually threatening portrayal of the licentious and aggressive Yellow Man lusting after the White Woman (Marchetti, 1993, p. 3). Heedful of the larger society's taboos against Asian male-white female sexual union, white male actors donning "yellowface"—instead of Asian male actors—are used in these "love scenes." Nevertheless, the message of the perverse and ani-malistic Asian male attacking helpless white women is clear (Wong, 1978). Though depicting sexual aggression, this image of the rapist, like that of the eunuch, casts Asian men as sexually undesirable. As Wong (1978) succinctly stated, in Asian male–white female relations, "There can be rape, but there cannot be romance" (p. 25). Thus, Asian males yield to the sexual superiority of the white males who are permitted filmically to maintain their sexual dominance over both white women and women of color. A young Vietnamese American man describes the damaging effect of these stereotypes on his self-image:

> Every day I was forced to look into a mirror created by white society and its media. As a young Asian man, I shrank before white eyes. I wasn't tall, I wasn't fair, I wasn't muscular, and so on. Combine that with the enormous insecurities any pubescent teenager feels, and I have no difficulty in knowing now why I felt naked before a mass of white people. (Nguyen, 1990, p. 23)

White cultural and institutional racism against Asian males is also reflected in the motion picture industry's preoccupation with the death of Asians—a filmic solution to the threats of the Yellow Peril. In a perceptive analysis of Hollywood's view of Asians in films made from the 1930s to the 1960s, Tom Engelhardt (1976) described how Asians, like Native Americans, are seen by the movie industry as inhuman invaders, ripe for extermination. He argued that the theme of the nonhumanness of Asians prepares the audience to accept, without flinching, "the levelling and near-obliteration of three Asian areas in the course of three decades" (Engelhardt, 1976, p. 273). The industry's death theme, though applying to all Asians, is mainly focused on Asian males, with Asian females reserved for sexual purposes (Wong, 1978, p. 35). Especially in war films, Asian males, however advantageous their initial position, inevitably perish at the hands of the superior white males (Wong, 1978, p. 34).

THE RACIAL CONSTRUCTION
OF ASIAN AMERICAN WOMANHOOD

Like Asian men, Asian women have been reduced to one-dimensional caricatures in Western representation. The condensation of Asian women's multiple differences into gross character types—mysterious, feminine, and non-white—obscures the social injustice of racial, class, and gender oppression (Marchetti, 1993, p. 71). Both Western film and literature promote dichotomous stereotypes of the Asian woman: Either she is the cunning Dragon Lady or the servile Lotus Blossom Baby (Tong, 1994, p. 197). Though connoting two extremes, these stereotypes are interrelated: Both eroticize Asian women as exotic "others"—sensuous, promiscuous, but untrustworthy. Whereas American popular culture denies "manhood" to Asian men, it endows Asian women with an excess of "womanhood," sexualizing them but also impugning their sexuality. In this process, both sexism and racism have been blended together to produce the sexualization of white racism (Wong, 1978, p. 260). Linking the controlling images of Asian men and women, Elaine Kim (1990) suggested that Asian women are portrayed as sexual for the same reasons that men are asexual: "Both exist to define the white man's virility and the white man's superiority" (p. 70).

As the racialized exotic "others," Asian American women do not fit the white-constructed notions of the feminine. Whereas white women have been depicted as chaste and dependable, Asian women have been represented as promiscuous and untrustworthy. In a mirror image of the evil Fu Manchu, the Asian woman was portrayed as the castrating Dragon Lady who, while puffing on her foot-long cigarette holder, could poison a man as easily as she could seduce him. "With her talon-like six-inch fingernails, her skin-tight satin dress slit to the thigh," the Dragon Lady is desirable, deceitful, and dangerous (Ling, 1990, p. 11). In the 1924 film *The Thief of Baghdad,* Anna May Wong, a pioneer Chinese American actress, played a handmaid who employed treachery to help an evil Mongol prince attempt to win the hand of the Princess of Baghdad (Tajima, 1989, p. 309). In so doing, Wong unwittingly popularized a common Dragon Lady social type: treacherous women who are partners in crime with men of their own kind. The publication of *Daughter of Fu Manchu* (1931) firmly entrenched the Dragon Lady image in white consciousness. Carrying on her father's work as the champion of Asian hegemony over the white race, Fah Lo Sue exhibited, in the words of American studies scholar, William F. Wu, "exotic sensuality, sexual availability to a white man, and a treacherous nature" (cited in Tong, 1994, p. 197). A few years later, in 1934, Milton Caniff inserted into his adventure comic strip *Terry and the Pirates* another version of the Dragon Lady who "combines all the best features of past moustache twirlers with the lure of the handsome wench" (Hoppenstand, 1983, p. 178). As such, Caniff's Dragon Lady fuses the image of the evil male Oriental mastermind with that of the Oriental prostitute first introduced some 50 years earlier in the dime novels.

At the opposite end of the spectrum is the Lotus Blossom stereotype, reincarnated throughout the years as the China Doll, the Geisha Girl, the War Bride, or the Vietnamese prostitute—many of whom are the spoils of the last three wars fought in Asia (Tajima, 1989, p. 309). Demure, diminutive, and deferential, the Lotus Blossom Baby is "modest, tittering behind her delicate ivory hand, eyes downcast, always walking ten steps behind her man, and, best of all, devot[ing] body and soul to serving him" (Ling, 1990, p. 11). Interchangeable in appearance and name, these women have no voice; their "nonlanguage" includes uninterpretable chattering, pidgin English, giggling, or silence (Tajima, 1989). These stereotypes of Asian women as submissive and dainty sex objects not only have impeded women's economic mobility but also have fostered an enormous demand for X-rated films and pornographic materials featuring Asian women in bondage, for "Oriental" bathhouse workers in U.S. cities, and for Asian mail-order brides (Kim, 1984, p. 64).

SEXISM, RACISM, AND LOVE

The racialization of Asian manhood and womanhood upholds white masculine hegemony. Cast as sexually available, Asian women become yet another possession of the white man. In motion pictures and network programs, interracial sexuality, though rare, occurs principally between a white male and an Asian female. A combination of sexism and racism makes this form of miscegenation more acceptable: Race mixing between an Asian male and a white female would upset not only racial taboos but those that attend patriarchal authority as well (Hamamoto, 1994, p. 39). Whereas Asian men are depicted as either the threatening rapist or the impotent eunuch, white men are endowed with the masculine attributes with which to sexually attract the Asian woman. Such popular television shows as *Gunsmoke* (1955–1975) and *How the West Was Won* (1978–1979) clearly articulate the theme of Asian female sexual possession by the white male. In these shows, only white males have the prerogative to cross racial boundaries and to choose freely from among women of color as sex partners. Within a system of racial and gender oppression, the sexual possession of women and men of color by white men becomes yet another means of enforcing unequal power relations (Hamamoto, 1994, p. 46).

The preference for white male-Asian female is also prevalent in contemporary television news broadcasting, most recently in the 1993–1995 pairing of Dan Rather and Connie Chung as coanchors of the *CBS Evening News*. Today, virtually every major metropolitan market across the United States today has at least one Asian American female newscaster (Hamamoto, 1994, p. 245). While female Asian American anchorpersons—Connie Chung, Tritia Toyota, Wendy Tokuda, and Emerald Yeh—are popular television news figures, there is a nearly total absence of Asian American men. Critics argue that this is so because the white male hiring establishment, and presumably the larger American public, feels more comfortable (i.e., less threatened) seeing a white male sitting next to a minority female at the anchor desk than the reverse. Stephen Tschida of WDBJ-TV (Roanoke, Virginia), one of only a handful of male Asian American television news anchors, was informed early in his career that he did not have the proper "look" to qualify for the anchorperson position. Other male broadcast news veterans have reported being passed over for younger, more beauteous, female Asian Americans (Hamamoto, 1994, p. 245). This gender imbalance sustains the construction of Asian American women as more successful, assimilated, attractive, and desirable than their male counterparts. . . .

CONCLUSION

Ideological representations of gender and sexuality are central in the exercise and maintenance of racial, patriarchal, and class domination. In the Asian American case, this ideological racism has taken seemingly contrasting forms: Asian men have been cast as both hypersexual and asexual, and Asian women have been rendered both superfeminine and masculine. Although in apparent disjunction, both forms exist to define, maintain, and justify white male supremacy. The racialization of Asian American manhood and womanhood underscores the interconnections of race, gender, and class. As categories of difference, race and gender relations do not parallel but intersect and confirm each other, and it is the complicity among these categories of difference that enables U.S. elites to justify and maintain their cultural, social, and economic power. Responding to the ideological assaults on their gender identities, Asian American cultural workers have engaged in a wide range of oppositional projects to defend Asian American manhood and womanhood. In the process, some have embraced a masculinist cultural nationalism, a stance that marginalizes Asian American women and their needs. Though sensitive to the emasculation of Asian American men, Asian American feminists have pointed out that Asian American nationalism insists on a fixed masculinist identity, thus obscuring gender differences. Though divergent, both the nationalist and feminist positions advance the dichotomous stance of man or woman, gender or race or class, without recognizing the complex relationality of these categories of oppression. It is only when Asian Americans recognize the intersections of race, gender, and class that we can transform the existing hierarchical structure.

References

Chin, F. (1972). Confessions of the Chinatown cowboy. *Bulletin of Concerned Asian Scholars, 4*(3), 66.

Chin. F., & Chan, J. P. (1972). Racist love. In R. Kostelanetz (Ed.), *Seeing through shuck* (pp. 65–79). New York: Ballantine.

Doane, M. A. (1991). *Femme fatales: Feminism, film theory, psychoanalysis.* New York: Routledge.

Engelhardt, T. (1976). Ambush at Kamikaze Pass. In E. Gee (Ed.), *Counterpoint: Perspectives on Asian America* (pp. 270–279). Los Angeles: University of California at Los Angeles, Asian American Studies Center.

Frankenberg, R. (1993). *White women, race matters: The social construction of whiteness.* Minneapolis: University of Minnesota Press.

Goellnicht, D. C. (1992). Tang Ao in America: Male subject positions in *China Men.* In S. G. Linn & A. Ling (Eds.), *Reading the literatures of Asian America* (pp. 191–212). Philadelphia: Temple University Press.

Hagedorn, J. (1993). Introduction: "Role of dead man require very little acting." In J. Hagedorn (Ed.), *Charlie Chan is dead: An anthology of contemporary Asian American fiction* (pp. xxi–xxx). New York: Penguin.

Hamamoto, D. Y. (1994). *Monitored peril: Asian Americans and the politics of representation.* Minneapolis: University of Minnesota Press.

Hoppenstand, G. (1983). Yellow devil doctors and opium dens: A survey of the yellow peril stereotypes in mass media entertainment. In C. D. Geist & J. Nachbar (Eds.), *The popular culture reader* (3rd ed., pp. 171–185). Bowling Green, OH: Bowling Green University Press.

Kim, E. (1984). Asian American writers: A bibliographical review. *American Studies International, 22,* 2.

Kim, E. (1990), "Such opposite creatures": Men and women in Asian American literature. *Michigan Quarterly Review, 29,* 68–93.

Ling, A. (1990). *Between worlds: Women writers of Chinese ancestry.* New York: Pergamon.

Marchetti, G. (1993). *Romance and the "Yellow Peril": Race, sex, and discursive strategies in Hollywood fiction.* Berkeley: University of California Press.

Mullings, L. (1994). Images, ideology, and women of color. In M. Baca Zinn & B. T. Dill (Eds.), *Women of color in U.S. society* (pp. 265–289). Philadelphia: Temple University Press.

Nguyen, V. (1990, December 7). Growing up in white America. *Asian Week,* p. 23.

Okihiro, G. Y. (1994). *Margins and mainstreams: Asians in American history and culture.* Seattle: University of Washington Press.

Okihiro, G. Y. (1995, November). *Reading Asian bodies, reading anxieties.* Paper presented at the University of California, San Diego Ethnic Studies Colloquium, La Jolla.

Quinsaat, J. (1976). Asians in the media. The shadows in the spotlight. In E. Gee (Ed.), *Counterpoint: Perspectives on Asian America* (pp. 264–269). Los Angeles: University of California at Los Angeles, Asian American Studies Center.

Said, E. (1979). *Orientalism.* New York: Random House.

Shah, S. (1994). Presenting the Blue Goddess: Toward a national, Pan-Asian Feminist agenda. In K. Aguilar-San Juan (Ed.), *The state of Asian America: Activism and resistance in the 1990s* (pp. 147–158). Boston: South End.

Tajima, R. (1989). Lotus blossoms don't bleed: Images of Asian women. In Asian Women United of California (Ed.), *Making waves: An anthology of writings by and about Asian American women* (pp. 308–317). Boston: Beacon.

Tong, B. (1994). *Unsubmissive women: Chinese prostitutes in nineteenth-century San Francisco.* Norman: University of Oklahoma Press.

Wang, A. (1988). Maxine Hong Kingston's reclaiming of America: The birthright of the Chinese American male. *South Dakota Review, 26,* 18–29.

Wong, E. F. (1978). *On visual media racism: Asians in the American motion pictures.* New York: Arno.

Wong, S.-L. C. (1993). *Reading Asian American literature: From necessity to extravagance.* Princeton, NJ: Princeton University Press.

Wu, W. F. (1982). *The Yellow Peril: Chinese Americans in American fiction 1850–1940.* Hamden, CT: Archon.

"J.A.P."-SLAPPING: *The Politics of Scapegoating*   23

Ruth Atkin and Adrienne Rich

Those who remember World War II may well recall the racist imagery and language levelled at Japanese people. The Japanese, formerly idealized as giving us exquisite art, magical paper toys, flower arranging, swiftly became the "Japs," to be "slapped" by American military force: yellow, toothy torturers with a genetic flair for cruelty, the dastardly bombers of Pearl Harbor; the people who would deserve the genocidal bombings of Hiroshima and Nagasaki. The word "Jap" held its own in the monosyllabic language of "kike," "wop," "spic," "chink," "bitch," "slut"—short, brutal sounds like the impact of a fist. "Slap That Jap" was a familiar wartime slogan.

These memories of the 1940s are part of the background some of us bring to the recent explosion of "Jewish-American Princess" stereotypes on Eastern college campuses. The Jewish feminist magazine *Lilith* first reported the phenomenon in its Fall 1987 issue (#17); since then, articles have appeared in the *New York Times* and the Jewish press. A column, "No Laughing Matter," by Suzanne Messing, appeared in the feminist paper *New Directions for Women.* On December 9, National Public Radio broadcast a segment on the spread of "J.A.P.-baiting," interviewing Eveyln Torton Beck, Professor of Women's Studies at the University of Maryland and editor of *Nice Jewish Girls: A Lesbian Anthology.*

"J.A.P."-baiting has taken a range of forms: novels by post–World War II American Jewish writers such as Herman Wouk's *Marjorie Morningstar;* the routines of Jewish comedians; negative stereotyping of middle-class Jewish women in greeting cards, jewelry, T-shirts, graffiti; and ritualized verbal assaults on Jewish women on college campuses. The Jewish woman is stereotyped as rich, spoiled, avidly materialistic, and solely out for herself. Most of

From: Originally published in *Gesher*, the feminist newsletter of New Jewish Agenda. January 1988, vol. 2, issue 2, pp. 4–5. Reprinted by permission of the authors.

the negative attributes are, of course, familiar anti-Jewish stereotypes: here they are pushed onto the Jewish woman. *Lilith* reported that at Syracuse University basketball games, the pep band would point at certain women who stood up and chant "JAP, JAP, JAP." On other campuses have appeared such graffiti as: "I tolerate JAPS for sex"; "All JAPS are sluts"; "Solution to the JAP question: when they go for their nose jobs, tie their tubes as well." (This last griffito is packed with implications: the "J.A.P." is trying to assimilate, to pass; Jewish women should be sterilized [as thousands were under Hitler]. It implies a knowledge of Nazi vocabulary and practice that belies the theory of "J.A.P."-baiting as ignorant fun and games.)

A different kind of hostility identifies the "J.A.P." not as a "slut" but as a "frigid" woman, unwilling to "put out" sexually. Messing quotes a greeting card (published by Noble Press, New York): "Why do JAPS close their eyes while having sex? So they can pretend they're shopping." National Public Radio reports a fun-fair booth: "Make Her Prove She's Not a JAP—Make Her Swallow."

"J.A.P." imagery has been acceptable in the Jewish community and continues to be. According to the Chicago *Jewish Sentinel*, the National Federation of Temple Sisterhoods adopted a resolution at their national convention this fall condemning "J.A.P." jokes and images, since what began as an object of sexist humor has now become a tool of the anti-Semite. The resolution called on member sisterhoods to discontinue the sale of "J.A.P. items" in their Judaica shops. But if the sisterhoods had challenged the stereotyping of Jewish women from the first, it might have stood less chance to become the tool of the anti-Semite, and within the Jewish community "JAP items" would not have received the endorsement of the National Federation. The issue is sometimes trivialized as a matter of humor ("we can laugh at ourselves"), or on the grounds that the negative stereotypes contain a "kernel of truth." We need to examine these responses.

The semiotics, or signifying power, of the "J.A.P." stereotype is complex. A clear feminist perception is needed to decipher the scapegoating of the women within a historically scapegoated group. Within the Jewish community, scapegoating and negative labelling of Jewish women may reflect tensions over gender roles and conflicts specific to the group. They also reveal how Jews participate in the sexism of the society at large.

"Kaleidoscopic" is Susan Schnur's term (in *Lilith*) for the "JAP theme." Rarely have two forms of social hatred—misogyny and anti-Semitism—been so explicitly joined: the "materialistic, pushy" Jew and the "princess," the selfish, privileged rich woman. Conflate these two identities and you have an easy target in a time when the presence of women on campuses is threatening to men, when jobs after college are at a premium, and any woman can be perceived by any man as a competitor for his future job. In fact, "J.A.P." is a conflation of three hated identities: Jew, woman, and those people who are seen, in a society of vast inequalities and injustice, as having "made it."

But to understand the "J.A.P."-baiting phenomenon fully we need an understanding of how the mechanisms of anti-Jewish thought operate. The "Jewish Mother" stereotype—of a too-assertive, domineering woman, devouring the lives of her children—a leftover of the community-building, survival orientation of immigrant culture, is followed by the "Jewish-American Princess." The next generation of epithets directed at Jewish women reflects the assimilation of the daughters into American society. As with any stereotype, a complex social pattern is crudely and simplistically caricatured. Young Jewish women are scapegoated for the material "success" of their parents' (usually their fathers') earning power. Scapegoating young Jewish women fits into the historic cyclical pattern of Jewish oppression, whereby some Jews have allowed a limited access to power (as tax-collectors, money-lenders, etc.), creating the illusion of Jews overall having power. Every period of toleration of Jews in host countries has been followed by periods of economic and social unrest when ruling interests have withdrawn "protection" and support of Jews, and have encouraged the general population to direct their resentments against Jews. This phase has been brutal in the extreme: Eastern European pogroms; the Nazi camps.

Increasing numbers of people in America today are without basic necessities and comforts. The current atmosphere of growing resentment of material success is fully justified. But its historic precedents, for Jews, are troubling. As the economic situation in the U.S. widens the gap between rich and poor, we need to be on the alert for expressions of anger and frustration which divert attention from the real sources of economic hardship—the prioritizing of death over life, of profit over the basic needs of people. This hardship is shared by many Jews, especially older Jewish women. It is not a coincidence that "J.A.P."-baiting is occurring on college campuses, perceived as places of privilege.

Jews have been perceived, and to a certain extent correctly, as a "successful" minority group in America. Writing in *Lilith*, Francine Klagsbrun asks: "Isn't it odd that the term JAP, referring to a spoiled, self-indulgent woman, should be so widely used at a time when women are working outside their homes in unprecedented numbers, struggling to balance their home lives and their work lives, to give as much of themselves as they can to everybody— their husbands, their kids, their bosses?" In the same issue, Susan Schnur notes that "the characterizations of JAPS and Yuppies are often identical." She sees the label of Yuppies as "neutral or even positive," but many a bitter, long-stored anti-Yuppie joke was heard when Wall Street crashed last October. And it is perhaps not coincidental that the acronym "JAP" fits so neatly into a growing anti-Asian racism that has accomplished the increased perception of Asians as a "successful" minority. Insofar as a fraternity house booth invites passers-by to "Slap a JAP" echoes the "Slap That Jap: Buy War Bonds" posters of World War II, it legitimizes anti-Semitism, misogyny, and anti-Asian racism simultaneously.

As the U.S. economy wavers, as American national identity itself wavers, anti-Semitism is one time-honored escape from critical thinking and political responsibility. Young Jewish women on college campuses may have received little in their education to help them interpret this double assault—especially since the "JAP" label can be applied to non-Jews as well. Some older Jewish women, too, as articles in both *Lilith* and *New Directions for Women* indicate, have reacted by accepting stereotyping, by suggesting that "We should be able to laugh at ourselves." Both Jewish men and women tell "J.A.P." jokes. But, according to Messing, "No one refers to herself as a JAP." Francine Klagsbrun observes, "When we put down other Jewish women, that is a form of self-hatred."

And yes, we do need to laugh at ourselves. But our humor cannot—for our own health—be founded on self-hatred. When we delight in ourselves as women, delight in ourselves as Jews, we can laugh out of the fullness of recognizing ourselves as necessarily flawed and sometimes ridiculous human beings. Our humor need not come out of the arsenal of those who would deny us our humanity.

NOTE

1. Thanks to *Lilith: The Jewish Women's Magazine*, 250 W. 57th Street, New York, NY 10107; *New Directions for Women*, 108 Palisade Ave., Englewood, NJ 07631; the Chicago *Jewish Sentinel*, 323 S. Franklin St., Rm. 501, Chicago, IL 60606.

A NEW VISION OF MASCULINITY   24

Cooper Thompson

I was once asked by a teacher in a suburban high school to give a guest presentation on male roles. She hoped that I might help her deal with four boys who exercised extraordinary control over the other boys in the class. Using ridicule and their status as physically imposing athletes, these four wrestlers had succeeded in stifling the participation of the other boys, who were reluctant to make comments in class discussions.

As a class we talked about the ways in which boys got status in that school and how they got put down by others. I was told that the most humiliating put-down was being called a "fag." The list of behaviors which could elicit ridicule filled two large chalkboards, and it was detailed and comprehensive; I got the sense that a boy in this school had to conform to rigid, narrow standards of masculinity to avoid being called a fag. I, too, felt this pressure and became very conscious of my mannerisms in front of the group. Partly from exasperation, I decided to test the seriousness of these assertions. Since one of the four boys had some streaks of pink in his shirt, and since he had told me that wearing pink was grounds for being called a fag, I told him that I thought he was a fag. Instead of laughing, he said, "I'm going to kill you."

Such is the stereotypic definition of strength that is associated with masculinity. But it is a very limited definition of strength, one based on dominance and control and acquired through the humiliation and degradation of others.

Contrast this with a view of strength offered by Pam McAllister in her introduction to *Reweaving the Web of Life:*

> The "Strength" card in my Tarot deck depicts, not a warrior going off to battle with his armor and his mighty sword, but a woman stroking a lion. The woman has not slain the lion nor maced it, not netted it, nor has she put on it a muzzle or a leash. And though the lion clearly has teeth and long sharp claws, the woman is not hiding, nor has she sought a protector, nor has she grown muscles. She doesn't appear to be talking to the lion nor flattering it, nor tossing it fresh meat to distract its hungry jaws.
>
> The woman on the "Strength" card wears a flowing white dress and a garland of flowers. With one hand she cups the lion's jaws, with the other she caresses its nose. The lion on the card has big yellow eyes and a long red

tongue curling out of its mouth. One paw is lifted and the mane falls in thick red curls across its broad torso. The woman. The lion. Together they depict strength.

This image of strength stands in direct contrast to the strength embodied in the actions of the four wrestlers. The collective strength of the woman and the lion is a strength unknown in a system of traditional male values. Other human qualities are equally foreign to a traditional conception of masculinity. In workshops I've offered on the male role stereotype, teachers and other school personnel easily generate lists of attitudes and behaviors which boys typically seem to not learn. Included in this list are being supportive and nurturant, accepting one's vulnerability and being able to ask for help, valuing women and "women's work," understanding and expressing emotions (except for anger), the ability to empathize with and empower other people, and learning to resolve conflict in nonaggressive, noncompetitive ways.

LEARNING VIOLENCE

All of this should come as no surprise. Traditional definitions of masculinity include attributes such as independence, price, resiliency, self-control, and physical strength. This is precisely the image of the Marlboro man, and to some extent, these are desirable attributes for boys and girls. But masculinity goes beyond these qualities to stress competitiveness, toughness, aggressiveness, and power. In this context, threats to one's status, however small, cannot be avoided or taken lightly. If a boy is called a fag, it means that he is perceived as weak or timid—and therefore not masculine enough for his peers. There is enormous pressure for him to fight back. Not being tough at these moments only proves the allegation.

Violence is learned not just as a way for boys to defend allegations that they are feminized, but as an effective, appropriate way for them to normally behave. In "The Civic Advocacy of Violence" [*M.*, Spring 1982] Wayne Ewing clearly states:

> I used to think that we simply tolerated and permitted male abusiveness in our society. I have now come to understand rather, that we advocate physical violence. Violence is presented as effective. Violence is taught as the normal, appropriate and necessary behavior of power and control. Analyses which interweave advocacy of male violence with "Super Bowl Culture" have never been refuted. Civic expectations—translated into professionalism, financial commitments, city planning for recreational space, the raising of male children for competitive sport, the corporate ethics of business ownership of athletic teams, profiteering on entertainment—all result in the monument of the National Football League, symbol and reality at once of the advocacy of violence.

Ultimately, violence is the tool which maintains what I believe are the two most crucial socializing forces in a boy's life: *homophobia*, the hatred of gay men (who are stereotyped as feminine) or those men believed to be gay, as well as the fear of being perceived as gay; and *misogyny*, the hatred of women. The two forces are targeted at different classes of victims, but they are really just the flip sides of the same coin. Homophobia is the hatred of feminine qualities in men while misogyny is the hatred of feminine qualities in women. The boy who is called a fag is the target of other boy's homophobia as well as the victim of his own homophobia. While the overt message is the absolute need to avoid being feminized, the implication is that females—and all that they traditionally represent—are contemptible. The United States Marines have a philosophy which conveniently combines homophobia and misogyny in the belief that "When you want to create a group of male killers, you kill 'the woman' in them."

The pressures of homophobia and misogyny in boys' lives have been poignantly demonstrated to me each time that I have repeated a simple yet provocative activity with students. I ask them to answer the question, "If you woke up tomorrow and discovered that you were the opposite sex from the one you are now, how would you and your life be different?" Girls consistently indicate that there are clear advantages to being a boy—from increased independence and career opportunities to decreased risks of physical and sexual assault—and eagerly answer the question. But boys often express disgust at this possibility and even refuse sometimes to answer the question. In her reports of a broad-based survey using this question, Alice Baumgartner reports the following responses as typical of boys: "If I were a girl, I'd be stupid and weak as a string"; "I would have to wear makeup, cook, be a mother and yuckky stuff like that"; "I would have to hate snakes. Everything would be miserable"; "If I were a girl, I'd kill myself."

THE COSTS OF MASCULINITY

The costs associated with a traditional view of masculinity are enormous, and the damage occurs at both personal and societal levels. The belief that a boy should be tough (aggressive, competitive, and daring) can create emotional pain for him. While a few boys experience short-term success for their toughness, there is little security in the long run. Instead, it leads to a series of challenges which few, if any, boys ultimately win. There is no security in being at the top when so many other boys are competing for the same status. Toughness also leads to increased chances of stress, physical injury, and even early death. It is considered manly to take extreme physical risks and voluntarily engage in combative, hostile activities.

The flip side of toughness—nurturance—is not a quality perceived as masculine and thus not valued. Because of this boys and men experience a greater emotional distance from other people and few opportunities to participate in meaningful interpersonal relationships. Studies consistently show that fathers spend very small amounts of time interacting with their children. In addition, men report that they seldom have intimate relationships with other men, reflecting their homophobia. They are afraid of getting too close and don't know how to take down the walls they have built between themselves.

As boys grow older and accept adult roles, the larger social costs of masculinity clearly emerge. Most women experience male resistance to an expansion of women's roles; one of the assumptions of traditional masculinity is the belief that women should be subordinate to men. The consequence is that men are often not willing to accept females as equal, competent partners in personal and professional settings. Whether the setting is a sexual relationship, the family, the streets, or the battlefield, men are continuously engaged in efforts to dominate. Statistics on child abuse consistently indicate that the vast majority of abusers are men, and that there is no "typical" abuser. Rape may be the fastest growing crime in the United States. And it is men, regardless of nationality, who provoke and sustain war. In short, traditional masculinity is life threatening.

NEW SOCIALIZATION FOR BOYS

Masculinity, like many other human traits, is determined by both biological and environmental factors. While some believe that biological factors are significant in shaping some masculine behavior, there is undeniable evidence that cultural and environmental factors are strong enough to override biological impulses. What is it, then, that we should be teaching boys about being a man in a modern world?

- Boys must learn to accept their vulnerability, learn to express a range of emotions such as fear and sadness, and learn to ask for help and support in appropriate situations.
- Boys must learn to be gentle, nurturant, cooperative and communicative, and in particular, learn nonviolent means of resolving conflicts.
- Boys must learn to accept those attitudes and behaviors which have traditionally been labeled feminine as necessary for full human development— thereby reducing homophobia and misogyny. This is tantamount to teaching boys to love other boys and girls.

Certain qualities like courage, physical strength, and independence, which are traditionally associated with masculinity, are indeed positive qualities for males, provided that they are not manifested in obsessive ways nor used to exploit or dominate others. It is not necessary to completely disregard or unlearn what is traditionally called masculine. I believe, however, that the three areas above are crucial for developing a broader view of masculinity, one which is healthier for all life.

These three areas are equally crucial for reducing aggressive, violent behavior among boys and men. Males must learn to cherish life for the sake of their *own* wholeness as human beings, not just *for* their children, friends, and lovers. If males were more nurturant, they would be less likely to hurt those they love.

Leonard Eron, writing in the *American Psychologist*, puts the issue of unlearning aggression and learning nurturance in clear-cut terms:

> Socialization is crucial in determining levels of aggression. No matter how aggression is measured or observed, as a group males always score higher than females. But this is not true for all girls. There are some girls who seem to have been socialized like boys who are just as aggressive as boys. Just as some females can learn to be aggressive, so males can learn *not* to be aggressive. If we want to reduce the level of aggression in society, we should also discourage boys from aggression very early on in life and reward them too for others' behaviors; in other words, we should socialize boys more like girls, and they should be encouraged to develop socially positive qualities such as tenderness, cooperation, and aesthetic appreciation. The level of individual aggression in society will be reduced only when male adolescents and young adults, as a result of socialization, subscribe to the same standards of behavior as have been traditionally encouraged for women.

Where will this change in socialization occur? In his first few years, most of a boy's learning about masculinity comes from the influences of parents, siblings and images of masculinity such as those found on television. Massive efforts will be needed to make changes here. But at older ages, school curriculum and the school environment provide powerful reinforcing images of traditional masculinity. This reinforcement occurs through a variety of channels, including curriculum content, role modeling, and extracurricular activities, especially competitive sports.

School athletics are a microcosm of the socialization of male values. While participation in competitive activities can be enjoyable and healthy, it too easily becomes a lesson in the need for toughness, invulnerability, and dominance. Athletes learn to ignore their own injuries and pain and instead try to injure and inflict pain on others in their attempts to win, regardless of the cost to themselves or their opponents. Yet the lessons learned in athletics are believed to be vital for full and complete masculine development, and as a model for problem-solving in other areas of life.

In addition to encouraging traditional male values, schools provide too few experiences in nurturance, cooperation, negotiation, nonviolent conflict resolution, and strategies for empathizing with and empowering others. Schools should become places where boys have the opportunity to learn these skills; clearly, they won't learn them on the street, from peers, or on television.

SETTING NEW EXAMPLES

Despite the pressures on men to display their masculinity in traditional ways, there are examples of men and boys who are changing. "Fathering" is one example of a positive change. In recent years, there has been a popular emphasis on child-care activities, with men becoming more involved in providing care to children, both professionally and as fathers. This is a clear shift from the more traditional view that child rearing should be delegated to women and is not an appropriate activity for men.

For all of the male resistance it has generated, the Women's Liberation Movement has at least provided a stimulus for some men to accept women as equal partners in most areas of life. These are the men who have chosen to learn and grow from women's experiences and together with women are creating new norms for relationships. Popular literature and research on male sex roles is expanding, reflecting a wider interest in masculinity. Weekly news magazines such as *Time* and *Newsweek* have run major stories on the "new masculinity," suggesting that positive changes are taking place in the home and in the workplace. Small groups of men scattered around the country have organized against pornography, battering, and sexual assault. Finally there is the National Organization for Changing Men which has a pro-feminist, pro-gay, pro–"new man" agenda, and its ranks are slowly growing.

In schools where I have worked with teachers, they report that years of efforts to enhance educational opportunities for girls have also had some positive effects on boys. The boys seem more tolerant of girls' participation in coed sports activities and in traditionally male shops and courses. They seem to have a greater respect for the accomplishments of women through women's contributions to literature and history. Among elementary school aged males, the expression of vulnerable feelings is gaining acceptance. In general, however, there has been far too little attention paid to redirecting male role development.

BOYS WILL BE BOYS

I think back to the four wrestlers and the stifling culture of masculinity in which they live. If schools were to radically alter this culture and substitute for it a new vision of masculinity, what would that look like? In this environment, boys would express a full range of behaviors and emotions without fear of being chastised. They would be permitted and encouraged to cry, to be afraid, to show joy, and to express love in a gentle fashion. Extreme concern for career goals would be replaced by a consideration of one's need for recreation, health, and meaningful work. Older boys would be encouraged to tutor and play with younger students. Moreover, boys would receive as much recognition for artistic talents as they do for athletics, and, in general, they would value leisure-time, recreational activities as highly as competitive sports.

In a system where maleness and femaleness were equally valued, boys might no longer feel that they have to "prove" themselves to other boys; they would simply accept the worth of each person and value those differences. Boys would realize that it is permissible to admit failure. In addition, they would seek out opportunities to learn from girls and women. Emotional support would be commonplace, and it would no longer be seen as just the role of the female to provide the support. Relationships between boys and girls would no longer be based on limited roles, but instead would become expressions of two individuals learning from and supporting one another. Relationships between boys would reflect their care for one another rather than their mutual fear and distrust.

Aggressive styles of resolving conflicts would be the exception rather than the norm. Girls would feel welcome in activities dominated by boys, knowing that they were safe from the threat of being sexually harassed. Boys would no longer boast of beating up another boy or of how much they "got off" of a girl the night before. In fact, the boys would be as outraged as the girls at rape or other violent crimes in the community. Finally, boys would become active in efforts to stop nuclear proliferation and all other forms of military violence, following the examples set by activist women.

The development of a new conception of masculinity based on this vision is an ambitious task, but one which is essential for the health and safety of both men and women. The survival of our society may rest on the degree to which we are able to teach men to cherish life.

III

Rethinking Institutions

Social institutions exert a powerful influence on our everyday lives. They are also powerful channels for societal penalties and privileges. The type of work you do, the structure of your family, the kind of education you receive, and how you are treated by the state are all shaped by the institutional structure of society. Because institutions are patterned by race, class, and gender, their effects differ, depending on who you are. We rely on institutions to meet our needs, although they do so better for some groups than others. When a specific institution (such as the economy) fails us, we often appeal to another institution (such as the state) for redress. In this sense, institutions are both sources of support and sources of oppression.

The concept of an institution is abstract, since there is no thing or object that one can point to as an institution. *Social institutions* are the established societal patterns of behavior organized around particular purposes. The economy is an institution, as are the family, the media, education, and the state—important societal institutions examined here. Each is organized around a specific purpose; in the case of the economy, for example, that purpose is the production, distribution, and consumption of goods and services. Within a given institution, there may be various patterns, such as different family structures, but as a whole, institutions are general patterns of behavior that emerge because of the specific societal conditions in which groups live. Institutions do change over time, both as societal conditions evolve and as groups challenge specific institutional structures, but they are also enduring and persistent, even in the face of active efforts to change them. Institutions confront us from birth and live on after we die.

Social institutions are the fundamental conduits for race, class, and gender oppression in this society, even though they are often presented as entities far removed from these experiences. The American creed portrays institutions as neutral in their treatment of different groups; indeed, the liberal framework of the law allegedly makes access to public institutions (like education and work) gender- and race-blind. Still, institutions differentiate on the basis of race, class, and gender. As the articles included here show, institutions are actually structured on the basis of race, class, and gender relations.

As an example, think of the economy. Economic institutions in this society are founded on capitalism—an economic system based on the pursuit of profit and the principle of private ownership. Such a system creates class inequality since, in simple terms, the profits of some stem from the exploitation of the labor of others. The U.S. capitalist economy is further divided by race and class, resulting in a *dual labor market*. The dual labor market includes (1) a primary labor market characterized by relatively high wages, opportunities for advancement, employee benefits, and rules of due process that protect workers' rights; and (2) a secondary labor market (where most women and minorities are located) characterized by low wages, little opportunity for advancement, few benefits, and little protection for workers.

One result of the dual labor market is the persistent wage gap between men and women (see Figure 1), and between Whites and people of color— even when they have the same level of education. Women tend to be clustered in jobs that employ mostly women workers; such jobs have been economically devalued as a result. Gender segregation and race segregation intersect in the dual labor market, so women of color are most likely to be working in occupations where most of the other workers are also women of color. At the same

Source: U.S. Bureau of the Census, 1996. *Historical Income Tables—Persons*. World Wide Web site: http://www.census.gov:80/hhes/income/histinc/p16.html

FIGURE 1 The Gender Gap in Income by Education.

time, men of color are segregated into particular segments of the market, too. Indeed, there is a direct connection between gender and race segregation and wages, since wages are lowest in occupations where women of color predominate (U.S. Department of Labor 1997).

The dual labor market is embedded in a larger economic institution that rests on race, class, and gender inequality. This is what it means to say that institutions are structured by race, class, and gender: Institutions are built from and then reflect the historical and contemporary patterns of race, class, and gender relations in society.

As a second example, think of the state. The *state* refers to the organized system of power and authority in society. This includes the government, the police, the military, and the law (as reflected in both social policy and the civil and criminal justice system). The state is supposed to protect all citizens, regardless of their race, class, and gender (as well as other characteristics, such as disability and age); yet, like other "gendered" institutions, the state can be described as "male" (MacKinnon 1982). This means not only that the majority of powerful people in the state are men (such as elected officials, judges, police, and the military) but, just as important, that the state works to protect men's interests. Policies about reproductive rights provide a good example. They are largely enacted by men, but have a particularly profound effect on women. Similarly, welfare policies designed to encourage people to work are based on the model of men's experiences, since they presume that staying home to care for one's children is not working. In this sense, the state is a "gendered" institution.

A gendered institution embeds the specific characteristics associated with gender into its structure (Acker 1992). The family provides a good example. Historically, the family has been presumed to be the world of women: the ideology of the family (i.e., dominant belief systems about the family) purports that families are places for nurturing, love, and support—characteristics that have been associated with women. This ideal identifies women with the private world of the family and men with the public sphere of work. In this sense, the family ideal identifies the family as a gendered institution. Family ideology, of course, only projects an ideal, since we know that few families actually fit the presumed ideal. Nonetheless, the ideology of the family provides a standard against which all families are judged.

This example demonstrates an important point: institutions are not only gendered, they are also structured by race and class. In the preceding example, the ideology of the family is class- and race-specific; that is, it ignores and distorts the family experiences of African Americans, Latinos, and most Whites. Bonnie Thornton Dill's essay, "Our Mothers' Grief," shows that for African American, Chinese American, and Mexican American women, family structure is deeply affected by the relationships of families to the structures of race, class, and gender.

Most people do not examine the institutional structure of society when thinking about race, class, and gender. The individualist framework of the dominant culture sees race, class, and gender as attributes of individuals, instead of seeing them as embedded in institutional structures. People do, of course, have race, class, and gender identities, and these identities have an enormous impact on individual experience. However, seeing race, class, and gender from an individualist viewpoint overlooks how profoundly embedded these identities are in the structure of American institutions.

In this section of the book we examine how institutions structure race, class, and gender experiences and, in turn, how race, class, and gender structure institutions. We look at four major institutions: work and the economic system, families, cultural institutions that reproduce ideas, and the state and social policy. Each can be shown to have a unique impact on different groups (such as the discriminatory treatment of African American men by the criminal justice system). At the same time, each institution and its interrelationship with other institutions can be seen as specifically structured through the dynamics of race, class, and gender relations. Moving historically marginalized groups to the center of analysis clarifies the importance of social institutions as links between individual experience and larger structures of race, class, and gender.

WORK AND ECONOMIC INSTITUTIONS

Structural transformations in the economy have dramatically changed the conditions under which people work. As Maxine Baca Zinn and D. Stanley Eitzen show in "Economic Restructuring and Systems of Inequality at Century's End," four basic transformations currently affect the character of work: the development of new technologies, global economic interdependence, capital flight, and the growth of the service sector. These changes have brought new opportunities for some groups—those positioned to benefit from the changes—while, for others, they have meant massive economic dislocation.

The articles in this section show that economic restructuring has unique effects on different groups. In "The Latino Population," Joan Moore and Raquel Pinderhughes document specific effects of economic restructuring on the urban Latino population. They point to the decline in traditional manufacturing and the growth of low-wage service and manufacturing industries (most notably, the electronics and garment industries) as most affecting the employment of Latino workers. These industries rely on using cheap labor, thus encouraging migration among Latinos. In addition, the growth of "global cities," where internationalization of the labor force occurs, creates a unique mix of high- and low-paid service jobs in major cities and encourages the development of urban labor markets with a distinct race, class, and gender structure.

In the midst of these changes, numerous myths abound regarding who succeeds and why. Deborah Woo, in "The Gap between Striving and Achieving," refutes one such myth: the recurring claim that current economic changes allow Asian Americans, the so-called model minority, to escape racial discrimination. Woo shows that the myth of the model minority obscures knowledge about the large number of Asian Americans in working-class jobs and the structural barriers to Asian American success. Taken together, these essays demonstrate the interactive relationship of race, class, and gender in shaping economic institutions.

One of the groups most affected by such changes, but also typically hidden from public view, is made up of the 30 million people who constitute the working poor. We have already seen (in the introduction to part II) that a large proportion of people living in poverty are employed, but at wages too low to bring their standard of living above the poverty level. Katherine Newman points out in "Working Poor, Working Hard" that the working poor, many of whom are mothers with children, seldom have either job benefits or the government supports provided to those with even less income. In the context of welfare reforms that require welfare recipients to work, the working poor are even more vulnerable. Under new federal welfare laws, most adults on welfare must spend thirty hours a week in a "work experience"; thus, at least 4 million new people will be competing for jobs in the lowest levels of the labor market. Companies can receive federal subsidies for hiring those on welfare, providing business owners financial incentives to displace the working poor and hire people from the welfare system at a lower wage (Cooper 1997). Mark and Linda Armstrong, in Steven VanderStaay's piece, put a human face on these issues. Despite their work histories, they were unable to find affordable housing for their family when Mark's company went out of business. Their struggles with homelessness illustrate the costs of economic restructuring.

FAMILIES

Families are another primary social institution profoundly influenced by systems of race, class, and gender. Bonnie Thornton Dill's historical analysis of racial-ethnic women and their families in "Our Mothers' Grief" examines diverse patterns of family organization directly influenced by a group's placement in the larger political economy. Just as the political economy of the nineteenth century affected women's experience in families, the political economy of the late twentieth century shapes family relations for women and men of all races.

The articles in this section illustrate several points that have emerged from feminist studies of families, as identified by Barrie Thorne (1992). First, the family is not monolithic. The now widely acknowledged diversity among families refutes the idea that there is a normative family: White, middle-class, with children, organized around a heterosexual married couple (preferably with the wife not employed), and needing little support from relatives or neighbors. As the experiences of African Americans, Latinos, lesbians, gays, Asian Americans, and others reveal, this so-called normal family actually represents a minority perspective. In "The Diversity of American Families,"

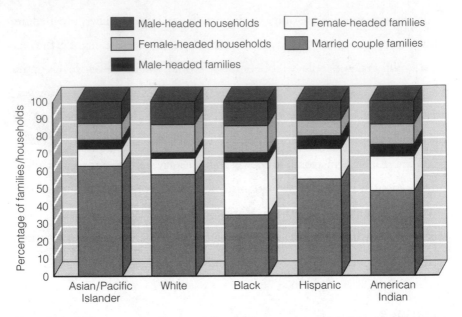

Legend:
- Male-headed households
- Female-headed households
- Male-headed families
- Female-headed families
- Married couple families

Y-axis: Percentage of families/households (0, 10, 20, 30, 40, 50, 60, 70, 80, 90, 100)

X-axis categories: Asian/Pacific Islander, White, Black, Hispanic, American Indian

Note: In the U.S. census, families are defined as two or more people living together and related by birth or marriage; households are residential units where people may or may not be related.

Source: U.S. Bureau of the Census, 1996. *Families by Type, Race, and Hispanic Origin: 1998, Series 3.* World Wide Web site: http://www.census.gov:80/population/socdemo/hh-fam/98pplb.txt

FIGURE 2 Diversity in U.S. Families and Households.

Eleanor Palo Stoller and Rose Campbell Gibson show how traditional myths about the American family mask the diversity of families in the United States (see also Figure 2). By focusing on older women, they also show us the different contexts of family experience of people in different generations.

Second, the best way to analyze families is to look at the underlying structures of "gender, generation, sexuality, race, and class" (Thorne 1992: 5). Families, for example, have been presumed to be formed around a heterosexual norm, as Stoller and Campbell point out, but gay and lesbian partners often form permanent relationships, sometimes including children. Although such partnerships are not legally recognized, they are part of the diversity among families. Raising children in diverse family environments so that they appreciate not only their own families, but also diverse ways of forming families, is a challenge in a society that devalues gays and lesbians and people of color.

Third, Thorne points out that the dominant ideology of the family has glorified the family, hiding the underlying conflicts that are embedded in family systems. Although we do not examine family violence directly here, we know that violence stems from the gender, race, and class conflicts that are encouraged in a sexist, racist, and class-based society. In addition, we think of family violence not only as that which occurs between family members, but also as what happens to families as they confront the institutional structures of race, class, and gender oppression.

Fourth, Thorne argues that the boundaries separating family, work, and other institutions are more fluid than was previously believed. No institution is isolated from another. Changes in the economy, for example, affect family structures; moreover, this effect is reciprocal, since changes in the family generate changes in the economy. We think the interrelationships among institutions are especially apparent when studied in the context of race, class, and gender. Race, class, and gender oppression rests on a network of interconnected social institutions. Understanding the interconnections between institutions helps us see that we are all part of one historically created system that finds structural form in interconnected social institutions.

Finally, Thorne's fifth point—that the presumed dichotomy between the public and private spheres is false—is especially evident in light of the experience of people of color. Racial-ethnic families have rarely been provided the protection and privacy that the alleged split between public and private assumes. From welfare policy to reproductive rights, this dichotomy is based on the myth that families are insulated from the society around them.

Recentering one's thinking about the family by understanding the interconnections of race, class, and gender reveals new understandings about families and the myths that have pervaded assumptions about family experience. Robin D. G. Kelley demonstrates this well in his essay on being a father to his young daughter. His "Countering the Conspiracy to Ignore Black Girls" takes on several longstanding myths—that African American fathers are uninvolved in the lives of their daughters and that the concerns of African American boys are more pressing than those of African American girls—and shows that they are untrue. His essay demonstrates that, contrary to the myth of the absent Black father, Kelley is very concerned about his daughter's well-being.

Just as Kelley's essay brings new perspectives to understanding father-daughter relationships in the context of race, class, and gender, Nazli Kibria generates new insights about how race, class, and gender structure family experiences. Despite the structural problems that systems of work and family produce, people are not just passive victims of these forces. Kibria's research ("Migration and Vietnamese American Women") shows how Vietnamese American women and men negotiate with each other to adjust to the specific experiences they face as immigrants. By examining gender roles in Vietnamese American families, Kibria shows how women rebuild families to provide economic and social support during the transition to a new community. Her analysis reminds us of how people shape viable family networks and support systems that enable them to survive even in the face of cultural, economic, and social assaults. Lynet Uttal's study of mothers shows the different concerns regarding child care that result from their racial locations. Taken as a whole, the articles in this section reveal the complex relationship of all families to systems of race, class, and gender oppression.

CULTURAL INSTITUTIONS AND THE PRODUCTION OF IDEAS

Work, family, and other social institutions are patterned by race, class, and gender, yet many people do not see these patterns and even may claim that they do not exist. The effects of economic restructuring on people of color and women and the differences manifested as Americans try to meet the American family ideal can be difficult to understand. How can race, class, and gender exert such a powerful influence on our everyday lives, yet remain so invisible?

The products of cultural institutions, such as movies, books, television, advertisements in the mass media, the statistics and documents produced by government, and the textbooks, curriculum materials, and teaching methods of schools, explain in part why race, class, and gender relations are obscured. These and other cultural institutions reproduce ideas by identifying which ideas are valuable, which are not, and which should not be heard at all. In this way, the ideas of groups that are privileged within race, class, and gender relations are routinely heard, whereas the ideas of groups who are disadvantaged are silenced.

In part, invisibility and silencing result from deeply entrenched ideas about race, class, and gender in the social fabric of the United States. Because beliefs about race, class, and gender are so ordinary, they often go unnoticed. Robert Moore points this out in his essay on "Racism in the English Language." Moore's analysis of the negative connotations associated with uses of the term "black" and the almost uniformly positive connotations that accompany the term "white" reveal a pattern that, for most people, is hidden in plain sight. In everyday social interaction, people invoke these negative and positive meanings associated with "black" and "white" without stopping to think about them at all. This everyday use obscures the historical origins of these meanings and makes the meanings of "black" and "white" appear to be natural and timeless rather than socially constructed.

Certain cultural institutions have gained greater importance in the context of global economic restructuring. With the emergence of a global, mass media that travels via television, music videos, cable, radio, and the Internet to all parts of the globe, ideas can travel quickly. Thus, those who control cultural institutions are in a position to shape the basic ideas of society that come to be seen as truth. Gregory Mantsios's essay "Media Magic: Making Class Invisible" explores how mass media have been central in shaping ideas about social class. His work identifies the growing significance of mass media in framing how people think about class, race, and gender. In a similar fashion, Gloria Steinem reminds us how pervasive male power is in shaping the value attached to all aspects of American society.

Other cultural institutions may appear to be less important than they once were, but they continue to reproduce ideas about race, class, and gender. Cultural institutions can be sources of support for social inequalities of race, class, and gender, but these same cultural institutions can be sites for challenging longstanding oppressions. In this sense, cultural institutions are rarely all good or all bad—more often, they are a little bit of both. Educational institutions fall into this category. Schools certainly have been central to reproducing ideas about race, class, and gender. At the same time, schools have also formed the focus of much activism by historically excluded groups who pushed for changes to school curricula. Schools are often the site of struggles between those who hold traditional views of race, class, and gender oppression as natural and inevitable and people of color, women, poor people, and other historically excluded groups who challenge these inequalities. Few winners or losers exist in these struggles. As John Garvey points out in his essay "My Problem with Multicultural Education," the record of school reform concerning the portrayal of race has been uneven.

Michael Messner's essay "Masculinities and Athletic Careers" explores how sport reproduces gender ideology. As a cultural institution, sport has a central place in the social lives of millions. Messner's study examines how boys from different racial and social class backgrounds learn about masculinity through their involvement in sport. Not only does sport play a major role in shaping American understandings of masculinity, it does so in ways that are race and class specific. Messner demonstrates that there is no one set of beliefs about masculinity to which all men subscribe. Instead, masculinity itself is constructed in race- and class-specific ways, with sport being very important in shaping these outcomes.

The articles in this section remind us that the actual ideas produced by these cultural institutions are far from benign. Judith Ortiz Cofer reminds us of how burdensome it can be to continually encounter the "Myth of the Latin Woman" wherever she goes. Ideas are not simply reproduced by cultural institutions, because there is no thing or object that one can point to as an institution. Because cultural institutions are established societal patterns of behavior, we all participate in reproducing these ideas all of the time.

STATE INSTITUTIONS AND SOCIAL POLICY

Finally, we include a section on the state and systems of social control. As we noted earlier, the state is the system of legitimated power and authority in society. Race, class, and gender are fundamental in the construction of the state and its policies, just as the state is fundamental in shaping and defining these categories. State policies determine people's rights; and as the history of Jim Crow legislation shows, the state has often been the basis for extreme exclusionary action. At the same time, the state has been an important site of protest against the exclusionary policies resulting from race, class, and gender patterns.

Matthew Snipp's essay "The First Americans" details the historical role of the state in forcing Native Americans from their homes and subordinating them to a new system of state control. Genocide, forced relocation, and regulation by state law have shaped Native American experience; state processes, whether in the form of war, legislation, or social policy, have contributed to the current place of Native Americans in U.S. society.

At the same time, as Snipp notes, groups are resilient as they face adversity and often turn to the state for assistance. The history of civil rights legislation shows that the state can be an invaluable resource for addressing the wrongs of race, class, and gender injustice. In this sense, the state is both a source of oppression *and* an avenue for seeking justice. For example, state policy has done much to eliminate earlier structures of inequality. At least in law (*de jure*), citizens' rights are race, class, and gender blind; in practice (*de facto*), however, these inequities continue.

Social policies can be developed on behalf of disadvantaged groups, and historically the state has had a significant role in developing such policies. The state can negotiate groups' rights and organize people's access to state and societal resources. States can solve problems that individuals cannot solve on their own, although many people are now cynical about the state's ability to do so. Public confidence in government has eroded, with many observers believing that the government is incapable of solving our social problems.

Indeed, in recent years, the state has been more involved in dismantling social supports than in providing assistance for those in need.

In this context, education has emerged as an important part of the state. Education has recently and frequently been described as an institution in crisis. People worry that children are not learning in school. High school dropout rates, especially among students from poor and working-class families, reveal deep problems in the system of education. The sheer cost of post-secondary education makes it inaccessible to many. All of these factors contribute to the continuing disparity in the educational attainment of different groups.

School violence indicates that the conflicts of race, class, and gender in the society at large are also played out within the schools. The persistence of inequality in educational opportunity because of race, class, and gender means that many disadvantaged groups are less able to succeed. All groups whose experience differs from the White norm are ignored and distorted in the educational curriculum. However they are described, the problems in education are a logical outgrowth of the race, class, and gender inequities that exist in society at large.

In "Can Education Eliminate Race, Class, and Gender Inequality?" Roslyn Arlin Mickelson and Stephen Samuel Smith show how schools promote inequalities of race, class, and gender. Their analysis reveals the interplay between school policies that perpetuate existing hierarchies (such as credential inflation) and belief systems about race, class, and gender that are embedded in the so-called hidden curriculum. Students encounter these structures and belief systems while young, when their identities assume major importance. Schools thus become key sites where the inequalities of race, class, and gender are fostered and resisted.

Finally, Alan Berkman's and Tim Blunk's analysis of political prisoners in "Thoughts on Class, Race, and Prison" shows how the state controls those judged to be a threat to the status quo. Their discussion highlights the fact that disproportionate numbers of Black, Latino, and Native American men are confined in prison. In fact, the criminal justice system reflects the differential treatment that individuals receive based on race, class, and gender.

Overall, institutions are powerful mechanisms for perpetuating the race, class, and gender inequities in society. Who controls them, who benefits from institutional resources, and who is best able to negotiate their way through institutional structures all reveal patterns of race, class, and gender inequity. Still, power does not operate only in a "top-down" fashion. Challenges to institutions come in many ways, but change begins with analysis.

References

Acker, Joan. 1992. "Gendered Institutions: From Sex Roles to Gendered Institutions." *Contemporary Sociology* 21 (September): 565–69.

Cooper, Marc. 1997. "When Push Comes to Shove: Who Is Welfare Reform Really Helping?" *Nation* 264 (June 2): 11–15.

MacKinnon, Catharine. 1982. "Feminism, Marxism, Method, and the State: An Agenda for Theory." *Signs* 7 (spring): 515–44.

Thorne, Barrie, with Marilyn Yalom. 1992. *Rethinking the Family: Some Feminist Questions.* Rev. ed. Boston: Northeastern University Press.

U.S. Department of Labor. January 1997. *Employment and Earnings.* Washington, D.C.: U.S. Government Printing Office.

Suggested Readings

Amott, Teresa L., and Julie Matthaei. 1991. *Race, Gender, and Work: A Multicultural Economic History of Women in the United States.* Boston: South End Press.

Coontz, Stephanie. 1992. *The Way We Never Were: American Families and the Nostalgia Trap.* New York: Basic Books.

Feagin, Joe R., Hernan Vera, and Nikitah Imani. 1996. *The Agony of Education: Black Students at White Colleges and Universities.* New York: Routledge.

Kelley, Robin D. G. 1994. *Race Rebels: Culture, Politics, and the Black Working Class.* New York: Free Press.

Quadagno, Jill. 1994. *The Color of Welfare: How Racism Undermined the War on Poverty.* New York: Oxford University Press.

Rose, Tricia. 1994. *Black Noise: Rap Music and Black Culture in Contemporary America.* Hanover, NH: Wesleyan University Press.

Squires, Gregory D. 1994. *Capital and Communities in Black and White: The Intersections of Race, Class, and Uneven Development.* Albany, NY: State University of New York Press.

Thorne, Barrie, and Marilyn Yalom, eds. 1992. *Rethinking the Family: Some Feminist Questions.* Boston: Northeastern University Press.

Van Dijk, Teun A. 1993. *Elite Discourse and Racism.* Newbury Park, CA: Sage.

InfoTrac College Edition: Search Terms

Use your access to the online library, InfoTrac College Edition, to learn more about subjects covered in this section. The following are some suggested terms for searches:

"Jim Crow" laws
"separate but equal" doctrine
Indian Self-Determination and Education Assistance Act (1975)
bilingual education
Bureau of Indian Affairs
comparable worth
compensatory education
corporate welfare/"wealthfare"
ethnocentrism
feminization of poverty
immigration laws (1965 and 1986)
labor market segmentation (primary and secondary labor markets)
living wage campaigns
North American Free Trade Agreement (NAFTA 1994)
school desegregation
sexual division of labor
Title IX (Higher Education Act of 1972)
tracking/ability grouping
U.S. Constitutional amendments (13th, 14th, 15th, and 19th)
underclass debate (urban underclass)

Wadsworth Sociology Resource Center: Virtual Society

For additional links, quizzes, and learning tools related to this section, see the Wadsworth Sociology Resource Center, Virtual Society, at **http://sociology. wadsworth.com**.

Work and Economic Transformation

ECONOMIC RESTRUCTURING AND SYSTEMS OF INEQUALITY AT CENTURY'S END

Maxine Baca Zinn and D. Stanley Eitzen

The present generation is in the midst of economic changes that are more far-reaching and are occurring faster than at any other time in human history. While all people in the United States are affected by the technological and economically based reorganization of society, the magnitude of this structural transformation is different throughout society. The old inequalities of class, race, and gender are thriving. New and subtle forms of discrimination are becoming prevalent throughout society as the economic base changes and settles.

Four factors are at work here: new technologies based primarily on the computer chip, global economic interdependence, capital flight, and the dominance of the information and service sectors over basic manufacturing industries. Together these factors have reinforced the unequal placement of individuals and families in the larger society. They have deepened patterns of social inequality, and they have formed new patterns of domination in which the affluent control the poor, whites dominate people of color, and men subjugate women.

The disproportionate effects of economic and industrial change are most visible in three trends: (1) structural unemployment; (2) the changing distribution and organization of jobs; and (3) the low income-generating capacity of jobs. Each of these three trends has significant consequences for the hierarchies of class, race, and gender.

CLASS

Two major developments stand out when the emerging class structure is examined. The first is the growing gap between the rich and the poor since 1970. The second is the decline of the middle class.

The distribution of income is very unequal and the gap is widening. From 1970 to 1993 the income share of the highest quintile rose from 43.3 to 48.2 percent, while the bottom fifth fell from 4.1 percent to 3.6 percent of all income (U.S. Bureau of the Census 1995: 41). While salaries and stock options plus a rising stock market have increased the wealth of those at the top, the wages of the majority have stagnated and benefits (medical and pensions) have declined.

Many Americans have experienced a slowdown of income growth. Since the early 1970s wages have fallen for 80 percent of the workforce, while the richest 20 percent have become richer by far. The following facts demonstrate the contours of this growing disparity:

- Median family income was $1,000 less in 1996 than in 1989 (Mishel, Bernstein, and Schmitt 1999).
- Since the 1970s, the top 1 percent of households have doubled their share of the national wealth. They now have more wealth than the entire bottom 95 percent (Collins, Leondar-Wright, and Sklar 1999).
- The typical middle-class family has nearly 3 percent less wealth in 1997 than in 1989, despite the stock market boom. This is because the richest 10 percent of households in the United States have reaped 85.8 percent of growth in the stock market since 1989 (Mishel, Bernstein, and Schmitt 1999).
- In 1977, the 2.7 million Americans in the top 1 percent of households had as much income, after federal taxes, as the bottom 49 million. In 1999, the top 2.7 million had as much as the bottom 100 million (Sklar 1999).
- One out of eight Americans, about 35 million, live below the official poverty line (about $13,000 for a three-person family). At the other end, there are 268 billionaires. Bill Gates, the principal owner of Microsoft, has more wealth than the bottom 45 percent of American households combined (Sklar 1999).
- The average chief executive officer (CEO) in *Business Week*'s annual survey made 326 times the pay of factory workers in 1997. In 1980, CEOs made 42 times as much (Collins, Leondar-Wright, and Sklar 1999).

In sum, many Americans have experienced a sharp slowdown in income with the advent of corporate downsizing, the increased use of temporary workers (who do not, typically, receive extra benefits such as medical insurance and pension plans), the loss by unions of membership and clout, the decline in the number of well-paid industry jobs, and the emergence of a bipolar wage structure in high-tech and service work. These data indicate a shrinkage of the middle class, a trend heretofore unknown in U.S. history. The changing of the economy, in effect, has closed many of the old avenues to social mobility, resulting, for the first time, in a rate of downward mobility that exceeds the rate of upward mobility.

RACE

Technology, foreign competition, and the changing distribution of jobs are having devastating effects on minority communities across the United States. The employment status of minorities is falling in all regions. It is worse, however, in areas of industrial decline and in segregated urban cores, where race and class intersect. Sociologist William Julius Wilson provides the data:

> In the ghetto census tracts of the nation's one hundred largest central cities, there were only 65.6 employed persons for every hundred adults who did not hold a job in a typical week in 1990. In contrast, the nonpoverty areas contained 182.3 employed persons for every hundred of those not working. In other words, the ratio of employed to jobless persons was three times greater in census tracts not marked by poverty (Wilson 1996: 19).

Race alone is significant because white job applicants continue to be disproportionately chosen over equally qualified minority ones. A 1991 study by the Urban Institute, for example, using carefully matched and trained pairs of white and black men applying for entry-level jobs, found that discrimination against blacks is "entrenched and widespread" (reported in Sklar 1993: 54). Similarly, studies in Chicago, Tampa, Atlanta, Denver, and other metropolitan areas found consistently that African Americans and Latinos face discrimination in housing, pay more than whites for similar housing, have greater difficulty than whites in receiving business and home loans, pay higher insurance rates, and pay more for consumer goods (Timmer, Eitzen, and Talley 1994: 94–95).

Latinos and African Americans have suffered disproportionately from industrial job loss, declining manufacturing employment, and low-wage production jobs. By every measure, including employment rates, occupational standing, and wage rates, the labor market status of racial minorities has deteriorated relative to whites. In 1998, for example, the official unemployment rate for Latinos was 7.2 percent compared with 8.9 percent for African Americans and 3.9 percent for whites (Nathan 1999). Not only are minorities twice as likely as whites to be unemployed, they are more likely to work in dead-end jobs. About a quarter of all African Americans and a fifth of all Latinos work at the low end of the occupational ladder, in poorly paid service jobs (Folbre 1995: 4–9).

GENDER

Women and men are affected differently by the transformation of the economy from its manufacturing base to a base in service and high technology. Industrial jobs, traditionally filled by men, are being replaced with service jobs that are increasingly filled by women. Since 1980, women have taken 80 percent of the new jobs created in the economy, but the overall degree of gender segregation has not changed much since 1900 (Herz and Wootton 1996: 56). Unlike other forms of inequality, sexism in U.S. society has not become more intense as a result of the economic transformation. Instead, sexism has taken new forms as women are propelled into the labor market. Women have continued to move from the private sphere (family) to public arenas, but they have done so under conditions of labor market discrimination that have always plagued women. Today, the "typical" job is a non-union, service sector, low-paying job occupied by a woman. Despite the growing feminization of the workforce, male domination has been more firmly entrenched in the social organization of work. The rise of the contingent workforce (including part-time work, temporary agencies, and subcontracted work) offers many advantages to employers but at considerable cost to women workers.

Women workers do not approach earnings parity with men even when they work in similar occupations and have similar levels of education. Current estimates are that women earn about 76 percent of the wage rate of men. The full impact of economic restructuring on women must take into account the relatively low wage levels and limited opportunities for advancement that characterize their work in the new economy.

NEW INTERSECTIONS
OF CLASS, RACE, AND GENDER

The hierarchies of class, race, and gender are simultaneous and interlocking systems. For this reason, they frequently operate with and through one another to produce social inequality. Not only are many existing inequalities exacerbated by the structural transformation of the economy, but the combined effects of class, race, and gender are producing new kinds of subordination and exclusion throughout society and especially the workplace. For example, the removal of manufacturing jobs has severely increased African American and Latino job loss. Just how much of this is due to class and how much is due to race remains an important question.

In contrast, many women of color have found their work opportunities expanded, albeit in poorly paid marginal work settings in service and high-tech jobs. Does such growth offer traditionally oppressed race/gender groups new mobility opportunities, or does the expansion of new kinds of work reproduce existing forms of inequality? The impact of economic restructuring on race and gender varies considerably. In some cases, it generates no jobs at all and displaces minority women workers. In other cases, minority women benefit by the creation of new jobs. Third-world immigrant women provide the bulk of the high-tech productive labor force in Silicon Valley (Hossfeld 1994, 1997). Yet a growing "underclass" in high tech consists of low-paid recent immigrant women from Mexico, Vietnam, Korea, and the Philippines. These examples reveal new labor systems as well as new forms of racial control based on class, race, and gender.

References

Collins, Chuck, Betsy Leondar-Wright, and Holly Sklar. 1999. *Shifting Fortunes: The Perils of the Growing Wealth Gap.* Boston: United for a Fair Economy.

Folbre, Nancy. 1995. *The New Field Guide to the U.S. Economy.* New York: New Press.

Herz, Diane E., and Barbara H. Wootton. 1996. "Women in the Workforce: An Overview." In Cynthia Costello and Barbara Kivimae Krimgold, eds., *The American Woman, 1996–1997*, pp. 44–78. New York: Norton.

Hossfeld, Karen J. 1994. "Hiring Immigrant Women: Silicon Valley's 'Simple Formula.'" In Maxine Baca Zinn and Bonnie Thornton Dill, eds., *Women of Color in U.S. Society*, pp. 65–93. Philadelphia: Temple University Press.

———. 1997. "'Their Logic Against Them': Contradictions in Sex, Race, and Class in Silicon Valley." In Maxine Baca Zinn, Pierrette Hondagneu-Sotelo, and Michael A. Messner, eds., *Through the Prism of Difference*, pp. 388–400. Boston: Allyn & Bacon.

Mishel, Lawrence, Jared Bernstein, and John Schmitt. 1999. *The State of Working America 1998–99.* Ithaca, NY: Cornell University Press.

Nathan, Sara. 1999. "Report: Minorities Earning More." *USA Today*, February 5, p. B1.

Sklar, Holly. 1999. "Brother, Can You Spare a Billion." *Z Magazine* 12 (December): 23–26.

Timmer, Doug A., D. Stanley Eitzen, and Kathryn D. Talley. 1994. *Paths to Homelessness: Extreme Poverty and the Urban Housing Crisis.* Boulder, CO: Westview Press.

U.S. Bureau of the Census. 1995. "Population Profile of the United States 1995." *Current Population Reports.* Series P23-189. Washington, DC: U.S. Government Printing Office.

Wilson, William Julius. 1996. *When Work Disappears: The World of the New Urban Poor.* New York: Knopf.

RACE, CLASS, GENDER, AND WOMEN'S WORKS

26

Teresa Amott and Julie Matthaei

What social and economic factors determine and differentiate women's work lives? Why is it, for instance, that the work experiences of African American women are so different from those of European American women? Why have some women worked outside the home for pay, while others have provided for their families through unpaid work in the home? Why are most of the wealthy women in the United States of European descent, and why are so many women of color poor? . . .

Throughout U.S. history, economic differences among women (and men) have been constructed and organized along a number of social categories. In our analysis, we focus on the three categories which we see as most central— gender, race-ethnicity, and class—with less discussion of others, such as age, sexual preference, and religion. We see these three social categories as inter-connected, historical processes of domination and subordination. Thinking about gender, race-ethnicity, and class, then, necessitates thinking historically about power and economic exploitation. . . .

GENDER, RACE-ETHNICITY, AND CLASS PROCESSES: HISTORICAL AND INTERCONNECTED

The concepts of gender, race-ethnicity, and class are neither trans-historical nor independent. Hence, it is artificial to discuss them outside of historical time and place, and separately from one another. At the same time, without such a set of concepts, it is impossible to make sense of women's disparate economic experiences.

Gender, race-ethnicity, and class are not natural or biological categories which are unchanging over time and across cultures. Rather, these categories are socially constructed: they arise and are transformed in history, and them-selves transform history. Although societies rationalize them as natural or god-given, ideas of appropriate feminine and masculine behavior vary widely across

From: Teresa Amott and Julie Matthaei, *Race, Gender, and Work: A Multicultural Economic History of Women in the United States*, 2d ed. (Boston: South End Press, 1996). Reprinted with permission of South End Press.

history and culture. Concepts and practices of race-ethnicity, usually justified by religion or biology, also vary over time, reflecting the politics, economics, and ideology of a particular time and, in turn, reinforcing or transforming politics, economics, and ideology. For example, nineteenth-century European biologists Louis Agassiz and Count Arthur de Gobineau developed a taxonomy of race which divided humanity into separate and unequal racial species; this taxonomy was used to rationalize European colonization of Africa and Asia, and slavery in the United States. Class is perhaps the most historically specific category of all, clearly dependent upon the particular economic and social constellation of a society at a point in time. Still, notions of class as inherited or genetic continue to haunt us, harkening back to earlier eras in which lowly birth was thought to cause low intelligence and a predisposition to criminal activity.

Central to the historical transformation of gender, race-ethnicity, and class processes have been the struggles of subordinated groups to redefine or transcend them. For example, throughout the development of capitalism, workers' consciousness of themselves as workers and their struggles against class oppression have transformed capitalist-worker relationships, expanding workers' rights and powers. In the nineteenth century, educated white women escaped from the prevailing, domestic view of womanhood by arguing that homemaking included caring for the sick and the needy through volunteer work, social homemaking careers, and political organizing. In the 1960s, the transformation of racial-ethnic identity into a source of solidarity and pride was essential to movements of people of color, such as the Black Power and American Indian movements.

Race-ethnicity, gender, and class are interconnected, interdetermining historical processes, rather than separate systems. This is true in two senses, which we will explore in more detail below. First, it is often difficult to determine whether an economic practice constitutes class, race, or gender oppression: for example, slavery in the U.S. South was at the same time a system of class oppression (of slaves by owners) and of racial-ethnic oppression (of Africans by Europeans). Second, a person does not experience these different processes of domination and subordination independently of one another; in philosopher Elizabeth Spelman's metaphor, gender, race-ethnicity, and class are not separate "pop-beads" on a necklace of identity. Hence, there is no generic gender oppression which is experienced by all women regardless of their race-ethnicity or class. As Spelman puts it:

> . . . in the case of much feminist thought we may get the impression that a woman's identity consists of a sum of parts neatly divisible from one another, parts defined in terms of her race, gender, class, and so on . . . On this view of personal identity (which might also be called pop-bead metaphysics), my being a woman means the same whether I am white or Black, rich or poor, French or Jamaican, Jewish or Muslim.[1]

The problems of "pop-bead metaphysics" also apply to historical analysis. In our reading of history, there is no common experience of gender across race-ethnicity and class, of race-ethnicity across class and gender lines, or of class across race-ethnicity and gender.

With these caveats in mind, let us examine the processes of gender, class, and race-ethnicity, their importance in the histories of women's works, and some of the ways in which these processes have been intertwined.

Gender

. . . Gender differences in the social lives of men and women are based on, but are not the same thing as, biological differences between the sexes. Gender is rooted in societies' beliefs that the sexes are naturally distinct and opposed social beings. These beliefs are turned into self-fulfilling prophecies through sex-role socialization: the biological sexes are assigned distinct and often unequal work and political positions, and turned into socially distinct genders.

Economists view the sexual division of labor as central to the gender differentiation of the sexes. By assigning the sexes to different and complementary tasks, the sexual division of labor turns them into different and complementary genders. . . . The work of males is at least partially, if not wholly, different from that of females, making "men" and "women" different economic and social beings. Sexual divisions of labor, not sexual difference alone, create difference and complementarity between "opposite" sexes. These differences, in turn, have been the basis for marriage in most societies. . . .

The concept of gender certainly helps us understand women's economic histories. . . . Each racial-ethnic group has had a sexual division of labor which has barred individuals from the activities of the opposite sex. Gender processes do differentiate women's lives in many ways from those of the men in their own racial-ethnic and class group. Further, gender relations in all groups tend to assign women to the intra-familial work of childrearing, as well as to place women in a subordinate position to the men of their class and racial-ethnic group.

But as soon as we have written these generalizations, exceptions pop into mind. Gender roles do not always correspond to sex. Some American Indian tribes allowed individuals to choose among gender roles: a female, for example, could choose a man's role, do men's work, and marry another female who lived out a woman's role. In the nineteenth century, some white females "passed" as men in order to escape the rigid mandates of gender roles. In many of these cases, women lived with and loved other women.

Even though childrearing is women's work in most societies, many women do not have children, and others do not perform their own child care or domestic work. Here, class is an especially important differentiating process. Upper-class women have been able to use their economic power to reassign some of the work of infant care—sometimes even breastfeeding—to lower-class women of their own or different racial-ethnic groups. These women, in turn, may have been forced to leave their infants alone or with relatives or friends. Finally, gender complementarity has not always led to social and economic inequality; for example, many American Indian women had real control over the home and benefited from a more egalitarian sharing of power between men and women.

Since the processes of sex-role socialization are historically distinct in different times and different cultures, they result in different conceptions of appropriate gender behavior. Both African American and Chicana girls, for instance, learn how to be women—but both must learn the specific gender roles which have developed within their racial-ethnic and class group and historical period. For example, for white middle-class homemakers in the 1950s, adherence to the concept of womanhood discouraged paid employment, while for poor Black women it meant employment as domestic servants for white middle-class women. Since racial-ethnic and class domination have differentiated the experiences of women, one cannot assume, as do many feminist theorists and activists, that all women have the same experience of gender oppression—or even that they will be on the same side of a struggle, not even when some women define that struggle as "feminist."

Not only is gender differentiation and oppression not a universal experience which creates a common "women's oppression," the sexual divisions of labor and family systems of people of color have been systematically disrupted by racial-ethnic and class processes. In the process of invasion and conquest, Europeans imposed their notions of male superiority on cultures with more egalitarian forms of gender relations, including many American Indian and African tribes. At the same time, European Americans were quick to abandon their notion of appropriate femininity when it conflicted with profits; for example, slave owners often assigned slave women to backbreaking labor in the fields.

Racial-ethnic and class oppression have also disrupted family life among people of color and the white working class. Europeans interfered with family relations within subordinated racial-ethnic communities through rape and forced cohabitation. Sometimes whites encouraged or forced reproduction, as when slaveowners forced slave women into sexual relations. On the other hand, whites have often used their power to curtail reproduction among peoples of color, and aggressive sterilization programs were practiced against Puerto Ricans and American Indians as late as the 1970s. Beginning in the late nineteenth century, white administrators took American Indian children from their parents to "civilize" them in boarding schools where they were forbidden to speak their own languages or wear their native dress. Slaveowners commonly split up slave families through sale to different and distant new owners. Nevertheless, African Americans were able to maintain strong family ties, and even augmented these with "fictive" or chosen kin. From the mid-nineteenth through the mid-twentieth centuries, many Asians were separated from their spouses or children by hiring policies and restrictions on immigration. Still, they maintained family life within these split households, and eventually succeeded in reuniting, sometimes after generations. Hence, for peoples of color, having children and maintaining families have been an essential part of the struggle against racist oppression. Not surprisingly, many women of color have rejected the white women's movement view of the family as the center of "women's oppression."

These examples reveal the limitations of gender as a single lens through which to view women's economic lives. Indeed, any attempt to understand women's experiences using gender alone cannot only cause misunderstanding, but can also interfere with the construction of broad-based movements against the oppressions experienced by women.

Race-Ethnicity

Like gender, race-ethnicity is based on a perceived physical difference, and rationalized as "natural" or "god-given." But whereas gender creates difference and inequality according to biological sex, race-ethnicity differentiates individuals according to skin color or other physical features.

In all of human history, individuals have lived in societies with distinct languages, cultures, and economic institutions; these ethnic differences have been perpetuated by intermarriage within, but rarely between, societies. However, ethnic differences can exist independently of a conception of race, and without a practice of racial-ethnic domination such as the Europeans practiced over the last three centuries. . . .

Does the concept of race-ethnicity help us understand the economic history of women in the United States? Certainly, for white racial-ethnic domination has been a central force in U.S. history. European colonization of North America entailed the displacement and murder of the continent's indigenous peoples, rationalized by the racist view that American Indians were savage heathens. The economy of the south was based on a racial-ethnic system, in which imported Africans were forced to work for white landowning families as slaves. U.S. military expansion in the nineteenth century brought more lands under U.S. control—the territories of northern Mexico (now the Southwest), the Philippines, and Puerto Rico—incorporating their peoples into the racial-ethnic hierarchy. And from the mid-nineteenth century onward, Asians were brought into Hawaii's plantation system to work for whites as semi-free laborers. In the twentieth century, racial-ethnic difference and inequality have been perpetuated by the segregation of people of color into different and inferior jobs, living conditions, schools, and political positions, and by the prohibition of intermarriage with whites in some states up until 1967.

Race-ethnicity is a key concept in understanding women's economic histories. But it is not without limitations. First, racial-ethnic processes have never operated independently of class and gender. In the previous section on gender, we saw how racial domination distorted gender and family relations among people of color. Racial domination has also been intricately linked to economic or class domination. As social scientists Michael Omi (Asian American) and Howard Winant (European American) explain, the early European arguments that people of color were without souls had direct economic meaning:

> At stake were not only the prospects for conversion, but the types of treatment to be accorded them. The expropriation of property, the denial of political rights, the introduction of slavery and other forms of coercive labor, as well as outright extermination, all presupposed a worldview which distinguished Europeans—children of God, human beings, etc.—from "others." Such a worldview was needed to explain why some should be "free" and others enslaved, why some had rights to land and property while others did not.[2]

Indeed, many have argued that racial theories only developed after the economic process of colonization had started, as a justification for white domination of peoples of color.

The essentially economic nature of early racial-ethnic oppression in the United States makes it difficult to isolate whether peoples of color were subordinated in the emerging U.S. economy because of their race-ethnicity or their economic class. Whites displaced American Indians and Mexicans to obtain their land. Whites imported Africans to work as slaves and Asians to work as contract laborers. Puerto Ricans and Filipinas/os were victims of further U.S. expansionism. Race-ethnicity and class intertwined in the patterns of displacement for land, genocide, forced labor, and recruitment from the seventeenth through the twentieth centuries. While it is impossible, in our minds, to determine which came first in these instances—race-ethnicity or class—it is clear that they were intertwined and inseparable.

Privileging racial-ethnic analysis also leads one to deny the existence of class differences, both among whites and among people of color, which complicate and blur the racial-ethnic hierarchy. A racial-ethnic analysis implies that all whites are placed above all peoples of color. . . .

. . . A minority of the dominated race is allowed some upward mobility and ranks economically above whites. At the same time, however, all whites have some people of color below them. For example, there are upper-class Black, Chicana, and Puerto Rican women who are more economically privileged than poor white women; however, there are always people of color who are less economically privileged than the poorest white woman. Finally, class oppression operates among women of the same racial-ethnic group.

A third problem with the analysis of racial domination is that such domination has not been a homogeneous process. Each subordinated racial-ethnic group has been oppressed and exploited differently by whites: for example, American Indians were killed and displaced, Africans were enslaved, and Filipinas/os and Puerto Ricans were colonized. Whites have also dominated whites; some European immigrant groups, particularly Southern and Eastern Europeans, were subjected to segregation and violence. In some cases, people of color have oppressed and exploited those in another group: Some American Indian tribes had African slaves; some Mexicans and Puerto Ricans displaced and murdered Indians and had African slaves. Because of these differences, racial oppression does not automatically bring unity of peoples of color across their own racial-ethnic differences, and feminists of color are not necessarily in solidarity with one another.

To sum up, we see that, as with gender, the concept of race-ethnicity is essential to our analysis of women's works. However, divorcing this concept from gender and class, again, leads to problems in both theory and practice.

Class

. . . We believe that the concepts of class and exploitation are crucial to understanding the work lives of women in early U.S. history, as well as in the modern, capitalist economy. Up through the nineteenth century, different class relations organized production in different regions of the United States. The south was dominated by slave agriculture; the Northeast by emerging industrial capitalism; the Southwest (then part of Mexico) by the *hacienda* system which carried over many elements of the feudal manor into large-scale production for the market; the rural Midwest by independent family farms that produced on a small scale for the market; and the American Indian West by a variety of tribal forms centered in hunting and gathering or agriculture, many characterized by cooperative, egalitarian economic relations. Living within these different labor systems, and in different class positions within them, women led very different economic lives.

By the late nineteenth century, however, capitalism had become the dominant form of production, displacing artisans and other small producers along with slave plantations and tribal economies. Today, wage labor accounts for over 90 percent of employment; self employment, including family businesses, accounts for the remaining share. With the rise of capitalism, women were brought into the same labor system, and polarized according to the capitalist-wage laborer hierarchy.

At the same time as the wage labor form specific to capitalism became more prevalent, capitalist class relations became more complex and less transparent. Owners of wealth (stocks and bonds) now rarely direct the production process; instead, salaried managers, who may or may not own stock in the company, take on this function. While the capitalist class may be less identifiable, it still remains a small and dominant elite. . . .

Class can be a powerful concept in understanding women's economic lives, but there are limits to class analysis if it is kept separate from race-ethnicity and gender. First, as we saw in the race section above, the class relations which characterized the early U.S. economy were also racial-ethnic and gender formations. Slave owners were white and mostly male, slaves were Black. The displaced tribal economies were the societies of indigenous peoples. Independent family farmers were whites who farmed American Indian lands; they organized production in a patriarchal manner, with women and children's work defined by and subordinated to the male household head and property owner. After establishing their dominance in the pre-capitalist period, white men were able to perpetuate and institutionalize this dominance in the emerging capitalist system, particularly through the monopolization of managerial and other high-level jobs.

Second, the sexual division of labor within the family makes the determination of a woman's class complicated—determined not simply by her relationship to the production process, but also by that of her husband or father. For instance, if a woman is not in the labor force but her husband is a capitalist, then we might wish to categorize her as a member of the capitalist class. But what if that same woman worked as a personnel manager for a large corporation, or as a salesperson in an elegant boutique? Clearly, she derives upper-class status and access to income from her husband, but she is also, in her own right, a worker. Conversely, when women lose their husbands through divorce, widowhood, or desertion, they often change their class position in a downward direction. A second gender-related economic process overlooked by class analysis is the unpaid household labor performed by women for their fathers, husbands, and children—or by other women, for pay.

Third, while all workers are exploited by capitalists, they are not equally exploited, and gender and race-ethnicity play important roles in this differentiation. Men and women of the same racial-ethnic group have rarely performed the same jobs—this sex-typing and segregation is the labor market form of the sexual division of labor we studied above. Further, women of different racial-ethnic groups have rarely been employed at the same job, at least not within the same workplace or region. This racial-ethnic typing and segregation has both reflected and reinforced the racist economic practices upon which the U.S. economy was built.

Thus, jobs in the labor force hierarchy tend to be simultaneously race-typed and gender-typed. Picture in your mind a registered nurse. Most likely, you thought of a white woman. Picture a doctor. Again, you imagined a person of a particular gender (probably a man), and a race (probably a white person). If you think of a railroad porter, it is likely that a Black man comes to mind. Almost all jobs tend to be typed in such a way that stereotypes make it difficult for persons of the "wrong" race and/or gender to train for or obtain the job. Of course, there are regional and historical variations in the typing of jobs. On the West Coast, for example, Asian men performed much of the paid domestic work during the nineteenth century because women were in such short supply. In states where the African American population is very small, such as South Dakota or Vermont, domestic servants and hotel chambermaids are typically white. Nonetheless, the presence of variations in race-gender typing does not contradict the idea that jobs tend to take on racial-ethnic and gender characteristics with profound effects on the labor market opportunities of job-seekers. . . .

. . . The racial-ethnic and gender processes operating in the labor market have transposed white and male domination from pre-capitalist structures into the labor market's class hierarchy. This hierarchy can be described by grouping jobs into different labor market sectors or segments: "primary," "secondary," and "underground." . . . The primary labor market—which has been monopolized by white men—offers high salaries, steady employment, and upward mobility. Its upper tier consists of white-collar salaried or self-employed workers with high status, autonomy, and, often, supervisory capacity. Wealth increases access to this sector, since it purchases elite education and provides helpful job connections. . . .

The lower tier of the primary sector, which still yields high earnings but involves less autonomy, contains many unionized blue-collar jobs. White working-class men have used union practices, mob violence, and intimidation to monopolize these jobs. By World War II, however, new ideologies of worker solidarity, embodied in the mass industrial unions, began to overcome the resistance of white male workers to the employment of people of color and white women in these jobs.

In contrast to both these primary tiers, the secondary sector offers low wages, few or no benefits, little opportunity for advancement, and unstable employment. People of color and most white women have been concentrated in these secondary sector jobs, where work is often part-time, temporary, or seasonal, and pay does not rise with increasing education or experience. Jobs in both tiers of the primary labor market have generally yielded family wages, earnings high enough to support a wife and children who are not in the labor force for pay. Men of color in the secondary sector have not been able to earn enough to support their families, and women of color have therefore participated in wage labor to a much higher degree than white women whose husbands held primary sector jobs.

Outside of the formal labor market is the underground sector, where the most marginalized labor force groups, including many people of color, earn their livings from illegal or quasi-legal work. This sector contains a great variety of jobs, including drug trafficking, crime, prostitution, work done by undocumented workers, and sweatshop work which violates labor standards such as minimum wages and job safety regulations. . . .

References

1. Elizabeth V. Spelman, *Inessential Woman: Problems of Exclusion in Feminist Thought* (Boston: Beacon Press, 1988).

2. Michael Omi and Howard Winant, *Racial Formation in the United States* (New York: Routledge & Kegan Paul, 1986), p. 58.

THE GAP BETWEEN STRIVING AND ACHIEVING

27

The Case of Asian American Women

Deborah Woo

Much academic research on Asian Americans tends to underscore their success, a success which is attributed almost always to a cultural emphasis on education, hard work, and thrift. Less familiar is the story of potential not fully realized. For example, despite the appearance of being successful and highly educated, Asian American women do not necessarily gain the kind of recognition or rewards they deserve.

The story of unfulfilled dreams remains unwritten for many Asian Americans. It is specifically this story about the gap between striving and achieving that I am concerned with here. Conventional wisdom obscures the discrepancy by looking primarily at whether society is adequately rewarding individuals. By comparing how minorities as disadvantaged groups are doing relative to each other, the tendency is to view Asian Americans as a "model minority." This practice programs us to ignore structural barriers and inequities and to insist that any problems are simply due to different cultural values or failure of individual effort.

Myths about the Asian American community derive from many sources. All ethnic groups develop their own cultural myths. Sometimes, however, they create myths out of historical necessity, as a matter of subterfuge and survival. Chinese Americans, for example, were motivated to create new myths because institutional opportunities were closed off to them. Succeeding in America meant they had to invent fake aspects of an "Oriental culture," which became the beginning of the Chinatown tourist industry.

What has been referred to as the "model minority myth," however, essentially originated from without. The idea that Asian Americans have been a successful group has been a popular news media theme for the last twenty years. It has become a basis for cutbacks in governmental support for all ethnic minorities—for Asian Americans because they apparently are already successful as a group; for other ethnic minorities because they are presumably not working as hard as Asian Americans or they would not need assistance. Critics of this view argue that the portrayal of Asian Americans as socially and economically successful ignores fundamental inequities. That is, the question "Why have Asians been successful vis-à-vis other minorities?" has been asked at the expense of another equally important question: "What has kept Asians from *fully* reaping the fruits of their education and hard work?"

The achievements of Asian Americans are part reality, part myth. Part of the reality is that a highly visible group of Asian Americans are college-educated, occupationally well-situated, and earning relatively high incomes. The myth, however, is that hard work reaps commensurate rewards. This essay documents the gap between the level of education and subsequent occupational or income gains.

THE ROOTS AND CONTOURS OF THE "MODEL MINORITY" CONCEPT

Since World War II, social researchers and news media personnel have been quick to assert that Asian Americans excel over other ethnic groups in terms of earnings, education, and occupation. Asian Americans are said to save more, study more, work more, and so achieve more. The reason given: a cultural emphasis on education and hard work. Implicit in this view is a social judgment and moral injunction: if Asian Americans can make it on their own, why can't other minorities?

While the story of Asian American women workers is only beginning to be pieced together, the success theme is already being sung. The image prevails that despite cultural and racial oppression, they are somehow rapidly assimilating into the mainstream. As workers, they participate in the labor force at rates higher than all others, including Anglo women. Those Asian American women who pursue higher education surpass other women, and even men, in this respect. Moreover, they have acquired a reputation for not only being conscientious and industrious but docile, compliant, and uncomplaining as well.

In the last few decades American women in general have been demanding "equal pay for equal work," the legitimation of housework as work that needs to be recompensed, and greater representation in the professional fields. These demands, however, have not usually come from Asian American women. From the perspective of those in power, this reluctance to complain is another feature of the "model minority." But for those who seek to uncover employment abuses, the unwillingness to talk about problems on the job is itself a problem. The garment industry, for example, is a major area of exploitation, yet it is also one that is difficult to investigate and control. In a 1983 report on the Concentrated Employment Program of the California Department of Industrial Relations, it was noted:

The major problem for investigators in San Francisco is that the Chinese community is very close-knit, and employers and employees cooperate in refusing to speak to investigators. In two years of enforcing the Garment Registration Act, the CEP has never received a complaint from an Asian employee. The few complaints received have been from Anglo or Latin workers.[1]

While many have argued vociferously either for or against the model minority concept, Asian Americans in general have been ambivalent in this regard. Asian Americans experience pride in achievement born of hard work and self-sacrifice, but at the same time, they resist the implication that all is well. Data provided here indicate that Asian Americans have not been successful in terms of benefitting fully (i.e., monetarily), from their education. It is a myth that Asian Americans have proven the American Dream. How does this myth develop?

The Working Consumer: Income and Cost of Living

One striking feature about Asian Americans is that they are geographically concentrated in areas where both income and cost of living are very high. . . . [Immigration] has not only produced dramatic increases, especially in the Filipino and Chinese populations, but has also continued the overwhelming tendency for these groups to concentrate in the same geographical areas, especially those in California.[2] Interestingly enough, the very existence of large Asian communities in the West has stimulated among more recent refugee populations what is now officially referred to as "secondary migration," that is, the movement of refugees away from their sponsoring communities (usually places where there was no sizeable Asian population prior to their own arrival) to those areas where there are well-established Asian communities.[3]

This residential pattern means that while Asian Americans may earn more by living in high-income areas, they also pay more as consumers. The additional earning power gained from living in San Francisco or Los Angeles, say, is absorbed by the high cost of living in such cities. National income averages which compare the income of Asian American women with that of the more broadly dispersed Anglo women systematically distort the picture. Indeed, if we compare women within the same area, Asian American women are frequently less well-off than Anglo American females, and the difference between women pales when compared with Anglo males, whose mean income is much higher than that of any group of women.[4]

When we consider the large immigrant Asian population and the language barriers that restrict women to menial or entry-level jobs, we are talking about a group that not only earns minimum wage or less, but one whose purchasing power is substantially undermined by living in metropolitan areas of states where the cost of living is unusually high.

Another striking pattern about Asian American female employment is the high rate of labor force participation. Asian American women are more likely than Anglo American women to work full time and year round. The model minority interpretation tends to assume that mere high labor force participation is a sign of successful employment. One important factor motivating minority women to enter the work force, however, is the need to supplement family resources. For Anglo American women some of the necessity for working is partly offset by the fact that they often share in the higher incomes of Anglo males, who tend not only to earn more than all other groups but, as noted earlier, also tend to receive higher returns on their education. Moreover, once regional variation is adjusted for, Filipino and Chinese Americans had a median annual income equivalent to black males in four mainland SMSAs—Chicago, Los Angeles/Long Beach, New York, San Francisco/Oakland.[5] Census statistics point to the relatively lower earning capacity of Asian males compared to Anglo males, suggesting that Asian American women enter the work force to help compensate for this inequality. Thus, the mere fact of high employment must be read cautiously and analyzed within a larger context.

The Different Faces of Immigration

Over the last decade immigration has expanded the Chinese population by 85.3 percent, making it the largest Asian group in the country at 806,027, and has swelled the Filipino population by 125.8 percent, making it the second largest at 774,640.* Hence at present the majority of Chinese American and Filipino American women are foreign-born. In addition the Asian American "success story" is misleading in part because of a select group of these immigrants: foreign-educated professionals.

Since 1965 U.S. immigration laws have given priority to seven categories of individuals. Two of the seven allow admittance of people with special occupational skills or services needed in the United States. Four categories facilitate family reunification, and the last applies only to refugees. While occupation is estimated to account for no more than 20 percent of all visas, professionals are not precluded from entering under other preference categories. Yet this select group is frequently offered as evidence of the upward mobility possible in America when Asian Americans who are born and raised in the United States are far less likely to reach the doctoral level in their education. Over two-thirds of Asians with doctorates in the United States are trained and educated abroad.[6]

Also overlooked in some analyses is a great deal of downward mobility among the foreign-born. For example, while foreign-educated health professionals are given preferential status for entry into this country, restrictive li-

---

*Editors' note: In 1990, the Chinese American population was 1,645,000, and the Filipino American population was 1,407,000—still the two largest Asian American groups.

censing requirements deny them the opportunity to practice or utilize their special skills. They are told that their educational credentials, experience, and certifications are inadequate. Consequently, for many the only alternatives are menial labor or unemployment.[7] Other highly educated immigrants become owner/managers of Asian businesses, which also suggests downward mobility and an inability to find jobs in their field of expertise.

"Professional" Obscures More Than It Reveals

Another major reason for the perception of "model minority" is that the census categories implying success, "professional-managerial" or "executive, administrative, managerial," frequently camouflage important inconsistencies with this image of success. As managers, Asian Americans, usually male, are concentrated in certain occupations. They tend to be self-employed in small-scale wholesale and retail trade and manufacturing. They are rarely buyers, sales managers, administrators, or salaried managers in large-scale retail trade, communications, or public utilities. Among foreign-born Asian women, executive-managerial status is limited primarily to auditors and accountants.[8]

In general, Asian American women with a college education are concentrated in narrow and select, usually less prestigious, rungs of the "professional-managerial" class. In 1970, 27 percent of native-born Japanese women were either elementary or secondary school teachers. Registered nurses made up the next largest group. Foreign-born Filipino women found this to be their single most important area of employment, with 19 percent being nurses. They were least represented in the more prestigious professions—physicians, judges, dentists, law professors, and lawyers.[9] In 1980 foreign-born Asian women with four or more years of college were most likely to find jobs in administrative support or clerical occupations.

Self-Help Through "Taking Care of One's Own"

Much of what is considered ideal or model behavior in American society is based on Anglo-Saxon, Protestant values. Chief among them is an ethic of individual self-help, of doing without outside assistance or governmental support. On the other hand, Asian Americans have historically relied to a large extent on family or community resources. Their tightly knit communities tend to be fairly closed to the outside world, even when under economic hardship. Many below the poverty level do not receive any form of public assistance.[10] Even if we include social security benefits as a form of supplementary income, the proportion of Asian Americans who use them is again very low, much lower than that for Anglo Americans.[11] Asian American families, in fact, are more likely than Anglo American families to bear economic hardships on their own.

While Asian Americans appear to have been self-sufficient as communities, we need to ask, at what personal cost? Moreover, have they as a group reaped rewards commensurate with their efforts? The following section presents data which document that while Asian American women may be motivated to achieve through education, monetary returns for them are less than for other groups.

THE NATURE OF INEQUALITY

The decision to use white males as the predominant reference group within the United States is a politically charged issue. When women raise and push the issue of "comparable worth," of "equal pay for equal work," they argue that women frequently do work equivalent to men's, but are paid far less for it. . . .

Another way of thinking about comparable worth is not to focus only on what individuals do on the job, but on what they bring to the job as well. Because formal education is one measure of merit in American society and because it is most frequently perceived as the means to upward mobility, we would expect greater education to have greater payoffs.

Asian American women tend to be extraordinarily successful in terms of attaining higher education. Filipino American women have the highest college completion rate of all women and graduate at a rate 50 percent greater than that of majority males. Chinese American and Japanese American women follow closely behind, exceeding both the majority male and female rate of college completion.[12] Higher levels of education, however, bring lower returns for Asian American women than they do for other groups.

While education enhances earnings capability, the return on education for Asian American women is not as great as that for other women, and is well below parity with white males. . . .

The fact that Asian American women do not reap the income benefits one might expect given their high levels of educational achievement raises questions about the reasons for such inequality. To what extent is this discrepancy based on outright discrimination? On self-imposed limitations related to cultural modesty? The absence of certain social or interpersonal skills required for upper managerial positions? Or institutional factors beyond their control? It is beyond the scope of this paper to address such concerns. However, the fact of inequality is itself noteworthy and poorly appreciated.

In general, Asian American women usually are overrepresented in clerical or administrative support jobs. While there is a somewhat greater tendency for foreign-born college-educated Asian women to find clerical-related jobs, both native- and foreign-born women have learned that clerical work is the area where they are most easily employed. . . . In addition Asian American women tend to be over-represented as cashiers, file clerks, office machine operators, and typists. They are less likely to get jobs as secretaries or reception-ists. The former occupations not only carry less prestige but generally have "little or no decision-making authority, low mobility, and low public contact." [13]

In short, education may improve one's chances for success, but it cannot promise the American Dream. For Asian American women education seems to serve less as an opportunity for upward mobility than as a protection against jobs as service or assembly workers, or as machine operatives—all areas where foreign-born Asian women are far more likely to find themselves.

CONCLUSION

In this essay I have attempted to direct our attention to the gap between achievement and reward, specifically the failure to reward monetarily those who have demonstrated competence. Asian American women, like Asian American men, have been touted as "model minorities," praised for their out-standing achievements. The concept of model minority, however, obscures the fact that one's accomplishments are not adequately recognized in terms of commensurate income or choice of occupation. By focusing on the achieve-ments of one minority in relation to another, our attention is diverted from larger institutional and historical factors which influence a group's success. Each ethnic group has a different history, and a simplistic method of model-ing which assumes the experience of all immigrants is the same ignores the so-ciostructural context in which a certain kind of achievement occurred. For ex-ample, World War II enabled many Asian Americans who were technically trained and highly educated to move into lucrative war-related industries. [14] More recently, Korean immigrants during the 1960s were able to capitalize on the fast-growing demand for wigs in the United States. It was not simply cul-tural ingenuity or individual hard work which made them successful in this enterprise, but the fact that Korean immigrants were in the unique position of being able to import cheap hair products from their mother country. [15]

Just as there are structural opportunities, so there are structural barriers. However, the persistent emphasis in American society on individual effort deflects attention away from such barriers and creates self-doubt among those who have not "made it." The myth that Asian Americans have succeeded as a group, when in actuality there are serious discrepancies between effort and achievement, and between achievement and reward, adds still further to this self-doubt.

While others have also pointed out the myth of the model minority, I want to add that myths do have social functions. It would be a mistake to dis-miss the model minority concept as merely a myth. Asian Americans are— however inappropriately—thrust into the role of being models for other minorities.

A closer look at the images associated with Asians as a model minority group suggests competing or contradictory themes. One image is that Asian Americans exemplify a competitive spirit, enabling them to overcome structural barriers through perseverance and ingenuity. On the other hand, they are also seen as complacent, content with their social lot, and expecting little in the way of outside help. A third image is that Asian Americans are experts at assimilation, demonstrating that this society still functions as a melting pot. Their values are sometimes equated with white, middle-class, Protestant values of hard work, determination, and thrift. Opposing this image, however, is still another, namely that Asian Americans have succeeded because they possess cultural values unique to them as a group—their family-centeredness and long tradition of reverence for scholarly achievement, for example.

Perhaps, then, this is why so many readily accept the myth, whose tenacity is due to its being vague and broad enough to appeal to a variety of different groups. Yet to the extent that the myth is based on misconceptions, we are called upon to reexamine it more closely in an effort to narrow the gap between striving and achieving.[16]

NOTES

1. Ted Bell, "Quiet Loyalty Keeps Shops Running," *Sacramento Bee*, 11 February 1985.

2. U.S. Bureau of the Census, *Race of the Population by States* (Washington, D.C., 1980). According to the census, 40 percent of all Chinese in America live in California, as well as 46 percent of all Filipinos, and 37 percent of all Japanese. New York ranks second for the number of Chinese residing there, and Hawaii is the second most populated state for Filipinos and Japanese.

3. Tricia Knoll, *Becoming Americans: Asian Sojourners, Immigrants, and Refugees in the Western United States* (Portland, Oreg.: Coast to Coast Books, 1982), 152.

4. U.S. Commission on Civil Rights, *Social Indicators of Equality for Minorities and Women* (Washington, D.C., 1978), 24, 50, 54, 58, 62.

5. David M. Moulton, "The Socioeconomic Status of Asian American Families in Five Major SMSAs" (Paper prepared for the Conference of Pacific and Asian American Families and HEW-related Issues, San Francisco, 1978). No comparative data were available on blacks for the fifth SMSA, Honolulu.

6. James E. Blackwell, *Mainstreaming Outsiders* (New York: General Hall, Inc., 1981), 306; and Commission on Civil Rights, *Social Indicators*, 9.

7. California Advisory Committee, "A Dream Unfulfilled: Korean and Pilipino Health Professionals in California" (Report prepared for submission to U.S. Commission on Civil Rights, May 1975), iii.

8. See Amado Y. Cabezas, "A View of Poor Linkages Between Education, Occupation and Earnings for Asian Americans" (Paper presented at the Third National Forum on Education and Work, San Francisco, 1977), 17; and Census of Population, PUS, 1980.

9. Census of the Population, PUS, 1970, 1980.

10. A 1977 report on California families showed that an average of 9.3 percent of Japanese, Chinese, and Filipino families were below the poverty level, but that only 5.4 percent of these families received public assistance. The corresponding figures for Anglos were 6.3 percent and 5.9 percent. From Harold T. Yee, "The General Level of Well-Being of Asian Americans" (Paper presented to U.S. government officials in partial response to Justice Department amicus).

11. Moulton, "Socioeconomic Status," 70–71.

12. Commission on Civil Rights, *Social Indicators*, 54.

13. Bob H. Suzuki, "Education and the Socialization of Asian Americans: A Revisionist Analysis of the 'Model Minority' Thesis," *Amerasia Journal* 4:2 (1977): 43. See also Fong and Cabezas, "Economic and Employment Status," 48–49; and Commission on Civil Rights, *Social Indicators*, 97–98.

14. U.S. Commission on Civil Rights, "Education Issues" in *Civil Rights Issues of Asian and Pacific Americans: Myths and Realities* (Washington, D.C., 1979), 370–376. This material was presented by Ling-chi Wang, University of California, Berkeley.

15. Illsoo Kim, *New Urban Immigrants: The Korean Community in New York* (Princeton, N.J.: Princeton University Press, 1981).

16. For further discussion of the model minority myth and interpretation of census data, see Deborah Woo, "The Socioeconomic Status of Asian American Women in the Labor Force: An Alternative View," *Sociological Perspectives* 28:3 (July 1985): 307–338.

THE LATINO POPULATION

28

The Importance of Economic Restructuring

Joan Moore and Raquel Pinderhughes

. . . American minorities have been incorporated into the general social fabric in a variety of ways. Just as Chicago's black ghettos reflect a history of slavery, Jim Crow legislation, and struggles for civil and economic rights, so the nation's Latino barrios reflect a history of conquest, immigration, and a struggle to maintain cultural identity.

In 1990 there were some 22 million Latinos residing in the United States, approximately 9 percent of the total population. Of these, 61 percent were

From: Joan Moore and Raquel Pinderhughes, eds., *In the Barrios: Latinos and the Underclass Debate* (New York: Russell Sage Foundation, 1993), pp. xvi–xxix. Copyright © 1993 Russell Sage Foundation. Reprinted by permission of Russell Sage Foundation.

Mexican in origin, 12 percent Puerto Rican, and 5 percent Cuban. These three groups were the largest, yet 13 percent of Latinos were of Central and South American origin and another 9 percent were classified as "other Hispanic." Latinos were among the fastest-growing segments of the American population, increasing by 7.6 million, or 53 percent, between 1980 and 1990. There are predictions that Latinos will outnumber blacks by the twenty-first century. If Latino immigration and fertility continue at their current rate, there will be over 54 million Latinos in the United States by the year 2020.

This is an old population: as early as the sixteenth century, Spanish explorers settled what is now the American Southwest. In 1848, Spanish and Mexican settlers who lived in that region became United States citizens as a result of the Mexican-American War. Although the aftermath of conquest left a small elite population, the precarious position of the masses combined with the peculiarities of southwestern economic development to lay the foundation for poverty in the current period (see Barrera 1979; Moore and Pachon 1985).

In addition to those Mexicans who were incorporated into the United States after the Treaty of Guadalupe Hidalgo, Mexicans have continually crossed the border into the United States, where they have been used as a source of cheap labor by U.S. employers. The volume of immigration from Mexico has been highly dependent on fluctuations in certain segments of the U.S. economy. This dependence became glaringly obvious earlier in this century. During the Great Depression of the 1930s state and local governments "repatriated" hundreds of thousands of unemployed Mexicans, and just a few years later World War II labor shortages reversed the process as Mexican contract-laborers (*braceros*) were eagerly sought. A little later, in the 1950s, massive deportations recurred when "operation Wetback" repatriated hundreds of thousands of Mexicans. Once again, in the 1980s, hundreds of thousands crossed the border to work in the United States, despite increasingly restrictive legislation.

High levels of immigration and high fertility mean that the Mexican-origin population is quite young—on the average, 9.5 years younger than the non-Latino population—and the typical household is large, with 3.8 persons, as compared with 2.6 persons in non-Latino households (U.S. Bureau of the Census 1991). Heavy immigration, problems in schooling, and industrial changes in the Southwest combine to constrain advancement. The occupational structure remains relatively steady, and though there is a growing middle class, there is also a growing number of very poor people.

The incorporation of Puerto Ricans into the United States began in 1898, when the United States took possession of Puerto Rico and Cuba during the Spanish-American War. Although Cuba gained its independence in 1902, Puerto Rico became a commonwealth of the United States in 1952. Thus Puerto Rican citizens are also citizens of the United States. The colonial relationship strongly influenced the structure of the Puerto Rican economy and the migration of Puerto Ricans to the mainland. As a result of the U.S. invasion, the island's economy was transformed from a diversified, subsistence economy, which emphasized tobacco, cattle, coffee, and sugar, to a one-crop sugar economy, of which more than 60 percent was controlled by absentee U.S. owners (Steward 1956). The constriction of the sugar economy in the 1920s resulted in high unemployment and widespread poverty, and propelled the first wave of Puerto Rican migration to the United States (Rodriguez 1989).

Puerto Rican migration to the mainland took place in roughly three periods. The first, 1900–1945, was marked by the arrival of rural migrants forced to leave the island to find work after some of these economic transformations. Many migrants directly responded to U.S. companies who valued Puerto Rican citizenship status and experience in agriculture and recruited Puerto Rican laborers for agriculture and industry in the United States (Morales 1986; Maldonado-Denis 1972). Almost all settled in New York City, most working in low-skilled occupations.

The second period, 1946–1964, is known as the "great migration" because it was during this period that the greatest number of Puerto Ricans migrated. This movement reflected factors that included the search for work, artificially low fares between the island and New York arranged by the island government, labor recruitment, and the emergence of Puerto Rican settlements on the mainland. Though Puerto Ricans were still relegated to low-wage jobs, they were employed in large numbers.

The period after 1965 has been characterized by a fluctuating pattern of net migration as well as greater dispersion to parts of the United States away from New York City (Rodriguez 1989). It is known as the "revolving-door migration": during most of this period the heavy flow from the island to the mainland was balanced by equally substantial flows in the opposite direction. However, since 1980 the net outflows from Puerto Rico have rivaled those experienced in the 1950s.

Over the past three decades the economic status of Puerto Ricans dropped precipitously. By 1990, 38 percent of all Puerto Rican families were below the poverty line. A growing proportion of these families were concentrated in poor urban neighborhoods located in declining industrial centers in the Northeast and Midwest, which experienced massive economic restructuring and diminished employment opportunities for those with less education and weaker skills. The rising poverty rate has also been linked to a dramatic increase in female-headed households. Recent studies show that the majority of recent migrants were not previously employed on the island. Many were single women who migrated with their young children (Falcon and Gurak 1991). Currently, Puerto Ricans are the most economically disadvantaged group of all Latinos. As a group they are poorer than African Americans.

Unlike other Latino migrants, who entered the United States as subordinate workers and were viewed as sources of cheap labor, the first large waves of Cuban refugees were educated middle- and upper-class professionals. Arriving in large numbers after Castro's 1959 revolution, Cubans were welcomed by the federal government as bona fide political refugees fleeing communism and were assisted in ways that significantly contributed to their economic well-being. Cubans had access to job-training programs and placement services, housing subsidies, English-language programs, and small-business loans. Federal and state assistance contributed to the growth of a vigorous enclave economy (with Cubans owning many of the businesses and hiring fellow Cubans) and also to the emergence of Miami as a center for Latin American trade. Cubans have the highest family income of all Latino groups. Nevertheless, in 1990, 16.9 percent of the Cuban population lived below the poverty line.

In recent years large numbers of Salvadorans and Guatemalans have come to the United States in search of refuge from political repression. But unlike Cubans, few have been recognized by the U.S. government as bona fide refugees. Their settlement and position in the labor market have been influenced by their undocumented (illegal) status. Dominicans have also come in large numbers to East Coast cities, many also arriving as undocumented workers. Working for the lowest wages and minimum job security, undocumented workers are among the poorest in the nation.

Despite their long history and large numbers, Latinos have been an "invisible minority" in the United States. Until recently, few social scientists and policy analysts concerned with understanding stratification and social problems in the United States have noticed them. Because they were almost exclusively concerned with relations between blacks and whites, social scientists were primarily concerned with generating demographic information on the nation's black and white populations, providing almost no information on other groups. Consequently, it has been difficult, sometimes impossible, to obtain accurate data about Latinos.

Latinos began to be considered an important minority group when census figures showed a huge increase in the population. By 1980 there were significant Latino communities in almost every metropolitan area in the nation. As a group, Latinos have low education, low family incomes, and are more clustered in low-paid, less-skilled occupations. Most Latinos live in cities, and poverty has become an increasing problem. On the whole, Latinos are more likely to live in poverty than the general U.S. population: poverty is widespread for all Latino subgroups except Cubans. They were affected by structural factors that influenced the socioeconomic status of all U.S. workers. In 1990, 28 percent were poor as compared with 13 percent of African Americans (U.S. Bureau of the Census 1991). Puerto Ricans were particularly likely to be poor. . . .

. . . The earliest evidence of a new and important economic change appeared in the 1970s. Jobs seemed to be relocating: they declined massively in some formerly prosperous parts of the country and grew quickly in other, formerly peripheral regions—especially the South and West (Perry and Watkins 1977). It became obvious that the nation as a whole was losing "good" manufacturing jobs as production became internationalized (AFL-CIO Industrial Union Department 1986; Bluestone and Harrison 1982). In the 1990s, white-collar employment began to be restructured as well.

By the late 1980s there was consensus that the geographical shift in the location of job growth was a manifestation of a second and more important aspect of economic restructuring—the shift from a manufacturing to a service economy, and of the increasing globalization of the economy. This was a major transformation, and it became obvious that traditional manufacturing was not going to revive. Jobs continued to be created in the new service and information economy, but many were disproportionately at either the high or the low end of the wage and salary distributions, and many of the new firms functioned without the internal differentiation that might permit workers to move up within the company.

Rustbelt manufacturing decline and Sunbelt growth have come to epitomize what economic restructuring means. But in reality things are a lot more subtle, a lot more complex, and demand a more elaborate conceptualization, especially as these trends affect Latino poverty. Elements of a more complex model are being developed by a number of researchers, but as of this writing none is yet adequate to understand the shifts that are evident in the cities represented in this volume. Several of these deserve particular emphasis.

First, there is the "Rustbelt in the Sunbelt" phenomenon. Some researchers have argued that deindustrialization has been limited to the Rustbelt, and that the causal chain adduced by Wilson therefore does not apply outside that region. But the fact is that many Sunbelt cities developed manufacturing industries, particularly during and after World War II. Thus Rustbelt-style economic restructuring—deindustrialization, in particular—has also affected them deeply. In the late 1970s and early 1980s cities like Los Angeles experienced a major wave of plant closings that put a fair number of Latinos out of work (Morales 1985; Soja, Morales, and Wolff 1983).

Second, there has been significant reindustrialization and many new jobs in many of these cities, a trend that is easily overlooked. Most of the expanding low-wage service and manufacturing industries, like electronics and garment manufacturing, employ Latinos (McCarthy and Valdez 1986; Muller and Espenshade 1986), and some depend almost completely on immigrant labor working at minimum wage (Fernandez-Kelly and Sassen 1991). In short, neither the Rustbelt nor the Sunbelt has seen uniform economic restructuring.

Third, Latinos are affected by the "global cities" phenomenon, particularly evident in New York and Chicago. This term refers to a particular mix of new jobs and populations and an expansion of both high- and low-paid service jobs (see Sassen-Koob 1984). When large multinational corporations centralize their service functions, upper-level service jobs expand. The growing corporate elite want more restaurants, more entertainment, more clothing, and more care for their homes and children, but these new consumer services usually pay low wages and offer only temporary and part-time work. The new service workers in turn generate their own demand for low-cost goods and services. Many of them are Latino immigrants and they create what Sassen calls a "Third World city . . . located in dense groupings spread all over the city": this new "city" also provides new jobs (1989, p. 70).

Los Angeles . . . has experienced many of these patterns. The loss of manufacturing jobs has been far less visible than in New York or Chicago, for although traditional manufacturing declined, until the 1990s high-tech manufacturing did not. Moreover, Los Angeles' international financial and trade functions flourished (Soja 1987). The real difference between Los Angeles on the one hand and New York and Chicago on the other was that more poor people in Los Angeles seemed to be working. In all three cities internationalization had similar consequences for the *structure* of jobs for the poor. More of the immigrants pouring into Los Angeles were finding jobs, while the poor residents of New York and Chicago were not.

Fourth, even though the deindustrialization framework remains of overarching importance in understanding variations in the urban context of Latino poverty, we must also understand that economic restructuring shows many different faces. It is different in economically specialized cities. Houston, for example, has been called "the oil capital of the world," and most of the devastating economic shifts in that city were due to "crisis and reorganization in the world oil-gas industry" (Hill and Feagin 1987, p. 174). Miami is another special case. The economic changes that have swept Miami have little to do with deindustrialization, or with Europe or the Pacific Rim, and much to do with the overpowering influence of its Cuban population, its important "enclave economy," and its "Latino Rim" functions (see Portes and Stepick 1993).

Finally, economic change has a different effect in peripheral areas. Both Albuquerque and Tucson are regional centers in an economically peripheral area. Historically, these two cities served the ranches, farms, and mines of their desert hinterlands. Since World War II, both became military centers, with substantial high-tech defense industrialization. Both cities are accustomed to having a large, poor Latino population, whose poverty is rarely viewed as a crisis. In Tucson, for example, unemployment for Mexican Americans has been low, and there is stable year-round income. But both cities remain marginal to the national economy, and this means that the fate of their poor depends more on local factors.

Laredo has many features in common with other cities along the Texas border, with its substantial military installations, and agricultural and tourist functions. All of these cities have been affected by general swings in the American and Texan economy. These border communities have long been the poorest in the nation, and their largely Mexican American populations have suffered even more from recent economic downturns. They are peripheral to the U.S. economy, but the important point is that their economic well-being is intimately tied to the Mexican economy. They were devastated by the collapse of the peso in the 1980s. They are also more involved than most American cities in international trade in illicit goods, and poverty in Laredo has been deeply affected by smuggling. Though Texas has a long history of discrimination against Mexican Americans, race is not an issue within Laredo itself, where most of the population—elite as well as poor—is of Mexican descent. This fact is of particular importance in evaluating the underclass debate.

THE INFORMAL AND ILLICIT ECONOMIES

The growth of an informal economy is part and parcel of late twentieth-century economic restructuring. Particularly in the global cities, a variety of "informal" economic activities proliferates—activities that are small-scale, informally organized, and largely outside government regulations (cf. Portes, Castells, and Benton 1989). Some low-wage reindustrialization, for example, makes use of new arrangements in well-established industries (like home work in the garment industry, as seamstresses take their work home with them). Small-scale individual activities such as street vending and "handyman" house repairs and alterations affect communities in peripheral as well as global cities. . . .

And, finally, there are illicit activities—most notoriously, a burgeoning drug market. There is not much doubt that the new poverty in the United States has often been accompanied by a resurgence of illicit economic activities. . . . Most . . . Latino communities . . . have been able to contain or encapsulate such activities so that they do not dominate neighborhood life. But in most of them there is also little doubt that illicit economic activities form an "expanded industry." They rarely provide more than a pittance for the average worker: but for a very small fraction of barrio households they are part of the battery of survival strategies. . . .

IMMIGRATION

Immigration—both international and from Puerto Rico—is of major significance for poor Latino communities in almost every city in every region of the country. Further, there is every reason to believe that immigration will continue to be important.

First, it has important economic consequences. Immigration is a central feature of the economic life of global cities: for example, Los Angeles has been called the "capital of the Third World" because of its huge Latino and Asian immigration (Rieff 1987). . . . Those cities most bound to world trends (New York, Los Angeles, Chicago, Houston, and Miami) experienced massive Latino immigration in the 1980s. In . . . Los Angeles, Houston, and Miami . . . , immigration is a major factor in the labor market, and the residents of the "second settlement" Puerto Rican communities . . . in New York and Chicago operate within a context of both racial and ethnic change and of increased Latino immigration. The restructured economy provides marginal jobs for immigrant workers, and wage scales seem to drop for native-born Latinos in areas where immigration is high. This is a more complicated scenario than the simple loss of jobs accompanying Rustbelt deindustrialization. Immigrants are ineligible for most government benefits, are usually highly motivated, and are driven to take even the poorest-paying jobs. They are also more vulnerable to labor-market swings.

These may be construed as rather negative consequences, but in addition, immigrants have been a constructive force in many cities. For example, [there is] the economic vitality of immigrant-serving businesses [and] the revival of language and of traditional social controls, the strengthening of networks, and the emergence of new community institutions. . . .

References

AFL-CIO Industrial Union Department 1986. *The Polarization of America*. Washington, D.C.: AFL-CIO Industrial Union Department.

Barrera, Mario 1979. *Race and Class in the Southwest*. Notre Dame, IN: University of Notre Dame Press.

Bluestone, Barry, and Bennett Harrison 1982. *The Deindustrialization of America*. New York: Basic Books.

Falcon, Luis, and Douglas Gurak 1991. "Features of the Hispanic Underclass: Puerto Ricans and Dominicans in New York." Unpublished manuscript.

Fernandez-Kelly, Patricia, and Saskia Sassen 1991. "A Collaborative Study of Hispanic Women in the Garment and Electronics Industries: Executive Summary." New York: New York University, Center for Latin American and Caribbean Studies.

Hill, Richard Child, and Joe R. Feagin 1987. "Detroit and Houston: Two Cities in Global Perspective." In Michael Peter Smith and Joe R. Feagin, eds. In *The Capitalist City*, pp. 155–177. New York: Basil Blackwell.

Maldonado-Denis, Manuel 1972. *Puerto Rico: A Sociohistoric Interpretation*. New York: Random House.

McCarthy, Kevin, and R. B. Valdez 1986. *Current and Future Effects of Mexican Immigration in California*. Santa Monica, CA: Rand Corporation.

Moore, Joan, and Harry Pachon 1985. *Hispanics in the United States*. Englewood Cliffs, NJ: Prentice Hall.

Morales, Julio 1986. *Puerto Rican Poverty and Migration: We Just Had to Try Elsewhere*. New York: Praeger.

Morales, Rebecca 1985. "Transitional Labor: Undocumented Workers in the Los Angeles Automobile Industry." *International Migration Review* 17:570–596.

Muller, Thomas, and Thomas J. Espenshade 1986. *The Fourth Wave*. Washington, D.C.: Urban Institute Press.

Perry, David, and Alfred Watkins 1977. *The Rise of the Sunbelt Cities*. Beverly Hills, CA: Sage.

Portes, Alejandro, Manuel Castells, and Lauren A. Benton 1989. *The Informal Economy*. Baltimore: Johns Hopkins University Press.

Portes, Alejandro, and Alex Stepick 1993. *City on the Edge: The Transformation of Miami*. Berkeley: University of California Press.

Rieff, David 1987. *Going to Miami: Exiles, Tourists, and Refugees in the New America*. Boston: Little Brown.

Rodriguez, Clara 1989. *Puerto Ricans: Born in the U.S.A.* Boston: Unwin Hyman.

Sassen, Saskia 1989. "New Trends in the Sociospatial Organization of the New York City Economy." In Robert Beauregard, ed. *Economic Restructuring and Political Response*. Newbury Park, CA: Sage.

Sassen-Koob, Saskia 1984. "The New Labor Demand in Global Cities." In Michael Smith, ed. *Cities in Transformation*. Beverly Hills, CA: Sage.

Soja, Edward 1987. "Economic Restructuring and the Internationalization of the Los Angeles Region." In Michael Peter Smith and Joe R. Feagin, eds. *The Capitalist City*, pp. 178–198. New York: Basil Blackwell.

Soja, Edward W., Rebecca Morales, and G. Wolff 1983. "Urban Restructuring: An Analysis of Social and Spatial Change in Los Angeles." *Economic Geography* 59:195–230.

Steward, Julian H. 1956. *The People of Puerto Rico*. Urbana, IL: University of Illinois Press.

U.S. Bureau of the Census 1991. *The Hispanic Population in the United States: March 1991*. Current Population Reports, Series P-20, No. 455. Washington, D.C.: U.S. Government Printing Office.

WORKING POOR, WORKING HARD

29

Katherine Newman

Conservatives insist that poor adults got where they are because they haven't the brains to do better, lack the moral fiber to restrain their sexual urges, or have succumbed to the easy out-of-state support that, we are told, puts people on the federal payroll for having children out of wedlock. What fails to register

From: *The Nation* 19 (July 29/August 5, 1996): 20–23. Reprinted by permission.

in the national imagination is the fact that the vast majority of poor people do work for a living. They hold the jobs that no one else really wants: the ones that pay the minimum wage, try the strength and patience of anyone who has ever tried to hold them, and subject their incumbents to a lingering stigma. Hamburger flippers, bedmakers, bedpan cleaners—these are the people Jesse Jackson once called attention to when he tried, in vain it seems, to elicit sympathy or at least recognition for the country's working poor.

There are approximately 30 million people in the United States who fill this bill. They are as far from the shiftless stereotype as one can imagine. Their full-time, year-round earnings are so meager that despite their best efforts they can't afford decent housing, diets, health care or child care. Apart from the Earned Income Tax Credit—perhaps the most important antipoverty program of the past twenty years, now threatened with dismemberment—we've devoted precious little attention to support of the working poor. We have been content to leave them to endure their struggle to survive, even though our best investment in poverty programs might well be to make sure the working poor can stay at work.

It is not surprising that we ignore the working poor. They do not impinge on the middle class; they are not poised to riot; and they are usually too busy trying to make ends meet to argue very loudly for a greater share of the public purse. Theirs is an invisible social problem, but a big one nonetheless. For the debilitating conditions that impinge on the working poor—substandard housing, crumbling schools, inaccessible health care—are hardly different from those that surround their non-working counterparts.

Indeed, for many these difficulties are measurably worse because the working poor lack access to many government supports like subsidized housing and medical care. Other benefits, like food stamps, are cut off at absurdly low levels and therefore unavailable to people who earn the minimum wage but work a forty-hour week. There isn't much of a safety net spread below the working poor, even though their struggle to survive can be as desperate as that of any family reliant on public support. We have put a great deal of energy into debating appropriate policy for the latter; we seem not to know the former exists.

But exist they do. In central Harlem—where I've been doing research on low-wage workers for the past three years—67 percent of households include at least one full-time worker. This, in a neighborhood where over 40 percent of the population exists below the poverty line and 29 percent receive public assistance, is the one number we never hear on the nightly news. The working people of central Harlem often find themselves subject to unstable hours— cut back with no notice because of a business downturn—or seasonal layoffs that hit their pocketbooks hard. Those who are part-time workers, most of whom are involuntary part-timers who would jump at the chance for a full-time position, are denied access to the unemployment insurance system. Hence, when the layoffs come or the hours shrink, there is no backstop save what is left of the welfare system.

Working mothers everywhere are faced with the problems of balancing the demands of a job and the responsibilities of child care. Poor mothers in Harlem who are working often find that their wages are so low that the best they can afford in the way of child care is of questionable quality and reliability. Even more problematic may be the arrangements for the care of the elderly, whose working adult children may be responsible for their care: there is no money to hire home aides or to make use of nursing homes, the strategies middle-aged middle-class families turn to (though at great cost).

Employers are less sympathetic, or less flexible, when faced with a store clerk who can't make it in today than they are when a high-priced accountant has to stay home. Vacation pay and sick pay are unknown benefits in the low-wage world. Instead, the working poor are deemed replaceable, and with good reason: there are indeed hundreds of people lining up to take their jobs, particularly in inner-city communities like Harlem, where we found the ratio of jobseekers to successful jobholders is 14 to 1.

Both child care and elder care obligations wreak havoc with the ability of a worker—especially a mother—to maintain her job when catastrophes or even garden-variety problems (the 5-year-old comes down with chicken pox) strike. The frequency with which these problems occur among poor families—working or not—is much higher than among those who are better off. Chronic asthma rates have doubled in the United States between 1980 and 1993, with over 5 million children presently suffering from this dangerous disease. Children in the ghetto are vastly overrepresented among asthma victims; medical researchers are unsure about the reasons. But like diabetes, tuberculosis and other chronic diseases, these are problems of poverty that are rising at alarming rates among ghetto residents. The working poor cannot earn their way out of crowded housing, exposure to toxic substances, inadequate diets and low birth weight babies—all conditions that contribute to disease. These health problems also set the stage for employment instability as parents struggle to cope with the endless rounds of hospitalization and doctors' visits that a chronic asthmatic requires. Many a working mother has found herself forced back to the welfare rolls because she can no longer manage these demands within the strictures of a low-wage job.

In recent years a new term has cropped up to describe ghetto dwellers: the urban underclass. Coined by the journalist Ken Auletta in an influential article in *The New Yorker*, the idea took on greater salience with the publication of William Julius Wilson's landmark volume *The Truly Disadvantaged* (see Adolph Reed Jr., "The Liberal Technocrat," February 6, 1988). The underclass literature paints a picture of the inner city as a public policy nightmare—a racially and economically segregated conglomeration of the welfare-dependent, criminals, broken families and children without stable roots or any understanding of how the employment world functions. Working people are erased from view; they are, presumably, living in better neighborhoods. What's wrong with this picture? There are, of course, millions of poor people on welfare in our ghettos. New York City, for example, has over 1 million people on A.F.D.C.* But my research in Harlem shows that no Berlin wall separates the welfare recipient from the working poor. More often than not, both kinds of poor people live under a single roof.

This will not surprise anyone who has ever tried to live on either an A.F.D.C. family budget or the proceeds of a "McJob." Neither will really float a family: women on welfare cannot possibly pay the rent, the food bill, utilities and other basic necessities (let alone any luxuries) on the stipend provided by A.F.D.C. They have to find additional resources, and most of them do: they work off the books, they receive "in kind" assistance from family members or friends, which has to be hidden from view. The working poor are in the same situation: they cannot pay the rent on their apartments out of the minimum wage. They frequently rely on another family member's subsidized housing and Medicare. America's poorest workers are often intertwined with relatives and close friends who are on welfare. The combination of the two income streams makes it possible to manage the basic necessities of life at a very low level.

Descriptions of inner-city communities that stress a dramatic separation between people who are gainfully employed and those who are on welfare fail to grasp this fundamental connection. This matters because any reforms or cuts the legislative enacts, aiming at welfare recipients, will have a profound effect on the working poor. Any move to rearrange the lives of those on welfare will ricochet back on the working poor. At the end of the day the nation may not be much better off in reducing the costs of welfare: we may simply push one group out and find another waiting on the doorstep. Credible policy begins by understanding how deeply intertwined the two kinds of poverty, working and non-, really are.

America's middle class used to seem remote from the daily problems of the poor. But the massive layoffs of the 1990s have left many a former middle manager scrambling for a job at K Mart where work conditions share some of the features that make low-wage jobs so problematic. Some analysts would see an optimistic aspect to this situation, hoping that the jarring experience of economic insecurity among the relatively advantaged would generate the

---

*Editors' note: A.F.D.C. (Aid to Families with Dependent Children)—the major federal program for public assistance to the poor—was eliminated by the Personal Responsibility and Work Reconciliation Act of 1996.

sympathy, the political will to reconsider the role of government in providing jobs, guaranteed income, health care and the other essentials in life. Most of us who have studied the shaken middle class believe we are very far from that kind of political reawakening. What middle-class insecurity seems to be fostering at the moment is a conservatism designed to punish.

Budget cuts will punish the poor who had the bad taste to get born into the wrong families at the wrong time in our economic and political history. But they will punish the rest of us too: the students who will be shut out of public universities, the elderly who will lose their home health aid (and their daughters who will have to forgo their jobs to care for them instead), the teachers who will be missing from classrooms that have already been stripped of books and pencils, and most of all the children who will inherit a labor market that is worsening steadily and a state sector that refuses to step in. And of course, the draconian legislation on the docket now will punish the very people who are among the strongest subscribers to the work ethic, the working poor and their families.

THE ARMSTRONGS

30

An Oral History of a Homeless American Family

Steven VanderStaay

The Armstrongs lived in Bellevue, a young, largely affluent city east of Seattle, until a medical emergency and the sudden loss of Mark's job forced the family to seek emergency housing.

Since Bellevue has little emergency housing, the Armstrongs were advised to seek shelter in nearby Seattle. Eventually, the family was moved to a large public housing project in the city's Central District. Each morning they awake at 5:00 for the long bus ride back to Bellevue for work and school.

Mark and Linda both work, as do their teenage children. Speaking to them, I am struck that they are the quintessential American family: hard-working, supportive,

From: Steven VanderStaay, *Street Lives: An Oral History of Homeless Americans* (Philadelphia, PA: New Society Publishers, 1992). Reprinted by permission of the author.

patriotic, loving. And now homeless. The Armstrongs' difficulties—underemployment, housing, grocery bills, health costs, insurance problems—mirror those of other homeless families driven from affluent communities.

They are African Americans in their early thirties.

Mark:

I designed and built conveyor belts, and was good at it. I was making over $15 an hour. And I can go back there right now and get you a letter of recommendation from the company and let you read what they wrote about me. That in itself tells you what kind of worker I am.

The company went out of business. Bang! Didn't even know it was coming. I was between jobs three or four months. I could have found work right away if I wanted to make minimum wage, but I got pretty high standards for myself. I don't even want to make what I'm making now. We could barely afford rent then, how can we now? But when you got kids to feed and bills to pay, you have to do the best you can.

But minimum wage—that's insulting. I don't knock it for high school students. They're getting training, learning about working, making their pocket money. That's fine. But you take a person . . . I got six kids. $3.35, $4 an hour, I spend more than that wage in a day's time on a grocery bill. I mean you can accept some setbacks, but you can't tell a person, "I don't care if you've been making $15 something an hour, the minimum is what you've got to make now." If I hand you this letter, give you my resumé, my military record, show you the kind of worker I am, talk about my family, how can you degrade me by offering me the minimum wage?

Then we had trouble with the house we were renting. And, well, the biggest part of it was hospital bills. My son had to have emergency surgery. Since the company was going out of business it let the insurance lapse, so I got stuck with the bill. Spent every penny we had saved and there's still fourteen hundred dollars on it. You would think by being medical that it wouldn't affect the credit, but it does.

Now I'm working with Safeway's warehouse. I work in the milk plant. Swing shift. Sometimes I'm off at 12:30, 1:00 at night, and then turn right around and go back at 8:30 the next morning. Yeah, it's hard sometimes. I'm not making half of what I used to. I'm a helper—I used to have people working for me. I'd worked my way up through the ranks. But like I was saying, you adjust, you do what you have to do. I'm the kind of person, I get with a company I want to stay, be a part of it. I like to get along with people and work, get my hands dirty. See something accomplished. I'm low man on the totem pole but I'll stay and work my way up.

The warehouse, it's refrigerated on one end and kind of hot on the other. They make their own milk cartons out of plastic so you have to deal with heat and cold. You have to know how to dress 'cause you're dealing with both extremes.

Linda:

I've been a custodian, nurse's aide; now I work at K-Mart. I still have to bus back to the East side [Bellevue] every day. It's okay but I'm looking for something else. You know, it's $4 an hour, and there's no benefits, no discounts at the store, nothing like that.

And I'm in school now, too. I'm going for business training, probably computers or administration. When school starts I'll either bring the little ones there with me or have one of the older ones bring them home.

Working full-time and going to school. Six kids, seventeen on down to twelve. Three in high school, three in grade school. Two of them work at Jack in the Box. They've been working the same shift but my oldest, he's on the football team, so he might be working at a different time than my daughter. And then there's the church, and those football games. Yes we're busy! Just an all-American family. One that's hit a string of bad luck, that's all.

The hardest thing is getting up early enough to bus back over there. As soon as school gets started that's really going to be a problem. It might be a couple of hours, both ways. And if they find out our kids are living here they'll want them in school in Seattle. But they like the schools there and I like them. They're better. And that's where we've lived, that's where we work.

But we get by. The kids, they cook, they clean, they wash and iron their own clothes. And the older ones, they all work. We're so proud of them. Oh, we have the same problems everybody else has, with teenagers and so forth. But we get through 'em. Just thank God they're not on drugs. That's the biggest problem here.

Mark:

When we had to move and lost the house, when I lost my job, we told the kids the truth, the flat out truth. With no misconception; none whatsoever. Kids are not dumb. If you lie to kids, why should they be honest with you? They know exactly what we're going through and they know why.

Same thing when we moved here—six kids, three rooms, writing all over the walls, the drugs and crime. We tried to avoid the move but we didn't have any choice. They knew exactly where we were moving to, as best as I could explain it. We told them we didn't want to come, but if it came down to it we were coming. And we did.

Now my worst fear . . . there's so much drugs in this area. And people think every apartment in the projects is a drug house. They knock on the doors, knock on the windows—they stop me out there and ask where it is. It's here, so close to us all the time. And all the shooting and fighting . . . You can look out the window any given night and see the police stopping people and searching everyone.

If I can't look out my door and see my kids, I send for 'em. And I'm afraid when I can't see 'em. 'Cause when they get to shootin' and fightin' and carryin'-on, a bullet don't got no names on it. Sometimes when I come in from work, three, four o'clock in the morning, I wonder just when they're going to get me. But my worst fear, my worst fear is the kids.

Linda:

Over in Bellevue they think if you can't afford it then you shouldn't be there. You know, who cares if you work there.

The first house that we had, we were the first blacks in the neighborhood. When I moved over there I said, "Where the black people?" [laughs, then moves her head from side to side as if searching] . . . no black people? Then the neighbors, they got to looking, came out, they were surprised, too. "Oooh, we got black people over here now" [laughs]. The kids were the only black kids around.

Mark:

People don't want to rent to a family. And you know the kind of rent they're asking over there in Bellevue, that's not easy to come up with. And you need first, last month's rent, security. . . . And then people automatically assess, they stereotype you. Maybe sometimes it's 'cause we're black—I'm not saying this is true, I'm saying that sometimes I *felt* that the reason we didn't get a place was because we were black. But most of the time it's the family. People would rather you have pets than kids these days.

One guy, he had six bedrooms in this house. But he didn't want a family. Why would you have six bedrooms if you didn't want to rent to a family? May not be legal, but they do that all the time.

Now there is some validity in what they say about children tearing up things. But the child is only as bad as you let him be. You're the parent, he's going to do exactly what you let him do and get away with. If my kids tear something up, I'll pay for it. But me, I tell my kids that if I have to replace something they've destroyed, then one of their sisters or brothers isn't going to get something they need. And when they do something they answer to me.

I'm not bitter . . . I mean I'm somewhat so. I'm not angry bitter. It's just that I don't like dragging my kids from one place to the next, and I don't think we've been treated right. We had to take places sight-unseen, just to get 'em. We paid $950 a month, and during the wintertime $300, $400 a month for electric and gas bills. Then bought food, kept my kids in clothes. How you supposed to save to get ahead with all that?

And the house, when we moved in the landlords said they'd do this and that, fix this and that. Said we would have an option to buy it. We said "Okay, and we'll do these things." We had an agreement.

We never got that chance to buy, and they never fixed those things. But we kept paying that $950 a month. They had a barrel over us: we needed some place to go. And they made a small fortune those years. A month after we moved out we went by: all those things they wouldn't do were done.

Before that the guy decided to sell his house, just like that, and we had to move. It was December, wintertime. For a while we were staying with her mother in a two-bedroom. Nine people. We had to be somewhere so we took that second place before we had even seen it.

Everybody has to have a place to live. And people will do what they have to do to survive. A long of things that you see going on around here are for survival [he sweeps his hand, indicating the housing projects]. I'm not taking up for them, there's a lot of things happening here that I oppose. But where there's a will there's a way, you know.

Families

OUR MOTHERS' GRIEF

Racial-Ethnic Women
and the Maintenance of Families

Bonnie Thornton Dill

31

REPRODUCTIVE LABOR[1] FOR WHITE WOMEN IN EARLY AMERICA

In eighteenth- and nineteenth-century America, the lives of white[2] women in the United States were circumscribed within a legal and social system based on patriarchal authority. This authority took two forms: public and private. The social, legal, and economic position of women in this society was controlled through the private aspects of patriarchy and defined in terms of their relationship to families headed by men. The society was structured to confine white wives to reproductive labor within the domestic sphere. At the same time, the formation, preservation, and protection of families among white settlers was seen as crucial to the growth and development of American society. Building, maintaining, and supporting families was a concern of the State and of those organizations that prefigured the State. Thus, while white women had few legal rights as women, they were protected through public forms of patriarchy that acknowledged and supported their family roles of wives, mothers, and daughters because they were vital instruments for building American society.

From: *Journal of Family History* 13 (1988): 415–31. Reprinted by permission.

The groundwork for public support of women's family roles was laid during the colonial period. As early as 1619, the London Company began planning for the importation of single women into the colonies to marry colonists, form families, and provide for a permanent settlement. The objective was to make the men "more settled and less moveable . . . instability would breed a dissolution, and so an overthrow of the Plantation" (cited in Spruill 1972, p. 8).

In accordance with this recognition of the importance of families, the London Company provided the economic basis necessary for the development of the family as a viable and essential institution within the nascent social structure of the colonies. Shares of land were allotted for both husbands and wives in recognition of the fact that "in a new plantation it is not known whether men or women be the most necessary" (cited in Spruill 1972, p. 9).

This pattern of providing an economic base designed to attract, promote, and maintain families was followed in the other colonial settlements. Lord Baltimore of Maryland ". . . offered to each adventurer a hundred acres for himself, a hundred for his wife, fifty for each child, a hundred for each man servant, and sixty for a woman servant. Women heads of families were treated just as men" (Spruill 1972, p. 11).

In Georgia, which appealed to poorer classes for settlers more than did Virginia or Maryland, ". . . among the advantages they offered men to emigrate was the gainful employment of their wives and children" (Spruill 1972, p. 16).

In colonial America, white women were seen as vital contributors to the stabilization and growth of society. They were therefore accorded some legal and economic recognition through a patriarchal family structure.

> While colonial life remained hard, . . . American women married earlier [than European women], were less restricted by dowries, and often had legal protection for themselves and their children in antenuptial contracts (Kennedy 1979, p. 7).

Throughout the colonial period, women's reproductive labor in the family was an integral part of the daily operation of small-scale family farms or artisan's shops. According to Kessler-Harris (1981), a gender-based division of labor was common, but not rigid. The participation of women in work that was essential to family survival reinforced the importance of their contributions to both the protection of the family and the growth of society.

Between the end of the eighteenth and mid-nineteenth century, what is labeled the "modern American family" developed. The growth of industrialization and an urban middle class, along with the accumulation of agrarian wealth among Southern planters, had two results that are particularly pertinent to this discussion. First, class differentiation increased and sharpened, and with it, distinctions in the content and nature of women's family lives. Second, the organization of industrial labor resulted in the separation of home and family and the assignment to women of a separate sphere of activity focused on childcare and home maintenance. Whereas men's activities became increasingly focused upon the industrial competitive sphere of work, "women's activities were increasingly confined to the care of children, the nurturing of the husband, and the physical maintenance of the home" (Degler 1980, p. 26).

This separate sphere of domesticity and piety became both an ideal for all white women as well as a source of important distinctions between them. As Matthaei (1982) points out, tied to the notion of wife as homemaker is a definition of masculinity in which the husband's successful role performance was measured by his ability to keep his wife in the homemaker role. The entry of white women into the labor force came to be linked with the husband's assumed inability to fulfill his provider role.

For wealthy and middle-class women, the growth of the domestic sphere offered a potential for creative development as homemakers and mothers. Given ample financial support from their husband's earnings, some of these women were able to concentrate their energies on the development and elaboration of the more intangible elements of this separate sphere. They were also able to hire other women to perform the daily tasks such as cleaning, laundry, cooking, and ironing. Kessler-Harris cautions, however, that the separation of productive labor from the home did not seriously diminish the amount of physical drudgery associated with housework, even for middle-class women.

> It did relegate the continuing hard work to second place, transforming the public image of the household by the 1820s and 1830s from a place where productive labor was performed to one whose main goals were the preservation of virtue and morality. . . . Many of the "well-run" homes of the pre–Civil War period seem to have been the dwelling of overworked women. Short of household help, without modern conveniences, and frequently pregnant, these women complained bitterly of their harsh existence (Kessler-Harris 1981, p. 39).

In effect, household labor was transformed from economic productivity done by members of the family group to home maintenance; childcare and moral uplift done by an isolated woman who perhaps supervised some servants.

Working-class white women experienced this same transformation but their families' acceptance of the domestic code meant that their labor in the home intensified. Given the meager earnings of working-class men, working-class families had to develop alternative strategies to both survive and keep the wives at home. The result was that working-class women's reproductive labor increased to fill the gap between family need and family income. Women increased their own production of household goods through things such as canning and sewing; and by developing other sources of income, including boarders and homework. A final and very important source of other income was wages earned by the participation of sons and daughters in the labor force. In fact, Matthaei argues that "the domestic homemaking of married women was supported by the labors of their daughters" (1982, p. 130).

The question arises: Why did white working-class families sacrifice other aspects of this nineteenth-century notion of family, such as privacy and the protection of children, to keep wives as homemakers within the home? Zaretsky (1978) provides a possible answer.

> The Victorian emphasis on the sanctity of the family and on the autonomy of women within the family marked an advance for women of all classes over the interdependent but male dominated subsistence farm of the 18th century . . . most of women's adult life was taken up with childrearing. As a result, a special respect for her place within the home, and particularly for her childrearing activities was appreciated by working-class women (p. 211).

Another way in which white women's family roles were socially acknowledged and protected was through the existence of a separate sphere for women. The code of domesticity, attainable for affluent women, became an ideal toward which nonaffluent women aspired. Notwithstanding the personal constraints placed on women's development, the notion of separate spheres promoted the growth and stability of family life among the white middle class and became the basis for working-class men's efforts to achieve a family wage, so that they could keep their wives at home. Also, women gained a distinct sphere of authority and expertise that yielded them special recognition.

During the eighteenth and nineteenth centuries, American society accorded considerable importance to the development and sustenance of European immigrant families. As primary laborers in the reproduction and maintenance of family life, women were acknowledged and accorded the privileges and protections deemed socially appropriate to their family roles. This argument acknowledges the fact that the family structure denied these women many rights and privileges and seriously constrained their individual growth and development. Because women gained social recognition primarily through their membership in families, their personal rights were few and privileges were subject to the will of the male head of the household. Nevertheless, the recognition of women's reproductive labor as an essential building block of the family, combined with a view of the family as the cornerstone of the nation, distinguished the experiences of the white, dominant culture from those of racial ethnics.

Thus, in its founding, American society initiated legal, economic, and social practices designed to promote the growth of family life among European colonists. The reception colonial families found in the United States contrasts sharply with the lack of attention given to the families of racial-ethnics. Although the presence of racial-ethnics was equally as important for the growth of the nation, their political, economic, legal, and social status was quite different.

REPRODUCTIVE LABOR AMONG RACIAL-ETHNICS IN EARLY AMERICA

Unlike white women, racial-ethnic women experienced the oppressions of a patriarchal society but were denied the protections and buffering of a patriarchal family. Their families suffered as a direct result of the organization of the labor systems in which they participated.

Racial-ethnics were brought to this country to meet the need for a cheap and exploitable labor force. Little attention was given to their family and community life except as it related to their economic productivity. Labor, and not the existence or maintenance of families, was the critical aspect of their role in building the nation. Thus they were denied the social structural supports necessary to make *their* families a vital element in the social order. Family membership was not a key means of access to participation in the wider society. The lack of social, legal, and economic support for racial-ethnic families intensified and extended women's reproductive labor, created tensions and strains in family relationships, and set the stage for a variety of creative and adaptive forms of resistance.

AFRICAN-AMERICAN SLAVES

Among students of slavery, there has been considerable debate over the relative "harshness" of American slavery, and the degree to which slaves were permitted or encouraged to form families. It is generally acknowledged that many slaveowners found it economically advantageous to encourage family formation as a way of reproducing and perpetuating the slave labor force. This became increasingly true after 1807 when the importation of African slaves was explicitly prohibited. The existence of these families and many aspects of their functioning, however, were directly controlled by the master. In other words, slaves married and formed families but these groupings were completely subject to the master's decision to let them remain intact. One study has estimated that about 32% of all recorded slave marriages were disrupted by sale, about 45% by death of a spouse, about 10 percent by choice, with the remaining 13 percent not disrupted at all (Blassingame 1972, pp. 90–92). African slaves thus quickly learned that they had a limited degree of control over the formation and maintenance of their marriages and could not be assured of keeping their children with them. The threat of disruption was perhaps the most direct and pervasive cultural assault[3] on families that slaves encountered. Yet there were a number of other aspects of the slave system which reinforced the precariousness of slave family life.

In contrast to some African traditions and the Euro-American patterns of the period, slave men were not the main provider or authority figure in the family. The mother-child tie was basic and of greatest interest to the slave-owner because it was critical in the reproduction of the labor force.

In addition to the lack of authority and economic autonomy experienced by the husband-father in the slave family, use of the rape of women slaves as a weapon of terror and control further undermined the integrity of the slave family.

> It would be a mistake to regard the institutionalized pattern of rape during slavery as an expression of white men's sexual urges, otherwise stifled by the specter of the white womanhood's chastity . . . Rape was a weapon of domination, a weapon of repression, whose covert goal was to extinguish slave women's will to resist, and in the process, to demoralize their men (Davis 1981, pp. 23–24).

The slave family, therefore, was at the heart of a peculiar tension in the master-slave relationship. On the one hand, slaveowners sought to encourage familial ties among slaves because, as Matthaei (1982) states: ". . . these provided the basis of the development of the slave into a self-conscious socialized human being" (p. 81). They also hoped and believed that this socialization process would help children learn to accept their place in society as slaves. Yet the master's need to control and intervene in the familial life of the slaves is indicative of the other side of this tension. Family ties had the potential for becoming a competing and more potent source of allegiance than the slavemaster himself. Also, kin were as likely to socialize children in forms of resistance as in acts of compliance.

It was within this context of surveillance, assault, and ambivalence that slave women's reproductive labor took place. She and her menfolk had the task of preserving the human and family ties that could ultimately give them a reason for living. They had to socialize their children to believe in the possibility of a life in which they were not enslaved. The slave woman's labor on behalf of the family was, as Davis (1971) has pointed out, the only labor the slave engaged in that could not be directly appropriated by the slaveowner for his own profit. Yet, its indirect appropriation, as labor crucial to the reproduction of the slaveowner's labor force, was the source of strong ambivalence for many slave women. Whereas some mothers murdered their babies to keep them from being slaves, many sought within the family sphere a degree of autonomy and creativity denied them in other realms of the society. The maintenance of a distinct African-American culture is testimony to the ways in which slaves maintained a degree of cultural autonomy and resisted the creation of a slave family that only served the needs of the master.

Gutman (1976) provides evidence of the ways in which slaves expressed a unique Afro-American culture through their family practices. He provides data on naming patterns and kinship ties among slaves that flies in the face of the dominant ideology of the period. That ideology argued that slaves were immoral and had little concern for or appreciation of family life.

Yet Gutman demonstrated that within a system which denied the father authority over his family, slave boys were frequently named after their fathers, and many children were named after blood relatives as a way of maintaining family ties. Gutman also suggested that after emancipation a number of slaves took the names of former owners in order to reestablish family ties that had been disrupted earlier. On plantation after plantation, Gutman found considerable evidence of the building and maintenance of extensive kinship ties among slaves. In instances where slave families had been disrupted, slaves in new communities reconstituted the kinds of family and kin ties that came to characterize black family life throughout the South. These patterns included, but were not limited to, a belief in the importance of marriage as a long-term commitment, rules of exogamy that included marriage between first cousins, and acceptance of women who had children outside of marriage. Kinship networks were an important source of resistance to the organization of labor that treated the individual slave, and not the family, as the unit of labor (Caulfield 1974).

Another interesting indicator of the slaves' maintenance of some degree of cultural autonomy has been pointed out by Wright (1981) in her discussion of slave housing. Until the early 1800s, slaves were often permitted to build their housing according to their own design and taste. During that period, housing built in an African style was quite common in the slave quarters. By 1830, however, slaveowners had begun to control the design and arrangement of slave housing and had introduced a degree of conformity and regularity to it that left little room for the slave's personalization of the home. Nevertheless, slaves did use some of their own techniques in construction and often hid it from their masters.

> Even the floors, which usually consisted of only tamped earth, were evidence of a hidden African tradition: slaves cooked clay over a fire, mixing in ox blood or cow dung, and then poured it in place to make hard dirt floors almost like asphalt . . . In slave houses, in contrast to other crafts, these signs of skill and tradition would then be covered over (Wright 1981, p. 48).

Housing is important in discussions of family because its design reflects sociocultural attitudes about family life. The housing that slaveowners provided for their slaves reflected a view of Black family life consistent with the stereotypes of the period. While the existence of slave families was acknowledged, it certainly was not nurtured. Thus, cabins were crowded, often containing more than one family, and there were no provisions for privacy. Slaves had to create their own.

> Slave couples hung up old clothes or quilts to establish boundaries; others built more substantial partitions from scrap wood. Parents sought to establish sexual privacy from children. A few ex-slaves described modified trundle beds designed to hide parental lovemaking . . . Even in one room cabins, sexual segregation was carefully organized (Wright 1981, p. 50).

Perhaps most critical in developing an understanding of slave women's reproductive labor is the gender-based division of labor in the domestic sphere. The organization of slave labor enforced considerable equality among men and women. The ways in which equality in the labor force was translated into the family sphere is somewhat speculative. Davis (1981), for example, suggests that egalitarianism between males and females was a direct result of slavery when she says:

> Within the confines of their family and community life, therefore, Black people managed to accomplish a magnificent feat. They transformed that negative equality which emanated from the equal oppression they suffered as slaves into a positive quality: the egalitarianism characterizing their social relations (p. 18).

It is likely, however, that this transformation was far less direct than Davis implies. We know, for example, that slave women experienced what has recently been called the "double day" before most other women in this society. Slave narratives (Jones 1985; White 1985; Blassingame 1977) reveal that women had primary responsibility for their family's domestic chores. They cooked (although on some plantations meals were prepared for all of the slaves), sewed, cared for their children, and cleaned house, all after completing a full day of labor for the master. Blassingame (1972) and others have pointed out that slave men engaged in hunting, trapping, perhaps some gardening, and furniture making as ways of contributing to the maintenance of their families. Clearly, a gender-based division of labor did exist within the family and it appears that women bore the larger share of the burden for housekeeping and child care.

By contrast to white families of the period, however, the division of labor in the domestic sphere was neither reinforced in the relationship of slave women to work nor in the social institutions of the slave community. The gender-based division of labor among the slaves existed within a social system that treated men and women as almost equal, independent units of labor.[4] Thus Matthaei (1982) is probably correct in concluding that

> Whereas . . . the white homemaker interacted with the public sphere through her husband, and had her work life determined by him, the enslaved

Afro-American homemaker was directly subordinated to and determined by
her owner . . . The equal enslavement of husband and wife gave the slave
marriage a curious kind of equality, an equality of oppression (p. 94).

Black men were denied the male resources of a patriarchal society and
therefore were unable to turn gender distinctions into female subordination,
even if that had been their desire. Black women, on the other hand, were denied support and protection for their roles as mothers and wives and thus had
to modify and structure those roles around the demands of their labor. Thus,
reproductive labor for slave women was intensified in several ways: by the demands of slave labor that forced them into the double-day of work; by the desire and need to maintain family ties in the face of a system that gave them
only limited recognition; by the stresses of building a family with men who
were denied the standard social privileges of manhood; and by the struggle to
raise children who could survive in a hostile environment.

This intensification of reproductive labor made networks of kin and
quasi-kin important instruments in carrying out the reproductive tasks of the
slave community. Given an African cultural heritage where kinship ties formed
the basis of social relations, it is not at all surprising that African American
slaves developed an extensive system of kinship ties and obligations (Gutman
1976; Sudarkasa 1981). Research on Black families in slavery provides considerable documentation of participation of extended kin in childrearing, child-
birth, and other domestic, social, and economic activities (Gutman 1976;
Blassingame 1972; Genovese and Miller 1974).

After slavery, these ties continued to be an important factor linking individual household units in a variety of domestic activities. While kinship ties
were also important among native-born whites and European immigrants,
Gutman (1976) has suggested that these ties

were comparatively more important to Afro-Americans than to lower-class native white and immigrant Americans, the result of their distinctive low economic
status, a condition that denied them the advantages of an extensive associa-
tional life beyond the kin group and the advantages and disadvantages resulting from mobility opportunities (p. 213).

His argument is reaffirmed by research on Afro-American families after
slavery (Shimkin et al. 1978; Aschenbrenner 1975; Davis 1981; Stack 1974).
Sudarkasa (1981) takes this argument one step further and links this pattern
to the African cultural heritage:

historical realities require that the derivation of this aspect of Black family organization be traced to its African antecedents. Such a view does not deny the
adaptive significance of consanguineal (kin) networks. In fact, it helps to clarify
why these networks had the flexibility they had and why, they, rather than conjugal relationships came to be the stabilizing factor in Black families (p. 49).

With individual households, the gender-based division of labor experienced some important shifts during emancipation. In their first real opportunity to establish family life beyond the controls and constraints imposed by a slavemaster, family life among Black sharecroppers changed radically. Most women, at least those who were wives and daughters of able-bodied men, withdrew from field labor and concentrated on their domestic duties in the home. Husbands took primary responsibility for the fieldwork and for relations with the owners, such as signing contracts on behalf of the family. Black women were severely criticized by whites for removing themselves from field labor because they were seen to be aspiring to a model of womanhood that was considered inappropriate for them. This reorganization of female labor, however, represented an attempt on the part of Blacks to protect women from some of the abuses of the slave system and to thus secure their family life. It was more likely a response to the particular set of circumstances that the newly freed slaves faced than a reaction to the lives of their former masters. Jones (1985) argues that these patterns were "particularly significant" because at a time when industrial development was introducing a labor system that divided male and female labor, the freed Black family was establishing a pattern of joint work and complementary tasks between males and females that was reminiscent of the preindustrial American families. Unfortunately, these former slaves had to do this without the institutional supports that white farm families had in the midst of a sharecropping system that deprived them of economic independence.

CHINESE SOJOURNERS

An increase in the African slave population was a desired goal. Therefore, Africans were permitted and even encouraged at times to form families subject to the authority and whim of the master. By sharp contrast, Chinese people were explicitly denied the right to form families in the United States through both law and social practice. Although male laborers began coming to the United States in sizable numbers in the middle of the nineteenth century, it was more than a century before an appreciable number of children of Chinese parents were born in America. Tom, a respondent in Nee and Nee's (1973) book, *Longtime Californ'* says: "One thing about Chinese men in America was you had to be either a merchant or a big gambler, have lot of side money to have a family here. A working man, an ordinary man, just can't!" (p. 80).

Working in the United States was a means of gaining support for one's family with an end of obtaining sufficient capital to return to China and purchase land. The practice of sojourning was reinforced by laws preventing Chinese laborers from becoming citizens, and by restrictions on their entry into this country. Chinese laborers who arrived before 1882 could not bring their wives and were prevented by law from marrying whites. Thus, it is likely that the number of Chinese-American families might have been negligible had it not been for two things: the San Francisco earthquake and fire in 1906, which destroyed all municipal records; and the ingenuity and persistence of the Chinese people who used the opportunity created by the earthquake to increase their numbers in the United States. Since relatives of citizens were permitted entry, American-born Chinese (real and claimed) would visit China, report the birth of a son, and thus create an entry slot. Years later the slot could be used by a relative or purchased. The purchasers were called "paper sons." Paper sons became a major mechanism for increasing the Chinese population, but it was a slow process and the sojourner community remained predominantly male for decades.

The high concentration of males in the Chinese community before 1920 resulted in a split-household form of family. As Glenn observes:

> In the split-household family, production is separated from other functions and is carried out by a member living far from the rest of the household. The rest—consumption, reproduction and socialization—are carried out by the wife and other relatives from the home village. . . . The split-household form makes possible maximum exploitation of the workers . . . The labor of prime-age male workers can be bought relatively cheaply, since the cost of reproduction and family maintenance is borne partially by unpaid subsistence work of women and old people in the home village (Glenn 1981, pp. 14–15).

The women who were in the United States during this period consisted of a small number who were wives and daughters of merchants and a larger percentage who were prostitutes. Hirata (1979) has suggested that Chinese prostitution was an important element in helping to maintain the split-household family. In conjunction with laws prohibiting intermarriage, Chinese prostitution helped men avoid long-term relationships with women in the United States and ensured that the bulk of their meager earnings would continue to support the family at home.

The reproductive labor of Chinese women, therefore, took on two dimensions primarily because of the split-household family form. Wives who remained in China were forced to raise children and care for in-laws on the meager remittances of their sojourning husband. Although we know few details about their lives, it is clear that the everyday work of bearing and maintaining children and a household fell entirely on their shoulders. Those women who immigrated and worked as prostitutes performed the more nurturant aspects of reproductive labor, that is, providing emotional and sexual companionship for men who were far from home. Yet their role as prostitute was more likely a means of supporting their families at home in China than a chosen vocation.

The Chinese family system during the nineteenth century was a patriarchal one wherein girls had little value. In fact, they were considered only temporary members of their father's family because when they married, they became members of their husband's families. They also had little social value: girls were sold by some poor parents to work as prostitutes, concubines, or servants. This saved the family the expense of raising them, and their earnings also became a source of family income. For most girls, however, marriages were arranged and families sought useful connections through this process.

With the development of a sojourning pattern in the United States, some Chinese women in those regions of China where this pattern was more prevalent would be sold to become prostitutes in the United States. Most, however, were married off to men whom they saw only once or twice in the 20- or 30-year period during which he was sojourning in the United States. Her status as wife ensured that a portion of the meager wages he earned would be returned to his family in China. This arrangement required considerable sacrifice and adjustment on the part of wives who remained in China and those who joined their husbands after a long separation.

Kingston (1977) tells the story of the unhappy meeting of her aunt, Moon Orchid, with her husband from whom she had been separated for 30 years.

> For thirty years she had been receiving money from him from America. But she had never told him that she wanted to come to the United States. She waited for him to suggest it, but he never did (p. 144).

His response to her when she arrived unexpectedly was to say:

> "Look at her. She'd never fit into an American household. I have important American guests who come inside my house to eat." He turned to Moon Orchid, "You can't talk to them. You can barely talk to me." Moon Orchid was so ashamed, she held her hands over her face. She wished she could also hide her dappled hands (p. 178).

Despite these handicaps, Chinese people collaborated to establish the opportunity to form families and settle in the United States. In some cases it took as long as three generations for a child to be born on United States soil.

> In one typical history, related by a 21 year old college student, great-grandfather arrived in the States in the 1890s as a "paper son" and worked for about 20 years as a laborer. He then sent for the grandfather, who worked alongside greatgrandfather in a small business for several years. Greatgrandfather subsequently returned to China, leaving grandfather to run the business and send remittance. In the 1940s, grandfather sent for father; up to this point, none of the wives had left China. Finally, in the late 1950s father returned to China and brought his wife back with him. Thus, after nearly 70 years, the first child was born in the United States (Glenn 1981, p. 14).

CHICANOS

Africans were uprooted from their native lands and encouraged to have families in order to increase the slave labor force. Chinese people were immigrant laborers whose "permanent" presence in the country was denied. By contrast, Mexican-Americans were colonized and their traditional family life was disrupted by war and the imposition of a new set of laws and conditions of labor. The hardships faced by Chicano families, therefore, were the result of the United States colonization of the indigenous Mexican population, accompanied by the beginnings of industrial development in the region. The treaty of Guadalupe Hidalgo, signed in 1848, granted American citizenship to Mexicans living in what is now called the Southwest. The American takeover, however, resulted in the gradual displacement of Mexicans from the land and their incorporation into a colonial labor force (Barrera 1979). In addition, Mexicans who immigrated into the United States after 1848 were also absorbed into the labor force.

Whether natives of Northern Mexico (which became the United States after 1848) or immigrants from Southern Mexico, Chicanos were a largely peasant population whose lives were defined by a feudal economy and a daily struggle on the land for economic survival. Patriarchal families were important instruments of community life and nuclear family units were linked together through an elaborate system of kinship and godparenting. Traditional life was characterized by hard work and a fairly distinct pattern of sex-role segregation.

> Most Mexican women were valued for their household qualities, men by their ability to work and to provide for a family. Children were taught to get up early, to contribute to the family's labor to prepare themselves for adult life . . . Such a life demanded discipline, authority, deference—values that cemented the working of a family surrounded and shaped by the requirements of Mexico's distinctive historical pattern of agricultural development, especially its pervasive debt peonage (Saragoza 1983, p. 8).

As the primary caretakers of hearth and home in a rural environment, *Las Chicanas* labor made a vital and important contribution to family survival. A description of women's reproductive labor in the early twentieth century can be used to gain insight into the work of the nineteenth-century rural women.

> For country women, work was seldom a salaried job. More often it was the work of growing and preparing food, of making adobes and plastering houses with mud, or making their children's clothes for school and teaching them the hymns and prayers of the church, or delivering babies and treating sicknesses with herbs and patience. In almost every town there were one or two women who, in addition to working in their own homes, served other fami-

lies in the community as *curanderas* (healers), *parteras* (midwives), and schoolteachers (Elasser and Vigil 1980, p. 10).

Although some scholars have argued that family rituals and community life showed little change before World War I (Saragoza 1983), the American conquest of Mexican lands, the introduction of a new system of labor, the loss of Mexican-owned land through the inability to document ownership, plus the transient nature of most of the jobs in which Chicanos were employed, resulted in the gradual erosion of this pastoral way of life. Families were uprooted as the economic basis for family life changed. Some immigrated from Mexico in search of a better standard of living and worked in the mines and railroads. Others who were native to the Southwest faced a job market that no longer required their skills and moved into mining, railroad, and agricultural labor in search of a means of earning a living. According to Camarillo (1979), the influx of Anglo[5] capital into the pastoral economy of Santa Barbara rendered obsolete the skills of many Chicano males who had worked as ranch-hands and farmers prior to the urbanization of that economy. While some women and children accompanied their husbands to the railroad and mine camps, they often did so despite prohibitions against it. Initially many of these camps discouraged or prohibited family settlement.

The American period (post-1848) was characterized by considerable transiency for the Chicano population. Its impact on families is seen in the growth of female-headed households, which was reflected in the data as early as 1860. Griswold del Castillo (1979) found a sharp increase in female-headed households in Los Angeles, from a low of 13 percent in 1844 to 31% in 1880. Camarillo (1979, p. 120) documents a similar increase in Santa Barbara from 15% in 1844 to 30 percent by 1880. These increases appear to be due not so much to divorce, which was infrequent in this Catholic population, but to widowhood and temporary abandonment in search of work. Given the hazardous nature of work in the mines and railroad camps, the death of a husband, father or son who was laboring in these sites was not uncommon. Griswold del Castillo (1979) reports a higher death rate among men than women in Los Angeles. The rise in female-headed households, therefore, reflects the instabilities and insecurities introduced into women's lives as a result of the changing social organization of work.

One outcome, the increasing participation of women and children in the labor force was primarily a response to economic factors that required the modification of traditional values. According to Louisa Vigil, who was born in 1890:

The women didn't work at that time. The man was supposed to marry that girl and take [care] of her . . . Your grandpa never did let me work for nobody.

He always had to work, and we never did have really bad times (Elasser and Vigil 1980, p. 14).

Señora Vigil's comments are reinforced in Garcia's (1980) study of El Paso. In the 393 households he examined in the 1900 census, he found 17.1% of the women to be employed. The majority of this group were daughters, mothers with no husbands, and single women. In the cases of Los Angeles and Santa Barbara, where there were even greater work opportunities for women than in El Paso, wives who were heads of household worked in seasonal and part-time jobs and lived from the earnings of children and relatives in an effort to maintain traditional female roles.

Slowly, entire families were encouraged to go to railroad workcamps and were eventually incorporated into the agricultural labor market. This was a response both to the extremely low wages paid to Chicano laborers and to the preferences of employers who saw family labor as a way of stabilizing the workforce. For Chicanos, engaging all family members in agricultural work was a means of increasing their earnings to a level close to subsistence for the entire group and of keeping the family unit together. Camarillo (1979, p. 93) provides a picture of the interplay of work, family, and migration in the Santa Barbara area in the following observation:

> The time of year when women and children were employed in the fruit cannery and participated in the almond and olive harvests coincided with the seasons when the men were most likely to be engaged in seasonal migratory work. There were seasons, however, especially in the early summer when the entire family migrated from the city to pick fruit. This type of family seasonal harvest was evident in Santa Barbara by the 1890s. As walnuts replaced almonds and as the fruit industry expanded, Chicano family labor became essential.

This arrangement, while bringing families together, did not decrease the hardships that Chicanas had to confront in raising their families. We may infer something about the rigors of that life from Jesse Lopez de la Cruz's description of the workday of migrant farm laborers in the 1940s. Work conditions in the 1890s were as difficult, if not worse.

> We always went where the women and men were going to work, because if it were just the men working it wasn't worth going out there because we wouldn't earn enough to support a family . . . We would start around 6:30 a.m. and work for four or five hours, then walk home and eat and rest until about three-thirty in the afternoon when it cooled off. We would go back and work until we couldn't see. Then I'd clean up the kitchen. I was doing the housework and working out in the fields and taking care of two children (quoted in Goldman 1981, pp. 119–120).

In the towns, women's reproductive labor was intensified by the congested and unsanitary conditions of the *barrios* in which they lived. Garcia (1980) described the following conditions in El Paso:

> Mexican women had to haul water for washing and cooking from the river or public water pipes. To feed their families, they had to spend time marketing, often in Ciudad Juarez across the border, as well as long, hot hours cooking meals and coping with the burden of desert sand both inside and outside their homes. Besides the problem of raising children, unsanitary living conditions forced Mexican mothers to deal with disease and illness in their families. Diphtheria, tuberculosis, typhus and influenza were never too far away. Some diseases could be directly traced to inferior city services . . . As a result, Mexican mothers had to devote much energy to caring for sick children, many of whom died (pp. 320–321).

While the extended family has remained an important element of Chicano life, it was eroded in the American period in several ways. Griswold del Castillo (1979), for example, points out that in 1845 about 71 percent of Angelenos lived in extended families and that by 1880, fewer than half did. This decrease in extended families appears to be a response to the changed economic conditions and to the instabilities generated by the new sociopolitical structure. Additionally, the imposition of American law and custom ignored and ultimately undermined some aspects of the extended family. The extended family in traditional Mexican life consisted of an important set of familial, religious, and community obligations. Women, while valued primarily for their domesticity, had certain legal and property rights that acknowledged the importance of their work, their families of origin and their children. In California, for example:

> Equal ownership of property between husband and wife had been one of the mainstays of the Spanish and Mexican family systems. Community-property laws were written into the civil codes with the intention of strengthening the economic controls of the wife and her relatives. The American government incorporated these Mexican laws into the state constitution, but later court decisions interpreted these statutes so as to undermine the wife's economic rights. In 1861, the legislature passed a law that allowed the deceased wife's property to revert to her husband. Previously it had been inherited by her children and relatives if she died without a will (Griswold del Castillo 1979, p. 69).

The impact of this and other similar court rulings was to "strengthen the property rights of the husband at the expense of his wife and children" (Griswold del Castillo 1979, p. 69).

In the face of the legal, social, and economic changes that occurred during the American period, Chicanas were forced to cope with a series of dislocations in traditional life. They were caught between conflicting pressures to maintain traditional women's roles and family customs and the need to participate in the economic support of their families by working outside the home. During this period the preservation of some traditional customs became an important force for resisting complete disarray.

According to Saragoza (1983), transiency, the effects of racism and segregation, and proximity to Mexico aided in the maintenance of traditional family practices. Garcia has suggested that women were the guardians of Mexican cultural traditions within the family. He cites the work of anthropologist Manuel Gamio, who identified the retention of many Mexican customs among Chicanos in settlements around the United States in the early 1900s.

> These included folklore, songs and ballads, birthday celebrations, saints' day, baptism, weddings, and funerals in the traditional style. Because of poverty, a lack of physicians in the barrios, and adherence to traditional customs, Mexicans continued to use medicinal herbs. Gamio also identified the maintenance of a number of oral traditions, and Mexican style cooking (Garcia 1980, p. 322).

Of vital importance to the integrity of traditional culture was the perpetuation of the Spanish language. Factors that aided in the maintenance of other aspects of Mexican culture also helped in sustaining the language. However, entry into English-language public schools introduced the children and their families to systematic efforts to erase their native tongue. Griswold del Castillo reports that in the early 1880s there was considerable pressure against the speaker of Spanish in the public school. He also found that some Chicano parents responded to this kind of discrimination by helping support independent bilingual schools. These efforts, however, were short-lived.

Another key factor in conserving Chicano culture was the extended family network, particularly the system of *compadrazgo* or godparenting. Although the full extent of the impact of the American period on the Chicano extended family is not known, it is generally acknowledged that this family system, though lacking many legal and social sanctions, played an important role in the preservation of the Mexican community (Camarillo 1979, p. 13). In Mexican society, godparents were an important way of linking family and community through respected friends or authorities. Named at the important rites of passage in a child's life, such as birth, confirmation, first communion, and marriage, *compadrazgo* created a moral obligation for godparents to act as guardians, to provide financial assistance in times of need, and to substitute in case of the death of a parent. Camarillo (1979) points out that in traditional society these bonds cut across class and racial lines.

> The rites of baptism established kinship networks between rich and poor—between Spanish, mestizo and Indian—and often carried with them political loyalty and economic-occupational ties. The leading California patriarchs in

> the pueblo played important roles in the compadrazgo network. They spon-
> sored dozens of children for their workers or poor relatives. The kindness of
> the *padrino* and *madrina* was repaid with respect and support from the pobla-
> dores (pp. 12–13).

The extended family network—which included godparents—expanded the support groups for women who were widowed or temporarily abandoned and for those who were in seasonal, part-, or full-time work. It suggests, therefore, the potential for an exchange of services among poor people whose income did not provide the basis for family subsistence. Griswold del Castillo (1979) argues that family organization influenced literacy rates and socioeconomic mobility among Chicanos in Los Angeles between 1850 and 1880. His data suggest that children in extended families (defined as those with at least one relative living in a nuclear family household) had higher literacy rates than those in nuclear families. He also argues that those in larger families fared better economically, and experienced less downward mobility. The data here are too limited to generalize to the Chicano experience as a whole but they do reinforce the actual and potential importance of this family form to the continued cultural autonomy of the Chicano community.

CONCLUSION: OUR MOTHERS' GRIEF

Reproductive labor for Afro-American, Chinese-American, and Mexican-American women in the nineteenth century centered on the struggle to maintain family units in the face of a variety of cultural assaults. Treated primarily as individual units of labor rather than as members of family groups, these women labored to maintain, sustain, stabilize, and reproduce their families while working in both the public (productive) and private (reproductive) spheres. Thus, the concept of reproductive labor, when applied to women of color, must be modified to account for the fact that labor in the productive sphere was required to achieve even minimal levels of family subsistence. Long after industrialization had begun to reshape family roles among middle-class white families, driving white women into a cult of domesticity, women of color were coping with an extended day. This day included subsistence labor outside the family and domestic labor within the family. For slaves, domestics, migrant farm laborers, seasonal factory-workers, and prostitutes, the distinctions between labor that reproduced family life and which economically sustained it were minimized. The expanded workday was one of the primary ways in which reproductive labor increased.

Racial-ethnic families were sustained and maintained in the face of various forms of disruption. Yet racial-ethnic women and their families paid a high price in the process. High rates of infant mortality, a shortened life span, the early onset of crippling and debilitating disease provided some insight into the costs of survival.

The poor quality of housing and the neglect of communities further increased reproductive labor. Not only did racial-ethnic women work hard outside the home for a mere subsistence, they worked very hard inside the home to achieve even minimal standards of privacy and cleanliness. They were continually faced with disease and illness that directly resulted from the absence of basic sanitation. The fact that some African women murdered their children to prevent them from becoming slaves is an indication of the emotional strain associated with bearing and raising children while participating in the colonial labor system.

We have uncovered little information about the use of birth control, the prevalence of infanticide, or the motivations that may have generated these or other behaviors. We can surmise, however, that no matter how much children were accepted, loved, or valued among any of these groups of people, their futures in a colonial labor system were a source of grief for their mothers. For those children who were born, the task of keeping them alive, of helping them to understand and participate in a system that exploited them, and the challenge of maintaining a measure—no matter how small—of cultural integrity, intensified reproductive labor.

Being a racial-ethnic woman in nineteenth-century American society meant having extra work both inside and outside the home. It meant having a contradictory relationship to the norms and values about women that were being generated in the dominant white culture. As pointed out earlier, the notion of separate spheres of male and female labor had contradictory outcomes for the nineteenth-century whites. It was the basis for the confinement of women to the household and for much of the protective legislation that subsequently developed. At the same time, it sustained white families by providing social acknowledgment and support to women in the performance of their family roles. For racial-ethnic women, however, the notion of separate spheres served to reinforce their subordinate status and became, in effect, another assault. As they increased their work outside the home, they were forced into a productive labor sphere that was organized for men and "desperate" women who were so unfortunate or immoral that they could not confine their work to the domestic sphere. In the productive sphere, racial-ethnic women faced exploitative jobs and depressed wages. In the reproductive sphere, however, they were denied the opportunity to embrace the dominant ideological definition of "good" wife or mother. In essence, they were faced with a double-bind situation, one that required their participation in the labor force to sustain family life but damned them as women, wives, and mothers because they did not confine their labor to the home. Thus, the conflict between ideology and reality in the lives of racial-ethnic women during the nineteenth century sets the stage for stereotypes, issues of self-esteem, and conflicts around gender-role prescriptions that surface more fully in the twentieth century. Further, the tensions and conflicts that characterized their lives during this period provided the impulse for community activism to jointly address the inequities, which they and their children and families faced.

ACKNOWLEDGMENTS

The research in this study is the result of the author's participation in a larger collaborative project examining family, community, and work lives of racial-ethnic women in the United States. The author is deeply indebted to the scholarship and creativity of members of the group in the development of this study. Appreciation is extended to Elizabeth Higginbotham, Cheryl Townsend Gilkes, Evelyn Nakano Glenn, and Ruth Zambrana (members of the original working group), and to the Ford Foundation for a grant that supported in part the work of this study.

NOTES

1. The term *reproductive labor* is used to refer to all of the work of women in the home. This includes but is not limited to: the buying and preparation of food and clothing, provision of emotional support and nurturance for all family members, bearing children, and planning, organizing, and carrying out a wide variety of tasks associated with their socialization. All of these activities are necessary for the growth of patriarchal capitalism because they maintain, sustain, stabilize, and *reproduce* (both biologically and socially) the labor force.

2. The term *white* is a global construct used to characterize peoples of European descent who migrated to and helped colonize America. In the seventeenth century, most of these immigrants were from the British Isles. However, during the time period covered by this article, European immigrants became increasingly diverse. It is a limitation of this article that time and space does not permit a fuller discussion of the variations in the white European immigrant experience. For the purposes of the argument made herein and of the contrast it seeks to draw between the experiences of mainstream (European) cultural groups and that of racial/ethnic minorities, the differences among European settlers are joined and the broad similarities emphasized.

3. Cultural assaults, according to Caulfield (1974), are benign and systematic attacks on the institutions and forms of social organization that are fundamental to the maintenance and flourishing of a group's culture.

4. Recent research suggests that there were some tasks that were primarily assigned to males and some others to females. Whereas some gender-role distinctions with regard to work may have existed on some plantations, it is clear that slave women were not exempt from strenuous physical labor.

5. This term is used to refer to white Americans of European ancestry.

References

Aschenbrenner, Joyce. 1975. *Lifelines: Black Families in Chicago*. New York, NY: Holt, Rinehart, and Winston.

Barrera, Mario. 1979. *Race and Class in the Southwest*. South Bend, IN: Notre Dame University Press.

Blassingame, John. 1972. *The Slave Community: Plantation Life in the Antebellum South*. New York: Oxford University Press.

———. 1977. *Slave Testimony: Two Centuries of Letters, Speeches, Interviews, and Autobiographies*. Baton Rouge, LA: Louisiana State University Press.

Camarillo, Albert. 1979. *Chicanos in a Changing Society*. Cambridge, MA: Harvard University Press.

Caulfield, Mina Davis. 1974. "Imperialism, the Family, and Cultures of Resistance." *Socialist Review* 4(2)(October): 67–85.

Davis, Angela. 1971. "The Black Woman's Role in the Community of Slaves." *Black Scholar* 3(4)(December): 2–15.

———. 1981. *Women, Race and Class*. New York: Random House.

Degler, Carl. 1980. *At Odds*. New York: Oxford University Press.

Elasser, Nan Kyle MacKenzie, and Yvonne Tixier Y. Vigil. 1980. *Las Mujeres*. New York: The Feminist Press.

Garcia, Mario T. 1980. "The Chicano in American History: The Mexican Women of El Paso, 1880–1920—A Case Study." *Pacific Historical Review* 49(2)(May): 315–358.

Genovese, Eugene D., and Elinor Miller, eds. 1974. *Plantation, Town, and County: Essays on the Local History of American Slave Society*. Urbana: University of Illinois Press.

Glenn, Evelyn Nakano. 1981. "Family Strategies of Chinese-Americans: An Institutional Analysis." Paper presented at the Society for the Study of Social Problems Annual Meetings.

Goldman, Marion S. 1981. *Gold Diggers and Silver Miners*. Ann Arbor: The University of Michigan Press.

Griswold del Castillo, Richard. 1979. *The Los Angeles Barrio: 1850–1890*. Los Angeles: The University of California Press.

Gutman, Herbert. 1976. *The Black Family in Slavery and Freedom: 1750–1925*. New York: Pantheon.

Hirata, Lucie Cheng. 1979. "Free, Indentured, Enslaved: Chinese Prostitutes in Nineteenth-Century America." *Signs* 5 (Autumn): 3–29.

Jones, Jacqueline. 1985. *Labor of Love, Labor of Sorrow*. New York: Basic Books.

Kennedy, Susan Estabrook. 1979. *If All We Did Was to Weep at Home: A History of White Working-Class Women in America*. Bloomington: Indiana University Press.

Kessler-Harris, Alice. 1981. *Women Have Always Worked*. Old Westbury: The Feminist Press.

Kingston, Maxine Hong. 1977. *The Woman Warrior*. New York: Vintage Books.

Matthaei, Julie. 1982. *An Economic History of Women in America*. New York: Schocken Books.

Nee, Victor G., and Brett de Bary Nee. 1973. *Longtime Californ'*. New York: Pantheon Books.

Saragoza, Alex M. 1983. "The Conceptualization of the History of the Chicano Family: Work, Family, and Migration in Chicanos." Research Proceedings of the Symposium on Chicano Research and Public Policy. Stanford, CA: Stanford University, Center for Chicano Research.

Shimkin, Demetri, E. M. Shimkin, and D. A. Frate, eds. 1978. *The Extended Family in Black Societies.* The Hague: Mouton.

Spruill, Julia Cherry. 1972. *Women's Life and Work in the Southern Colonies.* New York: W. W. Norton and Company (first published in 1938, University of North Carolina Press).

Stack, Carol S. 1974. *All Our Kin: Strategies for Survival in a Black Community.* New York: Harper and Row.

Sudarkasa, Niara. 1981. "Interpreting the African Heritage in Afro-American Family Organization." Pp. 37–53 in *Black Families,* edited by Harriette Pipes McAdoo. Beverly Hills, CA: Sage Publications.

White, Deborah Gray. 1985. *Ar'n't I a Woman?: Female Slaves in the Plantation South.* New York: W. W. Norton.

Wright, Gwendolyn. 1981. *Building the Dream: A Social History of Housing in America.* New York: Pantheon Books.

Zaretsky, Eli. 1978. "The Effects of the Economic Crisis on the Family." Pp. 209–218 in *U.S. Capitalism in Crisis,* edited by Crisis Reader Editorial Collective. New York: Union of Radical Political Economists.

THE DIVERSITY OF AMERICAN FAMILIES 32

Eleanor Palo Stoller and Rose Campbell Gibson

Our understanding of family, perhaps more than any other institution, is clouded by myth. Masking diversity among contemporary U.S. families is an ideology that describes the American family as "one man who goes off to earn the bacon, one woman who waits at home to fry it, and roughly 2.5 children poised to eat it" (Cole 1986, p. 11). This image of family-dominated U.S. culture during the decades following World War II, a period during which the majority of older people today experienced at least part of their childrearing

From: Eleanor Palo Stoller and Rose Campbell Gibson, eds., *Worlds of Difference: Inequality in the Aging Experience,* 3d ed. (Thousand Oaks, CA: Pine Forge Press, 2000). Reprinted by permission.

years. As described by Betty Friedan (1964) in *The Feminine Mystique*, this ideology told women that caring for their home and family was the path to fulfillment and gratification (Andersen 1997). The sociologist Talcott Parsons (1955) described the American family as an isolated, nuclear unit in which the husband, wife, and their dependent children live geographically and economically independent from other relatives. Families were viewed as safe havens from the competitiveness of the workplace, and both popular images and social scientific treatises emphasized the split between the public sphere of employment and the private sphere of home (Coontz 1992).

. . . We will explore the consequences of this idealized image of the American family on our efforts to understand the diversity of family experiences among older people today. Our exploration of older families will ask these questions:

1. How does the myth of the American family mask the diversity of families in which today's cohorts of elderly people grew up and grew old?
2. How do interlocking hierarchies based on gender, race, and class structure the family experiences of today's older Americans?
3. How do definitions of family based on the experiences of the dominant groups in society bias research on other older families?

HOW THE MYTH OF THE AMERICAN FAMILY MASKS THE DIVERSITY OF FAMILIES IN WHICH TODAY'S COHORTS OF ELDERLY PEOPLE GREW UP AND GREW OLD

There are a number of problems with the ideological view of the nuclear family as a key to understanding the family experiences of older people today. First, not all older people married, and not all married people had children. Of the people who are 65 and older today, 5% never married, 6% divorced or separated, and 20% do not have adult children. Marriage and divorce rates also vary by gender and ethnicity. Older American Indian and Asian American women are slightly less likely to have remained single throughout their lives than are other older people. Rates of divorce and separation for elderly Blacks, Hispanic Americans, American Indians, and Asian Americans are higher than rates for elderly Whites.

Second, the idealized view of the family glorified the role of the full-time housewife, wife, and mother. Married women who did not enter the paid labor force and worked full time at home often found that their lives did not correspond to the image fostered by popular culture. Many full-time mothers were troubled by the isolation of their daily lives, the repetitiveness of household tasks, and the invisibility of their accomplishments (Oakley 1974). Betty Friedan (1964) labeled the vague, unspoken anxiety experienced by the full-time housewives in her study as "the problem that has no name." According to popular ideology, these women should have been among the most happy and fulfilled. Their families came closest to the idealized American family. Yet Friedan's (1964) subjects shared doubts and dissatisfactions. Moreover, they felt responsible for this unease, because the ideology of the feminine mystique shifted the blame to women themselves if they were unsatisfied with their lives. Women were taught that

> [they] could desire no greater destiny than to glory in their femininity. . . . If a woman had a problem in the 1950s and 1960s, she knew that something must be wrong with her marriage and with herself. . . . What kind of woman was she if she did not feel this mysterious fulfillment waxing the kitchen floor? (1964, p. 19)

Not all women who opted for full-time work at home over paid work in the labor market were dissatisfied with their lives. Caring for a home and family offered opportunities for creativity and satisfaction. Because work at home provides freedom from supervision and some flexibility in organizing tasks, many women preferred it to the more alienating conditions they would have encountered in the paid positions available to them (Andersen 1997). Nevertheless, as the 1960s came to a close, the vague discontent described by Friedan began to crystallize into a feminist analysis that defined motherhood as a serious obstacle to women's fulfillment. This strain of feminist thought reflects the race and class position of its creators. In gathering data for *The Feminine Mystique*, Friedan interviewed her former classmates at Smith College, and her results reflect the experiences of these White, middle-class, college-educated women. bell hooks (1984) describes the bias of an analysis developed from the standpoint of this particular group:

> [They] argued that motherhood was a serious obstacle to women's liberation, a trap confining women to the home, keeping them tied to cleaning, cooking, and child care. . . . Had black women voiced their views on motherhood, [motherhood] would not have been named a serious obstacle to our freedom as women. Racism, availability of jobs, lack of skills or education, and a number of other issues would have been at the top of the list—but not motherhood. Black women would not have said motherhood prevented us from entering the world of paid work, because we have always worked. (p. 133)

. . . Not all of today's older women were able to choose whether or not they would stay out of the paid labor force when their children were young, despite the popular and scholarly rhetoric advocating full-time motherhood. Women rearing children alone because of single motherhood, divorce, or widowhood had little choice but to combine the nurturing roles assigned to mothers with the breadwinning responsibilities supposedly reserved for fathers. Furthermore, poor and working-class two-parent families often needed two incomes to survive. Women of color were more likely than White women to find themselves in this situation, as racial oppression denied many of these women sufficient economic resources to maintain nuclear family households (Collins 1990). Elderly Black women, for example, typically combined childrearing with paid work at a time when employment opportunities for women and for people of color were even more restricted than they are today.

The rigid gender-based division of labor that characterized popular constructions of the American family of the 1950s did not apply across all combinations of race and class. For example, the strict gender-role segregation within the domestic sphere applied more to White families than to Black families. Black couples have traditionally been more flexible in allocating family obligations, with parents sharing household tasks and childrearing as well as responsibility for earning a living (McAdoo 1986). Upper-class women, most of whom were White, retained personal responsibility for managing children and household, but rarely did the actual work themselves (Ostrander 1984). Rather, they supervised the work of paid domestic workers, who were usually poor or working-class women and often women of color (Cole 1986).

Upper-class women also had more resources with which to exercise their family responsibilities than less affluent women. Susan Ostrander's (1984) wealthy subjects wanted their children "to develop to their fullest potential, . . . to be 'the best'" (p. 75). They expressed concerns about their children's personal happiness and their future success. Most important, they had resources to facilitate these goals for their children. For example, if their children encountered academic difficulties or adjustment problems, the parents often sent them to private schools. Mrs. Miles, a woman now in her 70s, whose husband had been chairman of the board of a major bank, describes her decision to enroll her teenage daughter in a private boarding school: "She was a very shy child . . . so I thought . . . going away to school would be good for her, would give her some confidence and put her on her feet" (p. 85). As Ostrander explains, "Upper-class children . . . are not allowed to fail academically or personally. This gives them strong advantages" (p. 84). Parents from other social classes share many of the same dreams and concerns for their children expressed by the women Ostrander interviewed, but they do not share the same resources for helping their children realize these dreams.

Another aspect of the mythic American family that clouds our understanding of the family experiences of today's elderly people is the assumption of the nuclear family as isolated from other relatives. Contrary to this image of independent nuclear households, women have traditionally maintained family relationships across households through visiting, writing letters, organizing holiday gatherings, and remembering birthdays and anniversaries—activities that have been described as "kinship work" (DiLeonardo 1987; Rosenthal 1985). The work of "kinkeeping" can produce complex networks of female kin, who entrust confidences, pool resources, and share social activities. Furthermore, as social gerontologists have demonstrated, women are the primary caregivers of frail elderly people in their families.

Strong female-centered networks have also linked families and households among Blacks. Mothering responsibilities have traditionally been shared among women in Black communities. Boundaries distinguishing biological mothers from other women who care for children are less rigid within these communities, and women often feel a sense of obligation for "our children," a term that includes all of the children in their community. Patricia Hill Collins (1991) explains that

> Black communities recognized that vesting one person with full responsibility for mothering a child may not be wise or possible. As a result, "othermothers," women who assist bloodmothers by sharing mothering responsibilities, traditionally have been a central part of the institution of Black motherhood. (p. 47)

When children are orphaned, when parents are ill or at work, or when biological mothers are too young to care for their children alone, other women in the community take on child care responsibilities, sometimes temporarily but other times permanently.

These women-centered networks of bloodmothers and othermothers within Black communities have often been described as a reaction to the legacy of slavery and to generations of poverty and oppression. Some scholars have challenged this interpretation. The impact of racial oppression on Black families must be acknowledged, but it is also important to recognize the ways in which today's elderly Blacks evolved new definitions of family from their everyday experiences and cultural legacies. Networks of community-based child care, for example, provided supervision for children while biological parents worked to provide economic support. Alternative definitions of motherhood, emphasizing both emotional support and physical provision of care, were adapted from West African culture, which had been retained as a culture of resistance since slavery (Sudarkasa 1981). Building on this cultural heritage, Black women devised strategies for ensuring their children's physical survival within a racist society—ways of ensuring their physical survival without compromising their sense of self-worth (Collins 1991). The historian Elsa Barkley Brown (1991) describes this approach to mothering by explaining how her mother understood "the need to socialize me to live my life one way and, at the same time, to provide me with the tools I would need to live it differently" (p. 231). Like other Black women writing about family, Brown stresses the contributions of mothers and grandmothers in teaching the "delicate balance between conformity and resistance. . . . Black daughters must learn how to survive in interlocking structures of race, class, and gender oppression while rejecting and transcending these very same structures" (Collins 1991, p. 54).

Other examples also challenge the myth of self-reliance of isolated, nuclear households. Coontz (1992) points out that working-class and ethnic subcommunities "evolved mutual aid in finding jobs, surviving tough times, and pooling money for recreation" (p. 71). Immigrant groups developed infrastructures of churches, temperance societies, workers' associations, fraternal orders, and cooperatives that provided instrumental and emotional aid beyond the confines of the nuclear household. Godparenting created extrafamilial bonds among Catholic populations, bonds that often cut across social class boundaries, and as Coontz points out, "the notion of 'going for sisters' has long and still thriving roots in black communities" (p. 72). Extended networks of kin also characterize Latino families, in which child care responsibilities are often shared with older siblings, aunts, uncles, and grandparents. Ceremonial events frequently involve close friends linked to the family through *compadrazgo*, a network of kinlike ties among very close friends who exchange tangible assistance and social support (Heyck 1994).

The idealized image of the American family also assumes a heterosexual couple. Despite more recent attention to gay and lesbian rights, it is important to remember that today's cohorts of elderly gay men and lesbians grew up in a social environment in which they encountered strong pressures to hide their sexual orientation. They lived most of their lives during a historical period characterized by hostility toward homosexuality (Fullmer 1995). Many kept their relationships secret to avoid discriminatory treatment by their families, their employers, and their communities (D'Augelli & Hart 1987). Lesbians and gay men who revealed their relationships to others often needed to develop strategies for coping with negative attitudes and discriminatory treatment (Hooyman & Kiyak 1999). Indeed, there is some evidence that the experience of "coming out" strengthens the adaptive resources for meeting challenges of late life (Quan & Whitford 1992). Although marriage between gay and lesbian partners is not legally sanctioned, many couples establish long-term relationships (Peplau 1991). The absence of legal recognition creates a number of obstacles for these couples in late life. Many employers do not extend insurance or retirement benefits to unmarried partners, and social security does not extend survivor's benefits to gay men or lesbians whose partners have died. Although provision of domestic partnership benefits is increasing, these benefits were not available for current cohorts of gay or lesbian elders. Locating assisted living or nursing home environments receptive to gay or lesbian couples can also be difficult. When one partner is hospitalized, the other partner may be denied access to an intensive care unit or other contexts reserved for "next of kin." Without a medical power of attorney, hospital personnel do not recognize the authority of one partner to make health care decisions for his or her incapacitated partner. Gay or lesbian couples can try to protect each other's financial situations in their wills, but other family members sometimes contest the right of the surviving partner to an inheritance. . . .

Generalizing the image of the American family to all couples masks the complexity of family experiences and resources with which older Americans face the challenges of aging. Uncritically accepting dominant stereotypes of older families is like wearing blinders. Our understanding is limited, because we don't think to ask questions about dimensions of social reality that we overlook. We forget to ask how people who never married develop other relationships to meet their needs for companionship in old age. We forget to ask how gay and lesbian couples activate a support network to care for them when they are ill. We forget to ask how more fluid definitions of family and more flexible divisions of labor both within and beyond nuclear-family households influence strategies used by older Blacks in coping with disability in old age. These oversights are not intentional. They reflect limited views of social reality from particular standpoints. The poet Adrienne Rich (as quoted in West & Fenstermaker 1995) used the term *White solipsism* to refer to the process of thinking, imagining, and speaking "as if Whiteness described the world," resulting in a "tunnel-vision which simply does not see nonwhite experience or existence as precious or significant" (p. 306).

References

Andersen, M. L. (1997). *Thinking about women: Sociological perspectives on sex and gender* (4th ed.). Boston: Allyn & Bacon.

Brown, E. B. (1991). Mothers of mind. In P. Bell-Scott, B. Guy-Sheftall, J. Jones Royster, J. Sims-Wood, M. DeCosta-Willis, & L. Fultz (Eds.), *Double stitch: Black women write about mothers and daughters* (pp. 74–93). Boston: Beacon.

Cole, J. (1986). *All American woman: Lives that divide, ties that bind.* New York: Free Press.

Collins, P. H. (1990). *Black feminist thought: Knowledge, consciousness, and the politics of empowerment.* Boston: Unwin Hyman.

Collins, P. H. (1991). The meaning of motherhood in black culture and black mother-daughter relationships. In P. Bell-Scott, B. Guy-Sheftall, J. Jones Royster, J. Sims-Wood, M. DeCosta-Willis, & L. Fultz (Eds.), *Double stitch: Black women write about mothers and daughters* (pp. 42–60). Boston: Beacon.

Coontz, S. (1992). *The way we never were: American families and the nostalgia trap.* New York: Basic Books.

D'Augelli, A., & Hart, M. M. (1987). Gay women, men and families in rural settings: Toward the development of helping communities. *American Journal of Community Psychology, 15*(1), 79–93.

DiLeonardo, M. (1987). The female world of cards and holidays: Women, families, and the work of kinship. *Signs: Journal of Women in Culture and Society, 12,* 440–453.

Friedan, B. (1964). *The feminine mystique.* New York: Norton.

Fullmer, E. M. (1995). Challenging biases against families of older gays and lesbians. In G. C. Smith, S. Tobin, E. A. Robertson-Tchabo, & P. Power (Eds.), *Strengthening aging families: Diversity in practice and power.* Thousand Oaks, CA: Sage.

Heyck, D. L. D. (1994). *Barrios and borderlands: Cultures of Latinos and Latinas in the United States.* New York: Routledge.

hooks, b. (1984). *Feminist theory from margin to center.* Boston: South End Press.

Hooyman, N., & Kiyak, H. A. (1999). *Social gerontology: A multidisciplinary perspective* (5th ed.). Boston: Allyn & Bacon.

McAdoo, H. (1986). Societal stress: The black family. In J. Cole (Ed.), *All American women: Lines that divide, ties that bind* (pp. 187–197). New York: Free Press.

Oakley, A. (1974). *The sociology of housework.* Oxford: Martin Robertson.

Ostrander, S. (1984). Community volunteer. In *Women of the upper class* (pp. 111–139). Philadelphia: Temple University Press.

Parsons, T. (1955). The American family: Its relations to personality and the social structure. In T. Parsons & R. Bales (Eds.), *Family socialization and interaction process* (pp. 3–21). Glencoe, IL: Free Press.

Peplau, L. A. (1991). Lesbian and gay relationships. In J. C. Gonsiorek & J. D. Weinrich (Eds.), *Homosexuality: Research implications for public policy.* Newbury Park, CA: Sage.

Quan, J. K., & Whitford, G. (1992). Adaptation and age-related expectations of older gay and lesbian adults. *The Gerontologist, 32,* 367–374.

Rosenthal, C. J. (1985). Kinkeeping in the familial division of labor. *Journal of Marriage and the Family, 47,* 965–974.

Sudarkasa, N. (1981). Interpreting the African heritage in Afro-American family organizations. In H. McAdoo (Ed.), *Black families* (pp. 37–53). Beverly Hills, CA: Sage.

West, C., & Fenstermaker, S. (1995). Doing difference. *Gender & Society, 9*(1), 8–37.

COUNTERING THE CONSPIRACY TO IGNORE BLACK GIRLS

33

Robin D. G. Kelley

"Okay. Pretend I'm Kimberly and you're Tommy and, oh, you have to be Billy and Rocky, too. Anyway, pretend I'm the waitress in a restaurant and you see me for the first time and ask for the menu and then look up and then say, 'Kim-

From: Andre C. Willis, ed., *Faith of Our Fathers: African-American Men Reflect on Fatherhood* (New York: Dutton, 1996). Copyright © Robin D. G. Kelley.

berly, is that you?' Okay? and then you say, 'would you like to come to my pool party? All the Rangers will be there, and we'll have cake and ice cream.' And then Trini will get really mad because you didn't invite her and she'll be jealous, okay?"

This is how my five-year-old daughter, Elleza, imagines the lifestyles of *The Mighty Morphin Power Rangers*, a horrible, campy, excessively violent television show that has kids mesmerized and parents going broke on Power Rangers toys, clothes, and coloring books. We forbid her to watch the show and refuse to take her to see *Power Rangers—The Movie*, although she does own a couple of Power Rangers dolls and accessories. The Power Ranger craze is simply unavoidable; virtually every kid in the country has a general idea who these Morphin teens are and what color outfits each one wears.* However, Elleza has no detailed knowledge of the Power Rangers, besides the basic fact that this multicultural team of super adolescents fight "evil," derive their power from dinosaurs, and are experts in karate.

Because the Power Rangers are largely a mystery to her, she has to invent their world, their crises, their adventures. Although she is able to create fresh, highly imaginative tales about these dynamic teens dressed in colorful body suits, all of her narratives ultimately lead in the same direction: romance. Usually Billy, Tommy, Jason, or Rocky get in trouble, Kimberly comes to the rescue, and they get married. Occasionally Kimberly is in a bind and one of the boys saves her, but the outcome is usually the same—first love, then marriage, then Kimberly pushing a baby carriage. Romance is the dominant theme, yet in her mind the Power Rangers are not always teens; sometimes they're infants, other times they're toddlers or little kids who magically turn into adults with a snap of a finger. Those who are not romantically involved are usually siblings.

Of course, we try to do the P.C. thing. My wife, Diedra, and I encourage those narratives in which Kimberly rescues the boys rather than vice versa, and we constantly challenge her understanding of heterosexual relationships, which she derives from daily observation, daycare, fairy tales, Walt Disney, and perhaps a bit of instinct. We believe these are very serious issues, and we do the best we can to raise her with a healthy gender and sexual identity, to help her understand and challenge the sexist world she will inherit.

And yet I must confess that, for me at least, Elleza's style of play is far more enjoyable than being kicked in the face by an out-of-control "roundhouse" or karate-chopped in the stomach. Elleza is smart, strong, and outspoken when she's not feeing shy, but she is also strongly female-identified and takes pleasure in her girlhood. Yes, I know "girlhood" and "femininity" are

---

*For the uninitiated, I should point out that in the early version of Power Rangers, Zack, the only black member, wore a black suit and Trini, the only other minority, wore yellow. Yes, you guessed it: she is Asian American.

social constructions, and we are always reminding her that boys are not necessarily stronger, faster, more heroic, better leaders, or that they should be barred from wearing dresses, and that girls can have short hair, tattoos, big muscles, positions of power, or wear short skirts without inviting sexual assault. But having witnessed my nephews and cousins in action, it is hard for me to accept the notion that aggressive behavior among boys is entirely a product of socialization. Little boys, for example, will hurt themselves repeatedly by jumping off furniture or running into walls. It's as if they cannot comprehend the connection between their pain and their actions. On the other hand, most girls I've witnessed, Elleza included, only have to hurt themselves once in order to figure out that flying off the coffee table head first will result in excruciating pain. Indeed, Elleza was among that elite group of toddlers who came to that conclusion via a priori reasoning rather than experience.

Elleza has been described by friends as the classic girl, mainly because she tends to be nonviolent, cooperative, more verbal than physical, and deeply romantic to the point of bordering on utopianism. She has an astounding grasp of language that allows her to employ complex analogies and similes as well create stunning descriptions. When she was barely four years old, for example, she drew a small crowd at the Guggenheim Museum in SoHo when she started giving alternate names to works by Antoni Tapies, an abstract painter who usually titles his pieces by the materials or colors he uses. Elleza came up with evocative titles such as "Midnight Angel," "Rainy Night," "The Day the Sun Escaped," and "Peace."

Perhaps, as social psychologist Carol Gilligan suggests, this is the nature of girls' play.* But these were also the elements of my own boyhood I enjoyed most. My mother taught me to abhor violence, enjoy reading, and to use my powers of imagination to create a beautiful world rather than reproduce the reality surrounding us. I tried to do this while living on 156th Street between Amsterdam and Broadway in New York City, a neighborhood famous for male posturing and escalating violence. Although I spent a lot of time in the library, I made frequent visits to the local playgrounds and fire hydrants. Besides, my older sister's friends protected me from the baby thugs and saved me from the unmanly label of being a "pussy" ("sissy" simply wasn't in our vocabulary).

Yet, if the truth be told, I was never crazy about hanging out at the playground. Not that I disliked the playground: I still have fond memories of those hot summer days when I thought it couldn't get better than this, days when the music was blasting and everyone was laughing and joking on the sun-drenched concrete, stealing some shade on the other side of the handball court, using rocks, ballpoint pens, and matches to pop ten-cent rolls of "caps"

---

*See Carol Gilligan, *In a Different Voice: Psychological Theory and Women's Development* (Cambridge, Mass.: Harvard University Press, 1982).

(in our day, the phrase "bustin' caps" had a more benign meaning). But except for basketball and (later) tennis, I dreaded playing sports and felt extremely uncomfortable in gatherings of nappy-headed eight-year-old virgins bragging about the length of their "dicks" or which fourth-grader they claimed to have "fucked" in the coat room.

When I moved to Seattle to live with my father, "boy culture" (which some misguided social scientists wrongly label "street culture") was thrust upon me with a vengeance. My dad took it upon himself to turn me into a "man," by any means necessary. He insisted that I, not my sister, help him work on the car, he gave me clinics on "da mentals" of basketball (he took all the "fun" out of it), made me field fly balls, and sent me to a summer camp where boxing was strongly encouraged. My most traumatic memory was in the summer of 1974, when he signed me up to play for the Central Area Youth Association football team. I really didn't want to play football but was too afraid to tell him so. I went through the motions, expecting to get cut, but due to an unfortunate shortage of twelve-year-old players that year, everyone made the team. That the coming months would be spent in utter pain and agony hit me when my father took me to an athletic store to pick out my first jock strap and a protective cup.

To be fair, my father was not wholly responsible for my short-lived football career; I also succumbed to peer pressure from friends and relatives who also regarded organized contact sports as a male rite of passage. However, he did establish a climate at home in which becoming a man (i.e., conforming to established gender norms) and learning to respect authority was the raison d'etre for growing up. There was no give and take or open discussion about what we wanted to do or how we wanted to live our lives. He told us what to do and we did it, period. And like his father, he believed in discipline and followed the adage that to spare the rod (or the belt, the Hot Wheels track, the backhand slap) is to spoil the child. Rather than respect authority, we learned to fear it. Indeed, if I had to divide my life into neat historical epochs, I would call my five years in my father's house the "age of terror." To this day, I am afraid to tell him what I really think and dread the thought that he might accidentally discover this book while looking to buy me another one of those "inspirational" Christian fundamentalist paperbacks on how men should lead their families.

Although I lived with my father only a grand total of eight years,* I'm pretty sure his parenting style has had some impact on my own—what exactly, I'm not sure. Because I am raising a girl, most of his little maxims about what it means to be a man have no direct bearing on my parenting problems. On

---

*My mother and father split up when I was three years old. My sister and I ended up living with him and his second wife from 1971 to 1976, after which time we moved back with my mother.

the other hand, it is entirely possible that his utter paranoia about making me a man, manifested in his extreme misogynist and homophobic views, rendered his version of masculinity less than stable, if not downright comical. In other words, maybe his obsession with me becoming a man (i.e., not gay, not weak, not "pussy-whipped") exposed deep insecurities about his own masculinity and therefore revealed just how precarious "manhood" really is. A simpler, though more likely explanation is that my father, through his own example, taught me how not to raise a child. Instead of teaching us to respect authority, for example, his punishments merely demonstrated to me the futility of violence as a method of disciplining children. And the hierarchical manner in which he ran the household reinforced in my mind the limitations of patriarchy as a model for family life. I really do believe that my commitment to family based on shared authority, mutuality, and collective decision-making is largely an outgrowth of having lived—briefly—in a household where we were expected to follow orders and keep silent unless spoken to. I don't want my daughter to grow up like I did, feeling helpless and powerless, afraid to say what she thinks or fight for what she believes in. I don't want her to grow up in a family where men are the leaders, women and the children are followers, and all transgressors deviants who must be punished. Thus, long before I cracked open a book on the sociology of the family or on the case against patriarchy, I had concluded that my father's understanding of fatherhood was extremely dysfunctional.

Yet, within the current political discourse in African-American communities, which places a premium on saving black boys and puts the responsibility for doing so squarely on the shoulders of black men, my father should probably be regarded as a hero. According to certain popular schools of thought, the delicate balance of corporal punishment, steady work, family responsibilities, and father-son interaction on the playing field was the key to my success, not the "feminine" values my mother instilled into me when I lived with her.

I find this line of reasoning not only questionable but potentially damaging and shortsighted. It not only proposed a limited vision of masculinity, but more important, it signals that the only progressive, useful role black fathers ought to play is raising black boys. We see this discourse clear as day in films like John Singleton's *Boyz N the Hood* and in books such as Baba Zak A. Kondo's *For Homeboys Only: Arming and Strengthening Young Brothers for Black Manhood* and Jawanza Kunjufu's three-volume *Countering the Conspiracy to Destroy Black Boys.** We see it in the mushrooming of black male academies in innercity communities, where the curriculum places a heavy emphasis on promoting male role models in the classroom as well as in their reading assignments,

---

*Baba Zak A. Kondo, *For Homeboys Only: Arming and Strengthening Young Brothers for Black Manhood* (Washington, D.C.: Nubia Press, 1991); Jawanza Kunjufu, *Countering the Conspiracy to Destroy Black Boys* (Chicago: African American Images, 1985–86).

preparing boys for "leadership" roles, and building students' self-esteem and sense of masculinity through discipline and responsibility.[†]

Some of the same Afrocentric critics who support black male academies and insist that saving our sons and reestablishing black manhood is the key to liberation are also nudging women into more traditional roles or ignoring them altogether. Thus, while criticizing the media for what they believe are unduly negative images of black women, many contemporary black nationalists have invested more of their energy into reinstituting the traditional family and chastising black women for failing to support black men. Besides being anti-feminist, they tend to place the blame for the behavior of young black males squarely on the shoulders of single mothers, whom they characterize as irresponsible and incapable of disciplining their sons.

By implication, this limited focus on men raising boys not only renders my daughter invisible but makes me an inauthentic black father. There are far, far fewer guides on how black fathers ought to raise their daughters or popular texts on nurturing healthy, strong black girls. Likewise, books specifically for black mothers raising sons are also few and far between. And in my personal case, I'm worse than an inauthentic black father. I'm a traitor to my race and my gender. Why? Because I'm not raising a son, and I have no intention or desire to become a surrogate father to wayward boyz in the 'hood. Not that I'm suggesting that this sort of work isn't important. On the contrary, respect is due to the brothers out there trying to deal with these kids—boys who live their lives as if on a suicide mission.

Even if I had the desire and drive to take up the manly challenge of black fatherhood in the age of black male endangerment, I don't have a whole lot of confidence in my ability to bring a boy up in the manner to which our defenders of manhood are accustomed. I'm not good with my hands, I don't like baseball, fighting, or toy guns, and my wife can vouch for the fact that as a patriarch I couldn't rule myself out of a paper bag. Every time I'm asked to lecture at a boys detention center or neighborhood youth organization, the poets seem to identify with me much more than the regular homies. And during every family picnic hosted by my in-laws on Staten Island, I either end up playing with Elleza the whole time or swapping baby stories with Diedra's female cousins. I've never taken a seat inside the men's circle, where beer and sports are the order of the day. In short, to most black folks who subscribe to

[†]Clearly, the purpose of these institutions is not to eliminate or reduce misogyny among young black males, for if that was the goal one might expect to find a curriculum that emphasizes women's history, female role models, and issues of gender and sexism. Ironically, one of the most vicious of these attacks on black women generally and feminism in particular was written by a woman: Shahrazad Ali. Titled *The Blackman's Guide to Understanding the Blackwoman* (1990), this highly controversial and vastly popular book caricatured black women as selfish, power-hungry, aggressive, manipulating, and even dirty. She argued that true liberation required that black women return to their traditional roles as child-care givers and supporters of black men.

the notion that the role of black men is to save black boys, I'm probably not a very good male role model. Three decades ago, Senator Daniel Patrick Moynihan would have characterized me as one of those "dysfunctional" black men who lacked a healthy masculine self-image and needed to enlist in the army in order to attain one.

But the question remains: where is the concern for raising our daughters, and what are the issues and challenges fathers have to face? After all, even in today's world black women not only experience both race and gender discrimination but are potential victims of sexual harassment, rape, battery, incest, etc.—acts often committed by loved ones. Most African-American working women—not unlike other women—are still expected to put in double days, balancing their time between a full-time job, domestic work, and childcare. How should fathers help prepare their daughters for a world where black women are generally paid less than white men and white women, and in some circumstances less than black men, for the same job? How do we explain the underrepresentation of women in positions of authority, or help our daughters navigate a popular culture in which women are often portrayed as passive and weak or as sex objects for male gratification?

These are extremely critical issues whose political import ought to match that of, say, the rising black male incarceration rate in the U.S. Fathers (and mothers) simply cannot afford to ignore the complex problems confronting their offspring who are young, black, and female. Black girls, much more than boys, for example, constantly have to maintain their self-esteem and sense of beauty in the face of a racialist aesthetic that values white skin and straight hair. While this fact is certainly no revelation to African-Americans, we nonetheless unwittingly pass value-laden signals to our children about skin and hair. Besides the media, the point is sometimes made explicit by the way classmates decide who is ugly and who is beautiful, or family members making reference to "good hair" or to the "pretty babies" interracial couples supposedly produce. More often than not, the message is more subtle: a mother complaining about how difficult it is to do her daughter's hair, a father who is always admiring light-skinned women. Indeed, before Elleza turned three years old, she went through a brief phase when she wanted to be a little white girl. The phase passed quickly (at least for the time being), partly because we had always told her she was beautiful, partly because we never tried to compare her with anyone else. At the same time, we would not allow her to speak of someone else's physical appearance in a degrading fashion.

Battling the aesthetic assault on black girls and boosting their self-esteem in a racist world does carry a certain price. To be told incessantly that you're beautiful or cute or gorgeous while boys are told that they're strong, big, and smart reinforces the subordination of women while conveying the message that the only worthwhile possession girls have is their looks. With Elleza we try to teach her to love herself (including her body) while simultaneously playing down her appearance in order to emphasize her strength and intellect.

As most parents know, actions often speak louder than words. If we want to raise girls to break out of traditional gender conventions that reproduce female subordination and male dominance, dads need to be more cognizant of how our behavior and attitudes as men shape our children's understanding of the world. The way we speak to and interact with women and other men, the way decisions are made in the household, the way parenting responsibilities get defined—all of these factors affect our kids' identities. Daughters, for instance, need to see their fathers breaking traditional gender boundaries, but doing so without fanfare. Making a big deal out of transgressing the bounds of gender only reinforces the idea that traditional roles assigned to men and women are part of the "natural" order of things. The standard example is household work, although to make an impact men need to do at least half of all the work and should resist whining or making a big production out of it. Aside from household chores, dads should spend a lot more time with their daughters playing their games on *their* terms. Don't think for a minute that playing with dolls or makeup, hopscotch or jacks, ought to be Mom's domain, or that every Barbie needs a GI Joe. Those dads who feel uncomfortable playing girls' games ought to get over it or get some counseling. By refusing to play "girls' games," men and boys sometimes unwittingly degrade or ridicule girls' activities, which could have a damaging effect on their self-esteem. Besides, these intimate play moments are opportunities to listen to what your daughter has to say, to get a clearer sense of what she thinks about, and for her to know the many faces of Daddy.

Obviously, these brief and underdeveloped insights represent only the tip of an iceberg I'm only just beginning to explore myself. If there is any single lesson here, it is that arming our daughters for the twenty-first century is just as important as arming our sons. And the responsibility for doing so should not fall entirely on the shoulders of mothers (just as the task for turning boys into men should never be relegated to men alone). But what do I give my daughter to help prepare her for the future? What does she need to survive? Of course, there are the obvious things: unconditional love, affection, honesty, a sense of safety and security, independence, responsibility, and a right to her own private world. Hopefully, she'll leave the nest with enormous self-confidence; an unwavering love for herself as a woman and as an African-American; and a critical appreciation for her cultural heritage—again, as a woman, an African-descended person, and as a product of the modern world. I hope she grows up with a healthy and positive attitude toward sexuality as well as an analysis of society that will enable her to embrace and critically engage feminism(s). She needs to recognize that the sex-based limits placed in front of her are not natural but discriminatory barriers designed to maintain male dominance. She also must understand that these barriers are penetrable through struggle, and that a just society cannot exist until they are removed entirely. Finally, she should learn that valuing herself does not mean devaluing others, and that equality does not mean sameness.

Ironically, if Elleza ends up with a little brother I would probably arm him with the same principles. I will love him the same way I love his sister. I will flood him with affection, try to instill the same kinds of values, and place a great deal of emphasis on cooperation and nonviolence. He will learn to love his unique blackness, his cultural heritage with all of its multicultural roots, without apologetics or chauvinism. Better yet, through his big sister as well as his mother, he will learn to admire and take leadership from women, and vigilantly reject the idea that men are "superior" or that male dominance is the natural order of things. If we're successful, he too will grow up as a feminist. And like Elleza, I will teach him to love literature (from Toni Morrison to Oscar Ameringer), art (from Akan sculpture to Flemish painting), and music (from Monk to Debussy). If he wants a clinic in basketball or baseball, I'll certainly do everything in my power to encourage him. Given my limited athletic abilities, however, I'll have to send him to a summer program.

But if for some reason Power Rangers are still the rage by the time he hits three or four, I may have to bite the bullet and improve my karate skills.

RACIAL SAFETY AND CULTURAL MAINTENANCE

34

The Child Care Concerns of Employed Mothers of Color

Lynet Uttal

In the 1930s, doctors professed a single model of infant care that was promoted as superior to traditional ethnic infant care practices.[1] A similar movement is currently taking place in the 1990s in the field of paid child care services. Child care advocates are pressing for the professionalization of child care

From: *Ethnic Studies Review* 19, no. 1 (February 1996). Reprinted by permission.

work and the practice of a single model of developmentally appropriate care. Underlying this proposal is the assumption that child rearing can be stripped of cultural values and practices, and that the type of care a child receives can be offered independent of the social and cultural location of the child's family.

This model ignores how membership in historically subordinated racial ethnic groups creates a different experience of child care for people of color than for the White population. Child care research has identified systematic differences in preferences by racial ethnic groups. One difference frequently noted is that African American parents view child care as an educational setting more so than do White parents. White parents, especially middle-class ones, are more likely to view child care as an opportunity for their children to have social interactions with other children.[2] African American parents express a greater preference for child care that provides structured academic programs for preschool-aged children, whereas middle-class White parents prefer loosely structured activities that expose their children to different concepts through play. This high valuation of education is rooted in beliefs that early education will prepare children for kindergarten and create a stronger foundation for social mobility through education.[3]

One study found that African American parents expected the day care center's staff to be aware of and sensitive to racial issues and objected when the day care center's programming violated this expectation.[4] In another study, Chinese American parents expressed concern about the conflicting messages children get when what is taught at home differs from what is taught at their day cares,[5] such as differing beliefs about how to address elders and differing eating practices (e.g., whether picking up a bowl and eating from it is acceptable). These concerns are important to take into account because early childhood education research has shown that presentations of positive ethnic images are important in the formulation of children's self-images and for the transmission of cultural values.[6] Yet, when child care advocates propose a single model of developmentally appropriate child care, they ignore the significance of membership in a historically subordinated racial ethnic group and cultural values in how child care arrangements are viewed.

Racial group membership and cultural practices are important because they create a lens, or historical consciousness, through which child care is assessed. Historical consciousness, according to poet and scholar Janice Gould, is the awareness of one's historical identity.[7] In her discussion of Native American women, Gould states that historical consciousness is the collective awareness of five hundred years of internal colonialism and genocide. Although individual Native American women come from many different tribes and lead very different lives, Gould argues that their historical consciousness informs how individual women live out their lives on a daily basis. Their historical consciousness reflects their social histories as members of particular gender, race, ethnic, and class groups.

The historical consciousness of their status as members of historically subordinated racial ethnic groups informs the types of concerns employed mothers of color have about leaving their children in other people's care. . . . I explore two expressions of this historical consciousness in employed mothers' views of their child care arrangements: racial safety and cultural maintenance. The introduction of these two concepts is central to the understanding of why parents of color seek out child care providers who are members of their own racial ethnic group and of how they view childcare provided by persons who do not share their racial ethnic group membership or knowledge of their racial ethnic histories. Furthermore, this chapter not only identifies child care problems related to overt forms of racism but also discusses the problems that occur when well-intentioned White childcare providers lack experience with caring for children of different racial ethnic groups and with negotiating multicultural interactions. . . .

THE CONCERN FOR RACIAL SAFETY

. . . Awareness of racism in U.S. society was a common topic when mothers of color talked about their child care arrangements. Because of their own experiences with racism, they were concerned about how their children would be treated when the child care providers were White. Often times, mothers discovered these problems only after they had established child care arrangements. For example, Gloria Thomas, an African American waitress and mother of two children, observed behaviors that she defined as racist. Gloria said:

> I don't know if she was used to [Black people]. I think she was kind of narrow-minded. I didn't feel comfortable, me being Black. [And] she looked like she put more energy into the White kids than the Black kids. I think she felt that I was on to her, because she said in a couple days, or actually I said, "this isn't going to work," and she pretty much knew also that it wasn't going to work.

Gloria expected White child care providers to have knowledge of how to negotiate cross-racial interactions. She said,

> If you are dealing with my kids, I hope you do have some cultural skills. I don't like prejudiceness at all. . . . You have to be not dumb. Some white people can be really stupid. They say the stupidest things.

When it was clear that child care providers lacked these skills, mothers removed their children from the child care setting. Frances Trudeau, an African American lawyer and the mother of two children, responded this way when the school's teachers and administrators at her five year old son's school failed to acknowledge and address that the namecalling and chasing of African American children was racism. When she and other parents spoke to the director, they were told that the school could not develop a policy to address the problem because families came from so many different walks of life and the school did not want to tell people how to behave. This response reduced cross-racial interactions to individual interactions and personal disagreements and failed to acknowledge the more systemic nature of racism. Mothers of color found this kind of response inadequate and frustrating. Because they are aware of the pervasiveness of the problem of racism, they do not define unpleasant cross-racial interactions as occasional, individual disagreements even in child care settings.

Mothers of color also experienced racism when they used predominantly White child care settings. Gloria Thomas described one such encounter.

> This one woman was pretty annoying. She asked me this question and to this day I still want to ask her what did she mean by it. She said, "Oh, are you a single parent?" And I said, "yes." And she goes, "Oh, do you live around here?" And I said, "Yes, I live right around the corner." You could tell her mind was [thinking], "she goes to this day care? She's a single parent, Black, and she lives up here. How can she afford it?" It's really weird.

One of the strategies that mothers of color used to protect their children from racism was to find child care within their own racial ethnic communities. The use of kin and community networks protected the children and the mothers from having to deal with cross-racial interactions. When mothers of color were able to make child care arrangements with child care providers of their same racial ethnic group, the concerns about racial safety and cultural maintenance were eliminated. Yet, care within one's racial ethnic community did not guarantee a fit between the values and child rearing practices of mothers and child care providers. Often times, mothers had several relatives and acquaintances from which to choose. When this was the case, the mothers carefully discriminated between their choices based on what they considered to be a good environment and good care. After insuring their child's racial safety and exposure to traditional cultural practices and values, they invoked additional criteria to decide which child care setting was the best. Sylvia Rodriquez, an office manager and the mother of two children, chose a Mexican immigrant woman over her sister-in-law. She explained:

> It depends on who the relatives are. Like for example, you know, financially [my husband's sister] could have used watch[ing for pay] my son and my daughter at her house. She's real good about feeding them and things like that. But she has a lot of marital problems that I wouldn't want my kids to be around, watching the arguments and fights. I know they use bad language and that's another thing I don't like.

Like Sylvia, Lupe Gonzalez, an administrative assistant and the mother of an eleven-month-old, was discriminating in terms of which relative she chose to watch her young baby. She had two options: an elderly grandmother and an aunt who was the same age as herself. She was pleased that her aunt was available to care for her baby, though she would have left her baby in her grandmother's care if necessary. But her grandmother was elderly and was already watching several other grandchildren. Because of her grandmother's age, Lupe felt that she would not be as attentive or as physically able to pick up her baby. The advantage of care by the aunt was that her infant son would also be the only child for whom the aunt provided care.

Although Gloria Thomas had left a White child care provider because she felt the White provider was unable to negotiate the cross-racial interactions, she found that simply finding an African American child care provider did not necessarily create satisfactory child care arrangements. Gloria had found a family day care run by an African American woman, yet other factors prevented her from feeling comfortable with this arrangement. . . . Gloria and her provider had disagreements about what were appropriate disciplining practices. Gloria talked with her provider about these issues but felt that her preferences were not validated by the child care provider. She said:

> Well, I did, I said, I don't believe in hitting. And she said, "what do you mean by hitting." I said, "just swatting," and she said, "I do, you know, a slap on the hand." And I said, "pretty much even that, I don't want." But I could feel like that she didn't want to hear that.

Since Gloria also wanted something different from what she perceived as traditional African American child rearing practices, she moved her children into a day care center where she was the only African American parent, as well as of the lowest socioeconomic status and background. She often found herself irritated with what she perceived as a White style of interaction, yet she felt the social, educational, and environmental advantages of the day care center outweighed the need to have her child cared for by her previous African American child care provider.

Young mothers often opposed some of the traditional child rearing practices used by the older and more traditional women in their communities. For example, Maria Hernandez, a Mexican American office manager and the mother of a four year old, expressed dissatisfaction with the care provided by her Mexican American mother-in-law. She said:

> I don't really like the idea of them being yelled at or spanked. I think if there is a behavior problem, they should be able to tell [the parents] and for us to deal with it. Luckily, I have been in the situation where my kids is pretty mellow, but I've seen her spanking her other grandchildren. I wouldn't like that.

Occasionally, Maria would consider moving her child to a day care center. Yet, when Maria weighed out all factors (e.g., convenience, location, flexibility, cost, quality of care, being within the family for child care), she decided that this care by her mother-in-law was the best choice, in spite of the differences about disciplining practices. . . .

Another consideration was that simply being of the same race did not guarantee racial safety. Gloria felt that her African American child care provider was uncomfortable with the fact that her children's father was White. Being biracial located her children in a different category of race than simply "Black." Similarly, other mothers found that their searches for child care were complicated by having mixed-race children. Julie Lopez described how her background complicated her search for child care.

> I'm bilingual, but I'm not bicultural. My father was Black, my mother was White, my husband is Mexican. My child is half Mexican, Chicano. My grandparents are Jewish. We had all these different types of people all there and I picked parts of different cultures. . . . My child is going to get a different concept of different people. . . .

Several of the middle-class, predominantly White daycares had made a formal commitment to diversify their ethnic composition as well as to developing a multicultural curriculum. They offered full scholarships to children of color in order to diversify race and ethnicity. Yet, even when the daycare center had a formal commitment to a multiculturalism, childcare providers' behaviors and attitudes often demonstrated a lack of cultural competency that resulted in racially unsafe environments for children of color and their mothers. Racism ranged from outright hostile relations with child care staff and other parents at the day care to the interactions with well-intentioned White child care providers who lacked experience with caring for children of color and negotiating cross-cultural interactions. Aurora Garcia, a Mexican American mother, explained how this happens:

> They're all White, and they come from that perspective . . . And they have blind spots. I don't know how else to put it. They're coming from their perspectives and their reality, their experiences, and so to change that, you have to ask them to. You have to help them do it, too.

And indeed, one of the consequences of being a parent of a child of color in a majority White daycare was the increased need for parental involvement. Aurora negotiated her child's racial safety by becoming, informally, the day care center's multicultural consultant. She intervened when the staff at her daughter's day care center did not interrupt behavior that was racist and stereotypical, such as when a White child pretended to be an Indian and came to school stereotypically dressed in feathers and headbands, wielding a toy tomahawk and whooping war cries. First, she brought to their awareness that certain behaviors and practices were racist and stereotypical. In the case of the White boy who came to school dressed as a stereotypical American Indian, she told them that she objected to the child's practice as well as to the staff's encouragement of it by painting stereotypical American Indian war paint on him. When the day care center was responsive to her concerns and asked her to work with them on it, she talked to the children and staff and recommended multicultural readings. Aurora gave the day care staff credit for trying to improve, but at the same time she was aware that cross-cultural gaffs were going to be a regular part of being in a predominantly White day care. She added:

> They are very actively trying to deal with some of these issues, and to me that felt good, culturally, you know. They made some boo-boos. [Like] at one point one of these teachers was talking to one of the [Latino] kids in Spanish, and she said, "She's bilingual, right?" [She wasn't.] Then you have to decode what you are and [let them know that] not all Chicanos speak Spanish. So, on one level, it was like you could ignore it. But I had to talk to her and explain who I am, and this has been my experience, and people assume that if you're a particular ethnicity then you're going to do what they perceive are the stereotypical things of that ethnicity.

Because of their awareness of racism in U.S. society, mothers of color were acutely aware of whether their children would be racially safe in child care settings. When one is a member of a historically subordinated racial ethnic group, finding child care that provides children with racial safety is an important concern. Yet, the search is complicated by other racial-ethnic factors.

THE SEARCH FOR CULTURAL MAINTENANCE

Many of the mothers expressed interest in child care by racially and ethnically similar caregivers. For some, this was motivated by the desire to protect their children and have them in racially safe situations. For others, staying within one's own community was an explicit strategy to ensure that their children would learn about their cultural heritage and histories. Many of the mothers had been young adults at a time in history when racial ethnic groups began to take pride in claiming their cultural histories. Prior to the 1960s, historically subordinated racial ethnic groups were expected to socialize their children to the dominant Anglo Saxon Protestant values of U.S. society. As far back as the 1920s, child care services were used to "Americanize" immigrant children and their parents.[8] Mothers were aware of this bias and purposefully sought out culturally similar providers because they saw child care as a site that would influence their children's understandings of their cultural heritage.

Several Mexican American mothers sought Spanish-speaking Mexican or Mexican American caregivers for this reason. For example, when Elena Romero, a Mexican American nutritionist, first needed child care, she used this strategy and found a Spanish-speaking Mexican American child care provider. She said:

> We found out about this [family] day care that was run by a preschool teacher that had decided to open up her own day care. And she was Chicana and . . . I really wanted him to know Spanish. Since birth I had [talked] to him [in Spanish] . . . Anyway, so I went to this day care and I really was impressed with the day care center because . . . she was really organized . . . and I liked her right away, you know. Then she had like senoras mexicanas . . . come in and cook for her and like they would make a big ol' pot of albóndigas . . . a meatball soup, you know. So like they would make really good Mexican food.

Similarly, Aurora Garcia said:

> I was hoping that, given that my child would be in the household for a significant number of hours during the day, that there be some [ethnic] similarity, you know, not that I'm traditional, I don't consider myself traditional, but those values I wanted, kind of implanted, you know, issues of discipline, you know, being really caring and nurturing and her being familiar with Spanish.

In describing what she looked for in child care, Julie Lopez, an African American mother whose ex-husband and stepfather are Latino, said:

> There's a cultural thing . . . one of the things for me, and our family, it has been really important to have [my child] in a bilingual place where she can sit down with other kids and speak Spanish and have a teacher that speaks Spanish and they sit down at lunch and they speak Spanish together. And the writing they do is both in English and Spanish and the pictures on the walls and stuff, because that cultural thing to me is really important . . . I'm always more comfortable if they're bicultural as well, versus just being bilingual.

Thus, their concerns were not simply about the skills and types of food that their children would be eating but also addressed a broader understanding that shared cultural practices were expressions of shared cultural values.

Another issue that confronted employed mothers of color was whether to foster cultural maintenance and racial safety at the cost of educational opportunities. In particular, mothers who had been raised working class and were now middle class grappled with this problem. When Aurora Garcia switched her daughter from a family day care home with a Mexican American caregiver to a predominantly White day care center, she felt as if she had to make compromises. She said:

> I'm not getting the ideal. I can't find the ideal . . . there are very few children of color there. I think diversity to them is Jewish. That's being diverse culturally . . . I mean, the ideal to me would be that she be in a school where she would be learning Spanish, she would be learning those things. . . . And that's just a tradeoff for me right now . . . I think of all the skills she's learning right now, but there's a cultural context to them that would be nice to have.

Aurora acknowledged that because she used a predominantly White day care center, she was raising her child in a White environment. However, she pointed out that her daughter was exposed to traditional cultural values because of who her parents were. She said, "I'm very much entrenched in who I am and what my cultural values are and my experience, and my partner is in his." Similarly, Elena Romero reconciled herself to the fact that her children would learn about their culture and their history at home. She said:

> [My husband and I] are both real proud of being Mexicanos, Chicanos, you know. And we're both constantly involved in the Movement kind of things. And we both have friends who are bilingual and that have kids, and, you, our families. If we have a birthday party, we have a piñata and all that stuff. So we decided well, that they would get it from us.

Yet, Aurora and Elena both realized that placing children in White day cares removed them from being fully immersed in their traditional ethnic community. Aurora said:

> It's not the same for a child. I mean, it really is how you play, who you play with, what you play, it's what you eat, it's how people treat you, what they say to you. . . . [Her teachers] are going to present it from a white perspective because they don't have bilingual teachers. They don't have African American teachers. So for me, it's a trade off.

Clearly, choosing to move outside of one's culture into a predominantly White daycare was not an easy decision. When they made the decision to place their children in a predominantly White daycare, they continued to be conflicted about not being able to find a daycare for their children which would provide cultural maintenance and exposure to traditional cultural practices and values. Although on the surface it may appear that mothers of color who place their children in predominantly White daycare settings are rejecting their own cultural practices and turning their back on their racial ethnic group, this was not the case. They were highly self-conscious that their children's child care was not fulfilling one of their major criteria for their child care arrangements. By providing their children with the social opportunities and formal education which they had come to expect for any well-educated child of the middle class, they had to work harder at home to ensure that their children learned about their cultures and histories. Furthermore, by placing themselves in predominantly White settings, they more frequently encountered racism and, more frequently and at a younger age, had to explain to their young children about race relations with White society and how to navigate them.

Both of these concerns—racial safety and cultural maintenance—reflect how membership in specific racial ethnic groups influences views of what constitutes appropriate caregiving. The concern of mothers of color for racial safety addresses their awareness that their children can be the targets of racism by a society that has historically devalued their racial ethnic group. The concern for cultural maintenance reflects their preference to retain and/or retrieve traditional cultural practices and values. . . .

NOTES

1. Jacquelyn Litt, "Mothering, Medicalization, and Jewish Identity, 1928–1940," *Gender & Society* 10, no. 2 (1996): 185–198.

2. Carole E. Joffe, *Friendly Intruders: Childcare Professionals and Family Life* (Berkeley: University of California Press, 1977).

3. Mary Larner and Anne Mitchell, "Meeting the Child Care Needs of Low-Income Families," *Child and Youth Care Forum* 21, no. 5 (1992): 317–334. Katherine Brown Rosier and William A. Corsario, "Competent Parents, Complex Lives: Managing Parenthood in Poverty," *Journal of Contemporary Ethnography* 22, no. 2 (1993): 171–204.

4. Joffe, *Friendly Intruders*.

5. Stevanne Auerbach, "What Parents Want From Day Care," in *Child Care. A Comprehensive Guide: Philosophy, Programs, and Practices for the Creation of Quality Services for Children*, vol. 1, *Rationale for Child Care Services: Programs vs. Politics*, ed. Stevanne Auerbach with James A. Rivaldo (New York: Human Sciences Press, 1975), 137–152.

6. Janice Hale, "The Transmission of Cultural Values to Young African American Children," *Young Children* (September 1991): 7–14.

7. Janice Gould, "American Indian Women's Poetry: Strategies of Rage and Hope," *Signs* 20, no. 4 (1995): 797–817.

8. Julia Wrigley, "Different Care for Different Kids: Social Class and Child Care Policy," *Educational Policy* 3, no. 4 (1989): 421–439.

MIGRATION AND VIETNAMESE AMERICAN WOMEN

35

Remaking Ethnicity

Nazli Kibria

VIETNAMESE AMERICANS AND THE RISE IN WOMEN'S POWER

My research on the adaptive strategies of a community of Vietnamese refugees in Philadelphia revealed some of the ways in which women and men struggled and clashed with each other in efforts to shape the social organization of family and community life. From 1983 to 1985, I gathered information on family life and gender relations through participant observation in household and community settings, as well as in-depth interviews with women and men in the ethnic community.

The Vietnamese of the study were recent immigrants who had arrived in the United States during the late 1970s and early 1980s. Most were from urban, middle-class backgrounds in southern Vietnam. At the time of the study, over 30 percent of the adult men in the households of study were unemployed. Of the men who were employed, over half worked in low-paying, unskilled jobs in the urban service sector or in factories located in the outlying areas of the city. Women tended to work periodically, occupying jobs in the informal economic sector as well as in the urban service economy. Eight of the twelve households had members who collected public assistance. Both the family economy and informal community exchange networks were important means by which the households dealt with economic scarcities. Family and community were of tremendous economic salience to the group, as they were important resources for survival in the face of a rather inhospitable economic and social environment.

As suggested by the high rate of the men's unemployment, settlement in the United States had generated some shifts in power in favor of the women in the group. Traditional Vietnamese family and gender relations were modeled on Confucian principles, which placed women in subordination to men in every aspect of life. A key aspect of the social and economic oppression of women in traditional Vietnamese life was the patrilineal extended house-

From: Maxine Baca Zinn and Bonnie Thornton Dill, eds. *Women of Color in U.S. Society* (Philadelphia: Temple University Press, 1994), pp. 247–61. Reprinted by permission.

hold. Its organization dictated that women married at a young age, following which they entered the household of their husband's father. This structure ensured the concentration of economic resources in the hands of men and men's control of women through the isolation of women from their families of origin.[1]

It is important to note the deep-seated changes in traditional family and gender structures in Vietnam during this century. War and urbanization eroded the structure of the patrilineal extended household. While unemployment was high in the cities, men from middle-class backgrounds were able to take advantage of the expansion of middle-level positions in the government bureaucracy and army. Such occupational opportunities were more limited for women: the women study participants indicated that they engaged in seasonal and informal income-generating activities or worked in low-level jobs in the growing war-generated service sector in the cities. The transition from rural to urban life had generated a shift in the basis of men's control over economic and social resources. However, families relied on men's income to maintain a middle-class standard of living. Thus women remained in a position of economic subordination to men, a situation that served to sustain the ideals of the traditional family system and men's authority in the family. Restrictions on women's sexuality were important for middle-class families who sought to distinguish themselves from the lower social strata. My data suggest that families were especially conscious of the need to distance themselves from poorer "fallen" women who had become associated with the prostitution generated by the American military presence.

Within the Vietnamese American community of study, I found several conditions that were working to undermine the bases on which male authority had rested in Vietnam. Most important, for the Vietnamese men, the move to the United States had involved a profound loss of social economic status. Whereas in pre-1975 Vietnam the men held middle-class occupations, in the United States they had access to largely unskilled, low-status, and low-paying jobs. Also, because of their difficulties with English and their racial-ethnic status, the men found themselves disadvantaged within social arenas of the dominant society. Compounding these problems was the dearth of strong formal ethnic organizations in the community that could have served as a vehicle for the men's political assertion into the dominant society.

As a result of these losses, the comparative access of men and women to the resources of the dominant society had to some extent become equalized. In contrast to the experiences of the men, migration had not significantly altered the position of the women in the economy. As in Vietnam, the women tended to work sporadically, sometimes in family businesses or, more commonly, in temporary jobs in the informal and service sector economies of the city. However, the economic contributions of women to the family budget had risen in proportion to those of the men. I have suggested that in modern, urban South Vietnam the force and legitimacy of male authority had rested heavily on the ability of men to ensure a middle-class status and standard of living for their families. In the United States, the ability of men to fulfull this expectation had been eroded. Among the men, there was widespread concern about the consequences of this situation for their status in the family, as is revealed by the words of a former lieutenant of the South Vietnamese army: "In Vietnam, the man earns and everyone depends on him. In most families, one or two men could provide for the whole family. Here the man finds he can never make enough money to take care of the family. His wife has to work, his children have to work, and so they look at him in a different way. The man isn't strong anymore, like he was in Vietnam."

Such changes had opened up the possibilities for a renegotiation of gender relations, and were the cause of considerable conflict between men and women in the family and community. The shifts in power had also enhanced the ability of women to construct and channel familial and ethnic resources in ways that they chose. Previously I suggested that the changes in the balance of power between men and women generated by migration are crucial to understanding the manner and degree to which immigrant family and community reveal themselves to be gender contested. How, then, did the fairly drastic shift in the gender balance of power among the Vietnamese Americans reflect itself in the ability of the men and women in this group to influence family and community life? In the following section, I describe some of the ways in which gender interests and conflict shaped family and community life for the Vietnamese Americans.

FAMILY AND ETHNICITY AS GENDER CONTESTED

One of the most intriguing and important strategies of Vietnamese American adaptation that I observed was the rebuilding of kinship networks. Family ties had undergone tremendous disruption in the process of escape from Vietnam and resettlement in the United States. Despite this, the households of the group tended to be large and extended. The process by which this occurred was one in which the study participants actively worked to reconstruct family networks by building kin relationships. In order for this to take place, the criteria for inclusion in the family had become extremely flexible. Thus close friends were often incorporated into family groups as fictive kin. Also, relationships with relatives who were distant or vaguely known in Vietnam were elevated in importance. Perhaps most important for women, the somewhat greater significance traditionally accorded the husband's kin had receded in importance.[2] Given the scarcity of relatives in the United States, such distinctions were considered a luxury, and the demands of life made the rebuilding of family a valuable, if not a necessary, step in the process of adaptation to the dominant society.

While important for the group as a whole, the reconstruction of kinship as it took place had some special advantages for women. One consequence of the more varied and inclusive nature of the kinship network was that women were rarely surrounded exclusively by the husband's relatives and/or friends. As a result, they were often able to turn to close fictive kin and perhaps members of their families of origin for support during conflicts with men in the family. Another condition that enhanced the power of married women in the family was that few had to deal with the competing authority of their mother-in-law in the household, because elderly women have not been among those likely to leave Vietnam.

The reconstruction of kinship thus had important advantages for women, particularly as it moved the Vietnamese perhaps even further from the ideal model of the patrilineal extended household that it had been in the past. But women were not simply passive beneficiaries of the family rebuilding process. Rather, they played an active part in family reconstruction, attempting to shape family boundaries in ways that were to their advantage. I found women playing a vital part in creating fictive kin by forging close ties. And women were often important, if not central, "gatekeepers" to the family group and household. Thus the women helped to decide such matters as whether the marriage of a particular family member was a positive event and could be taken as an opportunity to expand kinship networks. At other times the women passed judgment on current or potential family members, as to whether they had demonstrated enough commitment to such important familial obligations as the sharing of economic and social resources with kin.

Although women undoubtedly played an important part in family reconstruction, their control over decisions about family membership was by no means exclusive or absolute. In fact, the question of who was legitimately included in the family group was often a source of tension within families, particularly between men and women. The frequency of disputes over this issue stemmed in part from the fluidity and subsequent uncertainty about family boundaries, as well as the great pressures often placed on individuals to subordinate their needs to those of the family collective. Beyond this, I also suggest that disputes over boundaries arose from the fundamental underlying gender divisions in the family. That is, the different interests of women and men in the family spurred efforts to shape the family in ways that were of particular advantage to them. For the reasons I have previously discussed, the Vietnamese American women had greater influence and opportunity in the shaping of family in the United States than they had in the past. The women tended to use this influence to construct family groups that extended their power in the family.

In one case that I observed, considerable tension developed between a couple named Nguyet and Phong concerning the sponsorship[3] of Nguyet's nephew and his family from a refugee camp in Southeast Asia. Nguyet and

Phong had been together with their three children (two from Nguyet's previous marriage) for about seven years, since they had met in a refugee camp in Thailand. Phong remained married to a woman who was still living in Vietnam with his children, a fact that was the source of some stress for Nguyet and Phong. The issue of the nephew's sponsorship seemed to exacerbate tensions in the relationship. Phong did not want to undertake the sponsorship because of the potentially heavy financial obligations it entailed. He also confessed that he was worried that Nguyet would leave him after the nephew's arrival, a threat often made by Nguyet during their quarrels. Finally, he talked of how Nguyet's relationship with the nephew was too distant to justify the sponsorship. Nguyet had never even met the nephew, who was the son of a first cousin rather than of a sibling.

Confirming some of Phong's fears, Nguyet saw the presence of the nephew and his family as a potentially important source of support for herself. She spoke of how she had none of "my family" in the country, in comparison with Phong, whose sister lived in the city. She agreed that she did not know much about her nephew, but nonetheless felt that his presence would ease her sense of isolation and also would provide a source of aid if her relationship with Phong deteriorated. Eventually she proceeded with the sponsorship, but only after a lengthy dispute with Phong.

While the issue of sponsorship posed questions about kinship in an especially sharp manner, there were other circumstances under which women and men clashed over family boundaries. When kin connections could not be questioned (for example, in the case of a sibling), what came under dispute was the commitment of the particular person involved to familial norms and obligations. One of my woman respondents fought bitterly with her older brother about whether their male cousin should live with them. Her brother objected to the cousin's presence in the household on the grounds that he had not responded to their request for a loan of money two years ago. The woman respondent wanted to overlook this breach of conduct because of her extremely close relationship with the cousin, who had been her "best friend" in Vietnam.

Regardless of the particular circumstances, gender conflict seemed an important part of the family reconstruction process. Women and men shared an interest in creating and maintaining a family group that was large and cohesive enough to provide economic and social support. However, their responses to the family reconstruction process were framed by their differing interests, as men and women, within the family. Men and women attempted to channel family membership in ways that were to their advantage, such that their control over the resources of the family group was enhanced.

Gender divisions and conflicts also entered into the community life of the group. The social networks of the Vietnamese American women were central to the dynamics and organization of the ethnic community. They served to organize and regulate exchange between households. While "hanging out" at informal social gatherings, I observed women exchanging information, money, goods, food, and tasks such as child care and cooking. Given the precarious economic situation of the group, these exchanges played an important role in ensuring the economic survival and stability of the households. The women's centrality to these social networks gave them the power not only to regulate household exchange but also to act as agents of social control in the community in a more general sense. I found that women, through the censure of gossip and the threat of ostracism, played an important part in defining community norms. In short, the relative rise in power that had accrued to the Vietnamese American women as a result of migration expressed itself in their considerable influence over the organization and dynamics of the ethnic community. Like kinship, community life was a negotiated arena, one over which women and men struggled to gain control.

The gender-contested quality of ethnic forms was also apparent in the efforts of women to reinterpret traditional Vietnamese familial ideologies on their own terms. In general, the Vietnamese American women continued to espouse and support traditional ideologies of gender relations as important ideals. For example, when asked during interviews to describe the "best" or ideal roles of men and women in the family, most of my respondents talked of a clear division of roles in which women assumed primary responsibility for maintaining the home and taking care of the children, and men for the economic support of the family. Most felt that household decisions should be made jointly, although the opinion of the man was seen to carry more weight. About half of those interviewed felt that a wife should almost always obey her husband. Even more widespread were beliefs in the importance of restrictions on female (but not male) sexuality before marriage.

While women often professed such beliefs, their relationship to traditional ideologies was active rather than passive and inflexible. In other words, the women tended to emphasize certain aspects of the traditional familial ideology over others. In particular, they emphasized parental authority and the obligation of men to sacrifice individual needs and concerns in order to fulfill the needs of the family, traditional precepts they valued and hoped to preserve in the United States. The women's selective approach to Vietnamese "tradition" emerged most clearly in situations of conflict between men and women in the family. In such disputes, women selectively used the traditional ideologies to protect themselves and to legitimate their actions and demands (Kibria 1990). Thus, husbands who were beating their wives were attacked by other women in the community on the grounds that they (the husbands) were inadequate breadwinners. The women focused not on the husband's treatment of his wife but on his failure to fulfill his family caretaker role. Through this selective emphasis, the women managed to condemn the delinquent husband without appearing to depart from "tradition." In short, for the Vietnamese American women, migration had resulted in a greater ability to shape family and community life.

CONCLUSION

For immigrant women, ethnic ties and institutions may be both a source of resistance and support, and of patriarchal oppression. Through an acknowledgment of this duality we can arrive at a fuller understanding of immigrant women's lives: one that captures the multifaceted constraints as well as the resistances that are offered by immigrant women to the oppressive forces in their lives. In patterns similar to those noted by studies of other racial-ethnic groups (Stack 1974; Baca Zinn 1975), the Vietnamese Americans presented in this [article] relied on family and community for survival and resistance. Their marginal status made the preservation of these institutions an important priority.

Like other racial-ethnic women, the ability of the Vietnamese American women to shape ethnicity was constrained by their social-structural location in the dominant society. These women saw the traditional family system as key to their cultural autonomy and economic security in American society. Migration may have equalized the economic resources of the men and women, but it had not expanded the economic opportunities of the women enough to make independence from men an attractive economic reality. The Vietnamese American women, as is true for other women of color, were especially constrained in their efforts to "negotiate" family and community in that they faced triple disadvantages (the combination of social class, racial-ethnic, and gender statuses) in their dealings with the dominant society.

Recognition of the role of ethnic institutions in facilitating immigrant adaptation and resistance is essential. However, it is equally important to not lose sight of gender divisions and conflicts, and the ways in which these influence the construction of ethnic institutions. Feminist scholars have begun to explore the diverse ways in which immigrant women manipulate family and community to enhance their own power, albeit in ways that are deeply constrained by the web of multiple oppressions that surround them (Andezian 1986; Bhachu 1986; Kibria 1990). Such work begins to suggest the complexity of immigrant women's relationship to ethnic structures, which is informed by both strength and oppression.

NOTES

1. Some scholars stress the fact that the reality of women's lives was far different from that suggested by these Confucian ideals. Women in traditional Vietnam also had a relatively favorable economic position in comparison with Chinese women due to Vietnamese women's rights of inheritance as well as their involvement in commercial activities (see Hickey 1964; Keyes 1977). Despite these qualifications, there is little to suggest that the economic and social subordination of women was not a fundamental reality in Vietnam.

2. Hy Van Luong (1984) has noted the importance of two models of kinship in Vietnamese life, one that is patrilineal-oriented and another in which bilateral kin are of significance. Thus the flexible, encompassing conceptions of family that I found among the group were not entirely new, but had their roots in Vietnamese life; however, they had acquired greater significance in the context of the United States.

3. Refugee resettlement in the United States involves a system of sponsorship by family members or other interested parties who agree to assume part of the responsibility for taking care of those sponsored for a period of time after their arrival.

References

Andezian, Sossie. 1986. "Women's Roles in Organizing Symbolic Life: Algerian Female Immigrants in France." Pp. 254–266 in *International Migration: The Female Experience*, edited by R. J. Simon and C. B. Brettell. Totowa, N.J.: Rowman and Allenheld.

Baca Zinn, Maxine. 1975. "Political Familism: Toward Sex Role Equality in Chicano Families." *Aztlan* 6, no. 1: 13–26.

Bhachu, Parminder K. 1986. "Work, Dowry and Marriage Among East African Sikh Women in the U.K." Pp. 241–254 in *International Migration: The Female Experience*, edited by R. J. Simon and C. B. Brettell. Totowa, N.J.: Rowman and Allenheld.

Hickey, Gerald C. 1964. *Village in Vietnam*. New Haven: Yale University Press.

Keyes, Charles F. 1977. *The Golden Peninsula*. New York: Macmillan.

Kibria, Nazli. 1990. "Power, Patriarchy and Gender Conflict in the Vietnamese Immigrant Community." *Gender and Society* 4, no. 1 (March): 9–24.

Luong, Hy Van. 1984. "'Brother' and 'Uncle': An Analysis of Rules, Structural Contradictions and Meaning in Vietnamese Kinship." *American Anthropologist* 86, no. 2: 290–313.

Stack, Carol. 1974. *All Our Kin*. New York: Harper & Row.

Cultural Institutions and the Production of Ideas

RACIST STEREOTYPING IN THE ENGLISH LANGUAGE

36

Robert B. Moore

LANGUAGE AND CULTURE

An integral part of any culture is its language. Language not only develops in conjunction with a society's historical, economic and political evolution; it also reflects that society's attitudes and thinking. Language not only *expresses* ideas and concepts but actually *shapes* thought.[1] If one accepts that our dominant white culture is racist, then one would expect our language—an indispensable transmitter of culture—to be racist as well. Whites, as the dominant group, are not subjected to the same abusive characterization by our language that people of color receive. Aspects of racism in the English language that will be discussed in this essay include terminology, symbolism, politics, ethnocentrism, and context.

Before beginning our analysis of racism in language we would like to quote part of a TV film review which shows the connection between language and culture.[2]

> Depending on one's culture, one interacts with time in a very distinct fashion. One example which gives some cross-cultural insights into the concept of

From: Paula S. Rothenberg (ed.), *Racism and Sexism: An Integrated Study* (New York: St. Martin's Press, 1988), pp. 269–279. Reprinted by permission of the Council on Interracial Books for Children c/o Lawrence Jordan Literary Agency, 345 West 121st Street, NY, NY 10027.

time is language. In Spanish, a watch is said to "walk." In English, the watch "runs." In German, the watch "functions." And in French, the watch "marches." In the Indian culture of the Southwest, people do not refer to time in this way. The value of the watch is displaced with the value of "what time it's getting to be." Viewing these five cultural perspectives of time, one can see some definite emphasis and values that each culture places on time. For example, a cultural perspective may provide a clue to why the negative stereotype of the slow and lazy Mexican who lives in the "Land of Manana" exists in the Anglo value system, where time "flies," the watch "runs" and "time is money."

A SHORT PLAY ON "BLACK" AND "WHITE" WORDS

Some may blackly (angrily) accuse me of trying to blacken (defame) the English language, to give it a black eye (a mark of shame) by writing such black words (hostile). They may denigrate (to cast aspersions; to darken) me by accusing me of being blackhearted (malevolent), of having a black outlook (pessimistic, dismal) on life, of being a blackguard (scoundrel)—which would certainly be a black mark (detrimental fact) against me. Some may black-brow (scowl at) me and hope that a black cat crosses in front of me because of this black deed. I may become a black sheep (one who causes shame or embarrassment because of deviation from the accepted standards), who will be blackballed (ostracized) by being placed on a blacklist (list of undesirables) in an attempt to blackmail (to force or coerce into a particular action) me to retract my words. But attempts to blackjack (to compel by threat) me will have a Chinaman's chance of success, for I am not a yellow-bellied Indian-giver of words, who will whitewash (cover up or gloss over vices or crimes) a black lie (harmful, inexcusable). I challenge the purity and innocence (white) of the English language. I don't see things in black and white (entirely bad or entirely good) terms, for I am a white man (marked by upright firmness) if there ever was one. However, it would be a black day when I would not "call a spade a spade," even though some will suggest a white man calling the English language racist is like the pot calling the kettle black. While many may be niggardly (grudging, scanty) in their support, others will be honest and decent—and to them I say, that's very white of you (honest, decent).

The preceding is of course a white lie (not intended to cause harm), meant only to illustrate some examples of racist terminology in the English language.

OBVIOUS BIGOTRY

Perhaps the most obvious aspect of racism in language would be terms like "nigger," "spook," "chink," "spic," etc. While these may be facing increasing social disdain, they certainly are not dead. Large numbers of white Americans continue to utilize these terms. "Chink," "gook," and "slant-eyes" were in common usage among U.S. troops in Vietnam. An NBC nightly news broadcast, in February 1972, reported that the basketball team in Pekin, Illinois, was called the "Pekin Chinks" and noted that even though this had been protested by Chinese Americans, the term continued to be used because it was easy, and meant no harm. Spiro Agnew's widely reported "fat Jap" remark and the "little Jap" comment of lawyer John Wilson, during the Watergate hearings, are surface indicators of a deep-rooted Archie Bunkerism.

Many white people continue to refer to Black people as "colored," as for instance in a July 30, 1975, *Boston Globe* article on a racist attack by whites on a group of Black people using a public beach in Boston. One white person was quoted as follows:

> We've always welcomed good colored people in South Boston but we will not tolerate radical blacks or Communists. . . . Good colored people are welcome in South Boston, black militants are not.

Many white people may still be unaware of the disdain many African Americans have for the term "colored," but it often appears that whether used intentionally or unintentionally, "colored" people are "good" and "know their place," while "Black" people are perceived as "uppity" and "threatening" to many whites. Similarly, the term "boy" to refer to African American men is now acknowledged to be a demeaning term, though still in common use. Other terms such as "the pot calling the kettle black" and "calling a spade a spade" have negative racial connotations but are still frequently used, as for example when President Ford was quoted in February 1976 saying that even though Daniel Moynihan had left the U.N., the U.S. would continue "calling a spade a spade."

COLOR SYMBOLISM

The symbolism of white as positive and black as negative is pervasive in our culture, with the black/white words used in the beginning of this essay only one of many aspects. "Good guys" wear white hats and ride white horses, "bad guys" wear black hats and ride black horses. Angels are white, and devils are black. The definition of *black* includes "without any moral light or goodness, evil, wicked, indicating disgrace, sinful," while that of *white* includes "morally pure, spotless, innocent, free from evil intent."

A children's TV cartoon program, *Captain Scarlet*, is about an organization called Spectrum, whose purpose is to save the world from an evil extraterrestrial force called the Mysterons. Everyone in Spectrum has a color name—Captain Scarlet, Captain Blue, etc. The one Spectrum agent who has been mysteriously taken over by the Mysterons and works to advance their evil aims is Captain Black. The person who heads Spectrum, the good organization out to defend the world, is Colonel White.

Three of the dictionary definitions of white are "fairness of complexion, purity, innocence." These definitions affect the standards of beauty in our culture, in which whiteness represents the norm. "Blondes have more fun" and "Wouldn't you really rather be a blonde" are sexist in their attitudes toward women generally, but are racist white standards when applied to third world women. A 1971 *Mademoiselle* advertisement pictured a curly-headed, ivory-skinned woman over the caption, "When you go blonde go all the way," and asked: "Isn't this how, in the back of your mind, you always wanted to look? All wide-eyed and silky blonde down to there, and innocent?" Whatever the advertising people meant by this particular woman's innocence, one must remember that "innocent" is one of the definitions of the word white. This standard of beauty when preached to all women is racist. The statement "Isn't this how, in the back of your mind, you always wanted to look?" either ignores third world women or assumes they long to be white.

Time magazine in its coverage of the Wimbledon tennis competition between the black Australian Evonne Goolagong and the white American Chris Evert described Ms. Goolagong as "the dusky daughter of an Australian sheepshearer," while Ms. Evert was "a fair young girl from the middle-class groves of Florida." *Dusky* is a synonym of "black" and is defined as "having dark skin; of a dark color; gloomy; dark; swarthy." Its antonyms are "fair" and "blonde." *Fair* is defined in part as "free from blemish, imperfection, or anything that impairs the appearance, quality, or character: pleasing in appearance, attractive; clean; pretty; comely." By defining Evonne Goolagong as "dusky," *Time* technically defined her as the opposite of "pleasing in appearance; attractive; clean; pretty; comely."

The studies of Kenneth B. Clark, Mary Ellen Goodman, Judith Porter and others indicate that this persuasive "rightness of whiteness" in U.S. culture affects children before the age of four, providing white youngsters with a false sense of superiority and encouraging self-hatred among third world youngsters.

ETHNOCENTRISM OR FROM A WHITE PERSPECTIVE

Some words and phrases that are commonly used represent particular perspectives and frames of reference, and these often distort the understanding of the reader or listener. David R. Burgest[3] has written about the effect of using the terms "slave" or "master." He argues that the psychological impact of the statement referring to "the master raped his slave" is different from the impact of the same statement substituting the words: "the white captor raped an African woman held in captivity."

> Implicit in the English usage of the "master-slave" concept is ownership of the "slave" by the "master," therefore, the "master" is merely abusing his property (slave). In reality, the captives (slave) were African individuals with human worth, right and dignity and the term "slave" denounces that human quality thereby making the mass rape of African women by white captors more acceptable in the minds of people and setting a mental frame of reference for legitimizing the atrocities perpetuated against African people.

The term slave connotes a less than human quality and turns the captive person into a thing. For example, two McGraw-Hill Far Eastern Publishers textbooks (1970) stated, "At first it was the slaves who worked the cane and they got only food for it. Now men work cane and get money." Next time you write about slavery or read about it, try transposing all "slaves" into "African people held in captivity," "Black people forced to work for no pay" or "African people stolen from their families and societies." While it is more cumbersome, such phrasing conveys a different meaning.

PASSIVE TENSE

Another means by which language shapes our perspective has been noted by Thomas Greenfield,[4] who writes that the achievements of Black people—and Black people themselves—have been hidden in

> the linguistic ghetto of the passive voice, the subordinate clause, and the "understood" subject. The seemingly innocuous distinction (between active/passive voice) holds enormous implications for writers and speakers. When it is effectively applied, the rhetorical impact of the passive voice—the art of making the creator or instigator of action totally disappear from a reader's perception—can be devastating.

For instance, some history texts will discuss how European immigrants came to the United States seeking a better life and expanded opportunities, but will note that "slaves *were brought* to America." Not only does this omit the destruction of African societies and families, but it ignores the role of northern merchants and southern slaveholders in the profitable trade in human beings. Other books will state that "the continental railroad *was built*," conveniently omitting information about the Chinese laborers who built much of it or the oppression they suffered.

Another example. While touring Monticello, Greenfield noted that the tour guide made all the black people of Monticello disappear through her use of the passive voice. While speaking of the architectural achievements of Jefferson in the active voice, she unfailingly shifted to passive when speaking of the work performed by Negro slaves and skilled servants.

Noting a type of door that after 166 years continued to operate without need for repair, Greenfield remarks that the design aspect of the door was much simpler than the actual skill and work involved in building and installing it. Yet his guide stated: "Mr. Jefferson designed these doors . . ." while "the doors were installed in 1809." The workers who installed those doors were African people whom Jefferson held in bondage. The guide's use of the passive tense enabled her to dismiss the reality of Jefferson's slaveholding. It also meant that she did not have to make any mention of the skills of those people held in bondage.

POLITICS AND TERMINOLOGY

"Culturally deprived," "economically disadvantaged" and "underdeveloped" are other terms which mislead and distort our awareness of reality. The application of the term "culturally deprived" to third world children in this society reflects a value judgment. It assumes that the dominant whites are cultured and all others without culture. In fact, third world children generally are bicultural, and many are bilingual, having grown up in their own culture as well as absorbing the dominant culture. In many ways, they are equipped with skills and experiences which white youth have been deprived of, since most white youth develop in a monocultural, monolingual environment. Burgest[5] suggests that the term "culturally deprived" be replaced by "culturally dispossessed," and that the term "economically disadvantaged" be replaced by "economically exploited." Both these terms present a perspective and implication that provide an entirely different frame of reference as to the reality of the third world experience in U.S. society.

Similarly, many nations of the third world are described as "underdeveloped." These less wealthy nations are generally those that suffered under colonialism and neo-colonialism. The "developed" nations are those that exploited their resources and wealth. Therefore, rather than referring to these countries as "underdeveloped," a more appropriate and meaningful designation might be "over exploited." Again, transpose this term next time you read about "underdeveloped nations" and note the different meaning that results.

Terms such as "culturally deprived," "economically disadvantaged" and "underdeveloped" place the responsibility for their own conditions on those being so described. This is known as "Blaming the Victim."[6] It places responsibility for poverty on the victims of poverty. It removes the blame from those in power who benefit from, and continue to permit, poverty.

Still another example involves the use of "non-white," "minority" or "third world." While people of color are a minority in the U.S., they are part of the vast majority of the world's population, in which white people are a distinct minority. Thus, by utilizing the term minority to describe people of color in the U.S., we can lose sight of the global majority/minority reality—a fact of some importance in the increasing and interconnected struggles of people of color inside and outside the U.S.

To describe people of color as "non-white" is to use whiteness as the standard and norm against which to measure all others. Use of the term "third world" to describe all people of color overcomes the inherent bias of "minority" and "non-white." Moreover, it connects the struggles of third world people in the U.S. with the freedom struggles around the globe.

The term third world gained increasing usage after the 1955 Bandung Conference of "non-aligned" nations, which represented a third force outside of the two world superpowers. The "first world" represents the United States, Western Europe and their sphere of influence. The "second world" represents the Soviet Union and its sphere. The "third world" represents, for the most part, nations that were, or are, controlled by the "first world" or West. For the most part, these are nations of Africa, Asia and Latin America.

"LOADED" WORDS AND NATIVE AMERICANS

Many words lead to a demeaning characterization of groups of people. For instance, Columbus, it is said, "discovered" America. The word *discover* is defined as "to gain sight or knowledge of something previously unseen or unknown; to discover may be to find some existent thing that was previously unknown." Thus, a continent inhabited by millions of human beings cannot be "discovered." For history books to continue this usage represents a Euroocentric (white European) perspective on world history and ignores the existence of, and the perspective of, Native Americans. "Discovery," as used in the Euro-American context, implies the right to take what one finds, ignoring the rights of those who already inhabit or own the "discovered" thing.

Eurocentrism is also apparent in the usage of "victory" and "massacre" to describe the battles between Native Americans and whites. *Victory* is defined in the dictionary as "a success or triumph over an enemy in battle or war; the decisive defeat of an opponent." *Conquest* denotes the "taking over of control by the victor, and the obedience of the conquered." *Massacre* is defined as "the unnecessary, indiscriminate killing of a number of human beings, as in barbarous warfare or persecution, or for revenge or plunder." *Defend* is described as "to ward off attack from; guard against assault or injury; to strive to keep safe by resisting attack."

Eurocentrism turns these definitions around to serve the purpose of distorting history and justifying Euro-American conquest of the Native American homelands. Euro-Americans are not described in history books as invading Native American lands, but rather as defending *their* homes against "Indian" attacks. Since European communities were constantly encroaching on land already occupied, then a more honest interpretation would state that it was the Native Americans who were "warding off," "guarding" and "defending" their homelands.

Native American victories are invariably defined as "massacres," while the indiscriminate killing, extermination and plunder of Native American nations by Euro-Americans is defined as "victory." Distortion of history by the choice of "loaded" words used to describe historical events is a common racist practice. Rather than portraying Native Americans as human beings in highly defined and complex societies, cultures and civilizations, history books use such adjectives as "savages," "beasts," "primitive," and "backward." Native people are referred to as "squaw," "brave," or "papoose" instead of "woman," "man," or "baby."

Another term that has questionable connotations is *tribe*. The Oxford English Dictionary defines this noun as "a race of people; now applied especially to a primary aggregate of people in a primitive or barbarous condition, under a headman or chief." Morton Fried,[7] discussing "The Myth of Tribe," states that the word "did not become a general term of reference to American Indian society until the nineteenth century. Previously, the words commonly used for Indian populations were 'nation' and 'people.'" Since "tribe" has assumed a connotation of primitiveness or backwardness, it is suggested that the use of "nation" or "people" replace the term whenever possible in referring to Native American peoples.

The term *tribe* invokes even more negative implications when used in reference to American peoples. As Evelyn Jones Rich[8] has noted, the term is "almost always used to refer to third world people and it implies a stage of development which is, in short, a put-down."

"LOADED" WORDS AND AFRICANS

Conflicts among diverse peoples within African nations are often referred to as "tribal warfare," while conflicts among the diverse peoples within European countries are never described in such terms. If the rivalries between the Ibo and the Hausa and Yoruba in Nigeria are described as "tribal," why not the rivalries between Serbs and Slavs in Yugoslavia, or Scots and English in Great Britain, Protestants and Catholics in Ireland, or the Basques and the Southern Spaniards in Spain? Conflicts among African peoples in a particular nation have religious, cultural, economic and/or political roots. If we can analyze the roots of conflicts among European peoples in terms other than "tribal warfare," certainly we can do the same with African peoples, including correct reference to the ethnic groups or nations involved. For example, the terms

"Kaffirs," "Hottentot" or "Bushmen" are names imposed by white Europeans. The correct names are always those by which a people refer to themselves. (In these instances Xhosa, Khoi-Khoin and San are correct.⁹)

The generalized application of "tribal" in reference to Africans—as well as the failure to acknowledge the religious, cultural and social diversity of African peoples—is a decidedly racist dynamic. It is part of the process whereby Euro-Americans justify, or avoid confronting, their oppression of third world peoples. Africa has been particularly insulted by this dynamic, as witness the pervasive "darkest Africa" image. This image, widespread in Western culture, evokes an Africa covered by jungles and inhabited by "uncivilized," "cannibalistic," "pagan," "savage" peoples. This "darkest Africa" image avoids the geographical reality. Less than 20 percent of the African continent is wooded savanna, for example. The image also ignores the history of African cultures and civilizations. Ample evidence suggests this distortion of reality was developed as a convenient rationale for the European and American slave trade. The Western powers, rather than exploiting, were civilizing and Christianizing "uncivilized" and "pagan savages" (so the rationalization went). This dynamic also served to justify Western colonialism. From Tarzan movies to racist children's books like *Doctor Dolittle* and *Charlie and the Chocolate Factory*, the image of "savage" Africa and the myth of "the white man's burden" has been perpetuated in Western culture.

A 1972 *Time* magazine editorial lamenting the demise of *Life* magazine, stated that the "lavishness" of *Life*'s enterprises included "organizing safaris into darkest Africa." The same year, the *New York Times*' C. L. Sulzberger wrote that Africa has "a history as dark as the skins of many of its people." Terms such as "darkest Africa," "primitive," "tribe" ("tribal") or "jungle," in reference to Africa, perpetuate myths and are especially inexcusable in such large circulation publications.

Ethnocentrism is similarly reflected in the term "pagan" to describe traditional religions. A February 1973 *Time* magazine article on Uganda stated, "Moslems account for only 500,000 of Uganda's 10 million people. Of the remainder, 5,000,000 are Christians and the rest pagan." *Pagan* is defined as "Heathen, a follower of a polytheistic religion; one that has little or no religion and that is marked by a frank delight in and uninhibited seeking after sensual pleasures and material goods." *Heathen* is defined as "Unenlightened; an unconverted member of a people or nation that does not acknowledge the God of the Bible. A person whose culture or enlightenment is of an inferior grade, especially an irreligious person." Now, the people of Uganda, like almost all Africans, have serious religious beliefs and practices. As used by Westerners, "pagan" connotes something wild, primitive and inferior—another term to watch out for.

The variety of traditional structures that African people live in are their "houses," not "huts." A *hut* is "an often small and temporary dwelling of simple construction." And to describe Africans as "natives" (noun) is derogatory terminology—as in, "the natives are restless." The dictionary definition of *native* includes: "one of a people inhabiting a territorial area at the time of its discovery or becoming familiar to a foreigner; one belonging to a people having a less complex civilization." Therefore, use of "native," like use of "pagan" often implies a value judgment of white superiority.

QUALIFYING ADJECTIVES

Words that would normally have positive connotations can have entirely different meanings when used in a racial context. For example, C. L. Sulzberger, the columnist of the *New York Times*, wrote in January 1975, about conversations he had with two people in Namibia. One was the white South African administrator of the country and the other a member of SWAPO, the Namibian liberation movement. The first is described as "Dirk Mudge, who as senior elected member of the administration is a kind of acting Prime Minister. . . ." But the second person is introduced as "Daniel Tijongarero, an intelligent Herero tribesman who is a member of SWAPO. . . ." What need was there for Sulzberger to state that Daniel Tijongarero is "intelligent"? Why not also state that Dirk Mudge was "intelligent"—or do we assume he wasn't?

A similar example from a 1968 *New York Times* article reporting on an address by Lyndon Johnson stated, "The President spoke to the well-dressed Negro officials and their wives." In what similar circumstances can one imagine a reporter finding it necessary to note that an audience of white government officials was "well-dressed"?

Still another word often used in a racist context is "qualified." In the 1960's white Americans often questioned whether Black people were "qualified" to hold public office, a question that was never raised (until too late) about white officials like Wallace, Maddox, Nixon, Agnew, Mitchell, et al. The question of qualifications has been raised even more frequently in recent years as white people question whether Black people are "qualified" to be hired for positions in industry and educational institutions. "We're looking for a qualified Black" has been heard again and again as institutions are confronted with affirmative action goals. Why stipulate that Blacks must be "qualified," when for others it is taken for granted that applicants must be "qualified"?

SPEAKING ENGLISH

Finally, the depiction in movies and children's books of third world people speaking English is often itself racist. Children's books about Puerto Ricans or Chicanos often connect poverty with a failure to speak English or to speak it well, thus blaming the victim and ignoring the racism which affects third world people regardless of their proficiency in English. Asian characters speak a stilted English ("Honorable so and so" or "Confucius say") or have a speech impediment ("roots or ruck," "very solly," "flied lice"). Native American characters speak another variation of stilted English ("Boy not hide. Indian take boy."), repeat certain Hollywood-Indian phrases ("Heap big" and "Many moons") or simply grunt out "Ugh" or "How." The repeated use of these language characterizations functions to make third world people seem less intelligent and less capable than the English-speaking white characters.

WRAP-UP

A *Saturday Review* editorial[10] on "The Environment of Language" stated that language

> . . . has as much to do with the philosophical and political conditioning of a society as geography or climate. . . . people in Western cultures do not realize the extent to which their racial attitudes have been conditioned since early childhood by the power of words to ennoble or condemn, augment or detract, glorify or demean. Negative language infects the subconscious of most Western people from the time they first learn to speak. Prejudice is not merely imparted or superimposed. It is metabolized in the bloodstream of society. What is needed is not so much a change in language as an awareness of the power of words to condition attitudes. If we can at least recognize the underpinnings of prejudice, we may be in a position to deal with the effects.

To recognize the racism in language is an important first step. Consciousness of the influence of language on our perceptions can help to negate much of that influence. But it is not enough to simply become aware of the effects of racism in conditioning attitudes. While we may not be able to change the language, we can definitely change our usage of the language. We can avoid using words that degrade people. We can make a conscious effort to use terminology that reflects a progressive perspective, as opposed to a distorting perspective. It is important for educators to provide students with opportunities to explore racism in language and to increase their awareness of it, as well as learning terminology that is positive and does not perpetuate negative human values.

NOTES

1. Simon Podair, "How Bigotry Builds Through Language," *Negro Digest*, March 1967.

2. Jose Armas, "Antonia and the Mayor: A Cultural Review of the Film," *The Journal of Ethnic Studies*, Fall 1975.

3. David R. Burgest, "The Racist Use of the English Language," *Black Scholar*, Sept. 1973.

4. Thomas Greenfield, "Race and Passive Voice at Monticello," *Crisis*, April 1975.

5. David R. Burgest, "Racism in Everyday Speech and Social Work Jargon," *Social Work*, July 1973.

6. William Ryan, *Blaming the Victim*, Pantheon Books, 1971.

7. Morton Fried, "The Myth of Tribe," *National History*, April 1975.

8. Evelyn Jones Rich, "Mind Your Language," *Africa Report*, Sept./Oct. 1974.

9. Steve Wolf, "Catalogers in Revolt Against LC's Racist, Sexist Headings," *Bulletin of Interracial Books for Children*, Vol. 6, Nos. 3&4, 1975.

10. "The Environment of Language," *Saturday Review*, April 8, 1967.

Also see:

Roger Bastide, "Color, Racism and Christianity," *Daedalus*, Spring 1967.

Kenneth J. Gergen, "The Significance of Skin Color in Human Relations," *Daedalus*, Spring 1967.

Lloyd Yabura, "Towards a Language of Humanism," *Rhythm*, Summer 1971.

UNESCO, "Recommendations Concerning Terminology in Education on Race Questions," June 1968.

MEDIA MAGIC

37

Making Class Invisible

Gregory Mantsios

Of the various social and cultural forces in our society, the mass media is arguably the most influential in molding public consciousness. Americans spend an average twenty-eight hours per week watching television. They also spend an undetermined number of hours reading periodicals, listening to the radio, and going to the movies. Unlike other cultural and socializing institutions, ownership and control of the mass media is highly concentrated. Twenty-three corporations own more than one-half of all the daily newspapers, magazines, movie studios, and radio and television outlets in the United States.[1] The number of media companies is shrinking and their control of the industry is expanding. And a relatively small number of media outlets is producing

From: Paula Rothenberg (ed.), *Race, Class, and Gender in the United States: An Integrated Study*, 4th ed. (New York: St. Martin's Press, 1998). Reprinted with permission of the author.

and packaging the majority of news and entertainment programs. For the most part, our media is national in nature and single-minded (profit-oriented) in purpose. This media plays a key role in defining our cultural tastes, helping us locate ourselves in history, establishing our national identity, and ascertaining the range of national and social possibilities. In this essay, we will examine the way the mass media shapes how people think about each other and about the nature of our society.

The United States is the most highly stratified society in the industrialized world. Class distinctions operate in virtually every aspect of our lives, determining the nature of our work, the quality of our schooling, and the health and safety of our loved ones. Yet remarkably, we, as a nation, retain illusions about living in an egalitarian society. We maintain these illusions, in large part, because the media hides gross inequities from public view. In those instances when inequities are revealed, we are provided with messages that obscure the nature of class realities and blame the victims of class-dominated society for their own plight. Let's briefly examine what the news media, in particular, tells us about class.

ABOUT THE POOR

The news media provides meager coverage of poor people and poverty. The coverage it does provide is often distorted and misleading.

The Poor Do Not Exist

For the most part, the news media ignores the poor. Unnoticed are forty million poor people in the nation—a number that equals the entire population of Maine, Vermont, New Hampshire, Connecticut, Rhode Island, New Jersey, and New York combined. Perhaps even more alarming is that the rate of poverty is increasing twice as fast as the population growth in the United States. Ordinarily, even a calamity of much smaller proportion (e.g., flooding in the Midwest) would garner a great deal of coverage and hype from a media usually eager to declare a crisis, yet less than one in five hundred articles in the *New York Times* and one in one thousand articles listed in the *Readers Guide to Periodic Literature* are on poverty. With remarkably little attention to them, the poor and their problems are hidden from most Americans.

When the media does turn its attention to the poor, it offers a series of contradictory messages and portrayals.

The Poor Are Faceless

Each year the Census Bureau releases a new report on poverty in our society and its results are duly reported in the media. At best, however, this coverage emphasizes annual fluctuations (showing how the numbers differ from previous years) and ongoing debates over the validity of the numbers (some argue the number should be lower, most that the number should be higher). Coverage like this desensitizes us to the poor by reducing poverty to a number. It ignores the human tragedy of poverty—the suffering, indignities, and misery endured by millions of children and adults. Instead, the poor become statistics rather than people.

The Poor Are Undeserving

When the media does put a face on the poor, it is not likely to be a pretty one. The media will provide us with sensational stories about welfare cheats, drug addicts, and greedy panhandlers (almost always urban and Black). Compare these images and the emotions evoked by them with the media's treatment of middle-class (usually white) "tax evaders," celebrities who have a "chemical dependency," or wealthy businesspeople who use unscrupulous means to "make a profit." While the behavior of the more affluent offenders is considered an "impropriety" and a deviation from the norm, the behavior of the poor is considered repugnant, indicative of the poor in general, and worthy of our indignation and resentment.

The Poor Are an Eyesore

When the media does cover the poor, they are often presented through the eyes of the middle class. For example, sometimes the media includes a story about community resistance to a homeless shelter or storekeeper annoyance with panhandlers. Rather than focusing on the plight of the poor, these stories are about middle-class opposition to the poor. Such stories tell us that the poor are an inconvenience and an irritation.

The Poor Have Only Themselves to Blame

In another example of media coverage, we are told that the poor live in a personal and cultural cycle of poverty that hopelessly imprisons them. They routinely center on the Black urban population and focus on perceived personality or cultural traits that doom the poor. While the women in these stories typically exhibit an "attitude" that leads to trouble or a promiscuity that leads to single motherhood, the men possess a need for immediate gratification that leads to drug abuse or an unquenchable greed that leads to the pursuit of fast money. The images that are seared into our mind are sexist, racist, and classist. Census figures reveal that most of the poor are white not Black or hispanic, that they live in rural or suburban areas not urban centers, and hold jobs at least part of the year.[2] Yet, in a fashion that is often framed in an understanding and sympathetic tone, we are told that the poor have inflicted poverty on themselves.

The Poor Are Down on Their Luck

During the Christmas season, the news media sometimes provides us with accounts of poor individuals or families (usually white) who are down on their luck. These stories are often linked to stories about soup kitchens or other charitable activities and sometimes call for charitable contributions. These "Yule time" stories are as much about the affluent as they are about the poor: they tell us that the affluent in our society are a kind, understanding, giving people—which we are not.* The series of unfortunate circumstances that have led to impoverishment are presumed to he a temporary condition that will improve with time and a change in luck.

Despite appearances, the messages provided by the media are not entirely disparate. With each variation, the media informs us what poverty is not (i.e., systemic and indicative of American society) by informing us what it is. The media tells us that poverty is either an aberration of the American way of life (it doesn't exist, it's just another number, it's unfortunate but temporary) or an end product of the poor themselves (they are a nuisance, do not deserve better, and have brought their predicament upon themselves).

By suggesting that the poor have brought poverty upon themselves, the media is engaging in what William Ryan has called "blaming the victim."[3] The media identifies in what ways the poor are different as a consequence of deprivation, then defines those differences as the cause of poverty itself. Whether blatantly hostile or cloaked in sympathy, the message is that there is something fundamentally wrong with the victims—their hormones, psychological makeup, family environment, community, race, or some combination of these—that accounts for their plight and their failure to lift themselves out of poverty.

But poverty in the United Stales is systemic. It is a direct result of economic. and political policies that deprive people of jobs, adequate wages, or legitimate support. It is neither natural nor inevitable: there is enough wealth in our nation to eliminate poverty if we chose to redistribute existing wealth or income. The plight of the poor is reason enough to make the elimination of poverty the nation's first priority. But poverty also impacts dramatically on the nonpoor. It has a dampening effect on wages in general (by maintaining a reserve army of unemployed and underemployed anxious for any job at any wage) and

---

*American households with incomes of less than $10,000 give an average of 5.5 percent of their earning to charity or to a religious organization, while those making more than $100,000 a year give only 2.9 percent. After changes in the 1986 tax code reduced the benefits of charitable giving, taxpayers earning $500,000 or more slashed their average donation by nearly one-third. Furthermore, many of these acts of benevolence do not help the needy. Rather than provide funding to social service agencies that aid the poor, the voluntary contributions of the wealthy go to places and institutions that entertain, inspire, cure, or educate wealthy Americans—art museums, opera houses, theaters, orchestras, ballet companies, private hospitals, and elite universities. (Robert Reich, "Secession of the Successful," *New York Times Magazine*, February 17, 1991, p. 43.)

breeds crime and violence (by maintaining conditions that invite private gain by illegal means and rebellion-like behavior, not entirely unlike the urban riots of the 1960s). Given the extent of poverty in the nation and the impact it has on us all, the media must spin considerable magic to keep the poor and the issue of poverty and its root causes out of the public consciousness.

ABOUT EVERYONE ELSE

Both the broadcast and the print news media strive to develop a strong sense of "we-ness" in their audience. They seek to speak to and for an audience that is both affluent and like-minded. The media's solidarity with affluence, that is, with the middle and upper class, varies little from one medium to another. Benjamin DeMott points out, for example, that the *New York Times* understands affluence to be intelligence, taste, public spirit, responsibility, and a readiness to rule and "conceives itself as spokesperson for a readership awash in these qualities."[4] Of course, the flip side to creating a sense of "we," or "us," is establishing a perception of the "other." The other relates back to the faceless, amoral, undeserving, and inferior "underclass." Thus, the world according to the news media is divided between the "underclass" and everyone else. Again the messages are often contradictory.

The Wealthy Are Us

Much of the information provided to us by the news media focuses attention on the concerns of a very wealthy and privileged class of people. Although the concerns of a small fraction of the populace, they are presented as though they were the concerns of everyone. For example, while relatively few people actually own stock, the news media devotes an inordinate amount of broadcast time and print space to business news and stock market quotations. Not only do business reports cater to a particular narrow clientele, so do the fashion pages (with $2,000 dresses), wedding announcements, and the obituaries. Even weather and sports news often have a class bias. An all news radio station in New York City, for example, provides regular national ski reports. International news, trade agreements, and domestic policies issues are also reported in terms of their impact on business climate and the business community. Besides being of practical value to the wealthy, such coverage has considerable ideological value. Its message: the concerns of the wealthy are the concerns of us all.

The Wealthy (as a Class) Do Not Exist

While preoccupied with the concerns of the wealthy, the media fails to notice the way in which the rich as a class of people create and shape domestic and foreign policy. Presented as an aggregate of individuals, the wealthy appear without special interests, interconnections, or unity in purpose. Out of public view are the class interests of the wealthy, the interlocking business links, the concerted actions to preserve their class privileges and business interests (by running for public office, supporting political candidates, lobbying, etc.). Corporate lobbying is ignored, taken for granted, or assumed to be in the public interest. (Compare this with the media's portrayal of the "strong arm of labor" in attempting to defeat trade legislation that is harmful to the interests of working people.) It is estimated that two-thirds of the U.S. Senate is composed of millionaires.[5] Having such a preponderance of millionaires in the Senate, however, is perceived to be neither unusual nor antidemocratic; these millionaire senators are assumed to be serving "our" collective interests in governing.

The Wealthy Are Fascinating and Benevolent

The broadcast and print media regularly provide hype for individuals who have achieved "super" success. These stories are usually about celebrities and superstars from the sports and entertainment world. Society pages and gossip columns serve to keep the social elite informed of each others' doings, allow the rest of us to gawk at their excesses, and help to keep the American dream alive. The print media is also fond of feature stories on corporate empire builders. These stories provide an occasional "insider's" view of the private and corporate life of industrialists by suggesting a rags to riches account of corporate success. These stories tell us that corporate success is a series of smart moves, shrewd acquisitions, timely mergers, and well thought out executive suite shuffles. By painting the upper class in a positive light, innocent of any wrongdoing (labor leaders and union organizations usually get the opposite treatment), the media assures us that wealth and power are benevolent. One person's capital accumulation is presumed to be good for all. The elite, then, are portrayed as investment wizards, people of special talent and skill, who even their victims (workers and consumers) can admire.

The Wealthy Include a Few Bad Apples

On rare occasions, the media will mock selected individuals for their personality flaws. Real estate investor Donald Trump and New York Yankees owner George Steinbrenner, for example, are admonished by the media for deliberately seeking publicity (a very un-upper class thing to do); hotel owner Leona Helmsley was caricatured for her personal cruelties; and junk bond broker Michael Milkin was condemned because he had the audacity to rob the rich. Michael Parenti points out that by treating business wrongdoings as isolated deviations from the socially beneficial system of "responsible capitalism," the media overlooks the features of the system that produce such abuses and the regularity with which they occur. Rather than portraying them as predictable and frequent outcomes of corporate power and the business system, the media treats abuses as if they were isolated and atypical. Presented as an occasional aberration, these incidents serve not to challenge, but to legitimate, the system.[6]

The Middle Class Is Us

By ignoring the poor and blurring the lines between the working people and the upper class, the news media creates a universal middle class. From this perspective, the size of one's income becomes largely irrelevant: what matters is that most of "us" share an intellectual and moral superiority over the disadvantaged. As *Time* magazine once concluded, "Middle America is a state of mind."[7] "We are all middle class," we are told, "and we all share the same concerns": job security, inflation, tax burdens, world peace, the cost of food and housing, health care, clean air and water, and the safety of our streets. While the concerns of the wealthy are quite distinct from those of the middle class (e.g., the wealthy worry about investments, not jobs), the media convinces us that "we [the affluent] are all in this together."

The Middle Class Is a Victim

For the media, "we" the affluent not only stand apart from the "other"—the poor, the working class, the minorities, and their problems—"we" are also victimized by the poor (who drive up the costs of maintaining the welfare roles), minorities (who commit crimes against us), and by workers (who are greedy and drive companies out and prices up). Ignored are the subsidies to the rich, the crimes of corporate America, and the policies that wreak havoc on the economic well-being of middle America. Media magic convinces us to fear, more than anything else, being victimized by those less affluent than ourselves.

The Middle Class Is Not a Working Class

The news media clearly distinguishes the middle class (employees) from the working class (i.e., blue collar workers) who are portrayed, at best, as irrelevant, outmoded, and a dying breed. Furthermore, the media will tell us that the hardships faced by blue collar workers are inevitable (due to progress), a result of bad luck (chance circumstances in a particular industry), or a product of their own doing (they priced themselves out of a job). Given the media's presentation of reality, it is hard to believe that manual, supervised, unskilled, and semiskilled workers actually represent more than 50 percent of the adult working population.[8] The working class, instead, is relegated by the media to "the other."

In short, the news media either lionizes the wealthy or treats their interests and those of the middle class as one in the same. But the upper class and the middle class do not share the same interests or worries. Members of the upper class worry about stock dividends (not employment), they profit from inflation and global militarism, their children attend exclusive private schools, they eat and live in a royal fashion, they call on (or are called upon by) personal physicians, they have few consumer problems, they can escape whenever they want from environmental pollution, and they live on streets and travel to other areas under the protection of private police forces.*[9]

The wealthy are not only a class with distinct life-styles and interests, they are a ruling class. They receive a disproportionate share of the country's yearly income, own a disproportionate amount of the country's wealth, and contribute a disproportionate number of their members to governmental bodies and decision-making groups—all traits that William Domhoff, in his classic work *Who Rules America*, defined as characteristic of a governing class.[10]

This governing class maintains and manages our political and economic structures in such a way that these structures continue to yield an amazing proportion of our wealth to a minuscule upper class. While the media is not above referring to ruling classes in other countries (we hear, for example, references to Japan's ruling elite),[11] its treatment of the news proceeds as though there were no such ruling class in the United States.

Furthermore, the news media inverts reality so that those who are working class and middle class learn to fear, resent, and blame those below, rather than those above them in the class structure. We learn to resent welfare, which accounts for only two cents out of every dollar in the federal budget (approximately $10 billion) and provides financial relief for the needy,** but learn little about the $11 billion the federal government spends on individuals with incomes in excess of $100,000 (not needy),[12] or the $17 billion in farm subsidies, or the $214 billion (twenty times the cost of welfare) in interest payments to financial institutions.

Middle-class whites learn to fear African Americans and Latinos, but most violent crime occurs within poor and minority communities and is neither interracial† nor interclass. As horrid as such crime is, it should not mask the destruction and violence perpetrated by corporate America. In spite of the fact that 14,000 innocent people are killed on the job each year, 100,000 die prematurely, 400,000 become seriously ill, and 6 million are injured from work-

---

*The number of private security guards in the United States now exceeds the number of public police officers. (Robert Reich, "Secession of the Successful," *New York Times Magazine*, February 17, 1991, p. 42.)

**A total of $20 billion is spent on welfare when you include all state funding. But the average state funding also comes to only two cents per state dollar.

†In 92 percent of the murders nationwide the assailant and the victim are of the same race (46 percent are white/white, 46 percent are black/black, 5.6 percent are black on white, and 2.4 percent are white on black. (FBI and Bureau of Justice Statistics, 1985–1986, quoted in Raymond S. Franklin, *Shadows of Race and Class*, University of Minnesota Press, Minneapolis, 1991, p. 108.)

related accidents and diseases, most Americans fear government regulation more than they do unsafe working conditions.

Through the media, middle-class—and even working-class—Americans learn to blame blue collar workers and their unions for declining purchasing power and economic security. But while workers who managed to keep their jobs and their unions struggled to keep up with inflation, the top 1 percent of American families saw their average incomes soar 80 percent in the last decade.[13] Much of the wealth at the top was accumulated as stockholders and corporate executives moved their companies abroad to employ cheaper labor (56 cents per hour in El Salvador) and avoid paying taxes in the United States. Corporate America is a world made up of ruthless bosses, massive layoffs, favoritism and nepotism, health and safety violations, pension plan losses, union busting, tax evasions, unfair competition, and price gouging, as well as fast buck deals, financial speculation, and corporate wheeling and dealing that serve the interests of the corporate elite, but are generally wasteful and destructive to workers and the economy in general.

It is no wonder Americans cannot think straight about class. The mass media is neither objective, balanced, independent, nor neutral. Those who own and direct the mass media are themselves part of the upper class, and neither they nor the ruling class in general have to conspire to manipulate public opinion. Their interest is in preserving the status quo, and their view of society as fair and equitable comes naturally to them. But their ideology dominates our society and justifies what is in reality a perverse social order—one that perpetuates unprecedented elite privilege and power on the one hand and widespread deprivation on the other. A mass media that did not have its own class interests in preserving the status quo would acknowledge that inordinate wealth and power undermines democracy and that a "free market" economy can ravage a people and their communities.

NOTES

1. Martin Lee and Norman Solomon, *Unreliable Sources*, Lyle Stuart (New York, 1990), p. 71. See also Ben Bagdikian, *The Media Monopoly*, Beacon Press (Boston, 1990).

2. Department of Commerce, Bureau of the Census, "Poverty in the United States: 92," *Current Population Reports, Consumer Income*, Series P60-185, pp. xi, xv, 1.

3. William Ryan, *Blaming the Victim*, Vintage (New York, 1971).

4. Benjamin Demott, *The Imperial Middle*, William Morrow (New York, 1990), p. 123.

5. Fred Barnes, "The Zillionaires Club," *The New Republic*, January 29, 1990, p. 24.

6. Michael Parenti, *Inventing Reality*, St. Martin's Press (New York, 1986), p. 109.

7. *Time*, January 5, 1979, p. 10.

8. Vincent Navarro, "The Middle Class—A Useful Myth," *The Nation*, March 23, 1992, p. 1.

9. Charles Anderson, *The Political Economy of Social Class*, Prentice Hall (Englewood Cliffs, N.J., 1974), p. 137.

10. William Domhoff, *Who Rules America*, Prentice Hall (Englewood Cliffs, N.J., 1967), p. 5.

11. Lee and Solomon, *Unreliable Sources*, p. 179.

12. *Newsweek*, August 10, 1992, p. 57.

13. *Business Week*, June 8, 1992, p. 86.

THE MYTH OF THE LATIN WOMAN

38

I Just Met a Girl Named María

Judith Ortiz Cofer

On a bus trip to London from Oxford University, where I was earning some graduate credits one summer, a young man, obviously fresh from a pub, spotted me and as if struck by inspiration went down on his knees in the aisle. With both hands over his heart he broke into an Irish tenor's rendition of "María" from *West Side Story*. My politely amused fellow passengers gave his lovely voice the round of gentle applause it deserved. Though I was not quite as amused, I managed my version of an English smile: no show of teeth, no extreme contortions of the facial muscles—I was at this time of my life practicing reserve and cool. Oh, that British control, how I coveted it. But María had followed me to London, reminding me of a prime fact of my life: you can leave the Island, master the English language, and travel as far as you can, but if you are a Latina, especially one like me who so obviously belongs to Rita Moreno's gene pool, the Island travels with you.

This is sometimes a very good thing—it may win you that extra minute of someone's attention. But with some people, the same things can make *you* an island—not so much a tropical paradise as an Alcatraz, a place nobody wants to visit. As a Puerto Rican girl growing up in the United States and wanting like most children to "belong," I resented the stereotype that my Hispanic appearance called forth from many people I met.

Our family lived in a large urban center in New Jersey during the sixties, where life was designed as a microcosm of my parents' casas on the island. We spoke in Spanish, we ate Puerto Rican food bought at the bodega, and we practiced strict Catholicism complete with Saturday confession and Sunday mass at a church where our parents were accommodated into a one-hour Spanish mass slot, performed by a Chinese priest trained as a missionary for Latin America.

As a girl I was kept under strict surveillance, since virtue and modesty were, by cultural equation, the same as family honor. As a teenager I was instructed on how to behave as a proper señorita. But it was a conflicting message girls got, since the Puerto Rican mothers also encouraged their daughters to look and act like women and to dress in clothes our Anglo friends and their mothers found too "mature" for our age. It was, and is, cultural, yet I often felt humiliated when I appeared at an American friend's party wearing a dress more suitable to a semiformal than to a playroom birthday celebration. At Puerto Rican festivities, neither the music nor the colors we wore could be too loud. I still experience a vague sense of letdown when I'm invited to a "party" and it turns out to be a marathon conversation in hushed tones rather than a fiesta with salsa, laughter, and dancing—the kind of celebration I remember from my childhood.

I remember Career Day in our high school, when teachers told us to come dressed as if for a job interview. It quickly became obvious that to the barrio girls, "dressing up" sometimes meant wearing ornate jewelry and clothing that would be more appropriate (by mainstream standards) for the company Christmas party than as daily office attire. That morning I had agonized in front of my closet, trying to figure out what a "career girl" would wear because, essentially, except for Marlo Thomas on TV, I had no models on which to base my decision. I knew how to dress for school: at the Catholic school I attended we all wore uniforms; I knew how to dress for Sunday mass, and I knew what dresses to wear for parties at my relatives' homes. Though I do not recall the precise details of my Career Day outfit, it must have been a composite of the above choices. But I remember a comment my friend (an Italian-American) made in later years that coalesced my impressions of that day. She said that at the business school she was attending the Puerto Rican girls always stood out for wearing "everything at once." She meant, of course, too much jewelry, too many accessories. On that day at school, we were simply made the negative models by the nuns who were themselves not credible fashion experts to any of us. But it was painfully obvious to me that to the others, in their tailored skirts and silk blouses, we must have seemed "hopeless" and "vulgar." Though I now know that most adolescents feel out of step much of the time,

I also know that for the Puerto Rican girls of my generation that sense was intensified. The way our teachers and classmates looked at us that day in school was just a taste of the culture clash that awaited us in the real world, where prospective employers and men on the street would often misinterpret our tight skirts and jingling bracelets as a come-on.

Mixed cultural signals have perpetuated certain stereotypes—for example, that of the Hispanic woman as the "Hot Tamale" or sexual firebrand. It is a one-dimensional view that the media have found easy to promote. In their special vocabulary, advertisers have designated "sizzling" and "smoldering" as the adjectives of choice for describing not only the foods but also the women of Latin America. From conversations in my house I recall hearing about the harassment that Puerto Rican women endured in factories where the "boss men" talked to them as if sexual innuendo was all they understood and, worse, often gave them the choice of submitting to advances or being fired.

It is custom, however, not chromosomes, that leads us to choose scarlet over pale pink. As young girls, we were influenced in our decisions about clothes and colors by the women—older sisters and mothers who had grown up on a tropical island where the natural environment was a riot of primary colors, where showing your skin was one way to keep cool as well as to look sexy. Most important of all, on the island, women perhaps felt freer to dress and move more provocatively, since, in most cases, they were protected by the traditions, mores, and laws of a Spanish/Catholic system of morality and machismo whose main rule was: *You may look at my sister, but if you touch her I will kill you.* The extended family and church structure could provide a young woman with a circle of safety in her small pueblo on the Island; if a man "wronged" a girl, everyone would close in to save her family honor.

This is what I have gleaned from my discussions as an adult with older Puerto Rican women. They have told me about dressing in their best party clothes on Saturday nights and going to the town's plaza to promenade with their girlfriends in front of the boys they liked. The males were thus given an opportunity to admire the women and to express their admiration in the form of *piropos:* erotically charged street poems they composed on the spot. I have been subjected to a few piropos while visiting the Island, and they can be outrageous, although custom dictates that they must never cross into obscenity. This ritual, as I understand it, also entails a show of studied indifference on the woman's part; if she is "decent," she must not acknowledge the man's impassioned words. So I do understand how things can be lost in translation. When a Puerto Rican girl dressed in her idea of what is attractive meets a man from the mainstream culture who has been trained to react to certain types of clothing as a sexual signal, a clash is likely to take place. The line I first heard based on this aspect of the myth happened when the boy who took me to my first formal dance leaned over to plant a sloppy overeager kiss painfully on my mouth, and when I didn't respond with sufficient passion said in a resentful tone: "I thought you Latin girls were supposed to mature early"—my first instance of being thought of as a fruit or vegetable—I was supposed to *ripen*, not just grow into womanhood like other girls.

It is surprising to some of my professional friends that some people, including those who should know better, still put others "in their place." Though rarer, these incidents are still commonplace in my life. It happened to me most recently during a stay at a very classy metropolitan hotel favored by young professional couples for their weddings. Late one evening after the theater, as I walked toward my room with my new colleague (a woman with whom I was coordinating an arts program), a middle-aged man in a tuxedo, a young girl in satin and lace on his arm, stepped directly into our path. With his champagne glass extended toward me, he exclaimed, "Evita!"

Our way blocked, my companion and I listened as the man half-recited, half-bellowed "Don't Cry for Me, Argentina." When he finished, the young girl said: "How about a round of applause for my daddy?" We complied, hoping this would bring the silly spectacle to a close. I was becoming aware that our little group was attracting the attention of the other guests. "Daddy" must have perceived this too, and he once more barred the way as we tried to walk past him. He began to shout-sing a ditty to the tune of "La Bamba"—except the lyrics were about a girl named María whose exploits all rhymed with her name and gonorrhea. The girl kept saying "Oh, Daddy" and looking at me with pleading eyes. She wanted me to laugh along with the others. My companion and I stood silently waiting for the man to end his offensive song. When he finished, I looked not at him but at his daughter. I advised her calmly never to ask her father what he had done in the army. Then I walked between them and to my room. My friend complimented me on my cool handling of the situation. I confessed to her that I really had wanted to push the jerk into the swimming pool. I knew that this same man—probably a corporate executive, well educated, even worldly by most standards—would not have been likely to regale a white woman with a dirty song in public. He would perhaps have checked his impulse by assuming that she could be somebody's wife or mother, or at least *somebody* who might take offense. But to him, I was just an Evita or a María: merely a character in his cartoon-populated universe.

Because of my education and my proficiency with the English language, I have acquired many mechanisms for dealing with the anger I experience. This was not true for my parents, nor is it true for the many Latin women working at menial jobs who must put up with stereotypes about our ethnic group such as: "They make good domestics." This is another facet of the myth of the Latin women in the United States. Its origin is simple to deduce. Work as domestics, waitressing, and factory jobs are all that's available to women with little English and few skills. The myth of the Hispanic menial has been sustained by the same media phenomenon that made "Mammy" from *Gone with the Wind* America's idea of the black woman for generations; María, the housemaid or counter girl, is now indelibly etched into the national psyche. The big and the little screens have presented us with the picture of the funny Hispanic maid, mispronouncing words and cooking up a spicy storm in a shiny California kitchen.

This media-engendered image of the Latina in the United States has been documented by feminist Hispanic scholars, who claim that such portrayals are partially responsible for the denial of opportunities for upward mobility among Latinas in the professions. I have a Chicana friend working on a Ph.D. in philosophy at a major university. She says her doctor still shakes his head in puzzled amazement at all the "big words" she uses. Since I do not wear my diplomas around my neck for all to see, I too have on occasion been sent to that "kitchen," where some think I obviously belong.

One such incident that has stayed with me, though I recognize it as a minor offense, happened on the day of my first public poetry reading. It took place in Miami in a boat-restaurant where we were having lunch before the event. I was nervous and excited as I walked in with my notebook in hand. An older woman motioned me to her table. Thinking (foolish me) that she wanted me to autograph a copy of my brand new slender volume of verse, I went over. She ordered a cup of coffee from me, assuming that I was the waitress. Easy enough to mistake my poems for menus, I suppose. I know that it wasn't an intentional act of cruelty, yet with all the good things that happened that day, I remember that scene most clearly, because it reminded me of what I had to overcome before anyone would take me seriously. In retrospect I understand that my anger gave my reading fire, that I have almost always taken doubts in my abilities as a challenge—and that the result is, most times, a feeling of satisfaction at having won a convert when I see the cold, appraising eyes warm to my words, the body language change, the smile that indicates that I have opened some avenue for communication. That day I read to that woman and her lowered eyes told me that she was embarrassed at her little faux pas, and when I willed her to look up to me, it was my victory, and she graciously allowed me to punish her with my full attention. We shook hands at the end of the reading, and I never saw her again. She has probably forgotten the whole thing but maybe not.

Yet I am one of the lucky ones. My parents made it possible for me to acquire a stronger footing in the mainstream culture by giving me the chance at an education. And books and art have saved me from the harsher forms of ethnic and racial prejudice that many of my Hispanic *compañeras* have had to endure. I travel a lot around the United States, reading from my books of poetry and my novel, and the reception I most often receive is one of positive interest by people who want to know more about my culture. There are, however, thousands of Latinas without the privilege of an education or the entrée into society that I have. For them life is a struggle against the misconceptions perpetuated by the myth of the Latina as whore, domestic, or criminal. We cannot change this by legislating the way people look at us. The transformation, as I see it, has to occur at a much more individual level. My personal goal in my public life is to try to replace the old pervasive stereotypes and myths about Latinas with a much more interesting set of realities. Every time I give a reading, I hope the stories I tell, the dreams and fears I examine in my work, can achieve some universal truth which will get my audience past the particulars of my skin color, my accent, or my clothes.

I once wrote a poem in which I called us Latinas "God's brown daughters." This poem is really a prayer of sorts, offered upward, but also, through the human-to-human channel of art, outward. It is a prayer for communication, and for respect. In it, Latin women pray "in Spanish to an Anglo God/with a Jewish heritage," and they are "fervently hoping/that if not omnipotent,/at least He be bilingual."

MASCULINITIES AND ATHLETIC CAREERS

39

Michael Messner

. . . It is now widely accepted in sport sociology that social institutions such as the media, education, the economy, and (a more recent and controversial addition to the list) the black family itself all serve to systematically channel disproportionately large numbers of young black men into football, basketball, boxing, and baseball, where they are subsequently "stacked" into low-prestige

Author's note: Parts of this article were presented as papers at the American Sociological Association Annual Meeting, Chicago, in August 1987, and at the North American Society for the Sociology of Sport Annual Meeting in Edmonton, Alberta, in November 1987. I thank Maxine Baca Zinn, Bob Blauner, Bob Dunn, Pierrette Hondagneu-Sotelo, Carol Jacklin, Michael Kimmel, Judith Lorber, Don Sabo, Barrie Thorne, and Carol Warren for constructive comments on earlier versions of this article.

From: *Gender & Society* 3 (March 1989): 71–88. Reprinted by permission of Sage Publications, Inc.

and high-risk positions, exploited for their skills, and finally, when their bodies are used up, excreted from organized athletics at a young age with no transferable skills with which to compete in the labor market (Edwards 1984; Eitzen and Purdy 1986; Eitzen and Yetman 1977).

While there are racial differences in involvement in sports, class, age, and educational differences seem more significant. Rudman's (1986) initial analysis revealed profound differences between whites' and blacks' orientations to sports. Blacks were found to be more likely than whites to view sports favorably, to incorporate sports into their daily lives, and to be affected by the outcome of sporting events. However, when age, education, and social class were factored into the analysis, Rudman found that race did not explain whites' and blacks' different orientations. Blacks' affinity to sports is best explained by their tendency to be clustered disproportionately in lower-income groups.

The 1980s has ushered in what Wellman (1986, p. 43) calls a "new political linguistics of race," which emphasizes cultural rather than structural causes (and solutions) to the problems faced by black communities. The advocates of the cultural perspective believe that the high value placed on sports by black communities has led to the development of unrealistic hopes in millions of black youths. They appeal to family and community to bolster other choices based upon a more rational assessment of "reality." Visible black role models in many other professions now exist, they say, and there is ample evidence which proves that sports careers are, at best, a bad gamble.

Critics of the cultural perspective have condemned it as conservative and victim blaming. But it can also be seen as a response to the view of black athletes as little more than unreflexive dupes of an all-powerful system, which ignores the importance of agency. Gruneau (1983) has argued that sports must be examined within a theory that views human beings as active subjects who are operating within historically constituted structural constraints. Gruneau's reflexive theory rejects the simplistic views of sports as either a realm of absolute oppression or an arena of absolute freedom and spontaneity. Instead, he argues, it is necessary to construct an understanding of how and why participants themselves actively make choices and construct and define meaning and a sense of identity within the institutions that they find themselves.

None of these perspectives considers the ways that gender shapes men's definitions of meaning and choices. Within the sociology of sport, gender as a process that interacts with race and class is usually ignored or taken for granted — except when it is *women* athletes who are being studied. Sociologists who are attempting to come to grips with the experiences of black men in general, and in organized sports in particular, have almost exclusively focused their analytic attention on the variable "black," while uncritically taking "men" as a given. Hare and Hare (1984), for example, view masculinity as a biologically determined tendency to act as a provider and protector that is thwarted for black men by socioeconomic and racist obstacles. Staples (1982) does view masculinity largely as a socially produced script, but he accepts this script as a given, preferring to focus on black men's blocked access to male role fulfillment. These perspectives on masculinity fail to show how the male role itself, as it interacts with a constricted structure of opportunity, can contribute to locking black men into destructive relationships and life-styles (Franklin 1984; Majors 1986).

This article will examine the relationships among male identity, race, and social class by listening to the voices of former athletes. I will first briefly describe my research. Then I will discuss the similarities and differences in the choices and experiences of men from different racial and social class backgrounds. Together, these choices and experiences help to construct what Connell (1987) calls "the gender order." Organized sports, it will be suggested, is a practice through which men's separation from and power over women is embodied and naturalized at the same time that hegemonic (white, heterosexual, professional-class) masculinity is clearly differentiated from marginalized and subordinated masculinities.

DESCRIPTION OF RESEARCH

Between 1983 and 1985, I conducted 30 open-ended, in-depth interviews with male former athletes. My purpose was to add a critical understanding of male gender identity to Levinson's (1978) conception of the "individual life-course"—specifically, to discover how masculinity develops and changes as a man interacts with the socially constructed world of organized sports. Most of the men I interviewed had played the U.S. "major sports"—football, basketball, baseball, track. At the time of the interview, each had been retired from playing organized sports for at least 5 years. Their ages ranged from 21 to 48, with the median, 33. Fourteen were black, 14 were white, and 2 were Hispanic. Fifteen of the 16 black and Hispanic men had come from poor or working-class families, while the majority (9 of 14) of the white men had come from middle-class or professional families. Twelve had played organized sports through high school, 11 through college, and 7 had been professional athletes. All had at some time in their lives based their identities largely on their roles as athletes and could therefore be said to have had athletic careers.

MALE IDENTITY AND ORGANIZED SPORTS

... For the men in my study, the rule-bound structure of organized sports became a context in which they struggled to construct a masculine positional identity.

All of the men in this study described the emotional salience of their earliest experiences in sports in terms of relationships with other males. It was not winning and victories that seemed important at first; it was something "fun" to do with fathers, older brothers or uncles, and eventually with same-aged peers. As a man from a white, middle-class family said, "The most important thing was just being out there with the rest of the guys—being friends." A 32-year-old man from a poor Chicano family, whose mother had died when he was 9 years old, put it more succinctly:

> What I think sports did for me is it brought me into kind of an instant family. By being on a Little League team, or even just playing with kids in the neighborhood, it brought what I really wanted, which was some kind of closeness.

Though sports participation may have initially promised "some kind of closeness," by the ages of 9 or 10, the less skilled boys were already becoming alienated from—or weeded out of—the highly competitive and hierarchical system of organized sports. Those who did experience some early successes received recognition from adult males (especially fathers and older brothers) and held higher status among peers. As a result, they began to pour more and more of their energies into athletic participation. It was only after they learned that they would get recognition from other people for being a good athlete—indeed, that this attention was contingent upon *being a winner*—that performance and winning (the dominant values of organized sports) became extremely important. For some, this created pressures that served to lessen or eliminate the fun of athletic participation (Messner 1987a, 1987b).

While feminist psychoanalytic and developmental theories of masculinity are helpful in explaining boys' early attraction and motivations in organized sports, the imperatives of core gender identity do not fully determine the contours and directions of the life course. As Rubin (1985) and Levinson (1978) have pointed out, an understanding of the lives of men must take into account the processual nature of male identity as it unfolds through interaction between the internal (psychological ambivalences) and the external (social, historical, and institutional) contexts.

To examine the impact of the social contexts, I divided my sample into two comparison groups. In the first group were 10 men from higher-status backgrounds, primarily white, middle-class, and professional families. In the second group were 20 men from lower-status backgrounds, primarily minority, poor, and working-class families. While my data offered evidence for the similarity of experiences and motivations of men from poor backgrounds, independent of race, I also found anecdotal evidence of a racial dynamic that operates independently of social class. However, my sample was not large enough to separate race and class, and so I have combined them to make two status groups.

In discussing these two groups, I will focus mainly on the high school years. During this crucial period, the athletic role may become a master status for a young man, and he is beginning to make assessments and choices about his future. It is here that many young men make a major commitment to—or begin to back away from—athletic careers.

Men from Higher-Status Backgrounds

The boyhood dream of one day becoming a professional athlete—a dream shared by nearly all the men interviewed in this study—is rarely realized. The sports world is extremely hierarchical. The pyramid of sports careers narrows very rapidly as one climbs from high school, to college, to professional levels of competition (Edwards 1984; Harris and Eitzen 1978; Hill and Lowe 1978). In fact, the chances of attaining professional status in sports are approximately 4/100,000 for a white man, 2/100,000 for a black man, and 3/100,000 for a Hispanic man in the United States (Leonard and Reyman 1988). For many young athletes, their dream ends early when coaches inform them that they are not big enough, strong enough, fast enough, or skilled enough to compete at the higher levels. But six of the higher-status men I interviewed did not wait for coaches to weed them out. They made conscious decisions in high school or in college to shift their attentions elsewhere—usually toward educational and career goals. Their decision not to pursue an athletic career appeared to them in retrospect to be a rational decision based on the growing knowledge of how very slim their chances were to be successful in the sports world. For instance, a 28-year-old white graduate student said:

> By junior high I started to realize that I was a good player—maybe even one of the best in my community—but I realized that there were all these people all over the country and how few will get to play pro sports. By high school, I still dreamed of being a pro—I was a serious athlete, I played hard—but I knew it wasn't heading anywhere. I wasn't going to play pro ball.

A 32-year-old white athletic director at a small private college had been a successful college baseball player. Despite considerable attention from professional scouts, he had decided to forgo a shot at a baseball career and to enter graduate school to pursue a teaching credential. As he explained this decision:

> At the time I think I saw baseball as pissing in the wind, really. I was married, I was 22 years old with a kid. I didn't want to spend 4 or 5 years in the minors with a family. And I could see I wasn't a superstar; so it wasn't really worth it. So I went to grad school. I thought that would be better for me.

Perhaps most striking was the story of a high school student body president and top-notch student who was also "Mr. Everything" in sports. He was named captain of his basketball, baseball, and football teams and achieved All-League honors in each sport. This young white man from a middle-class family received attention from the press and praise from his community and peers for his athletic accomplishments, as well as several offers of athletic scholarships from universities. But by the time he completed high school, he had already decided to quit playing organized sports. As he said:

> I think in my own mind I kind of downgraded the stardom thing. I thought that was small potatoes. And sure, that's nice in high school and all that, but on a broad scale, I didn't think it amounted to all that much. So I decided that my goal's to be a dentist, as soon as I can.

In his sophomore year of college, the basketball coach nearly persuaded him to go out for the team, but eventually he decided against it:

> I thought, so what if I can spend two years playing basketball? I'm not going to be a basketball player forever and I might jeopardize my chances of getting into dental school if I play.

He finished college in three years, completed dental school, and now, in his mid-30s, is again the epitome of the successful American man: a professional with a family, a home, and a membership in the local country club.

How and why do so many successful male athletes from higher-status backgrounds come to view sports careers as "pissing in the wind," or as "small potatoes"? How and why do they make this early assessment and choice to shift from sports and toward educational and professional goals? The white, middle-class institutional context, with its emphasis on education and income, makes it clear to them that choices exist and that the pursuit of an athletic career is not a particularly good choice to make. Where the young male once found sports to be a convenient institution within which to construct masculine status, the postadolescent and young adult man from a higher-status background simply *transfers* these same strivings to other institutional contexts: education and careers.

For the higher-status men who had chosen to shift from athletic careers, sports remained important on two levels. First, having been a successful high school or college athlete enhances one's adult status among other men in the community—but only as a badge of masculinity that is *added* to his professional status. In fact, several men in professions chose to be interviewed in their offices, where they publicly displayed the trophies and plaques that attested to their earlier athletic accomplishments. Their high school and college athletic careers may have appeared to them as "small potatoes," but many successful men speak of their earlier status as athletes as having "opened doors" for them in their present professions and in community affairs. Similarly, Farr's (1988) research on "Good Old Boys Sociability Groups" shows how sports, as part of the glue of masculine culture, continues to facilitate "dominance bonding" among privileged men long after active sports careers end. The college-educated, career-successful men in Farr's study rarely express overtly sexist, racist, or classist attitudes; in fact, in their relationships with women, they "often engage in expressive intimacies" and "make fun of exaggerated 'machismo'" (p. 276). But though they outwardly conform more to what Pleck (1982) calls "the modern male role," their informal relationships within their sociability groups, in effect, affirm their own gender and class status by constructing and clarifying the boundaries between themselves and women and lower-status men. This dominance bonding is based largely upon ritual forms of sociability (camaraderie, competition), "the superiority of which was first affirmed in the exclusionary play activities of young boys in groups" (Farr 1988, p. 265).

In addition to contributing to dominance bonding among higher-status adult men, sports remains salient in terms of the ideology of gender relations. Most men continued to watch, talk about, and identify with sports long after their own disengagement from athletic careers. Sports as a mediated spectacle provides an important context in which traditional conceptions of masculine superiority—conceptions recently contested by women—are shored up. As a 32-year-old white professional-class man said of one of the most feared professional football players today:

> A woman can do the same job as I can do—maybe even be my boss. But I'll be *damned* if she can go out on the football field and take a hit from Ronnie Lott.

Violent sports as spectacle provide linkages among men in the project of the domination of women, while at the same time helping to construct and clarify differences among various masculinities. The statement above is a clear identification with Ronnie Lott *as a man*, and the basis of the identification is the violent male body. As Connell (1987, p. 85) argues, sports is an important organizing institution for the embodiment of masculinity. Here, men's power over women becomes naturalized and linked to the social distribution of violence. Sports, as a practice, suppresses natural (sex) similarities, constructs differences, and then, largely through the media, weaves a structure of symbol and interpretation around these differences that naturalizes them (Hargreaves 1986, p. 112). It is also significant that the man who made the above statement about Ronnie Lott was quite aware that he (and perhaps 99 percent of the rest of the U.S. male population) was probably as incapable as most women of taking a "hit" from someone like Lott and living to tell of it. For middle-class men, the "tough guys" of the culture industry—the Rambos, the Ronnie Lotts who are fearsome "hitters," who "play hurt"—are the heroes who "prove" that "we men" are superior to women. At the same time, they play the role of the "primitive other," against whom higher-status men define themselves as "modern" and "civilized."

Sports, then, is important from boyhood through adulthood for men from higher-status backgrounds. But it is significant that by adolescence and early adulthood, most of these young men have concluded that sports *careers* are not for them. Their middle-class cultural environment encourages them to decide to shift their masculine strivings in more "rational" directions: education and nonsports careers. Yet their previous sports participation continues to be very important to them in terms of constructing and validating their status within privileged male peer groups and within their chosen professional careers. And organized sports, as a public spectacle, is a crucial locus around which ideologies of male superiority over women, as well as higher-status men's superiority over lower-status men, are constructed and naturalized.

Men from Lower-Status Backgrounds

For the lower-status young men in this study, success in sports was not an added proof of masculinity; it was often their only hope of achieving public masculine status. A 34-year-old black bus driver who had been a star athlete in three sports in high school had neither the grades nor the money to attend college, so he accepted an offer from the U.S. Marine Corps to play on their baseball team. He ended up in Vietnam, where a grenade blew four fingers off his pitching hand. In retrospect, he believed that his youthful focus on sports stardom and his concomitant lack of effort in academics made sense:

> You can go anywhere with athletics—you don't have to have brains. I mean, I didn't feel like I was gonna go out there and be a computer expert, or something that was gonna make a lot of money. The only thing I could do and live comfortably would be to play sports—just to get a contract—doesn't matter if you play second or third team in the pros, you're gonna make big bucks. That's all I wanted, a confirmed livelihood at the end of my ventures, and the only way I could do it would be through sports. So I tried. It failed, but that's what I tried.

Similar, and even more tragic, is the story of a 34-year-old black man who is now serving a life term in prison. After a career-ending knee injury at the age of 20 abruptly ended what had appeared to be a certain road to professional football fame and fortune, he decided that he "could still be rich and famous" by robbing a bank. During his high school and college years, he said, he was nearly illiterate:

> I'd hardly ever go to classes and they'd give me *Cs*. My coaches taught some of the classes. And I felt, "So what? They *owe* me that! I'm an *athlete!* I thought that was what I was born to do—to play sports—and everybody understood that.

Are lower-status boys and young men simply duped into putting all their eggs into one basket? My research suggested that there was more than "hope for the future" operating here. There were also immediate psychological reasons that they chose to pursue athletic careers. By the high school years, class and ethnic inequalities had become glaringly obvious, especially for those who attended socioeconomically heterogeneous schools. Cars, nice clothes, and other signs of status were often unavailable to these young men, and this contributed to a situation in which sports took on an expanded importance for them in terms of constructing masculine identities and status. A white, 36-year-old man from a poor, single-parent family who later played professional baseball had been acutely aware of his low-class status in his high school:

> I had one pair of jeans, and I wore them every day. I was always afraid of what people thought of me—that this guy doesn't have anything, that he's wearing the same Levi's all the time, he's having to work in the cafeteria for his lunch. What's going on? I think that's what made me so shy. . . . But boy, when I got into sports, I let it all hang out—[laughs]—and maybe that's why I became so good, because I was frustrated, and when I got into that element, they gave me my uniform in football, basketball, and baseball, and I didn't have to worry about how I looked, because then it was *me* who was coming out, and not my clothes or whatever. And I think that was the drive.

Similarly, a 41-year-old black man who had a 10-year professional football career described his insecurities as one of the few poor blacks in a mostly white, middle-class school and his belief that sports was the one arena in which he could be judged solely on his merit:

> I came from a poor family, and I was very sensitive about that in those days. When people would say things like "Look at him—he has dirty pants on," I'd think about it for a week. [But] I'd put my pants on and I'd go out on the football field with the intention that I'm gonna do a job. And if that calls on me to hurt you, I'm gonna do it. It's as simple as that. I demand respect just like everybody else.

"Respect" was what I heard over and over when talking with the men from lower-status backgrounds, especially black men. I interpret this type of respect to be a crystallization of the masculine quest for recognition through public achievement, unfolding within a system of structured constraints due to class and race inequities. The institutional context of education (sometimes with the collusion of teachers and coaches) and the constricted structure of opportunity in the economy made the pursuit of athletic careers appear to be the most rational choice to these young men.

The same is not true of young lower-status women. Dunkle (1985) points out that from junior high school through adulthood, young black men are far more likely to place high value on sports than are young black women, who are more likely to value academic achievement. There appears to be a gender dynamic operating in adolescent male peer groups that contributes toward their valuing sports more highly than education. Franklin (1986, p. 161) has argued that many of the normative values of the black male peer group (little respect for nonaggressive solutions to disputes, contempt for nonmaterial culture) contribute to the constriction of black men's views of desirable social positions, especially through education. In my study, a 42-year-old black man who did succeed in beating the odds by using his athletic scholarship to get a college degree and eventually becoming a successful professional said:

> By junior high, you either got identified as an athlete, a thug, or a bookworm. It's very important to be seen as somebody who's capable in some area. And you *don't* want to be identified as a bookworm. I was very good with books, but I was kind of covert about it. I was a closet bookworm. But with sports, I was *somebody;* so I worked very hard at it.

For most young men from lower-status backgrounds, the poor quality of their schools, the attitudes of teachers and coaches, as well as the antieducation environment within their own male peer groups, made it extremely unlikely that they would be able to succeed as students. Sports, therefore, became *the* arena in which they attempted to "show their stuff." For these lower-status men, as Baca Zinn (1982) and Majors (1986) argued in their respective studies of Chicano men and black men, when institutional resources that signify masculine status and control are absent, physical presence, personal style, and expressiveness take on increased importance. What Majors (1986, p. 6) calls "cool pose" is black men's expressive, often aggressive, assertion of masculinity. This self-assertion often takes place within a social context in which the young man is quite aware of existing social inequities. As the black bus driver, referred to above, said of his high school years:

> See, the rich people use their money to do what they want to do. I use my ability. If you wanted to be around me, if you wanted to learn something about sports, I'd teach you. But you're gonna take me to lunch. You're gonna let me use your car. See what I'm saying? In high school I'd go where I wanted to go. I didn't have to be educated. I was well-respected. I'd go somewhere, and they'd say, "Hey, that's Mitch Harris,[1] yeah, that's a bad son of a bitch!"

Majors (1986) argues that although "cool pose" represents a creative survival technique within a hostile environment, the most likely long-term effect of this masculine posturing is educational and occupational dead ends. As a result, we can conclude, lower-status men's personal and peer-group responses to a constricted structure of opportunity—responses that are rooted, in part, in the developmental insecurities and ambivalences of masculinity—serve to lock many of these young men into limiting activities such as sports.

SUMMARY AND CONCLUSIONS

This research has suggested that within a social context that is stratified by social class and by race, the choice to pursue—or not to pursue—an athletic career is explicable as an individual's rational assessment of the available means to achieve a respected masculine identity. For nearly all of the men from lower-status backgrounds, the status and respect that they received through sports was temporary—it did not translate into upward mobility. Nonetheless, a strategy of discouraging young black boys and men from involvement in sports is probably doomed to fail, since it ignores the continued existence of structural constraints. Despite the increased number of black role models in nonsports professions, employment opportunities for young black males have actually deteriorated. . . .

But it would be a mistake to conclude that we simply need to breed socioeconomic conditions that make it possible for poor and minority men to mimic the "rational choices" of white, middle-class men. If we are to build an appropriate understanding of the lives of all men, we must critically analyze white middle-class masculinity, rather than uncritically taking it as a normative standard. To fail to do this would be to ignore the ways in which organized sports serve to construct and legitimate gender differences and inequalities among men and women.

Feminist scholars have demonstrated that organized sports gives men from all backgrounds a means of status enhancement that is not available to young women. Sports thus serve the interests of all men in helping to construct and legitimize their control of public life and their domination of women (Bryson 1987; Hall 1987; Theberge 1987). Yet concrete studies are suggesting that men's experiences within sports are not all of a piece. Brian Pronger's (1990) research suggests that gay men approach sports differently than straight men do, with a sense of "irony." And my research suggests that although sports are important for men from both higher- and lower-status backgrounds, there are crucial differences. In fact, it appears that the meaning that most men give to their athletic strivings has more to do with competing for status among men than it has to do with proving superiority over women. How can we explain this seeming contradiction between the feminist claim that sports links all men in the domination of women and the research findings that different groups of men relate to sports in very different ways?

. . . Connell's (1987) concept of the "gender order" is useful. The gender order is a dynamic process that is constantly in a state of play. Moving beyond static gender-role theory and reductionist concepts of patriarchy that view men as an undifferentiated group which oppresses women, Connell argues that at any given historical moment, there are competing masculinities—some hegemonic, some marginalized, some stigmatized. Hegemonic masculinity (that definition of masculinity which is culturally ascendant) is constructed in relation to various subordinated masculinities as well as in relation to femininities. The project of male domination of women may tie all men together, but men share very unequally in the fruits of this domination.

These are key insights in examining the contemporary meaning of sports. Utilizing the concept of the gender order, we can begin to conceptualize how hierarchies of race, class, age, and sexual preference among men help to construct and legitimize men's overall power and privilege over women. And how, for some black, working-class, or gay men, the false promise of sharing in the fruits of hegemonic masculinity often ties them into their marginalized and subordinate statuses within hierarchies of intermale dominance. For instance, black men's development of what Majors (1986) calls "cool pose" within sports can be interpreted as an example of creative resistance to one form of social domination (racism); yet it also demonstrates the limits of an agency that adopts other forms of social domination (masculinity) as its vehicle. As Majors (1990) points out:

> Cool Pose demonstrates black males' potential to transcend oppressive conditions in order to express themselves *as men.* [Yet] it ultimately does not put black males in a position to live and work in more egalitarian ways with women, nor does it directly challenge male hierarchies.

Indeed, as Connell's (1990) analysis of an Australian "Iron Man" shows, the commercially successful, publicly acclaimed athlete may embody all that is valued in present cultural conceptions of hegemonic masculinity—physical strength, commercial success, supposed heterosexual virility. Yet higher-status men, while they admire the public image of the successful athlete, may also look down on him as a narrow, even atavistic, example of masculinity. For these higher-status men, their earlier sports successes are often status enhancing and serve to link them with other men in ways that continue to exclude women. Their decisions not to pursue athletic careers are equally important signs of their status vis-à-vis other men. Future examinations of the contemporary meaning and importance of sports to men might take as a fruitful point of departure that athletic participation, and sports as public spectacle, serve to provide linkages among men in the project of the domination of women, while at the same time helping to construct and clarify differences and hierarchies among various masculinities.

NOTE

1. "Mitch Harris" is a pseudonym.

References

Baca Zinn, M. 1982. "Chicano Men and Masuclinity." *Journal of Ethnic Studies* 10:29–44.

Bryson, L. 1987. "Sport and the Maintenance of Masculine Hegemony." *Women's Studies International Forum* 10:349–60.

Connell, R. W. 1987. *Gender and Power.* Stanford, CA: Stanford University Press.

———. 1990. "An Iron Man: The Body and Some Contradictions of Hegemonic Masculinity." In *Sport, Men, and the Gender Order: Critical Feminist Perspectives,* edited by M. A. Messner and D. S. Sabo. Champaign, IL: Human Kinetics.

Dunkle, M. 1985. "Minority and Low-Income Girls and Young Women in Athletics." *Equal Play* 5 (Spring-Summer): 12–13.

Edwards, H. 1984. "The Collegiate Athletic Arms Race: Origins and Implications of the 'Rule 48' Controversy." *Journal of Sport and Social Issues* 8:4–22.

Eitzen, D. S. and D. A. Purdy. 1986. "The Academic Preparation and Achievement of Black and White College Athletes." *Journal of Sport and Social Issues* 10:15–29.

Eitzen, D. S. and N. B. Yetman. 1977. "Immune From Racism?" *Civil Rights Digest* 9:3–13.

Farr, K. A. 1988. "Dominance Bonding Through the Good Old Boys Sociability Group." *Sex Roles* 18:259–77.

Franklin, C. W. II. 1984. *The Changing Definition of Masculinity.* New York: Plenum.

———. 1986. "Surviving the Institutional Decimation of Black Males: Causes, Consequences, and Intervention." in *The Making of Masculinities: The New Men's Studies,* edited by H. Brod, pp. 155–70. Winchester, MA: Allen & Unwin.

Gruneau, R. 1983. *Class, Sports, and Social Development.* Amherst: University of Massachusetts Press.

Hall, M. A. (ed.). 1987. "The Gendering of Sport, Leisure, and Physical Education." *Women's Studies International Forum* 10:361–474.

Hare, N. and J. Hare. 1984. *The Endangered Black Family: Coping with the Unisexualization and Coming Extinction of the Black Race.* San Francisco, CA: Black Think Tank.

Hargreaves, J. A. 1986. "Where's the Virtue? Where's the Grace? A Discussion of the Social Production of Gender Through Sport." *Theory, Culture and Society* 3:109–21.

Harris, D. S. and D. S. Eitzen. 1978. "The Consequences of Failure in Sport." *Urban Life* 7:177–88.

Hill, P. and B. Lowe. 1978. "The Inevitable Metathesis of the Retiring Athlete." *International Review of Sport Sociology* 9:5–29.

Leonard, W. M. II and J. M. Reyman. 1988. "The Odds of Attaining Professional Athlete Status: Refining the Computations." *Sociology of Sport Journal* 5:162–69.

Levinson, D. J. 1978. *The Seasons of a Man's Life*. New York: Ballantine.

Majors, R. 1986. "Cool Pose: The Proud Signature of Black Survival." *Changing Men: Issues in Gender, Sex, and Politics* 17:5–6.

————. 1990. "Cool Pose: Black Masculinity in Sports." In *Sport, Men, and the Gender Order: Critical Feminist Perspectives*, edited by M. A. Messner and D. S. Sabo. Champaign, IL: Human Kinetics.

Messner, M. 1987a. "The Meaning of Success: The Athletic Experience and the Development of Male Identity." In *The Making of Masculinities: The New Men's Studies*, edited by H. Brod, pp. 193–209. Winchester, MA: Allen & Unwin.

————. 1987b. "The Life of a Man's Seasons: Male Identity in the Lifecourse of the Athlete." in *Changing Men: New Directions in Research on Men and Masculinity*, edited by M. S. Kimmel, pp. 53–67. Newbury Park, CA: Sage.

Pleck, J. H. 1982. *The Myth of Masculinity*. Cambridge: MIT Press.

Pronger, B. 1990. "Gay Jocks: A Phenomenology of Gay Men in Athletics." In *Sport, Men, and the Gender Order: Critical Feminist Perspectives*, edited by M. A. Messner and D. S. Sabo. Champaign, IL: Human Kinetics.

Rubin, L. B. 1985. *Just Friends: The Role of Friendship in Our Lives*. New York: Harper & Row.

Rudman, W. J. 1986. "The Sport Mystique in Black Culture." *Sociology of Sport Journal* 3:305–19.

Staples, Robert. 1982. *Black Masculinity*. New York: Black Scholar Press.

Theberge, N. 1987. "Sport and Women's Empowerment." *Women's Studies International Forum* 10:387–93.

Wellman, D. 1986. "The New Political Linguistics of Race." *Socialist Review* 87/88:43–62.

MY PROBLEM WITH MULTI-CULTURAL EDUCATION

40

John Garvey

"Daddy, what are we?"

"What do you mean?"

"You know, where are we from? Are we Italian, Irish, Jewish; you know, like that?"

"Well, we're from here; we're Americans."

"Daddy!!! What am I going to say in school?"

More than once, my now nine-year-old daughter and I have had this conversation. I think I understand my daughter's frustration. After all, for the better part of my grammar school and high school life, I knew who I was—a Catholic and Irish. But, definitely, more Catholic than Irish. My sisters and I can still joke that the reason why we went to parochial school rather than public school was that only "public" children went to public school. We had not a clue what such "public" schools might be like; but we knew they weren't Catholic.

Being Catholic meant getting up two hours early on school days and going to Mass every day for weeks on end; it meant becoming an altar boy and dreaming of the sacred power invested in the priesthood; it meant seriously considering the priesthood until the end of grammar school. Being Catholic meant real fear when you went to confession on Saturday—even though the worst you had done was inconsequential.

Being Irish was not an everyday, living and breathing thing. Being Irish meant watching the St. Patrick's Day Parade on television; it meant being part of an annual school play where all the children dressed in green; it meant, for my sisters, taking dancing lessons where they learned jigs and reels (but stopped dancing them soon enough). Being Irish meant going to Rockaway (a beach-front peninsula, inside New York City limits, frequented by those of Irish origin or ancestry) for summer vacation once or twice and learning there that an old family friend had one of those school custodian jobs that allowed him to be almost rich. Apparently, the "public" schools were good for something.

Later, when I went way off to the Bronx, from Brooklyn, for college, I cringed whenever someone referred to anyone as "BIC"—variously Bronx or Brooklyn Irish Catholic. They intended it to mean someone who was sexually

From: Noel Ignatiev and John Garvey, eds., *Race Traitor* (New York: Routledge, 1996).

timid and alcoholically bold. Most of those who were so labelled resented it, but, as time went on, I heard more than a few proudly claim the label for themselves. My daughter, in spite of her dismay at us not being anything useful in school, would not know what to make of "BIC."

Once I stopped being Catholic, it was not too long before I, more or less absentmindedly, stopped feeling very Irish. Giving up the Catholic part was hard; the Irish barely an after-thought. (Giving up whiteness came much later still.)

Let me go back to the beginning of this story. My daughter really wants to know "Who was the first person?" and "Where did he come from?" Unlike her questions about the origins of the human species, her questions about her social identity seldom come from her own desires to know or to understand. They come from her school, a school which is explicitly committed to providing a multi-cultural education for a diverse student body. They are usually part of an assignment from a teacher attempting to discover, with the children, the varied roots of the kids in the class. The places of family origin, back a generation or two, are located on maps; family trees are constructed; biographies are written. How could I object?

But object I have. Earlier this year, upon learning that my daughter would be studying immigration in fourth grade, I told her teacher, someone I've known for many years, that I didn't like the theme, that it misconstrued the essentials of America and that it placed the black children in the class in a profoundly disadvantaged place. Too many of those black children would have no tales of immigrant suffering and triumph to share with their classmates. The teacher was, I think, genuinely surprised by my objections. She reminded me that the school traditionally celebrated Black History Month by studying topics associated with the black struggle for freedom. I wasn't satisfied. I suggested that the theme of "Movement" might allow her to explore some of the same topics without as many problems. To my pleasant surprise, the eventual class theme was revised to include forced migration along with immigration.

Since then, my daughter has indeed written an autobiography which includes information on my grandparents' origins in the Irish countryside. But she has also written a report on Frederick Douglass in which she interpreted his escape from slavery as a form of migration. By any measure, it's much better than what I was doing in fourth grade—or, for that matter, in much of my formal education through sixteen years of Catholic schools and colleges.

When I went to college, I had never read an assigned text by or about black folks in America. In my senior year in high school, I had independently read *The Fire Next Time* by James Baldwin and had written a review essay for the high school literary magazine. In college, I took more than twenty required courses in history, theology, philosophy, art, literature. Although we spent a good deal of time exploring the origins of civilization in the Near and Middle East, mostly we re-traced an imagined history of Europe—a lot of emphasis on the achievements of high culture and international conflict, hardly any on social conflict. As I recall, I don't think we were so much encouraged to see Egypt, for example, as a European civilization. Instead, we were encouraged to see that Europe had wisely borrowed from the great achievements of those other civilizations. At the same time, we didn't spend a moment on the civilizations of Asia and Africa outside the Near and Middle East. I read Plato, Aristotle, Sophocles, and Euripides; I read the Old and the New Testament; I read Kant, Hegel, and Marx. In many ways, I was well educated. But, I didn't read any American literature. I didn't study any American history. For that matter, I didn't study any Irish history either, although I did read Yeats and Joyce.

As is with others of my generation, events had their own demands to make on my academic development. In 1968, as rebellions shook the streets of America's cities and as Black Power became a household expression, some friends and I participated in an uncredited Black History seminar with a sympathetic history professor. I don't remember all that we read but it included Stanley Elkins's *Slavery* and C. Vann Woodward's *The Strange Career of Jim Crow*. In spite of this, I left college remarkably ignorant of much that I now hold to be essential. I knew virtually nothing of the pre-Columbian American civilizations. My only knowledge of Reconstruction consisted of grammar school phrases about carpetbaggers and scalawags.

So why am I complaining? After all, my daughter already knows more than a little about Frederick Douglass. What's so bad about schools fostering an appreciation of the different habits and customs of people from different parts of the world? Well, nothing is wrong about that—unless some of those habits and customs are themselves objectionable or if the appreciation of some results in the obscurance of others. (Last year, I saw a movie on videotape about a Romanian war criminal who had emigrated to America and was all involved in the appreciation of things Romanian here in the United States. His college-educated daughter could not imagine what the celebration had to do with the crime and, more important, could not imagine him being the criminal.) What we need to talk about is not so much appreciation or celebration but rather critical examination. After all, how do we know if a habit or custom is objectionable or not?

Too often, the multi-cultural education being promoted across American schools relies on a superficial notion of culture. Ralph W. Nicholas put the matter well for me when he wrote that culture "refers to all the habits, patterns, and ways of thinking that human beings acquire as an *extragenetic* inheritance" (emphasis added). Given the preoccupation with studying multiple cultures *through the prism of continental or national origin*, it seems to me that many children and older students are being encouraged to understand culture as a genetic inheritance. Immigration is, after all, one of the most common and most common-sensical of the ways in which the diversity of the American people is described and understood. It allows teachers and students to appreciate how difficult is the adjustment to new ways. But, as a way of understanding America, it is deeply flawed.

The focus on immigration as the central category of historical study of America usually results in the understanding of "making it" as the central economic category and of small businesses as the central economic institution. In New York City, children visit neighborhood shops and restaurants and interview the shopkeepers—why did they come, how hard have they worked, what kind of food is that. They walk by walls covered with graffiti; they walk by teenagers with pants hanging down upon their ankles; they walk by schoolyards with basketballs bouncing. But they are not asked to interview the teenagers—to find out why.

Last April, I visited San Francisco for the first time. On the highway in from the airport, the first thing I noticed was the stylized writing of tags on the pillars of the overpasses. How did the kids of San Francisco learn from the kids of New York to write their tags in the same way? Or did the kids in New York learn from the kids in San Francisco? Or did they both learn from kids in Chicago? Put simply, sauerkraut, lasagna, and bagels do not a culture make. Basketball (played a certain way), clothes (worn in a certain style) and lyrics (sung in a certain rhythm) do so much more. Within the predominant multicultural paradigm, the cultures that children are encouraged to appreciate are, or will be, marginal to the world they will live in as adults. That world is being made, not out of nostalgia for customs of lands far away, but of events and personalities close by. And the culture that has made America what it is and what it might be is not the accumulation of more or less equal contributions by various immigrant groups as such.

All those who have been here and all those who are here now are part of what we are and might become. But, we need to be clear about what we are and what we want to become. The characteristic practices of multi-cultural education, as evidenced in my daughter's study of immigration, suggest that we have accomplished more than we have and that there is less to do than there is. Multi-cultural education tends to discount the significance of present-day oppression or if it does acknowledge it, tends to present it as oppression without oppressors. I may be wrong. For example, it may be that, in some multicultural education environments, students are encouraged to examine not only the hardships endured by European immigrants, but also their relative willingness to become white in America.

I would suggest that multi-cultural education is a project of defeat. Those who are in the forefront of efforts to multi-culturalize the curriculum are, often enough, intellectual and personal products of the upsurge of the 1960s. But they have abandoned hope in the utopian desire of the 1960s and have substituted, for that desire, the social/political/educational equivalent of managed care. More than anything else, that utopian desire was given initial expression by the black struggles of the '50s and '60s. And it struck deep into the minds and hearts of white people. There was a time when thousands of white households were being rocked by debates between children and parents over the issue of race. But, I would guess, not too much of that goes on now. The abandonment of the struggle over race has been fueled by a conviction that those considered white are not, after all, capable of joining unequivocally in the fight for black liberation and their own freedom.

It was the struggle over race that was the defining issue in the large and small episodes of the 1960s. I played a part in the battles of that era too small to include in a footnote. But I am glad that I did. It was not always easy—arguing when no one else appeared to have the same point of view. It was not always easy when relatives would tell me of the time when "No Irish Need Apply"—as if they had the day before experienced discrimination because of their Irishness. I'm glad that I didn't have too much of an appreciation for their Irishness because, to me, it seemed then, and mostly seems still now, inseparable from their whiteness.

The multi-culturalist vision has a limited social goal—people should learn to live and let live. But what the proponents of the multi-culturalist creed often overlook is that in America living and letting live is premised on a continued complicity with the reproduction of race distinctions. So long as those distinctions are left intact, it is unlikely that multi-cultural education will do much towards changing the persistent refusal of many thousands of young blacks to participate enthusiastically in school. And it is unlikely that multi-cultural education will do much towards changing the common-sense views of whites, no matter the part of the globe they or their ancestors came from.

IF MEN COULD MENSTRUATE

41

Gloria Steinem

A white minority of the world has spent centuries conning us into thinking that a white skin makes people superior—even though the only thing it really does is make them more subject to ultraviolet rays and to wrinkles. Male human beings have built whole cultures around the idea that penis-envy is "natural"

From: *Ms.* VII (October 1978): 110. Copyright © Gloria Steinem. Reprinted by permission.

to women—though having such an unprotected organ might be said to make men vulnerable, and the power to give birth makes womb-envy at least as logical.

In short, the characteristics of the powerful, whatever they may be, are thought to be better than the characteristics of the powerless—and logic has nothing to do with it.

What would happen, for instance, if suddenly, magically, men could menstruate and women could not?

The answer is clear—menstruation would become an enviable, boast-worthy, masculine event:

Men would brag about how long and how much.

Boys would mark the onset of menses, that longed-for proof of manhood, with religious ritual and stag parties.

Congress would fund a National Institute of Dysmenorrhea to help stamp out monthly discomforts.

Sanitary supplies would be federally funded and free. (Of course, some men would still pay for the prestige of commercial brands such as John Wayne Tampons, Muhammad Ali's Rope-a-dope Pads, Joe Namath Jock Shields— "For Those Light Bachelor Days," and Robert "Baretta" Blake Maxi-Pads.)

Military men, right-wing politicians, and religious fundamentalists would cite menstruation ("*men*-struation") as proof that only men could serve in the Army ("you have to give blood to take blood"), occupy political office ("can women be aggressive without that steadfast cycle governed by the planet Mars?"), be priests and ministers ("how could a woman give her blood for our sins?"), or rabbis ("without the monthly loss of impurities, women remain un-clean").

Male radicals, left-wing politicians, and mystics, however, would insist that women are equal, just different; and that any woman could enter their ranks if only she were willing to self-inflict a major wound every month ("you *must* give blood for the revolution"), recognize the preeminence of menstrual issues, or subordinate her selfness to all men in the Cycle of Enlightenment.

Street guys would brag ("I'm a three-pad man") or answer praise from a buddy ("Man, you lookin' *good!*") by giving fives and saying, "Yeah, man, I'm on the rag!"

TV shows would treat the subject at length. ("Happy Days": Richie and Potsie try to convince Fonzie that he is still "The Fonz," though he has missed two periods in a row.) So would newspapers. (SHARK SCARE THREAT-ENS MENSTRUATING MEN. JUDGE CITES MONTHLY STRESS IN PARDONING RAPIST.) And movies. (Newman and Redford in "Blood Brothers"!)

Men would convince women that intercourse was *more* pleasurable at "that time of the month." Lesbians would be said to fear blood and therefore life itself—though probably only because they needed a good menstruating man.

Of course, male intellectuals would offer the most moral and logical arguments. How could a woman master any discipline that demanded a sense of time, space, mathematics, or measurement, for instance, without that in-built gift for measuring the cycles of the moon and planets—and thus for measuring anything at all? In the rarefied fields of philosophy and religion, could women compensate for missing the rhythm of the universe? Or for their lack of symbolic death-and-resurrection every month?

Liberal males in every field would try to be kind: the fact that "these people" have no gift of measuring life or connecting to the universe, the liberals would explain, should be punishment enough.

And how would women be trained to react? One can imagine traditional women agreeing to all these arguments with a staunch and smiling masochism. ("The ERA would force housewives to wound themselves every month": Phyllis Schafly. "Your husband's blood is as sacred as that of Jesus—and so sexy, too!": Marabel Morgan.) Reformers and Queen Bees would try to imitate men, and *pretend* to have a monthly cycle. All feminists would explain endlessly that men, too, needed to be liberated from the false idea of Martian aggressiveness, just as women needed to escape the bonds of menses-envy. Radical feminists would add that the oppression of the nonmenstrual was the pattern for all other oppressions. ("Vampires were our first freedom fighters!") Cultural feminists would develop a bloodless imagery in art and literature. Socialist feminists would insist that only under capitalism would men be able to monopolize menstrual blood. . . .

In fact, if men could menstruate, the power justifications could probably go on forever.

If we let them.

State Institutions and Social Policy

THE FIRST AMERICANS

American Indians

C. Matthew Snipp

42

By the end of the nineteenth century, many observers predicted that American Indians were destined for extinction. Within a few generations, disease, warfare, famine, and outright genocide had reduced their numbers from millions to less than 250,000 in 1890. Once a self-governing, self-sufficient people, American Indians were forced to give up their homes and their land, and to subordinate themselves to an alien culture. The forced resettlement to reservation lands or the Indian Territory (now Oklahoma) frequently meant a life of destitution, hunger, and complete dependency on the federal government for material needs.

Today, American Indians are more numerous than they have been for several centuries. While still one of the most destitute groups in American society, tribes have more autonomy and are now more self-sufficient than at any time since the last century. In cities, modern pan-Indian organizations have been successful in making the presence of American Indians known to the larger community, and have mobilized to meet the needs of their people (Cornell 1988; Nagel 1986; Weibel-Orlando 1991). In many rural areas, American Indians and especially tribal governments have become increasingly more important and increasingly more visible by virtue of their growing political and

From: Silvia Pedraza and Rubén G. Rumbaut, eds., *Origins and Destinies: Immigration, Race, and Ethnicity in America*. (Belmont, CA: Wadsworth, 1996), pp. 390–403. Reprinted by permission.

economic power. The balance of this [reading] is devoted to explaining their unique place in American society.

THE INCORPORATION OF AMERICAN INDIANS

The current political and economic status of American Indians is the result of the process by which they were incorporated into Euro-American society (Hall 1989). This amounts to a long history of efforts aimed at subordinating an otherwise self-governing and self-sufficient people that eventually culminated in widespread economic dependency. The role of the U.S. government in this process can be seen in the five major historical periods of federal Indian relations: removal, assimilation, the Indian New Deal, termination and relocation, and self-determination.

Removal

In the early nineteenth century, the population of the United States expanded rapidly at the same time that the federal government increased its political and military capabilities. The character of Indian-American relations changed after the War of 1812. The federal government increasingly pressured tribes settled east of the Appalachian Mountains to move west to the territory acquired in the Louisiana purchase. Numerous treaties were negotiated by which the tribes relinquished most of their land and eventually were forced to move west.

Initially the federal government used bargaining and negotiation to accomplish removal, but many tribes resisted (Prucha 1984). However, the election of Andrew Jackson by a frontier constituency signaled the beginning of more forceful measures to accomplish removal. In 1830 Congress passed the Indian Removal Act, which mandated the eventual removal of the eastern tribes to points west of the Mississippi River, in an area which was to become the Indian Territory and is now the state of Oklahoma. Dozens of tribes were forcibly removed from the eastern half of the United States to the Indian Territory and newly created reservations in the west, a long process ridden with conflict and bloodshed.

As the nation expanded beyond the Mississippi River, tribes of the plains, southwest, and west coast were forcibly settled and quarantined on isolated reservations. This was accompanied by the so-called Indian Wars—a bloody chapter in the history of Indian-White relations (Prucha 1984; Utley 1984). This period in American history is especially remarkable because the U.S. government was responsible for what is unquestionably one of the largest forced migrations in history.

The actual process of removal spanned more than a half-century and affected nearly every tribe east of the Mississippi River. Removal often meant extreme hardships for American Indians, and in some cases this hardship reached legendary proportions. For example, the Cherokee removal has become known as the "Trail of Tears." In 1838, nearly 17,000 Cherokees were ordered to leave their homes and assemble in military stockades (Thornton 1987, p. 117). The march to the Indian Territory began in October and continued through the winter months. As many as 8,000 Cherokees died from cold weather and diseases such as influenza (Thornton 1987, p. 118).

According to William Hagan (1979), removal also caused the Creeks to suffer dearly as their society underwent a profound disintegration. The contractors who forcibly removed them from their homes refused to do anything for "the large number who had nothing but a cotton garment to protect them from the sleet storms and no shoes between them and the frozen ground of the last stages of their hegira. About half of the Creek nation did not survive the migration and the difficult early years in the West" (Hagan 1979, p. 77–81). In the West, a band of Nez Perce men, women, and children, under the leadership of Chief Joseph, resisted resettlement in 1877. Heavily outnumbered, they were pursued by cavalry troops from the Wallowa valley in eastern Oregon and finally captured in Montana near the Canadian border. Although the Nez Perce were eventually captured and moved to the Indian Territory, and later to Idaho, their resistance to resettlement has been described by one historian as "one of the great military movements in history" (Prucha 1984, p. 541).

Assimilation

Near the end of the nineteenth century, the goal of isolating American Indians on reservations and the Indian Territory was finally achieved. The Indian population also was near extinction. Their numbers had declined steadily throughout the nineteenth century, leading most observers to predict their disappearance (Hoxie 1984). Reformers urged the federal government to adopt measures that would humanely ease American Indians into extinction. The federal government responded by creating boarding schools and the allotment acts—both were intended to "civilize" and assimilate American Indians into American society by Christianizing them, educating them, introducing them to private property, and making them into farmers. American Indian boarding schools sought to accomplish this task by indoctrinating Indian children with the belief that tribal culture was an inferior relic of the past and that Euro-American culture was vastly superior and preferable. Indian children were forbidden to wear their native attire, to eat their native foods, to speak their native language, or to practice their traditional religion. Instead, they were issued Euro-American clothes, and expected to speak English and become Christians. Indian children who did not relinquish their culture were punished by school authorities. The curriculum of these schools taught vocational arts along with "civilization" courses.

'The impact of allotment policies is still evident today. The 1887 General Allotment Act (the Dawes Severalty Act) and subsequent legislation mandated that tribal lands were to be allotted to individual American Indians in fee simple title, and the surplus lands left over from allotment were to be sold on the open market. Indians who received allotted tribal lands also received citizenship, farm implements, and encouragement from Indian agents to adopt farming as a livelihood (Hoxie 1984, Prucha 1984).

For a variety of reasons, Indian lands were not completely liquidated by allotment, many Indians did not receive allotments, and relatively few changed their lifestyles to become farmers. Nonetheless, the allotment era was a disaster because a significant number of allottees eventually lost their land. Through tax foreclosures, real estate fraud, and their own need for cash, many American Indians lost what for most of them was their last remaining asset (Hoxie 1984).

Allotment took a heavy toll on Indian lands. It caused about 90 million acres of Indian land to be lost, approximately two-thirds of the land that had belonged to tribes in 1887 (O'Brien 1990). This created another problem that continues to vex many reservations: "checkerboarding." Reservations that were subjected to allotment are typically a crazy quilt composed of tribal lands, privately owned "fee" land, and trust land belonging to individual Indian families. Checkerboarding presents reservation officials with enormous administrative problems when trying to develop land use management plans, zoning ordinances, or economic development projects that require the construction of physical infrastructure such as roads or bridges.

The Indian New Deal

The Indian New Deal was short-lived but profoundly important. Implemented in the early 1930s along with the other New Deal programs of the Roosevelt administration, the Indian New Deal was important for at least three reasons. First, signaling the end of the disastrous allotment era as well as a new respect for American Indian tribal culture, the Indian New Deal repudiated allotment as a policy. Instead of continuing its futile efforts to detribalize American Indians, the federal government acknowledged that tribal culture was worthy of respect. Much of this change was due to John Collier, a long-time Indian rights advocate appointed by Franklin Roosevelt to serve as Commissioner of Indian Affairs (Prucha 1984).

Like other New Deal policies, the Indian New Deal also offered some relief from the Great Depression and brought essential infrastructure development to many reservations, such as projects to control soil erosion and to build hydroelectric dams, roads, and other public facilities. These projects created jobs in New Deal programs such as the Civilian Conservation Corps and the Works Progress Administration.

An especially important and enduring legacy of the Indian New Deal was the passage of the Indian Reorganization Act (IRA) of 1934. Until then, Indian self-government had been forbidden by law. This act allowed tribal governments, for the first time in decades, to reconstitute themselves for the purpose of overseeing their own affairs on the reservation. Critics charge that this law imposed an alien form of government, representative democracy, on traditional tribal authority. On some reservations, this has been an on-going source of conflict (O'Brien 1989). Some reservations rejected the IRA for this reason, but now have tribal governments authorized under different legislation.

Termination and Relocation

After World War II, the federal government moved to terminate its long-standing relationship with Indian tribes by settling the tribes' outstanding legal claims, by terminating the special status of reservations, and by helping reservation Indians relocate to urban areas (Fixico 1986). The Indian Claims Commission was a special tribunal created in 1946 to hasten the settlement of legal claims that tribes had brought against the federal government. In fact, the Indian Claims Commission became bogged down with prolonged cases, and in 1978 the commission was dissolved by Congress. At that time, there were 133 claims still unresolved out of an original 617 that were first heard by the commission three decades earlier (Fixico 1986, p. 186). The unresolved claims that were still pending were transferred to the Federal Court of Claims.

Congress also moved to terminate the federal government's relationship with Indian tribes. House Concurrent Resolution (HCR) 108, passed in 1953, called for steps that eventually would abolish all reservations and abolish all special programs serving American Indians. It also established a priority list of reservations slated for immediate termination. However, this bill and subsequent attempts to abolish reservations were vigorously opposed by Indian advocacy groups such as the National Congress of American Indians. Only two reservations were actually terminated, the Klamath in Oregon and the Menominee in Wisconsin. The Menominee reservation regained its trust status in 1975 and the Klamath reservation was restored in 1986.

The Bureau of Indian Affairs (BIA) also encouraged reservation Indians to relocate and seek work in urban job markets. This was prompted partly by the desperate economic prospects on most reservations, and partly because of the federal government's desire to "get out of the Indian business." The BIA's relocation programs aided reservation Indians in moving to designated cities, such as Los Angeles and Chicago, where they also assisted them in finding housing and employment. Between 1952 and 1972, the BIA relocated more than 100,000 American Indians (Sorkin 1978). However, many Indians returned to their reservations (Fixico 1986). For some American Indians, the return to the reservation was only temporary; for example, during periods when seasonal employment such as construction work was hard to find.

Self-Determination

Many of the policies enacted during the termination and relocation era were steadfastly opposed by American Indian leaders and their supporters. As these programs became stalled, critics attacked them for being harmful, ineffective, or both. By the mid-1960s, these policies had very little serious support. Perhaps inspired by the gains of the Civil Rights movement, American Indian leaders and their supporters made "self-determination" the first priority on their political agendas. For these activists, self-determination meant that Indian people would have the autonomy to control their own affairs, free from the paternalism of the federal government.

The idea of self-determination was well received by members of Congress sympathetic to American Indians. It also was consistent with the "New Federalism" of the Nixon administration. Thus, the policies of termination and relocation were repudiated in a process that culminated in 1975 with the passage of the American Indian Self-Determination and Education Assistance Act, a profound shift in federal Indian policy. For the first time since this nation's founding, American Indians were authorized to oversee the affairs of their own communities, free of federal intervention. In practice, the Self-Determination Act established measures that would allow tribal governments to assume a larger role in reservation administration of programs for welfare assistance, housing, job training, education, natural resource conservation, and the maintenance of reservation roads and bridges (Snipp and Summers 1991). Some reservations also have their own police forces and game wardens, and can issue licenses and levy taxes. The Onondaga tribe in upstate New York have taken their sovereignty one step further by issuing passports that are internationally recognized. Yet there is a great deal of variability in terms of how much autonomy tribes have over reservation affairs. Some tribes, especially those on large and well-organized reservations have nearly complete control over their reservations, while smaller reservations with limited resources often depend heavily on BIA services. . . .

CONCLUSION

Though small in number, American Indians have an enduring place in American society. Growing numbers of American Indians occupy reservation and other trust lands, and equally important has been the revitalization of tribal governments. Tribal governments now have a larger role in reservation affairs than ever in the past. Another significant development has been the urbanization of American Indians. Since 1950, the proportion of American Indians in cities has grown rapidly. These American Indians have in common with reservation Indians many of the same problems and disadvantages, but they also face other challenges unique to city life.

The challenges facing tribal governments are daunting. American Indians are among the poorest groups in the nation. Reservation Indians have substantial needs for improved housing, adequate health care, educational opportunities, and employment, as well as developing and maintaining reservation infrastructure. In the face of declining federal assistance, tribal governments are assuming an ever-larger burden. On a handful of reservations, tribal governments have assumed completely the tasks once performed by the BIA.

As tribes have taken greater responsibility for their communities, they also have struggled with the problems of raising revenues and providing economic opportunities for their people. Reservation land bases provide many reservations with resources for development. However, these resources are not always abundant, much less unlimited, and they have not always been well managed. It will be yet another challenge for tribes to explore ways of efficiently managing their existing resources. Legal challenges also face tribes seeking to exploit unconventional resources such as gambling revenues. Their success depends on many complicated legal and political contingencies.

Urban American Indians have few of the resources found on reservations, and they face other difficult problems. Preserving their culture and identity is an especially pressing concern. However, urban Indians have successfully adapted to city environments in ways that preserve valued customs and activities—powwows, for example, are an important event in all cities where there is a large Indian community. In addition, pan-Indianism has helped urban Indians set aside tribal differences and forge alliances for the betterment of urban Indian communities.

These alliances are essential, because unlike reservation Indians, urban American Indians do not have their own form of self-government. Tribal governments do not have jurisdiction over urban Indians. For this reason, urban Indians must depend on other strategies for ensuring that the needs of their community are met, especially for those new to city life. Coping with the transition to urban life poses a multitude of difficult challenges for many American Indians. Some succumb to these problems, especially the hardships of unemployment, economic deprivation, and related maladies such as substance abuse, crime, and violence. But most successfully overcome these difficulties, often with help from other members of the urban Indian community.

Perhaps the greatest strength of American Indians has been their ability to find creative ways for dealing with adversity, whether in cities or on reservations. In the past, this quality enabled them to survive centuries of oppression and persecution. Today this is reflected in the practice of cultural traditions that Indian people are proud to embrace. The resilience of American Indians is an abiding quality that will no doubt ensure that they will remain part of the ethnic mosaic of American society throughout the twenty-first century and beyond.

References

Cornell, Stephen. 1988. *The Return of the Native: American Indian Political Resurgence.* New York: Oxford University Press.

Fixico, Donald L. 1986. *Termination and Relocation: Federal Indian Policy, 1945–1960.* Albuquerque, NM: University of New Mexico Press.

Hagan, William P. 1977. *American Indians.* Chicago, IL: University of Chicago Press.

Hall, Thomas D. 1989. *Social Change in the Southwest, 1350–1880.* Lawrence, KS: University Press of Kansas.

Hoxie, Frederick E. 1984. *A Final Promise: The Campaign to Assimilate the Indians, 1880–1920.* Lincoln, NE: University of Nebraska Press.

Nagel, Joanne. 1989. "American Indian Repertoires of Contention." Paper presented at the annual meeting of the American Sociological Association, San Francisco, CA.

O'Brien, Sharon. 1990. *American Indian Tribal Governments.* Norman, OK: University of Oklahoma Press.

Prucha, Francis Paul. 1984. *The Great Father.* Lincoln, NE: University of Nebraska Press.

Snipp, C. Matthew and Gene F. Summers. 1991. "American Indian Development Policies," pp. 166–180 in *Rural Policies for the 1990s*, edited by Cornelia Flora and James A. Christenson. Boulder, CO: Westview Press.

Sorkin, Alan L. 1978. *The Urban American Indian.* Lexington, MA: Lexington Books.

Thornton, Russell. 1987. *American Indian Holocaust and Survival: A Population History since 1942.* Norman, OK: University of Oklahoma Press.

Utley, Robert M. 1963. *The Last Days of the Sioux Nation.* New Haven: Yale University Press.

Weibel-Orlando, Joan. 1991. *Indian Country, L.A.* Urbana, IL: University of Illinois Press.

CAN EDUCATION ELIMINATE RACE, CLASS, AND GENDER INEQUALITY?

43

Roslyn Arlin Mickelson and Stephen Samuel Smith

INTRODUCTION

Parents, politicians, and educational policy makers share the belief that a "good education" is *the* meal ticket. It will unlock the door to economic opportunity and thus enable disadvantaged groups or individuals to improve their lot dramatically.[1] This belief is one of the assumptions that has long been part of the American Dream. According to the putative dominant ideology, the United States is basically a meritocracy in which hard work and individual effort are rewarded, especially in financial terms.[2] Related to this central belief are a series of culturally enshrined misconceptions about poverty and wealth. The central one is that poverty and wealth are the result of individual inadequacies or strengths rather than the results of the distributive mechanisms of the capitalist economy. A second misconception is the belief that everyone is the master of her or his own fate. The dominant ideology assumes that American society is open and competitive, a place where an individual's status depends on talent and motivation, not inherited position, connections, or privileges linked to ascriptive characteristics like gender or race. To compete fairly, everyone must have access to education free of the fetters of family background, gender, and race. Since the middle of this century, the reform policies of the federal government have been designed, at least officially, to enhance individuals' opportunities to acquire education. The question we will explore in this essay is whether expanding educational opportunity is enough to reduce the inequalities of race, social class, and gender which continue to characterize U.S. society.

We begin by discussing some of the major educational policies and programs of the past forty-five years that sought to reduce social inequality through expanding equality of educational opportunity. This discussion highlights the success and failures of programs such as school desegregation, compensatory education, Title IX, and job training. We then focus on the barriers these programs face in actually reducing social inequality. Our point is that inequality is so deeply rooted in the structure and operation of the U.S. polit-

---

Printed by permission of the authors.

ical economy, that, at best, educational reforms can play only a limited role in ameliorating such inequality. In fact, there is considerable evidence that indicates that, for poor and many minority children, education helps legitimate, if not actually reproduce, significant aspects of social inequality in their lives. Finally, we speculate about education's potential role in individual and social transformation.

First, it is necessary to distinguish among equality, equality of opportunity, and equality of educational opportunity. The term *equality* has been the subject of extensive scholarly and political debate, much of which is beyond the scope of this essay. Most Americans reject equality of life conditions as a goal, because it would require a fundamental transformation of our basic economic and political institutions, a scenario most are unwilling to accept. As Ralph Waldo Emerson put it, "The genius of our country has worked out our true policy—opportunity."

The distinction between equality of opportunity and equality of outcome is important. Through this country's history, equality has most typically been understood in the former way. Rather than a call for the equal distribution of money, property, or many other social goods, the concern over equality has been with equal opportunity in pursuit of these goods. In the words of Jennifer Hochschild, "So long as we live in a democratic capitalist society—that is, so long as we maintain the formal promise of political and social equality while encouraging the practice of economic inequality—we need the idea of equal opportunity to bridge that otherwise unacceptable contradiction."[3] To use a current metaphor: If life is a game, the playing field must be level; if life is a race, the starting line must be in the same place for everyone. For the playing field to be level, many believe education is crucial because it gives individuals the wherewithal to compete in the allegedly meritocratic system. In America, then, *equality* is really understood to mean *equality of opportunity*, which itself hinges on *equality of educational opportunity*.

THE SPOTTY RECORD OF FEDERAL EDUCATIONAL REFORMS

In the past forty-five years, a series of educational reforms initiated at the national level has been introduced into local school systems. All of the reforms aimed to move education closer to the ideal of equality of educational opportunity. Here we discuss several of these reforms, and how the concept of equality of educational opportunity has evolved. Given the importance of race and racism in U.S. history, many of the federal education policies during this period attempted to redress the most egregious forms of inequality based on race.

School Desegregation

Although American society has long claimed to be based on equality of opportunity, the history of race relations suggests the opposite. Perhaps the most influential early discussion of this disparity was Gunnar Myrdal's *An American Dilemma*, published in 1944. The book vividly exposed the contradictions between the ethos of freedom, justice, equality of opportunity and the actual experiences of African Americans in the United States.[4]

The links among desegregation, expanded educational opportunity, and the larger issue of equality of opportunity are very clear from the history of the desegregation movement. This movement, whose first phase culminated in the 1954 *Brown* decision outlawing *de jure* segregation in school, was the first orchestrated attempt in U.S. history to directly address inequality of educational opportunity. The NAACP strategically chose school segregation to be the camel's nose under the tent of the Jim Crow (segregated) society. That one of the nation's foremost civil rights organizations saw the attack on segregated schools as the opening salvo in the battle against society-wide inequality is a powerful example of the American belief that education has a pivotal role in promoting equality of opportunity.

Has desegregation succeeded? This is really three questions: First, to what extent are the nation's schools desegregated? Second, have desegregation efforts enhanced students' academic outcomes? Third, what are the long-term outcomes of desegregated educational experiences?

Since 1954, progress toward the desegregation of the nation's public schools has been uneven and limited. Blacks experienced little progress in desegregation until the mid-1960s when, in response to the civil rights movement, a series of federal laws, executive actions, and judicial decisions resulted in significant gains, especially in the South. Progress continued until 1988, when the effects of a series of federal court decisions and various local and national political developments precipitated marked trends toward the resegregation of Black students. Nationally, in 1994–1995, 33 percent of Black students attended majority White schools compared with the approximately 37 percent who attended majority White schools for much of the 1980s.[5]

Historically, Latinos were relatively less segregated than African Americans. However, from the mid-1960s to the mid-1990s there was a steady increase in the percentage of the Latino students who attended segregated schools. As a result, education for Latinos is now more segregated than it is for Blacks.

Given the long history of legalized segregation in the south, it is ironic that the South's school systems are now generally the country's most *de*segregated, while those in the northeast are the most intensely segregated. However, even desegregated schools are often resegregated at the classroom level by tracking or ability grouping. There is a strong relationship between race and social class, and racial isolation is often an outgrowth of residential seg-regation and socioeconomic background.

Has desegregation helped to equalize educational outcomes? A better question might be which desegregation programs under what circumstances accomplish which goals? Evidence from recent desegregation research sug-gests that, overall, children benefit academically and socially from well-run programs. Black students enjoy modest academic gains, while the academic achievement of White children is not hurt, and in some cases is helped, by de-segregation. In school systems which have undergone desegregation efforts, the racial gap in educational outcomes has generally been reduced, but not eliminated.

More important than short-term academic gains are the long-term con-sequence of desegregation for Black students. Compared to those who at-tended racially isolated schools, Black adults who experienced desegregated education as children are more likely to attend multiracial colleges and grad-uate from them, work in higher-status jobs, live in integrated neighborhoods, assess their abilities more realistically when choosing an occupation, and to report interracial friendships.[6]

Despite these modest, but positive, outcomes, in the last decade of the twentieth century, most American children attend schools segregated by race, ethnicity, and social class. Consequently, forty-five years of official federal in-terventions aimed at achieving equality of educational opportunity through school desegregation have only made small steps toward achieving that goal; children from different race and class backgrounds continue to receive segre-gated and, in many respects, unequal educations.

The Coleman Report

Largely because evidence introduced in the 1954 *Brown* case showed that re-sources in segregated Black and White schools were grossly unequal, Con-gress mandated in 1964 a national study of the "lack of availability of equality of educational opportunity for individuals due to race, color, religious, or na-tional origin in public schools." The authors of the subsequent study, James Coleman and his associates, expected to find glaring disparities in educational resources available to African-American and White students and that these differences would explain the substantial achievement differences between majority and minority students.

Instead, the Coleman Report, released in 1966, produced some very un-expected findings which became the underpinning for many subsequent edu-cational policies and programs. The researchers found that twelve years after *Brown*, most Americans still attended segregated schools but that the char-acteristics of Black and White schools (e.g., facilities, books, labs, teacher experience, and expenditures) were surprisingly similar. Apparently, segregated Southern districts had upgraded Black educational facilities in the wake of the *Brown* decision. Coleman and his colleagues also found that variations in school resources had relatively little to do with the variations in students' school performance. Instead, they found that family background influenced an individual's school achievement more than any other factor, including school characteristics.[7] Subsequent research has provided a better understanding of when, where, and how resources and school characteristics influence student outcomes.

However, at the time, the Coleman Report had dramatic and long-lasting effects. The report tended to deflect attention away from how schools operated and instead focused public policy upon poor and minority children and their families as the ultimate sources of unequal school outcomes. Numerous observers concluded incorrectly that schools had little to do with Black-White educational differences because they paid insufficient attention to another of the report's findings that implicated schools in inequality of educational outcomes. That finding showed that African-American and White achievement differences increased with every year of schooling. That is, the achievement gap between Black and White first graders was much smaller than the gap between twelfth graders. This finding suggested that, at best, schools reinforce the disadvantages of race and class and, at worst, are themselves a major source of educational inequality.

Although published over thirty years ago, the Coleman Report remains one of the most important and controversial pieces of social research ever completed in the United States. One of its many lasting results was a redefinition of the concept of equality of educational opportunity. The report made it clear that putting greater resources into schools, in and of itself, was not necessarily associated with greater student achievement or with eliminating the racial gap in school outcomes. In other words, resource levels alone were no longer considered a satisfactory measure of equality of educational opportunity. As a result, the Coleman Report helped reconceptualize the notion of equality of educational opportunity. It became a matter of equality of educational outcomes, measured in terms of academic achievement (performance) and attainment (amount of schooling completed) irrespective of race, gender, and socioeconomic background. This goal has yet to be reached in the United States.

Compensatory Education

A second outcome of the Coleman Report was widespread support for compensatory education. Policy makers interpreted the finding that family background was the strongest predictor of students' achievement as evidence of "cultural deprivation" among poor and minority families. This interpretation gave impetus to an education movement designed to compensate for the alleged cultural deficiencies of families that were neither middle class nor White, so that when so-called disadvantaged children came to school, they could compete without the handicaps of their background.

Beginning with the passage of the Elementary and Secondary Education Act in 1965, a series of educational programs offered low-income and underachieving children developmental preschool followed by a host of individualized programs in math, reading, and language arts once they arrived in elementary school. Examples of compensatory education programs include:

- Early childhood education such as Head Start
- Follow Through, where Head Start children, now in elementary school, continue to receive special programs
- Title I (formerly called Chapter I), which provides language arts and math programs plus food, medicine, and clothing to needy children in primary schools
- Guidance and counseling in secondary schools

Compensatory education programs have had a controversial history. Critics from the left charge that the underlying premise of compensatory education—that poor and minority families are deficient relative to middle-class White families—is racist and elitist. Critics on the right argue that compensatory education is a waste of time and money because the lower achievement scores of minority and poor children are due to their inferior intelligence. Policy critics charge that it is impossible to judge the effectiveness of compensatory education programs unless they are fully funded and implemented so that all eligible children receive services. Since the inception of compensatory education programs, less than half of eligible students have received services.

Despite criticism from such diverse quarters, the compensatory education movement survived the past thirty years. The Head Start program, for example, is currently embraced by a wide range of Americans who consider it a cost-effective strategy to help poor children do better in school. A growing body of research demonstrates the existence of both cognitive and social benefits from early childhood education for low-income and minority children. However, the achievement gaps between minority and White, and between working- and middle-class, children remain. Furthermore, evaluations of Title I and Follow Through have been unable to demonstrate unambiguous benefits. One must conclude that compensatory education, like desegregated education, has neither leveled the playing field nor eliminated racial or social class inequality in educational outcomes.

Human Capital Theory and Workforce Education Programs

The widely held belief that a good education is *the* meal ticket to reducing inequality receives its most sophisticated exposition in human capital theory, which holds that greater levels of education are investments in human beings' productive capacities. People who are poor, according to this theory, have had inadequate investments in their education. Over many decades, numerous education and training programs have been implemented, but the school-to-work transition remains problematic for many noncollege-bound youth. During the last third of this century, specific programs linked to anti-poverty efforts were implemented and eventually scrapped for failing to provide low-income youth with what they needed. While the Comprehensive Education and Training Act (CETA) and its successor, the Job Training and Partnership Act (JTPA), two of the best known programs, gave skill training to low-income youth, the jobs needed to employ them were simply not there. Moreover, JTPA graduates were no more likely to obtain a job than those without such training.

A variety of workforce education programs exist today in America's schools. These are attempts to provide broad-based technical skills to students, although they have not completely displaced the more traditional vocational education programs. However, current programs are of questionable value for reducing inequality for a number of reasons. First, there is a striking absence of bridges from schools to workplaces. Other than tapping into their personal networks, youth usually do not know alternative options for obtaining jobs. Schools rarely have outreach programs, and employers who hire entry-level workers only occasionally check grades and transcripts. The federal government's initiative for community-based one-stop job centers, where potential workers and employers can match their availabilities via computerized databases, may prove useful in the future by providing the necessary bridges and pathways from school to work. But they are only in their infancy.

A second reason to question the utility of these programs is that the human capital approach views the problem of inequality as a lack of worker skill, not a paucity of well-paying jobs. The poor often have a great deal of skills and education. What they lack are well-paying jobs in which to invest their skills. In fact, many studies indicate there is an adequate match between skill requirements of current jobs and those possessed by the workforce. Rather, the complaints of most employers are that entry-level new hires lack a strong work ethic, a problem human capital theory does not address.

The third reason to question the utility of workforce development education for reducing inequality has to do with the changing nature of the post-industrial economy. There is little certain knowledge of what the restructuring and globalization of the economy will mean for future workers. It is entirely possible that workforce education will prepare people for jobs which have been relocated to Mexico, Thailand, or India. Certainly, there is already evidence of such a trend. And the relocation of these jobs has more to do with the cost of labor in these nations than with the education or skill levels of Americans. It is not surprising, then, that educational reforms based on human capital theory have not, and cannot, substantially narrow race, class, and gender differences in equality of opportunity in this society.

Title IX

Title IX of the 1972 Higher Education Act is the primary federal law prohibiting sex discrimination in education. It states, "No person in the United States shall, on the basis of sex, be excluded from participation in, be denied benefit of, or be subjected to discrimination under any program or activity receiving Federal financial assistance." Until Title IX's passage, gender inequality in educational opportunity received minimal legislative attention. The act mandates gender equality of treatment in admission, courses, financial aid, counseling services, employment, and athletics.

The effect of Title IX upon college athletics has been especially controversial. While women constitute 53 percent of undergraduates, they are only 37 percent of college athletes. This is undoubtedly due to the complex interaction between institutional practices and gender-role socialization over the life course. Certainly, the fact that the vast majority of colleges spend much more money on recruiting and scholarships for male athletes contributes to the disparities.

In spring 1997, the U.S. Supreme Court refused to review a lower court's ruling in *Brown v. Cohen* that states in essence that Title IX requires universities to provide equal athletic opportunities for male and female students regardless of cost. Courts have generally upheld the following three-pronged test for compliance: (1) the percentage of athletes who are females should reflect the percentage of students who are female; (2) there must be a continuous record of expanding athletic opportunities for females athletes; and (3) schools must accommodate the athletic interests and abilities of female students. As of the ruling, very few universities were in compliance with the law.

Gender discrimination exists in other areas of education where it takes a variety of forms. For example, in K–12 education official curricular materials frequently feature a preponderance of male characters. Male and female characters typically exhibit traditional gender roles. Vocational education at the high school and college level remains gender-segregated to some degree. School administrators at all levels are overwhelmingly male although most teachers in elementary and secondary schools are female. In higher education, the situation is more complex. Faculty women in academia are found disproportionately in the lower ranks, are less likely to be promoted, and continue to earn less than their male colleagues.

Like the laws and policies aimed at eliminating race differences in school processes and outcomes, those designed to eliminate gender differences in educational opportunities have, at best, only narrowed them. Access to educational opportunity in the United States remains unequal for people of different gender, race, ethnic, and socioeconomic backgrounds.

EQUALITY OF EDUCATIONAL OPPORTUNITY AND EQUALITY OF INCOME

Despite the failures of these many programs to eliminate the inequality of educational opportunity over the past 45 years, there is one indicator of substantial progress: measured in median years, the gap in educational attainment between Blacks and Whites, and between males and females, has all but disappeared. In 1997, the median educational attainment of most groups was slightly more than twelve years. In the 1940s, by contrast, White males and females had a median educational attainment of just under nine years, African American males about five years, and African American women about six.

However, the main goal of educational reform is not merely to give all groups the opportunity to receive the same quality and quantity of education. According to the dominant ideology, the ultimate goal of these reforms is to provide equal educational opportunity in order to facilitate equal access to jobs, housing, and various other aspects of the American dream. It thus becomes crucial to examine whether the virtual elimination of the gap in educational attainment has been accompanied by a comparable decrease in other measures of inequality.

Of the various ways inequality can be measured, income is one of the most useful. Much of a person's social standing and access to the good things in life depends on his or her income.[8] Unfortunately, the dramatic progress in narrowing the gap in educational attainment has not been matched by a comparable narrowing of the gap in income inequality. Median individual earnings by race and gender indicate that White men still earn significantly more than any other group. Black men trail White men, and all women earn significantly less than all men. Even when occupation, experience, and level of education are controlled, women earn less than men, and Black men earn less than White men. It is only Black and White women with comparable educational credentials in similar jobs who earn about the same.

The discrepancy between the near elimination of the gap in median educational attainment and the ongoing gaps in median income is further evidence that addressing the inequality of educational opportunity is woefully insufficient for addressing broader sources of inequality throughout society.

This discrepancy can be explained by the nature of the U.S. political economy. The main cause of income inequality is the structure and operation of U.S. capitalism, a set of institutions which scarcely have been affected by the educational reforms discussed earlier. Greater equality of educational opportunity has not led to a corresponding decrease in income inequality because educational reforms do not create more good-paying jobs, affect gender-segregated and racially segmented occupational structures, or limit the mobility of capital either between regions of the country or between the United States and other countries. For example, no matter how good an education White working-class or minority youth may receive, it does nothing to alter the fact that thousands of relatively good paying manufacturing jobs have left northern inner cities for northern suburbs, the sunbelt, or foreign countries.

Many argue that numerous service jobs remain or that new manufacturing positions have been created in the wake of this capital flight. But these pay less than the departed manufacturing jobs, are often part-time or temporary, and frequently do not provide benefits. Even middle-class youth are beginning to fear the nature of the jobs which await them once they complete their formal education. Without changes in the structure and operation of the capitalist economy, educational reforms alone cannot markedly improve the social and economic position of disadvantaged groups. This is the primary reason that educational reforms do little to affect the gross social inequalities that inspired them in the first place.

BEYOND ATTAINMENT: THE PERSISTENCE OF EDUCATIONAL INEQUALITY

Educational reforms have not led to greater overall equality for several additional reasons. While race and gender gaps in educational attainment have narrowed considerably, educational achievement remains highly differentiated by social class, gender, and race. Many aspects of school processes and curricular content are deeply connected to race, social class, and gender inequality. But gross measures of educational outputs, such as median years of schooling completed, mask these indicators of inequality.

Not all educational experiences are alike. Four years of public high school in Beverly Hills are quite different from four years in an inner-city school. Family background, race, and gender have a great deal to do with whether a person goes to college and which institution of higher education she or he attends. The more privileged the background, the more likely a person is to attend an elite private university.

For example, according to Jacobs, women trail men slightly in representation in high status institutions of higher education because women are less likely to attend engineering programs and are more likely to be part-time students (who are themselves more likely to attend lower status institutions such as community colleges). Gender segregation in fields of study remains marked, with women less likely than men to study in scientific and mathematical fields. Furthermore, there is substantial race and ethnic segregation between institutions of higher education. Asian-Americans and Latinos are more segregated from Whites than are African-Americans. Whites and Asian-Americans are more likely to attend higher status universities than are African-Americans and Latinos.[9]

These patterns of race and gender segregation in higher education have direct implications for gender and race gaps in occupational and income attainment. Math and science degree recipients are more likely to obtain more lucrative jobs. A degree from a state college is not as competitive as one from an elite private university. Part of the advantage of attending more prestigious schools comes from the social networks to which a person has access and can join.

Another example of persistent inequality of educational opportunity is credential inflation. Even though women, minorities, and members of the working class now obtain higher levels of education than they did before, members of more privileged social groups gain even higher levels of education. At the same time, the educational requirements for the best jobs (those with the highest salaries, benefits, agreeable working conditions, autonomy, responsibility) are growing. Those with the most education from the best schools tend to be the top candidates for the best jobs. Because people from more privileged backgrounds are almost always in a better position to gain these desirable educational credentials, members of the working class, women, and minorities are still at a competitive disadvantage. Due to the dynamics of credential inflation, educational requirements previously necessary for the better jobs and now within the reach of many dispossessed groups are inadequate and insufficient in today's labor market. The credential inflation process keeps the already privileged one step (educational credential) ahead of the rest of the job seekers.[10]

One additional aspect of the persistent inequalities in educational opportunities concerns what sociologists of education call the hidden curriculum. This concept refers to two separate but related processes. The first is that the content and process of education differ for children according to their race, gender, and class. The second is that these differences reflect and thus help reproduce the inequalities based on race, gender, and class that characterize U.S. society as a whole.

One aspect of the hidden curriculum is the formal curriculum's ideological content. Anyon's work on U.S. history texts demonstrates that children from more privileged backgrounds are more likely to be exposed to rich, sophisticated, and complex materials than are their working-class counter-parts.[11] Another aspect of the hidden curriculum concerns the social organization of the school and the classroom. Some hidden curriculum theorists suggest that tracking, ability grouping, and conventional teacher-centered classroom interactions contribute to the reproduction of the social relations of production at the workplace. Lower-track classrooms are disproportionately filled with working-class and minority students. Students in lower tracks are more likely than those in higher tracks to be assigned repetitive exercises with low levels of cognitive challenge. Lower-track students are likely to work individually and to lack classroom experience with problem solving or other independent, creative activities. Such activities are more conducive to preparing students for working-class jobs than for professional and managerial positions. Correspondence principle theorists argue that educational experiences from preschool to high school are designed to differentially prepare students for their ultimate positions in the work force, and that a student's placement in various school programs is strongly related to her or his race and class origin. Critics charge that the correspondence principle has been applied in too deterministic and mechanical a fashion. Evidence abounds of student resistance to class, gender, and race differentiated education.[12] This is undoubtedly why so many students drop out or graduate from high school with minimal levels of literacy and formal skills. Nonetheless, hidden curriculum theory offers a compelling contribution to explanations of how and why school processes and outcomes are so markedly different according to the race, gender, and social class of students.

CONCLUSION

In this [essay] we have argued that educational reforms alone cannot reduce inequality. Nevertheless, education remains important to any struggle to reduce inequality. Moreover, education is more than a meal ticket; it is intrinsically worthwhile and crucially important for the survival of democratic society. Many of the programs discussed in this essay contribute to the enhancement of individuals' cognitive growth and thus promote important nonsexist, nonracist attitudes and practices. Many of these programs also make schools somewhat more humane places for adults and children. Furthermore, education, even reformist liberal education, contains the seeds of individual and social transformation. Those of us committed to the struggle against inequality cannot be paralyzed by the structural barriers that make it impossible for education to eliminate inequality. We must look upon the schools as arenas of struggle against race, gender, and social class inequality.

NOTES

1. This essay draws on an article by Roslyn Arlin Mickelson that appeared as "Education and the Struggle Against Race, Class and Gender Inequality," *Humanity and Society* 11(4) (1987): 440–64.

2. Ascertaining whether a set of beliefs constitutes the dominant ideology in a particular society involves a host of difficult theoretical and empirical questions. For this reason we use the term *putative dominant ideology*. For discussion of these questions, see Nicholas Abercrombie et al., *The Dominant Ideology Thesis* (London: George Allen & Unwin, 1980); James C. Scott, *Weapons of the Weak* (New Haven: Yale University Press, 1985); Stephen Samuel Smith, "Political Acquiescence and Beliefs About State Coercion" (unpublished Ph.D. dissertation, Stanford University, 1990).

3. Jennifer Hochschild, "The Double-Edged Sword of Equal Educational Opportunity." Paper presented at the meeting of the American Education Research Association, Washington, D.C., April 22, 1987.

4. Gunnar Myrdal, *An American Dilemma: The Negro Problem and Modern Democracy* (New York: Harper & Row, 1944).

5. Gary Orfield, Mark D. Bachmeier, David R. James, and Tamela Eitle, "Deepening Segregation in American Public Schools" (Cambridge, MA: Harvard Project on School Desegregation, 1997).

6. Amy Stuart Wells and Robert L. Crain, "Perpetuation Theory and the Long-Term Effects of School Desegregation," *Review of Educational Research* 64(4) (1994): 531–55.

7. J. S. Coleman et al., *Equality of Educational Opportunity* (Washington, D.C.: Government Printing Office, 1966).

8. To be sure, income does not measure class-based inequality, but there is a positive correlation between income and class. Income has the additional advantage of being easily quantifiable. Were we to use another measure of inequality, e.g., wealth, the disjuncture between it and increases in educational attainment would be even larger. Although the distribution of wealth in U.S. society has remained fairly stable since the Depression, the gap between rich and poor increased in the 1980s and 1990s. Although accurate data are difficult to obtain, a 1992 study by the Federal Reserve found that in 1989 the top one-half of one percent of households held 29 percent of the wealth held by all households.

9. Jerry A. Jacobs, "Gender and Race Segregation Between and Within Colleges" (paper presented at the Eastern Sociological Society, Boston, MA, April 1996).

10. Randall Collins, *The Credential Society* (New York: Academic Press, 1979).

11. Jean Anyon, "Social Class and the Hidden Curriculum of Work," *Journal of Education* 162(1) (1980): 67–92; Jean Anyon, "Social Class and School Knowledge," *Curriculum Inquiry* 10 (1981): 3–42.

12. Samuel Bowles and Herbert Gintis, *Schooling in Capitalist America: Educational Reform and the Contradictions of Economic Life* (New York: Basic Books, 1976); Roslyn Arlin Mickelson, "The Case of the Missing Brackets: Teachers and Social Reproduction," *Journal of Education* 169(2) (1987): 78–88.

THE SHREDDED NET

The End of Welfare as We Knew It

44

Valerie Polakow

As a Democratic president and a Republican-controlled House and Senate joined forces to end welfare for the "good of the poor," one of the last remaining vestiges of the federal social safety net—a minimal guarantee of public assistance for poor children—was decisively shredded. In a society where child poverty and family homelessness have become endemic characteristics, the signing of the new welfare legislation and its passage into law on 22 August 1996 was the culmination of a continuing decades-long public policy assault on poor single mothers with dependent children. However, this legislation, which repeals Title IVa of the Social Security Act of 1935, is the most far-reaching and radical of any antiwelfare initiative, which Senator Daniel Patrick Moynihan characterized as "the first step in dismantling a social contract that has been in place in the United States since at least the 1930s. Do not doubt that social security itself . . . will be next. . . . We would care for the elderly, the unemployed, the dependent children. Drop the latter; watch the others fall." [1]

In a "residual" welfare state such as the United States, market sovereignty is the foundation for the argument that the state should play a minimal role in the distribution of welfare and that individuals are essentially responsible for contracting their own welfare. [2] During the past decade, the boundaries of the public space have contracted, with narrowed public commitments and a discourse that has fostered "self-reliance." Limited public benefits have always been organized in means-tested assistance schemes that target particular segments of the population in stigmatizing ways. In such a residual welfare state, women alone—divorced, separated, or unmarried mothers—are a constituency at risk, disproportionately poor and facing an alarming array of obstacles and impediments to their autonomy. [3]

Furthermore, the impact of global capitalism on domestic infrastructures has been far-reaching; exporting jobs, downsizing, outsourcing, and increasing numbers of nonunionized contract workers all represent the face of the meaner, leaner, global economy. The North American Free Trade Agreement (NAFTA), which was implemented in 1994, caused seventy-five thousand

From: *Sage Race Relations Abstracts* 22, no. 3 (1997).

U.S. workers to lose jobs and displaced more than a million and a half Mexican workers. In addition, as corporations sell the notion that international competition requires greater "flexibility," more and more part-time workers without benefits are hired, and corporate lobbying of lawmakers promotes government deregulation, the cutting of overtime pay, and the gutting of union shops. In all three NAFTA countries—the United States, Canada, and Mexico—real wages are actually far below increases in productivity. In Mexico real wages in May 1996 were 35 percent below pre-1994 levels, and in Canada and the United States real wages have stagnated and the proportion of full-time workers in poverty continues to grow.[4] While public infrastructures crumble and income inequality soars, powerful global corporations have expanded beyond the boundaries of the nation-state, and, increasingly, beyond the boundaries of governments. Korten points out that between 1980 and 1994 the *Fortune* 500 companies shed 4.4 million jobs, while sales increased 1.4 times and assets increased 2.3 times! Hence, he argues, in an unfettered market economy, "which responds to money, not needs, the rich win this competition every time. . . . The average CEO of a large corporation now receives a compensation package of more than 3.7 million per year. Those same corporations employ 1/20th of 1% of the world's population, but they control 25% of the world's output and 70% of world trade. Of the world's hundred largest economies, fifty are now corporations."[5]

Within the United States, the march toward privatization inexorably continues—schools, prisons, city services, transportation—and, since the passage of the new welfare law, privatized welfare, in which giant corporations vie for contracts to run welfare-to-work programs, is creating what the *New York Times* described as "the business opportunity of a lifetime."[6] The new law permits states to buy both welfare services and gatekeepers who screen eligibility and determine benefits. Lockheed Martin, the formidable $30-billion "giant of the weapons industry" and a major beneficiary of corporate welfare subsidies, plans to close one of its plants in New Jersey; as one congressman put it, "They would be getting a subsidy to lay off these folks and then could be getting additional money from the government to help these people get off welfare."[7]

As such "wealthfare" flourishes and public entitlements are reduced or eliminated, what happens to those who live in the broadening swath of the Other America? What is life like under a shredded net?

LIFE UNDER THE SHREDDED NET

I lived in public housing in Detroit, I stayed there for two years, and I know the debilitating factors that it takes just to survive. People have tried and tried and tried to find jobs; it's a vicious circle and after you get the door slammed in your face, you don't have the will to go out there and fight anymore. . . . I got a little slip in my son's pocket saying I owed $900 in child care and saying don't bring my children back until that is paid. . . . I couldn't do it so I tried to go back on welfare. It was either pay my rent or pay child care . . . so I called social services and asked them about getting my benefits again and my worker said I had to wait two months, so I stopped work in November and she said I wouldn't get any benefits until January. I asked my worker, "How'm I supposed to live?" and she said, "It's not for me to tell you!"

—Tanya, a single mother of two young children[8]

At the present time in the United States, 30 percent of all families with children under eighteen are single-parent families, with single-mother families constituting the vast majority, or 82 percent. In addition, more than 40 percent of single-mother families are living in poverty.[9] However, the largest constituency of poor Americans is children: in 1995, 15.3 million children lived in poverty in the United States, and the younger in age, the higher the risk. While 21 percent of children under eighteen are classified as living in poverty, 25 percent of children under six and 27 percent under three live in poverty, the majority of whom reside in poor, single-mother households.[10]

The term *feminization of poverty* has been widely used to describe the particular plight of women in the United States who experience occupational segregation and workplace discrimination, disproportionately occupy part-time service-sector jobs with few or no benefits, perform unpaid domestic work at home and retain primary care of children. As single mothers, they are disproportionately poor and face an alarming array of obstacles that threaten their family stability.[11] By the late 1980s women and their children had become a significant majority of America's poor.[12] Unmet needs in housing, health care, and child care have coalesced to form a triple crisis where single mothers, as both providers for and nurturers of their children, cannot sustain family viability when they are low-wage earners, with no family support provisions in place to act as a buffer against the ravages of the market economy. In 1995, a full-time minimum wage salary was $8,800 a year—$3,000 less than under the federal poverty line for a single-mother family of three. And while the minimum wage was raised by 50 cents to $4.75 an hour in October 1996, full-time minimum wage work still yields a wage well below the poverty line. The child care crisis compounds the situation, with many low-wage mothers unable to afford the high costs of private child care.

Single mothers also make up 70–90 percent of homeless families nationwide,[13] and more than 50 percent of homeless families become homeless because the mother flees domestic violence.[14] One in four homeless persons is now a child younger than eighteen.[15] Furthermore, reports from the Food and Research Action Center indicate that four million children under twelve go hungry during part of each month, and there are now ten million children who have no health insurance coverage.

It is clear that the increasing economic vulnerability of the single-mother family represents a child welfare crisis of growing magnitude that has been further exacerbated by recent welfare repeal legislation. Mothers now struggling to survive on public assistance are being ordered to pay their dues and take up paid or unpaid work—part of the punitive rehabilitation of the "welfare culture" that defines the new "opportunity society," promoted by Newt Gingrich and his fellow Republican supporters, in which the poor are to assume personal responsibility for their family's poverty. Practically speaking, that means that mothers with dependent children are coerced into taking up low-wage jobs, or "voluntary" indentured servitude, as a condition for receiving any benefits, with no guarantee of adequate child care services or subsidies. The blatant failure of the new personal-responsibility legislation to address the daily survival needs of economically vulnerable single mothers clearly threatens their children's basic physical, social, and emotional development.

Unlike other industrialized democracies, the United States, as a residual welfare state, has no national health care system and no universal family support policies such as paid maternity and parental leave, national child/family allowances, or a national subsidized child care system for infants and preschool children.[16] Head Start, the national early childhood intervention program for poor children developed during the "War on Poverty" of the 1960s, was available to only 36 percent of income-eligible children during 1995.[17]

Despite the dismal record of the United States in developing public policies that provide for the basic health, shelter, and daily living needs of its most vulnerable citizens—poor women and their children—female and child poverty is still cast as a "moral" problem, tied to public rhetoric about "family values" and "family breakdown," which in turn is used to rationalize further cuts in public assistance. The structural evidence of poverty wages, contingent no-benefit jobs, corporate downsizing, racial and gender discrimination, and the growing number of job-poor isolated and destitute communities[18] is ignored in favor of "blaming the victim" discourses that reduce poor women to caricatured public parasites or promiscuous sluts, living it up at taxpayer expense. Rarely are their grim survival struggles chronicled, or their children's traumatic lives examined, as part of the consequences of a trickle-down market economy that offers few protections to those who live in the other America.[19]

While Social Security for elderly Americans is still considered an earned entitlement, a Social Security system for children (who in turn must depend on their parents' benefits) forms part of a completely different discourse in the United States, because the parents, specifically poor mothers of dependent children, are viewed as undeserving of government support. The discourse about poor mothers and their children is couched in "moral" and "personal responsibility" frames and, more recently, in terms of "productive work." Taking care of one's own children, however, is not viewed as productive work if one is poor, and having children when poor is perceived as both irresponsible and/or immoral.

It is significant to note that during the House debates in 1995 on the original welfare reform bill, ironically titled the Personal Responsibility Act, which was proposed as part of the Republican's Contract with America, poor mothers receiving public assistance were publicly vilified by Republican lawmakers as "breeding mules," as "alligators," and as "monkeys." Earlier, House Ways and Means chair Representative Clay Shaw Jr., who shepherded welfare repeal legislation through the House, stated, "It may be like hitting a mule with a two-by-four, but you've got to get their attention."[20] When the bill reached the Senate, Senator Phil Gramm demanded, "We've got to get a provision that denies more and more cash benefits to women who have more and more babies while on welfare."[21]

The antiwelfare and "underclass" punitive discourses that have targeted single mothers and pregnant teens have promoted a continuing public perception of poverty as a private and behavioral condition leading to proliferating racialized and sexualized fictions about *them;* the causes of family poverty are seen as rooted in failed and fallen women, failed children, and a failed work ethic—but not in the actual consequence of public policies that produce family poverty by omission and commission. The ravages of a market economy; the lack of affordable, quality child care; the lack of safe and affordable family housing; the absence of universal health care; and the traumas of domestic violence—all coalesce to create a tangled web of obstacles that entrap poor single mothers in poverty, destitution, and homelessness. Hence, a national family policy (or absence thereof) is a potent force in women's lives, either weaving a safety net to support family viability or shredding the net and destabilizing family existence.

In the Scandinavian countries, for example, where family policies are comparatively strong and where universal entitlements such as paid parental leave, health care, child care, absent-parent child support, and housing subsidies are in place, chronic single mother and child poverty has largely been eliminated.[22] Yet, despite the evidence of abysmal life conditions for the poorest Americans, the minimal safety net that formerly existed in the United States has now been dismantled.

The welfare repeal law that passed the House and Senate with bipartisan support in 1996 could hardly be more emblematic of a postmodern market individualism—eliminating "big government" and public responsibility in favor of the surreal privatized self—where to have is to be. . . .

NOTES

1. *New York Times,* 2 August 1996.
2. Gösta Esping-Anderson and Walter Korpi, "From Poor Relief to Institutional Welfare States: The Development of Scandinavian Social Policy," in *The Scandinavian*

Model: Welfare States and Welfare Research, ed. R. Erikson, E. J. Hansen, S. Ringen, and H. Uusitalo (Armonk, N.Y.: M. E. Sharpe, 1987), 39–74.

3. Valerie Polakow, "Savage Distributions: Welfare Myths and Daily Lives," *Sage Race Relations Abstracts* 19, no. 4 (1994): 3–29.

4. Sarah Anderson, John Cavanagh, and David Ranney, "NAFTA: Trinational Fiasco," *Nation*, 15/22 July 1996, 26–28.

5. David C. Korten, "The Limits of the Earth," *Nation*, 15/22 July 1996, 16, 18.

6. *New York Times*, 15 September 1996.

7. Ibid., A14.

8. Excerpt from an interview conducted by the author and published in *Nation*, 1 May 1995.

9. U.S. Bureau of the Census, "Poverty in the United States," *Current Population Reports*. Series P60-194 (Washington, D.C.: Government Printing Office, 1995).

10. Children's Defense Fund, *The State of America's Children: Yearbook* (Washington, D.C.: Children's Defense Fund, 1996).

11. Barbara Ehrenreich and Frances Fox Piven, "The Feminization of Poverty: When the Family Wage System Breaks Down," *Dissent* 31 (Summer 1984): 162–68; Gertrude S. Goldberg and Eleanor Kremen, *The Feminization of Poverty: Only in America?* (New York: Greenwood Press 1990); Linda Gordon, ed., *Women, the State and Welfare* (Madison: University of Wisconsin Press 1990); Diana Pearce, "The Feminization of Poverty: Women, Work and Welfare," *Urban and Social Change Review* 11, nos. 1–2 (1978): 28–36; Valerie Polakow, *Lives on the Edge: Single Mothers and their Children in the Other America* (Chicago: University of Chicago Press, 1993); Valerie Polakow, "On a Tightrope without a Net," *Nation*, May 1995, 590–92.

12. U.S. Bureau of the Census, "Poverty in the United States," *Current Population Reports*. Series P60-163 (Washington, D.C.: Government Printing Office, 1989).

13. Ellen L. Bassuk, "Who Are the Homeless Families? Characteristics of Sheltered Mothers and Children," *Community Mental Health Journal* 26 (1990): 425–34; Marcia Steinbock, "Homeless Female-headed Families: Relationships at Risk," *Marriage and Family Review* 20 (1995): 143–59.

14. National Clearinghouse for the Defense of Battered Women, *Statistics Packet*, 3rd ed. (Philadelphia: National Clearinghouse for the Defense of Battered Women, 1994).

15. National Law Center on Homelessness and Poverty, *A Foot in the Schoolhouse Door* (Washington, D.C.: National Law Center on Homelessness and Poverty, 1995).

16. Sheila B. Kamerman and Alfred J. Kahn, eds., *Child Care, Parental Leave, and the Under 3's: Policy Innovation in Europe* (New York: Auburn House, 1991); Sheila B. Kamerman and Alfred J. Kahn, *Starting Right: How America Neglects Its Youngest Children and What We Can Do about It* (New York: Oxford University Press, 1995); Polakow, *Lives on the Edge*.

17. Children's Defense Fund, *The State of America's Children: Yearbook* (1996).

18. James Jennings, "Persistent Poverty in the United States: Review of Theories and Explanations," *Sage Race Relations Abstracts* 19, no. 1 (1994): 5–34; William J. Wilson, "Work," *New York Times Magazine*, 18 August 1996.

19. Polakow, "Savage Distributions."

20. Quoted in Jason DeParle, "Momentum Builds for Cutting Back Welfare System," *New York Times*, 13 November 1994.

21. Quoted in Robin Toner, "Senate Passes Bill to Abolish Guarantees of Aid for the Poor," *New York Times*, 20 September 1995.

22. Sheila Kamerman and Alfred Kahn, *Child Care, Parental Leave, and the Under 3's;* Kamerman and Kahn, *Starting Right;* Valerie Polakow, "Family Policy in the United States and Denmark: A Cross-national Study of Discourse and Practice," *Early Education and Development* 8, no. 3 (1997) 242–60.

AID TO DEPENDENT CORPORATIONS   45

Exposing Federal Handouts to the Wealthy

Chuck Collins

In 1992 rancher J. R. Simplot of Grandview, Idaho, paid the U.S. government $87,000 for grazing rights on federal lands, about one-quarter the rate charged by private landowners. Simplot's implicit subsidy from U.S. taxpayers, $261,000, would have covered the welfare costs of about 60 poor families. With a net worth exceeding $500 million, it's hard to argue that Simplot needed the money.

Since 1987, American Barrick Resources Corporation has pocketed $8.75 billion by extracting gold from a Nevada mine owned by the U.S. government. But Barrick has paid only minimal rent to the Department of the Interior. In 1992 Barrick's founder was rewarded for his business acumen with a $32 million annual salary.

Such discounts are only one form of corporate welfare, dubbed "wealthfare" by some activists, that U.S. taxpayers fund. At a time when Congress is attempting to slash or eliminate the meager benefits received by the poor, we are spending far more to subsidize wealthy corporations and individuals. Wealthfare comes in five main varieties: discounted user fees for public resources; direct grants; corporate tax reductions and loopholes; giveaways of publicly funded research and development (R&D) to private profit-making companies; and tax breaks for wealthy individuals.

Within the Clinton administration Secretary of Labor Robert Reich and Budget Director Alice Rivlin have attacked "welfare for the rich." Armed with

From: *Dollars & Sense* 1 (May/June 1995): 15–17, 40. Reprinted by permission.

a study from the Progressive Policy Institute, the Democratic Leadership Council's think tank, Reich floated the notion that over $200 billion in corporate welfare could be trimmed over the next five years. In a sign of the problems with our two-party system, Clinton discouraged Reich from taking this campaign further, for fear of alienating big Democratic Party funders.

TAX AVOIDANCE

The largest, yet most invisible, part of wealthfare is tax breaks for corporations and wealthy individuals. The federal Office of Management and Budget (OMB) estimates that these credits, deductions, and exemptions, called "tax expenditures," will cost $440 billion in fiscal 1996. This compares, for example, to the $16 billion annual federal cost of child support programs.

Due both to lower basic tax rates and to myriad loopholes, corporate taxes fell from one-third of total federal revenues in 1953 to less than 10% today (see "Disappearing Corporate Taxes," *Dollars & Sense*, July 1994). Were corporations paying as much tax now as they did in the 1950s, the government would take in another $250 billion a year—more than the entire budget deficit.

The tax code is riddled with tax breaks for the natural resource, construction, corporate agri-business, and financial industries. Some serve legitimate purposes, or did at one time. Others have been distorted to create tax shelters and perpetuate bad business practices. During the 1993 budget battle, New Jersey Senator Bill Bradley attacked the "loophole writing" industry in Washington, where inserting a single sentence into the tax laws can save millions, even billions, in taxes for a corporate client.

Depreciation on equipment and buildings, for example, is a legitimate business expense. But the "accelerated depreciation" rule allows corporations to take this deduction far faster than their assets are wearing out. This simply lets businesses make billions of dollars in untaxed profits. One estimate is that this loophole will cost $164 billion over the next five years.

One particularly generous tax break is the foreign tax credit, which allows U.S.-based multinational corporations to deduct from their U.S. taxes the income taxes they pay to other nations. Donald Bartlett and James Steele, authors of *America: Who Really Pays the Taxes*, say that by 1990 this writeoff was worth $25 billion a year.

While in many cases this credit is a valid method of preventing double taxation on profits earned overseas, the oil companies have used it to avoid most of their U.S. tax obligations. Until 1950, Saudi Arabia had no income tax, but charged royalties on all oil taken from their wells. Such royalties are a payment for use of a natural resource. They are a standard business expense, payable *before* a corporation calculates the profits on which it will pay taxes.

These royalties were a major cost to ARAMCO, the oil consortium op erating there (consisting of Exxon, Mobil, Chevron, and Texaco). But since royalties are not income taxes, they could not be used to reduce Exxon and friends' tax bills back home.

When King Saud decided to increase the royalty payments, ARAMCO convinced him to institute a corporate income tax and to substitute this for the royalties. The tax was a sham, since it applied only to ARAMCO, not to any other business in Saudi Arabia's relatively primitive economy. The result was that the oil companies avoided hundreds of millions of dollars in their American taxes. Eventually the other oil-producing nations, including Kuwait, Iraq, and Nigeria, followed suit, at huge cost to the U.S. Treasury.

In contrast to the ARAMCO problem, many corporate executive salaries should not be counted as deductible expenses. These salaries and bonuses are often so large today that they constitute disguised profits. Twenty years ago the average top executive made 34 times the wages of the firm's lowest paid workers. Today the ratio is 140 to 1. The Hospital Corporation of America, for example, paid its chairman $127 million in 1992—$61,000 an hour! In 1993 the Clinton administration capped the deductibility of salaries at $1 million, but the law has several loopholes that allow for easy evasion.

CHICKEN McNUGGETS
AND OTHER VITAL MATTERS

Taxes are but one form of wealthfare. Subsidized use of public resources, as with J. R. Simplot's grazing and American Barrick's mining, is also widespread. Barrick's profit-making was allowed by the General Mining Law of 1872. Just last year the government finally put a one-year moratorium on this resource-raiding.

In a manner similar to the mining situation, the U.S. Forest Service under-charges timber companies for the logs they take from publicly owned land. The Forest Service also builds roads and other infrastructure needed by the timber industry, investing $140 million last year.

Many corporations also receive direct payments from the federal government. The libertarian Cato Institute argues that every cabinet department "has become a conduit for government funding of private industry. Within some cabinet agencies, such as the U.S. Department of Agriculture and the Department of Commerce, almost every spending program underwrites private business."

Agriculture subsidies typically flow in greater quantities the larger is the recipient firm. Of the $1.4 billion in annual sugar price supports, for example, 40% of the money goes to the largest 1% of firms, with the largest ones receiving more than $1 million each.

The Agriculture Department also spends $110 million a year to help U.S. companies advertise abroad. In 1992 Sunkist Growers got $10 million, Gallo Wines $4.5 million, M&M/Mars $1.1 million, McDonalds $466,000 to promote Chicken McNuggets, and American Legend Fur Coats $1.2 million.

The Progressive Policy Institute estimates that taxpayers could save $114 billion over five years by eliminating or restricting such direct subsidies. Farm subsidies, for example, could be limited to only small farmers.

The government also pays for scientific research and development, then allows the benefits to be reaped by private firms. This occurs commonly in medical research. One product, the anti-cancer drug Taxol, cost the U.S. government $32 million to develop as part of a joint venture with private industry. But in the end the government gave its share to Bristol-Myers Squibb, which now charges cancer patients almost $1,000 for a three-week supply of the drug.

WHO IS ENTITLED?

Beyond corporate subsidies, the government also spends far more than necessary to help support the lifestyles of wealthy individuals. This largess pertains to several of the most expensive and popular "entitlements" in the federal budget, such as Social Security, Medicare, and the deductibility of interest on home mortgages. As the current budget-cutting moves in Congress demonstrate, such universal programs have much greater political strength than do programs targeted solely at low-income households.

While this broad appeal is essential to maintain, billions of dollars could be saved by restricting the degree to which the wealthy benefit from universal programs. If Social Security and Medicare payments were denied to just the richest 3% of households this would reduce federal spending by $30 to $40 billion a year—more than the total federal cost of food stamps.

Similarly, mortgage interest is currently deductible up to $1 million per home, justifying the term "mansion subsidy" for its use by the rich. The government could continue allowing everyone to use this deduction, but limit it to $250,000 per home. This would affect only the wealthiest 5% of Americans, but would save taxpayers $10 billion a year.

Progressive organizations have mounted a renewed focus on the myriad handouts to the corporate and individual rich. One effort is the Green Scissors coalition, an unusual alliance of environmental groups such as Friends of the Earth, and conservative taxcutters, such as the National Taxpayers Union. Last January Green Scissors proposed cutting $33 billion over the next ten years in subsidies that they contend are wasteful and environmentally damaging. These include boondoggle water projects, public land subsidies, highways, foreign aid projects, and agricultural programs.

Another new organization, Share the Wealth, is a coalition of labor, religious, and economic justice organizations. It recently launched the "Campaign for Wealth-Fare Reform," whose initial proposal targets over $35 billion in annual subsidies that benefit the wealthiest 3% of the population. The campaign rejects the term "corporate welfare" because it reinforces punitive anti-welfare sentiments. Welfare is something a humane society guarantees to people facing poverty, unemployment, low wages, and racism. "Wealthfare," in contrast, is the fees and subsidies extracted from the public by the wealthy and powerful—those who are least in need.

Today's Congress is not sympathetic to such arguments. But the blatant anti-poor, pro-corporate bias of the Republicans has already begun to awaken a dormant public consciousness. This will leave more openings, not less, for progressives to engage in public education around the true nature of government waste.

References

Bartlett, Donald, and James Steele. 1994. *America: Who Really Pays the Taxes?* New York: Simon & Schuster.

Crittendon, Anne. 1993. *Killing the Sacred Cows.* New York: Penguin Books.

Friends of the Earth. 1995. *Green Scissors Report: Cutting Wasteful and Environmentally Harmful Spending and Subsidies.* Washington, DC: Green Scissors Campaign of Citizens United to Terminate Subsidies.

Shapiro, Robert. 1994. *Cut-and-Invest to Compete and Win: A Budget Strategy for American Growth.* Washington, DC: Progressive Policy Institute.

Shields, Janice C. 1994. *Aid to Dependent Corporations.* Washington, DC: Essential Information.

THOUGHTS ON CLASS, RACE, AND PRISON

46

Alan Berkman and Tim Blunk

Having been locked up as political prisoners for the past five years, we have found a lot in several recent articles which was familiar and thought provoking. Certain descriptions of ping-ponging from jail to jail could be a log of some of our own trips conducted by the Bureau of Prisons (BoP), and we can verify accounts of how prisoners typically support one another. Perhaps most importantly, we strongly agree with the view—best expressed in an article by Sam Day published in the October 13, 1989 issue of *Isthmus*—that the threat of prison should not deter political activists from acting. We are concerned, though, that in so vividly portraying his own experience and utilizing it to demystify prison life, he may have played into some common misrepresentations of life in U.S. prisons.

First, a word about our own experiences. We've each spent time in prison for a variety of politically motivated acts. One of us (Alan Berkman) spent two years in a number of county jails in the Philadelphia area. The other (Tim Blunk) spent a year in New York's Riker's Island. We've both been in a number of federal prisons, including the BoP's most repressive facility at Marion, Illinois. For the past eighteen months, we've been together in the equivalent of a county jail in Washington, D.C., where we and four women activists face federal charges of resisting U.S. war crimes through "violent and illegal means" (we call this the Resistance Conspiracy Case). Tim is presently serving a fifty-eight year sentence; Alan, twelve years. Having spent considerable time in the whole range of penal institutions, from county jails where most prisoners are pre-trial to Marion, where the average sentence is forty years, we've been struck by how directly prisons reflect the social and economic realities of society as a whole.

We live in a country where large numbers of people, particularly young Afro-American, Latino, and Native American women and men, have been written off by society. Government leaders look at the human devastation caused by their policies and declare war on the victims (the "war on drugs"). The racism and malignant neglect that permeate the schools, the labor mar-

From: Alan Berkman and Tim Blunk, "Thoughts on Class, Race, and Prison," in *Cages of Steel: The Politics of Imprisonment in the United States*, eds. Ward Churchill and J. J. Vanderwell (Washington, DC: Maisonnueve Press, 1992), pp. 190–93. Reprinted by permission.

ket, the welfare system and social services of the Third World, and poor white neighborhoods of our cities bear their inevitable fruit in the prisons. In prison, though, even the usual facade of "fairness" and "justice" by which such inequity is usually accompanied is dropped.

There are almost a million people in U.S. jails, state and federal prisons. More than ninety percent of these prisoners are in county jails and state prisons. D.C. jail, for example, is filled to capacity with poor, mis-educated, profoundly alienated young Afro-American men and women. It's a warehouse. There are no programs, no contact visiting, no privacy, and most importantly, no justice.

Particularly for political activists who are white and middle class, prison can be one of the few places where we look at America from the bottom up. We can understand poverty differently when we live with young people who've never had $20 in their pocket and who are constantly bombarded with the Gucci ads, the BMWs on *Miami Vice,* and the idea of free trips to Rio on *The Price is Right.* In a consumer society, if you've got nothing, you're considered to be nothing, and the frustration of this reality leads people into crime and drugs. You can see the deadness and despair in the eyes of too many of the people around you as they realize the American Dream is not for them now, and probably wasn't from the day they were born into the ghetto, the barrio or the reservation. And you'll get a feeling in your gut about the rage racism and poverty generate in the hearts of the oppressed. In fact, if you allow yourself, you'll learn quite a lot about the feelings that accompany that word, "oppressed."

What we've come to understand ever more deeply from our experience as prisoners is that the essence of oppression lies in dehumanization and disrespect. Being oppressed isn't just being a bit poorer or having a rougher life than your oppressor; it means being treated as if you're less of a human being than they are. For instance, we've consistently experienced the fact that you can be getting along okay with the guards and prison officials when they suddenly do something which is not only totally outrageous, but often a complete violation of their own supposed rule structure. You call them on it, and their response is to look at you—*through* you would be more accurate—as if you just weren't there. It doesn't matter a bit whether you're right or wrong. They deny that you have the right even to hold an opinion on the matter. It cuts at the very core of your sense of humanity and self-worth. It is infuriating and degrading.

Self-worth. Dignity. Self-respect. These are the feelings prison consciously or unconsciously is designed to destroy. These are the same feelings that racism and economic inequality in society work to destroy in the poor and people of color. This is why we believe Sam and others err when they reduce prison life to "three hots [meals] and a cot" and other minor indignities. It's like reducing chattel slavery to hard work, bad pay and poor living conditions. It leaves out the truth of the human dimension of oppression. And it leaves out the human reaction to prison conditions: rebellion. Prison "riots" are fundamentally slave rebellions.

Over the past few weeks, there have been one major and two minor prison uprisings in the Pennsylvania prison system. At Camp Hill, where prisoners destroyed much of the prison, the precipitating event seems trivial: the prison cancelled the semi-annual family day picnics where prisoners' relatives can bring home-cooked food and eat with their loved ones out on the yard. What's the big deal about two afternoons per year? Well, at one level, when you don't have much, even a *little* more deprivation hurts rather badly, especially when that deprivation concerns those precious bits of time you can spend with those closest to you and when you manage to feel most fully human. At a deeper level, the arbitrariness of the prison officials' decision in Pennsylvania gave the prisoners a clear message that they had nothing at all coming to them: *everything* is a "privilege," *nothing* is a right. The oppressor giveth, the oppressor taketh away. The oppressed have nothing to say in the matter, one way or the other. The oppressed—the prisoner in this instance—is a cipher, a statistic, nothing more than an animal whose basic needs of calories, shelter and waste disposal must (usually) be met. No more.

The "senseless violence" of burning buildings and smashing equipment which marked the Camp Hill rebellion—and which has marked prison uprisings from Attica to Atlanta, New Mexico, Los Angeles, and elsewhere—is, perhaps paradoxically, the most basic assertion of human dignity and self-respect. "We do have a say," the prisoners are insisting. "We will exercise our rights as human beings one way or another, either as reasonable human beings in a reasonable situation, or this way if you insist the situation remain unreasonable. But either way you can ultimately do nothing to provide our demonstration of the fact that *we are people*." It is a very human response to a very inhuman situation, the same impulse which led to the great ghetto uprisings of Watts, Detroit and Newark during the '60s, and which has led to similar phenomena in places like Miami during the '80s.

Political activists who come to jail and are able to keep their eyes and hearts open will learn an enormous amount, both about themselves and about the world they live in. How do we deal with our own race/class biases to build principled relationships with those we live with? If we're white, how do we respond when the Aryan Brotherhood tells us they'll kick our ass if we eat with Afro-American, Latino or American Indian prisoners in the *de facto* segregated mess hall? How do we struggle against the pervasive and intense sexism in men's prisons? How do we remain caring and giving people without allowing ourselves to be taken advantage of and disrespected? How do we decide when to directly confront the power of the officials, and when not to? When do we get involved in other people's beefs, whether among prisoners or between prisoners and guards?

There's a lot to learn in prison, although it's certainly not the only, or even necessarily the best, place to learn it. Whatever else may be said, time spent behind bars—no more or less than any other sort of time—need never be "wasted." We agree with Sam and others when they say that fear of prison should never be paralyzing. While locked up, you'll more than likely get in shape, have the opportunity to read many of the books you always meant to plow through but never managed to get around to, learn to write letters which say more than just "howdy-do." Most importantly, you'll finally have the chance to identify with the oppressed on a gut level which is typically absent from the life experiences of most Euro-Americans. You'll come to understand power relationships in a new and far more meaningful way. And we're willing to bet that you'll come out more committed than ever to the need for fundamental social change.

IV

Analyzing Social Issues

In the United States, public debates about issues such as multicultural education, abortion, school prayer, and welfare reform all reflect race, class, and gender arrangements in society. Race, class, and gender are systemic features of American society and do not change rapidly; however, the issues they generate change over time. Thinking inclusively about race, class, and gender can help us analyze contemporary social issues in at least three ways.

First, themes that emerge as social issues—affirmative action, immigration, and welfare reform, among others—are products of social institutions and institutional policies reflecting race, class, and gender arrangements. Since social institutions themselves are framed by race, class, and gender politics, social issues reflect these institutional politics. The organization of health care in the United States offers a compelling instance of how the politics of race, class, and gender operate. Depending on their placement in the race, class, and gender system, different groups have widely varying patterns of health and illness. Something as fundamental as who gets to live and who is left to die reflects the politics of race, class, and gender. Death rates for diabetes, for example—a disease exacerbated by poor nutrition and health care—are noticeably higher among African American, Latina, and Native American women than among Asian Americans and Whites. Access to health care also reflects the politics of race, class, and gender. People of color are much less likely than Whites to have health insurance. About 10 percent of Whites report they have no health coverage, compared to 17 percent of Asians, 20 percent of African Americans and Native Americans, and 33 percent of Latinos (O'Hare 1992: 17). Race, class, and gender also shape the contours of health research and health care delivery. For example, differences in funding for breast cancer research and heart disease research speak to the differential power of men and women in the health care system. Similarly, funding for infertility treatments for middle-class White couples is quite different from ongoing efforts to control the fertility of poor women via funding for sterilization.

Second, how social issues are presented and understood also operates within a race-, class-, and gender-inclusive framework. Media representations of homelessness provide an example of how dominant ideologies frame American understandings of important social issues. Increasing levels of underemployment coupled with a housing shortage of affordable, low-income housing pushed many people into poverty in the 1980s. The result was a large increase in the number of homeless people in the United States. But while the social issue of homelessness affected individuals and families across race, class, and gender groups, not all segments of the homeless population were seen as equally worthy of assistance. Building on longstanding notions of the deserving and undeserving poor, newly homeless families—especially women with dependent children—garnered more sympathy than groups long seen as part of the undeserving poor—namely, single men, persons with addictions, veterans, and the mentally ill. Moreover, racial politics intersected with class and gender to subdivide the homeless further: White families were seen as more deserving of aid than people of color, especially African Americans. Moreover, despite the centrality of ideologies of race, class, and gender in shaping understandings of homelessness, the importance of race, class, and gender to these understandings typically remains hidden. This is because the same social institutions that are organized through race, class, and gender simultaneously use ideologies to obscure how homelessness and other social issues reflect the politics of race, class, and gender.

Third, since current arrangements of race, class, and gender create social issues, an inclusive framework is required to effectively address such issues. It is not enough to critique existing social structures; we must also use our understanding of race, class, and gender to analyze existing social issues. For example, how might the United States redesign health care to make it equitable and responsive to all citizens? How might American communities provide safe, affordable housing so that everyone has a home? Not only do social institutions structure and legitimate existing race, class, and gender power relations, but individuals and groups use these same social institutions as sites of struggle. Thinking inclusively allows us to create alternative analyses of social issues and more effectively use our social locations to effect change.

As an example, consider the environment. Thinking narrowly about the environment leaves many people of color with the perception that the environmental movement is more concerned with protecting animals and other wildlife than with protecting people. In which types of communities do polluting industries locate? What is the least desirable land, and who is forced to live there? Some observers argue that communities with high concentrations of poor people and/or people of color incur more of the negative costs associated with industrial development than do more affluent communities. A more broadly defined environmental movement—such as the environmental justice movement, a national coalition of grassroots organizations from all types of communities—recognizes that uses of natural resources reflect institutional decision making, and it takes into account all people and their relationship to the environment.

In part IV, we include readings on three significant social issues that are currently contested in the United States: American national identity, sexuality, and violence. Although these three issues are not the only ones meriting attention, they remain prominent issues of public debate in the United States, and they can be fully understood only if they are located within a race, class, and gender analysis. Contemporary discussions about what constitutes American identity and culture, about the changing meaning of sexuality, and about the significance of violence are framed by implicit and explicit assumptions that stem from competing ideologies of race, class, and gender. How do race, class, and gender help our analysis of these important social issues? Conversely, how do these issues aid our understanding of the politics of race, class, and gender?

RETHINKING AMERICAN NATIONAL IDENTITY

Despite the ideology of the "melting pot," American national identity has been closely linked to a history of racial privilege. As Lillian Rubin points out in "Is This a White Country, or What?" the term "American" is assumed to mean White. Other types of "Americans," such as African Americans and Asian Americans, become distinguished from the "real" Americans by virtue of their race. "To be an 'all-American' is, by definition, *not* to be an Asian American, Pacific American, American Indian, Latino, Arab American, or African American," observes political theorist Manning Marable (Marable 1995: 364). More importantly, certain benefits are reserved for those deemed to be deserving "Americans."

This longstanding view of American national identity and of the social rewards that should accompany American citizenship is being challenged by the changing contours of the U.S. population. The overall percentage of the American population consisting of people of color is changing. Between 1900 and 1960, this percentage increased slightly, from 13.1 to 14.9 percent; between 1960 and 1990, it nearly doubled, to approximately 25 percent. In 1992, the combined population of Native Americans, African Americans, Latinos, and Asian Americans was estimated at 64.3 million; moreover, the composition of people of color in the United States is also undergoing substantial change. Just a few generations ago, African Americans were by far the largest "minority" group. Although still the most numerous, African Americans now account for less than half of all people of color, and their share continues to decline. Latino and Asian American populations are growing more rapidly than African American and Native American populations (O'Hare 1992: 9).

Longstanding perceptions of American national identity have also been challenged by profound global changes. You need only consult an atlas from the 1980s to get a sense of the widespread changes that characterize the late twentieth century. Political, economic, and social trends such as the dismantling of the Soviet Union, the increasing importance of Pacific Rim nations in global economic development, the rise of nationalisms of all sorts, and the erosion and collapse of socialism and communism have all affected the United States. The emergence of transnational corporations promises to dramatically change all societies, including the United States. Civil wars, rebellions, and economic hardships have led to shifts in national borders.

Changes of this magnitude both within and outside formal American borders raise fundamental questions about American national identity. How will America define itself as a nation-state in the changing global context? How will the increased visibility and vocality of people of color in the United States, in Latin America, in Africa, in Asia, and within the borders of former European colonial powers shape this process? Who will control the cultural representations and institutions that define American culture and transport it across the globe? How can such a diverse American population craft one country from so much difference created by race, class, and gender arrangements? What will it mean to be "American"?

Several themes emerge in rethinking American national identity via the lens of race, class, and gender. One is the issue of Americans who never "melted" into the melting pot. Many people think that race is like ethnicity and that the failure of people of color to shed their cultures and assimilate into the mainstream as White ethnic groups purportedly have done represents an unwillingness to embrace American national identity. But as Mary Waters points out in "Optional Ethnicities: For Whites Only?" this view seriously misreads the meaning of both race and ethnicity in shaping American national identity.

Waters suggests that White Americans of European ancestry have a great deal of choice in terms of their ethnic identities and that ethnicity does not influence later-generation White ethnics' lives unless they want it to. Waters contrasts this individualistic *symbolic ethnic identity* among many Whites with a socially enforced and imposed racial identity among African Americans. Because race operates as a physical marker in the United States, intersections of race and ethnicity operate differently for Whites and for people of color.

For Native Americans, the seeming failure to assimilate into the dominant national culture takes on special meaning. Placing his analysis in a global human rights context, Ward Churchill discusses how American national identity has been constructed against the interests of Native Americans. He suggests that, while Native American symbolism and imagery is ubiquitous in the United States, the use of Native American mascots and the like for sports teams continues to harm Native Americans. Ironically, while the original "Americans" experienced and continue to experience genocidal policies, distorted ideas about Native American culture remain in use as symbols in constructing American national identity.

Current trends in African American culture can also be seen as a response to this theme of being an unmeltable racial-ethnic group within contemporary American national identity. Dominant ideologies about race, class, and gender and ideologies of resistance developed by subordinated groups gain institutional expression in language, the media, humor, and music. Institutional structures of racism have restricted Black access to wealth, power, and prestige; African Americans have lacked opportunities to assimilate, to "melt" into the American identity; yet, the continued racial segregation of African Americans has simultaneously provided community structures with their own outcomes. Many young Black people in particular see bleak futures for themselves, are warehoused in deteriorating neighborhoods and schools, and in response have created various cultures of resistance. The refusal to "melt" or assimilate is often accomplished by holding on to culture.

Ironically, while Native Americans and African Americans struggle to broaden definitions of "American" to include their experiences, Asians and

Latinos migrate to the United States, in part, in search of an American identity. This leads to a second theme regarding American national identity — namely, the impact that immigration and changing population patterns are having on American culture. Many people of color see the United States as a land of opportunity, and their arrival and struggles to fit into existing structures of race, class, and gender reveal both the tenacity of these structures and how the structures are being changed. For example, Sucheng Chan's description of her experiences of immigration and of "becoming an American" and Magdoline Asfahani's efforts to negotiate an Arab American identity reveal how American identity looks different to those choosing to migrate and to those lacking these choices. Recent migrations by people of color have fostered a corresponding discussion of the rights that accrue to citizens. What happens if citizens are defined as "White" and if English is the only "American" language? Which benefits should be reserved for American citizens, and which citizens should receive these benefits? In the United States, this process is profoundly affected by race, class, and gender.

While many social issues intersect with this overarching theme of rethinking American national identity, two social issues present particularly difficult challenges within this process. These challenges are raised by the changing nature of sexuality and the role of violence in American national identity and culture.

SEXUALITY

As a critical part of structures of race, class, and gender, sexuality in American culture has emerged as a central social issue in contemporary American life. Sexuality links systems of race, class, and gender, and can be seen as a dimension of each. For example, constructing images about Black sexuality was central to maintaining institutional racism. Similarly, beliefs about women's sexuality operate in structuring gender oppression. At the same time, sexuality operates as a system of oppression comparable to the systems of race, class, and gender. *Heterosexism*, the institutionalized structures and beliefs that define and enforce heterosexual behavior as the only natural and permissible form of sexual expression, can be seen as a system of oppression that affects everyone. These two meanings of sexuality are linked: Manipulating sexualities in structuring systems of race, class, and gender occurs in conjunction with making assumptions of heterosexism and establishing definitions of so-called normal sexuality.

Currently, both meanings of sexuality—namely, sexuality as a dimension of race, class, and gender oppression and the rethinking of sexualities via challenges to heterosexism—are being contested in American culture. June Jordan refers to this situation as the "politics of sexuality" and posits that it "subsumes all of the different ways in which some of us seek to dictate to others of us what we should do, what we should desire, what we should dream about, and how we should behave ourselves, generally." For Jordan, race, class, gender, and sexuality are linked: challenging one necessarily involves challenging the rest. As she points out, "Freedom is indivisible, and either we are working for freedom or you are working for the sake of your self-interests and I am working for mine."

The interview by Amy Gluckman and Betsy Reed with longtime activist Barbara Smith explores race, class, and gender in the context of sexual oppressions. Challenging views that collapse race, class, gender, and sexuality into one another as interchangeable substitutes, Smith carefully identifies some of the ways in which race and sexuality, for example, are not similar. Smith notes that racial oppression is historically and structurally embedded in the founding of the United States, whereas lesbian and gay oppression was not. Differences in historical paths and varying structural arrangements should not blind us, however, to the similarities that link targets of racial oppression and homophobia. Smith notes that similar strategies are used to oppress people by race and by sexuality. As she succinctly puts it, "Our enemies are the same. That to me is the major thing that should be pulling us together."

In "The Beauty Myth," Naomi Wolf analyzes how sexuality is linked to the social-class system. As she points out, women's sexuality is used to sell products and is itself turned into a commodity for sale on the open market. Wolf emphasizes how the commodification and marketing of women's sexuality works to limit fully human, erotic love relationships among women and men. By keeping heterosexual men and women estranged and fearful concerning their heterosexual identities, businesses create a market for their products.

Dana Takagi's article problematizes the question of sexuality within Asian American groups as constructed under heterosexism and racism. Using the term *sexualities* to refer to the "variety of practices and identities that range from homoerotic to heterosexual desire," Takagi opens up the kind of conceptual space for discussion of sexualities called for by June Jordan. By focusing on issues shaping the construction of a lesbian and Asian identity, Takagi uses this particular social location to question how a broader conceptualization of sexuality might be constructed within the confines of racism and heterosexism.

In "Getting Off on Feminism," Jason Schultz takes on a similar question. Where Takagi focuses on lesbian sexuality and Asian American populations, Schultz questions White heterosexual male sexualities. He points to the narrow range of sexualities that are available to men, especially middle-class White men, under heterosexism. "Just as hetero women are often forced to choose between the images of the virgin and the whore, modern straight men are caught in a cultural tug-of-war between the Marlboro Man and the Wimp," Schultz observes. Rather than bemoan this dilemma, Schultz describes how he and his male friends tried to explore new ways of thinking about heterosexual masculinity.

VIOLENCE AND SOCIAL CONTROL

The escalating level of violence permeating the United States has emerged as another social issue that challenges the very terms of American national identity. Rather than being the spontaneous result of individual acts, violence represents a device of social control used to maintain systems of race, class, gender, and sexual inequality. Within social institutions organized around the politics of race, class, and gender, actual or threatened violence has long been essential in maintaining oppression. When people resist, violence is often used to keep them in their place.

Many of the current forms of violence are directly linked to inequality. For example, many people argue that pornography is a form of violence against women: it represents the link between commodified sexuality and violence, because both sell products. Joining sexuality and violence in this particular commodity fuels the social-class system's ongoing search for new consumer markets. The fact that women and children are used in this industry further reflects inequalities of gender and age. Moreover, Helen Zia's "Where Race and Gender Meet: Racism, Hate Crimes, and Pornography" reminds us that pornography is also linked to racism.

The arming of America via gun sales and promotion offers another example of the marketing of violence within American culture and invites inquiry into the consequences of this practice. Unfortunately, violence often hurts the most vulnerable segments of society. For example, violence against children has reached alarming proportions. Homicide is the fourth leading cause of death for children one to four years old and the third leading cause of death for five- to fourteen-year-olds. These data are heightened for African American children; homicide is the second leading cause of death for Black children of ages one to fourteen; a Black child dies from a gunshot wound every six hours (Robinson and Briggs 1993).

It is important to see violence not as acts of individual social deviance but as one outcome of how the politics of race, class, and gender permeates a range of social institutions. Violent acts, the threat of violence, and more generalized policies based on the use of force find organizational homes in designated institutions of social control—primarily the police, the military, and the criminal justice system. Violence simultaneously permeates a range of other social institutions. Some social institutions are known for their use of force, while others are less peaceful than they appear. Men's violence against women and children (whether physical, emotional, or sexual) in families of all social classes and racial/ethnic compositions contradicts the dominant belief that the home is a place of tranquility and love. Sexual harassment on the job as a dimension of social control belies the belief that men and women encounter a similar work environment. In the media, depicting rape as pleasurable to women and portraying violence against Native Americans, Asian Americans, and African Americans in numerous movies as justified contributes to a generalized belief system condoning violence. Thus, violence is simultaneously concentrated and diffuse.

One prominent theme in the readings on "Violence and Social Control" involves the links between individual acts of violence and more routinized, systemic violence. Lynchings of African American men can be seen as the random acts of unruly mobs; yet, the failure to arrest, prosecute, and convict those who did the lynching is powerful testament to public endorsement of these seemingly individual acts of violence. For example, rape appears to be a private act, but rapes occur as part of a generalized climate that condones violence against women. Although violence may be experienced individually, it occurs in specific organizational and institutional contexts. Race, class, and gender are fundamental determinants of organizational policies that foster social control. As Elijah Anderson's work points out, African American men's experience with the police exemplifies the differential treatment that individuals receive based on race, class, and gender.

Investigating violence and social control also reveals the interconnected nature of dominant ideologies of masculinity, the individualized and systemic forms of violence they justify, and the mechanisms of social control that support masculinity. "More Power Than We Want: Masculine Sexuality and Violence," by Bruce Kokopeli and George Lakey, investigates these links. Although we include no articles on violence against gays and lesbians, homophobic violence and violence against women are both ways of enforcing interlocking belief systems concerning heterosexism and masculinity. Violence based on race, gender, and heterosexism are parts of one system of social control: all of these types of violence aim to reinforce systems of privilege.

In a sense, the escalating violence within American society is a curious outcome of these same conditions of inequality. Renegotiating a new American national identity and culture that no longer has the certainty of fixed race, class, and gender categories creates change, confusion, and often violence. When people are wronged, they may use violence as a weapon. Conflict that escalates into violence can characterize relationships among groups disadvantaged within existing race, class, and gender arrangements—sometimes with tragic consequences, as was the case with the Los Angeles riot in 1992. Sumi Cho's article "Korean Americans vs. African Americans: Conflict and Construction" examines some of the tensions between Black people and Koreans. She grounds her analysis in the politics of race, class, and gender, helping us rethink American national identity and culture.

Sexuality and violence are but two of the social issues that intertwine with the need to rethink American national identity in the context of globalization. How can the United States build a national community that acknowledges the differences within its population created by race, ethnicity, class, gender, sexuality, and citizenship status? This final and in some ways most central theme to rethinking American national identity requires avoiding two problematic stances to social change. On the one hand, structures where Whiteness, masculinity, and wealth set the standards by which everyone else is judged cannot continue. Although this way of building community—namely, placing one group in the center and requiring everyone else to try to be like them—can foster a sense of certainty within the American national community, it is unjust. Social issues such as oppressive sexualities and societal violence emerge in this context. On the other hand, the politics of self-interest, where each group lobbies only for itself and cares little about the American national community as a whole, is equally undesirable. Crafting new views of community that take race, class, and gender relations, among others, into account while aiming to construct an American national identity in which democracy is fully realized is a vital task that promises to engage us all for some time.

References

Marable, Manning. 1995. "Beyond Racial Identity Politics: Toward a Liberation Theory for Multicultural Democracy." In *Race, Class, and Gender: An Anthology*. 2d ed. Eds. Margaret L. Andersen and Patricia Hill Collins. Belmont, CA: Wadsworth.

O'Hare, William P. 1992. "America's Minorities—The Demographics of Diversity." *Population Bulletin* 47, no. 4 (December). Washington, DC: Population Reference Bureau.

Robinson, Lori S., and Jimmie Briggs. 1993. "Kids and Violence." *Emerge* 5 (November): 44–50.

Suggested Readings

Berry, Mary Frances. 1994 [1971]. *Black Resistance, White Law: A History of Constitutional Racism in America.* New York: Penguin.

Canada, Geoffrey. 1995. *Fist Stick Knife Gun: A Personal History of Violence in America.* Boston: Beacon Press.

Collins, Patricia Hill. 1998. *Fighting Words: Black Women and the Search for Social Justice.* Minneapolis: University of Minnesota Press.

Ferber, Abby. 1998. *White Man Falling: Race, Gender, and White Supremacy.* Lanham, MD: Rowman & Littlefield.

Hacker, Andrew. 1992. *Two Nations: Black and White, Separate, Hostile, Unequal.* New York: Ballantine.

Jordan, June. 1992. *Technical Difficulties: African-American Notes on the State of the Union.* New York: Pantheon.

Williams, Patricia J. 1991. *The Alchemy of Race and Rights: Diary of a Law Professor.* Cambridge, MA: Harvard University Press.

InfoTrac College Edition: Search Terms

Use your access to the online library, InfoTrac College Edition, to learn more about subjects covered in this section. The following are some suggested terms for searches:

1992 Los Angeles riots
African Americans and the criminal justice system
Arab world
assimilation
bisexuality
"coming out" experience
gays, lesbians, and the military
hate crimes
inter-ethnic group conflict
Islam
Judeo-Christian tradition
Native Americans and genocide
pornography
queer identity/nation/theory
rape and warfare

Rodney King verdict
sex education
sexual desire
sexual identity
sexual socialization
sexual terrorism
street harassment

Wadsworth Sociology Resource Center: Virtual Society

For additional links, quizzes, and learning tools related to this section, see the Wadsworth Sociology Resource Center, Virtual Society, at **http://sociology. wadsworth.com**.

American Identities

"IS THIS A WHITE COUNTRY, OR WHAT?"   47

Lillian Rubin

"They're letting all these coloreds come in and soon there won't be any place left for white people," broods Tim Walsh, a thirty-three-year-old white construction worker. "It makes you wonder: Is this a white country, or what?"

It's a question that nags at white America, one perhaps that's articulated most often and most clearly by the men and women of the working class. For it's they who feel most vulnerable, who have suffered the economic contractions of recent decades most keenly, who see the new immigrants most clearly as direct competitors for their jobs.

It's not whites alone who stew about immigrants. Native-born blacks, too, fear the newcomers nearly as much as whites—and for the same economic reasons. But for whites the issue is compounded by race, by the fact that the newcomers are primarily people of color. For them, therefore, their economic anxieties have combined with the changing face of America to create a profound uneasiness about immigration—a theme that was sounded by nearly 90 percent of the whites I met, even by those who are themselves first-generation, albeit well-assimilated, immigrants.

Sometimes they spoke about this in response to my questions; equally often the subject of immigration arose spontaneously as people gave voice to their concerns. But because the new immigrants are dominantly people of color, the discourse was almost always cast in terms of race as well as immigration, with the talk slipping from immigration to race and back again as if these are not two separate phenomena. "If we keep letting all them foreigners in, pretty soon there'll be more of them than us and then what will this country be like?" Tim's wife, Mary Anne, frets. "I mean, this is *our* country, but the way things are going, white people will be the minority in our own country. Now does that make any sense?"

Such fears are not new. Americans have always worried about the strangers who came to our shores, fearing that they would corrupt our society, dilute our culture, debase our values. So I remind Mary Anne, "When your ancestors came here, people also thought we were allowing too many foreigners into the country. Yet those earlier immigrants were successfully integrated into the American society. What's different now?"

"Oh, it's different, all right," she replies without hesitation. "When my people came, the immigrants were all white. That makes a big difference." . . .

Listening to Mary Anne's words I was reminded again how little we Americans look to history for its lessons, how impoverished is our historical memory. For, in fact, being white didn't make "a big difference" for many of those earlier immigrants. The dark-skinned Italians and the eastern European Jews who came in the late nineteenth and early twentieth centuries didn't look very white to the fair-skinned Americans who were here then. Indeed, the same people we now call white—Italians, Jews, Irish—were seen as another race at that time. Not black or Asian, it's true, but an alien other, a race apart, although one that didn't have a clearly defined name. Moreover, the racist fears and fantasies of native-born Americans were far less contained then than they are now, largely because there were few social constraints on their expression.

When, during the nineteenth century, for example, some Italians were taken for blacks and lynched in the South, the incidents passed virtually unnoticed. And if Mary Anne and Tim Walsh, both of Irish ancestry, had come to this country during the great Irish immigration of that period, they would have found themselves defined as an inferior race and described with the same language that was used to characterize blacks: "low-browed and savage, grovelling and bestial, lazy and wild, simian and sensual."[1] Not only during that period but for a long time afterward as well, the U.S. Census Bureau counted the Irish as a distinct and separate group, much as it does today with the category it labels "Hispanic."

But there are two important differences between then and now, differences that can be summed up in a few words: the economy and race. Then, a growing industrial economy meant that there were plenty of jobs for both immigrant and native workers, something that can't be said for the contracting economy in which we live today. True, the arrival of the immigrants, who were more readily exploitable than native workers, put Americans at a disadvantage and created discord between the two groups. Nevertheless, work was available for both.

Then, too, the immigrants—no matter how they were labeled, no matter how reviled they may have been—were ultimately assimilable, if for no other reason than that they were white. As they began to lose their alien ways, it became possible for native Americans to see in the white ethnics of yesteryear a reflection of themselves. Once this shift in perception occurred, it was possible for the nation to incorporate them, to take them in, chew them up, digest them, and spit them out as Americans—with subcultural variations not always to the liking of those who hoped to control the manners and mores of the day, to be sure, but still recognizably white Americans.

Today's immigrants, however, are the racial other in a deep and profound way. . . . And integrating masses of people of color into a society where race conciousness lies at the very heart of our central nervous system raises a whole new set of anxieties and tensions. . . .

The increased visibility of other racial groups has focused whites more self-consciously than ever on their own racial identification. Until the new immigration shifted the complexion of the land so perceptibly, whites didn't think of themselves as white in the same way that Chinese know they're Chinese and African-Americans know they're black. Being white was simply a fact of life, one that didn't require any public statement, since it was the definitive social value against which all others were measured. "It's like everything's changed and I don't know what happened," complains Marianne Bardolino. "All of a sudden you have to be thinking all the time about these race things. I don't remember growing up thinking about being white like I think about it now. I'm not saying I didn't know there was coloreds and whites; it's just that I didn't go along thinking, *Gee, I'm a white person.* I never thought about it at all. But now with all the different colored people around, you have to think about it because they're thinking about it all the time."

"You say you feel pushed now to think about being white, but I'm not sure I understand why. What's changed?" I ask.

"I told you," she replies quickly, a small smile covering her impatience with my question. "It's because they think about what they are, and they want things their way, so now I have to think about what I am and what's good for me and my kids." She pauses briefly to let her thoughts catch up with her tongue, then continues. "I mean, if somebody's always yelling at you about being black or Asian or something, then it makes you think about being white. Like, they want the kids in school to learn about their culture, so then I think about being white and being Italian and say: What about my culture? If they're going to teach about theirs, what about mine?"

To which America's racial minorities respond with bewilderment. "I don't understand what white people want," says Gwen Tomalson. "They say if black kids are going to learn about black culture in school, then white people want their kids to learn about white culture. I don't get it. What do they think kids have been learning about all these years? It's all about white people and how they live and what they accomplished. When I was in school you wouldn't have thought black people existed for all our books ever said about us."

As for the charge that they're "thinking about race all the time," as Marianne Bardolino complains, people of color insist that they're forced into it by a white world that never lets them forget. "If you're Chinese, you can't forget it, even if you want to, because there's always something that reminds you," Carol Kwan's husband, Andrew, remarks tartly. "I mean, if Chinese kids get good grades and get into the university, everybody's worried and you read about it in the papers."

While there's little doubt that racial anxieties are at the center of white concerns, our historic nativism also plays a part in escalating white alarm. The new immigrants bring with them a language and an ethnic culture that's vividly expressed wherever they congregate. And it's this also, the constant reminder of an alien presence from which whites are excluded, that's so troublesome to them.

The nativist impulse isn't, of course, given to the white working class alone. But for those in the upper reaches of the class and status hierarchy— those whose children go to private schools, whose closest contact with public transportation is the taxi cab—the immigrant population supplies a source of cheap labor, whether as nannies for their children, maids in their households, or workers in their businesses. They may grouse and complain that "nobody speaks English anymore," just as working-class people do. But for the people who use immigrant labor, legal or illegal, there's a payoff for the inconvenience—a payoff that doesn't exist for the families in this study but that sometimes costs them dearly. For while it may be true that American workers aren't eager for many of the jobs immigrants are willing to take, it's also true that the presence of a large immigrant population—especially those who come from developing countries where living standards are far below our own—helps to make these jobs undesirable by keeping wages depressed well below what most American workers are willing to accept. . . .

It's not surprising, therefore, that working-class women and men speak so angrily about the recent influx of immigrants. They not only see their jobs and their way of life threatened, they feel bruised and assaulted by an environment that seems suddenly to have turned color and in which they feel like strangers in their own land. So they chafe and complain: "They come here to take advantage of us, but they don't really want to learn our ways," Beverly Sowell, a thirty-three-year old white electronics assembler, grumbles irritably. "They live different than us; it's like another world how they live. And they're so clannish. They keep to themselves, and they don't even *try* to learn English. You go on the bus these days and you might as well be in a foreign country; everybody's talking some other language, you know, Chinese or Spanish or something. Lots of them have been here a long time, too, but they don't care; they just want to take what they can get."

But their complaints reveal an interesting paradox, an illuminating glimpse into the contradictions that beset native-born Americans in their relations with those who seek refuge here. On the one hand, they scorn the immigrants;

on the other, they protest because they "keep to themselves." It's the same contradiction that dominates black-white relations. Whites refuse to integrate blacks but are outraged when they stop knocking at the door, when they move to sustain the separation on their own terms—in black theme houses on campuses, for example, or in the newly developing black middle-class suburbs.

I wondered, as I listened to Beverly Sowell and others like her, why the same people who find the lifeways and languages of our foreign-born population offensive also care whether they "keep to themselves."

"Because like I said, they just shouldn't, that's all," Beverly says stubbornly. "If they're going to come here, they should be willing to learn our ways—you know what I mean, be real Americans. That's what my grandparents did, and that's what they should do."

"But your grandparents probably lived in an immigrant neighborhood when they first came here, too," I remind her.

"It was different," she insists. "I don't know why; it was. They wanted to be Americans; these here people now, I don't think they do. They just want to take advantage of this country. . . .

"Everything's changed, and it doesn't make sense. Maybe you get it, but I don't. We can't take care of our own people and we keep bringing more and more foreigners in. Look at all the homeless. Why do we need more people here when our own people haven't got a place to sleep?"

"Why do we need more people here?"—a question Americans have asked for two centuries now. Historically, efforts to curb immigration have come during economic downturns, which suggests that when times are good, when American workers feel confident about their future, they're likely to be more generous in sharing their good fortune with foreigners. But when the economy falters, as it did in the 1990s, and workers worry about having to compete for jobs with people whose standard of living is well below their own, resistance to immigration rises. "Don't get me wrong; I've got nothing against these people," Tim Walsh demurs. "But they don't talk English, and they're used to a lot less, so they can work for less money than guys like me can. I see it all the time; they get hired and some white guy gets left out."

It's this confluence of forces—the racial and cultural diversity of our new immigrant population; the claims on the resources of the nation now being made by those minorities who, for generations, have called America their home; the failure of some of our basic institutions to serve the needs of our people; the contracting economy, which threatens the mobility aspirations of working-class families—all these have come together to leave white workers feeling as if everyone else is getting a piece of the action while they get nothing. "I feel like white people are left out in the cold," protests Diane Johnson, a twenty-eight-year-old white single mother who believes she lost a job as a bus driver to a black woman. "First it's the blacks; now it's all those other colored people, and it's like everything always goes their way. It seems like a white person doesn't have a chance anymore. It's like the squeaky wheel gets the grease, and they've been squeaking and we haven't," she concludes angrily.

Until recently, whites didn't need to think about having to "squeak"—at least not specifically as whites. They have, of course, organized and squeaked at various times in the past—sometimes as ethnic groups, sometimes as workers. But not as whites. As whites they have been the dominant group, the favored ones, the ones who could count on getting the job when people of color could not. Now suddenly there are others—not just individual others but identifiable groups, people who share a history, a language, a culture, even a color—who lay claim to some of the rights and privileges that formerly had been labeled "for whites only." And whites react as if they've been betrayed, as if a sacred promise has been broken. They're white, aren't they? They're *real* Americans, aren't they? This is their country, isn't it?

The answers to these questions used to be relatively unambiguous. But not anymore. Being white no longer automatically assures dominance in the politics of a multiracial society. Ethnic group politics, however, has a long and fruitful history. As whites sought a social and political base on which to stand, therefore, it was natural and logical to reach back to their ethnic past. Then they, too, could be "something"; they also would belong to a group; they would have a name, a history, a culture, and a voice. "Why is it only the blacks or Mexicans or Jews that are 'something'?" asks Tim Walsh. "I'm Irish, isn't that something, too? Why doesn't that count?"

In reclaiming their ethnic roots, whites can recount with pride the tribulations and transcendence of their ancestors and insist that others take their place in the line from which they have only recently come. "My people had a rough time, too. But nobody gave us anything, so why do we owe them something? Let them pull their share like the rest of us had to do," says Al Riccardi, a twenty-nine-year-old white taxi driver.

From there it's only a short step to the conviction that those who don't progress up that line are hampered by nothing more than their own inadequacies or, worse yet, by their unwillingness to take advantage of the opportunities offered them. "Those people, they're hollering all the time about discrimination," Al continues, without defining who "those people" are. "Maybe once a long time ago that was true, but not now. The problem is that a lot of those people are lazy. There's plenty of opportunities, but you've got to be willing to work hard."

He stops a moment, as if listening to his own words, then continues, "Yeah, yeah, I know there's a recession on and lots of people don't have jobs. But it's different with some of those people. They don't really want to work, because if they did, there wouldn't be so many of them selling drugs and getting in all kinds of trouble."

"You keep talking about 'those people' without saying who you mean," I remark.

"Aw c'mon, you know who I'm talking about," he says, his body shifting uneasily in his chair. "It's mostly the black people, but the Spanish ones, too."

In reality, however, it's a no-win situation for America's people of color, whether immigrant or native born. For the industriousness of the Asians comes in for nearly as much criticism as the alleged laziness of other groups. When blacks don't make it, it's because, whites like Al Riccardi insist, their culture doesn't teach respect for family; because they're hedonistic, lazy, stupid, and/or criminally inclined. But when Asians demonstrate their ability to overcome the obstacles of an alien language and culture, when the Asian family seems to be the repository of our most highly regarded traditional values, white hostility doesn't disappear. It just changes its form. Then the accomplishments of Asians, the speed with which they move up the economic ladder, aren't credited to their superior culture, diligence, or intelligence—even when these are granted—but to the fact that they're "single minded," "untrustworthy," "clannish drones," "narrow people" who raise children who are insufficiently "well rounded."[2] . . .

Not surprisingly, as competition increases, the various minority groups often are at war among themselves as they press their own particular claims, fight over turf, and compete for an ever-shrinking piece of the pie. In several African-American communities, where Korean shopkeepers have taken the place once held by Jews, the confrontations have been both wrenching and tragic. A Korean grocer in Los Angeles shoots and kills a fifteen-year-old black girl for allegedly trying to steal some trivial item from the store.[3] From New York City to Berkeley, California, African-Americans boycott Korean shop owners who, they charge, invade their neighborhoods, take their money, and treat them disrespectfully.[4] But painful as these incidents are for those involved, they are only symptoms of a deeper malaise in both communities— the contempt and distrust in which the Koreans hold their African-American neighbors, and the rage of blacks as they watch these new immigrants surpass them.

Latino-black conflict also makes headlines when, in the aftermath of the riots in South Central Los Angeles, the two groups fight over who will get the lion's share of the jobs to rebuild the neighborhood. Blacks, insisting that they're being discriminated against, shut down building projects that don't include them in satisfactory numbers. And indeed, many of the jobs that formerly went to African-Americans are now being taken by Latino workers. In an article entitled "Black vs. Brown," Jack Miles, an editorial writer for the *Los Angeles Times*, reports that "janitorial firms serving downtown Los Angeles have almost entirely replaced their unionized black work force with non-unionized immigrants."[5] . . .

But the disagreements among America's racial minorities are of little interest or concern to most white working-class families. Instead of conflicting groups, they see one large mass of people of color, all of them making claims that endanger their own precarious place in the world. It's this perception that has led some white ethnics to believe that reclaiming their ethnicity alone is not enough, that so long as they remain in their separate and distinct groups, their power will be limited. United, however, they can become a formidable countervailing force, one that can stand fast against the threat posed by minority demands. But to come together solely as whites would diminish their impact and leave them open to the charge that their real purpose is simply to retain the privileges of whiteness. A dilemma that has been resolved, at least for some, by the birth of a new entity in the history of American ethnic groups—the "European-Americans."[6] . . .

At the University of California at Berkeley, for example, white students and their faculty supporters insisted that the recently adopted multicultural curriculum include a unit of study of European-Americans. At Queens College in New York City, where white ethnic groups retain a more distinct presence, Italian-American students launched a successful suit to win recognition as a disadvantaged minority and gain the entitlements accompanying that status, including special units of Italian-American studies.

White high school students, too, talk of feeling isolated and, being less sophisticated and wary than their older sisters and brothers, complain quite openly that there's no acceptable and legitimate way for them to acknowledge a white identity. "There's all these things for all the different ethnicities, you know, like clubs for black kids and Hispanic kids, but there's nothing for me and my friends to join," Lisa Marshall, a sixteen-year-old white high school student, explains with exasperation. "They won't let us have a white club because that's supposed to be racist. So we figured we'd just have to call it something else, you know, some ethnic thing, like Euro-Americans. Why not? They have African-American clubs."

Ethnicity, then, often becomes a cover for " white," not necessarily because these students are racist but because racial identity is now such a prominent feature of the discourse in our social world. In a society where racial consciousness is so high, how else can whites define themselves in ways that connect them to a community and, at the same time, allow them to deny their racial antagonisms?

Ethnicity and race—separate phenomena that are now inextricably entwined. Incorporating newcomers has never been easy, as our history of controversy and violence over immigration tells us.[7] But for the first time, the new immigrants are also people of color, which means that they tap both the nativist and racist impulses that are so deeply a part of American life. As in the past, however, the fear of foreigners, the revulsion against their strange customs and seemingly unruly ways, is only part of the reason for the anti-immigrant attitudes that are increasingly being expressed today. For whatever xenophobic suspicions may arise in modern America, economic issues play a critical role in stirring them up.

NOTES

1. David R. Roediger, *The Wages of Whiteness* (New York: Verso, 1991), p. 133.

2. These were, and often still are, the commonly held stereotypes about Jews. Indeed, the Asian immigrants are often referred to as "the new Jews."

3. Soon Ja Du, the Korean grocer who killed fifteen-year-old Latasha Harlins, was found guilty of voluntary manslaughter, for which he was sentenced to four hundred hours of community service, a $500 fine, reimbursement of funeral costs to the Harlins family, and five years' probation.

4. The incident in Berkeley didn't happen in the black ghetto, as most of the others did. There, the Korean grocery store is near the University of California campus, and the woman involved in the incident is an African-American university student who was Maced by the grocer after an argument over a penny.

5. Jack Miles, "Blacks vs. Browns," *Atlantic Monthly* (October 1992), pp. 41–68.

6. For an interesting analysis of what he calls "the transformation of ethnicity," see Richard D. Alba, *Ethnic Identity* (New Haven, CT: Yale University Press, 1990).

7. In the past, many of those who agitated for a halt to immigration were immigrants or native-born children of immigrants. The same often is true today. As anti-immigrant sentiment grows, at least some of those joining the fray are relatively recent arrivals. One man in this study, for example—a fifty-two-year-old immigrant from Hungary— is one of the leaders of an anti-immigration group in the city where he lives.

References

Alba, Richard D. *Ethnic Identity.* New Haven: Yale University Press, 1990.

Roediger, David R. *The Wages of Whiteness.* New York: Verso, 1991.

BLACK HISPANICS
The Ties That Bind

48

Vivian Brady

At the bottom of the Spring semester course selection sheet is an optional question: students are requested to supply the college with their ethnicity for federal reporting requirements. Six categories are provided: White non-Hispanic,

From: *Centro*, Journal of the Center for Puerto Rican Studies, Hunter College, NY.

Hispanic, Black non-Hispanic, Puerto Rican, Hispanic other, Asian/Pacific Islander and Native American/Alaskan. Students must choose only one category, the one that best describes them.

I have always found the restriction to only one choice incredibly frustrating. As someone who describes herself as Black–Puerto Rican, there never seems to be any category that acknowledges the strong African heritage of Hispanic people in the Caribbean and Latin America. We, as Hispanics, are isolated as if we were a separate race unto ourselves. Unlike English and French-speaking people of the Caribbean, the kinship ties of Puerto Ricans to the Black American community are often ignored or denied. Our common bond of African heritage, as people of color in this hemisphere, and our implicit sisterhood and brotherhood are often left unrecognized, even on my course selection sheet.

My recognition of myself as a Black–Puerto Rican may be facilitated by the fact that my parents come from two different islands. My mother is from Puerto Rico and my father from St. Thomas, VI, but I have met many Hispanics who do not have mixed parentage who see themselves as I do. My mother emigrated to this country from Puerto Rico when she was three years old. The economic situation in Puerto Rico during the War was harsh and her family came to find a better life, settling in *El Barrio*, East Harlem. She has always viewed herself as a Black woman, a brave and independent stance to take in the 1940s and 50s. To my mother, separating the communities was a dangerous thing. She believes that it strengthens us to find our commonalities and stand united because the price of separation can be great in the face of racist oppression.

The "West Side Story" of my mother's time was more the relationship between the newly arrived Puerto Ricans and American Blacks than the romanticized tensions between the Italians and the Puerto Ricans of that musical's fame. An imaginary line was drawn on Lenox Avenue creating two insular communities, one Black and one Puerto Rican, and even though their lives and experiences were startlingly similar there was ambivalence. This ambivalence still survives today and divides us. Both groups fell into the trap of believing what the racist dogma of the day heralded. Many Puerto Ricans accepted on face value that Black was synonymous with inferiority. They believed the stereotypes about Blacks being "bad" and shied away from building a relationship with them, not wanting to be tainted by their status. Black Americans also fell into the mire of white racism; Puerto Ricans were loud, heavy drinkers and the men were womanizing Latinos. It seems funny to list these ridiculous images, yet they live on. I know because I have lived on both sides of the issue, red faced and embarrassed at how glibly we apply these stereotypes to each other; the multitudes of accusatory general statements not based on direct knowledge. Underneath it all is a wealth of strength that can help us discard the pervasive racism that our country is shackled to, but it must be a combined effort.

Our shared experience is not just the oppression that we have had to survive in this country, although it is of crucial importance and should serve to bind us together politically in order to create change and support each other's self-determination. We live together in some of the poorest communities, are racked by a drug epidemic, inadequate housing, and an educational system that leaves us unqualified and intellectually stifled. We ride the subways together every day, feeling much the same anger and despair, yet there is uncertainty between us. We are determined to see our cultural differences as insurmountable even though we have a shared heritage. The core of this uncertainty and divisiveness is ignorance.

My grandmother lives in Ceiba, a sleepy town near the Navy base in Puerto Rico where all the houses are painted in tropical pastels and one can hear the war games being executed along the coast. I see in her brown face my African heritage. Slaves were imported into Puerto Rico like the other neighboring islands for their cheap labor. They were exploited in the sugar cane fields under the hot sun. They brought with them their music, spirit and culture, enriching Puerto Rico. Black people in the Spanish-speaking Caribbean and in Latin America have left us with great legacies: The quilombo leader Ganga Zambi in Brazil, the African rhythms of the *merengue* and the spiritual influences in our religions. My grandmother would never call herself Black though; she is firstly and lastly Puerto Rican. Most Puerto Ricans describe their country like a rainbow, a mixture and blend of African, European and Indian. The manner in which they view their "blackness" is directly related to their environment and culture.

I have often heard Black Americans alienated by this concept; they see a woman as dark as my grandmother not identifying herself as Black and conclude that "Puerto Ricans don't know what they are" or that they seek to deny their blackness. Sadly enough this is true for some. I certainly don't wish to obscure the issues of race, color and class among Puerto Ricans. We are afflicted by these prejudices, much like Black Americans. It is Puerto Rican to recognize our mixed heritage. It is a mulatto country, not the stark Black and White of the United States.

When I learn about Afro-American history I treat it as my own, as part of my identity as a Black woman. I see the accomplishments and survival as a testimony to all people of color. I hope that Black Americans can find pride and strength in Puerto Rican and other Afro-Latin histories, but I know that it will take time for people to see this global Pan-Africanist view.

Things are not simple though, and viewing the situation perched on the edge of both communities I see that though we may socialize, form committees and lobby together, we must learn more about each other to see the merits of standing nonjudgmentally side by side. A good place to begin is to examine our histories.

I recently asked some of my Black American friends, "What if Michael Griffith* were Puerto Rican? Would you fight racist aggression in Howard Beach if the lynch mob were out to kill 'dirty spics' with bats and pipes?" Most said their response would have been tempered by the fact that the victim was Hispanic and that they would not be as passionate. By the same token I would have liked to see a stronger voice made by the Hispanic community during the case. We do not yet see that the enemy and the issue are the same: we must both be energized to see the struggle.

I have been told that it is impossible for me to continue being both Puerto Rican and Black and that I will inevitaby need to choose sides, perhaps as a way to show my allegiance to my chosen community. But I, like many other Hispanics, know that the blood I share with Afro-Americans links me to the survival and work necessary in both communities equally.

OPTIONAL ETHNICITIES
For Whites Only?

Mary C. Waters

49

What does it mean to talk about ethnicity as an option for an individual? To argue that an individual has some degree of choice in their ethnic identity flies in the face of the commonsense notion of ethnicity many of us believe in—that one's ethnic identity is a fixed characteristic, reflective of blood ties and given at birth. However, social scientists who study ethnicity have long concluded that while ethnicity is based on a *belief* in a common ancestry, ethnic-

---

*Michael Griffith was a young Black man who, in the summer of 1986, was chased through the streets of Howard Beach, Queens (New York), by young White men who struck him repeatedly with baseball bats and chased him onto a highway where he was struck by a car and killed instantly.

From: Silvia Pedraza and Rubén G. Rumbaut, eds. *Origins and Destinies: Immigration, Race and Ethnicity in America* (Belmont, CA: Wadsworth, 1996), pp. 444–54. Reprinted by permission.

ity is primarily a *social* phenomenon, not a biological one (Alba 1985, 1990; Barth 1969; Weber [1921] 1968, p. 389). The belief that members of an ethnic group have that they share a common ancestry may not be a fact. There is a great deal of change in ethnic identities across generations through intermarriage, changing allegiances, and changing social categories. There is also a much larger amount of change in the identities of individuals over their lives than is commonly believed. While most people are aware of the phenomenon known as "passing"—people raised as one race who change at some point and claim a different race as their identity—there are similar life course changes in ethnicity that happen all the time and are not given the same degree of attention as "racial passing."

White Americans of European ancestry can be described as having a great deal of choice in terms of their ethnic identities. The two major types of options White Americans can exercise are (1) the option of whether to claim any specific ancestry, or to just be "White" or American, [Lieberson (1985) called these people "unhyphenated Whites"] and (2) the choice of which of their European ancestries to choose to include in their description of their own identities. In both cases, the option of choosing how to present yourself on surveys and in everyday social interactions exists for Whites because of social changes and societal conditions that have created a great deal of social mobility, immigrant assimilation, and political and economic power for Whites in the United States. Specifically, the option of being able to not claim any ethnic identity exists for Whites of European background in the United States because they are the majority group—in terms of holding political and social power, as well as being a numerical majority. The option of choosing among different ethnicities in their family backgrounds exists because the degree of discrimination and social distance attached to specific European backgrounds has diminished over time. . . .

SYMBOLIC ETHNICITIES FOR WHITE AMERICANS

What do these ethnic identities mean to people and why do they cling to them rather than just abandoning the tie and calling themselves American? My own field research with suburban Whites in California and Pennsylvania found that later-generation descendants of European origin maintain what are called "symbolic ethnicities." Symbolic ethnicity is a term coined by Herbert Gans (1979) to refer to ethnicity that is individualistic in nature and without real social cost for the individual. These symbolic identifications are essentially leisure-time activities, rooted in nuclear family traditions and reinforced by the voluntary enjoyable aspects of being ethnic (Waters 1990). Richard Alba (1990) also found later-generation Whites in Albany, New York, who chose to keep a tie with an ethnic identity because of the enjoyable and voluntary aspects to those identities, along with the feelings of specialness they entailed. An example of symbolic ethnicity is individuals who identify as Irish, for example, on occasions such as Saint Patrick's Day, on family holidays, or for vacations. They do not usually belong to Irish American organizations, live in Irish neighborhoods, work in Irish jobs, or marry other Irish people. The symbolic meaning of being Irish American can be constructed by individuals from mass media images, family traditions, or other intermittent social activities. In other words, for later-generation White ethnics, ethnicity is not something that influences their lives unless they want it to. In the world of work and school and neighborhood, individuals do not have to admit to being ethnic unless they choose to. And for an increasing number of European-origin individuals whose parents and grandparents have intermarried, the ethnicity they claim is largely a matter of personal choice as they sort through all of the possible combinations of groups in their genealogies. . . .

RACE RELATIONS AND SYMBOLIC ETHNICITY

However much symbolic ethnicity is without cost for the individual, there is a cost associated with symbolic ethnicity for the society. That is because symbolic ethnicities of the type described here are confined to White Americans of European origin. Black Americans, Hispanic Americans, Asian Americans, and American Indians do not have the option of a symbolic ethnicity at present in the United States. For all of the ways in which ethnicity does not matter for White Americans, it does matter for non-Whites. Who your ancestors are does affect your choice of spouse, where you live, what job you have, who your friends are, and what your chances are for success in American society, if those ancestors happen not to be from Europe. The reality is that White ethnics have a lot more choice and room for maneuver than they themselves think they do. The situation is very different for members of racial minorities, whose lives are strongly influenced by their race or national origin regardless of how much they may choose not to identify themselves in terms of their ancestries.

When White Americans learn the stories of how their grandparents and great-grandparents triumphed in the United States over adversity, they are usually told in terms of their individual efforts and triumphs. The important role of labor unions and other organized political and economic actors in their social and economic successes are left out of the story in favor of a generational story of individual Americans rising up against communitarian, Old World intolerance, and New World resistance. As a result, the "individualized" voluntary, cultural view of ethnicity for Whites is what is remembered.

One important implication of these identities is that they tend to be very individualistic. There is a tendency to view valuing diversity in a pluralist environment as equating all groups. The symbolic ethnic tends to think that all groups are equal; everyone has a background that is their right to celebrate and pass on to their children. This leads to the conclusion that all identities are equal and all identities in some sense are interchangeable—"I'm Italian American, you're Polish American. I'm Irish American, you're African American." The important thing is to treat people as individuals and all equally. However, this assumption ignores the very big difference between an individualistic symbolic ethnic identity and a socially enforced and imposed racial identity.

My favorite example of how this type of thinking can lead to some severe misunderstandings between people of different backgrounds is from the *Dear Abby* advice column. A few years back a person wrote in who had asked an acquaintance of Asian background where his family was from. His acquaintance answered that this was a rude question and he would not reply. The bewildered White asked Abby why it was rude, since he thought it was a sign of respect to wonder where people were from, and he certainly would not mind anyone asking HIM about where his family was from. Abby asked her readers to write in to say whether it was rude to ask about a person's ethnic background. She reported that she got a large response, that most non-Whites thought it was a sign of disrespect, and Whites thought it was flattering:

> Dear Abby,
> I am 100 percent American and because I am of Asian ancestry I am often asked "What are you?" It's not the personal nature of this question that bothers me, it's the question itself. This query seems to question my very humanity. "What am I? Why I am a person like everyone else!"
>
> Signed, A REAL AMERICAN

> Dear Abby,
> Why do people resent being asked what they are? The Irish are so proud of being Irish, they tell you before you even ask. Tip O'Neill has never tried to hide his Irish ancestry.
>
> Signed, JIMMY.

In this exchange Jimmy cannot understand why Asians are not as happy to be asked about their ethnicity as he is, because he understands his ethnicity and theirs to be separate but equal. Everyone has to come from somewhere— his family from Ireland, another's family from Asia—each has a history and each should be proud of it. But the reason he cannot understand the perspective of the Asian American is that all ethnicities are not equal; all are not symbolic, costless, and voluntary. When White Americans equate their own symbolic ethnicities with the socially enforced identities of non-White Americans, they obscure the fact that the experiences of Whites and non-Whites have been qualitatively different in the United States and that the current identities of individuals partly reflect that unequal history.

In the next section I describe how relations between Black and White students on college campuses reflect some of these asymmetries in the understanding of what a racial or ethnic identity means. While I focus on Black and White students in the following discussion, you should be aware that the myriad other groups in the United States—Mexican Americans, American Indians, Japanese Americans—all have some degree of social and individual influences on their identities, which reflect the group's social and economic history and present circumstance.

RELATIONS ON COLLEGE CAMPUSES

Both Black and White students face the task of developing their race and ethnic identities. Sociologists and psychologists note that at the time people leave home and begin to live independently from their parents, often ages eighteen to twenty-two, they report a heightened sense of racial and ethnic identity as they sort through how much of their beliefs and behaviors are idiosyncratic to their families and how much are shared with other people. It is not until one comes in close contact with many people who are different from oneself that individuals realize the ways in which their backgrounds may influence their individual personality. This involves coming into contact with people who are different in terms of their ethnicity, class, religion, region, and race. For White students, the ethnicity they claim is more often than not a symbolic one—with all of the voluntary, enjoyable, and intermittent characteristics I have described above.

Black students at the university are also developing identities through interactions with others who are different from them. Their identity development is more complicated than that of Whites because of the added element of racial discrimination and racism, along with the "ethnic" developments of finding others who share their background. Thus Black students have the positive attraction of being around other Black students who share some cultural elements, as well as the need to band together with other students in a reactive and oppositional way in the face of racist incidents on campus.

Colleges and universities across the country have been increasing diversity among their student bodies in the last few decades. This has led in many cases to strained relations among students from different racial and ethnic backgrounds. The 1980s and 1990s produced a great number of racial incidents and high racial tensions on campuses. While there were a number of racial incidents that were due to bigotry, unlawful behavior, and violent or vicious attacks, much of what happens among students on campuses involves a low level of tension and awkwardness in social interactions.

Many Black students experience racism personally for the first time on campus. The upper-middle-class students from White suburbs were often isolated enough that their presence was not threatening to racists in their high schools. Also, their class background was known by their residence and this may have prevented attacks being directed at them. Often Black students at the university who begin talking with other students and recognizing racial slights will remember incidents that happened to them earlier that they might not have thought were related to race.

Black college students across the country experience a sizeable number of incidents that are clearly the result of racism. Many of the most blatant ones that occur between students are the result of drinking. Sometimes late at night, drunken groups of White students coming home from parties will yell slurs at single Black students on the street. The other types of incidents that happen include being singled out for special treatment by employees, such as being followed when shopping at the campus bookstore, or going to the art museum with your class and the guard stops you and asks for your I.D. Others involve impersonal encounters on the street—being called a nigger by a truck driver while crossing the street, or seeing old ladies clutch their pocketbooks and shake in terror as you pass them on the street. For the most part these incidents are not specific to the university environment, they are the types of incidents middle-class Blacks face every day throughout American society, and they have been documented by sociologists (Feagin 1991).

In such a climate, however, with students experiencing these types of incidents and talking with each other about them, Black students do experience a tension and a feeling of being singled out. It is unfair that this is part of their college experience and not that of White students. Dealing with incidents like this, or the ever-present threat of such incidents, is an ongoing developmental task for Black students that takes energy, attention, and strength of character. It should be clearly understood that this is an asymmetry in the "college experience" for Black and White students. It is one of the unfair aspects of life that results from living in a society with ongoing racial prejudice and discrimination. It is also very understandable that it makes some students angry at the unfairness of it all, even if there is no one to blame specifically. It is also very troubling because, while most Whites do not create these incidents, some do, and it is never clear until you know someone well whether they are the type of person who could do something like this. So one of the reactions of Black students to these incidents is to band together.

In some sense then, as Blauner (1992) has argued, you can see Black students coming together on campus as both an "ethnic" pull of wanting to be together to share common experiences and community, and a "racial" push of banding together defensively because of perceived rejection and tension from Whites. In this way the ethnic identities of Black students are in some sense similar to, say, Korean students wanting to be together to share experiences.

And it is an ethnicity that is generally much stronger than, say, Italian Americans. But for Koreans who come together there is generally a definition of themselves as "different from" Whites. For Blacks reacting to exclusion, there is a tendency for the coming together to involve both being "different from" but also "opposed to" Whites.

The anthropologist John Ogbu (1990) has documented the tendency of minorities in a variety of societies around the world, who have experienced severe blocked mobility for long periods of time, to develop such oppositional identities. An important component of having such an identity is to describe others of your group who do not join in the group solidarity as devaluing and denying their very core identity. This is why it is not common for successful Asians to be accused by others of "acting White" in the United States, but it is quite common for such a term to be used by Blacks and Latinos. The oppositional component of a Black identity also explains how Black people can question whether others are acting "Black enough." On campus, it explains some of the intense pressures felt by Black students who do not make their racial identity central and who choose to hang out primarily with non-Blacks. This pressure from the group, which is partly defining itself by not being White, is exacerbated by the fact that race is a physical marker in American society. No one immediately notices the Jewish students sitting together in the dining hall, or the one Jewish student sitting surrounded by non-Jews, or the Texan sitting with the Californians, but everyone notices the Black student who is or is not at the "Black table" in the cafeteria.

An example of the kinds of misunderstandings that can arise because of different understandings of the meanings and implications of symbolic versus oppositional identities concerns questions students ask one another in the dorms about personal appearances and customs. A very common type of interaction in the dorm concerns questions Whites ask Blacks about their hair. Because Whites tend to know little about Blacks, and Blacks know a lot about Whites, there is a general asymmetry in the level of curiosity people have about one another. Whites, as the numerical majority, have had little contact with Black culture; Blacks, especially those who are in college, have had to develop bicultural skills—knowledge about the social worlds of both Whites and Blacks. Miscommunication and hurt feelings about White students' questions about Black students' hair illustrate this point. One of the things that happens freshman year is that White students are around Black students as they fix their hair. White students are generally quite curious about Black students' hair—they have basic questions such as how often Blacks wash their hair, how they get it straightened or curled, what products they use on their hair, how they comb it, etc. Whites often wonder to themselves whether they should ask these questions. One thought experiment Whites perform is to ask themselves whether a particular question would upset them. Adopting the "do unto others" rule, they ask themselves, "If a Black person was curious about my hair would I get upset?" The answer usually is "No, I would be happy to tell them."

Another example is an Italian American student wondering to herself, "Would I be upset if someone asked me about calamari?" The answer is no, so she asks her Black roommate about collard greens, and the roommate explodes with an angry response such as, "Do you think all Black people eat watermelon too?" Note that if this Italian American knew her friend was Trinidadian American and asked about peas and rice the situation would be more similar and would not necessarily ignite underlying tensions.

Like the debate in *Dear Abby*, these innocent questions are likely to lead to resentment. The issue of stereotypes about Black Americans and the assumption that all Blacks are alike and have the same stereotypical cultural traits has more power to hurt or offend a Black person than vice versa. The innocent questions about Black hair also bring up a number of asymmetries between the Black and White experience. Because Blacks tend to have more knowledge about Whites than vice versa, there is not an even exchange going on, the Black freshman is likely to have fewer basic questions about his White roommate than his White roommate has about him. Because of the differences historically in the group experiences of Blacks and Whites there are some connotations to Black hair that don't exist about White hair. (For instance, is straightening your hair a form of assimilation, do some people distinguish between women having "good hair" and "bad hair" in terms of beauty and how is that related to looking "White"?) Finally, even a Black freshman who cheerfully disregards or is unaware that there are these asymmetries will soon slam into another asymmetry if she willingly answers every innocent question asked of her. In a situation where Blacks make up only 10 percent of the student body, if every non-Black needs to be educated about hair, she will have to explain it to nine other students. As one Black student explained to me, after you've been asked a couple of times about something so personal you begin to feel like you are an attraction in a zoo, that you are at the university for the education of the White students.

INSTITUTIONAL RESPONSES

Our society asks a lot of young people. We ask young people to do something that no one else does as successfully on such a wide scale—that is to live together with people from very different backgrounds, to respect one another, to appreciate one another, and to enjoy and learn from one another. The successes that occur every day in this endeavor are many, and they are too often overlooked. However, the problems and tensions are also real, and they will not vanish on their own. We tend to see pluralism working in the United States in much the same way some people expect capitalism to work. If you put together people with various interests and abilities and resources, the "invisible hand" of capitalism is supposed to make all the parts work together in an economy for the common good.

There is much to be said for such a model—the invisible hand of the market can solve complicated problems of production and distribution better than any "visible hand" of a state plan. However, we have learned that unequal power relations among the actors in the capitalist marketplace, as well as "externalities" that the market cannot account for, such as long-term pollution, or collusion between corporations, or the exploitation of child labor, means that state regulation is often needed. Pluralism and the relations between groups are very similar. There is a lot to be said for the idea that bringing people who belong to different ethnic or racial groups together in institutions with no interference will have good consequences. Students from different backgrounds will make friends if they share a dorm room or corridor, and there is no need for the institution to do any more than provide the locale. But like capitalism, the invisible hand of pluralism does not do well when power relations and externalities are ignored. When you bring together individuals from groups that are differentially valued in the wider society and provide no guidance, there will be problems. In these cases the "invisible hand" of pluralist relations does not work, and tensions and disagreements can arise without any particular individual or group of individuals being "to blame." On college campuses in the 1990s some of the tensions between students are of this sort. They arise from honest misunderstandings, lack of a common background, and very different experiences of what race and ethnicity mean to the individual.

The implications of symbolic ethnicities for thinking about race relations are subtle but consequential. If your understanding of your own ethnicity and its relationship to society and politics is one of individual choice, it becomes harder to understand the need for programs like affirmative action, which recognize the ongoing need for group struggle and group recognition, in order to bring about social change. It also is hard for a White college student to understand the need that minority students feel to band together against discrimination. It also is easy, on the individual level, to expect everyone else to be able to turn their ethnicity on and off at will, the way you are able to, without understanding that ongoing discrimination and societal attention to minority status makes that impossible for individuals from minority groups to do. The paradox of symbolic ethnicity is that it depends upon the ultimate goal of a pluralist society, and at the same time makes it more difficult to achieve that ultimate goal. It is dependent upon the concept that all ethnicities mean the same thing, that enjoying the traditions of one's heritage is an option available to a group or an individual, but that such a heritage should not have any social costs associated with it.

As the Asian Americans who wrote to *Dear Abby* make clear, there are many societal issues and involuntary ascriptions associated with non-White identities. The developments necessary for this to change are not individual but societal in nature. Social mobility and declining racial and ethnic sensitivity are closely associated. The legacy and the present reality of discrimination on the basis of race or ethnicity must be overcome before the ideal of a pluralist society, where all heritages are treated equally and are equally available for individuals to choose or discard at will, is realized.

References

Alba, Richard D. 1985. *Italian Americans: Into the Twilight of Ethnicity*. Englewood Cliffs, NJ: Prentice-Hall.

————. 1990. *Ethnic Identity: The Transformation of White America*. New Haven: Yale University Press.

Barth, Frederick. 1969. *Ethnic Groups and Boundaries*. Boston: Little, Brown.

Blauner, Robert. 1992. "Talking Past Each Other: Black and White Languages of Race." *American Prospect* (Summer): 55–64.

Feagin, Joe R. 1991. "The Continuing Significance of Race: Anti-Black Discrimination in Public Places." *American Sociological Review* 56: 101–17.

Gans, Herbert. 1979. "Symbolic Ethnicity: The Future of Ethnic Groups and Cultures in America." *Ethnic and Racial Studies* 2: 1–20.

Lieberson, Stanley. 1985. *Making It Count: The Improvement of Social Research and Theory*. Berkeley: University of California Press.

Ogbu, John. 1990. "Minority Status and Literacy in Comparative Perspective." *Daedalus* 119: 141–69.

Waters, Mary C. 1990. *Ethnic Options: Choosing Identities in America*. Berkeley: University of California Press.

Weber, Max. [1921]/1968. *Economy and Society: An Outline of Interpretive Sociology*. Eds. Guenther Roth and Claus Wittich, trans. Ephraim Fischoff. New York: Bedminister Press.

CRIMES AGAINST HUMANITY   **50**

Ward Churchill

If nifty little "pep" gestures like the "Indian Chant" and the "Tomahawk Chop" are just good clean fun, then let's spread the fun around, shall we?

During the past couple of seasons, there has been an increasing wave of controversy regarding the names of professional sports teams like the Atlanta "Braves," Cleveland "Indians," Washington "Redskins," and Kansas City

From: Ward Churchill, "Crimes Against Humanity," *Z Magazine* 6 (March 1993): 43–47. Reprinted by permission of the author.

"Chiefs." The issue extends to the names of college teams like Florida State University "Seminoles," University of Illinois "Fighting Illini," and so on, right on down to high school outfits like the Lamar (Colorado) "Savages." Also involved have been team adoption of "mascots," replete with feathers, buckskins, beads, spears, and "warpaint" (some fans have opted to adorn themselves in the same fashion), and nifty little "pep" gestures like the "Indian Chant" and "Tomahawk Chop."

A substantial number of American Indians have protested that use of native names, images, and symbols as sports team mascots and the like is, by definition, a virulently racist practice. Given the historical relationship between Indians and non-Indians during what has been called the "Conquest of America," American Indian Movement leader (and American Indian Anti-Defamation Council founder) Russell Means has compared the practice to contemporary Germans naming their soccer teams the "Jews," "Hebrews," and "Yids," while adorning their uniforms with grotesque caricatures of Jewish faces taken from the Nazis' anti-Semitic propaganda of the 1930s. Numerous demonstrations have occurred in conjunction with games—most notably during the November 15, 1992 match-up between the Chiefs and Redskins in Kansas City—by angry Indians and their supporters.

In response, a number of players—especially African Americans and other minority athletes—have been trotted out by professional team owners like Ted Turner, as well as university and public school officials, to announce that they mean not to insult but to honor native people. They have been joined by the television networks and most major newspapers, all of which have editorialized that Indian discomfort with the situation is "no big deal," insisting that the whole thing is just "good, clean fun." The country needs more such fun, they've argued, and "a few disgruntled Native Americans" have no right to undermine the nation's enjoyment of its leisure time by complaining. This is especially the case, some have argued, "in hard times like these." It has even been contended that Indian outrage at being systematically degraded—rather than the degradation itself—creates "a serious barrier to the sort of intergroup communication so necessary in a multicultural society such as ours."

Okay, let's communicate. We are frankly dubious that those advancing such positions really believe their own rhetoric, but, just for the sake of argument, let's accept the premise that they are sincere. If what they say is true, then isn't it time we spread such "inoffensiveness" and "good cheer" around among *all* groups so that *everybody* can participate *equally* in fostering the round of national laughs they call for? Sure it is—the country can't have too much fun or "intergroup involvement"—so the more, the merrier. Simple consistency demands that anyone who thinks the Tomahawk Chop is a swell pastime must be just as hearty in their endorsement of the following ideas— by the logic used to defend the defamation of American Indians—should help us all really start yukking it up.

First, as a counterpart to the Redskins, we need an NFL team called "Niggers" to honor Afro-Americans. Half-time festivities for fans might include a simulated stewing of the opposing coach in a large pot while players and cheerleaders dance around it, garbed in leopard skins and wearing fake bones in their noses. This concept obviously goes along with the kind of gaiety attending the Chop, but also with the actions of the Kansas City Chiefs, whose team members—prominently including black team members—lately appeared on a poster looking "fierce" and "savage" by way of wearing Indian regalia. Just a bit of harmless "morale boosting," says the Chiefs' front office. You bet.

So that the newly formed Niggers sports club won't end up too out of sync while expressing the "spirit" and "identity" of Afro-Americans in the above fashion, a baseball franchise—let's call this one the "Sambos"—should be formed. How about a basketball team called the "Spearchuckers"? A hockey team called the "Jungle Bunnies"? Maybe the "essence" of these teams could be depicted by images of tiny black faces adorned with huge pairs of lips. The players could appear on TV every week or so gnawing on chicken legs and spitting watermelon seeds at one another. Catchy, eh? Well, there's "nothing to be upset about," according to those who love wearing "war bonnets" to the Super Bowl or having "Chief Illiniwik" dance around the sports arenas of Urbana, Illinois.

And why stop there? There are plenty of other groups to include. Hispanics? They can be "represented" by the Galveston "Greasers" and San Diego "Spics," at least until the Wisconsin "Wetbacks" and Baltimore "Beaners" get off the ground. Asian Americans? How about the "Slopes," "Dinks," "Gooks," and "Zipperheads?" Owners of the latter teams might get their logo ideas from editorial page cartoons printed in the nation's newspapers during World War II: slant-eyes, buck teeth, big glasses, but nothing racially insulting or derogatory, according to the editors and artists involved at the time. Indeed, this Second World War–vintage stuff can be seen as just another barrel of laughs, at least by what current editors say are their "local standards" concerning American Indians.

Let's see. Who's been left out? Teams like the Kansas City "Kikes," Hanover "Honkies," San Leandro "Shylocks," Daytona "Dagos," and Pittsburgh "Polacks" will fill a certain social void among white folk. Have a religious belief? Let's all go for the gusto and gear up the Milwaukee "Mackerel Snappers" and Hollywood "Holy Rollers." The Fighting Irish of Notre Dame can be rechristened the "Drunken Irish" or "Papist Pigs." Issues of gender and sexual preferences can be addressed through creation of teams like the St. Louis "Sluts," Boston "Bimbos," Detroit "Dykes," and the Fresno "Fags." How about the Gainesville "Gimps" and Richmond "Retards," so the physically and mentally impaired won't be excluded from our fun and games?

Now, don't go getting "overly sensitive" out there. None of this is demeaning or insulting, at least not when it's being done to Indians. Just ask the folks who are doing it, or their apologists like Andy Rooney in the national media. They'll tell you—as in fact they *have* been telling you—that there's been no harm done, regardless of what their victims think, feel, or say. The situation is exactly the same as when those with precisely the same mentality used to insist that Step 'n' Fetchit was okay, or Rochester on the Jack Benny Show, or Amos and Andy, Charlie Chan, the Frito Bandito, or any of the other cutesy symbols making up the lexicon of American racism. Have we communicated yet?

Let's get just a little bit real here. The notion of "fun" embodied in rituals like the Tomahawk Chop must be understood for what it is. There's not a single non-Indian example used above which can be considered socially acceptable in even the most marginal sense. The reasons are obvious enough. So why is it different where American Indians are concerned? One can only conclude that, in contrast to the other groups at issue, Indians are (falsely) perceived as being too few, and therefore too weak, to defend themselves effectively against racist and otherwise offensive behavior.

Fortunately, there are some glimmers of hope. A few teams and their fans have gotten the message and have responded appropriately. Stanford University, which opted to drop the name "Indians" from Stanford, has experienced no resulting drop-off in attendance. Meanwhile, the local newspaper in Portland, Oregon, recently decided its long-standing editorial policy prohibiting use of racial epithets should include derogatory team names. The Redskins, for instance, are now referred to as "the Washington team," and will continue to be described in this way until the franchise adopts an inoffensive moniker (newspaper sales in Portland have suffered no decline as a result).

Such examples are to be applauded and encouraged. They stand as figurative beacons in the night, proving beyond all doubt that it is quite possible to indulge in the pleasure of athletics without accepting blatant racism into the bargain.

NUREMBERG PRECEDENTS

On October 16, 1946, a man named Julius Streicher mounted the steps of a gallows. Moments later he was dead, the sentence of an international tribunal composed of representatives of the United States, France, Great Britain, and the Soviet Union having been imposed. Streicher's body was then cremated, and—so horrendous were his crimes thought to have been—his ashes dumped into an unspecified German river so that "no one should ever know a particular place to go for reasons of mourning his memory."

Julius Streicher had been convicted at Nuremberg, Germany, of what were termed "Crimes Against Humanity." The lead prosecutor in his case—Justice Robert Jackson of the United States Supreme Court—had not argued that the defendant had killed anyone, nor that he had personally committed any especially violent act. Nor was it contended that Streicher had held any particularly important position in the German government during the period in which the so-called Third Reich had exterminated some 6,000,000 Jews, as well as several million Gypsies, Poles, Slavs, homosexuals, and other untermenschen (subhumans).

The sole offense for which the accused was ordered put to death was in having served as publisher/editor of a Bavarian tabloid entitled *Der Sturmer* during the early-to-mid 1930s, years before the Nazi genocide actually began. In this capacity, he had penned a long series of virulently anti-Semitic editorials and "news" stories, usually accompanied by cartoons and other images graphically depicting Jews in extraordinarily derogatory fashion. This, the prosecution asserted, had done much to "dehumanize" the targets of his distortion in the mind of the German public. In turn, such dehumanization had made it possible—or at least easier—for average Germans to later indulge in the outright liquidation of Jewish "vermin." The tribunal agreed, holding that Streicher was therefore complicit in genocide and deserving of death by hanging.

During his remarks to the Nuremberg tribunal, Justice Jackson observed that, in implementing its sentences, the participating powers were morally and legally binding themselves to adhere forever after to the same standards of conduct that were being applied to Streicher and the other Nazi leaders. In the alternative, he said, the victorious allies would have committed "pure murder" at Nuremberg—no different in substance from that carried out by those they presumed to judge—rather than establishing the "permanent benchmark for justice" which was intended.

Yet in the United States of Robert Jackson, the indigenous American Indian population had already been reduced, in a process which is ongoing to this day, from perhaps 12.5 million in the year 1500 to fewer than 250,000 by the beginning of the 20th century. This was accomplished, according to official sources, "largely through the cruelty of [Euro-American] settlers," and an informal but clear governmental policy which had made it an articulated goal to "exterminate these red vermin," or at least whole segments of them.

Bounties had been placed on the scalps of Indians—any Indians—in places as diverse as Georgia, Kentucky, Texas, the Dakotas, Oregon, and California, and had been maintained until resident Indian populations were decimated or disappeared altogether. Entire peoples such as the Cherokee had been reduced to half their size through a policy of forced removal from their homelands east of the Mississippi River to what were then considered less preferable areas in the West.

Others, such as the Navajo, suffered the same fate while under military guard for years on end. The United States Army had also perpetrated a long series of wholesale massacres of Indians at places like Horseshoe Bend, Bear

River, Sand Creek, the Washita River, the Marias River, Camp Robinson, and Wounded Knee.

Through it all, hundreds of popular novels—each competing with the next to make Indians appear more grotesque, menacing, and inhuman—were sold in the tens of millions of copies in the U.S. Plainly, the Euro-American public was being conditioned to see Indians in such a way as to allow their eradication to continue. And continue it did until the Manifest Destiny of the U.S.—a direct precursor to what Hitler would subsequently call Lebensraum-politik (the politics of living space)—was consummated.

By 1900, the national project of "clearing" Native Americans from their land and replacing them with "superior" Anglo-American settlers was complete: the indigenous population had been reduced by as much as 98 percent while approximately 97.5 percent of their original territory had "passed" to the invaders. The survivors had been concentrated, out of sight and mind of the public, on scattered "reservations," all of them under the self-assigned "plenary" (full) power of the federal government. There was, of course, no Nuremberg-style tribunal passing judgment on those who had fostered such circumstances in North America. No U.S. official or private citizen was ever imprisoned—never mind hanged—for implementing or propagandizing what had been done. Nor had the process of genocide afflicting Indians been completed. Instead, it merely changed form.

Between the 1880s and the 1980s, nearly half of all Native American children were coercively transferred from their own families, communities, and cultures to those of the conquering society. This was done through compulsory attendance at remote boarding schools, often hundreds of miles from their homes, where native children were kept for years on end while being systematically "deculturated" (indoctrinated to think and act in the manner of Euro-Americans rather than Indians). It was also accomplished through a pervasive foster home and adoption program—including "blind" adoptions, where children would be permanently denied information as to who they were/are and where they'd come from—placing native youths in non-Indian homes.

The express purpose of all this was to facilitate a U.S. governmental policy to bring about the "assimilation" (dissolution) of indigenous societies. In other words, Indian cultures as such were to be caused to disappear. Such policy objectives are directly contrary to the United Nations 1948 Convention on Punishment and Prevention of the Crime of Genocide, an element of international law arising from the Nuremberg proceedings. The forced "transfer of the children" of a targeted "racial, ethnical, or religious group" is explicitly prohibited as a genocidal activity under the Convention's second article.

Article II of the Genocide Convention also expressly prohibits involuntary sterilization as a means of "preventing births among" a targeted population. Yet, in 1975, it was conceded by the U.S. government that its Indian Health

Service (IHS), then a subpart of the Bureau of Indian Affairs (BIA), was even then conducting a secret program of involuntary sterilization that had affected approximately 40 percent of all Indian women. The program was allegedly discontinued, and the IHS was transferred to the Public Health Service, but no one was punished. In 1990, it came out that the IHS was inoculating Inuit children in Alaska with Hepatitis-B vaccine. The vaccine had already been banned by the World Health Organization as having a demonstrated correlation with the HIV-Syndrome which is itself correlated to AIDS. As this is written, a "field test" of Hepatitis-A vaccine, also HIV-correlated, is being conducted on Indian reservations in the northern plains region.

The Genocide Convention makes it a "crime against humanity" to create conditions leading to the destruction of an identifiable human group, as such. Yet the BIA has utilized the government's plenary prerogatives to negotiate mineral leases "on behalf of" Indian peoples paying a fraction of standard royalty rates. The result has been "super profits" for a number of preferred U.S. corporations. Meanwhile, Indians, whose reservations ironically turned out to be in some of the most mineral-rich areas of North America, which makes us, the nominally wealthiest segment of the continent's population, live in dire poverty.

By the government's own data in the mid-1980s, Indians received the lowest annual and lifetime per capita incomes of any aggregate population group in the United States. Concomitantly, we suffer the highest rate of infant mortality, death by exposure and malnutrition, disease, and the like. Under such circumstances, alcoholism and other escapist forms of substance abuse are endemic in the Indian community, a situation which leads both to a general physical debilitation of the population and a catastrophic accident rate. Teen suicide among Indians is several times the national average.

The average life expectancy of a reservation-based Native American man is barely 45 years; women can expect to live less than three years longer.

Such itemizations could be continued at great length, including matters like the radioactive contamination of large portions of contemporary Indian Country, the forced relocation of traditional Navajos, and so on. But the point should be made: genocide, as defined in international law, is a continuing fact of day-to-day life (and death) for North America's native peoples. Yet there has been—and is—only the barest flicker of public concern about, or even consciousness of, this reality. Absent any serious expression of public outrage, no one is punished and the process continues.

A salient reason for public acquiescence before the ongoing holocaust in Native North America has been a continuation of the popular legacy, often through more effective media. Since 1925, Hollywood has released more than 2,000 films, many of them rerun frequently on television, portraying Indians as strange, perverted, ridiculous, and often dangerous things of the past. Moreover, we are habitually presented to mass audiences one-dimensionally, devoid of recognizable human motivations and emotions; Indians thus serve as props, little more. We have thus been thoroughly and systematically dehumanized.

Nor is this the extent of it. Everywhere, we are used as logos, as mascots, as jokes: "Big-Chief" writing tablets, "Red Man" chewing tobacco, "Winnebago" campers, "Navajo" and "Cherokee" and "Pontiac" and "Cadillac" pickups and automobiles. There are the Cleveland "Indians," the Kansas City "Chiefs," the Atlanta "Braves" and the Washington "Redskins" professional sports teams—not to mention those in thousands of colleges, high schools, and elementary schools across the country—each with their own degrading caricatures and parodies of Indians and/or things Indian. Pop fiction continues in the same vein, including an unending stream of New Age manuals purporting to expose the inner works of indigenous spirituality in everything from pseudo-philosophical to do-it-yourself styles. Blond yuppies from Beverly Hills amble about the country claiming to be reincarnated 17th century Cheyenne Ushamans ready to perform previously secret ceremonies.

In effect, a concerted, sustained, and in some ways accelerating effort has gone into making Indians unreal. It is thus of obvious importance that the American public begin to think about the implications of such things the next time they witness a gaggle of face-painted and war-bonneted buffoons doing the "Tomahawk Chop" at a baseball or football game. It is necessary that they think about the implications of the grade-school teacher adorning their child in turkey feathers to commemorate Thanksgiving. Think about the significance of John Wayne or Charlton Heston killing a dozen "savages" with a single bullet the next time a western comes on TV. Think about why Land-o-Lakes finds it appropriate to market its butter with the stereotyped image of an "Indian princess" on the wrapper. Think about what it means when non-Indian academics profess—as they often do—to "know more about Indians than Indians do themselves." Think about the significance of charlatans like Carlos Castaneda and Jamake Highwater and Mary Summer Rain and Lynn Andrews churning out "Indian" bestsellers, one after the other, while Indians typically can't get into print.

Think about the real situation of American Indians. Think about Julius Streicher. Remember Justice Jackson's admonition. Understand that the treatment of Indians in American popular culture is not "cute" or "amusing" or just "good, clean fun."

Know that it causes real pain and real suffering to real people. Know that it threatens our very survival. And know that this is just as much a crime against humanity as anything the Nazis ever did. It is likely that the indigenous people of the United States will never demand that those guilty of such criminal activity be punished for their deeds. But the least we have the right to expect—indeed, to demand—is that such practices finally be brought to a halt.

YOU'RE SHORT, BESIDES!

51

Sucheng Chan

When asked to write about being a physically handicapped Asian American woman, I considered it an insult. After all, my accomplishments are many, yet I was not asked to write about any of them. Is being handicapped the most salient feature about me? The fact that it might be in the eyes of others made me decide to write the essay as requested. I realized that the way I think about myself may differ considerably from the way others perceive me. And maybe that's what being physically handicapped is all about.

I was stricken simultaneously with pneumonia and polio at the age of four. Uncertain whether I had polio of the lungs, seven of the eight doctors who attended me—all practitioners of Western medicine—told my parents they should not feel optimistic about my survival. A Chinese fortune teller my mother consulted also gave a grim prognosis, but for an entirely different reason: I had been stricken because my name was offensive to the gods. My grandmother had named me "grandchild of wisdom," a name that the fortune teller said was too presumptuous for a girl. So he advised my parents to change my name to "chaste virgin." All these pessimistic predictions notwithstanding, I hung onto life, if only by a thread. For three years, my body was periodically pierced with electric shocks as the muscles of my legs atrophied. Before my illness, I had been an active, rambunctious, precocious, and very curious child. Being confined to bed was thus a mental agony as great as my physical pain. Living in war-torn China, I received little medical attention; physical therapy was unheard of. But I was determined to walk. So one day, when I was six or seven, I instructed my mother to set up two rows of chairs to face each other so that I could use them as I would parallel bars. I attempted to walk by holding my body up and moving it forward with my arms while dragging my legs along behind. Each time I fell, my mother gasped, but I badgered her until she let me try again. After four nonambulatory years, I finally walked once more by pressing my hands against my thighs so my knees wouldn't buckle.

My father had been away from home during most of those years because of the war. When he returned, I had to confront the guilt he felt about my condition. In many East Asian cultures, there is a strong folk belief that a person's physical state in this life is a reflection of how morally or sinfully he or she lived in previous lives. Furthermore, because of the tendency to view the family as a single unit, it is believed that the fate of one member can be caused by the behavior of another. Some of my father's relatives told him that my illness had doubtless been caused by the wild carousing he did in his youth. A well-meaning but somewhat simple man, my father believed them.

Throughout my childhood, he sometimes apologized to me for having to suffer retribution for his former bad behavior. This upset me; it was bad enough that I had to deal with the anguish of not being able to walk, but to have to assuage his guilt as well was a real burden! In other ways, my father was very good to me. He took me out often, carrying me on his shoulders or back, to give me fresh air and sunshine. He did this until I was too large and heavy for him to carry. And ever since I can remember, he has told me that I am pretty.

After getting over her anxieties about my constant falls, my mother decided to send me to school. I had already learned to read some words of Chinese at the age of three by asking my parents to teach me the sounds and meaning of various characters in the daily newspaper. But between the ages of four and eight, I received no education since just staying alive was a full-time job. Much to her chagrin, my mother found no school in Shanghai, where we lived at the time, which would accept me as a student. Finally, as a last resort, she approached the American School, which agreed to enroll me only if my family kept an *amah* (a servant who takes care of children) by my side at all times. The tuition at the school was twenty U.S. dollars per month—a huge sum of money during those years of runaway inflation in China—and payable only in U.S. dollars. My family afforded the high cost of tuition and the expense of employing a full-time *amah* for less than a year.

We left China as the Communist forces swept across the country in victory. We found an apartment in Hong Kong across the street from a school run by Seventh-Day Adventists. By that time I could walk a little, so the principal was persuaded to accept me. An *amah* now had to take care of me only during recess when my classmates might easily knock me over as they ran about the playground.

After a year and a half in Hong Kong, we moved to Malaysia, where my father's family had lived for four generations. There I learned to swim in the lovely warm waters of the tropics and fell in love with the sea. On land I was a cripple; in the ocean I could move with the grace of a fish. I liked the freedom of being in the water so much that many years later, when I was a graduate student in Hawaii, I became greatly enamored with a man just because he called me a "Polynesian water nymph."

As my overall health improved, my mother became less anxious about all aspects of my life. She did everything possible to enable me to lead as normal a life as possible. I remember how once some of her colleagues in the high school where she taught criticized her for letting me wear short skirts. They felt my legs should not be exposed to public view. My mother's response was, "All girls her age wear short skirts, so why shouldn't she?"

The years in Malaysia were the happiest of my childhood, even though I was constantly fending off children who ran after me calling, "*Baikah! Baikah!*" ("Cripple! Cripple!" in the Hokkien dialect commonly spoken in Malaysia.) The taunts of children mattered little because I was a star pupil. I won one award after another for general scholarship as well as for art and public speaking. Whenever the school had important visitors, my teacher always called on me to recite in front of the class.

A significant event that marked me indelibly occurred when I was twelve. That year my school held a music recital and I was one of the students chosen to play the piano. I managed to get up the steps to the stage without any problem, but as I walked across the stage, I fell. Out of the audience, a voice said loudly and clearly, "Ayah! A *baikah* shouldn't be allowed to perform in public." I got up before anyone could get on stage to help me and, with tears streaming uncontrollably down my face, I rushed to the piano and began to play. Beethoven's "Für Elise" had never been played so fiendishly fast before or since, but I managed to finish the whole piece. That I managed to do so made me feel really strong. I never again feared ridicule.

In later years I was reminded of this experience from time to time. During my fourth year as an assistant professor at the University of California at Berkeley, I won a distinguished teaching award. Some weeks later I ran into a former professor who congratulated me enthusiastically. But I said to him, "You know what? I became a distinguished teacher by *limping* across the stage of Dwinelle 155!" (Dwinelle 155 is a large, cold classroom that most colleagues of mine hate to teach in.) I was rude not because I lacked graciousness but because this man, who had told me that my dissertation was the finest piece of work he had read in fifteen years, had nevertheless advised me to eschew a teaching career.

"Why?" I asked.

"Your leg . . . " he responded.

"What about my leg?" I said, puzzled.

"Well, how would you feel standing in front of a large lecture class?"

"If it makes any difference, I want you to know I've won a number of speech contests in my life, and I am not the least bit self-conscious about speaking in front of large audiences. . . . Look, why don't you write me a letter of recommendation to tell people how brilliant I am, and let *me* worry about my leg!"

This incident is worth recounting only because it illustrates a dilemma that handicapped persons face frequently: those who care about us sometimes get so protective that they unwittingly limit our growth. This former professor of mine had been one of my greatest supporters for two decades. Time after time, he had written glowing letters of recommendation on my behalf. He had spoken as he did because he thought he had my best interests at heart; he thought that if I got a desk job rather than one that required me to be a visible, public person, I would be spared the misery of being stared at.

Americans, for the most part, do not believe as Asians do that physically handicapped persons are morally flawed. But they are equally inept at interacting with those of us who are not able-bodied. Cultural differences in the perception and treatment of handicapped people are most clearly expressed by adults. Children, regardless of where they are, tend to be openly curious about people who do not look "normal." Adults in Asia have no hesitation in asking visibly handicapped people what is wrong with them, often expressing their sympathy with looks of pity, whereas adults in the United States try desperately to be polite by pretending not to notice.

One interesting response I often elicited from people in Asia but have never encountered in America is the attempt to link my physical condition to the state of my soul. Many a time while living and traveling in Asia people would ask me what religion I belonged to. I would tell them that my mother is a devout Buddhist, that my father was baptized a Catholic but has never practiced Catholicism, and that I am an agnostic. Upon hearing this, people would try strenuously to convert me to their religion so that whichever God they believed in could bless me. If I would only attend this church or that temple regularly, they urged, I would surely get cured. Catholics and Buddhists alike have pressed religious medallions into my palm, telling me if I would wear these, the relevant deity or saint would make me well. Once while visiting the tomb of Muhammad Ali Jinnah in Karachi, Pakistan, an old Muslim, after finishing his evening prayers, spotted me, gestured toward my legs, raised his arms heavenward, and began a new round of prayers, apparently on my behalf.

In the United States adults who try to act "civilized" towards handicapped people by pretending they don't notice anything unusual sometimes end up ignoring handicapped people completely. In the first few months I lived in this country, I was struck by the fact that whenever children asked me what was the matter with my leg, their adult companions would hurriedly shush them up, furtively look at me, mumble apologies, and rush their children away. After a few months of such encounters, I decided it was my responsibility to educate these people. So I would say to the flustered adults, "It's okay, let the kid ask." Turning to the child, I would say, "When I was a little girl, no bigger than you are, I became sick with something called polio. The muscles in my leg shrank up and I couldn't walk very well. You're much luckier than I am because now you can get a vaccine to make sure you never get my disease. So don't cry when your mommy takes you to get a polio vaccine, okay?" Some adults and their little companions I talked to this way were glad to be rescued from embarrassment; others thought I was strange.

Americans have another way of covering up their uneasiness: they become jovially patronizing. Sometimes when people spot my crutch, they ask if I've had a skiing accident. When I answer that unfortunately it is something less glamorous than that, they say, "I bet you *could* ski if you put your mind to it!" Alternately, at parties where people dance, men who ask me to dance with them get almost belligerent when I decline their invitation. They say, "Of course you can dance if you *want* to!" Some have given me pep talks about how if I would only develop the right mental attitude, I would have more fun in life.

Different cultural attitudes toward handicapped persons came out clearly during my wedding. My father-in-law, as solid a representative of middle America as could be found, had no qualms about objecting to the marriage on racial grounds, but he could bring himself to comment on my handicap only indirectly. He wondered why his son, who had dated numerous high school and college beauty queens, couldn't marry one of them instead of me. My mother in-law, a devout Christian, did not share her husband's prejudices, but she worried aloud about whether I could have children. Some Chinese friends of my parents, on the other hand, said that I was lucky to have found such a noble man, one who would marry me despite my handicap. I, for my part, appeared in church in a white lace wedding dress I had designed and made myself—a miniskirt!

How Asian Americans treat me with respect to my handicap tells me a great deal about their degree of acculturation. Recent immigrants behave just like Asians in Asia; those who have been here longer or who grew up in the United States behave more like their white counterparts. I have not encountered any distinctly Asian American pattern of response. What makes the experience of Asian American handicapped people unique is the duality of responses we elicit.

Regardless of racial or cultural background, most handicapped people have to learn to find a balance between the desire to attain physical independence and the need to take care of ourselves by not overtaxing our bodies. In my case, I've had to learn to accept the fact that leading an active life has its price. Between the ages of eight and eighteen, I walked without using crutches or braces but the effort caused my right leg to become badly misaligned. Soon after I came to the United States, I had a series of operations to straighten out the bones of my right leg; afterwards though my leg looked straighter and presumably better, I could no longer walk on my own. Initially my doctors fitted me with a brace, but I found wearing one cumbersome and soon gave it up. I could move around much more easily—and more important, faster—by using one crutch. One orthopedist after another warned me that using a single crutch was a bad practice. They were right. Over the years my spine developed a double-S curve and for the last twenty years I have suffered from severe, chronic back pains, which neither conventional physical therapy nor a lighter work load can eliminate.

The only thing that helps my backaches is a good massage, but the soothing effect lasts no more than a day or two. Massages are expensive, especially when one needs them three times a week. So I found a job that pays better, but at which I have to work longer hours, consequently increasing the physical strain on my body—a sort of vicious circle. When I was in my thirties, my doctors told me that if I kept leading the strenuous life I did, I would be in a wheelchair by the time I was forty. They were right on target: I bought myself a wheelchair when I was forty-one. But being the incorrigible character that I am, I use it only when I am *not* in a hurry!

It is a good thing, however, that I am too busy to think much about my handicap or my backaches because pain can physically debilitate as well as cause depression. And there are days when my spirits get rather low. What has helped me is realizing that being handicapped is akin to growing old at an accelerated rate. The contradiction I experience is that often my mind races along as though I'm only twenty while my body feels about sixty. But fifteen or twenty years hence, unlike my peers who will have to cope with aging for the first time, I shall be full of cheer because I will have already fought, and I hope won, that battle long ago.

Beyond learning how to be physically independent and, for some of us, living with chronic pain or other kinds of discomfort, the most difficult thing a handicapped person has to deal with, especially during puberty and early adulthood, is relating to potential sexual partners. Because American culture places so much emphasis on physical attractiveness, a person with a shriveled limb, or a tilt to the head, or the inability to speak clearly, experiences great uncertainty—indeed trauma—when interacting with someone to whom he or she is attracted. My problem was that I was not only physically handicapped, small, and short, but worse, I also wore glasses and was smarter than all the boys I knew! Alas, an insurmountable combination. Yet somehow I have managed to have intimate relationships, all of them with extraordinary men. Not surprisingly, there have also been countless men who broke my heart—men who enjoyed my company "as a friend," but who never found the courage to date or make love with me, although I am sure my experience in this regard is no different from that of many able-bodied persons.

The day came when my backaches got in the way of having an active sex life. Surprisingly that development was liberating because I stopped worrying about being attractive to men. No matter how headstrong I had been, I, like most women of my generation, had had the desire to be alluring to men ingrained into me. And that longing had always worked like a brake on my behavior. When what men think of me ceased to be compelling, I gained greater freedom to be myself.

I've often wondered if I would have been a different person had I not been physically handicapped. I really don't know, though there is no question that being handicapped has marked me. But at the same time I usually do not *feel* handicapped—and consequently, I do not *act* handicapped. People are therefore less likely to treat me as a handicapped person. There is no doubt, however, that the lives of my parents, sister, husband, other family members, and some close friends have been affected by my physical condition. They have had to learn not to hide me away at home, not to feel embarrassed by how I look or react to people who say silly things to me, and not to resent me for the extra demands my condition makes on them. Perhaps the hardest thing for those who live with handicapped people is to know when and how to offer help. There are no guidelines applicable to all situations. My advice is, when in doubt, ask, but ask in a way that does not smack of pity or embarrassment. Most important, please don't talk to us as though we are children.

So, has being physically handicapped been a handicap? It all depends on one's attitude. Some years ago, I told a friend that I had once said to an affirmative action compliance officer (somewhat sardonically since I do not believe in the head count approach to affirmative action) that the institution which employs me is triply lucky because it can count me as nonwhite, female and handicapped. He responded, "Why don't you tell them to count you four times? . . . Remember, you're short, besides!"

TIME TO LOOK AND LISTEN

52

Magdoline Asfahani

I love my country as many who have been here for generations cannot. Perhaps that's because I'm the child of immigrants, raised with a conscious respect for America that many people take for granted. My parents chose this country because it offered them a new life, freedom and possibilities. But I learned at a young age that the country we loved so much did not feel the same way about us.

Discrimination is not unique to America. It occurs in any country that allows immigration. Anyone who is unlike the majority is looked at a little suspiciously, dealt with a little differently. The fact that I wasn't part of the majority never occurred to me. I knew that I was an Arab and a Muslim. This meant nothing to me. At school I stood up to say the Pledge of Allegiance every day. These things did not seem incompatible at all. Then everything changed for me, suddenly and permanently, in 1985. I was only in seventh grade, but that was the beginning of my political education.

That year a TWA plane originating in Athens was diverted to Beirut. Two years earlier the U.S. Marine barracks in Beirut had been bombed. That seemed to start a chain of events that would forever link Arabs with terrorism. After the hijacking, I faced classmates who taunted me with cruel names, attacking my heritage and my religion. I became an outcast and had to apologize for myself constantly.

After a while, I tried to forget my heritage. No matter what race, religion or ethnicity, a child who is attacked often retreats. I was the only Arab I knew of in my class, so I had no one in my peer group as an ally. No matter what my parents tried to tell me about my proud cultural history, I would ignore it. My classmates told me I came from an uncivilized, brutal place, that Arabs were by nature anti-American, and I believed them. They did not know the hours my parents spent studying, working, trying to preserve part of their old lives while embracing, willingly, the new.

I tried to forget the Arabic I knew, because if I didn't I'd be forever linked to murderers. I stopped inviting friends over for dinner, because I thought the food we ate was "weird." I lied about where my parents had come from. Their accents (although they spoke English perfectly) humiliated me. Though Islam is a major monotheistic religion with many similarities to Judaism and Christianity, there were no holidays near Chanukah or Christmas, nothing to tie me to the "Judeo-Christian" tradition. I felt more excluded. I slowly began to turn into someone without a past.

Civil war was raging in Lebanon, and all that Americans saw of that country was destruction and violence. Every other movie seemed to feature Arab terrorists. The most common questions I was asked were if I had ever ridden a camel or if my family lived in tents. I felt burdened with responsibility. Why should an adolescent be asked questions like "Is it true you hate Jews and you want Israel destroyed?" I didn't hate anybody. My parents had never said anything even alluding to such sentiments. I was confused and hurt.

As I grew older and began to form my own opinions, my embarrassment lessened and my anger grew. The turning point came in high school. My grandmother had become very ill, and it was necessary for me to leave school a few days before Christmas vacation. My chemistry teacher was very sympathetic until I said I was going to the Middle East. "Don't come back in a body bag," he said cheerfully. The class laughed. Suddenly, those years of watching movies that mocked me and listening to others who knew nothing about Arabs and Muslims except what they saw on television seemed like a bad dream. I knew then that I would never be silent again.

I've tried to reclaim those lost years. I realize now that I come from a culture that has a rich history. The Arab world is a medley of people of different religions; not every Arab is a Muslim, and vice versa. The Arabs brought tremendous advances in the sciences and mathematics, as well as creating a literary tradition that has never been surpassed. The language itself is flexible and beautiful, with nuances and shades of meaning unparalleled in any language. Though many find it hard to believe, Islam has made progress in women's rights. There is a specific provision in the Koran that permits women to own property and ensures that their inheritance is protected—although recent events have shown that interpretation of these laws can vary.

My youngest brother, who is 12, is now at the crossroads I faced. When initial reports of the Oklahoma City bombing pointed to "Arab-looking individuals" as the culprits, he came home from school crying. "Mom, why do Muslims kill people? Why are the Arabs so bad?" She was angry and broken hearted, but tried to handle the situation in the best way possible: through education. She went to his class, armed with Arabic music, pictures, traditional dress and cookies. She brought a chapter of the social-studies book to life, and the children asked intelligent, thoughtful questions, even after the class was over. Some even asked if she was coming back. When my brother came home, he was excited and proud instead of ashamed.

I only recently told my mother about my past experience. Maybe if I had told her then, I would have been better equipped to deal with the thoughtless teasing. But, fortunately, the world is changing. Although discrimination and stereotyping still exist, many people are trying to lessen and end it. Teachers, schools and the media are showing greater sensitivity to cultural issues. However, there is still much that needs to be done, not for the sake of any particular ethnic or cultural group but for the sake of our country.

The America that I love is one that values freedom and the differences of its peoples. Education is the key to understanding. As Americans we need to take a little time to look and listen carefully to what is around us and not rush to judgment without knowing all the facts. And we must never be ashamed of our pasts. It is our collective differences that unite us and make us unique as a nation. It's what determines our present and our future.

Sexuality

THE GENDER OF SEXUALITY

53

Pepper Schwartz and Virginia Rutter

The gender of the person you desire is a serious matter seemingly fundamental to the whole business of romance. And it isn't simply a matter of whether someone is male or female; how well the person fulfills a lover's expectations of masculinity or femininity is of great consequence, as two examples from the movies illustrate.

In the movie *The Truth about Cats & Dogs* (1996), a man (Brian, played by Ben Chaplin) falls in love with a woman (Abby, played by Janeane Garofalo) over the phone, and she with him. They find each other warm, clever, charming, and intriguing. But she, thinking herself too plain, asks her beautiful friend (Noelle, played by Uma Thurman) to impersonate her when the man and woman are scheduled to meet. The movie continues as a comedy of errors. Although the man becomes very confused about which woman he really desires, in the end the telephone lovers are united. The match depended on social matters far more than physical matters.

In the British drama *The Crying Game* (1994), Fergus, an Irish Republican Army underling, meets and falls in love with the lover (Dil) of Jody, a British soldier whom Fergus befriended prior to being ordered to execute him. The movie was about passionate love, war, betrayal, and, in the end, loyalty and commitment. Fergus seeks out Jody's girlfriend in London out of guilt and curiosity. But Fergus's guilt over Jody's death turns into love, and the pair become romantically and sexually involved. In the end, although Fergus is jailed for terrorist activities, Fergus and Dil have solidified their bond and are committed and, it seems, in love. The story of sexual conquest and love is familiar, but this particular story grabbed imaginations because of a single, crucial detail. Jody's girlfriend Dil, Fergus discovers, turns out to be (physically) a man. Although Fergus is horrified when he discovers his lover is biologically different from what he had expected, in the end their relationship survives.

These movies raise an interesting point about sexual desire. Although sex is experienced as one of the most basic and biological of activities, in human beings it is profoundly affected by things other than the body's urges. Who we're attracted to and what we find sexually satisfying is not just a matter of the genital equipment we're born with. . . .

On one level, sex can be regarded as having both a biological and a social context. The biological (and physiological) refers to how people use their genital equipment to reproduce. In addition, as simple as it seems, bodies make the experience of sexual pleasure available—whether the pleasure involves other bodies or just one's own body and mind. It should be obvious, however, that people engage in sex even when they do not intend to reproduce. They have sex for fun, as a way to communicate their feelings to each other, as a way to satisfy their ego, and for any number of other reasons relating to the way they see themselves and interact with others.

Another dimension of sex involves both what we do and how we think about it. Sexual behavior refers to the sexual acts that people engage in. These acts involve not only petting and intercourse but also seduction and courtship. Sexual behavior also involves the things people do alone for pleasure and stimulation and the things they do with other people. Sexual desire, on the other hand, is the motivation to engage in sexual acts. It relates to what turns people on. A person's sexuality consists of both behavior and desire.

The most significant dimension of sexuality is gender. Gender relates both to the biological and social contexts of sexual behavior and desire. People tend to believe they know whether someone is a man or a woman not because we do a physical examination and determine that the person is biologically male or biologically female. Instead, we notice whether a person is masculine or feminine. Gender is a social characteristic of individuals in our society that is only sometimes consistent with biological sex. Thus, animals, like people, tend to be identified as male and female in accordance with the reproductive function, but only people are described by their gender, as a man or woman.

When we say something is gendered we mean that social processes have determined what is appropriately masculine and feminine and that gender has thereby become integral to the definition of the phenomenon. For example, marriage is a gendered institution: The definition of marriage involves a masculine part (husband) and a feminine part (wife). Gendered phenomena, like marriage, tend to appear "naturally" so. But, as recent debates about same-sex marriage underscore, the role of gender in marriage is the product of social processes and beliefs about men, women, and marriage. In examining how gender influences sexuality, moreover, you will see that gender rarely operates alone: Class, culture, race, and individual differences also combine to influence sexuality. . .

DESIRE: ATTRACTION AND AROUSAL

The most salient fact about sex is that nearly everybody is interested in it. Most people like to have sex, and they talk about it, hear about it, and think about it. But some people are obsessed with sex and willing to have sex with anyone or anything. Others are aroused only by particular conditions and hold exacting criteria. For example, some people will have sex only if they are positive that they are in love, that their partner loves them, and that the act is sanctified by marriage. Others view sex as not much different from eating a sandwich. They neither love nor hate the sandwich; they are merely hungry, and they want something to satisfy that hunger. What we are talking about here are differences in desire. As you have undoubtedly noticed, people differ in what they find attractive, and they are also physically aroused by different things. . . .

Many observers argue that when it comes to sex, men and women have fundamentally different biological wiring. Others use the evidence to argue that culture has produced marked sexual differences among men and women. We believe, however, that it is hard to tease apart biological differences and social differences. As soon as a baby enters the world, it receives messages about gender and sexuality. In the United States, for example, disposable diapers come adorned in pink for girls and blue for boys. In case people aren't sure whether to treat the baby as masculine or feminine in its first years of life, the diaper signals them. The assumption is that girl babies really are different from boy babies and the difference ought to be displayed. This different treatment continues throughout life, and therefore a sex difference at birth becomes amplified into gender difference as people mature.

Gendered experiences have a great deal of influence on sexual desire. As a boy enters adolescence, he hears jokes about boys' uncontainable desire. Girls are told the same thing and told that their job is to resist. These gender messages have power not only over attitudes and behavior (such as whether a person grows up to prefer sex with a lover rather than a stranger) but also over physical and biological experience. For example, a girl may be discouraged from vigorous competitive activity, which will subsequently influence how she develops physically, how she feels about her body, and even how she relates to the adrenaline rush associated with physical competition. Hypothetically, a

person who is accustomed to adrenaline responses experiences sexual attraction differently from one who is not. . . .

THE BIOLOGY OF DESIRE: NATURE'S EXPLANATION

Biology is admittedly a critical factor in sexuality. Few human beings fall in
love with fish or sexualize trees. Humans are designed to respond to other humans. And human activity is, to some extent, organized by the physical equipment humans are born with. Imagine if people had fins instead of arms or laid
eggs instead of fertilizing them during intercourse. Romance would look quite
different.

Although biology seems to be a constant (i.e., a component of sex that is
fixed and unchanging), the social world tends to mold biology as much as biology shapes humans' sexuality. Each society has its own rules for sex. Therefore, how people experience their biology varies widely. In some societies,
women act intensely aroused and active during sex; in others, they have no concept of orgasm. In fact, women in some settings, when told about orgasm, do
not even believe it exists, as anthropologists discovered in some parts of Nepal.
Clearly, culture—not biology—is at work, because we know that orgasm is
physically possible, barring damage to or destruction of the sex organs. Even
ejaculation is culturally dictated. In some countries, it is considered healthy to
ejaculate early and often; in others, men are told to conserve semen and ejaculate as rarely as possible. The biological capacity may not be so different, but
the way bodies behave during sex varies according to social beliefs.

Sometimes the dictates of culture are so rigid and powerful that the so-
called laws of nature can be overridden. Infertility treatment provides an example: For couples who cannot produce children "naturally," a several billion
dollar industry has provided technology that can, in a small proportion of
cases, overcome this biological problem (Rutter 1996). Recently, in California,
a child was born to a 63-year-old woman who had been implanted with fertil-
ized eggs. The cultural emphasis on reproduction and parenthood, in this case,
overrode the biological incapacity to produce children. . . .

The Social Origins of Desire

Your own experience should indicate that biology and genetics alone do not
shape human sexuality. From the moment you entered the world, cues from
the environment were telling you which desires and behaviors were "normal"
and which were not. The result is that people who grow up in different circumstances tend to have different sexualities. Who has not had their sexual

behavior influenced by their parents' or guardians' explicit or implicit rules? You may break the rules or follow them, but you can't forget them. On a societal level, in Sweden, for example, premarital sex is accepted, and people are expected to be sexually knowledgeable and experienced. Swedes are likely to associate sex with pleasure in this "sex positive" society. In Ireland, however, Catholics are supposed to heed the Church's strict prohibitions against sex outside of marriage, birth control, and the expression of lust. In Ireland the experience of sexuality is different from the experience of sexuality in Sweden because the rules are different. Certainly, biology in Sweden is no different from biology in Ireland, nor is the physical capacity to experience pleasure different. But in Ireland, nonmarital sex is clandestine and shameful. Perhaps the taboo adds excitement to the experience. In Sweden, nonmarital sex is acceptable. In the absence of social constraint, it may even feel a bit mundane. These culturally specific sexual rules and experiences arise from different norms, the well-known, unwritten rules of society.

Another sign that social influences play a bigger role in shaping sexuality than does biology is the changing notions historically of male and female differences in desire. Throughout history, varied explanations of male and female desire have been popular. At times, woman was portrayed as the stormy temptress and man the reluctant participant, as in the Bible story of Adam and Eve. At other times, women were seen as pure in thought and deed while men were voracious sexual beasts, as the Victorians would have it.

These shifting ideas about gender are the social "clothing" for sexuality. The concept of gender typically relies on a dichotomy of male versus female sexual categories, just as the tradition of women wearing dresses and men wearing pants has in the past made the shape of men and women appear quite different. Consider high heels, an on-again-off-again Western fashion. Shoes have no innate sexual function, but high heels have often been understood to be "sexy" for women, even though (or perhaps because) they render women less physically agile. (Of course, women cope. As Ginger Rogers, the 1940s movie star and dancing partner to Fred Astaire, is said to have quipped, "I did everything Fred did, only backwards and in high heels.") Social norms of femininity have at times rendered high heels fashionable. So feminine are high heels understood to be that a man in high heels, in some sort of visual comedy gag, guarantees a laugh from the audience. Alternatively, high heels are a required emblem of femininity for cross-dressing men.

Such distinctions are an important tool of society; they provide guidance to human beings about how to be a "culturally correct" male or female. Theoretically, society could "clothe" its members with explicit norms of sexuality that de-emphasize difference and emphasize similarity or even multiplicity. Picture unisex hairstyles and men and women both free to wear skirts or pants, norms that prevail from time to time in some subcultures. What is remarkable about dichotomies is that even when distinctions, like male and female norms of fashion, are reduced, new ways to assert an ostensibly essential difference between men and women arise. Societies' rules, like clothes, are changeable. But societies' entrenched taste for constructing differences between men and women persists.

The Social Construction of Sexuality

Social constructionists believe that cues from the environment shape human beings from the moment they enter the world. The sexual customs, values, and expectations of a culture, passed on to the young through teaching and by example, exert a powerful influence over individuals. . . .

In a heterogeneous and individualistic culture like North America, sexual socialization is complex. A society creates an "ideal" sexuality, but different families and subcultures have their own values. For example, even though contemporary society at large may now accept premarital sexuality, a given family may lay down the law: Sex before marriage is against the family's religion and an offense against God's teaching. A teenager who grows up in such a household may suppress feelings of sexual arousal or channel them into outlets that are more acceptable to the family. Or the teenager may react against her or his background, reject parental and community opinion, and search for what she or he perceives to be a more "authentic" self. Variables like birth order or observations of a sibling's social and sexual expression can also influence a person's development.

As important as family and social background are, so are individual differences in response to that background. In the abstract, people raised to celebrate their sexuality must surely have a different approach to enjoying their bodies than those who are taught that their bodies will betray them and are a venal part of human nature. Yet whether or not a person is raised to be at ease with physicality does not always help predict adult sexual behavior. Sexual sybarites and libertines may have grown up in sexually repressive environments, as did pop culture icon and Catholic-raised Madonna. Sometimes individuals whose families promoted sex education and free personal expression are content with minimal sexual expression.

Even with the nearly infinite variety of sexuality that individual experience produces, social circumstances shape sexual patterns. For example, research shows that people who have had more premarital sexual intercourse are likely to have more extramarital intercourse, or sex with someone other than their spouse (Blumstein and Schwartz 1983). Perhaps early experience creates a desire for sexual variety and makes it harder for a person to be monogamous. On the other hand, higher levels of sexual desire may generate both the premarital and extramarital propensities. Or perhaps nonmonogamous, sexually active individuals are "rule breakers" in other areas also, and resist not only the traditional rules of sex but also other social norms they encounter. Sexual history is useful for predicting sexual future, but it does not provide a complete explanation. . . .

Social Control of Sexuality

So powerful are norms as they are transmitted through both social structures and everyday life that it is impossible to imagine the absence of norms that control sexuality. In fact, most images of "liberated" sexuality involve breaking a social norm—say, having sex in public rather than in private. The social norm is always the reference point. Because people are influenced from birth by the social and physical contexts of sexuality, their desires are shaped by those norms. There is no such thing as a truly free sexuality. For the past two centuries in North America, people have sought "true love" through personal choice in dating and mating (D'Emilio and Freedman 1988). Although this form of sexual liberation has generated a small increase in the number of mixed pairs—interracial, interethnic, interfaith pairs—the rule of homogamy, or marrying within one's class, religion, and ethnicity, still constitutes one of the robust social facts of romantic life. Freedom to choose the person one loves turns out not to be as free as one might suppose.

Despite the norm of true love currently accepted in our culture, personal choice and indiscriminate sexuality have often been construed across cultures and across history as socially disruptive. Disruptions to the social order include liaisons between poor and rich; between people of different races, ethnicities, or faiths; and between members of the same sex. Traditional norms of marriage and sexuality have maintained social order by keeping people in familiar and "appropriate" categories. Offenders have been punished by ostracism, curtailed civil rights, or in some societies, death. Conformists are rewarded with social approval and material advantages. Although it hardly seems possible today, mixed-race marriage was against the law in the United States until 1967. Committed same-sex couples continue to be denied legal marriages, . . . income tax breaks, and health insurance benefits; heterosexual couples take these social benefits for granted.

Some social theorists observe that societies control sexuality through construction of a dichotomized or gendered (male-female) sexuality (Foucault 1978). Society's rules about pleasure seeking and procreating are enforced by norms about appropriate male and female behavior. For example, saying that masculinity is enhanced by sexual experimentation while femininity is demeaned by it gives men sexual privilege (and pleasure) and denies it to women. Furthermore, according to Foucault, sexual desire is fueled by the experience of privilege and taboo regarding sexual pleasure. That is, the very rules that control sexual desire shape it and even enhance it. The social world could just as plausibly concentrate on how much alike are the ways that men and women experience sex and emphasize how broadly dispersed sexual conduct is across genders. However, social control turns pleasure into a scarce resource and endows leaders who regulate the pleasure of others with power. . . .

Society's interest in controlling sexuality is expressed in the debates regarding sex education. Debates about sex education in grade school and high school illustrate the importance to society of both the control of desire and its social construction. The debates raise the question, does formal learning about sex increase or deter early sexual experimentation? The point is, opponents and proponents of sex education all want to know how to control sexuality in young people. Those who favor sex education hold that children benefit from early, comprehensive information about sex, in the belief that people learn about sexuality from birth and are sexual at least from the time of puberty. Providing young people with an appropriate vocabulary and accurate information both discourages early sexual activity and encourages safe sexual practices for those teenagers who, according to the evidence, will not be deterred from sexual activity (Sexuality Information and Education Council of the United States [SIECUS] 1995). On the other hand, opponents of sex education are intensely committed to the belief that information about sex changes teenagers' reactions and values and leads to early, and what they believe are inappropriate, sexual behaviors (Whitehead 1994). Conservative groups hold that sex education, if it occurs at all, should emphasize abstinence as opposed to practical information.

These conflicting points of view about sex education are both concerned with managing adolescent sexual desire. Conservatives fear that education creates desire; liberals feel that information merely enables better decision making. So who is correct? In various studies, a majority of both conservative and liberal sex education programs have demonstrated little effect on behavior. Conservatives believe these results prove the programs' lack of worth. Liberals believe the studies prove that many programs are not good enough, usually because they do not include the most important content. Furthermore, liberals point out that sex education has increased contraceptive (including condom) use, which is crucial to public health goals of reducing sexually transmitted disease and unwanted pregnancy. Other research indicates that comprehensive sex education actually tends to delay the age of first intercourse and does not intensify desire or escalate sexual behavior. There is no evidence that comprehensive sex education promotes or precipitates early teen sexual activity (Kirby et al. 1994).

The passionate debate about sex education is played out with high emotions. Political ideology, parental fears, and the election strategies of politicians all influence this mode of social control. In the final analysis, however, teaching about sex clearly does not have an intense impact on the pupil. Students' response to sex education varies tremendously at the individual level. In terms of trends within groups, however, it appears that sex education tends to delay sexual activity and makes teenage sex safer when it happens.

To summarize, social constructionists believe that a society influences sexual behavior through its norms. Some norms are explicit, such as laws against adult sexual activity with minors. Others are implicit, such as norms of fidelity and parental responsibility. In a stable, homogeneous society, it is relatively easy to understand such rules. But in a changing, complex society like the United States, the rules may be in flux or indistinct. Perhaps this ambiguity is what makes some issues of sexuality so controversial today. . . .

Sexual Identity and Orientation

. . . Sexual identity and sexual orientation . . . are used to mean a variety of things. We use these terms to refer to how people tend to classify themselves sexually—either as gay, lesbian, bisexual, or straight. Sexual behavior and sexual desire may or may not be consistent with sexual identity. That is, people may identify themselves as heterosexual, but desire people of the same sex— or vice versa.

It is hard to argue with the observation that human desire is, after all, organized. Humans do not generally desire cows or horses (with, perhaps, the exception of Catherine the Great, the Russian czarina who purportedly came to her demise while copulating with a stallion). More to the point, humans are usually quite specific about which sex is desirable to them and even whether the object of their desire is short or tall, dark or light, hairy or sleek.

In the United States, people tend to be identified as either homosexual or heterosexual. Other cultures (and prior eras in the United States) have not distinguished between these two sexual orientations. However, our culture embraces the perspective that, whether gay or straight, one has an essential, inborn desire, and it cannot change. Many people seem convinced that homosexuality is an essence rather than a sexual act. . . . People tend to assume that the object of desire is a matter of the gender of the object. That is, they think even homosexual men desire someone who is feminine and that homosexual women desire someone who is masculine. In other words, even among gay men and lesbians, it is assumed that they will desire opposite-gendered people, even if they are of the same sex.

Historians have chronicled in Western culture the evolution of homosexuality from a behavior into an identity (e.g., D'Emilio and Freedman 1988). In the past, people might engage in same-gender sexuality, but only in the twentieth century has it become a well-defined (and diverse) lifestyle and self-definition. Nevertheless, other evidence shows that homosexual identity has existed for a long time. The distinguished historian John Boswell (1994) believes that homosexuals as a group and homosexuality as an identity have existed from the very earliest of recorded history. He used evidence of early Christian same-sex "marriage" to support his thesis. Social scientist Fred Whitman (1983) has looked at homosexuality across cultures and declared that the evidence of a social type, including men who use certain effeminate gestures and have diverse sexual tastes, goes far beyond any one culture. Geneticist Dean Hamer provides evidence that sexual attraction may be genetically programmed, suggesting that it has persisted over time and been passed down through generations.

On the other side of the debate is the idea that sexuality has always been invented and that sexual orientations are socially created. A gay man's or lesbian's sexual orientation has been created by a social context. Although this creation takes place in a society that prefers dichotomous, polarized categories, the social constructionist vision of sexuality at least poses the possibility that sexuality could involve a continuum of behavior that is matched by a continuum of fantasy, ability to love, and sense of self.

References

Blumstein, P. and P. Schwartz. 1983. *American Couples: Money, Work, and Sex.* New York: William Morrow.

Boswell, J. 1994. *Same-Sex Unions in Pre-Modern Europe.* New York: Villard.

D'Emilio, J. D. and E. Freedman. 1988. *Intimate Matters: A History of Sexuality in America.* New York: Harper & Row.

Foucault, M. 1978. *A History of Sexuality: Vol. 1. An Introduction.* New York: Pantheon.

Kirby, D., L. Short, J. Collins, D. Rugg, L. Kolbe, M. Howard, B. Miller, F. Sonenstein, and L. S. Zabin. 1994. "School-Based Programs to Reduce Sexual Risk Behaviors: A Review of Effectiveness." *Public Health Reports* 109: 339–60.

Rutter, V. 1996. "Who Stole Fertility?" *Psychology Today*, March/April, pp. 44–70.

Sexuality Information and Education Council of the United States. 1995. *A Report on Adolescent Sexuality.* New York: SIECUS.

Whitehead, B. D. 1994. "The Failure of Sex Education." *Atlantic Monthly*, October, pp. 55–80.

Whitman, F. 1983 "Culturally Invariable Properties of Male Homosexualities: Tentative Conclusions from Cross-Cultural Research. *Archives of Sexual Behavior* 12: 207–26.

A NEW POLITICS OF SEXUALITY

54

June Jordan

As a young worried mother, I remember turning to Dr. Benjamin Spock's *Common Sense Book of Baby and Child Care* just about as often as I'd pick up the telephone. He was God. I was ignorant but striving to be good: a good Mother. And so it was there, in that best-seller pocketbook of do's and don't's, that I came upon this doozie of a guideline: Do not wear miniskirts or other provocative clothing because that will upset your child, especially if your child happens to be a boy. If you give your offspring "cause" to think of you as a sexual being, he will, at the least, become disturbed; you will derail the equilibrium of his notions about your possible identity and meaning in the world.

It had never occurred to me that anyone, especially my son, might look upon me as an asexual being. I had never supposed that "asexual" was some kind of positive designation I should, so to speak, lust after. I was pretty surprised by Dr. Spock. However, I was also, by habit, a creature of obedience. For a couple of weeks I actually experimented with lusterless colors and dowdy tops and bottoms, self-consciously hoping thereby to prove myself as a lusterless and dowdy and, therefore, excellent female parent.

Years would have to pass before I could recognize the familiar, by then, absurdity of a man setting himself up as the expert on a subject that presupposed women as the primary objects for his patriarchal discourse—on motherhood, no less! Years passed before I came to perceive the perversity of dominant power assumed by men, and the perversity of self-determining power ceded to men by women.

A lot of years went by before I understood the dynamics of what anyone could summarize as the Politics of Sexuality.

I believe the Politics of Sexuality is the most ancient and probably the most profound arena for human conflict. Increasingly, it seems clear to me that deeper and more pervasive than any other oppression, than any other bitterly contested human domain, is the oppression of sexuality, the exploitation of the human domain of sexuality for power.

This essay was adopted from the author's keynote address to the Bisexual, Gay, and Lesbian Student Association at Stanford University on April 29, 1991. It was published in *The Progressive*, July 1991.

When I say sexuality, I mean gender: I mean male subjugation of human beings because they are female. When I say sexuality, I mean heterosexual institutionalization of rights and privileges denied to homosexual men and women. When I say sexuality, I mean gay or lesbian contempt for bisexual modes of human relationship.

The Politics of Sexuality therefore subsumes all of the different ways in which some of us seek to dictate to others of us what we should do, what we should desire, what we should dream about, and how we should behave ourselves, generally. From China to Iran, from Nigeria to Czechoslovakia, from Chile to California, the politics of sexuality—enforced by traditions of state-sanctioned violence plus religion and the law—reduces to male domination of women, heterosexist tyranny, and, among those of us who are in any case deemed despicable or deviant by the powerful, we find intolerance for those who choose a different, a more complicated—for example, an interracial or bisexual—mode of rebellion and freedom.

We must move out from the shadows of our collective subjugation—as people of color/as women/as gay/as lesbian/as bisexual human beings.

I can voice my ideas without hesitation or fear because I am speaking, finally, about myself. I am black and I am female and I am a mother and I am bisexual and I am a nationalist and I am an antinationalist. And I mean to be fully and freely all that I am!

Conversely, I do not accept that any white or black or Chinese man—I do not accept that, for instance, Dr. Spock—should presume to tell me, or any other woman, how to mother a child. He has no right. He is not a mother. My child is not his child. And, likewise, I do not accept that anyone—any woman or any man who is not inextricably part of the subject he or she dares to address—should attempt to tell any of us, the objects of her or his presumptuous discourse, what we should do or what we should not do.

Recently, I have come upon gratuitous and appalling pseudoliberal pronouncements on sexuality. Too often, these utterances fall out of the mouths of men and women who first disclaim any sentiment remotely related to homophobia, but who then proceed to issue outrageous opinions like the following:

- That it is blasphemous to compare the oppression of gay, lesbian, or bisexual people to the oppression, say, of black people, or of the Palestinians.
- That the bottom line about gay or lesbian or bisexual identity is that you can conceal it whenever necessary and, so, therefore, why don't you do just that? Why don't you keep your deviant sexuality in the closet and let the rest of us—we who suffer oppression for reasons of our ineradicable and always visible components of our personhood such as race or gender—get on with our more necessary, our more beleaguered struggle to survive?

Well, number one: I believe I have worked as hard as I could, and then harder than that, on behalf of equality and justice—for African-Americans, for the Palestinian people, and for people of color everywhere.

And no, I do not believe it is blasphemous to compare oppressions of sexuality to oppressions of race and ethnicity: freedom is indivisible or it is nothing at all besides sloganeering and temporary, short-sighted, and short-lived advancement for a few. Freedom is indivisible, and either we are working for freedom or you are working for the sake of your self-interests and I am working for mine.

If you can finally go to the bathroom wherever you find one, if you can finally order a cup of coffee and drink it wherever coffee is available, but you cannot follow your heart—you cannot respect the response of your own honest body in the world—then how much of what kind of freedom does any one of us possess?

Or, conversely, if your heart and your honest body can be controlled by the state, or controlled by community taboo, are you not then, and in that case, no more than a slave ruled by outside force?

What tyranny could exceed a tyranny that dictates to the human heart, and that attempts to dictate the public career of an honest human body?

Freedom is indivisible; the Politics of Sexuality is not some optional "special-interest" concern for serious, progressive folk.

And, on another level, let me assure you: if every single gay or lesbian or bisexual man or woman active on the Left of American politics decided to stay home, there would be *no* Left left.

One of the things I want to propose is that we act on that reality: that we insistently demand reciprocal respect and concern from those who cheerfully depend upon our brains and our energies for their, and our, effective impact on the political landscape.

Last spring, at Berkeley, some students asked me to speak at a rally against racism. And I did. There were four or five hundred people massed on Sproul Plaza, standing together against that evil. And, on the next day, on that same plaza, there was a rally for bisexual and gay and lesbian rights, and students asked me to speak at that rally. And I did. There were fewer than seventy-five people stranded, pitiful, on that public space. And I said then what I say today: That was disgraceful! There should have been just one rally. One rally: freedom is indivisible.

As for the second, nefarious pronouncement on sexuality that now enjoys mass-media currency: the idiot notion of keeping yourself in the closet—that is very much the same thing as the suggestion that black folks and Asian-Americans and Mexican-Americans should assimilate and become as "white" as possible—in our walk/talk/music/food/values—or else. Or else? Or else we should, deservedly, perish.

Sure enough, we have plenty of exposure to white everything so why would we opt to remain our African/Asian/Mexican selves? The answer is that suicide is absolute, and if you think you will survive by hiding who you really are, you are sadly misled: there is no such thing as partial or intermittent suicide. You can only survive if you—who you really are—do survive.

Likewise, we who are not men and we who are not heterosexist—we, sure enough, have plenty of exposure to male-dominated/heterosexist this and that.

But a struggle to survive cannot lead to suicide: suicide is the opposite of survival. And so we must not conceal/assimilate/integrate into the would-be dominant culture and political system that despises us. Our survival requires that we alter our environment so that we can live and so that we can hold each other's hands and so that we can kiss each other on the streets, and in the daylight of our existence, without terror and without violent and sometimes fatal reactions from the busybodies of America.

Finally, I need to speak on bisexuality. I do believe that the analogy is interracial or multiracial identity. I do believe that the analogy for bisexuality is a multicultural, multi-ethnic, multiracial world view. Bisexuality follows from such a perspective and leads to it, as well.

Just as there are many men and women in the United States whose parents have given them more than one racial, more than one ethnic identity and cultural heritage to honor; and just as these men and women must deny no given part of themselves except at the risk of self-deception and the insanities that must issue from that; and just as these men and women embody the principle of equality among races and ethnic communities; and just as these men and women falter and anguish and choose and then falter again and then anguish and then choose yet again how they will honor the irreducible complexity of their God-given human being—even so, there are many men and women, especially young men and women, who seek to embrace the complexity of their total, always-changing social and political circumstance.

They seek to embrace our increasing global complexity on the basis of the heart and on the basis of an honest human body. Not according to ideology. Not according to group pressure. Not according to anybody's concept of "correct."

This is a New Politics of Sexuality. And even as I despair of identity politics—because identity is given and principles of justice/equality/freedom cut across given gender and given racial definitions of being, and because I will call you my brother, I will call you my sister, on the basis of what you *do* for justice, what you *do* for equality, what you *do* for freedom and *not* on the basis of you who are, even so I look with admiration and respect upon the new, bisexual politics of sexuality.

This emerging movement politicizes the so-called middle ground: bisexuality invalidates either/or formulation, either/or analysis. Bisexuality means

I am free and I am as likely to want and to love a woman as I am likely to want and to love a man, and what about that? Isn't that what freedom implies?

If you are free, you are not predictable and you are not controllable. To my mind, that is the keenly positive, politicizing significance of bisexual affirmation:

To insist upon complexity, to insist upon the validity of all of the components of social/sexual complexity, to insist upon the equal validity of all of the components of social/sexual complexity.

This seems to me a unifying, 1990s mandate for revolutionary Americans planning to make it into the twenty-first century on the basis of the heart, on the basis of an honest human body, consecrated to every struggle for justice, every struggle for equality, every struggle for freedom.

WHERE HAS GAY LIBERATION GONE? 55
An Interview with Barbara Smith

Amy Gluckman and Betsy Reed

The links between homophobia and sexism have been analyzed a lot, but the linkages between homophobia and other forms of oppression, especially class and race oppression, haven't been thought about or analyzed as much. What connections do you see between, first of all, gay oppression and our economic system, and issues of class?

I think that's really a very complicated issue. I often say that, unlike racial oppression, lesbian and gay oppression is not economically linked, and is not structurally and historically linked, to the founding of this country and of capitalism in the United States. This country was not founded on homophobia; it was founded on slavery and racism and, before that, prior to the importation of slaves, it was founded on the genocide of the indigenous people who lived here, which also had profound racial consequences and rationales. I think that sometimes, certain lesbians and gay men get very upset when I and

From: Amy Gluckman and Betsy Reed, eds., *Homo Economics, Capitalism, Community, and Lesbian and Gay Life* (New York: Routledge, 1997), pp. 195–207. Reprinted by permission.

others—I'm not the only person who would say it—put that kind of analysis out because they think it means that I'm saying that lesbian and gay oppression is not serious. That's not what I'm saying at all.

Do you think that extends into the future? In other words, would you say that capitalism could go along its merry way and assimilate gay people and provide gay rights, but otherwise remain the same?

. . . As with all groups, I think that our economic system has the most implications for lesbians and gay men when their class position makes them vulnerable to that economic system. So in other words, it's not that in general being lesbian or gay puts you into a critical relationship to capitalism, it's that a large proportion of lesbians and gay men are poor or working class, but of course they're completely invisible the way the movement's politics are defined now.

So much of this society is about consumerism. As long as lesbians and gay men are characterized as people who have huge amounts of disposable income and who are kind of fun and trendy—nice entertainment type people, k. d. langs and Martinas, just a little on the edge but not really that threatening—as long as they're characterized in that way, probably capitalism can incorporate them. If they begin to think about how extending lesbian and gay rights fully might shake up the patriarchal nuclear family and the economic arrangements that are tied to that, then that might be the point at which capitalists would say, "Well no, I don't think we can include that." As long as it's about k. d. lang and Cindy Crawford on the cover of *Vanity Fair*, capitalism doesn't have any problem with that because that's nothing but an image. . . .

. . . Right-wing organizations have used inflated income information about gays and lesbians to try to drum up homophobia, which is almost a direct appeal to people's economic frustration. As an organizer, have you encountered that? To what extent do you think that the backlash against lesbian and gay rights has to do with the degree to which people in this country under capitalism are economically exploited and might seek a hateful outlet for that?

What they say is that these people do not qualify as a disenfranchised group because look at their income levels, as if the only way you could be disenfranchised is by income or lack of access to it. When they tell the untruth that all of us are economically privileged, of course that fans it. I can't say that I have personally seen that myth being picked up. When I come into contact with straight people, it's usually Black people. And it's usually around Black issues.

I don't know that the economic thing is such an issue for heterosexual Black communities; I think it's the moral thing. It's not so much that those white gays are rich, it's that those white gays are sinners, they're going against

God. And they're also white, so they must be racist. And if you are a Black lesbian or gay man, then you must be a racial traitor. Those are the kinds of things that I hear, not so much that they're so rich. But I think there's an assumption on the part of most people of color that *most* white people are better off than we are anyway. It's an assumption that in some cases is accurate and in some cases is a myth that is perpetuated to keep people apart who should be in solidarity with each other because of class. It's a myth that keeps people away from each other, because there are some real commonalities between white and poor and being of color and poor. . . .

Can you say more about the links that you see between racism and gay oppression?

All of the different kinds of oppression are tied to each other, particularly when it comes to the kinds of repression and oppression that are practiced against different groups of people. When you look at a profile of how people who are oppressed experience their oppression, you see such similar components: demonization, scapegoating, police brutality, housing segregation, lack of access to certain jobs and employment, even the taking away of children—custody. They have done that to poor women of color and to poor women from time out of mind. This is not a new phenomenon that women who had children couldn't keep them because the state intervened. It's just that this group of people—lesbians and some gay men—are now experiencing the same thing. There are many similarities in what we experience. And also the same people who are hounding the usual scapegoat target groups, they're hounding the lesbian and gay community too. Our enemies are the same. That to me is the major thing that should be pulling us together.

The militant right wing in this country has targeted the lesbian and gay community, but they have targeted other groups, too. And they're really being quite successful during this time period. Does the Oklahoma City bombing have anything to do with the fate of the lesbian and gay community? Absolutely it does! The Oklahoma bombing epitomizes what dire straits the country is in as a whole, and if we had a responsible lesbian/gay/bisexual/transgendered people movement, it would be asking questions like, "Okay, what is our movement supposed to be doing now, post–Oklahoma City?" That really should have been a wake-up call.

We need to look at why those people are so antigovernment. The press never explains; all it gave us after the bombing was, "They're antigovernment and they're very upset over Waco." The reason those people are so antigovernment is that they think this government is a Zionist conspiracy that privileges Black savages. That's what they think. It's never explained that the reason they're so antigovernment is because they're white supremacists, they're anti-Semitic, they're homophobic, and they're definitely opposed to women's freedom too.

You asked about race and lesbian and gay oppression. One of the things that I wanted to say early on is that the clearest responses that I have to that are out of my own experience as a person who has those identities linked. I think that the clearest answers come from those of us who simultaneously experience these oppressions; however, identity politics has been so maligned during this period that I almost hesitate to bring it up, because I don't want people to think I'm saying that the only reason it makes a difference is because it's bothering *me*. Of course, I am concerned about these issues because in my own life and experience I know what struggle is about, I know what oppression is about, and I have seen and experienced suffering myself.

That's not the only reason I am an activist, though. I care about everyone who is under siege. Some people think that because I'm so positively pro Black and because I speak out against racism at every turn, that I don't really care if white people are suffering. Quite to the contrary. I care about all people who are not getting a fair shake, who are not getting an equal chance to fulfill their maximum potential and to live without fear and to have the basic things that every human needs: shelter, clothing, quality health care, meaningful and fairly compensated work, love and caring and freedom to express and to create, all those things that make life worth living. How limited would my politics be if I was only concerned about people like me! Given who I am as a Black woman and a lesbian and a person from a working-class home who is a socialist opposed to the exploitation of capitalism, well maybe that isn't so narrow. But what if I only cared about other Black lesbians? I would be sitting on the head of a pin.

The best heroes and the best heroines that we have throughout history have been those people who have gone beyond the narrow expectations that their demographic profile would lead you to expect. . . .

Those privileged, white gay men you mentioned that you view as setting the agenda currently—suppose homophobia could be eased in some ways. What stake do they have in other forms of oppression being ended?

The systems of oppression really do tie together. The plans and the strategies for oppressing and repressing our various groups are startlingly similar, and a society that is unjust, it's like cancer or a bleeding ulcer or something. You can't contain it. I guess it was Martin Luther King who said that when you have injustice anywhere, you really have it everywhere. It poisons the body politic of the society as a whole, and therefore you can't have singular solutions. Those white gay men who have disposable income and who think that all they need to do is get rid of the most blatant homophobia in corporate, government, and military settings, in the legal system and on TV, and everything else will fall into place, that they'll have a nice life in their little enclaves— they're dreaming. Let's say they got rid of homophobia in those places that I mentioned—which is not really getting rid of homophobia, it's getting rid of it in places that make their lives difficult—but suppose they were able to do that. If they were living in or near a city that has imploded, like Los Angeles, because of racial and economic exploitation and oppression, then how free are they going to be? I don't know why people can't understand how interconnected our fates are as creatures on the planet. . . .

One of the arguments people make for single-issue activism is that the gay community is too diverse to agree on an entire multi-issue agenda. They say, "We'll never get anywhere if we have to agree on everything else, so we're just going to work on one thing that we do agree about."

. . . If gay rights were put in place tomorrow, my behind would still be on fire. I would still be in ultimate danger here, because racism is still in the saddle. And so is class oppression, and so is sexual oppression. So getting a middle-of-the-road, mainstream gay rights agenda passed, how's that going to stop me from being raped? How's that going to help me not get breast cancer? How is it going to help the environment not get poisoned? How is it going to help the children of my community to have a chance for a decent life?

THE BEAUTY MYTH

56

Naomi Wolf

. . . Beauty pornography looks like this: The perfected woman lies prone, pressing down her pelvis. Her back arches, her mouth is open, her eyes shut, her nipples erect; there is a fine spray of moisture over her golden skin. The position is female superior; the stage of arousal, the plateau phase just preceding orgasm. On the next page, a version of her, mouth open, eyes shut, is about to tongue the pink tip of a lipstick cylinder. On the page after, another version kneels in the sand on all fours, her buttocks in the air, her face pressed into a towel, mouth open, eyes shut. The reader is looking through an ordinary women's magazine. In an ad for Reebok shoes, the woman sees a naked female torso, eyes averted. In an ad for Lily of France lingerie, she sees a naked female torso, eyes shut; for Opium perfume, a naked woman, back and buttocks bare, falls facedown from the edge of a bed; for Triton showers, a naked woman, back arched, flings her arms upward; for Jogbra sports bras, a naked female torso is cut off at the neck. In these images, where the face is visible, it is expressionless in a rictus of ecstasy. The reader understands from them that she will have to look like that if she wants to feel like that.

Beauty sadomasochism is different: In an ad for Obsession perfume, a well-muscled man drapes the naked, lifeless body of a woman over his shoulder. In an ad for Hermès perfume, a blond woman trussed in black leather is hanging upside down, screaming, her wrists looped in chains, mouth bound. In an ad for Fuji cassettes, a female robot with a playmate's body, but made of steel, floats with her genitals exposed, her ankles bolted and her face a steel mask with slits for the eyes and mouth. In an ad for Erno Laszlo skin care products, a woman sits up and begs, her wrists clasped together with a leather leash that is also tied to her dog, who is sitting up in the same posture and begging. In an American ad for Newport cigarettes, two men tackle one woman and pull another by the hair; both women are screaming. In another Newport ad, a man forces a woman's head down to get her distended mouth around a length of spurting hose gripped in his fist; her eyes are terrified. In an ad for Saab automobiles, a shot up a fashion model's thighs is captioned, "Don't worry. It's ugly underneath." In a fashion layout in *The Observer* (London), five men in black menace a model, whose face is in shock, with scissors and hot iron rods. In *Tatler* and *Harper's* and *Queen*, "designer rape sequences (women beaten, bound and abducted, but immaculately turned out and artistically photographed)" appear. In Chris von Wangenheim's *Vogue* layout, Doberman pinschers attack a model. Geoffrey Beene's metallic sandals are displayed against a background of S and M accessories. The woman learns from these images that no matter how assertive she may be in the world, her private submission to control is what makes her desirable. . . .

Sexual "explicitness" is not the issue. We could use a lot more of that, if explicit meant honest and revealing; if there were a full spectrum of erotic images of uncoerced real women and real men in contexts of sexual trust, beauty pornography could theoretically hurt no one. Defenders of pornography base their position on the idea of freedom of speech, casting pornographic imagery as language. Using their own argument, something striking emerges about the representation of women's bodies: the representation is heavily censored. Because we see many versions of the naked Iron Maiden, we are asked to believe that our culture promotes the display of female sexuality. It actually shows almost none. It censors representations of women's bodies, so that only the official versions are visible. Rather than seeing images *of* female desire or that cater *to* female desire, we see mock ups of living mannequins, made to contort and grimace, immobilized and uncomfortable under hot lights, professional set-pieces that reveal little about female sexuality. In the United States and Great Britain, which have no tradition of public nakedness, women rarely—and almost never outside a competitive context—see what other *women* look like naked; we see only identical humanoid products based loosely on women's bodies. . . .

. . . Leaving aside the issue of what violent sexual imagery does, it is still apparent that there is an officially enforced double standard for men's and women's nakedness in mainstream culture that bolsters power inequities.

The practice of displaying breasts, for example, in contexts in which the display of penises would be unthinkable, is portrayed as trivial because breasts are not "as naked" as penises or vaginas; and the idea of half exposing men in a similar way is moot because men don't have body parts comparable to breasts. But if we think about how women's genitals are physically concealed, unlike men's, and how women's breasts are physically exposed, unlike men's, it can be seen differently: women's breasts, then correspond to men's penises as the vulnerable "sexual flower" on the body, so that to display the former and conceal the latter makes women's bodies vulnerable while men's are protected. Cross-culturally, unequal nakedness almost always expresses power relations: in modern jails, male prisoners are stripped in front of clothed prison guards; in the antebellum South, young black male slaves were naked while serving the clothed white masters at table. To live in a culture in which women are routinely naked where men aren't is to learn inequality in little ways all day long. So even if we agree that sexual imagery is in fact a language, it is clearly one that is already heavily edited to protect men's sexual—and hence social—confidence while undermining that of women. . . .

Why this flood of images now? They do not arise simply as a market response to deep-seated, innate desires already in place. They arise also—and primarily—to set a sexual agenda and to *create* their versions of desire. The way to instill social values, writes historian Susan G. Cole, is to eroticize them. Images that turn women into objects or eroticize the degradation of women have arisen to counterbalance women's recent self-assertion. They are welcome and necessary because the sexes have come too close for the comfort of the powerful; they act to keep men and women apart, wherever the restraints of religion, law, and economics have grown too weak to continue their work of sustaining the sex war.

Heterosexual love, before the women's movement, was undermined by women's economic dependence on men. Love freely given between equals is the child of the women's movement, and a very recent historical possibility, and as such very fragile. It is also the enemy of some of the most powerful interests of this society.

If women and men in great numbers were to form bonds that were equal, nonviolent, and sexual, honoring the female principle no less or more than the male, the result would be more radical than the establishment's worst nightmares of homosexual "conversions." A mass heterosexual deviation into tenderness and mutual respect would mean real trouble for the status quo since heterosexuals are the most powerful sexual majority. The power structure would face a massive shift of allegiances: from each relationship might emerge a doubled commitment to transform society into one based publicly on what have traditionally been women's values, demonstrating all too well the appeal for both sexes of a world rescued from male dominance. The good news would get out on the street: free women have more fun; worse, so do free men.

Male-dominated institutions—particularly corporate interests—recognize the dangers posed to them by love's escape. Women who love themselves are threatening; but men who love real women, more so. Women who have broken out of gender roles have proved manageable: those few with power are being retrained as men. But with the apparition of numbers of men moving into passionate, sexual love of real women, serious money and authority could defect to join forces with the opposition. Such love would be a political upheaval more radical than the Russian Revolution and more destabilizing to the balance of world power than the end of the nuclear age. It would be the downfall of civilization as we know it—that is, of male dominance; and for heterosexual love, the beginning of the beginning.

Images that flatten sex into "beauty," and flatten the beauty into something inhuman, or subject her to eroticized torment, are politically and socioeconomically welcome, subverting female sexual pride and ensuring that men and women are unlikely to form common cause against the social order that feeds on their mutual antagonism, their separate versions of loneliness.

Barbara Ehrenreich, Elizabeth Hess, and Gloria Jacobs, in *Re-Making Love*, point out that the new market of sexual products demands quick-turnover sexual consumerism. That point applies beyond the sexual accessories market to the entire economy of consumption. The last thing the consumer index wants men and women to do is to figure out how to love one another: the $1.5-trillion retail-sales industry depends on sexual estrangement between men and women, and is fueled by sexual dissatisfaction. Ads do not sell sex—that would be counterproductive, if it meant that heterosexual women and men turned to one another and were gratified. What they sell is sexual discontent.

Though the survival of the planet depends on women's values balancing men's, consumer culture depends on maintaining a broken line of communication between the sexes and promoting matching sexual insecurities. Harley-Davidsons and Cuisinarts stand in for maleness and femaleness. But sexual satisfaction eases the stranglehold of materialism, since status symbols no longer look sexual, but irrelevant. Product lust weakens where emotional and sexual lust intensifies. The price we pay for artificially buoying up this market is our heart's desire. The beauty myth keeps a gap of fantasy between men and women. That gap is made with mirrors; no law of nature supports it. It keeps us spending vast sums of money and looking distractedly around us, but its smoke and reflection interfere with our freedom to be sexually ourselves.

Consumer culture is best supported by markets made up of sexual clones, men who want objects and women who want to be objects, and the object desired ever-changing, disposable, and dictated by the market. The beautiful object of consumer pornography has a built-in obsolescence, to ensure that as few men as possible will form a bond with one woman for years or for a lifetime, and to ensure that women's dissatisfaction with themselves will grow rather than diminish over time. Emotionally unstable relationships, high divorce rates, and a large population cast out into the sexual marketplace are good for business in a consumer economy. Beauty pornography is intent on making modern sex brutal and boring and only as deep as a mirror's mercury, antierotic for both men and women.

But even more powerful interests than the consumer index depend on heterosexual estrangement and are threatened by heterosexual accord. The military is supported by nearly one third of the United States government's budget; militarism depends on men choosing the bond with one another over the bond with women and children. Men who loved women would shift loyalties back to the family and community from which becoming a man is one long exile. Serious lovers and fathers would be unwilling to believe the standard propaganda of militarism: that their wives and children would benefit from their heroic death. Mothers don't fear mothers; if men's love for women and for their own children led them to define themselves first as fathers and lovers, the propaganda of war would fall on deaf ears: the enemy would be a father and partner too. This percentage of the economy is at risk from heterosexual love. Peace and trust between men and women who are lovers would be as bad for the consumer economy and the power structure as peace on earth for the military-industrial complex.

Heterosexual love threatens to lead to political change: an erotic life based on nonviolent mutuality rather than domination and pain teaches firsthand its appeal beyond the bedroom. A consequence of female self-love is that the woman grows convinced of social worth. Her love for her body will be unqualified, which is the basis of female identification. If a woman loves her own body, she doesn't grudge what other women do with theirs; if she loves femaleness, she champions its rights. It's true what they say about women: Women *are* insatiable. We *are* greedy. Our appetites do need to be controlled if things are to stay in place. If the world were ours too, if we believed we could get away with it, we *would* ask for more love, more sex, more money, more commitment to children, more food, more care. These sexual, emotional, and physical demands *would* begin to extend to social demands: payment for care of the elderly, parental leave, child care, etc. The force of female desire would be so great that society would truly have to reckon with what women want, in bed and in the world.

The economy also depends on a male work structure that denies the family. Men police one another's sexuality, forbidding each other to put sexual love and family at the center of their lives; women define themselves as successful according to their ability to sustain sexually loving relationships. If too many men and women formed common cause, that definition of success would make its appeal to men, liberating them from the echoing wind-tunnel of competitive masculinity. Beauty pornography is useful in preventing that eventuality: when aimed at men, its effect is to keep them from finding peace in sexual love. The fleeting chimera of the airbrushed centerfold, always receding before him, keeps the man destabilized in pursuit, unable to focus on the beauty of the woman—known, marked, lined, familiar—who hands him the paper every morning.

The myth freezes the sexual revolution to bring us full circle, evading sexual love with its expensive economic price tag. The nineteenth century constrained heterosexuality in arranged marriages; today's urban overachievers sign over their sexual fate to dating services, and their libido to work: one survey found that many yuppie couples share mutual impotence. The last century kept men and women apart in rigid gender stereotypes, as they are now estranged through rigid physical stereotypes. In the Victorian marriage market, men judged and chose; in the stakes of the beauty market, men judge and choose. It is hard to love a jailer, women knew when they had no legal rights. But it is not much easier to love a judge. Beauty pornography is a war-keeping force to stabilize the institutions of a society under threat from an outbreak of heterosexual love. . . .

When they discuss [their bodies], women lean forward, their voices lower. They tell their terrible secret. It's my breasts, they say. My hips. It's my thighs. I hate my stomach. This is not aesthetic distaste, but deep sexual shame. The parts of the body vary. But what each woman who describes it shares is the conviction that *that* is what the pornography of beauty most fetishizes. Breasts, thighs, buttocks, bellies; the most sexually central parts of women, whose "ugliness" therefore becomes an obsession. Those are the parts most often battered by abusive men. The parts that sex murderers most often mutilate. The parts most often defiled by violent pornography. The parts that beauty surgeons most often cut open. The parts that bear and nurse children and feel sexual. A misogynist culture has succeeded in making women hate what misogynists hate. . . .

MAIDEN VOYAGE   57

Excursion into Sexuality and Identity Politics

in Asian America

Dana Y. Takagi

The topic of sexualities—in particular, lesbian, gay, and bisexual identities—
is an important and timely issue in that place we imagine as Asian America. All
of us in Asian American Studies ought to be thinking about sexuality and
Asian American history for at least two compelling reasons.

One, while there has been a good deal of talk about the "diversity" of Asian
American communities, we are relatively uninformed about Asian American
subcultures organized specifically around sexuality. There are Asian American
gay and lesbian social organizations, gay bars that are known for Asian clientele, conferences that have focused on Asian American lesbian and gay experiences, and . . . electronic bulletin boards catering primarily to gay Asians,
their friends, and their lovers. I use the term "subcultures" here rather loosely
and not in the classic sociological sense, mindful that the term is somewhat inaccurate since gay Asian organizations are not likely to view themselves as a
gay subculture within Asian America any more than they are likely to think of
themselves as an Asian American subculture within gay America. If anything,
I expect that many of us view ourselves as on the margins of both communities. That state of marginalization in both communities is what prompts this
essay and makes the issues raised in it all the more urgent for all of us—gay,
straight, or somewhere-in-between. . . .

To be honest, it is not clear to me exactly how we ought to be thinking
about these organizations, places, and activities. On the one hand, I would argue that an organization like the Association of Lesbians and Gay Asians
(ALGA) ought to be catalogued in the annals of Asian American history. But
on the other hand, having noted that ALGA is as Asian American as Sansei
Live! or the National Coalition for Redress and Reparation, the very act of including lesbian and gay experiences in Asian American history, which seems
important in a symbolic sense, produces in me a moment of hesitation. Not

My special thanks to Russell Leong for his encouragement and commentary on this essay.

From: Russell Leong, ed., *Asian American Sexualities: Dimensions of the Gay and Lesbian Experience*
(New York: Routledge, 1996), pp. 21–35. Reprinted by permission.

because I do not think that lesbian and gay sexualities are deserving of a place in Asian American history, but rather, because the inscription of non-straight sexualities in Asian American history immediately casts theoretical doubt about how to do it. As I will suggest, the recognition of different sexual practices and identities that also claim the label Asian American presents a useful opportunity for rethinking and reevaluating notions of identity that have been used, for the most part, unproblematically and uncritically in Asian American Studies.

The second reason, then, that we ought to be thinking about gay and lesbian sexuality and Asian American Studies is for the theoretical trouble we encounter in our attempts to situate and think about sexual identity and racial identity. Our attempts to locate gay Asian experiences in Asian American history render us "uninformed" in an ironic double sense. On the one hand, the field of Asian American Studies is mostly ignorant about the multiple ways that gay identities are often hidden or invisible within Asian American communities. But the irony is that the more we know, the less we know about the ways of knowing. On the other hand, just at the moment that we attempt to rectify our ignorance by adding say, the lesbian, to Asian American history, we arrive at a stumbling block, an ignorance of how to add her. Surely the quickest and simplest way to add her is to think of lesbianism as a kind of ad hoc subject-position, a minority within a minority. But efforts to think of sexuality in the same terms that we think of race, yet simultaneously different from race in certain ways, and therefore, the inevitable "revelation" that gays/lesbians/bisexuals are like minorities but also different too, is often inconclusive, frequently ending in "counting" practice. While many minority women speak of "triple jeopardy" oppression—as if class, race, and gender could be disentangled into discrete additive parts—some Asian American lesbians could rightfully claim quadruple jeopardy oppression—class, race, gender, and sexuality. Enough counting. Marginalization is not as much about the quantities of experiences as it is about qualities of experience. And, as many writers, most notably feminists, have argued, identities whether sourced from sexual desire, racial origins, languages of gender, or class roots, are simply not additive.[1]

NOT COUNTING

A discussion of sexualities is fraught with all sorts of definition conundrums. What exactly does it mean, sexualities? The plurality of the term may be unsettling to some who recognize three (or two, or one) forms of sexual identity: gay, straight, bisexual. But there are those who identify as straight, but regularly indulge in homoeroticism, and, of course, there are those who claim the identity gay/lesbian, but engage in heterosexual sex. In addition, some people identify themselves sexually but do not actually have sex, and, there are those who claim celibacy as a sexual practice. For those who profess a form of sexual identity that is, at some point, at odds with their sexual practice or sexual desire, the idea of a single, permanent, or even stable sexual identity is confining and inaccurate. Therefore, in an effort to capture the widest possible range of human sexual practices, I use the term sexualities to refer to the variety of practices and identities that range from homoerotic to heterosexual desire. In this essay, I am concerned mainly with homosexual desire and the question of what happens when we try to locate homosexual identities in Asian American history.

Writing, speaking, acting queer. Against a backdrop of lotus leaves, sliding shoji panels, and the mountains of Guilin. Amid the bustling enclaves of Little Saigon, Koreatown, Chinatown, and Little Tokyo. Sexual identity, like racial identity, is one of many types of recognized "difference." If marginalization is a qualitative state of being and not simply a quantitative one, then what is it about being "gay" that is different from "Asian American?"

The terms "lesbian" and "gay," like "Third World," "woman," and "Asian American," are political categories that serve as rallying calls and personal affirmations. In concatenating these identities we create and locate ourselves in phrases that seem a familiar fit: black gay man, Third World woman, working-class Chicana lesbian, Asian American bisexual, etc. But is it possible to write these identities—like Asian American gay—without writing oneself into the corners that are either gay and only gay, or, Asian American and only Asian American? Or, as Trinh T. Minh-ha put it, "How do you inscribe difference without bursting into a series of euphoric narcissistic accounts of yourself and your own kind?"[2]

It is vogue these days to celebrate difference. But underlying much contemporary talk about difference is the assumption that differences are comparable things. For example, many new social movements activists, including those in the gay and lesbian movement, think of themselves as patterned on the "ethnic model."[3] And for many ethnic minorities, the belief that "gays are oppressed too" is a reminder of a sameness, a common political project in moving margin to center, that unites race-based movements with gays, feminists, and greens. The notion that our differences are "separate but equal" can be used to call attention to the specificity of experiences or to rally the troops under a collective banner. Thus, the concept of difference espoused in identity politics may be articulated in moments of what Spivak refers to as "strategic essentialism" or in what Hall coins "positionalities." But in the heat of local political struggles and coalition building, it turns out that not all differences are created equally. For example, Ellsworth recounts how differences of race, nationality, and gender, unfolded in the context of a relatively safe environment, the university classroom:

> Women found it difficult to prioritize expressions of racial privilege and oppression when such prioritizing threatened to perpetuate their gender op- pression. Among international students, both those who were of color and those who were White found it difficult to join their voices with those of U.S. students of color when it meant a subordination of their oppressions as people living under U.S. imperialist policies and as students for whom English was a sec- ond language. Asian American women found it difficult to join their voices with other students of color when it meant subordinating their specific oppressions as Asian Americans. I found it difficult to speak as a White woman about gen- der oppression when I occupied positions of institutional power relative to all students in the class, men and women, but positions of gender oppression relative to students who were White men, and in different terms, relative to stu- dents who were men of color.[4]

The above example demonstrates the tensions between sameness and differ- ence that haunt identity politics.

There are numerous ways that being "gay" is not like being "Asian." Two broad distinctions are worth noting. The first . . . is the relative invisibility of sexual identity compared with racial identity. While both can be said to be so- cially constructed, the former are performed, acted out, and produced, often in individual routines, whereas the latter tends to be more obviously "written" on the body and negotiated by political groups.[5] Put another way, there is a quality of voluntarism in being gay/lesbian that is usually not possible as an Asian American. One has the option to present oneself as "gay" or "lesbian," or alternatively, to attempt to "pass," or, to stay in "the closet," that is, to hide one's sexual preference.[6] However, these same options are not available to most racial minorities in face-to-face interactions with others.

As Asian Americans, we do not think in advance about whether or not to present ourselves as "Asian American," rather, that is an identification that is worn by us, whether we like it or not, and which is easily read off of us by others.

A second major reason that the category "gay" ought to be distinguished from the category "Asian American" is for the very different histories of each group. Studying the politics of being "gay" entails on the one hand, an analy- sis of discursive fields, ideologies, and rhetoric about sexual identity, and on the other hand, knowledge of the history of gays/lesbians as subordinated mi- norities relative to heterosexuals. Similarly, studying "Asian America" re- quires analysis of semantic and rhetorical discourse in its variegated forms, racist, apologist, and paternalist, and requires in addition, an understanding of the specific histories of the peoples who recognize themselves as Asian or Asian American. But the specific discourses and histories in each case are quite different. Even though we make the same intellectual moves to approach each form of identity, that is, a two-tracked study of ideology on the one hand, and history on the other, the particular ideologies and histories of each are very different.[7]

In other words, many of us experience the worlds of Asian America and gay America as separate places—emotionally, physically, intellectually. We sustain the separation of these worlds with our folk knowledge about the family-centeredness and supra-homophobic beliefs of ethnic communities. Moreover, it is not just that these communities know so little of one another, but, we frequently take great care to keep those worlds distant from each other. What could be more different than the scene at gay bars like "The End Up" in San Francisco, or "Faces" in Hollywood, and, on the other hand, the annual Buddhist church bazaars in the Japanese American community or Filipino revivalist meetings?[8] These disparate worlds occasionally collide through individuals who manage to move, for the most part, stealthily, between these spaces. But it is the act of deliberately bringing these worlds closer together that seems unthinkable. Imagining your parents, clutching bento box lunches, thrust into the smoky haze of a South of Market leather bar in San Francisco is no less strange a vision than the idea of Lowie taking Ishi, the last of his tribe, for a cruise on Lucas' Star Tours at Disneyland. "Cultural strain," the anthropologists would say. Or, as Wynn Young, laughing at the prospect of mixing his family with his boyfriend, said, "Somehow I just can't picture this conversation at the dinner table, over my mother's homemade barbecued pork: 'Hey, Ma. I'm sleeping with a sixty-year-old white guy who's got three kids, and would you please pass the soy sauce?'"[9]

Thus, "not counting" is a warning about the ways to think about the relationship of lesbian/gay identities to Asian American history. While it may seem politically efficacious to toss the lesbian onto the diversity pile, adding one more form of subordination to the heap of inequalities, such a strategy glosses over the particular or distinctive ways sexuality is troped in Asian America. Before examining the possibilities for theorizing "gay" and "Asian American" as nonmutually exclusive identities, I turn first to a fuller description of the chasm of silence that separates them.

SILENCES

The concept of silence is a doggedly familiar one in Asian American history. For example, Hosokawa characterized the Nisei as "Quiet Americans" and popular media discussions of the "model minority" typically describe Asian American students as "quiet" along with "hard working" and "successful." In the popular dressing of Asian American identity, silence has functioned as a metaphor for the assimilative and positive imagery of the "good" minorities. More recently, analysis of popular imagery of the "model minority" suggests that silence ought to be understood as an adaptive mechanism to a racially discriminatory society rather than as an intrinsic part of Asian American culture.[10]

If silence has been a powerful metaphor in Asian American history, it is also a crucial element of discussions of gay/lesbian identity, albeit in a somewhat different way. In both cases, silence may be viewed as the oppressive cost of a racially biased or heterosexist society. For gays and lesbians, the act of coming out takes on symbolic importance, not just as a personal affirmation of "this is who I am," but additionally as a critique of expected norms in society, "we are everywhere." While "breaking the silence" about Asian Americans refers to crashing popular stereotypes about them, and shares with the gay act of "coming out" the desire to define oneself rather than be defined by others, there remains an important difference between the two.

The relative invisibility of homosexuality compared with Asian American identity means that silence and its corollary space, the closet, are more ephemeral, appear less fixed as boundaries of social identities, less likely to be taken-for-granted than markers of race, and consequently, more likely to be problematized and theorized in discussions that have as yet barely begun on racial identity. Put another way, homosexuality is more clearly seen as constructed than racial identity.[11] Theoretically speaking, homosexual identity does not enjoy the same privileged stability as racial identity. The borders that separate gay from straight, and, "in" from "out," are so fluid that in the final moment we can only be sure that sexual identities are . . . "less a matter of final discovery than a matter of perpetual invention."[12]

Thus, while silence is a central piece of theoretical discussions of homosexuality, it is viewed primarily as a negative stereotype in the case of Asian Americans. What seems at first a simple question in gay identity of being "in" or "out" is actually laced in epistemological knots.

For example, a common question asked of gays and lesbians by one another, or by straights, is, "Are you out?" The answer to that question (yes and no) is typically followed by a list of who knows and who does not (e.g., my coworkers know, but my family doesn't . . .). But the question of who knows or how many people know about one's gayness raises yet another question, "how many, or which, people need to know one is gay before one qualifies as 'out'?" Or as Fuss says, "To be out, in common gay parlance, is precisely to be no longer out; to be out is to be finally outside of exteriority and all the exclusions and deprivations such outsider-hood imposes. Or, put another way, to be out is really to be in—inside the realm of the visible, the speakable, the culturally intelligible."[13]

Returning to the issue of silence and homosexuality in Asian America, it seems that topics of sex, sexuality, and gender are already diffused through discussions of Asian America.[14] For example, numerous writers have disclosed, and challenged, the panoply of contradictory sexually charged images of Asian American women as docile and subservient on the one hand, and as ruthless mata-hari, dragon-lady aggressors on the other. And of course, Frank Chin's tirades against the feminization of Asian American men has been one reaction to the particular way in which Asian Americans have been historically (de)sexualized as racial subjects. Moving from popular imagery of Asian Americans, the people, to Asia, the nation, Rey Chow uses Bertolucci's blockbuster film, *The Last Emperor*, to illustrate what she calls, "the metaphysics of feminizing the other (culture)" wherein China is predictably cast as a "feminized, eroticized, space."[15]

That the topic of homosexuality in Asian American studies is often treated in whispers, if mentioned at all, should be some indication of trouble. It is noteworthy, I think, that in the last major anthology on Asian American women, *Making Waves*, the author of the essay on Asian American lesbians was the only contributor who did not wish her last name to be published.[16] Of course, as we all know, a chorus of sympathetic bystanders is chanting about homophobia, saying, "she was worried about her job, her family, her community . . ." Therefore, perhaps a good starting point to consider lesbian and gay identities in Asian American studies is by problematizing the silences surrounding homosexuality in Asian America.

It would be easy enough for me to say that I often feel a part of me is "silenced" in Asian American Studies. But I can hardly place all of the blame on my colleagues. Sometimes I silence myself as much as I feel silenced by them. And my silencing act is a blaring welter of false starts, uncertainties, and anxieties. For example, on the one hand, an omnipresent little voice tells me that visibility is better than invisibility, and therefore, coming out is an affirming social act. On the other hand, I fear the awkward silences and struggle for conversation that sometimes follow the business of coming out. One has to think about when and where to time the act since virtually no one has ever asked me, "Are you a lesbian?" Another voice reminds me that the act of coming out, once accomplished, almost always leaves me wondering whether I did it for myself or them. Not only that, but at the moment that I have come out, relief that is born of honesty and integrity quickly turns to new uncertainty. This time, my worry is that someone will think that in my coming out, they will now have a ready-made label for me, lesbian. The prospect that someone may think that they know me because they comprehend the category lesbian fills me with stubborn resistance. The category lesbian calls up so many different images of women who love other women that I do not think that anyone— gay or straight—could possibly know or find me through that category alone. No wonder that I mostly find it easier to completely avoid the whole issue of sexual identity in discussions with colleagues.

There are so many different and subtle ways to come out. I am not much of a queer nation type, an "in your face" queer—I catalogue my own brand of lesbian identity as a kind of Asian American "take" on gay identity. I do not wear pink triangles, have photos of girls kissing in my living room, or, make a point of bringing up my girlfriend in conversation. In effect, my sexual identity is often backgrounded or stored somewhere in between domains of public and private. I used to think that my style of being gay was dignified and polite—sophisticated, civilized, and genteel. Work was work and home was home. The separation of work and home has been an easy gulf to maintain, less simple to bridge. Recently, however, I have come to think otherwise.

But all this talk about me is getting away from my point, which is that while it would be easy enough for me to say many of us feel "silenced," which alone might argue for inclusion of gay sexualities in discourse about the Asian American experience, that is not enough. Technically speaking then, the terms "addition" and "inclusion" are misleading. I'm afraid that in using such terms, the reader will assume that by adding gay/lesbian experiences to the last week's topics in a course on Asian American contemporary issues, or, by including lesbians in a discussion of Asian women, the deed is done. Instead, I want to suggest that the task is better thought of as just begun, that the topic of sexualities ought to be envisioned as a means, not an end, to theorizing about the Asian American experience.

NOTES

1. See Teresa de Lauretis, "Feminist Studies/Critical Studies: Issues, Terms, and Contexts," in *Feminist Studies/Critical Studies*, ed. Teresa de Lauretis (Bloomington: Indiana University Press, 1986), 1–19; bell hooks, *Yearning: Race, Gender and Cultural Politics* (Boston: South End Press, 1990); Trinh T. Minh-ha, *Woman, Native, Other* (Bloomington: Indiana University Press, 1989); Chandra Talpade Mohanty, "Under Western Eyes: Feminist Scholarship and Colonialist Discourses," in *Third World Women and the Politics of Feminism*, eds. Chandra Talpade Mohanty, Ann Russo, and Lourdes Torres (Bloomington: Indiana University Press, 1991), 52–80; Linda Alcoff, "Cultural Feminism versus Post-Structuralism: The Identity Crisis in Feminist Theory," *Signs*, 13: 3 (1988): 405–37.

2. Trin T. Minh-ha, 28.

3. Epstein (1987). Jeffrey Escoffier, editor of *Outlook* magazine made this point in a speech at the American Educational Research Association meetings in San Francisco, April 24, 1992.

4. See Elizabeth Ellsworth, "Why Doesn't This Feel Empowering? Working through the Repressive Myths of Critical Pedagogy," 59: 3 (1989): 297–324.

5. Of course there are exceptions, for example, blacks that "pass" and perhaps this is where homosexuality and racial identity come closest to one another, amongst those minorities who "pass" and gays who can also "pass."

6. I do not mean to suggest that there is only one presentation of self as lesbian. For example, one development recently featured in the *Los Angeles Times* is the evolution of "lipstick lesbians" (Van Gelder, 1991). The fashion issue has also been discussed in gay/lesbian publications. For example, Stein (1988) writing for *Outlook* has commented on the lack of correspondence between fashion and sexual identity, "For many, you can dress as femme one day and a butch the next. . . ."

7. Compare for example the histories: Ronald Takaki's *Strangers from a Different Shore: A History of Asian Americans* (Boston: Little, Brown, 1989) with Jonathan Katz's *Gay*

American History (New York: Meridian, 1992), Michel Foucault's *The History of Sexuality* (New York: Vintage, 1980), and David Greenberg, *The Construction of Homosexuality* (Chicago: University of Chicago Press, 1988).

8. See Steffi San Buenaventura, "The Master and the Federation : A Filipino-American Social Movement in California and Hawaii," *Social Process in Hawaii* 33 (1991): 169–93.

9. Wynn Young, "Poor Butterfly," *Amerasia Journal* 17:2 (1991): 118.

10. See Keith Osajima, "Asian Americans as the Model Minority: An Analysis of the Popular Press Image in the 1960s and 1980s," *Reflections on Shattered Windows: Promises and Prospects for Asian American Studies*, eds. Gary Y. Okihiro, Shirley Hune, Arthur A. Hansen, and John M. Liu (Pullman: Washington State University Press, 1988), 165–74.

11. See Judith Butler, *Gender Trouble* (New York: Routledge, 1990).

12. Diana Fuss, "Inside/Out," *inside/out*, ed. Diana Fuss (New York: Routledge, 1991), 1–10.

13. Ibid.

14. Consider for example debates in recent times over intermarriage patterns, the controversy over Asian Americans dating white men, the Asian Men's calendar, and the continuation of discussions started over a decade ago about gender, assimilation, and nativism in Asian American literature.

15. See Rey Chow, *Woman and Chinese Modernity* (Minneapolis: University of Minnesota Press, 1991).

16. See Asian Women United, *Making Waves* (Boston: Beacon Press, 1989).

GETTING OFF ON FEMINISM

58

Jason Schultz

Minutes after my best friend told me he was getting married, I casually offered to throw a bachelor party in his honor. Even though such parties are notorious for their degradation of women, I didn't think this party would be much of a problem. Both the bride and groom considered themselves feminists, and I figured that most of the men attending would agree that sexism had no place in the celebration of this union. In fact, I thought the bachelor party would be a great opportunity to get a group of men together for a social event that didn't

From: Rebecca Walker, ed., *To Be Real: Telling the Truth and Changing the Face of Feminism* (New York: Anchor Books, 1995), pp. 107–26. Reprinted by permission.

degenerate into the typical antiwomen, homophobic male-bonding thing. Still, ending one of the most sexist traditions in history—even for one night— was a lot tougher than I envisioned.

I have to admit that I'm not a *complete* iconoclast: I wanted to make the party a success by including at least some of the usual elements, such as good food and drink, great music, and cool things to do. At the same time, I was determined not to fall prey to traditional sexist party gimmicks such as prostitutes, strippers jumping out of cakes, or straight porn. But after nixing all the traditional lore, even *I* thought it sounded boring. What were we going to do except sit around and think about women?

"What about a belly dancer?" one of the ushers suggested when I confided my concerns to him. "That's not as bad as a stripper." I sighed. This was supposed to be an occasion for the groom and his male friends to get together, celebrate the upcoming marriage, and affirm their friendship and connection with each other as men. "What . . . does hiring a female sex worker have to do with any of that?" I shouted into the phone. I quickly regained my calm, but his suggestion still stung. We had to find some other way.

I wanted my party to be as "sexy" as the rest of them, but I had no idea how to do that in the absence of female sex workers. There was no powerful alternative image in our culture from which I could draw. I thought about renting some gay porn, or making it a cross-dressing party, but many of the guests were conservative, and I didn't want to scare anyone off. Besides, what would it say about a bunch of straight men if all we could do to be sexy was act queer for a night?

Over coffee on a Sunday morning, I asked some of the other guys what they thought was so "sexy" about having a stripper at a bachelor party.

"Well," David said, "it's just a gag. It's something kinda funny and sexy at the same time."

"Yeah," A.J. agreed. "It's not all that serious, but it's something special to do that makes the party cool."

"But *why* is it sexy and funny?" I asked. "Why can't we, as a bunch of guys, be sexy and funny ourselves?"

"'Cause it's easier to be a guy with other guys when there's a chick around. It gives you all something in common to relate to."

"Hmm. I think I know what you mean," I said. "When I see a stripper, I get turned on, but not in the same way I would if I was with a lover. It's more like going to a show or watching a flick together. It's enjoyable, stimulating, but it's not overwhelming or intimate in the same way that sex is. Having the stripper provides a common emotional context for us to feel turned on. But we don't have to do anything about it like we would if we were with a girlfriend, right?"

"Well, my girlfriend would kill me if she saw me checking out this stripper," Greg replied. "But because it's kind of a male-bonding thing, it's not as threatening to our relationship. It's not because it's the stripper over her, it's because it's just us guys hanging out. It doesn't go past that."

Others agreed. "Yeah. You get turned on, but not in a serious way. It makes you feel sexy and sexual, and you can enjoy feeling that way with your friends. Otherwise, a lot of times, just hanging out with the guys is pretty boring. Especially at a bachelor party. I mean, that's the whole point, isn't it—to celebrate the fact that we're bachelors, and he"—referring to Robert, the groom—"isn't!"

Through these conversations, I realized that having a female sex worker at the party would give the men permission to connect with one another without becoming vulnerable. When men discuss sex in terms of actions—who they "did," and how and where they did it—they can gain recognition and validation of their sexuality from other men without having to expose their *feelings* about sex.

"What other kinds of things make you feel sexy like the stripper does?" I asked several of the guys.

"Watching porn sometimes, or a sexy movie."

A. J. said, "Just getting a look from a girl at a club. I mean, she doesn't even have to talk to you, but you still feel sexy and you can still hang out with your friends."

Greg added, "Sometimes just knowing that my girlfriend thinks I'm sexy, and then talking about her with friends, makes me feel like I'm the man. Or I'll hear some other guy talk about his girlfriend in a way that reminds me of mine, and I'll still get that same feeling. But that doesn't happen very often, and usually only when talking with one other guy.

This gave me an idea. "I've noticed that same thing, both here and at school with my other close guy friends. Why doesn't it happen with a bunch of guys, say at a party?"

"I don't know. It's hard to share a lot of personal stuff with guys," said Adam, "especially about someone you're seeing, if you don't feel comfortable. Well, not comfortable, because I know most of the guys who'll be at the party, but it's more like I don't want them to hassle me, or I might say something that freaks them out."

"Or you're just used to guys talking shit about girls," someone else added. "Like at a party or hanging out together. They rag on them, or pick out who's the cutest or who wants to do who. That's not the same thing as really talking about what makes you feel sexy."

"Hmm," I said. "So it's kind of like if I were to say that I liked to be tied down to the bed, no one would take me seriously. You guys would probably crack up laughing, make a joke or two, but I'd never expect you to actually join in and talk about being tied up in a serious way. It certainly wouldn't feel 'sexy,' would it? At least not as much as the stripper."

"Exactly. You talking about being tied down here is fine, 'cause we're into the subject of sex on a serious kick and all. But at a party, people are bullshitting each other and gabbing, and horsing around. The last thing most of us want is to trip over someone's personal taste or start thinking someone's a little queer."

"You mean queer as in homosexual?" I asked.

"Well, not really, 'cause I think everyone here is straight. But more of queer in the sense of perverted or different. I mean, you grow up in high school thinking that all guys are basically the same. You all want the same thing from girls in the same way. And when someone like you says you like to be tied down, it's kinda weird—almost like a challenge. It makes me have to respond in a way that either shows me agreeing that I also like to be tied down or not. And if someone's a typical guy and he says that, it makes you think he's different—not the same guy you knew in high school. And if he's not the same guy, then it challenges you to relate to him on a different level."

"Yeah, I guess in some ways it's like relating to someone who's gay," Greg said. "He can be cool and all, and you can get along totally great. But there's this barrier that's hard to cross over. It kinda keeps you apart. And that's not what you want to feel toward your friends, especially at a party like this one, where you're all coming together to chill."

As the bachelor party approached, I found myself wondering whether my friends and I could "come together to chill"—and affirm our status as sexual straight men—without buying into homophobic or sexist expressions. At the same time, I was doing a lot of soul-searching on how we could challenge the dominant culture's vision of male heterosexuality, not only by deciding against having a stripper at our party, but also by examining and redefining our own relationships with women.

SEX AND THE SENSITIVE MAN

According to the prevailing cultural view, "desirable" hetero men are inherently dominant, aggressive, and, in many subtle and overt ways, abusive to women. To be sexy and powerful, straight men are expected to control and contrive a sexuality that reinforces their authority. Opposing these notions of power subjects a straight guy to being branded "sensitive," submissive, or passive—banished to the nether regions of excitement and pleasure, the unmasculine, asexual, "vanilla" purgatory of antieroticism. Just as hetero women are often forced to choose between the images of the virgin and the whore, modern straight men are caught in a cultural tug-of-war between the Marlboro Man and the Wimp.

So where does that leave straight men who want to reexamine what a man is and change it? Can a good man be sexy? Can a sexy man be good? What is good sex, egalitarian sex? More fundamentally, can feminist women and men coexist comfortably, even happily, within the same theoretical framework— or the same bedroom?

Relationships with men remain one of the most controversial topics among feminists today. Having sex, negotiating emotional dependency, and/or raising children force many hetero couples to balance their desire to be together with the oppressive dynamics of sexism. In few other movements are the oppressor group and the oppressed group so intimately linked.

But what about men who support feminism? Shouldn't it be okay for straight feminist women to have sex with them? Straight men aren't always oppressive in their sexuality, are they?

You may laugh at these questions, but they hold serious implications for straight feminist sex. I've seen many relationships between opposite-sex activists self-destruct because critical assumptions about power dynamics and desires were made in the mind, but not in the bed. I've even been told that straight male feminists can't get laid without (A) feeling guilty; (B) reinforcing patriarchy; or (C) maintaining complete passivity during sexual activity. Each of these three options represents common assumptions about the sexuality of straight men who support feminism. Choice A, "feeling guilty," reflects the belief that straight male desire inherently contradicts the goals of feminism and fails to contribute to the empowerment of women. It holds that any man who enjoys sex with a woman must be benefiting from sexist male privilege, not fighting against it. In other words, hot sex becomes a zero-sum game where if men gain, feminism loses.

Choice B represents the assumption that hetero male sex is inherently patriarchal. Beyond merely being of no help, as in Choice A, straight male sexuality is seen as part of the problem. Within this theory, one often hears statements such as "all heterosexual sex is rape." Even though these statements are usually taken out of context, the ideas behind them are problematic. In essence, they say that you can never have a male/female interaction that isn't caught up in oppressive dynamics. Men and women can never be together, especially in such a vulnerable exchange as sexuality, without being subject to the misdistribution of power in society.

The third choice, "maintaining complete passivity," attempts a logical answer to the above predicament. In order to come even close to achieving equality in heterosexuality (and still get laid), men must "give up" all their power through inactivity. A truly feminist man should take no aggressive or dominant position. He should, in fact, not act at all; he should merely lie back and allow the woman to subvert male supremacy through her complete control of the situation. In other words, for a man and a woman to share sexuality on a "level playing field," the man must remove all symptoms of his power through passivity, even though the causes of that inequality (including his penis!) still exist. . . .

Does it have to be this way? Must male heterosexuality always pose a threat to feminism? What about the sensitive guy? Wasn't that the male cry (whimper) of the nineties? Sorry, but all the media hype about sensitivity never added up to significant changes in behavior. Straight male sexuality still re-mains one of the most underchallenged areas of masculinity in America. Some men *did* propose a different kind of sexuality for straight men in the 1970s, one that emphasizes feelings and sensitivity and emotional connection. But these efforts failed to affect our ideas in any kind of revolutionary way. Now, instead of a "sexy" sensitive guy, men's magazines are calling for the emergence of the "Post-Sensitive Man," while scientific studies tell us that women prefer Clint Eastwood over Michael Bolton.

Why did sensitivity fail? Were straight women, even feminists, lying to men about what they wanted? The answer is "yes" and "no." I don't think sen-sitivity was the culprit. I think the problem was men's passivity, or more spe-cifically, men's lack of assertiveness and power.

In much of our understanding, power is equated with oppression: images of white supremacists dominating people of color, men dominating women, and the rich dominating the poor underline the histories of many cultures and societies. But power need not always oppress others. One can, I believe, be powerful in a nonoppressive way.

In order to find this sort of alternative, we need to examine men's experi-ence with power and sexuality further. Fortunately, queer men and women have given us a leg up on the process by reenergizing the debate about what is good sex and what is fair sex. Gay male culture has a long history of exploring nontraditional aspects of male sexuality, such as cross-dressing, bondage and dominance, and role playing. These dynamics force gay men to break out of a singular experience of male sexual desire and to examine the diversity within male sexuality in the absence of gender oppression. Though gay men's culture still struggles with issues such as the fetishizing of men of color and body fas-cism, it does invite greater exploration of diversity than straight male culture. Gay culture has broader and more inclusive attitudes about what is sexy and a conception of desire that accommodates many types of sex for many types of gay men. For straight men in our culture, there is such a rigid definition of "sexy" that it leaves us few options besides being oppressive, overbearing, or violent.

Part of the success that gay male culture enjoys in breaking out of mono-lithic notions of male sexuality lies in the acceptance it receives from its part-ners and peers. Camp, butch, leather, drag-queen culture is constantly affirm-ing the powerful presence of alternative sexualities. Straight male culture, on the other hand, experiences a lack—a void of acceptance—whenever it tries to assert some image other than the sexist hetero male. Both publicly and in many cases privately, alternative straight male sexualities fail to compete for attention and acceptance among hetero men and women. . . .

We need to assert a new feminist sexuality for men, one that competes with the traditional paradigm but offers a more inviting notion of how hetero men can be sexual while tearing apart the oppressive and problematic ways in which so many of us have experienced sexuality in the past. We need to find new, strong values and ideas of male heterosexuality instead of passive identities that try to distance us from sexist men. We need to stop trying to avoid powerful straight sexuality and work to redefine what our power means and does. We need to find strength and desire outside of macho, antiwomen ways of being masculine. . . .

Gay men and lesbians have engaged in a cultural dialogue around sexuality over the last twenty-five years; straight women are becoming more and more vocal. But straight men have been almost completely silent. This silence, I think, stems in large part from fear: our cultures tell us that being a "real" man means not being feminine, not being gay, and not being weak. They warn us that anyone who dares to stand up to these ideas becomes a sitting target to have his manhood shot down in flames.

BREAKING THE SILENCE

Not becoming a sitting target to have *my* manhood shot down was high on my mind when the evening of my best friend's bachelor party finally arrived. But I was determined not to be silent about how I felt about the party and about new visions for straight men within our society.

We decided to throw the party two nights before the wedding. We all gathered at my house, each of us bringing a present to add to the night's activities. After all the men had arrived, we began cooking dinner, breaking open beer and champagne, and catching up on where we had left off since we last saw each other.

During the evening, we continued to talk off and on about why we didn't have a stripper or prostitute for the party. After several rounds of margaritas and a few hands of poker, tension started to build around the direction I was pushing the conversation.

"So what don't you like about strippers?" David asked me.

This was an interesting question. I was surprised not only by the guts of David to ask it, but also by my own mixed feelings in coming up with an answer. "It's not that I don't like being excited, or turned on, per se," I responded. "In fact, to be honest, watching a female stripper is an exciting and erotic experience for me. But at the same time, it's a very uncomfortable one. I get a sense when I watch her that I'm participating in a misuse of pleasure, if that makes sense."

I looked around at my friends. I couldn't tell whether the confused looks on their faces were due to the alcohol, the poker game, or my answer, so I continued. "Ideally, I would love to sit back and enjoy watching someone express herself sexually through dance, seduction, flirtation—all the positive elements I associate with stripping," I said. "But at the same time, because so many strippers are poor and forced to perform in order to survive economically, I feel like the turn-on I get is false. I feel like I get off easy, sitting back as the man, paying for the show. No one ever expects me to get up on stage.

"And in that way, it's selling myself short sexually. It's not only saying very little about the sexual worth of the woman on stage, but the sexual worth of me as the viewer as well. By *only* being a viewer—just getting off as a member of the audience—the striptease becomes a very limiting thing, an imbalanced dynamic. If the purpose is for me to feel sexy and excited, but not to act on those feelings, I'd rather find a more honest and direct way to do it. So personally, while I would enjoy watching a stripper on one level, the real issues of economics, the treatment of women, and the limitation of my own sexual personae push me to reject the whole stripper thing in favor of something else."

"But what else do you do to feel sexy?" A. J. asked.

"That's a tough question," I said. "Feeling sexy often depends on the way other people act toward you. For me, right now, you guys are a huge way for me to feel sexy. [Some of the men cringe.] I'm not saying that we have to challenge our sexual identities, although that's one way. But we can cut through a lot of this locker-room macho crap and start talking with each other about how we feel sexually, what we think, what we like, etc. Watching the stripper makes us feel sexy because we get turned on through the dynamic between her performance and our voyeurism. We can find that same erotic connection with each other by re-creating that context between us. In such a case, we're still heterosexual—we're no more having sex with each other than we are with the stripper. But we're not relying on the imbalanced dynamic of sex work to feel pleasure as straight men." . . .

The guys were silent for a few seconds, but soon afterwards, the ice seemed to break. . . . They agreed that, as heterosexual men, we should be able to share with each other what we find exciting and shouldn't *need* a female stripper to feel sexy. In some ways it may have been the desire to define their own sexuality that changed their minds; in others it may have been a traditionally masculine desire to reject any dependency on women. In any case, other men began to speak of their own experiences with pleasure and desire, and we continued to talk throughout the night, exploring the joys of hot sex, one-night stands, and even our preferences for certain brands of condoms. We discussed the ups and down of monogamy versus "open" dating and the pains of long-distance relationships.

Some men continued to talk openly about their desire for straight pornography or women who fit the traditional stereotype of feminity. But others contradicted this, expressing their wish to move beyond that image of women in their lives. The wedding, which started out as the circumstance for our gathering, soon fell into the background of our thoughts as we focused away from institutional ideas of breeder sexuality and began to find common ground through our real-life experiences and feelings as straight men. In the end, we all toasted the groom, sharing stories, jokes, and parts of our lives that many of us had never told. Most importantly, we were able to express ourselves sexually without hiding who we were from each other.

Thinking back on the party, I realized that the hard part was figuring out what we all wanted and how to construct a different way of finding that experience. The other men there wanted it just as much as I did. The problem was that we had no ideas of what a different kind of bachelor party might look like. Merely eliminating the old ways of relating (i.e., the female sex workers) left a gap, an empty space which in many ways *felt* worse than the sexist connection that existed there before; we felt passive and powerless. Yet we found a new way of interacting—one that embraced new ideas and shared the risk of experiencing them.

Was the party sexy? Did we challenge the dominance of oppressive male sexuality? Not completely, but it was a start. I doubt anyone found my party as "sexy" as traditional ones might be, but the dialogue has to start somewhere. It's going to take a while to generate the language and collective tension to balance the cultural image of heterosexual male sexuality with true sexual diversity. Still, one of my friends from high school—who's generally on the conservative end of most issues—told me as he was leaving that of all the bachelor parties he had been to, this was by far the best one. "I had a great time," he said. "Even without the stripper." . . .

When it comes to sex, feminist straight men must become participants in the discourse about our own sexuality. We have to fight the oppressive images of men as biological breeders and leering animals. We must find ways in which to understand our diverse backgrounds, articulate desires that are not oppressive, and acknowledge the power we hold. We must take center stage when it comes to articulating our views in a powerful voice. I'm not trying to prescribe any particular form of sexuality or specify what straight men should want. But until we begin to generate our own demands and desires in an honest and equitable way for feminist straight women to hear, I don't think we can expect to be both good *and* sexy any time soon.

Violence and Social Control

THE HARM THAT HAS NO NAME

Street Harassment, Embodiment, and African American Women

Deirdre E. Davis

In her article *Street Harassment and the Informal Ghettoization of Women*, law professor Cynthia Grant Bowman explores street harassment as a harm and the necessity of legally recognizing street harassment's oppressive effects.[1] This chapter explores the idea that "[w]e cannot hope to understand the meaning of a person's experiences, including her experiences of oppression, without first thinking of her as embodied, and second thinking about the particular meanings assigned to that embodiment"[2] in the context of street harassment and African American women. Street harassment silences women. Similarly, racism has silenced and continues to silence African American women. Writing about street harassment and African American women legitimizes and recognizes the existence and importance of both.

THE MECHANICS OF STREET HARASSMENT

There are three ways to define and understand street harassment. Specifically, particular acts constitute street harassment. Normatively, the following characteristics identify particular acts of street harassment: the locale; the gender

From: *UCLA Women's Law Journal* 133 (1994).

of and the relationship between the harasser and the target; the unacceptabil-
ity of "thank you" as a response; and the reference to body parts. Systematically, street harassment can be understood as an element of a larger system of
sexual terrorism.

Specific Acts of Street Harassment

Cheris Kramarae, professor of speech communication and sociology, and
Elizabeth Kissling describe street harassment as "verbal and nonverbal mark-
ers . . . wolf-whistles, leers, winks, grabs, pinches, catcalls and street remarks."[3]
Specific remarks commonly include "Hey, pretty," "Hey, whore," "What ya
doin' tonight?" "Look at them legs," "Wanna fuck?" "Are you working?"
"Great legs," "Hey, cunt," "Smile," "Smile for me, baby," "Smile, bitch,"
"Come here, girl," and "I'll be back when you get a little older, baby." When
these acts occur on a public street, street harassment takes place.[4]

Street Harassment's Role in Sexual Terrorism

Recognizing street harassment's role in sexual terrorism is crucial to understanding its potential to harm. Carole Sheffield defines sexual terrorism as
men's systematic control and domination of women through actual and implied
violence.[5] She views sexual terrorism as both the objective condition of wom-
en's existence and the theoretical framework that creates and maintains social
orders.[6] Sexual terrorism and violence play crucial roles in the ongoing process
of female subordination.[7] Violence is not one particular act, nor is it static;
rather, it is a continuum of behavior in which street harassment must be placed
if we are to understand the depth and pervasiveness of sexual terrorism.[8]

Street harassment "frightens women and reinforces fears of rape and other
acts of terrorism."[9] Rape is generally viewed as a violent act of power occurring in a context limited to particular individuals or situations. However, rape
may begin with an act of street harassment. Potential rapists can test the accessibility of a victim by making derogatory sexual comments to determine
whether she can be intimidated.[10] As a result, street harassment plays a definite role in the objective condition of women fearing bodily harm on a day-
to-day basis.

Women also experience the connection between rape and street harassment on a subjective level. Regardless of whether there is the possibility of actual rape, when women endure street harassment, they fear the possibility of
rape.[11] That one of every eight adult women has been raped makes rape a constant possibility on a subjective level.[12] The sexual content of street harassment "reminds women of their vulnerability to violent attack in American urban centers, and to sexual violence in general" and intensifies the fear of the
possibility of rape.[13] As a precursor to rape and an escalator of the fear of rape,
street harassment entraps women in a sexually terroristic environment.

Within the framework of sexual terrorism, the specific acts and normative characteristics of street harassment identify the range of behavior that
constitutes street harassment. Once it is realized that "street harassment is not
a product of a sexually terroristic culture, but an active factor in creating such
a culture," then the ability of an act of street harassment to cause harm becomes clearer.[14]

GENDERIZATION OF THE STREET: THE EFFECTS
AND CONTEXT OF STREET HARASSMENT

Street harassment genderizes the street by distributing power in such a way
that perpetuates male supremacy and female subordination.[15] Consequently,
street harassment transforms the street into yet another forum that perpetuates and reinforces the gender hierarchy.

In order for the social effects of street harassment to occur, a preexisting
context must exist that enables street harassment. Psychological oppression
serves as the context that allows street harassment to genderize the street.

Despite street harassment's clear socially and psychologically oppressive
effects, street harassment remains invisible as a harm. Because men do not suffer street harassment to the extent women do, street harassment is characterized as something other than harassment. Acts that are legally cognizable
harms gain recognition "as an injury of the systematic abuse of power in hierarchies [when it is an exercise of] power men recognize."[16] Men view street
harassment as innocuous, trivial, "boys will be boys" type of behavior and
blame women for attaching negative meanings to their acts. Street harassment
remains invisible because it is not a harm men suffer, and therefore it is not a
harm men, or society as a whole, recognize.

While some women view street harassment as a trivial part of their everyday lives, they can still suffer extreme consequences. First, because street harassment has been trivialized, women do not talk about it and are thus silenced.
This reinforces the invisibility of street harassment and its effects. Moreover,
when a woman thinks about ending the silence, she may have a lot of doubt,
given that street harassment—a pervasive part of everyday life—is so trivialized. Ignoring street harassment causes women to become complicit supporters of a system of sexual terrorism.[17] Finally, the failure to perceive street harassment as a harm causes women to "transform the pain into something else,
such as, for example, punishment, or flattery, or transcendence, or unconscious pleasure."[18]

Giving a harm a name is the first step in making the harm visible. Given
that "an injury uniquely sustained by a disempowered group will *lack a name*,
a history, and in general *a linguistic reality*," it is crucial for the targets of street
harassment to name the harm.[19] Naming is not a random or neutral process,

but is biased. One need only look at workplace sexual harassment, date rape, domestic violence, and marital rape to understand the importance of naming a harm. While these harms have been a part of society for a long time, once they had a name, their visibility, both as acts and as harms, increased and led to the possibility of redress.

It is important for women to name the harms they suffer, because "[b]y taking the power of naming for themselves [and gaining cultural autonomy], women can determine with what bias street harassment will be encoded."[20] Discussing and naming street harassment are crucial steps toward erasing a constant source of women's pain and making street harassment visible as a harm.

INCLUDING AFRICAN AMERICAN WOMEN IN THE DISCOURSE ON STREET HARASSMENT: GENDERIZATION AND RACIALIZATION OF THE STREET

African American Women and Street Harassment: Recurring Images of Slavery

By refusing to acknowledge difference, street harassment discourse has excluded African American women's experiences. Many have argued that street harassment just "is," and that race, class, and sexual orientation are irrelevant: "In fact, women will sometimes comment that they think that women of all races, classes, and ages are subject to attacks from men—of all races, classes, and ages."[21] This statement relies on the idea that street harassment is primarily based on gender domination. Consequently, this statement implies that, because all women experience street harassment, it has no significance beyond its gender meaning: "[T]he women who do find street remarks disturbing, disgusting, or dangerous evidently hear them as more sexist than racist or classist."[22] The race of the harassers has also been disregarded: "You can say what you like about class and race. Those differences are real. But in this everyday scenario, any man on earth, no matter what his color or class is, has the power to make any woman who is exposed to him hate herself and her body."[23] This nuanced treatment of race ignores the relevant inquiry: the issue is not the act's independence from these differences, but the fact that the act occurs in spite of the differences. Abstracting the categories of identity limits understanding of the dynamics of street harassment.

All women are subjected to street harassment and, consequently, street harassment is a form of gender subordination. However, when African American women are subjected to street harassment, street harassment is, at the very least, genderized and racialized. This is not to say that street harassment has one meaning for African American women and a different meaning for all other women. Given the various histories of women of differing races and ethnicities, including white women, street harassment is both genderized and racialized for every woman; but the racial aspect is set in the particular historical context to which the particular woman belongs.

During and as a result of slavery, African American women have experienced the preexisting context that enables street harassment to be a factor in our sexually terroristic environment. Consequently, the psychological oppression of street harassment has a different—not a double—impact on African American women given their embodiment as indivisible beings. Street harassment forces African American women to realize that the ideologies of slavery still exist.

Although slavery has been legally eradicated, the racist ideology perpetuated during the slave era still exists with a different fate. While the "formal barriers and symbolic manifestations of subordination"[24] have disappeared, "[t]he white norm . . . has not disappeared; it has only been submerged in popular consciousness."[25] White men struggle to maintain their hierarchical position in a social structure that is constantly being challenged, questioned, and chiseled away.

Street harassment is a forum that allows white men, in the absence of slavery, to maintain the boundaries of their relationship with black women and to perpetuate the image of African American women as "blackwomen." The legal and cultural invisibility of street harassment gives white men a way of oppressing African American women that replaces the historical slave/master structure.

The Cult of True Womanhood: The White Woman as Paradigm

Street harassment oppresses women because it denies women an authentic choice of self and mandates conformance to gender stereotypes. Such oppression also formed the basis of the slave era's dominant gender ideology. In her work *Reconstructing Womanhood*, English and African American studies professor Hazel Carby explores women slaves' relationship to the predominant ideology of the "cult of true [white] womanhood."[26] Based on notions of motherhood and womanhood, the cardinal tenets of piety, purity (sexual and nonsexual), submissiveness, and domesticity characterized the cult of true womanhood.[27]

The ideology had two cultural effects: "[I]t was dominant, in the sense of being the most subscribed to convention governing female behavior, but it was also clearly recognizable as a dominating image, describing the parameters within which women were measured and declared to be, or not to be, women."[28] White men used the cult of true womanhood to establish the normative ideal for white women and to establish the boundaries outside of which slave women were placed.[29] Despite the opposing definitions of motherhood and womanhood for white women and slave women, the definitions were dependent on one another.[30]

The cult of true womanhood also illustrates how stereotypes obscure women's reality by focusing on men's interpretations. During slavery, slave owners and buyers perceived some characteristics as negative in white women, yet as positive, economic assets in slave women. For example, "[s]trength and ability to bear fatigue, argued to be so distasteful a presence in a white woman, were positive features to be emphasized in the promotion and selling of a black female field hand at a slave auction."[31]

African American slave women internalized the underlying ideological beliefs; "[b]y completely accepting the female role as defined by patriarchy, enslaved blackwomen embraced and upheld an oppressive sexist social order and became (along with their white sisters) both accomplices in the crimes perpetuated against women and the victims of those crimes."[32] Consequently, cultural domination has led African American women to believe that street harassment is an acceptable, natural part of everyday life, given the slave culture.

The Controlling Image of Jezebel: African American Woman as (White) Man's Temptress   During slavery, white men developed a racist ideology particular to slave women, which consisted of four "interrelated, socially constructed controlling images."[33] Created by white men to justify, maintain, and perpetuate the subordination of African American women, the most powerful of these controlling images is that of the female slave as a Jezebel. The Jezebel image—the slave woman as "whore, sexually aggressive wet nurse," and "sexual temptress"—served two functions. First, it justified white men's sexual abuse of slave women. Second, it justified the inapplicability of the cult of true womanhood to slave women—if a slave woman was seen as a sexual animal, then she was not a real woman. The hypersexual Jezebel image dehumanized black women and justified their exploitation in the fields. White men used the controlling image of Jezebel, in conjunction with other images, to create and maintain the existing slave/master social and economic structure.

Multiple Subordination: The Intersection of White Men's and African American Men's Objectification of African American Women   While "[r]acism has always been a divisive force separating black men and white men, [it has been] sexism [that] has been a force that unites the two groups."[34] Like white men, African American men have been socialized to exercise their male status to oppress women: "As Americans, they [African American men] had not been taught to really believe that social equality was an inherent right all people possess, but they had been socialized to believe that it is the nature of males to desire and have access to power and privilege."[35] One of the entitlements of being a member of the male gender is the ability to exercise dominance over women. During the slavery era, the African American man, "though obviously deprived of the social status that would enable him to protect and provide for himself and others, had a higher status than the black female slave based solely on his being male." [36] Again, the binary framework of racism and sexism ignores the fact that "[r]acism does not prevent black men from absorbing the same sexist socialization white men are inundated with." [37] As a result of the intersection of race and gender, while racism "cause[s] white men to make blackwomen targets," [38] "sexism . . . causes all men to think they can verbally or physically assault women sexually with impunity." [39]

When African American Men Seek a Position of Whiteness: The Experience of Intraracial Harassment   Given the pervasiveness of the controlling images of African American womanhood created and perpetuated by white men, African American men also view African American women "as nothing more than mammies, matriarchs, or Jezebels." As bell hooks points out, "[a]s sexist ideology has been accepted by black people, these negative myths and stereotypes have effectively transcended class and race boundaries and affected the way black women [are] perceived by members of their own race." [40]

African American men exercise the power implicit in sexism from a "position of whiteness." A position of whiteness consists of the "historically derived constellation of privileges associated with white [male] racial domination." [41] A person acting from a position of whiteness creates a racial hierarchy and produces and reinforces stereotypical images. This position of whiteness is not limited to white men, but can be seen as a position of authority attended by the privileges associated with authority.

Whereas white men assign and invoke the Jezebel image of African American women in order to maintain dominance, African American men use the same image in order to try to obtain that which white men have—the power to define the position of whiteness. As bell hooks has noted, "[t]heir [black men's] expressions of rage and anger are less a critique of the white male patriarchal social order and more a reaction against the fact that *they have not been allowed full participation in the power game.*" [42] Engaging in any form of oppression when you are a member of a marginalized group may make a person feel more powerful and less oppressed. Nevertheless, the established social order, though possibly capable of change, is still relative. Consequently, "men of color are not able to reap the material and social rewards for their participation in patriarchy. In fact they often suffer from blindly and passively acting out a myth of masculinity that is life-threatening. Sexist thinking blinds them to this reality. They become victims of the patriarchy." [43]

Some have argued that street harassment does not harm African American women because "[i]n many African American communities, men and women engage in sexually oriented banter in public." [44] Even if this rapping does exist between African American men and women, the speech rights are asymmetrical because "although many African American women respond assertively to rapping, they typically do not initiate it."[45] Furthermore, the fact that some African American women may engage in rapping does not negate the fact that

> [b]lack leaders, male and female, have been unwilling to acknowledge black male sexist oppression of black women because they do not want to acknowledge that racism is not the only oppressive force in our lives. *Nor do they wish to complicate efforts to resist racism by acknowledging that black men can be victimized by racism but at the same time act as sexist oppressors of black women.*[46]

Finally, characterizing street harassment as an African American cultural phenomenon ignores the intersection of race and gender by "overlook[ing] the way in which this sexual discourse reflects a differential power relationship between men and women."[47] This characterization also allows society to avoid examining "the different means by which these [African American cultural] practices are maintained and legitimated," thereby perpetuating the subordination of African American women.[48]

Multiple Consciousness and Street Harassment: Incorporating African American Women's Experience

Including African American women's experiences in the street harassment discourse enlightens women to their multiple consciousness and provides all women with a tool that enables them to cope with the social and psychologically oppressive effects of street harassment. By embracing the multiplicitous self, African American women, as the descendants of slaves, have learned how to handle the multiple forms of oppression, including gender and racial oppression. Recognizing a multiple consciousness helps women deconstruct and accept their experiences with street harassment. By embracing the multiple parts of self and moving away from a binary construction of "self," we also recognize the possibility for internal contradiction.

African American women have historically and consistently existed in a zone of dissonance. African American women, as society's "other," are disenfranchised and excluded from society in many ways. At the same time, African American women are "essential for [society's] survival because those individuals who stand at the margins of society clarify its boundaries. African American women, by not belonging, emphasize the significance of belonging."[49]

The multiple consciousness is yet another site of identity, where both the subjective self and the objective self coexist. Recognizing this site of identity will allow women to shift their energies from deconstructing and understanding women's response to street harassment, to eradicating street harassment.

A New Definition for the Effects of Street Harassment: Spirit-Murder

Including African American women's experiences in street harassment discourse provides a fuller understanding of how all women may experience street harassment. This inclusion also provides access to a broader term that may more fully reflect street harassment's invidious role in terrorizing all women. Law professor Patricia Williams states that "[a] fundamental part of ourselves and of our dignity is dependent upon the uncontrollable, powerful, external observers who constitute society."[50] Engaging in racist behavior, which is the overt expression of the internalized "system of formalized distortions of thought,"[51] leads to the "disregard for others whose lives qualitatively depend on our regard."[52] Williams terms this disregard "spirit-murder," a phenomenon that creates and perpetuates social structures that are defined by hate and fear, and give unexpressed feeling an outlet. While Williams's discussion of spirit-murder encompasses only race, Adrien Wing incorporates sexism into the concept of spirit-murder.[53] While spirit-murder is the cumulative effect, it is made up of micro aggressions, "[h]undreds, if not thousands of spirit injuries and assaults—some major, some minor—the cumulative effect of which is the slow death of the psyche, the soul and the persona."[54] In the context of street harassment, it is easy to understand spirit-murder as being subjected to many incidences of street harassment each day. To gain a fuller understanding of street harassment and its impact on African American women, it is necessary to place street harassment in the continuum of behavior that includes spirit-murder. Using these terms, one can understand the full extent to which all women are terrorized.

Redefining street harassment as spirit-murder benefits not only African American women, but all women. It allows for recognition of the "other" harms that women suffer, which may or may not be due to their gender. Furthermore, defining street harassment as "spirit-murder" both helps to give street harassment a name and identifies the harasser's wrong instead of focusing on the target. An objective definition of street harassment focuses on the harasser's actions as a form of intrusion instead of "looking to" or blaming the female target. When African American women's experiences are incorporated into the street harassment discourse, women are empowered with a terminology that fully portrays the depth of women's experiences with street harassment.

The first step in recognizing an act as a harm is the accurate construction of that act. Once street harassment is constructed and understood to be a harm that plays a role in the sexual terrorism that governs women's lives by genderizing the street n order to perpetuate female subordination, street harassment becomes visible as a harm. In order to address, deconstruct, and eradicate a harm, we must give the harm a name. Employing the term "street harassment" to describe the type of behavior is one step toward breaking the silence and misconceptions that surround street harassment.

Including African American women's experiences within street harassment and recognizing the different ways African American women experience street harassment due to their experiences with slavery broaden street harassment discourse. This inclusion provides both access to a term, multiple consciousness, that defines the site in which the harm occurs, and a broader meaning of the effects of street harassment, spirit-murder. These terms give women a fuller understanding of the harm street harassment causes.

Naming the harm gives all women the tools with which street harassment can be dismantled and gives them the strength to speak out, up, and loud in response to street harassment.

NOTES

1. Cynthia G. Bowman, *Street Harassment and the Informal Ghettoization of Women*, 106 Harv. L. Rev. 517 (1993).

2. Elizabeth V. Spelman, Inessential Woman: Problems of Exclusion in Feminist Thought 129–30 (1988).

3. Elizabeth A. Kissling & Cheris Kramarae, *Stranger Compliments: The Interpretation of Street Remarks*, 14 Women's Stud. Comm. 75, 75–76 (1991) (reporting results from a computer notes file discussion on street harassment).

4. I focus on the street/sidewalk as the situs. I exclude places like buses, bus stations, taxis, stores, and other public accommodations to highlight the arbitrariness of street harassment. Although I choose to focus on the street, harassment can and does occur in other places.

5. Carole J. Sheffield, *Sexual Terrorism: The Social Control of Women*, *in* Analyzing Gender 171, 171 (Beth B. Hess & Myra Marx Ferree eds., 1987).

6. *Id.* at 172. The manifestations of sexual terrorism include wife-battering, sexual harassment in the workplace, incest, sexual slavery, prostitution, and rape. *Id.* at 171.

7. *Id.* at 172.

8. There is an "unstated relationship [between] compliments, verbal hostility and physical attack." Kissling & Kramarae, *supra* note 3, at 78; *see also* Cristina Del Sesto, *Our Mean Streets: D.C.'s Women Walk Through Verbal Combat Zones*, Wash. Post, Mar. 18, 1990, at B1 ("I'm afraid everyday that a verbal assault is going to turn into a physical one.").

9. Elizabeth A. Kissling, *Street Harassment: The Language of Sexual Terrorism*, 2 Discourse & Soc'y 451, 456 (1991).

10. *See* Bowman, *supra* note 1, at 536.

11. Kissling & Kramarae, *supra* note 3, at 84–85.

12. Bowman, *supra* note 1, at 536 n.86 (quoting *Study: Rapes Far Underestimated*, Chi. Trib., Apr. 24, 2991 § 1, at 3).

13. Kissling & Kramarae, *supra* note 3, at 76.

14. *See* Kissling, *supra* note 9, at 456.

15. *See* Catharine A. MacKinnon, *Difference and Dominance: On Discrimination, in* Feminism Unmodified: Discourses on Life and Law 32, 40 (1987).

16. Catharine A. MacKinnon, *Sexual Harassment: Its First Decade in Court, in* Feminism Unmodified, *supra* note 15, at 103, 107.

17. Kissling, *supra* note 9, at 456.

18. Robin West, *The Difference in Women's Hedonic Lives: A Phenomenological Critique of Feminist Legal Theory*, 3 Wis. Women's L.J. 81, 85 (1987). This is also something the street harasser does.

19. *Id.* (emphasis added).

20. *See* Kissling, *supra* note 9, at 457.

21. Kissling & Kramarae, *supra* note 3, at 90.

22. *Id.* It would be helpful to know the race, sexual orientation, and economic status of the women commentators.

23. Meredith Tax, *Women and Her Mind: The Story of Everyday Life, in* Radical Feminism 23, 28 (Anne Koedt et al., eds., 1973). While this may be true, there is still a power differential among men based on race.

24. Kimberlé W. Crenshaw, *Race, Reform, and Retrenchment: Transformation and Legitimation in Antidiscrimination Law*, 101 Harv. L. Rev. 1331, 1378 (1988).

25. *Id.* at 1379.

26. Hazel V. Carby, Reconstructing Womanhood: The Emergence of the Afro-American Woman Novelist 23 (1987).

27. *Id.* at 20–39.

28. *Id.*

29. Hazel V. Carby, Lecture in Class on Black Women Writers at Wesleyan University (Sept. 9, 1987).

30. For example, although all women "had" to reproduce, white women were responsible for producing heirs and slave women were responsible for producing property for the heirs to inherit. Carby, *supra* note 29.

31. Carby, *supra* note 26, at 25.

32. bell hooks, Ain't I a Woman? Black Women and Feminism 49 (1981).

33. Patricia Hill Collins, Black Feminist Thought: Knowledge, Consciousness, and the Politics of Empowerment 71 (1991). The other controlling images of African American womanhood are the "mammy," the "matriarch," and the "welfare mother." *See Id.* at 71–77.

34. bell hooks, Feminist Theory: From Margin to Center 99 (1984).

35. *Id.* at 98.

36. *Id.* at 88–89.

37. *Id.* at 101–102.

38. *Id.* at 68.

39. *Id.* at 68–69 (emphasis added).

40. hooks, *supra* note 32, at 70.

41. Neil Gotanda, "Race-ing" Racial Non-Recognition, and Racial Stratification: Re-Reading Judge Joyce Karlin's Sentencing Colloquy in *People v. Soon Ja Du* 23 (Mar. 12, 1993) (unpublished manuscript).

42. hooks, *supra* note 32, at 94 (emphasis added).

43. bell hooks, *Reflections on Race and Sex, in* Yearning Race, Gender and Cultural Politics 57, 63 (1990).

44. Bowman, *supra* note 1, at 532. This type of banter has been referred to as "rapping."

45. *Id.* at 532.

46. hooks, *supra* note 32, at 88 (emphasis added).

47. Kimberlé W. Crenshaw, *Whose Story Is It Anyway? Feminist and Antiracist Appropriations of Anita Hill, in* Race-ing Justice, Engendering Power: Essays on Anita Hill, Clarence Thomas, and the Construction of Social Reality 402, 429 (Toni Morrison ed., 1992).

48. *Id.* at 431.

49. Collins, *supra* note 33, at 68.

50. Patricia J. Williams, *Spirit-Murdering the Messenger: The Discourse of Fingerpointing as the Law's Response to Racism*, 42 U. Miami L. Rev. 127, 151 (1987) (also chapter 28 in this volume).

51. *Id.*

52. *Id.*

53. Adrien K. Wing, *Brief Reflections toward a Multiplicative Theory and Praxis of Being*, 6 Berkeley Women's L.J. 181, 186 (1990–91) (also chapter 3 in this volume).

54. *Id.*

MORE POWER THAN WE WANT   60

Masculine Sexuality and Violence

Bruce Kokopeli and George Lakey

Masculine sexuality involves the oppression of women, competition among men, and homophobia (fear of homosexuality). Patriarchy, the systematic domination of women by men through unequal opportunities, rewards, pun-

From: *Off Their Backs . . . and on Our Own Two Feet* (Philadelphia: New Society Publishers, 1983), pp. 17–24. Reprinted by permission.

ishments, and the internalization of unequal expectations through sex role differentiation, is the institution which organizes these behaviors. Patriarchy is men having more power, both personally and politically, than women of the same rank. This imbalance of power is the core of patriarchy, but definitely not the extent of it.

Sex inequality cannot be routinely enforced through open violence or even blatant discriminatory agreements—patriarchy also needs its values accepted in the minds of people. If as many young *women* wanted to be physicians as men, and as many young men *wanted* to be nurses as women, the medical schools and the hospitals would be hard put to maintain the masculine domination of health care; open struggle and the naked exercise of power would be necessary. Little girls, therefore, are encouraged to think "nurse" and boys to think "doctor."

Patriarchy assigns a list of human characteristics according to gender: women should be nurturant, gentle, in touch with their feelings, etc.; men should be productive, competitive, super-rational, etc. Occupations are valued according to these gender-linked characteristics, so social work, teaching, housework, and nursing are of lower status than business executive, judge, or professional football player.

When men do enter "feminine" professions, they disproportionately rise to the top and become chefs, principals of schools, directors of ballet, and teachers of social work. A man is somewhat excused from his sex role deviation if he at least dominates within the deviation. Domination, after all, is what patriarchy is all about.

Access to powerful positions by women (i.e., those positions formerly limited to men) is contingent on the women adopting some masculine characteristics, such as competitiveness. They feel pressure to give up qualities assigned to females (such as gentleness) because those qualities are considered inherently weak by patriarchal culture. The existence, therefore, of a woman like Indira Gandhi in the position of a dictator in no way undermines the basic sexist structure which allocates power to those with masculine characteristics.

Patriarchy also shapes men's sexuality so it expresses the theme of domination. Notice the masculine preoccupation with size. The size of a man's body has a lot to say about his clout or his vulnerability, as any junior high boy can tell you. Many of these schoolyard fights are settled by who is bigger than whom, and we experience in our adult lives the echoes of intimidation and deference produced by our habitual "sizing up" of the situation.

Penis size is part of this masculine preoccupation, this time directed toward women. Men want to have large penises because size equals power, the ability to make a woman "really feel it." The imagery of violence is close to the surface here, since women find penis size irrelevant to sexual genital pleasure. "Fucking" is a highly ambiguous word, meaning both intercourse and exploitation/assault.

It is this confusion that we need to untangle and understand. Patriarchy tells men that their need for love and respect can only be met by being masculine, powerful, and ultimately violent. As men come to accept this, their sexuality begins to reflect it. Violence and sexuality combine to support masculinity as a character ideal. To love a woman is to have power over her and to treat her violently if need be. The Beatles' song "Happiness Is a Warm Gun" is but one example of how sexuality gets confused with violence and power. We know one man who was discussing another man who seemed to be highly fertile—he had made several women pregnant. "That guy," he said, "doesn't shoot any blanks."

Rape is the end logic of masculine sexuality. Rape is not so much a sexual act as an act of violence expressed in a sexual way. The rapist's mind-set—that violence and sexuality *can* go together—is actually a product of patriarchal conditioning, for most of us men understand the same, however abhorrent rape may be to us personally.

In war, rape is astonishingly prevalent even among men who "back home" would not do it. In the following description by a marine sergeant who witnessed a gang rape in Vietnam, notice that nearly all the nine-man squad participated:

> They were supposed to go after what they called a Viet Cong whore. They went into her village and instead of capturing her, they raped her—every man raped her. As a matter of fact, one man said to me later that it was the first time he had ever made love to a woman with his boots on. The man who led the platoon, or the squad, was actually a private. The squad leader was a sergeant but he was a useless person and he let the private take over his squad. Later he said he took no part in the raid. It was against his morals. So instead of telling his squad not to do it, because they wouldn't listen to him anyway, the sergeant went into another side of the village and just sat and stared bleakly at the ground, feeling sorry for himself. But at any rate, they raped the girl, and then, the last man to make love to her, shot her in the head. [Vietnam Veterans Against the War, statement by Michael McClusker in *The Winter Soldier Investigation: An Inquiry Into American War Crimes.*]

Psychologist James Prescott adds to this account:

> What is it in the American psyche that permits the use of the word "love" to describe rape? And where the act of love is completed with a bullet in the head! [*Bulletin of the Atomic Scientists*, November 1975, p. 17.]

MASCULINITY AGAINST MEN: THE MILITARIZATION OF EVERYDAY LIFE

Patriarchy benefits men by giving us a class of people (women) to dominate and exploit. Patriarchy also oppresses men, by setting us at odds with each other and shrinking our life space.

The pressure to win starts early and never stops. Working-class gangs fight over turf; rich people's sons are pushed to compete on the sports field. British military officers, it is said, learned to win on the playing fields of Eton.

Competition is conflict held within a framework of rules. When the stakes are really high, the rules may not be obeyed; fighting breaks out. We men mostly relate through competition, but we know what is waiting in the wings. John Wayne is not a cultural hero by accident.

Men compete with each other for status as masculine males. Because masculinity equals power, this means we are competing for power. The ultimate proof of power/masculinity is violence. A man may fail to "measure up" to the macho stereotype in important ways, but if he can fight successfully with the person who challenges him on his deviance, he is still all right. The television policeman Baretta is strange in some ways: he is gentle with women and he cried when a man he loved was killed. However, he has what are probably the largest biceps in television and he proves weekly that he can beat up the toughs who come his way.

The close relationship between violence and masculinity does not need much demonstration. War used to be justified partly because it promoted "manly virtue" in a nation. Those millions of people in the woods hunting deer, in the National Rifle Association, and cheering on the bloodiest hockey teams are overwhelmingly men.

The world situation is so much defined by patriarchy that what we see in the wars of today is competition between various patriarchal ruling classes and governments breaking into open conflict. Violence is the accepted masculine form of conflict resolution. Women at this time are not powerful enough in the world situation for us to see mass overt violence being waged on them. But the violence is in fact there; it is hidden through its legitimization by the state and by culture.

In everyday middle-class life, open violence between men is of course rare. The defining characteristics of masculinity, however, are only a few steps removed from violence. Wealth, productivity, or rank in the firm or institution translate into power—the capacity (whether or not exercised) to dominate. The holders of power in even polite institutions seem to know that violence is at their fingertips, judging from the reactions of college presidents to student protest in the 1960s. We know of one urban "pacifist" man, the head of a theological seminary, who was barely talked out of calling the police to deal with a nonviolent student sit-in at "his" seminary!

Patriarchy teaches us at very deep levels that we can never be safe with other men (or perhaps with anyone!), for the guard must be kept up lest our vulnerability be exposed and we be taken advantage of. At a recent Quaker conference in Philadelphia, a discussion group considered the value of personal sharing and openness in the Quaker Meeting. In almost every case the women advocated more sharing and the men opposed it. Dividing by gender on that issue was predictable; men are conditioned by our life experience of masculinity to distrust settings where personal exposure will happen, especially if men are present. Most men find emotional intimacy possible only with women; many with only one woman; some men cannot be emotionally intimate with anyone.

Patriarchy creates a character ideal—we call it masculinity—and measures everyone against it. Many men as well as women fail the test and even men who are passing the test today are carrying a heavy load of anxiety about tomorrow. Because masculinity is a form of domination, no one can really rest secure. The striving goes on forever unless you are actually willing to give up and find a more secure basis for identity.

MASCULINITY AGAINST GAY MEN: PATRIARCHY FIGHTS A REAR GUARD ACTION

Homophobia is the measure of masculinity. The degree to which a man is thought to have gay feelings is the degree of his unmanliness. Because patriarchy presents sexuality as men over women (part of the general dominance theme), men are conditioned to have only that in mind as a model of sexual expression. Sex with another man must mean being dominated, which is very scary. A nonpatriarchal model of sexual expression as the mutuality of equals doesn't seem possible; the transfer of the heterosexual model to same-sex relations can at best be "queer," at worst, "perverted."

In the recent book *Blue Collar Aristocrats*, by E. E. LeMasters, a working-class tavern is described in which the topic of homosexuality sometimes comes up. Gayness is never defended. In fact, the worst thing you can call a man is homosexual. A man so attacked must either fight or leave the bar.

Notice the importance of violence in defending yourself against the charge of being a "pansy." Referring to your income or academic degrees or size of your car is no defense against such a charge. Only fighting will re-establish your respect as a masculine male. Because "gay" appears to mean "powerless," one needs to go to the masculine source of power—violence—for adequate defense.

Last year, the Argentinian government decided to persecute gays on a systematic basis. The Ministry of Social Welfare offered the rationale for this policy in an article in its journal, which also attacked lesbians, concluding that they should be put in jail or killed:

> As children they played with dolls. As they grew up, violent sports horrified them. As was to be expected, with the passage of time and the custom of listening to foreign mulattos on the radio, they became conscientious objectors. [*El Caudillo*, February 1975, excerpted in *Peace News*, July 11, 1975, p. 5]

The Danish government, by contrast with Argentina, has liberal policies on gay people. There is no government persecution and all government jobs are open to gays—except in the military and the diplomatic service! Two places where the nation-state is most keen to assert power are places where gays are excluded as a matter of policy.

We need not go abroad to see the connections between violence and homophobia. In the documentary film *Men's Lives*, a high school boy is interviewed on what it is like to be a dancer. While the interview is conducted, we see him working out, with a very demanding set of acrobatic exercises. The boy mentions that other boys think he must be gay. "Why is that?" the interviewer asks. "Dancers are free and loose," he replies; they are not big like football players; and "you're not trying to kill anybody."

Different kinds of homosexual behavior bring out different amounts of hostility, curiously enough. That fact gives us further clues to violence and female oppression. In prisons, for example, men can be respected if they fuck other men, but not if they are themselves fucked. (We use the word "fucked" intentionally for its ambiguity.) Often prison rapes are done by men who identify as heterosexual; one hole substitutes for another in this scene, for sex is in either case an expression of domination for the masculine mystique.

But for a man to be entered sexually, or to use effeminate gestures and actions, is to invite attack in prison and hostility outside. Effeminate gay men are at the bottom of the totem pole because they are *most like women*, which is nothing less than treachery to the Masculine Cause. Even many gay men shudder at drag queens and vigilantly guard against certain mannerisms because they, too, have internalized the masculinist dread of effeminacy.

John Braxton's report of prison life as a draft resister is revealing on this score. The other inmates knew immediately that John was a conscientious objector because he did not act tough. They also assumed he was gay, for the same reason. (If you are not masculine, you must be a pacifist and gay, for masculinity is a package which includes both violence and heterosexuality.)

A ticket of admission to masculinity, then, is sex with women, and bisexuals can at least get that ticket even if they deviate through having gay feelings as well. This may be why bisexuality is not feared as much as exclusive gayness among men. Exclusively gay men let down the Masculine Cause in a very important way—those gays do not participate in the control of women through sexuality. Control through sexuality matters because it is flexible; it usually is mixed with love and dependency so that it becomes quite subtle. (Women often testify to years of confusion and only the faintest uneasiness at their submissive role in traditional heterosexual relationships and the role sex plays in that.)

Now we better understand why women are in general so much more supportive of gay men than nongay men are. Part of it of course is that heterosexual men are often paralyzed by fear. Never very trusting, such men find gayness one more reason to keep up the defenses. But heterosexual women are drawn to active support for the struggles of gay men because there is a common enemy—patriarchy and its definition of sexuality as domination. Both heterosexual women and gay men have experienced first hand the violence of sexism; we all have experienced its less open forms such as put-downs and discrimination, and we all fear its open forms such as rape and assault.

Patriarchy, which links characteristics (gentleness, aggressiveness, etc.) to gender, shapes sexuality as well, in such a way as to maintain male power. The Masculine Cause draws strength from homophobia and resorts habitually to violence in its battles on the field of sexual politics. It provides psychological support for the military state and is in turn stimulated by it.

THE POLICE AND THE BLACK MALE   61

Elijah Anderson

The police, in the Village-Northton [neighborhood] as elsewhere, represent society's formal, legitimate means of social control. Their role includes protecting law-abiding citizens from those who are not law-abiding by preventing crime and by apprehending likely criminals. Precisely how the police fulfill the public's expectations is strongly related to how they view the neighborhood and the people who live there. On the streets, color-coding often works to confuse race, age, class, gender, incivility, and criminality, and it expresses itself most concretely in the person of the anonymous black male. In doing their job, the police often become willing parties to this general color-coding of the public environment, and related distinctions, particularly those of skin color and gender, come to convey definite meanings. Although such coding may make the work of the police more manageable, it may also fit well with their own presuppositions regarding race and class relations, thus shaping officers' perceptions of crime "in the city." Moreover, the anonymous black male is usually an ambiguous figure who arouses the utmost caution and is generally considered dangerous until he proves he is not. . . .

To be white is to be seen by the police—at least superficially—as an ally, eligible for consideration and for much more deferential treatment than that

Editors' note: This article is based on the author's field research in two city neighborhoods he calls Village-Northton.

From: Elijah Anderson, *Streetwise* (Chicago: University of Chicago Press, 1990), pp. 190–206. Copyright © 1990 University of Chicago Press. Reprinted by permission of the publisher and author.

accorded to blacks in general. This attitude may be grounded in the back-grounds of the police themselves. Many have grown up in . . . "ethnic" neigh-borhoods. They may serve what they perceive as their own class and neigh-borhood interests, which often translates as keeping blacks "in their place"—away from neighborhoods that are socially defined as "white." In try-ing to do their job, the police appear to engage in an informal policy of mon-itoring young black men as a means of controlling crime, and often they seem to go beyond the bounds of duty. . . .

On the streets late at night, the average young black man is suspicious of others he encounters, and he is particularly wary of the police. If he is dressed in the uniform of the "gangster," such as a black leather jacket, sneakers, and a "gangster cap," if he is carrying a radio or a suspicious bag (which may be confiscated), or if he is moving too fast or too slow, the police may stop him. As part of the routine, they search him and make him sit in the police car while they run a check to see whether there is a "detainer" on him. If there is noth-ing, he is allowed to go on his way. After this ordeal the youth is often left afraid, sometimes shaking, and uncertain about the area he had previously taken for granted. He is upset in part because he is painfully aware of how close he has come to being in "big trouble." He knows of other youths who have gotten into a "world of trouble" simply by being on the streets at the wrong time or when the police were pursuing a criminal. In these circumstances, particularly at night, it is relatively easy for one black man to be mistaken for another. Over the years, while walking through the neighborhood I have on occasion been stopped and questioned by police chasing a mugger, but after explaining myself I was released.

Many youths, however, have reason to fear such mistaken identity or ha-rassment, since they might be jailed, if only for a short time, and would have to post bail money and pay legal fees to extricate themselves from the mess. . . . When law-abiding blacks are ensnared by the criminal justice system, the sce-nario may proceed as follows. A young man is arbitrarily stopped by the po-lice and questioned. If he cannot effectively negotiate with the officer(s), he may be accused of a crime and arrested. To resolve this situation he needs fi-nancial resources, which for him are in short supply. If he does not have money for any attorney, which often happens, he is left to a public defender who may be more interested in going along with the court system than in fighting for a poor black person. Without legal support, he may well wind up "doing time" even if he is innocent of the charges brought against him. The next time he is stopped for questioning he will have a record, which will make detention all the more likely.

Because the young black man is aware of many cases when an "innocent" black person was wrongly accused and detained, he develops an "attitude" to-ward the police. The street word for police is "the man," signifying a certain machismo, power, and authority. He becomes concerned when he notices "the man" in the community or when the police focus on him because he is outside his own neighborhood. The youth knows, or soon finds out, that he exists in a legally precarious state. Hence he is motivated to avoid the police, and his public life becomes severely circumscribed. . . .

Such scrutiny and harassment by local police make black youths see them as a problem to get beyond, to deal with, and their attempts affect their overall behavior. To avoid encounters with the man, some streetwise young men camouflage themselves, giving up the urban uniform and emblems that identify them as "legitimate" objects of police attention. They may adopt a more conventional presentation of self, wearing chinos, sweat suits, and generally more conservative dress. Some youths have been known to "ditch" a favorite jacket if they see others wearing one like it, because wearing it increases their chances of being mistaken for someone else who may have committed a crime.

But such strategies do not always work over the long run and must be constantly modified. For instance, because so many young ghetto blacks have begun to wear Fila and Adidas sweat suits as status symbols, such dress has become incorporated into the public image generally associated with young black males. These athletic suits, particularly the more expensive and colorful ones, along with high-priced sneakers, have become the leisure dress of successful drug dealers, and other youths will often mimic their wardrobe to "go for bad" in the quest for local esteem. Hence what was once a "square" mark of distinction approximating the conventions of the wider culture has been adopted by a neighborhood group devalued by that same culture. As we saw earlier, the young black male enjoys a certain power over fashion: whatever the collective peer group embraces can become "hip" in a manner the wider society may not desire. . . . These same styles then attract the attention of the agents of social control.

THE IDENTIFICATION CARD

Law-abiding black people, particularly those of the middle class, set out to approximate middle-class whites in styles of self-presentation in public, including dress and bearing. Such middle-class emblems, often viewed as "square," are not usually embraced by young working-class blacks. Instead, their connections with and claims on the institutions of the wider society seem to be symbolized by the identification card. The common identification card associates its holder with a firm, a corporation, a school, a union, or some other institution of substance and influence. Such a card, particularly from a prominent establishment, puts the police and others on notice that the youth is "somebody," thus creating an important distinction between a black man who can claim a connection with the wider society and one who is summarily judged as "deviant." Although blacks who are established in the middle class might take such cards for granted, many lower-class blacks, who continue to find it necessary to campaign for civil rights denied them because of skin color, believe that carrying an identification card brings them better treatment than is meted out to their less fortunate brothers and sisters. For them this link to the wider society, though often tenuous, is psychically and socially important. . . .

"DOWNTOWN" POLICE AND LOCAL POLICE

In attempting to manage the police—and by implication to manage themselves—some black youths have developed a working connection of the police in certain public areas of the Village-Northton. Those who spend a good amount of their time on these corners, and thus observing the police, have come to distinguish between the "downtown" police and the "regular" local police.

The local police are the ones who spend time in the area; normally they drive around in patrol cars, often one officer to a car. These officers usually make a kind of working peace with the young men on the streets; for example, they know the names of some of them and may even befriend a young boy. Thus they offer an image of the police department different from that displayed by the "downtown" police. The downtown police are distant, impersonal, and often actively looking for "trouble." They are known to swoop down arbitrarily on gatherings of black youths standing on a street corner; they might punch them around, call them names, and administer other kinds of abuse, apparently for sport. A young Northton man gave the following narrative about his experiences with the police.

> And I happen to live in a violent part. There's a real difference between the violence level in the Village and the violence level in Northton. In the nighttime it's more dangerous over there.
>
> It's so bad now, they got downtown cops over there now. They doin' a good job bringin' the highway patrol over there. Regular cops don't like that. You can tell that. They even try to emphasize to us the certain category. Highway patrol come up, he leave, they say somethin' about it. "We can do our job over here." We call [downtown police] Nazis. They about six feet eight, seven feet. We walkin', they jump out. "You run, and we'll blow your nigger brains out." I hate bein' called a nigger. I want to say somethin' but get myself in trouble.
>
> When a cop do somethin', nothing happen to 'em. They come from downtown. From what I heard some of 'em don't even wear their real badge numbers. So you have to put up with that. Just keep your mouth shut when they stop you, that's all. Forget about questions, get against the wall, just obey 'em. "Put all that out right there"—might get rough with you now. They snatch you by the shirt, throw you against the wall, pat you hard, and grab you by the arms, and say, "Get outta here." They call you nigger this and little black this, and things like that. I take that. Some of the fellas get mad. It's a whole different world. . . .
>
> You call a cop, they don't come. My boy got shot, we had to take him to the hospital ourselves. A cop said, "You know who did it?" We said no. He said,

"Well, I hope he dies if y'all don't say nothin'." What he say that for? My boy said, "I hope your mother die," he told the cop right to his face. And I was grabbin' another cop, and he made a complaint about that. There were a lot of witnesses. Even the nurse behind the counter said the cop had no business saying nothin' like that. He said it loud, "I hope he dies." Nothin' like that should be comin' from a cop.

Such behavior by formal agents of social control may reduce the crime rate, but it raises questions about social justice and civil rights. Many of the old-time liberal white residents of the Village view the police with some ambivalence. They want their streets and homes defended, but many are convinced that the police manhandle "kids" and mete out an arbitrary form of "justice." These feelings make many of them reluctant to call the police when they are needed, and they may even be less than completely cooperative after a crime has been committed. They know that far too often the police simply "go out and pick up some poor black kid." Yet they do cooperate, if ambivalently, with these agents of social control. . . .

. . . Stories about police prejudice against blacks are often traded at Village get-togethers. Cynicism about the effectiveness of the police mixed with community suspicion of their behavior toward blacks keeps middle-class Villagers from embracing the notion that they must rely heavily on the formal means of social control to maintain even the minimum freedom of movement they enjoy on the streets.

Many residents of the Village, especially those who see themselves as the "old guard" or "old-timers," who were around during the good old days when antiwar and antiracist protest was a major concern, sigh and turn their heads when they see the criminal justice system operating in the ways described here. They express hope that "things will work out," that tensions will ease, that crime will decrease and police behavior will improve. Yet as incivility and crime become increasing problems in the neighborhood, whites become less tolerant of anonymous blacks and more inclined to embrace the police as their heroes. . . .

Gentrifiers and the local old-timers who join them, and some traditional residents continue to fear, care more for their own safety and well-being than for the rights of young blacks accused of wrong-doing. Yet reliance on the police, even by an increasing number of former liberals, may be traced to a general feeling of oppression at the hands of street criminals, whom many believe are most often black. As these feelings intensify and as more yuppies and students inhabit the area and press the local government for services, especially police protection, the police may be required to "ride herd" more stringently on the youthful black population. Thus young black males are often singled out as the "bad" element in an otherwise healthy diversity, and the tensions between the lower-class black ghetto and the middle- and upper-class white community increase rather than diminish.

KOREAN AMERICANS VS. AFRICAN AMERICANS

62

Conflict and Construction

Sumi K. Cho

The violence and destruction that followed the Rodney King verdict again exploded the myth of a shared consensus around American justice and democracy. The blind injustice of the Simi Valley "not guilty" verdict produced a rainbow coalition of people—old, young, of all colors—who had few or no reservations about looting stores owned primarily by Koreans and Latinos. It soon became clear that the nation's professional, academic, political, and business elite were ill-equipped to deal with the complexity of issues before them, captured in the simple but straightforward plea by Rodney King: "Can we all get along?"

King's question hints at the real question confronting U.S. society: who is the "we" that must get along? For too long, the political and academic tradition has defined U.S. race relations in terms of a Black/white binary opposition. For example, a CNN–*Time Magazine* poll taken immediately after the verdict surveyed "Americans" on their opinions regarding the verdict and the violence that followed. Yet the poll only sought the views of African Americans and whites regarding the future of race relations. The Black/white framing of race issues must give way to a fuller, more differentiated understanding of a multiracial, multiethnic society divided along the lines of race, class, gender, and other axes in order to explicate effectively the Los Angeles explosion and to contribute to the long-term empowerment of those who, for a short time, exercised the power of their own agency.

Dominating the current debate within the Black/white racial paradigm are, on the one hand, the human-capital theorists[1] who assert that the degradation of "family values" caused the fires in L.A. Dan Quayle's now infamous Murphy Brown speech, for example, pointed the finger at a television sitcom for contributing to the social and moral decay which lie behind the problems

Author's note: I would like to thank Gil Gott, Pedro Noguera, Susan Lee, Ronnie Stevenson, Ann Park, Evageline Ordaz, Christopher Burroughs, and Bob Gooding-Williams for their helpful comments on this essay.

From: Sumi Cho, "Korean Americans vs. African Americans: Conflict and Construction," in *Reading Rodney King/Reading Urban Uprising*, ed. Robert Gooding-Williams (New York: Routledge, 1993), pp. 196–211. Reprinted by permission of the author.

in South Central L.A. by portraying the single motherhood of a white woman from the professional class. On the other hand, there are structuralists[2] proposing that the U.S. adopt a "Marshall Plan" for its cities to address the institutional lockout of people of color from economic development.

While the structural explanations provide more illuminating insights than human-capital theories, they cannot fully explain the myriad of events in Los Angeles, particularly those that affected the Korean-American community. The portrayal of Asian Americans as the paragons of socioeconomic success contributed to the targeting of Korean Americans as a scapegoat by those above and below Koreans on the socioeconomic ladder during the L.A. riots. The King verdict and the failure of the U.S. economy to provide jobs and a decent standard of living for all of its peoples, the ostensible root causes of the rioting, were not the fault of Korean (or Latino) shopowners. If, as some have suggested, the Willie Horton imagery[3] is the myth and Rodney King's beating the practice, then likewise, the casting of Asian Americans as a model minority is the myth, and the looting and burning of Koreatown and Korean-owned stores is the practice.

Manipulation of Korean Americans into a "model minority" contributed to their "triple scapegoating" following the King verdict. The first layer of attack came from those who targeted Korean-owned stores for looting and arson. The second layer consisted of those in positions of power who were responsible for the sacrifice of Koreatown, Pico Union, and South Central Los Angeles to ensure the safety of wealthier, whiter communities. The final scapegoating came at the hands of the media, eager to sensationalize the events by excluding Korean perspectives from coverage and stereotyping the immigrant community. These three forces combined to blame the Korean-American community for the nation's most daunting economic and socio-political problems.

Rodney King's spontaneous reaction upon seeing the varied groups of color pitted against each other in L.A. reflected a deeper understanding of the commonalities among those groups than many intellectuals and politicians have shown: "I love people of color," he declared, although almost all the mainstream media edited out this statement. Further, his plea can be read as a challenge to the academic community and intellectual activists of racial and ethnic politics: "We're all stuck here for awhile. . . . Let's try to work it out."

Race-relations theorists must accept this challenge and go beyond the standard structuralist critique of institutional racism to incorporate the most difficult issues presented by the aftermath of the not-guilty verdicts in the Rodney King case. Specifically, intellectual activists must devise a new approach to understanding interethnic conflict between subordinated groups and work toward a proactive theory of social change. Such a theory would examine the structural conditions that influence patterns of conflict or cooperation between groups of color, racial ideologies, and how they influence group prejudices, as well as the roles of human agency, community education, and political leadership and accountability. Such a theory should strive to explain and resolve interethnic conflicts to unite subordinated groups.

KOREAN AMERICANS IN L.A.:
MODEL MINORITY MYTH AND PRAXIS

The View from Below: The Politics of Resentment

The deteriorated socioeconomic conditions of neglected inner cities have led scholars to compare ghettos like South Central Los Angeles (which includes the Southeast and South Central city-planning areas) to South African "bantu-stans" that serve solely as "holding space for blacks and browns no longer of use to the larger economy."[4] According to 1990 census data, African Americans constitute 24.5 percent of South Central's residents, and Latinos account for 46 percent (with a rapidly growing Latino population). Only 3.6 percent of the total land mass is zoned for industry.[5] South Central residents lack self-determination and political-economic power. In this context, Korean Americans who open stores in the neighborhood are resented by long-deprived residents and are seen as "outsiders" exerting unfair control and power in the community. The interaction between the two racial groups is structured strictly by market relationships: one is the consumer, the other is the owner. This market structuring of group relations has influenced the "Korean/Black conflict" and contributed to the course of events following the not-guilty verdicts.

Koreans first were scapegoated by rioters of all colors who looted stores and later set them afire. Reports of the early activity following the not-guilty verdict in the Rodney King beating centered around a crowd that had gathered in front of Tom's Liquor Store at Florence and Normandie in the late afternoon of 29 April 1992. One of the first targets of the group was the "swap meets" because they were Korean-owned. The swap meets were essentially indoor flea markets that operated every day during the week and offered discounted prices on consumer items such as electronics and clothing. Whether these stores provided a service to an underserved community by offering low-priced goods where megaretailers refused to tread or whether they shamelessly promoted consumerism to an economically disadvantaged population was not at issue. The most oft-stated reason for the targeting of these stores and Korean stores in general was a familiar refrain: Korean owners were rude to African-American and Latino customers. One Latino interviewed on television was asked why people were looting Koreans. "Because we hate 'em. Everybody hates them," he responded.

Much has been said about the rudeness of Korean owners. Some of the major media outlets that covered the tensions between African Americans and Korean Americans attempted to reduce the conflict to "cultural differences" such as not smiling enough, not looking into another person's eyes, not placing change in a person's hands. Although Koreans wanted very badly to believe in this reductionism, one making an honest assessment must conclude that far too many Korean shopowners had accepted widespread stereotypes about African Americans as lazy, complaining criminals.

The dominant U.S. racial hierarchy and its concomitant stereotypes are transferred worldwide to every country that the United States has occupied militarily. Korean women who married American GIs and returned to the United States after the Korean War quickly discovered the social significance of marrying a white versus an African-American GI. American racial hierarchies were telegraphed back home. When Koreans immigrate to the U.S., internationalized stereotypes are reinforced by negative depictions of African Americans in U.S. films, television shows, and other popular forms of cultural production. This stereotype, combined with the high crime rate inherent in businesses such as liquor or convenience stores (regardless of who owns them), produced the prejudiced, paranoid, bunker mentality of Soon Ja Du who shot Latasha Harlins, a 15-year-old African-American girl, in the back of the neck during a dispute over a bottle of orange juice. Since 1 January 1990, at least 25 Korean merchants have been killed by non-Korean gunmen.[6]

On the other hand, many African Americans also internalize stereotypes of Korean Americans. Asian Americans walk a fine line between being seen as model minorities and callous unfair competitors. The result is a split image of success and greed that goes together with callousness and racial superiority. Distinctions between Asian ethnicities are often blurred as are distinctions between Asians and Asian Americans. "Sins of the neighbor" are passed on to Koreans in the United States. For example, when then prime minister Yasuhiro Nakasone of Japan made his blundering remarks in 1986 that "the level of intelligence in the United States is lowered by the large number of Blacks, Puerto Ricans, and Mexicans who live there,"[7] this comment was often applied generally to represent the views of all Asians, including Koreans, although Korea has a long history of colonization at the hands of the Japanese.

In rationalizing the violence that followed the verdict, African-American leaders often repeated the myth that Korean immigrants unfairly compete with aspiring entrepreneurs from the Black community because Korean Americans receive preferential treatment over African Americans for bank and government loans. "Until banks make loans available to Blacks as much as other people, there's going to be resentment," observed John Murray of Cal-Pac, a Black liquor-store-owners' association.[8] In reality, however, banks and government lenders uniformly reject loan applications for businesses located in poor, predominantly minority neighborhoods such as South Central Los Angeles, regardless of the applicant's color. Korean immigrants rarely receive traditional financing. Those who open liquor stores and small businesses often come over with some capital and/or borrow from family and friends. At times, groups of Koreans will act as their own financial institutions through informal rotating credit associations known as "kyes" (pronounced "keh").

Thus, the ability to open stores largely depends upon a class variable, as opposed to a racial one. In fact, Korean merchants at times purchased their liquor and grocery stores from African-American owners. Prior to the Watts riot in 1965, most of the liquor-store owners in South Central Los Angeles were Jewish. After the riots, many Jewish owners wanted out. The easing of government-backed loans and the low selling price of the stores in the mid-1960s opened the way for African-American entrepreneurs. The labor-intensive, high-risk nature of work combined with the deregulation of liquor pricing in 1978 and subsequent price wars that drove many small stores out of business led to a sell-off of liquor stores by African Americans in the late 1970s and early 1980s. The sell-off coincided with a large increase in Korean immigration to the U.S. during the same time period. African-American merchants often made a solid profit selling to Koreans.[9] Korean immigrants, many of whom held college degrees, could not find jobs commensurate with their training and education in the new country due to structural discrimination, occupational downgrading, and general antiforeign sentiment. A disproportionate number of Korean families turned to small businesses as a living. According to U.S. Census Bureau statistics, the rate of self-employment among Koreans is higher than that of any other ethnic group.[10] This self-employment, or "self-exploitation" as some have termed the practice, extends not only to the "head of the household," but often to the entire family, including children. Given the high educational background of this group, high self-employment rates in mom-and-pop grocery stores can hardly be viewed as "success."[11]

Nevertheless, the politics of resentment painted Koreans as callous and greedy invaders who got easy bank loans. As this depiction ran unchecked, it became increasingly easy to consider violence against such a contemptible group. The popular rap artist, Ice Cube, warned Korean shopowners in his song entitled "Black Korea" (on his *Death Certificate* album) to "pay respect to the black fist, or we'll burn your store right down to a crisp." The scene was set for disaster and required simply a spark to ignite a highly flammable situation. When the scorching injustice of the verdict was announced, Korean-owned businesses were scapegoated as the primary target for centuries of racial injustice against African Americans—injustice that predated the bulk of Korean immigration which occurred only after the lifting of discriminatory immigration barriers in 1965.

The View from Above: "Racist Love" and the Model Minority

The police nonresponse to the initial outbreak of violence represented a conscious sacrificing of South Central Los Angeles and Koreatown, largely inhabited by African Americans, Chicanos, Latinos, and Korean Americans, to ensure the safety of affluent white communities. The LAPD's intentional neglect in failing to respond to the initial outbreak of rioting set up a foreseeable conflict between African Americans, Chicanos, Latinos, and Korean Americans with destructive and deadly consequences. When it became evident that no police would come to protect Koreatown, Koreans took up arms in self-defense against other minority groups. Rather than focus on whether these actions by the Korean community were right or wrong, one should question the allocation of police-protection resources and the absolute desertion of Koreatown and South Central L.A. by the police. When Deputy Chief Matthew Hunt, who commands officers in South Los Angeles, asked Chief of Police Daryl Gates for greater preparation prior to the announcement of the verdicts, the chief refused, claiming smugly that such preparations were unnecessary.

It was a badly kept secret that angry mobs bent upon destruction and violence would be descending on Koreatown. When Korean Americans called the LAPD and local and state officials for assistance and protection, there was no response. It was very clear that Koreatown was on its own. In the absence of police protection, the community harnessed its resources through Radio Korea (KBLA) in Los Angeles to coordinate efforts to defend stores from attack. People from as far away as San Bernardino and Orange County came to help. Radio Korea reported on the movement of the crowds and instructed volunteers where to go. In short, the radio station and individual volunteers served as the police force for Koreatown. It is bitterly ironic that some Koreans defending stores were later arrested by police for weapon-permit violations.

In stark contrast, when looters began to work over major shopping malls such as the Fox Hills Mall in Culver City, they were quickly stopped by the police, with "merchants and residents praising [police] efforts."[12] Likewise, the police made sure that the downtown business interests were secured. The west-side edition of the *Los Angeles Times* even boasted that the police forces in the predominantly white communities of Santa Monica, Beverly Hills, and West Hollywood "emerged remarkably unscathed by the riots."[13] Other areas, especially communities of color such as South Central, Pico Union, and Koreatown, effectively became a "no-person's-land." Enter at your own risk. There was no protection for these areas. Although residents paid taxes for police protection, the LAPD made a conscious choice to stay out of the neighborhoods of color that were most at risk during the postverdict rioting.

Although Korean Americans donated substantial amounts of money to the election campaigns of state and local officials, no political assistance was forthcoming in their time of need. "We've made significant contributions to the city council, as well as county, state and federal politicians, and they failed us," said Bong Hwan Kim, executive director of the L.A. Korean Youth Center.[14] Attempts to contact Governor Wilson for help from the National Guard were in vain. The National Guard did not arrive on the scene until there was little left to do. Wilson's explanation was that the National Guard was late be-

cause they had run out of ammunition.[15] During the initial outbreak of violence, it is now known Chief Gates was attending an expensive fundraiser on
the west side while these communities burned. In response, he later stated at
his first press conference following the verdict that police were needed to protect the firefighters. Unfortunately for Gates, the fire department was unwilling to go along with this excuse. In a stinging report to the Fire Commission,
L.A. Fire Chief Donald Manning complained that the LAPD dismissed their
requests for protection during the outbreak of violence as "not a top priority,"
thereby delaying fire-department responses to the fires.[16] Moreover, Gates was
stumped by an *L.A. Times* reporter who pressed him about the hours prior to
the arsons, when some of the most sensationalized violence occurred outside
of Tom's Liquor Store.

Many Koreans mistakenly believed that they would be taken care of if
they worked hard, did not complain, and contributed handsomely to powerful politicians such as Governor Wilson and local officials. One hard lesson to
be learned from the aftermath of the King verdict and the Korean-American
experience is that a model minority is expediently forgotten and dismissed if
white dominance or security is threatened. This point was also demonstrated
through the Asian-American admissions scandals at the nation's premier institutions of higher education when Asian-American students began to outper-
form white students on SATs and GPAs. The rules of the game of "meritocracy" had to be changed to put a ceiling on Asian-American admissions, thereby
producing the largest unstated affirmative-action policy benefiting whites.

The easy dismissal of Korean-American pleas for help is rooted in the relationship between the dominant power brokers and the model-minority
group. The model-minority "thesis," popularized during the late 1960s and the
mid-1980s during the Reagan administration, represents a political backlash
to civil rights struggles. It is critical to understand that the model-minority
thesis is no compliment for Asian Americans. It has been historically constructed to discipline activists in the Black Power, Black Panther, American
Indian, United Farm Workers, and other radical social movements demanding institutional change.[17] Because it has this genesis, the embrace of Asian
Americans as a model minority is an embrace of "racist love."[18] The basis of
that love has a racist origin: to provide a public rationale for the ongoing subordination of non-Asian people of color. Because the embrace or love is not
genuine, one cannot reasonably expect the architects truly to care about the
health or well-being of the model minority. . . .

NOTES

1. The human-capital model is a variant of neoclassical economic theory applied to
labor-market economics. The model attempts to explain a dependent variable such as
income inequality as derivative of independent variables such as educational attainment,

work experience, total number of hours worked per year, marital status, and English proficiency, among others. It explains Asian Americans' advancement by foregrounding their investments in human capital such as educational attainment. It would also explain the lack of mobility of certain groups such as Southeast Asians or African Americans who had not yet invested appropriately in human capital.

2. Structuralists emphasize the basic characteristics or "structures" of a social system. For example, internal colonial theory places the U.S. historical and contemporary actualities of race in the context of international colonialism that connects the Third World abroad with the Third World within the U.S. This framework emphasizes similarities in the patterns of racial domination and exploitation experienced by people of color and distinguishes their incorporation into the U.S. from the processes of immigration and assimilation by which European Americans are incorporated into a nation. See Robert Blauner, "Colonized and Immigrant Minorities," *Racial Oppression in America* (New York: Harper and Row, 1972), 51–82.

3. President Bush's 1988 television campaign centered around an ad attacking Michael Dukakis for being "soft on crime." To support this claim, the TV ads played upon white fears by focusing on close-up "mug" shots of Willie Horton, an African-American convict who committed subsequent crimes while on an early-release program implemented by Dukakis, then governor of Massachusetts.

4. Cynthia Hamilton, *Apartheid in an American City: The Case of the Black Community in Los Angeles* (Van Nuys, CA: Labor Community Strategy Center, 1991), 1.

5. Ibid. Internal colonial theory is useful in viewing South Central as a Third World colony, within a First World nation, that lacks political and economic self-determination, similar to the relationship between Third World nations abroad and First World ones.

6. Eui-Young Yu, "We Saw Our Dreams Burn for No Reason," *San Francisco Examiner*, 24 May 1992, editorial page.

7. Robert C. Toh, "Blacks Pressing Japanese to Halt Slurs, Prejudice," *Los Angeles Times*, 13 December 1990.

8. Susan Moffat, "Shopkeepers Fight Back," *Los Angeles Times*, 15 May 1992.

9. Ibid.

10. At 17 percent, self-employment rates of foreign-born Korean men top those of white men (10 percent) and other people of color. U.S. Bureau of the Census, 1980 Census of Population, vol. 2, Subject Reports, *Asian and Pacific Islander Population in the United States: 1980*, table 45A. A 1990 survey conducted by California State University sociologist Eui-Young Yu found that nearly 40 percent of Korean families own a business.

11. The long hours worked by more members of the family under dangerous conditions, combined with the high educational levels of those owning businesses, calls into question the definition of success applied to Korean Americans. Some have suggested that a blue-collar union job offers better working conditions and a more reliable income than engaging in small businesses.

12. Nancy Hill-Holtzman and Mathis Chazanov, "Police Credited for Heading Off Spread of Riots," *Los Angeles Times*, 7 May 1992.

13. Ibid.

14. Steven Chin, "Innocence Lost: L.A.'s Koreans Fight to be Heard," *San Francisco Examiner*, 9 May 1992.

15. California National Guard Brigadier General Daniel Brennan stated that bullets and grenades were not loaded for transport to L.A. because there were no lights on the

parade ground where the ammunition is stored. Daniel Weintraub, "National Guard Official Cites Series of Delays," *Los Angeles Times*, 7 May 1992.

16. Rich Connell and Richard Simon, "Top LAPD Officer, Fire Chief Cite Flaws in Police Response," *Los Angeles Times*, 8 May 1992.

17. *"At a time when it is being proposed that hundreds of billions be spent to uplift Negroes and other minorities,* the nation's 300,000 Chinese are moving ahead on their own . . . with no help from anyone else. Still being taught in Chinatown is the old idea that people should depend on their own efforts . . . not a welfare check . . . in order to reach America's 'promised land'" (emphasis added). "Success Story of One Minority Group in U.S.," *U.S. News and World Report*, 26 December 1966, 73. Similarly, scholar Thomas Sowell argues in *Race and Economics* (New York: McKay and Co., 1975) that historic exclusion from U.S. political institutions paradoxically benefits Jews and Asian Americans. "[T]hose American ethnic groups that have succeeded best politically have not usually been the same as those who succeeded best economically. . . . [T]hose minorities that have pinned their greatest hopes on political action—the Irish and the Negroes, for example—have made some of the slower economic advances."

18. Frank Chin and Jeffrey Paul Chan, "Racist Love," in *Seen through Shuck* ed. Richard Kostelanetz (New York: Ballantine Books, 1972), 65–79.

WHERE RACE AND GENDER MEET

63

Racism, Hate Crimes, and Pornography

Helen Zia

There is a specific area where racism, hate crimes, and pornography intersect, and where current civil rights law fails: racially motivated, gender-based crimes against women of color. This area of bias-motivated sexual assault has been called "ethnorape"; I refer to it as "hate rape."

I started looking into this issue after years of organizing against hate killings of Asian Americans. After a while, I noticed that all the cases I could name concerned male victims. I wondered why. Perhaps it was because Asian-American men came into contact with perpetrator types more often or because they are more hated and therefore more often attacked by racists. But

From: Laura Lederer and Richard Delgado, eds., *The Price We Pay: The Case against Racist Speech, Hate Propaganda and Pornography*. Copyright © 1995 by Laura J. Lederer.

the subordination and vulnerability of Asian-American women, who are thought to be sexually exotic, subservient, and passive, argued against that interpretation. So where were the Asian-American women hate-crime victims?

Once I began looking, I found them, in random news clippings, in footnotes in books, through word of mouth. Let me share with you some examples I unearthed of bias-motivated attacks and sexual assaults:

- In February 1984, Ly Yung Cheung, a nineteen-year-old Chinese woman who was seven months pregnant, was pushed in front of a New York City subway train and decapitated. Her attacker, a white male high school teacher, claimed he suffered from "a phobia of Asian people" and was overcome with the urge to kill this woman. He successfully pleaded insanity. If this case had been investigated as a hate crime, there might have been more information about his so-called phobia and whether it was part of a pattern of racism. But it was not.
- On December 7, 1984, fifty-two-year-old Japanese American Helen Fukui disappeared in Denver, Colorado. Her decomposed body was found weeks later. Her disappearance on Pearl Harbor Day, when anti-Asian speech and incidents increase dramatically, was considered significant in the community. But the case was not investigated as a hate crime and no suspects were ever apprehended.
- In 1985 an eight-year-old Chinese girl named Jean Har-Kaw Fewel was found raped and lynched in Chapel Hill, North Carolina—two months after *Penthouse* featured pictures of Asian women in various poses of bondage and torture, including hanging bound from trees. Were epithets or pornography used during the attack? No one knows—her rape and killing were not investigated as a possible hate crime.
- Recently a serial rapist was convicted of kidnapping and raping a Japanese exchange student in Oregon. He had also assaulted a Japanese woman in Arizona, and another in San Francisco. He was sentenced to jail for these crimes, but they were never pursued as hate crimes, even though California has a hate statute. Was hate speech or race-specific pornography used? No one knows.
- At Ohio State University, two Asian women were gang raped by fraternity brothers in two separate incidents. One of the rapes was part of a racially targeted game called the "Ethnic Sex Challenge," in which the fraternity men followed an ethnic checklist indicating what kind of women to gang rape. Because the women feared humiliation and ostracism by their communities, neither reported the rapes. However, campus officials found out about the attacks, but did not take them up as hate crimes, or as anything else.

All of these incidents could have been investigated and prosecuted either as state hate crimes or as federal civil rights cases. But they were not. To have done so would have required one of two things: awareness and interest on the part of police investigators and prosecutors—who generally have a poor track record on race and gender issues—or awareness and support for civil rights charges by the Asian-American community—which is generally lacking on issues surrounding women, gender, sex, and sexual assault. The result is a double-silencing effect on the assaults and deaths of these women, who become invisible because of their gender and their race.

Although my research centers on hate crimes and Asian women, this silence and this failure to provide equal protection have parallels in all of the other classes protected by federal civil rights and hate statutes. That is, all other communities of color have a similar prosecution rate for hate crimes against the women in their communities—namely, zero. This dismal record is almost as bad in lesbian and gay antiviolence projects: the vast preponderance of hate crimes reported, tracked, and prosecuted concern gay men—very few concern lesbians. So where are all the women?

The answer to this question lies in the way our justice system was designed, and the way women are mere shadows in the existing civil rights framework. But in spite of this history, federal and state law do offer legal avenues for women to be heard. Federal civil rights prosecutions, for example, can be excellent platforms for high-visibility community education on the harmful impact of hate speech and behavior. When on June 19, 1982, two white auto workers in Detroit screamed racial epithets at Chinese-American Vincent Chin and said, "It's because of you motherfuckers that we're out of work," a public furor followed, raising the level of national discourse on what constitutes racism toward Asian Americans. Constitutional law professors and members of the American Civil Liberties Union and the National Lawyers Guild had acted as if Asian Americans were not covered by civil rights law. Asian Americans emphatically corrected that misconception.

Hate crimes remedies can be used to force the criminal justice bureaucracy to adopt new attitudes. Patrick Purdy went to an elementary school in Stockton, California, in which 85 percent of the students came from Southeast Asia. When he selected that school as the place to open fire with his automatic weapon and killed five eight-year-olds and wounded thirty other children, the police and the media did not think it was a bias-motivated crime. Their denial reminds me of the response by the Montreal officials to the antifeminist killings of fourteen women students there. But an outraged Asian-American community forced a state investigation into the Purdy incident and uncovered hate literature in the killer's effects. As a result, the community was validated, and, in addition, the criminal justice system and the media acquired a new level of understanding.

Imagine if a federal civil rights investigation had been launched in the case of the African-American student at St. John's University who was raped and sodomized by white members of the school lacrosse team, who were later acquitted. Investigators could have raised issues of those white men's attitudes toward the victim as a black woman, found out whether hate speech or race-specific pornography was present, investigated the overall racial climate on campus, and brought all of the silenced aspects of the incident to the public eye. Community discourse could have been raised to a high level.

Making these investigations happen will not be an easy road. Hate-crime efforts are generally expended on blatant cases, with high community consensus, not ones that bring up hard issues like gender-based violence. Yet these intersections of race and gender hatred are the very issues we must give voice to.

There is a serious difficulty with pushing for use of federal and state hate remedies. Some state statutes have been used against men of color: specifically, on behalf of white rape victims against African-American men. We know that the system, if left unchecked, will try to use antihate laws to enforce unequal justice. On the other hand, state hate statutes could be used to prosecute men of color who are believed to have assaulted women of color of another race—interminority assaults are increasing. Also, if violence against women generally were made into a hate crime, women of color could seek prosecutions against men in their own community for their gender-based violence—even if this would make it harder to win the support of men in communities of color, and of women in those communities who would not want to be accused of dividing the community

But at least within the Asian-American antiviolence community, this discourse is taking place now. Asian-American feminists in San Francisco have prepared a critique of the Asian movement against hate crimes and the men of that movement are listening. Other communities of color should also examine the nexus between race and gender for women of color, and by extension, for all women.

The legal system must expand the boundaries of existing law to include the most invisible women. There are hundreds of cases involving women of color waiting to be filed. Activists in the violence-against-women movement must reexamine current views on gender-based violence. Not all sexual assaults are the same. Racism in a sexual assault adds another dimension to the pain and harm inflicted. By taking women of color out of the legal shadows, out of invisibility, all women make gains toward full human dignity and human rights.

V

Making a Difference

What in your life do you care about so much that it would spur you to work for social change? Is it your family, your children, your neighborhood, a concern for a social issue, or an ethical framework that requires not just talk but action? Most people think that people who work for social change must be somehow extraordinary like Martin Luther King or other heroic leaders. But most people who engage in social activism are ordinary, everyday people who decide to take action about something that touches their lives.

Why don't we know more about these people? Dominant social institutions and the ideologies that defend them obscure the individual and collective political activism of everyday individuals. By making the political activism of everyday people from historically marginalized groups invisible, social institutions suppress the strength of these groups and render them more easily exploited. Investigating forms of power used by historically marginalized groups offers one way of rethinking social change and reconceptualizing how people work to make a difference. African Americans, Native Americans, women, Latinos, gays and lesbians, and members of the poor and working class have never been powerless. The question is how to identify and use forms of power that often go unrecognized.

The political activism of individuals from historically privileged groups is hidden as well. Many people who currently benefit within existing race, class, and gender arrangements have little interest in studying—much less show-casing—the ideas and actions of those who not only see the unfairness of race, class, and gender relations in the United States, but who try to make a differ-ence. The expected political protest from those harmed by existing race, class, and gender relations is routinely discredited. Stereotyping people of color, women, working-class and poor people, and gays, lesbians, and bisexuals as angry minorities, strident feminists, disgruntled trade unionists, or hyper-sensitive homosexuals effectively recasts political protest in negative terms and works to strip their protest of meaning. These tactics remain less effective against those who benefit from existing structures of race, class, gender, and sexuality but who decide to use their privilege in new ways. In some ways, in-dividuals who are White, middle class, male, and/or straight and who reject current social arrangements that privilege them may be more threatening than other groups because they often have the power to make change. Con-sider how different things would be if White American children learned ways to be "White" different from those they are routinely taught or if men learned models of masculinity that do not demean women. Relegating political protest of this sort to the margins remains vitally important to dominant interests.

Despite their invisibility on both sides of privilege, most of the people who try to make a difference are people just like you. Often some sort of cat-alyst spurs them to action. The needless death of a relative, the placement of a toxic dump site in their neighborhood, losing a job when an employer closes shop, a police beating, or hearing a sermon about Christian brotherhood one Sunday morning in the familiarity of a racially segregated church have all been catalysts for activism. Because people engaging in social activism come from all walks of life, their paths into social activism can be quite unexpected, and the strategies they select for making a difference can be richly diverse. The articles in "Making a Difference" explore the various ways that people across race, class, and gender groups participate in social activism. They also provide new visions about what is possible. Collectively, these authors offer inclusive thinking, reconstructed knowledge, and a distinctive perspective on the kinds of questions we might consider in working to make a difference.

WHO ARE THE ACTIVISTS?

When we ask students in our classes to describe an "activist," they often think of a "radical"-looking young person, typically with strange hair and unusual clothing, who gives fiery speeches and engages in losing causes. People who work for social change rarely fit this stereotype and actually reflect a much broader spectrum of folks. Often they remain invisible because we do not label their activities as activism.

There is no "typical" activist. Almost anyone can make a difference in the context of her or his everyday life. Celene Krauss's article "Women of Color on the Front Line" describes how the majority of participants in the environmental justice movement are mothers who became involved out of concern for their children's health. Her article highlights how women often become politically involved—through concerns over family, children, and quality of life in their neighborhoods. Still, women's activism often is overlooked. Although academic credentials, positions of authority, and economic resources can do much to help individuals challenge hierarchies of race, class, and gender, Krauss suggests that the individual and collective actions of ordinary people form the bedrock for many social movements.

Charon Asetoyer's article "From the Ground Up" points to how much women and men can accomplish through persistence. When Asetoyer found herself moving to the Yankton Sioux reservation in South Dakota, she did not explicitly search out activist activities. Instead, they found her. Through conversations with her few neighbors, she learned of problems that women and children were having in her new community. Health issues came up first, and these were the issues that she and others initially addressed. Over time, the informal discussions about women's health issues on the reservation grew to the point where her group was able to purchase a building and organize the Native Women's Reproductive Rights Coalition, involving women from eight states. Asetoyer's article provides an historical overview of how one individual decided to respond in the context of her everyday life, instead of throwing up her hands in defeat.

WORKING FOR CHANGE IN MANY PLACES

People decide to work for change from diverse social locations. Workplaces, families, schools, and the government—some of the social institutions we examined in part III—all represent potential locations for social activism. The media, health care organizations, the penal system, and recreational organizations also constitute potential sites of social activism.

People often think that, without a group of some sort, they cannot make a difference. Again, this narrow view of activists and activism obscures the tremendous impact that even one individual can have when she or he tries. Enid Lee's efforts as one teacher developing an antiracist, multicultural curriculum within her own classroom reflect this choice to work from a position of authority inside an existing social institution. In Barbara Miner's interview with Lee, Lee offers some solid advice to teachers who want to make a difference in their own classrooms. While acknowledging the difficulties of working in conditions with inadequate funding and uncooperative colleagues, Lee firmly believes that attitude and commitment still matter. As she points out, "If you don't take multicultural education or antiracist education seriously, you are actually promoting a monocultural or racist education. There is no neutral ground on this issue."

Whether by choice or by necessity, other individuals and groups work outside workplaces, schools, and other formal social institutions. Members of "The Boys and Girls of (Union) Summer" spent their time confronting what they deemed unjust labor conditions in workplaces where they themselves were not employed. The familiar boycotts, picketing, leafleting, and other direct-action strategies long associated with social movements of all types typically constitute actions taken outside some institution. Although activities such as these can be trivialized in the media, it is important to remember that direct action from outsider locations represents one important way to make a difference.

Sometimes institutional policies and practices become the focus of change. Because existing institutions are structured around race, class, and gender oppression, there are limits to the kinds of change that can be achieved from inside them. Furthermore, even when African Americans, Native Americans, women, Asian Americans, the poor, gays and lesbians, Latinos, and other historically marginalized groups gain power within them, change does not automatically follow. Replacing one type of dominant group with another of a different color or gender may improve the lives of some people without addressing the fundamental inequalities that pervade existing social institutions.

At other times, the goal is to enlist support from these same social institutions for a social agenda. This acknowledges that some social problems cannot be solved by ordinary citizens: institutional involvement is often needed. Despite the cynicism that many people express regarding the proper role of government, many social issues cannot be addressed without government intervention of some sort. Thus, actions of the federal government were required to desegregate the American South in the 1950s and 1960s. While government cannot solve social issues created through current race, class, and gender arrangements, social issues such as homelessness, environmental concerns, violence against children, poverty, racial discrimination, and gender discrimination often require government partnership of some sort to support the actions of everyday citizens who care about these problems. At other times, actions of the government may be part of the problem, and people must find other means of challenging oppressive institutional arrangements.

STRATEGIES: WHAT WORKS?

We are often asked, what strategies make a difference? The range of strategies that individuals and groups use in working for social change is immense. Some engage in individualistic strategies. One well-placed individual with a clear sense of what is possible and why it is important to try can accomplish amazing things. Others engage in collective actions where a small group of like-minded individuals organize around some concern that is important to them. By engaging in strategic resistance, a few people can make a big difference if they use their resources wisely. Charon Asetoyer's article on building Native American health services from the ground up illustrates this process. Still other activists participate in national and global mass movements.

Regardless of the strategies selected, one important issue that surfaces repeatedly involves the importance of building coalitions and working across differences. Bringing ordinary people together who have long been separated by race, class, and gender (among other barriers) raises the necessity of building coalitions across differences—and the difficulty of doing so. Using the image of the barred room in "Coalition Politics: Turning the Century," Bernice Johnson Reagon explores the creation of nurturing spaces and communities where individuals try and recover from the damaging effects of race, class, and gender oppression. "Nationalism is crucial to a people if you are going to ever impact as a group in your interest," suggests Reagon. On some college campuses, African American organizations, for example, offer a space where Black students can retreat from the difficulties of desegregating what many experience as hostile White campuses, learn ways of supporting one another, and identify the positive qualities of difference based on group identity. These spaces are valuable, but Reagon also points to the limits of their value. Nationalism and the celebration of difference that may accompany it become limiting if a group does not look beyond its own "room" and learn to appreciate differences of other groups. Within the category African American student, as with Latinos, Asian Americans, and Native Americans, tremendous heterogeneity exists. Flattening differences within groups to create a unidimensional unity can rob Black student organizations of their creativity. Moreover, over time, if it fails to build coalitions with other campus and community groups, even the most dedicated group may find itself increasingly isolated and ineffective.

Coalition building operates best when individuals and groups share a concern for a social issue while recognizing the diversity of ways that people experience, think about, and want to deal with that issue. People from across race, class, and gender categories engage in a range of social issues. Part IV of this volume explored American identities, sexuality, and violence as three important social issues that benefited from a race-, class-, and gender-inclusive analysis. There are many more such issues, and working for change involves bringing an inclusive framework to ideas and actions that address these social issues.

As Reagon also points out, coalition building requires hard work that creates tensions and discomforts. This tension can be further aggravated when groups of different power within hierarchies of race, class, and gender try to build coalitions. As the concrete suggestions in John Anner's article, "Having the Tools at Hand: Building Successful Multicultural Social Justice Organizations," remind us, people can learn to work together across all sorts of differences. Through case studies of several grassroots groups who realized that their political effectiveness would be increasingly compromised if they didn't learn to deal with difference, Anner develops a list of models and mechanisms that can be used to build successful multicultural social justice organizations. Despite the difficulties, "change means growth, and growth can be painful," observes Audre Lorde in her essay included in part II of this volume. "But we sharpen self-definition by exposing the self in work and struggle together with those whom we define as different from ourselves, although sharing the same goals."

TOWARD A POLITICS OF EMPOWERMENT

Power is typically equated with domination and control over people or things. Social institutions depend on this version of power to reproduce hierarchies of race, class, and gender. Exploration of the experiences of African Americans, Latinos, women, Native Americans, Asian Americans, and the poor reveals much about how dominant groups exercise power, but centering on the experiences of historically marginalized groups also reveals much about resistance, because members of these groups engage in individual acts of resistance and organized political activism to challenge race, class, and gender oppression.

Re-envisioning and exercising power to bring about social change requires a sense of purpose and a vision that encourages us to look beyond what already exists. We must learn to imagine what is possible. For example, what type of environmental policies would result if working-class White women and women of color were central in the environmental movement's decision-making processes? If teachers tried to implement antiracist education from kindergarten through post-graduate education, how might American national identity be different? How might health care be organized if Native American women's ideas were central to planning? If men and women truly learned to work together, how might economic security be better provided for all?

Trying to make a difference takes time. One can take the long view or focus on the here and now. These are not either/or choices but two ways of looking at the same thing. Many people become cynical because they expect change to be immediate and dramatic rather than long-term and continual. How people deal with this disappointment is revealing. The White working-class women who became concerned about the effects of environmental dumping on their children initially trusted the government to provide solutions. When it did not, they could easily have become cynical and thrown in the towel. Instead, they tried to find another way because too much was at stake. Their initial idealism became tempered by pragmatism. Taking a long view, seeing the connectedness among all sorts of people, and involving people across race, class, and gender—and beyond—will be necessary to bringing lasting change. Clearly this will not happen tomorrow. But if people do not try to make a difference, "it doesn't just happen" at all.

Suggested Readings

Bannerji, Himani. 1995. *Thinking Through: Essays on Feminism, Marxism, and Anti-Racism*. Toronto: Women's Press.

Bullard, Robert D. 1994. *Unequal Protection: Environmental Justice and Communities of Color*. San Francisco: Sierra Club Books.

Caraway, Nancie. 1991. *Segregated Sisterhood: Racism and the Politics of American Feminism*. Knoxville: University of Tennessee Press.

Cleage, Pearl. 1993. *Deals with the Devil and Other Reasons to Riot*. New York: Ballantine.

D'Emilio, John. 1998. *Sexual Politics/Sexual Communities: The Making of a Homosexual Minority in the United States, 1940–1970*. Chicago: University of Chicago Press.

Espiritu, Yen Le. 1992. *Asian-American Pan-Ethnicity: Bridging Institutions and Identities*. Philadelphia: Temple University Press.

Freeman, Jo, and Victoria Johnson. 1999. *Waves of Protest: Social Movements since the Sixties*. Totowa, NJ: Rowman & Littlefield.

Morris, Aldon D. 1986. *The Origins of the Civil Rights Movement: Black Communities Organize for Change*. New York: Free Press.

InfoTrac College Edition: Search Terms

Use your access to the online library, InfoTrac College Edition, to learn more about some of the subjects covered in this section. The following are some suggested terms for searches:

Black power movement
civil rights movement
community activism
environmental racism
feminist movement
feminist organizations
grassroots organizations
identity politics
La Raza
multiracial coalitions
multiracial organizations
Union Summer

Wadsworth Sociology Resource Center: Virtual Society

For additional links, quizzes, and learning tools related to this section, see the Wadsworth Sociology Resource Center, Virtual Society, at **http://sociology.wadsworth.com.**

Making a Difference

COALITION POLITICS

64

Turning the Century

Bernice Johnson Reagon

I've never been this high before. I'm talking about the altitude. There is a lesson in bringing people together where they can't get enough oxygen, then having them try to figure out what they're going to do when they can't think properly. I'm serious about that. There probably are some people here who can breathe, because you were born in high altitudes and you have big lung cavities. But when you bring people in who have not had the environmental conditioning, you got one group of people who are in a strain—and the group of people who are feeling fine are trying to figure out why you're staggering around, and that's what this workshop is about this morning.

I wish there had been another way to graphically make me feel it because I belong to the group of people who are having a very difficult time being here. I feel as if I'm gonna keel over any minute and die. That is often what it feels like if you're *really* doing coalition work. Most of the time you feel threatened to the core and if you don't, you're not really doing no coalescing.

I'm Bernice Reagon. I was born in Georgia, and I'd like to talk about the fact that in about twenty years we'll turn up another century. I believe that we are positioned to have the opportunity to have something to do with what

Based on a presentation at the West Coast Women's Music Festival 1981, Yosemite National Forest, California.

From: Barbara Smith, ed., *Home Girls: A Black Feminist Anthology* (New York: Kitchen Table Press, 1983), pp. 356–68. Reprinted by permission.

makes it into the next century. And the principles of coalition are directly related to that. You don't go into coalition because you just *like* it. The only reason you would consider trying to team up with somebody who could possibly kill you, is because that's the only way you can figure you can stay alive.

A hundred years ago in this country we were just beginning to heat up for the century we're in. And the name of the game in terms of the dominant energy was technology. We have lived through a period where there have been things like railroads and telephones, and radios, TVs and airplanes, and cars, and transistors, and computers. And what this has done to the concept of human society and human life is, to a large extent, what we in the latter part of this century have been trying to grapple with. With the coming of all that technology, there was finally the possibility of making sure no human being in the world would be unreached. You couldn't find a place where you could hide if somebody who had access to that technology wanted to get to you. Before the dawning of that age you had all these little cute villages and the wonderful homogeneous societies where everybody looked the same, did things the same, and believed the same things, and if they didn't, you could just kill them and nobody would even ask you about it.

We've pretty much come to the end of a time when you can have a space that is "yours only"—just for the people you want to be there. Even when we have our "women-only" festivals, there is no such thing. The fault is not necessarily with the organizers of the gathering. To a large extent it's because we have just finished with that kind of isolating. There is no hiding place. There is nowhere you can go and only be with people who are like you. It's over. Give it up.

Now every once in awhile there is a need for people to try to clean out corners and bar the doors and check everybody who comes in the door, and check what they carry in and say, "Humph, inside this place the only thing we are going to deal with is X or Y or Z." And so only the X's or Y's or Z's get to come in. That place can then become a nurturing place or a very destructive place. Most of the time when people do that, they do it because of the heat of trying to live in this society where being an X or Y or Z is very difficult, to say the least. The people running the society call the shots as if they're still living in one of those little villages, where they kill the ones they don't like or put them in the forest to die. (There are some societies where babies are born and if they are not wanted for some reason they are put over in a corner. They do that here too, you know, put them in garbage cans.) When somebody else is running a society like that, and you are the one who would be put out to die, it gets too hard to stay out in that society all the time. And that's when you find a place, and you try to bar the door and check all the people who come in. You come together to see what you can do about shouldering up all of your energies so that you and your kind can survive.

There is no chance that you can survive by staying *inside* the barred room. (Applause) That will not be tolerated. The door of the room will just be painted red and then when those who call the shots get ready to clean house, they have easy access to you.

But that space while it lasts should be a nurturing space where you sift out what people are saying about you and decide who you really are. And you take the time to try to construct within yourself and within your community who you would be if you were running society. In fact, in that little barred room where you check everybody at the door, you act out community. You pretend that your room is a world. It's almost like a play, and in some cases you actually grow food, you learn to have clean water, and all of that stuff, you just try to do it all. It's like, "If *I* was really running it, this is the way it would be."

Of course the problem with the experiment is that there ain't nobody in there but folk like you, which by implication means you wouldn't know what to do if you were running it with all of the other people who are out there in the world. Now that's nationalism. I mean it's nurturing, but it is also nationalism. At a certain stage nationalism is crucial to a people if you are going to ever impact as a group in your own interest. Nationalism at another point becomes reactionary because it is totally inadequate for surviving in the world with many peoples. (Applause)

Sometimes you get comfortable in your little barred room, and you decide you in fact are going to live there and carry out all of your stuff in there. And you gonna take care of everything that needs to be taken care of in the barred room. If you're white and in the barred room and if everybody's white, one of the first things you try to take care of is making sure that people don't think that the barred room is a racist barred room. So you begin to talk about racism and the first thing you do is say, "Well, maybe we better open the door and let some Black folks in the barred room." Then you think, "Well, how we gonna figure out whether they're X's or not?" Because there's nothing in the room but X's. (Laughter) You go down the checklist. You been working a while to sort out who you are, right? So you go down the checklist and say, "If we can find Black folk like that we'll let them in the room." You don't really want Black folks, you are just looking for yourself with a little color to it.

And there are those of us Black folk who are like that. So if you're lucky you can open the door and get one or two. Right? And everything's wonderful. But no matter what, there will be one or two of us who have not bothered to be like you and you know it. We come knocking on your door and say, "Well, you let them in, you let me in too." And we will break your door down trying to get in. (Laughter) As far as we can see we are also X's. Cause you didn't say, "THIS BARRED ROOM IS FOR WHITE X'S ONLY." You just said it was for X's. So everybody who thinks they're an X comes running to get into the room. And because you trying to take care of everything in this room, and you know you're not racist, you get pressed to let us all in.

The first thing that happens is that the room don't feel like the room any-more. (Laughter) And it ain't home no more. It is not a womb no more. And you can't feel comfortable no more. And what happens at that point has to do with trying to do too much in it. You don't do no coalition building in a womb. It's just like trying to get a baby used to taking a drink when they're in your womb. It just don't work too well. Inside the womb you generally are very soft and unshelled. You have no covering. And you have no ability to handle what happens if you start to let folks in who are not like you.

Coalition work is not work done in your home. Coalition work has to be done in the streets. And it is some of the most dangerous work you can do. And you shouldn't look for comfort. Some people will come to a coalition and they rate the success of the coalition on whether or not they feel good when they get there. They're not looking for a coalition; they're looking for a home! They're looking for a bottle with some milk in it and a nipple, which does not happen in a coalition. You don't get a lot of food in a coalition. You don't get fed a lot in a coalition. In a coalition you have to give, and it is different from your home. You can't stay there all the time. You go to the coalition for a few hours and then you go back and take your bottle wherever it is, and then you go back and coalesce some more.

It is very important not to confuse them—home and coalition. Now when it comes to women—the organized women's movement—this recent thrust—we all have had the opportunity to have some kind of relationship with it. The women's movement has perpetuated a myth that there is some common expe-rience that comes just cause you're women. And they're throwing all these fes-tivals and this music and these concerts happen. If you're the same kind of women like the folk in that little barred room, it works. But as soon as some other folk check the definition of "women" that's in the dictionary (which you didn't write, right?) they decide that they can come because they are women, but when they do, they don't see or hear nothing that is like them. Then they charge, "This ain't no women's thing!" (Applause) Then if you try to address that and bring them in, they start to play music that ain't even women's music! (Laughter and hoots) And you try to figure out what happened to your won-derful barred room. It comes from taking a word like "women" and using it as a code. There is an in-house definition so that when you say "women only" most of the time that means you had better be able—if you come to this place—to handle lesbianism and a lot of folks running around with no clothes on. And I'm being too harsh this morning as I talk to you, but I don't want you to miss what I'm trying to say. Now if you come and you can't handle that, there's an-other term that's called "woman-identified." They say you might be a woman but you're not woman-identified, and we only want women who are "woman-identified." That's a good way to leave a lot of women out of your room.

So here you are and you grew up and you speak English and you know about this word "woman" and you know you one, and you walk into this "woman-only" space and you ain't there. (Laughter) Because "woman" in that space does not mean "woman" from your world. It's a code word and it traps, and the people that use the word are not prepared to deal with the fact that if you put it out, everybody that thinks they're a woman may one day want to seek refuge. And it ain't no refuge place! And it's not safe! It should be a coalition! It may have been that in its first year the Michigan National "Women-Only" festival was a refuge place. By the fourth year it was a place of coalition, and it's not safe anymore. (Applause) It ain't safe for nobody who comes. When you walk in there you in trouble—and everybody who comes is trying to get to their home there. At this festival [Yosemite] they said: whatever you drink, bring it with you—tea, honey, you know, whatever it is—and we will provide hot water. Now I understand that you got here and there was no hot water. Can't get nothing! That is the nature of coalition. (Laughter) You have to give it all. It is not to feed you; you have to feed it. And it's a monster. It never gets enough. It always wants more. So you better be sure you got your home someplace for you to go to so that you will not become a martyr to the coalition. Coalition *can* kill people; however, it is not by nature fatal. You do not have to die because you are committed to coalition. I'm not so old, and I don't know nothing else. But you do have to know how to pull back, and you do have to have an old-age perspective. You have to be beyond the womb stage.

None of this matters at all very much if you die tomorrow—that won't even be cute. It only matters if you make a commitment to be around for another fifty more years. There are some grey haired women I see running around occasionally, and we have to talk to those folks about how come they didn't commit suicide forty years ago. Don't take everything they say because some of the stuff they gave up to stay around ain't worth considering. But be sure you get on your agenda some old people and try to figure out what it will be like if you are a raging radical fifty years from today.

Think about yourself that way. What would you be like if you had white hair and had not given up your principles? It might be wise as you deal with coalition efforts to think about the possibilities of going for fifty years. It calls for some care. I'm not gonna be suicidal, if I can help it. Sometimes you don't even know you just took a step that could take your head off cause you can't know everything when you start to coalesce with these people who sorta look like you in just one aspect but really they belong to another group. That is really the nature of women. It does not matter at all that biologically we have being women in common. We have been organized to have our primary cultural signals come from some other factors than that we are women. We are not from our base acculturated to be women people, capable of crossing our first people boundaries—Black, White, Indian, etc.

Now if we are the same women from the same people in this barred room, we never notice it. That stuff stays wherever it is. It does not show up until somebody walks into the room who happens to be a woman but really is also somebody else. And then out comes who we really are. And at that point you are not a woman. You are Black or you are Chicana or you are Disabled or you are Racist or you are White. The fact that you are a woman is not important at all and it is not the governing factor to your existence at that moment. I am now talking about bigotry and everybody's got it. I am talking about turning the century with some principles intact. Today wherever women gather together it is not necessarily nurturing. It is coalition building. And if you feel the strain, you may be doing some good work. (Applause) So don't come to no women's festival looking for comfort unless you brought it in your little tent. (Laughter) And then if you bring it in your tent don't be inviting everybody in because everybody ain't your company, and then you won't be able to stand the festival. Am I confusing you? Yes, I am. If coalition is so bad, and so terrible, and so uncomfortable, why is it necessary? That's what you're asking. Because the barred rooms will not be allowed to exist. They will all be wiped out. That is the plan that we now have in front of us.

Now these little rooms were created by some of the most powerful movements we have seen in this country. I'm going to start with the Civil Rights movement because of course I think that that was the first one in the era we're in. Black folks started it, Black folks did it, so everything you've done politically rests on the efforts of my people—that's my arrogance! Yes, and it's the truth; it's my truth. You can take it or leave it, but that's the way I see it. So once we did what we did, then you've got women, you've got Chicanos, you've got the Native Americans, and you've got homosexuals, and you got all of these people who also got sick of somebody being on their neck. And maybe if they come together, they can do something about it. And I claim all of you as coming from something that made me who I am. You can't tell me that you ain't in the Civil Rights movement. You are in the Civil Rights movement that we created that just rolled up to your door. But it could not stay the same, because if it was gonna stay the same it wouldn't have done you no good. Some of you would not have caught yourself dead near no Black folks walking around talking about freeing themselves from racism and lynching. So by the time our movement got to you it had to sound like something you knew about. Like if I find out you're gay, you gonna lose your job.

There were people who came South to work in the movement who were not Black. Most of them were white when they came. Before it was over, that category broke up—you know, some of them were Jewish, not simply White, and some others even changed their names. Say if it was Mary when they came South, by the time they were finished it was Maria, right? It's called finding yourself. At some point, you cannot be fighting oppression and be oppressed yourself and not feel it. Within the Black movement there was also all of the evils of the society, so that anything that was happening to you in New York or the West Coast probably also happened to you in another way, within the movement. And as you became aware of that you tried to talk to these movement people about how you felt. And they say, "Well let's take that up next week. Because the most important thing now is that Black people are being oppressed and we must work with that." Watch these mono-issue people. They ain't gonna do you no good. I don't care who they are. And there are people who prioritize the cutting line of the struggle. And they say the cutting line is this issue, and more than anything we must move on this issue and that's automatically saying that whatever's bothering you will be put down if you bring it up. You have to watch these folks. Watch these groups that can only deal with one thing at a time. On the other hand, learn about space within coalition. You can't have everybody sitting up there talking about everything that concerns you at the same time or you won't get no place. . . .

It must become necessary for all of us to feel that this is our world. And that we are here to stay and that anything that is here is ours to take and to use in our image. And watch that "our"—make it as big as you can—it ain't got nothing to do with that barred room. The "our" must include everybody you have to include in order for you to survive. You must be sure you understand that you ain't gonna be able to have an "our" that don't include Bernice Johnson Reagon, cause I don't plan to go nowhere! That's why we have to have coalitions. Cause I ain't gonna let you live unless you let me live. Now there's danger in that, but there's also the possibility that we can both live—if you can stand it. . . .

THE BOYS AND GIRLS OF (UNION) SUMMER

65

Marc Cooper

Twenty-one-year-old Nicola Grunthal is no less than a living 4-foot, 10-inch trophy for the newly invigorated A.F.L.-C.I.O. It was only two summers ago that she was on the fast track to a lifetime of privilege, studying to be a diplomat and spending her vacation interning at the White House. But now she's changed her plans. She still wants to finish Harvard Law School, but "no way I'm going into corporate America," she says. "I want to work with labor de-

---

From: *The Nation* 19 (August 12/19, 1996): 18–20. Reprinted with permission.

signing international campaigns against multinational corporations. I'm juiced on that idea. Really juiced."

Grunthal had been slowly drifting toward a career in social activism since her self-described "disillusionment" with mainstream politics, but her new direction jelled only as she was completing her three-week stint in the A.F.L.-C.I.O.'s first-ever "Union Summer." That program—often compared to the civil rights movement's Freedom Summer of 1964—has thrust more than 1,000 mostly young people onto the front lines of the U.S. labor movement. In forty-one separate three-week "waves" in twenty-two different cities coast to coast, the new recruits are given a place to sleep, a light varnishing of labor history, a stipend of $210 a week and are then thrown raw into local organizing drives.

"Put simply, we want to inject a massive dose of class consciousness into youth politics," says Andy Levin, the 36-year-old head of Union Summer, himself a grad of Harvard Law. "Yes, we want to recruit new blood. But more important, we want to transform the politics of the next generation of activists." Since the days of Vietnam, says Levin, "most young progressives have been either antilabor or have ignored labor," falling into single-issue or strict identity politics. "Our message is that labor is where it's at in the fight for social justice in the nineties."

A bitter, protracted campaign by the United Steelworkers against Japanese-owned Bridgestone/Firestone, based here in Nashville, is where Grunthal and nine other Union Summer (U/S) enlistees were sent to test their mettle. In July 1994, more than 4,000 members of the United Rubber Workers went on strike after the company demanded rotating twelve-hour shifts, cuts in benefits and lower pay for new hires. A half-year later the company permanently replaced about half the strikers—a move recently deemed illegal by the National Labor Relations Board (but still being contested by Bridgestone). Ten months after the strike began, the union saw no option but to return to work without a contract, though not everyone was taken back.

Shortly afterward, the cash-flush Steelworkers merged with the defeated rubber union and things began to turn around. A tenacious worldwide corporate campaign and consumer boycott were launched to embarrass and pressure Bridgestone/Firestone. Slowly, some striking workers were hired back. But as the second anniversary of the walkout loomed, some 500 workers were still out of a job, the company continued to refuse union terms for a contract and the Steelworkers were escalating their fight.

When I met Grunthal and the rest of the "Nashville Ten"—as these Union Summer kids call themselves—they were in their final week of service, feverishly working for a successful conclusion to the Steelworkers' July 12–13 "International Days of Rage." Of the Union Summer group, eight are between 18 and 21, the youngest having just graduated from high school. One is 22; the oldest, a schoolteacher, is 27. And there they were, front and center in what Steelworkers corporate campaign organizer Doug Niehouse calls "the

biggest coordinated international hit ever on a corporation." During the Days
of Rage, Argentine and Brazilian Bridgestone workers were to stage stoppages, while other unions in France, Italy, Japan and Turkey would be protest-
ing company policy. Throughout the United States, union workers planned to
set up picket lines around 950 Bridgestone-owned MasterCare garages. In
Nashville alone, there would be protests at sixteen separate MasterCares, a
march on company headquarters and a rally the following day to be keynoted
by the new A.F.L.-C.I.O. president, John Sweeney.

"That's why we're working fifteen hours a day," says 20-year-old Amanda
Johnson, a junior at the University of New Mexico. "It's exciting and immediate. You know you are doing something right there."

Far from being simple grunts, the U/S kids have been given tangible organizing responsibilities. One group has been charged with pulling together
a prayer breakfast to recruit local clergy into the campaign. Another has organized two neighborhood "blitzes," where the entire group will be going door
to door in areas where Bridgestone/Firestone execs live, asking their neighbors to call the company and urge a settlement. They're out every morning at
7:30 leafleting customers at the MasterCare centers. At night they listen to
"educational modules"—talks and videos on labor history and organizing
techniques. In between it all, at 9:30 sharp each morning, they sit in as equals
in Local 1055's "war room," where campaign strategy and logistics are ham-
mered out. Bunked in collectively at a Vanderbilt University chapel, they take
turns spending the night in sleeping bags in the union-run tent city outside
the doors of the company headquarters.

It's a lot of responsibility, but the consensus is that the Nashville Ten are
holding up admirably. "I'd trade these kids in one minute for most of our own
union organizers," says Dick Blin, on loan from the Paperworkers to handle
media. "There's so much deadwood around us, so-called organizers who make
a hundred Gs a year and can't remember the last time they talked to a worker.
These kids, on the other hand, are great, fearless and full of energy."

Perhaps this Nashville site is extraordinary compared with others, its success owing to the militancy and professionalism of the union Local. The
achievement of this group is no doubt also facilitated by its immediate supervisor, a powerhouse named Joe Geevarghese, himself only 23 and now a full-
time Steelworkers staff organizer (after graduating from Vanderbilt last year
as student body president). Andy Levin admits that at least one site fell apart in
internecine squabbling and that not all have had such meaty work to do as here
in Nashville (even among this group one college junior decided to go home
five days early, upset over the "confrontational" tactic of the neighborhood
blitz). But after I called around to other sites and looked over the first-person
report faxed around the U/S network, it seems safe to say that in general Union
Summer has been successful in bringing young people into meaningful organizing work.

In Los Angeles, the youth activists were so adept at organizing county home-care workers that when the program was over, four U/S participants were hired to keep working for the Service Employees International Union. In Watsonville, California, U/S detachments are involved in the country's largest single organizing effort, the drive to unionize 20,000 strawberry workers. In Akron, Ohio, an all-female contingent worked with the Service Employees to help foster a community-based poor people's organization. In posh Hilton Head, South Carolina, U/S activists worked in a campaign to unionize low-wage hotel workers. Some of those same students are already pulling together other U/S alumni from several Southern states to head a regional campaign to fight privatization of government service jobs. Union Summer volunteers are signed up for a train ride through the South aimed at organizing textile workers. In Washington, D.C., a couple dozen Union Summer recruits wound up working on political campaigns for the left-of-center New Party.

For all the media comparisons with Freedom Summer, Union Summer, in principle, has much more in common with the community organizing program started in 1963, at Tom Hayden's urging, by the incipient Students for a Democratic Society. After receiving an initial grant of $5,000 from the United Auto Workers, the early student radicals came up with the Economic Research and Action Project (ERAP). The concept was to deploy in a dozen urban centers during summer vacation groups of ten to twenty students who would organize impoverished residents around a host of social justice issues. For two years the ERAPs came and went with little tangible success, until they disappeared completely when S.D.S. shifted its focus to the horrors of Vietnam. Even so, the experience deeply marked the core group of 500 or so ERAP activists. "Hardly anyone on the 'outside' can imagine the completeness of transformation or the depth of [the students'] commitment," wrote Andrew Kopkind after visiting the Newark site in 1965. In fact, in the turbulent handful of years that immediately followed, much of the cream of the radical movement grew directly out of the ERAP projects.

These are, of course, different times and a different generation of students. "The problem is, there's no transference between generations," says Geevarghese, the Steelworkers' organizer. That analysis was borne out by hours of conversation I had with the Nashville U/S group during the week I spent with them. There was an unquestionable sense of disjuncture with history, even their own personal histories. Four of the ten had come from union families, but all four said that until this experience they had never known what their union parent really did. Nor was there much evidence of the ideological fervor that drove the original S.D.S.ers.

By contrast with the mood of their sixties forerunners, this group's is one of quiet skepticism and sincere confusion and curiosity about the present and the future rather than anger and indignation. Then again, thirty years ago the disillusionment provoked by Bull Connor's fire hoses and Lyndon Johnson's B-52s was shockingly fresh and created a sense of betrayal that was immediately radicalizing. With the exception of the schoolteacher, the Nashville participants were all born after Nixon's resignation and were preschoolers or in kindergarten when the Great Communicator was sworn in.

A majority of Union Summer participants are women, 52 percent are of color and just under half come from union families. But the lure of labor work seems strong, even on top-drawer college campuses. Almost two dozen A.F.L.-C.I.O. recruiters combed more than a hundred campuses this past spring, and union officials predict that as many as 1,000 students will eventually apply this year to become full-time organizers—more than twice the number of 1995. At Swarthmore alone, thirty applications were filed.

The Union Summer program and the stepped-up recruitment of young organizers is central to the strategic plan of the new A.F.L.-C.I.O. leadership under Sweeney. Indeed, Union Summer was part of Sweeney's election platform and is integral to his vow to create a new "culture of organizing" inside America's flagging labor movement. The decline in union membership to its current level of only 10.4 percent of the private-sector work force can be traced not only to aggressive corporate strategy and a stacked legislative deck but also to a sort of narcolepsy that has beset the official union culture in recent decades.

Now, Sweeney has brought the seven-year-old Organizing Institute into the heart of the labor federation and has named its respected leader, Richard Bensinger, to head the newly created A.F.L.-C.I.O. Organizing Department. Armed with a $20 million budget, Bensinger has a mandate to jump-start massive campaigns that will bring tens of thousands of new, mostly young workers into unions.

"But don't think for a moment that it's all clear sailing within the A.F.L.," says one veteran organizer. "There's still plenty of tension within the A.F.L. between Sweeney and the old guard, who still have plenty of sinecures and power. And there's plenty of tension within the Sweeney camp as well about how far they are really going to go. Don't forget, Sweeney himself is hardly a radical. No doubt, however, a successful Union Summer is going to give a lot of ammo to those who want to take organizing seriously."

In any case, the mathematics are daunting. U/S head Andy Levin estimates that to just stand still at 10 percent of the labor force, unions will have to recruit 300,000 new members a year. To get back to unionization levels of a few decades ago, a million or more new union members a year for several years would be needed. "That's why Union Summer is so crucial," he says. "The people we are bringing in—youth, women, minorities—look a lot more like the work force we need to organize than the older generation does. They're our future."

Is the A.F.L.-C.I.O., however, the best future for a new generation of radical youth? While Sweeney's administration is a world removed from the dinosaur regime of predecessor Lane Kirkland, there are real limits to how far a "reformed" labor movement might be willing to go. "In most union activity it's still taboo to focus on social class," says Joe Geevarghese. But it's also understood that Sweeney is a transitional figure whose program will either fail and let the A.F.L. drift back to sleep, or will in the relatively near future open the door to a more militant leadership under a younger group of supporters he has brought in. The more space that younger allies like Levin are given, and the better they perform, the better chance there is for the more hopeful course of the federation. But no matter where the A.F.L.-C.I.O. eventually goes, Union Summer has to be viewed as positive. The contemporary left is too quick to politicize the way goods are consumed (choosing politically correct coffee, cosmetics and culture) rather than the way they are produced. Union Summer begins to reverse the focus.

It's the final day of the Steelworkers' Days of Rage campaign, and everything has gone like clockwork. Faxed reports confirm the international work stoppages and protests against Bridgestone/Firestone. The previous afternoon, the Nashville Union Summer activists helped lead a raucous march of union members and supporters onto the corporate campus. This morning, each U/S activist led a protest at a local MasterCare garage. And now with 2,500 or so union members rallying under a stifling sun at a lakeside campsite, the Union Summer crew has been invited into an air-conditioned cabin for a private meeting with John Sweeney. The air inside the room is electric. Certainly not because they are meeting with the suspendered and balding 62-year-old leader of the A.F.L.-C.I.O., who thanks them for their hard work. But rather because the kids themselves are charged up and downright giddy.

It's the charge you get from directly confronting power, no matter on how small or symbolic a scale. And for most, if not all, of the activists in the room, the morning's MasterCare demonstrations had been their baptism in direct action. As Sweeney went around the room asking the organizers to relate their personal experience, they bubbled. Acting on their own authority, at least four of the nine activists "went in"—led their groups past police lines into brief, nonviolent occupations of the targeted MasterCare service centers. It didn't change the world. The coolheaded Nashville police force didn't even arrest anyone, but a psychic barricade has been crossed. "What a rush," said Grunthal. "What an unbelievable rush."

FROM THE GROUND UP

66

Charon Asetoyer

My husband is Dakota Sioux from the Yankton Sioux reservation, located in the South Central part of South Dakota. His father passed away in 1983, and in 1985 we moved to his reservation in order to fulfill our traditional commitment. It is a tradition to hold a memorial on the anniversary of a loved one's death for the following four years. It was to be a temporary stay, until our commitment was over. We had planned to move to Oklahoma so I could work for my tribe.

After we had moved to South Dakota, I applied for a job with the Yankton Sioux Tribe. The tribe is small and jobs were held by members of the tribe; it was not likely that I would be hired. I was turned down. But word got around that Clarence Rockboy had married a Comanche woman and had returned home with her, and people were curious to meet me.

Women in particular started to drop by, and I took that opportunity to invite others to come and talk. Before long a group of women were meeting regularly in my home to talk about "women's things." We moved the meetings to an empty bedroom in our basement. Out conversations centered around problems that women and children were having in the community and what we might do to address them.

By 1986 we were incorporated as a nonprofit organization. My small basement bedroom turned into an office. Women would stop in to have coffee and talk about their problems at home. Early one morning a woman came by to ask me what I knew about Fetal Alcohol Syndrome (FAS). She told me that she had gone on drinking during her pregnancy and that her child, now a teenager, was having many learning problems. She wanted to know where she could get the child tested for FAS. She was frustrated and had nowhere to turn for support or help. Before long we were meeting on a regular basis; she began bringing other mothers to join in. Soon we had a community task force on FAS, the beginning of our first project, "Women and Children in Alcohol."

It was natural that health issues should come up first: in reservation communities across the U.S., health problems are devastating, and some of the worst are on the Yankton Sioux Reservation. The infant mortality rate has been as high as 23.8 per thousand. Diabetes affects 70 percent of the people over

From: *Women's Review of Books* 11 (July 1994): 22. Reprinted by permission.

the age of 40, and the rates of secondary health conditions caused by diabetes, such as kidney failure, heart attacks, stroke, amputations and blindness, are alarmingly high. Alcoholism is out of control and contributes to many of these health problems, including domestic abuse and fetal alcohol births—one out of four children has FAS. Many health problems are related to poor nutrition, caused by years and even generations of eating government commodity foods that are high in salt, sugars and fat and low in fiber.

Native activists have brought the Indian Health Service under fire for years for their neglect and mistreatment of Native women. In the 1960s sterilization abuses surfaced, as they did again in the eighties when it was revealed that the Indian Health Service had used Depo-Provera on Native women who were developmentally disabled before it was FDA approved. Today the Indian Health Service is still abusing Native women's reproductive rights by limiting our contraception choices. They are promoting contraceptives like Depo Provera and Norplant, as well as sterilization. When the Hyde Amendment took away federal funding for abortion, Native women lost their access to abortion altogether: the Indian Health Service, our primary health care provider, is a division of the U.S. Public Service—that is, the Federal government.

The direction our programs have taken has been determined by the women who have come through our doors. I was sitting at my desk one afternoon working on an article for our newsletter when the phone rang. "Is it true that a tubal ligation can be temporary and that I can have it reversed when I want to have a child?" the caller asked. When I asked her why she wanted the information, she said an Indian Health Service doctor had recommended that she have her tubes tied. The procedure, he told her, could be reversed later if she wanted. Incidents like this spurred us to create a reproductive health program.

Other issues evolved after we started doing workshops in the community. One Saturday morning a young woman came to my front door, banging for someone to let her in. I opened the door and she ran in. I recognized the look of fright and helplessness on her face, and locked the door behind her. During my first marriage I too had been a victim of domestic violence. There I was, standing in the hallway of my home faced with something that I had wanted to leave behind. Only this time I was not the one in need of someone to take me in.

In the course of time we created a program to assist women like this one and their children. We started out with a safe house program, sheltering women in local motels. In 1991, after a long court battle over zoning, the Native American Community Board opened a shelter for women and children fleeing from domestic violence and sexual assault. It now houses eighteen women and children and has provided services for over 900 women and children over the past two and a half years.

As more concerns were brought forward, we needed additional programming and additional staff. The office had grown too small for the organization. Several months earlier I had visited the National Black Women's Health Project in Atlanta, Georgia. The Project was located in a large house which seemed ideal: there was room to grow in, space for program work, a kitchen, a yard, and a strong sense of pride among the staff in their unique working environment. It all seemed so right: why not for us too? We wanted to do nutrition work to address diabetics, so we needed a place to prepare food; we wanted to work with children, so we needed space for them as well as for office work. And if we could buy a house we would no longer have to pay rent to a landlord.

Owning our own place seemed like a good idea but no more than a dream at that point, so I put it in the back of my mind. Who would fund a group of women to buy a house anyway, especially a group of Native American women living on a reservation in South Dakota? I had no idea what the cost of real estate might be in Lake Andes, South Dakota. But I kept thinking about the idea. A friend mentioned a small house she knew of, a fixer-upper, around $5,000 to $7,000. I went to look at it: it did seem to suit our needs.

Shortly after, I was invited to a conference sponsored by the National Women's Health Network, a health advocacy organization based in Washington, D.C. At a networking reception the first evening, I met another woman of color, Luz Alveolus Martinets, the director of the National Latina Health Organization. We talked about the work we were doing, and I eventually told her about our dream of buying a house for our project. When I told her what it would cost, she thought I meant the down payment. But $6,000 was the price for the entire house.

Luz told me that most of the women attending the conference were working women and could afford to make a contribution toward the house. All I had to do was to get up during lunch the next day, when we all had to introduce ourselves, and make an appeal for donations. At lunch I tried to avoid Luz: it seemed too hard to stand up in a crowded room of women I really did not know and ask for money. But Luz found me. Still, when it was my turn to introduce myself, I started to sit down without making my request for donations. Luz kept encouraging me to go ahead and make my request. Before long, all the women in the room wanted to know what we were arguing about. So I went ahead and asked for their help. Then I saw Byllye Avery of the National Black Women's Health Project, across the room, reach into her pocketbook and pull out her checkbook. Byllye held up the first check and announced to the room, "I donate $100." The pocketbooks opened and the checks piled up. It was like a dream: the house was soon to become a reality. I left the conference with about half of the money we needed.

Soon after we purchased the house, people from the community came to help clean, paint and panel the walls. A few weeks of hard work transformed the little brick house across from my home into a warm environment where women and children could come together to share in health education activities and to organize around issues confronting our community. In February 1988, the doors opened on the first Native American Women's Health Education Resource Center based on a reservation, located in Lake Andes, South Dakota, on the Yankton Sioux Reservation.

Not long after ther Resource Center opened a young Yankton Sioux woman walked in, introduced herself and asked if she could do her college internship with us. She was interested in working with children. It was time, we decided, for us to examine how we could provide services for children with special needs. The Child Development Program was our answer.

The Program brought children with special needs together to work, play and learn in an after-school program. Fetal alcohol-affected children, latchkey children, gifted children, and children from highly stressed families participate in the program. Today the program has evolved into a Dakota Cultural program in which elders of the Yankton Sioux tribe work with children, teaching them Dakota language, values and spirituality.

An Adult Education Program was not something we had even thought about developing—until one day a call came in from one of the local high school counselors, asking if a sixteen-year-old pregnant student could continue her schooling at the Resource Center with tutoring from our staff. "She's getting too big to sit in class all day long," he said. We said "Sure," and the next week we had a student. Soon after that a mother of one of the children in our Child Development Program asked if we could show her how to use a computer. She said that she already knew how to type, and she could get a job if she knew how to use a computer. This was the beginning of a program that offered job readiness skills and GED completion.

As more women heard about the work and the services that the Resource Center was providing, a feeling of trust was established. Women turned to us for help concerning sterilization abuse, and for information about sexually transmitted diseases, AIDS, family planning and abortion. A high school student came into the Resource Center one afternoon wanting information about pregnancy, AIDS and condoms. She asked if we could get her a home pregnancy test kit, since she thought that she might be pregnant, but if she went down to the local drugstore for it, the clerk would recognize her and call her mother.

It was not long before we were going into the schools with AIDS and contraception information, and conducting AIDS workshops in the community. We hired four high school students, two girls and two boys, and trained them to be AIDS peer counselors, so they could go back into the community and schools to give out accurate information to other young people.

It became obvious to us that no one else in our community, and no other Native women's groups on other reservations, were doing this kind of work.

As women turned to us for information about abortion and issues of reproductive health, we knew that we needed to organize our reproductive health work more formally. Our next move was to bring Native women together in a project that would address our unmet health care needs and the reproductive abuses committed by the Indian Health Service. In 1990, 36 Native women met in Pierre, South Dakota, to form the first Native Women's Reproductive Rights Coalition. The Coalition has developed a reproductive rights agenda that defines the issues of reproductive rights and health as Native women ourselves understand them.

Over the past three years the Native Women's Reproductive Rights Coalition has grown to involve over 150 women from eight states, and it continues to grow each year. It organizes Native women to address such concerns as Norplant and Depo-Provera abuse, environmental issues, abortion, and the oppressive effects of organized religion in reservation communities.

Another central part of the Coalition's work has been to include the teachings of our elders. The passing down of traditional methods of birthing, child spacing, abortion, parenting and "becoming a woman" ceremonies is an important issue for Native women and has become a major mission of the Coalition. Through its work, combined with the direct services of our Resource Center, we can bring into the national and international arena practices and policies that we ourselves have shaped and that truly represent the issues confronting us.

TAKING MULTICULTURAL, ANTIRACIST EDUCATION SERIOUSLY   67

An Interview with Enid Lee

Barbara Miner

What do you mean by a multicultural education?

The term *multicultural education* has a lot of different meanings. The term I use most often is *antiracist education*.

From: David Levine, Robert Lowe, Bob Peterson, and Rita Tenorio, eds., *Rethinking Schools: An Agenda for Change* (New York: New Press, 1995), pp. 9–16. Reprinted by permission.

Multicultural or antiracist education is fundamentally a perspective. It's a point of view that cuts across all subject areas, and addresses the histories and experiences of people who have been left out of the curriculum. Its purpose is to help us deal equitably with all the cultural and racial differences that you find in the human family. It's also a perspective that allows us to get at explanations for why things are the way they are in terms of power relationships, in terms of equality issues.

So when I say multicultural or antiracist education, I am talking about equipping students, parents, and teachers with the tools needed to combat racism and ethnic discrimination, and to find ways to build a society that includes all people on an equal footing.

It also has to do with how the school is run in terms of who gets to be involved with decisions. It has to do with parents and how their voices are heard or not heard. It has to do with who gets hired in the school.

If you don't take multicultural education or antiracist education seriously, you are actually promoting a monocultural or racist education. There is not neutral ground on this issue.

Why do you use the term antiracist education instead of multicultural education?

Partly because in Canada, multicultural education often has come to mean something that is quite superficial: the dances, the dress, the dialect, the dinners. And it does so without focusing on what those expressions of culture mean: the values, the power relationships that shape the culture.

I also use the term *antiracist education* because a lot of multicultural education hasn't looked at discrimination. It has the view, "People are different and isn't that nice," as opposed to looking at how some people's differences are looked upon as deficits and disadvantages. In antiracist education, we attempt to look at—and change—those things in school and society that prevent some differences from being valued.

Oftentimes, whatever is white is treated as normal. So when teachers choose literature that they say will deal with a universal theme or story, like childhood, all the people in the stories are of European origin; it's basically white culture and civilization. That culture is different from others, but it doesn't get named as different. It gets named as normal.

Antiracist education helps us move that European perspective over to the side to make room for other cultural perspectives that must be included.

What are some ways your perspective might manifest itself in a kindergarten classroom, for example?

It might manifest itself in something as basic as the kinds of toys and games that you select. If all the toys and games reflect the dominant culture and race and language, then that's what I call a monocultural classroom even if you have kids of different backgrounds in the class.

I have met some teachers who think that just because they have kids from different races and backgrounds, they have a multicultural classroom. Bodies of kids are not enough.

It also gets into issues such as what kind of pictures are up on the wall? What kinds of festivals are celebrated? What are the rules and expectations in the classroom in terms of what kinds of languages are acceptable? What kinds of interactions are encouraged? How are the kids grouped? These are just some of the concrete ways in which a multicultural perspective affects a classroom.

How does one implement a multicultural or antiracist education?

It usually happens in stages. Because there's a lot of resistance to change in schools, I don't think it's reasonable to expect to move straight from a monocultural school to a multiracial school.

First there is this surface stage in which people change a few expressions of culture in the school. They make welcome signs in several languages and have a variety of foods and festivals. My problem is not that they start there. My concern is that they often stop there. Instead, what they have to do is move very quickly and steadily to transform the entire curriculum. For example, when we say classical music, whose classical music are we talking about? European? Japanese? And what items are on the tests? Whose culture do they reflect? Who is getting equal access to knowledge in the school? Whose perspective is heard? Whose is ignored?

The second stage is transitional and involves creating units of study. Teachers might develop a unit on Native Americans, or Native Canadians, or people of African background. And they have a whole unit that they study from one period to the next. But it's a separate unit and what remains intact is the main curriculum, the main menu. One of the ways to assess multicultural education in your school is to look at the school organization. Look at how much time you spend on which subjects. When you are in the second stage you usually have a two- or three-week unit on a group of people or an area that's been omitted in the main curriculum.

You're moving into the next stage of structural change when you have elements of that unit integrated into existing units. Ultimately, what is at the center of the curriculum gets changed in its prominence. For example, civilizations. Instead of just talking about Western civilization, you begin to draw on what we need to know about India, Africa, China. We also begin to ask different questions about why and what we are doing. Whose interest is it in that we study what we study? Why is it that certain kinds of knowledge get hidden? In mathematics, instead of studying statistics with sports and weather numbers, why not look at employment in light of ethnicity?

Then there is the social change stage, when the curriculum helps lead to changes outside of the school. We actually go out and change the nature of the community we live in. For example, kids might become involved in how the media portray people and start a letter-writing campaign about news that is negatively biased. Kids begin to see this as a responsibility that they have to change the world.

I think about a group of elementary school kids who wrote to the manager of the store about the kinds of games and dolls that they had. That's a long way from having some dinner and dances that represent an "exotic" form of life.

In essence, in antiracist education we use knowledge to empower people and to change their lives.

Teachers have limited money to buy new materials. How can they begin to incorporate a multicultural education even if they don't have a lot of money?

We do need money and it is a pattern to underfund antiracist intiatives so that they fail. We must push for funding for new resources because some of the information we have is downright inaccurate. But if you have a perspective, which is really a set of questions that you ask about your life, and you have the kids ask, then you can begin to fill in the gaps.

Columbus is a good example. It turns the whole story on its head when you have the children try to find out what the people who were on this continent might have been thinking and doing and feeling when they were being "discovered," tricked, robbed, and murdered. You might not have that information on hand, because that kind of knowledge is deliberately suppressed. But if nothing else happens, at least you shift your teaching, to recognize the native peoples as human beings, to look at things from their view.

There are other things you can do without new resources. You can include, in a sensitive way, children's backgrounds and life experiences. One way is through interviews with parents and with community people, in which they can recount their own stories, especially their interactions with institutions like schools, hospitals, and employment agencies. These are things that often don't get heard.

I've seen schools inviting grandparents who can tell stories about their own lives, and these stories get to be part of the curriculum later in the year. It allows excluded people, it allows humanity, back into the schools. One of the ways that discrimination works is that it treats some people's experiences, lives, and points of view as though they don't count, as though they are less valuable than other people's.

I know we need to look at materials. But we can also take some of the existing curriculum and ask kids questions about what is missing, and whose interest is being served when things are written in the way they are. Both teachers and students must alter that material.

How can a teacher who knows little about multiculturalism be expected to teach multiculturally?

I think the teachers need to have the time and encouragement to do some reading and to see the necessity to do so. A lot has been written about multiculturalism. It's not like there's no information.

You also have to look around at what people of color are saying about their lives and draw from those sources. You can't truly teach this until you reeducate yourself from a multicultural perspective. But you can begin. It's an ongoing process.

Most of all, you have to get in touch with the fact that your current education has a cultural bias, that it is an exclusionary, racist bias and that it needs to be purged. A lot of times people say, "I just need to learn more about those other groups." And I say, "No, you need to look at how the dominant culture and biases affect your view of nondominant groups in society." You don't have to fill your head with little details about what other cultural groups eat and dance. You need to take a look at your culture, what your idea of normal is, and realize it is quite limited and is in fact just reflecting a particular experience. You have to realize that what you recognize as universal is, quite often, exclusionary. To be really universal, you must begin to learn what Africans, Asians, Latin Americans, the aboriginal peoples, and all silenced groups of Americans have had to say about the topic.

How can one teach multiculturally without making white children feel guilty or threatened?

Perhaps a sense of being threatened or feeling guilty will occur. But I think it is possible to have kids move beyond that.

First of all, recognize that there have always been white people who have fought against racism and social injustice. White children can proudly identify with these people and join in that tradition of fighting for social justice.

Second, it is in their interest to be opening their minds and finding out how things really are. Otherwise, they will constantly have an incomplete picture of the human family.

The other thing is, if we don't make clear that some people benefit from racism, then we are being dishonest. What we have to do is talk about how young people can use that from which they benefit to change the order of things so that more people will benefit.

If we say we are all equally discriminated against on the basis of racism, or sexism, that's not accurate. We don't need to be caught up in the guilt of our benefit, but should use our privilege to help change things.

I remember a teacher telling me last summer that after she listened to me on the issue of racism, she felt ashamed of who she was. And I remember wondering if her sense of self was founded on a sense of superiority. Because if that's true, then she is going to feel shaken. but if her sense of self is founded on working with people of different colors to change things, then there is no need to feel guilt or shame.

Where does an antisexist perspective fit into a multicultural perspective?

In my experience, when you include racism as just another of the "isms," it tends to get sidetracked or omitted. That's because people are sometimes uncomfortable with racism, although they may be comfortable with class and gender issues. I like to put racism in the foreground, and then include the others by example and analysis.

I certainly believe that sexism—and ageism and heterosexism and class issues—have to be taken up. But in my way of thinking I don't list them under multicultural education.

For me, the emphasis is race. I've seen instances where teachers have replaced a really sexist set of materials with nonsexist materials—but the new resources included only white people. In my judgment, more has been done in the curriculum in terms of sexism that in terms of racism.

Of course, we must continue to address sexism in all its forms, no question about that. But we cannot give up on the fight against racism either. As a black woman, both hurt my heart. . . .

What can school districts do to further multicultural education?

Many teachers will not change the curriculum if they have no administrative support. Sometimes, making these changes can be scary. You can have parents on your back, kids who can be resentful. You can be told you are making the curriculum too political.

What we are talking about here is pretty radical; multicultural education is about challenging the status quo and the basis of power. You need administrative support to do that.

In the final analysis, multicultural or antiracist education is about allowing educators to do the things they have wanted to do in the name of their profession: to broaden the horizons of the young people they teach, to give them skills to change a world in which the color of their skin defines their opportunities, where some human beings are treated as if they are just junior children.

Maybe teachers don't have this big vision all the time. But I think those are the things that a democratic society is supposed to be about.

When you look at the state of things in the United States and Canada, it's almost as if many parts of the society have given up on decency, doing the right thing, and democracy in any serious way. I think that antiracist education gives us an opportunity to try again.

Unfortunately, I feel that this educational movement is going to face a serious challenge. The 1980s were marked by very conservative attitudes, and some of the gains of the social change movements in the 1960s and 1970s were rolled back.

A major struggle is taking place in the 1990s to regain those victories of the 1960s and 1970s. I think that antiracist education can help us do that. But the conservative forces are certainly not going to allow this to happen without a battle. So we'd better get ready to fight.

WOMEN OF COLOR ON THE FRONT LINE

68

Celene Krauss

Toxic waste disposal is a central focus of women's grass-roots environmental activism. Toxic waste facilities are predominantly sited in working-class and low-income communities and communities of color, reflecting the disproportionate burden placed on these communities by a political economy of growth that distributes the costs of economic growth unequally. Spurred by the threat that toxic wastes pose to family health and community survival, female grass-roots activists have assumed the leadership of community environmental struggles. As part of a larger movement for environmental justice, they constitute a diverse constituency, including working-class housewives and secretaries, rural African American farmers, urban residents, Mexican American farm workers, and Native Americans.

These activists attempt to differentiate themselves from what they see as the white, male, middle-class leadership of many national environmental organizations. Unlike the more abstract, issue-oriented focus of national groups, women's focus is on environmental issues that grow out of their concrete, immediate experiences. Female blue-collar activists often share a loosely defined ideology of environmental justice and a critique of dominant social institutions and mainstream environmental organizations, which they believe do not address the broader issues of inequality underlying environmental hazards. At the same time, these activists exhibit significant diversity in their conceptual-

From: Robert D. Bullard, ed., *Unequal Protection: Environmental Justice and Communities of Color* (San Francisco: Sierra Club Books, 1994), pp. 256–71. Reprinted by permission.

ization of toxic waste issues, reflecting different experiences of class, race, and ethnicity.

This [essay] looks at the ways in which different working-class women formulate ideologies of resistance around toxic waste issues and the process by which they arrive at a concept of environmental justice. Through an analysis of interviews, newsletters, and conference presentations, I show the voices of white, African American, and Native American female activists and the resources that inform and support their protests. What emerges is an environmental discourse that is mediated by subjective experiences and interpretations and rooted in the political truths women construct out of their identities as housewives, mothers, and members of communities and racial and ethnic groups.

THE SUBJECTIVE DIMENSION OF GRASS-ROOTS ACTIVISM

Grass-roots protest activities have often been trivialized, ignored, and viewed as self-interested actions that are particularistic and parochial, failing to go beyond a single-issue focus. This view of community grass-roots protests is held by most policymakers as well as by many analysts of movements for progressive social change.

In contrast, the voices of blue-collar women engaged in protests regarding toxic waste issues tell us that single-issue protests are about more than the single issue. They reveal a larger world of power and resistance, which in some measure ends up challenging the social relations of power. This challenge becomes visible when we shift the analysis of environmental activism to the experiences of working-class women and the subjective meanings they create around toxic waste issues.

In traditional sociological analysis, this subjective dimension of protest has often been ignored or viewed as private and individualistic. Feminist theory, however, helps us to see its importance. For feminists, the critical reflection on the everyday world of experience is an important subjective dimension of social change. Feminists show us that experience is not merely a personal, individualistic concept. It is social. People's experiences reflect where they fit in the social hierarchy. Thus, blue-collar women of differing backgrounds interpret their experiences of toxic waste problems within the context of their particular cultural histories, starting from different assumptions and arriving at concepts of environmental justice that reflect broader experiences of class and race.

Feminist theorists also challenge a dominant ideology that separates the "public" world of policy and power from the "private" and personal world of everyday experience. By definition, this ideology relegates the lives and concerns of women relating to home and family to the private, nonpolitical arena, leading to invisibility of their grass-roots protests about issues such as toxic wastes. As Ann Bookman has noted in her important study of working-class women's community struggles, women's political activism in general, and working-class political life at the community level in particular, remain "peripheral to the historical record . . . where there is a tendency to privilege male political activity and labor activism."[1] The women's movement took as its central task the reconceptualization of the political itself, critiquing this dominant ideology and constructing a new definition of the political located in the everyday world of ordinary women rather than in the world of public policy. Feminists provide a perspective for making visible the importance of particular, single-issue protests regarding toxic wastes by showing how ordinary women subjectively link the particulars of their private lives with a broader analysis of power in the public sphere.

Social historians such as George Rudé have pointed out that it is often difficult to understand the experience and ideologies of resistance because ordinary working people appropriate and reshape traditional beliefs embedded within working-class culture, such as family and community. This point is also relevant for understanding the environmental protests of working-class women. Their protests are framed in terms of the traditions of motherhood and family; as a result, they often appear parochial or even conservative. As we shall see, however, for working-class women, these traditions become the levers that set in motion a political process, shaping the language and oppositional meanings that emerge and providing resources for social change.

Shifting the analysis of toxic waste issues to the subjective experience of ordinary women makes visible a complex relationship between everyday life and the larger structures of public power. It reveals the potential for human agency that is hidden in a more traditional sociological approach and provides us with a means of seeing "the sources of power which subordinated groups have created."[2]

The analysis presented in this [essay] is based on the oral and written voices of women involved in toxic waste protests. Interviews were conducted at environmental conferences such as the First National People of Color Environmental Leadership Summit, Washington, D.C., 1991, and the World Women's Congress for a Healthy Planet, Miami, Florida, 1991, and by telephone. Additional sources include conference presentations, pamphlets, books, and other written materials that have emerged from this movement. This research is part of an ongoing comparative study that will examine the ways in which experiences of race, class, and ethnicity mediate women's environmental activism. Future research includes an analysis of the environmental activism of Mexican American women in addition to that of the women discussed here.

TOXIC WASTE PROTESTS
AND THE RESOURCE OF MOTHERHOOD

Blue-collar women do not use the language of the bureaucrat to talk about environmental issues. They do not spout data or marshal statistics in support of their positions. In fact, interviews with these women rarely generate a lot of discussion about the environmental problem per se. But in telling their stories about their protest against a landfill or incinerator, they ultimately tell larger stories about their discovery or analysis of oppression. Theirs is a political, not a technical, analysis.

Working-class women of diverse racial and ethnic backgrounds identify the toxic waste movement as a women's movement, composed primarily of mothers. Says one woman who fought against an incinerator in Arizona and subsequently worked on other anti-incinerator campaigns throughout the state, "Women are the backbone of the grass-roots groups; they are the ones who stick with it, the ones who won't back off." By and large, it is women, in their traditional role as mothers, who make the link between toxic wastes and their children's ill health. They discover the hazards of toxic contamination: multiple miscarriages, birth defects, cancer deaths, and so on. This is not surprising, as the gender-based division of labor in a capitalist society gives working-class women the responsibility for the health of their children.

These women define their environmental protests as part of the work that mothers do. Cora Tucker, an African American activist who fought against uranium mining in Virginia and who now organizes nationally, says:

> It's not that I don't think that women are smarter, [she laughs] but I think that we are with the kids all day long. . . . If Johnny gets a cough and Mary gets a cough, we try to discover the problem.

Another activist from California sums up this view: "If we don't oppose an incinerator, we're not doing our work as mothers."

For these women, family serves as a spur to action, contradicting popular notions of family as conservative and parochial. Family has a very different meaning for these women than it does for the middle-class nuclear family. Theirs is a less privatized, extended family that is open, permeable, and attached to community. This more extended family creates the networks and resources that enable working-class communities to survive materially given few economic resources. The destruction of working-class neighborhoods by economic growth deprives blue-collar communities of the basic resources of survival; hence the resistance engendered by toxic waste issues. Working-class women's struggles over toxic waste issues are, at root, issues about survival. Ideologies of motherhood, traditionally relegated to the private sphere, become political resources that working-class women use to initiate and justify their resistance. In the process of protest, working-class women come to reject the dominant ideology, which separates the public and private arenas.

Working-class women's extended network of family and community serves as the vehicle for spreading information and concern about toxic waste issues. Extended networks of kinship and friendship become political resources of opposition. For example, in one community in Detroit, women discovered patterns of health problems while attending Tupperware parties. Frequently, a mother may read about a hazard in a newspaper, make a tentative connection between her own child's ill health and the pollutant, and start telephoning friends and family, developing an informal health survey. Such a discovery process is rooted in what Sarah Ruddick has called the everyday practice of mothering.[3] Through their informal networks, they compare notes and experiences and develop an oppositional knowledge used to resist the dominant knowledge of experts and the decisions of government and corporate officials.

These women separate themselves from "mainstream" environmental organizations, which are seen as dominated by white, middle-class men and concerned with remote issues. Says one woman from Rahway, New Jersey: "The mainstream groups deal with safe issues. They want to stop incinerators to save the eagle, or they protect trees for the owl. But we say, what about the people?"

Another activist implicitly criticizes the mainstream environmental groups when she says of the grass-roots Citizens' Clearinghouse for Hazardous Wastes:

> Rather than oceans and lakes, they're concerned about kids dying. Once you've had someone in your family who has been attacked by the environment—I mean who has had cancer or some other disease—you get a keen sense of what's going on.

It is the traditional, "private" women's concerns about home, children, and family that provide the initial impetus for blue-collar women's involvement in issues of toxic waste. The political analyses they develop break down the public-private distinction of dominant ideology and frame a particular toxic waste issue within broader contexts of power relationships.

THE ROLE OF RACE, ETHNICITY, AND CLASS

Interviews with white, African American, and Native American women show that the starting places for and subsequent development of their analyses of toxic waste protests are mediated by issues of class, race, and ethnicity.

White working-class women come from a culture in which traditional women's roles center on the private arena of family. They often marry young; although they may work out of financial necessity, the primary roles from which they derive meaning and satisfaction are those of mothering and taking care of family. They are revered and supported for fulfilling the ideology of a patriarchal family. And these families often reflect a strong belief in the existing political system. The narratives of white working-class women involved in toxic waste issues are filled with the process by which they discover the injustice of their government, their own insecurity about entering the public sphere of politics, and the constraints of the patriarchal family, which, ironically prevent them from becoming fully active in the defense of their family, especially in their protest. Their narratives are marked by a strong initial faith in "their" government, as well as a remarkable transformation as they become disillusioned with the system. They discover "that they never knew what they were capable of doing in defense of their children."

For white working-class women, whose views on public issues are generally expressed only within family or among friends, entering a more public arena to confront toxic waste issues is often extremely stressful. "Even when I went to the PTA," says one activist, "I rarely spoke. I was so nervous." Says another: "My views have always been strong, but I expressed them only in the family. They were not for the public." A strong belief in the existing political system is characteristic of these women's initial response to toxic waste issues. Lois Gibbs, whose involvement in toxic waste issues started at Love Canal, tells us, "I believed if I had a problem I just had to go to the right person in government and he would take care of it."

Initially, white working-class women believe that all they have to do is give the government the facts and their problem will be taken care of. They become progressively disenchanted with what they view as the violation of their rights and the injustice of a system that allows their children and family to die. In the process, they develop a perspective of environmental justice rooted in issues of class, the attempt to make democracy real, and a critique of the corporate state. Says one activist who fought the siting of an incinerator in Sumter County, Alabama: "We need to stop letting economic development be the true God and religion of this country. We have to prevent big money from influencing our government."

A recurring theme in the narratives of these women is the transformation of their beliefs about government and power. Their politicization is rooted in the deep sense of violation, betrayal, and hurt they feel when they find that their government will not protect their families. Lois Gibbs sums up this feeling well:

> I grew up in a blue-collar community. We were very into democracy. There is something about discovering that democracy isn't democracy as we know it.

> When you lose faith in your government, it's like finding out your mother was fooling around on your father. I was very upset. It almost broke my heart because I really believed in the system. I still believe in the system, only now I believe that democracy is of the people and by the people, that people have to move it, it ain't gonna move by itself.

Echoes of this disillusionment are heard from white blue-collar women throughout the country. One activist relates:

> We decided to tell our elected officials about the problems of incineration because we didn't think they knew. Surely if they knew that there was a toxic waste dump in our county they would stop it. I was politically naive. I was real surprised because I live in an area that's like the Bible Belt of the South. Now I think the God of the United States is really economic development, and that has got to change.

Ultimately, these women become aware of the inequities of power as it is shaped by issues of class and gender. Highly traditional values of democracy and motherhood remain central to their lives. But in the process of politicization through their work on toxic waste issues, these values become transformed into resources of opposition that enable women to enter the public arena and challenge its legitimacy. They justify their resistance as a way to make democracy real and to protect their children.

White blue-collar women's stories are stories of transformations: transformations into more self-confident and assertive women; into political activists who challenge the existing system and feel powerful in that challenge; into wives and mothers who establish new relationships with their spouses (or get divorced) and new, empowering relationships with their children as they provide role models of women capable of fighting for what they believe in.

African American working-class women begin their involvement in toxic waste protests from a different place. They bring to their protests a political awareness that is grounded in race and that shares none of the white blue-collar women's initial trust in democratic institutions. These women view government with mistrust, having been victims of racist policies throughout their lives. Individual toxic waste issues are immediately framed within a broader political context and viewed as environmental racism. Says an African American activist from Rahway, New Jersey:

> When they sited the incinerator for Rahway, I wasn't surprised. All you have to do is look around my community to know that we are a dumping ground for all kinds of urban industrial projects that no one else wants. I knew this was about environmental racism the moment that they proposed the incinerator.

An African American woman who fought the siting of a landfill on the South Side of Chicago reiterates this view: "My community is an all-black community isolated from everyone. They don't care what happens to us." She describes her community as a "toxic doughnut":

> We have seven landfills. We have a sewer treatment plant. We have the Ford Motor Company. We have a paint factory. We have numerous chemical companies and steel mills. The river is just a few blocks away from us and is carrying water so highly contaminated that they say it would take seventy-five years or more before they can clean it up.

This activist sees her involvement in toxic waste issues as a challenge to traditional stereotypes of African American women. She says, "I'm here to tell the story that all people in the projects are not lazy and dumb!"

Some of these women share experiences of personal empowerment through their involvement in toxic waste issues. Says one African American activist:

> Twenty years ago I couldn't do this because I was so shy. . . . I had to really know you to talk with you. Now I talk. Sometimes I think I talk too much. I waited until my fifties to go to jail. But it was well worth it. I never went to no university or college, but I'm going in there and making speeches.

However, this is not a major theme in the narratives of female African American activists, as it is in those of white blue-collar women. African American women's private work as mothers has traditionally extended to a more public role in the local community as protectors of the race. As a decade of African American feminist history has shown, African American women have historically played a central role in community activism and in dealing with issues of race and economic injustice. They receive tremendous status and recognition from their community. Many women participating in toxic waste protests have come out of a history of civil rights activism, and their environmental protests, especially in the South, develop through community organizations born during the civil rights movement. And while the visible leaders are often male, the base of the organizing has been led by African American women, who, as Cheryl Townsend Gilkes has written, have often been called "race women," responsible for the "racial uplift" of their communities.[4]

African American women perceive that traditional environmental groups only peripherally relate to their concerns. As Cora Tucker relates:

> This white woman from an environmental group asked me to come down to save a park. She said that they had been trying to get black folks involved and that they won't come. I said, "Honey, it's not that they aren't concerned, but when their babies are dying in their arms they don't give a damn about a park." I said, "They want to save their babies. If you can help them save their babies, then in turn they can help you save your park." And she said, "But this is a real immediate problem." And I said, "Well, these people's kids dying is immediate."

Tucker says that white environmental groups often call her or the head of the NAACP at the last minute to participate in an environmental rally because they want to "include" African Americans. But they exclude African Americans from the process of defining the issues in the first place. What African American communities are doing is changing the agenda.

Because the concrete experience of African Americans' lives is the experience and analysis of racism, social issues are interpreted and struggled with within this context. Cora Tucker's story of attending a town board meeting shows that the issue she deals with is not merely the environment but also the disempowerment she experiences as an African American woman. At the meeting, white women were addressed as Mrs. So-and-So by the all-white, male board. When Mrs. Tucker stood up, however, she was addressed as "Cora":

> One morning I got up and I got pissed off and I said, "What did you call me?" He said, "Cora," and I said, "The name is Mrs. Tucker." And I had the floor until he said "Mrs. Tucker." He waited five minutes before he said "Mrs. Tucker." And I held the floor. I said, "I'm Mrs. Tucker," I said, "Mr. Chairman, I don't call you by your first name and I don't want you to call me by mine. My name is Mrs. Tucker. And when you want me, you call me Mrs. Tucker." It's not that— I mean it's not like you gotta call me Mrs. Tucker, but it was the respect.

In discussing this small act of resistance as an African American woman, Cora Tucker is showing how environmental issues may be about corporate and state power, but they are also about race. For female African American activists, environmental issues are seen as reflecting environmental racism and linked to other social justice issues, such as jobs, housing, and crime. They are viewed as part of a broader picture of social inequity based on race. Hence, the solution articulated in a vision of environmental justice is a civil rights vision— rooted in the everyday experience of racism. Environmental justice comes to mean the need to resolve the broad social inequities of race.

The narratives of Native American women are also filled with the theme of environmental racism. However, their analysis is laced with different images. It is a genocidal analysis rooted in the Native American cultural identification, the experience of colonialism, and the imminent endangerment of their culture. A Native American woman from North Dakota, who opposed a landfill, says:

> Ever since the white man came here, they keep pushing us back, taking our lands, pushing us onto reservations. We are down to 3 percent now, and I see this as just another way for them to take our lands, to completely annihilate our races. We see that as racism.

Like that of the African American women, these women's involvement in toxic waste protests is grounded from the start in race and shares none of the white blue-collar women's initial belief in the state. A Native American woman from southern California who opposed a landfill on the Rosebud Reservation in South Dakota tells us:

> Government did pretty much what we expected them to do. They supported the dump. People here fear the government. They control so many aspects of our life. When I became involved in opposing the garbage landfill, my people told me to be careful. They said they annihilate people like me.

Another woman involved in the protest in South Dakota describes a government official's derision of the tribe's resistance to the siting of a landfill:

> If we wanted to live the life of Mother Earth, we should got a tepee and live on the Great Plains and hunt buffalo.

Native American women come from a culture in which women have had more empowered and public roles than is the case in white working-class culture. Within the Native American community, women are revered as nurturers. From childhood, boys and girls learn that men depend on women for their survival. Women also play a central role in the decision-making process within the tribe. Tribal council membership is often equally divided between men and women; many women are tribal leaders and medicine women. Native American religions embody a respect for women as well as an ecological ethic based on values such as reciprocity and sustainable development: Native Americans pray to Mother Earth, as opposed to the dominant culture's belief in a white, male, Anglicized representation of divinity.

In describing the ways in which their culture integrates notions of environmentalism and womanhood, one woman from New Mexico says:

> We deal with the whole of life and community; we're not separated, we're born into it—you are it. Our connection as women is to the Mother Earth, from the time of our consciousness. We're not environmentalists. We're born into the struggle of protecting and preserving our communities. We don't separate ourselves. Our lifeblood automatically makes us responsible; we are born with it. Our teaching comes from a spiritual base. This is foreign to our culture. There isn't even a word for dioxin in Navajo.

In recent years, Native American lands have become common sites for commercial garbage dumping. Garbage and waste companies have exploited the poverty and lack of jobs in Native American communities and the fact that Native American lands, as sovereign nation territories, are often exempt from local environmental regulations. In discussing their opposition to dumping, Native American women ground their narratives in values about land that are inherent in the Native American community. They see these projects as violating tribal sovereignty and the deep meaning of land, the last resource they have. The issue, says a Native American woman from California, is protection of the land for future generations, not really as a mother, but for the health of the people, for survival. Our tribe bases its sovereignty on our land base, and if we lose our land base, then we will be a lost people. We can't afford to take this trash and jeopardize our tribe.

If you don't take care of the land, then the land isn't going to take care of you. Because everything we have around us involves Mother Earth. If we don't take care of the land, what's going to happen to us?

In the process of protest, these women tell us, they are forced to articulate more clearly their cultural values, which become resources of resistance in helping the tribe organize against a landfill. While many tribal members may not articulate an "environmental" critique, they well understand the meaning of land and their religion of Mother Earth, on which their society is built.

CONCLUSION

The narratives of white, African American, and Native American women involved in toxic waste protests reveal the ways in which their subjective, particular experiences lead them to analyses of toxic waste issues that extend beyond the particularistic issue to wider worlds of power. Traditional beliefs about home, family, and community provide the impetus for women's involvement in these issues and become a rich source of empowerment as women reshape traditional language and meanings into an ideology of resistance. These stories challenge traditional views of toxic waste protests as parochial, self-interested, and failing to go beyond a single-issue focus. They show that single-issue protests are ultimately about far more and reveal the experiences of daily life and resources that different groups use to resist. Through environmental protests, these women challenge, in some measure, the social relations of race, class, and gender.

These women's protests have different beginning places, and their analyses of environmental justice are mediated by issues of class and race. For white blue-collar women, the critique of the corporate state and the realization of a more genuine democracy are central to a vision of environmental justice. The definition of environmental justice that they develop becomes rooted in the issue of class. For women of color, it is the link between race and environment, rather than between class and environment, that characterizes definitions of environmental justice. African American women's narratives strongly link environment justice to other social justice concerns, such as jobs, housing, and crime. Environmental justice comes to mean the need to resolve the broad social inequities of race. For Native American women, environmental justice is bound up with the sovereignty of the indigenous peoples.

In these women's stories, their responses to particular toxic waste issues are inextricably tied to the injustice they feel as mothers, as working-class women, as African Americans, and as Native Americans. They do not talk about their protests in terms of single issues. Thus, their political activism has implications far beyond the visible, particularistic concern of a toxic waste dump site or the siting of a hazardous waste incinerator.

NOTES

1. Sandra Morgen, "'It's the Whole Power of the City Against Us!': The Development of Political Consciousness in a Women's Health Care Coalition," in *Women and the Politics of Empowerment*, eds. Ann Bookman and Sandra Morgen (Philadelphia: Temple University Press, 1988), p. 97.

2. Sheila Rowbotham, *Women's Consciousness, Man's World* (New York: Penguin, 1973).

3. See Sara Ruddick, *Maternal Thinking: Towards a Politics of Peace* (New York: Ballantine, 1989).

4. Cheryl Townsend Gilkes, "Building in Many Places: Multiple Commitments and Ideologies in Black Women's Community Work," in *Women and the Politics of Empowerment*, op. cit.

HAVING THE TOOLS AT HAND

69

Building Successful Multicultural

Social Justice Organizations

John Anner

The long-awaited age of the true international city is fully upon us, although not quite in the cheerful Disney World format expected by the advocates of multiculturalism. Urban America has become a staggeringly diverse melange

From: John Anner, ed., *Beyond Identity Politics: Emerging Social Justice Movements in Communities of Color* (Boston: South End Press, 1996), pp. 153–66. Reprinted by permission.

of cultures and languages; it's no longer hyperbole to talk about the "global village," not with millions of the global villagers themselves living just down the street.

The changing demographic composition of many areas of the country is coupled with other shifts in the global political economy that are having severe negative effects on both urban and rural America. In brief, the unrestrained ability of international corporations to shift production and jobs just about anywhere in the world has meant disrupted communities, declining wages, and lower standards of living for most Americans—and increasing social decay and conflict.

Social justice organizations and movements have to contend with new constituents and new conditions. They have to figure out how to mobilize and organize people who may share geographic proximity and hard times but little else, in a political climate that has shifted the blame for worsening economic conditions onto the immigrants, the poor, and the powerless. And they have to figure out how to develop effective strategies for defending their constituents in an era in which progressive government-financed social legislation is close to politically impossible.

On the whole, the traditional defenders of low-income and working-class Americans have done a very poor job of building a sophisticated multicultural response to the changes outlined above, which is one reason things are so terrible. Unions, long the main bulwark against attacks on people's livelihoods, are barely awakening from a long period of political sleep. Progressive academics, professionals, leaders of national civil rights organizations, advocates, lobbyists, and politicians appear to be helpless, timid, and out of ideas, endlessly fighting symbolic battles. And for whatever reason, there is no credible leftist political party in America.

It's more or less an article of faith among progressive political thinkers that we need a new mass-based struggle for social justice featuring leadership from people of color and a diverse membership. I believe . . . that there is an emerging "second generation" of grass-roots community and labor organizations that have developed over the past five to ten years. . . . The energy and mutual respect characteristic of the politics of identity have been used to revitalize and strengthen class-based organizing and to build strong relations between communities normally divided by race, language, and culture.

NO MYSTERY TO MULTICULTURALISM

There is no mystery to building effective multicultural social justice organizations, say many activists and organizers. A variety of organizations provide training and consultations, and, as this [essay] indicates, there are specific methods available to activists and organizers. "What matters most of all," says diversity trainer Guadalupe Guajardo, of Technical Assistance for Community Services (TACS) in Portland, Oregon, "is being able to listen and learn, and having the tools at hand to make changes."

This [essay] focuses on the specific tactics and strategies that social justice organizers use to build multicultural organizations. . . . Organizers can begin to confront the larger economic and political forces devastating low- and middle-income communities by building social justice organizations that can adapt to rapid changes in the demographic and cultural environment. While these organizations may not lead a national social justice movement, if and when it develops, they will train its political leaders, provide models of effective organizing methods, educate and develop memberships, keep people involved on a regular basis in community work, and test the local power structure for weak points.

A movement can draw on this base and use it to inspire large numbers of people to take action. This phenomenon occurred in California's anti-Proposition 187 movement. Established community, student, labor, civil rights, professional, and other groups sounded the alarm and laid the groundwork, but in the end a movement exploded outside the boundaries these organizations created. Indeed, one of the biggest protest marches, which took place in Los Angeles, occurred despite attempts by some "Stop 187" organizations to prevent it. A movement, when one develops, pulls in political, community, and labor organizations, but also inspires large numbers of previously uninvolved people.

At the same time, the efficacy and longevity of a movement rests on the foundation created through the daily back-breaking work of local grass-roots organizing. This work must include constant attention to developing multicultural memberships and alliances.

The models and mechanisms being used to build successful multicultural social justice organizations include:

- Building personal relationships between members from different backgrounds.
- Actively engaging in solidarity campaigns, actions, and activities with social justice organizations in other communities.
- Challenging bigoted statements and attitudes when they arise.
- Holding regular discussions, forums, "educationals," and workshops to enhance people's understandings of other communities and individuals.
- Working to change the culture of the organization so that members see themselves as "members of the community" first instead of members of a particular part of the community.
- Developing issues, tactics, and campaigns that are relevant to different communities and that reveal fundamental areas of common interest.

- Conducting antiracism training to get people to confront and deal with their biases.
- Examining and changing the organization's practices in order to hire, promote, and develop people of color.
- Confronting white privilege and nationalism.
- Hiring, recruiting, and training more people of color for leadership positions.

IT DOESN'T JUST HAPPEN

Elsa Barboza is an organizer with South Los Angeles–based Action for Grass-roots Empowerment and Neighborhood Development Alternatives (AGENDA). AGENDA has generally focused on the African-American community, and most of the staff and organizers are African-American. In 1994, says Barboza, "we decided to move towards organizing in the Latino community for the simple reason that we have a lot of new immigrants from Central America in the neighborhoods. We wanted to [make AGENDA] an authentic multicultural organization, but we learned an important lesson: it doesn't just happen."

AGENDA organizers quickly found that bringing monolingual Spanish-speaking members to the general membership and committee meetings was not effective in involving the new Latino members. AGENDA staff decided instead to form a separate organization known as the Latino Organizing Committee. The plan is to build leadership in the Committee, take on a few organizing campaigns around issues of particular concern to those members, and "agitate and educate" the South Los Angeles Latino community. "In the beginning we used the same strategies and tactics for everyone," says Barboza, but it simply didn't work in terms of attracting more Latinos to the group.

One solution is to define issues and campaigns so as to make them relevant to all members of the organization. For example, People United for a Better Oakland (PUEBLO) conducted a campaign in 1994 to force Highland Hospital to hire more professional translators. At first glance, this would not seem to be an issue of major concern to the native English speakers in the group. However, PUEBLO organizers and leaders successfully argued that nobody can get adequate medical care if some doctors and nurses are being called away from their duties in order to translate for a patient who doesn't speak English.

AGENDA has taken a different tack, working instead to research and develop campaigns that are of particular concern to the Spanish-speaking members. At some point in the future, when the Latino Organizing Committee has had enough experience organizing, the two organizations will be merged. In the meantime, AGENDA is conducting what they call "educationals" with all their African-American members to "demystify" the changing demographics of Los Angeles, and show how low income communities of color face similar challenges and problems.

In terms of specific mechanisms to overcome prejudice-based resistance on the part of current members, "we don't have any 'diversity training' going on just yet," says Barboza, "but we'll probably need it in the future." She says that people get past any initial resistance pretty quickly, however, and see through to the larger self-interest that unites people of color. All the members come together for general membership meetings and selected planning meetings. Translation is conducted by an interpreter who sits with the Spanish-speaking members.

. . . [A]nother community group that started out all African-American and gradually changed as the demographics of the neighborhood changed is Direct Action for Rights and Equality (DARE) in Providence, Rhode Island. DARE is a powerful ten-year-old organization well known at City Hall; part of that power, say staff members, comes from the group's representative membership. In the beginning, however, the few Latino and Asian members seldom participated in DARE's activities. Looking back, says former organizer Libero Della Piana, three things stand out as "holding back" other members: language, culture, and the issues DARE worked on.

In contrast to AGENDA, DARE set out from the beginning to avoid creating two different organizations. "We did have a Comité Latino where meetings are conducted only in Spanish," says Della Piana, "but we didn't want it to become a separate group because we didn't think we'd be able to later turn it into a cohesive organization."

Della Piana says that organizers who want to build multicultural organizations have to ask themselves if they are making everyone feel welcome and wanted. Translating all written materials is critical, he says, because it not only makes all members feel part of the organization but is a way of visibly showing that the group is serious about being multiracial. At this point, Providence is changing again, experiencing a big influx of immigrants from South Asia, and DARE "desperately needs" an organizer who speaks one or more of the languages of the Indian subcontinent.

IN THE HEAT OF THE STRUGGLE

Perhaps the most common way that multicultural groups deal with diversity in their memberships is through a political ideology that emphasizes how the struggle at hand transcends differences of race, age, gender, or sexuality. The Committee Against Anti-Asian Violence (CAAAV) is a New York-based community group that has been active and visible on issues ranging from hate crimes to police brutality and economic exploitation. The group's 2,500 members are diverse, but all Asian. "We are a pan-Asian organization," says staff organizer Saleem Osman, "so in our group there is no hostility, only solidarity, because we are all working together for the same things." Although it is certainly true that there is a good deal of mutual dislike and often active hostility among the large variety of immigrant communities that have found themselves living side by side in urban America, it does seem to be the case that these differences can be set aside in the heat of the struggle.

An additional factor might be that the members of multicultural groups tend to be self-selecting. If someone is really not happy being part of a diverse membership organization, they tend to simply not join in the first place, or leave as the group changes. Finally, differences that seemed of intense importance in the region of origin (Chinese versus Japanese, Salvadoran versus Honduran, North Indian versus South Indian) start to lose their meaning once the reality of life in the United States sinks in and the different groups find that more unites them than separates them.

On the other hand, says Osman, working in coalition with other groups requires a lot of internal education. "Our members, who are taxi drivers, garment workers, and vendors mostly, need to be challenged to look at [their prejudices]." Prejudice against Latinos and African Americans among CAAAV members was clearly revealed during city council hearings on a bill that would have granted taxi drivers the right to refuse to pick up any individual based on their appearance. CAAAV organizers knew that drivers were supportive of the bill because it gave them the right to refuse rides to African-American men.

"We had to do a lot of work with the members on that one," says Osman. "That was a law aimed directly at African-Americans. So we said 'no, we won't support it because it's racist.' But first we put together a video and used it to educate drivers" in day-long training sessions.

CAAAV then took the issue one step further, appearing at public hearings to argue against the law, sometimes surprising African-American civil rights groups. "The best way to overcome prejudices between [communities of color]," says Osman, "is to work together in solidarity with each other to build unity." For this reason, says Osman, CAAAV has actively sought to build a working relationship with Puerto Rican and African-American groups active in the fight against police brutality.

Organizations such as CAAAV, AGENDA, and PUEBLO frequently are called upon by other local groups to attend public hearings or demonstrations or turn out their members for community events. Wendall Chin, an organizer for a multiracial group called San Francisco Anglers for Environmental Rights (SAFER) says that an important way to overcome racial prejudices is to get the members involved in soliciting secondary support from other groups and in joining those groups' actions. SAFER is an environmental justice organization sponsored by Communities for a Better Environment that organizes low-income anglers who fish in the San Francisco Bay for food as opposed to sport. SAFER has joined forces with Texas-based Fuerza Unida in their campaign against the Levi Strauss Company, which is headquartered in San Francisco. Similarly, they have been actively involved with PUEBLO and Asian Immigrant Women Advocates (AIWA), both of which are located in Oakland, not too far from SAFER's main area of operations.

The relationship between external and internal politics is not always as easy and obvious as staff and leaders would like; this is especially true when the senior staff is white. "One of the reasons we had such trouble with the NTC [National Toxics Coalition]," says Sonia Peña, "is that the people in charge figured that because they were part of the struggle and did good political work, they therefore could not be considered racist or sexist or authoritarian or any of those things and didn't have to deal with the issues when they came up in the organization." Peña was on the NTC board at the time of its demise due to intractable internal problems in 1993; she is the lead organizer for the multiracial community group Denver Action for a Better Community.

The anti-AIDS activist group ACT UP and the gay visibility network Queer Nation also started to come apart at the seams in the mid-1990s, in part because of their inability to cope with demands by members of color that the particular needs of their communities receive greater attention. Similarly, at the 1995 National People's Action (NPA) conference in Washington, D.C., a group of Latino delegates stormed the stage and took over the microphone from executive director Gale Cinotta. Led by Juan Mireles, they demanded that the NPA start translating meetings and conference plenaries into Spanish and that a minimum of 25 percent of the delegates to the next year's convention be Latino. Mireles told freelance writer Daniel Cordes that part of the problem is that the NPA—as a predominantly white and African-American organization—doesn't see the need to organize around issues of particular concern to Latinos or to figure out mechanisms to bring in a more diverse membership.

For both NPA and NTC, shared concerns among the membership about declining neighborhoods, redlining, and economic justice were not enough to paper over conflicts among staff and/or members of different races. Some formal mechanism is needed for "surfacing" these conflicts, letting them come out into the open, and resolving them as a group.

This can be as simple as not letting bigoted comments pass without comment. When prejudices are aired openly in a meeting or other event, say organizers, it can poison relations unless it is dealt with openly. "I remember one time at a meeting where we had whites, Blacks, and three or four Mexican members," says SAFER organizer Wendell Chin," and an outspoken white leader commented that she was glad that [the anti-immigrant California ballot initiative] Proposition 187 had passed because of the problems too many immigrants were causing. I looked over at the Mexican [members] and they weren't saying anything. So I had to step in and intervene."

"It's always better if the challenge comes from inside the membership of the group," says PUEBLO organizer Danny HoSang, "because then the members who are being challenged don't feel like they are being singled out by the staff. But if nobody speaks up, the staff organizer has to do it. It's not only about consciousness-raising. All the members of the group need to feel like they are welcome and valued."

Sometimes a more involved process is required. When tensions surfaced between Asian and Black participants in a year-long program called A New Collaboration for Hands-On Relationships (ANCHOR), program director Rinku Sen decided to skip the actual program for that week and hold a series of discussions about the differences between the two communities. "Just because we call ourselves people of color doesn't mean we have the same backgrounds," says Sen. "Someone who was born in Cambodia and moved into a Black neighborhood in Oakland might experience racism as a daily fact of life. But that experience itself might be different than it would be for a Black person, and of course it is filtered through their history and current expectations."

SPEAKING MY LANGUAGE

Multicultural organizations are usually multilingual. PUEBLO, DARE, and other community groups have invested in a number of simultaneous translating machines. "They are a costly but highly effective tool," says PUEBLO lead organizer Rosi Reyes. The machines allow members to be seated anywhere in the room, instead of being segregated in one area, while the translator speaks quietly into a transmitter worn over the head. Receivers are smaller than a pack of cigarettes, with tiny earphones.

Some groups break meetings into segments, with some parts translated and others held in one language. Monica Russo, an organizer with a Florida local of the UNITE, uses this technique with a membership that speaks English, Creole, and Spanish. Day-long trainings, for example, feature monolingual sessions combined with collective meals and informal periods.

Most organizers warn, however, that translation demands more than simply literally transcribing what is being said. In order to transmit the real meaning and invite participation, says Peter Cervantes-Gautschi, director of the Portland, Oregon Workers Organizing Committee, "the critical thing is that the [translator] has to be into the movement. Because if [that person] doesn't really understand what we're trying to accomplish, then they are not going to get it right."

FROM WHITE TO RAINBOW

"There are two main obstacles to building multiracial social justice movements," says Libero Della Piana, who edits *Race File* at the Applied Research Center, "nationalism and white racism." Although many barriers divide people of color from each other, diversifying white organizations presents a different and more difficult set of challenges. "People of color generally understand racism as institutional," says Guadalupe Guajardo, "while to white people white privilege is virtually invisible, and they see prejudice as being something personal.

"Sometimes the hardest thing is to get people to face the reality that racism does exist even though polite people don't make racist comments anymore. But the only way to reach people and get them to examine how they benefit [from white privilege] is to start from the assumption that people are basically good. If you call folks racist, you will just make them defensive and won't get anywhere."

When working with an all white group that wants to become multicultural, TACS trainers lay out five concrete areas to examine and consider changing: (1) the recruitment process, including where it is done and what the qualification requirements are; (2) planning, i.e., who is at the table when plans are being made; (3) decisionmaking, i.e., who is involved when decisions are made, both in formal and informal settings; (4) resource allocation, including money, access, and power; (5) promotion and leadership. Promoting people of color to leadership positions is vital, but only if these individuals have a base of support, are going to be given power and resources, and are held accountable.

"People need solutions," says Guajardo. "We help them find a new model based on an alliance-building or partnership idea, instead of seeing diversity as a win/lost kind of thing."

A number of other organizations around the country conduct similar trainings, ranging from "racial awareness training" to "diversity management," "prejudice reduction," and "coalition building."

CHANGING THE MIX

A criticism frequently directed at national community organizing networks is that the staff organizers and directors are mostly white, while the people they organize are predominantly people of color. This is certainly true for NPA, the Association of Community Organizations for Reform Now (ACORN), and to a lesser extent the Industrial Areas Foundation (IAF). The same criticism is leveled at labor organizations and the progressive press. There are more people of color working at the average metropolitan daily newspaper than at all the left-wing magazines in the country combined.

This situation—at least on the community organizing side of things—is responsible for at least three significant trends in grass-roots social justice organizing that appeared in the 1980s and developed throughout the 1990s. First is the rapid growth of independent organizations in communities of color not connected to any of the community organizing networks or unions. . . .

Second is the formation of organizer training programs specifically designed to train organizers of color to work in community and labor organizations comprised of people of color. Of these, by far the most prominent is the Center for Third World Organizing (CTWO), which has trained several hundred organizers of color through ten years of programs such as the Minority Activist Apprenticeship Program (MAAP) and the Community Partnership Program. Along with the organizer training programs, CTWO has also developed a model of community organizing that relies on organizers of color.

Finally, many emerging social justice organizations have made an explicit commitment to leadership diversity. The New Party constitution, for example, states that 50 percent or more of the leaders of local chapters must be people of color and 50 percent must be women. Greater diversity in the organizing staff can bring immediate rewards for community and labor organizations; it is now pretty much accepted by labor leaders that white men are the least effective organizers.

Teamsters Local 175 in Seattle, Washington, wanted to organize Asian women working in private postal facilities. The notion that these women could not be organized, says organizer Michael Laslett, was partly due to the fact that nobody had ever tried, and partly due to the expected barriers of culture, race, and language. He brought on two Asian-American interns from the AFL-CIO Organizing Institute to go into one particular shop, which resulted in a victorious union drive. "Having Asian organizers is what made organizing this company possible," he said.

In 1994, the United Electrical Workers (UE) were able to organize Mexican workers at a SteelTech factory in Milwaukee by importing an organizer from a sister union in Mexico. Labor organizers of color can be pretty scarce. A perhaps apocryphal story has it that the Oil, Chemical, and Atomic Workers Union at one time employed the only Vietnamese labor organizer in the country, and used to lend him out to other unions that needed a Vietnamese-speaking organizer.

FLUID IDENTITIES

The strategies for diversifying that work with this generation may not work with the next one, however. According to Libero Della Piana, when push comes to shove, the color of the organizer matters less than the person's commitment, especially when working with youth. "Of course it helps to have a diverse organizing staff," he comments, "but in the end that's not what it's about. Members respect the staff that's willing to do the work. It's a delicate balance."

In fact, say some youth organizers, most of what has been outlined above is based on strict definitions that don't fit with the mixed identities and intensely multicultural lives of urban youth. These young people don't need to be taught how to get along with other cultures, nor do they necessarily identify with the racial categories that guide the previous generation.

"It's pretty wild," says Next Generation co-director Mike Perez, who used to work at the Oakland-based youth program Encampment for Citizenship. "Race and class intersect in different ways for young people than they do for their parents." Many young people believe they can choose their racial identity based on how they feel. "I didn't have enough attitude to be a Black girl," one white high school student told *YO!* editor Nell Bernstein, explaining why she dressed like a *cholita*, or Latina gangsta girl.

"You have white kids coming in saying they are just as much a 'nigga' as any Black kid since they come from the same 'hood," says Perez. "You have Asian kids dressing hip hop and talking [African-American dialect]. Other Black kids talk and act 'white,' in the eyes of their friends. Identities are very fluid, but it's what being young is about now."

Della Piana agrees: "During the campaign to stop Prop 187, the main organizations active in Oakland tried to define it as a Latino issue. The high school and junior high students who organized and marched in the streets refused to see it that way. Their notion of what the fight was about was based on who was in and who was out.

"Kids base their identity on the basis of a complicated formula of territory, race, class, and aspirations," he continues. "There's a connection between kids that nobody understands; they can relate to each other [across racial boundaries] in some way adults have a hard time with."

It is probably true, as some youth organizers argue, that the intense problems that race, gender, and sexuality caused for older political groups and movements will not be as much in evidence as younger people start to move into leadership positions in social justice organizations. Perhaps "the fire next time" will burn brightly in rainbow patterns. But if we want social justice organizing to move beyond the limitations of identity struggles into an enlightened next phase, with justice, community, democracy, and true solidarity on the top of the agenda, we would do well to remember what Elsa Barboza said: It doesn't just happen.

Index

Acker, Joan, 8, 175, 216
Activism: grass-roots activism, 562–573; meaning of, 8–9; and social change, 531–534
Additive model, 4, 5
African Americans: and athletics, 347–348, 349, 351, 354–357; and class, 4, 36, 121, 128, 151, 156–167, 241–242, 340, 516–517, 518; and coalition politics, 544, 545; and diversity, 55; and education, 147, 152, 156, 158, 305, 362, 363, 377–380, 383, 385; and employment, 147, 150, 151, 152, 159–160, 231–232, 233, 239, 357; and ethnicity, 432, 434–436; and family, 156, 216, 219, 221–222, 237, 272–277, 285, 286, 290, 293, 296–304, 300; and gangs, 150, 151; and gender, 36, 237; and hate crimes, 529–530; and health issues, 405, 406; as Hispanic, 427–430; and history, 35–36, 39–40, 55–56, 61; and income, 76, 77, 82, 83, 384; and Jews, 57–58, 59; and knowledge construction, 13, 14, 15; and Korean Americans, 425, 519–527; and language, 223, 323, 324–327, 329–331; and Latinos, 425; and mass media, 522; and men, 146–155, 172, 217, 415, 514–518; and multiculturalism, 20; and national identity, 55, 59, 60, 408, 410, 419, 421, 425; and oppression, 31, 59, 110, 178, 181; and police, 415, 514–518; population of, 1, 2, 54, 408–409, 521; and poverty, 67, 68, 78, 79, 80, 86, 87, 123, 141, 335; and prisons, 266, 400, 401, 402; and Puerto Ricans, 428–430; and race, 4, 67, 74, 436; and racism, 72, 75, 82, 93, 109, 110, 111, 112, 113–115, 119–124, 152, 153–154, 240, 435, 519, 568; and rap music, 152–153; and sexism, 148, 190; and sexual orientation, 471–472; and sexuality, 411; and social activism, 562, 566, 568–570, 572; and social institutions, 147, 217; and social justice organizations, 575–577, 579; and violence, 414, 415; and wealth, 76, 77, 78, 134, 138, 156; and white privilege, 96; and women, 148, 171, 175, 296–304, 497–508
Age: and antiracist education, 560; as category of experience, 17; and diversity, 1, 3; and gender, 169, 177–184; and oppression, 5, 110, 178, 190; and privilege, 103; and racism, 76, 92; and women, 172, 179–180
Allen, Paula Gunn, 18–19
American Indians. *See* Native Americans

Andersen, Margaret L., 100, 290, 291
Anderson, Elijah, 415
Anner, John, 537
Arab Americans, 54, 113, 408, 411, 453–455
Asetoyer, Charon, 533–534, 536
Asfahani, Magdoline, 411
Asian Americans: and class, 4, 128, 241; and education, 18, 244, 247, 249, 385, 525; and employment, 218, 239, 243–251; and ethnicity, 432, 433, 438; and family, 219, 238, 290; and gender, 85; and hate crimes, 527–530; and health issues, 406; and history, 61; and income, 82, 83; and knowledge construction, 13, 14; and language, 332; and men, 194–196, 198–199; and national identity, 53, 55, 56, 408, 410–412, 447–453; and oppression, 32, 59; population of, 1, 2, 54, 56, 110, 408, 409, 521; and poverty, 67, 78, 79, 141; and race, 4, 54, 74; and racism, 92, 111, 112, 113, 122, 191–201, 203–204; and sexism, 191–192; and sexuality, 413, 480–488; and social justice organizations, 577–578, 579, 582; and violence, 415; and wealth, 76, 78; and women, 171, 196–198, 199, 243–251
Asian Indians: and national identity, 56; and poverty, 78
Atkin, Ruth, 85
Auletta, Ken, 261

Baca Zinn, Maxine, 84, 171, 217, 320, 356
Baldwin, James, 362
Banfield, Edward C., 143
Barrera, Mario, 252, 280
Bartlett, Donald, 396
Baumgartner, Alice, 207
Beck, Evelyn Torton, 201
Berkman, Alan, 226
Bernstein, Jared, 83, 230
Bisexuals, 85, 171, 464, 467, 469–470, 480–488
Black nationalism, 121
Blacks. *See* African Americans
Blassingame, John, 272, 275, 276
Blauner, Robert, 71, 110, 435
Blood, Peter, 84–85
Bluestone, Barry, 255
Blunk, Tim, 226